CLARENDON LAW SERIES

Edited by
TONY HONORÉ
AND
JOSEPH RAZ

CLARENDON LAW SERIES

Some Recent Titles in this Series

LABOUR LEGISLATION AND PUBLIC POLICY

A Contemporary History

PAUL DAVIES

and

MARK FREEDLAND

CLARENDON PRESS · OXFORD
1993

Oxford University Press, Walton Street, Oxford OX2 6DP

Oxford New York Toronto
Delhi Bombay Calcutta Madras Karachi
Kucla Lumpur Singapore Hong Kong Tokyo
Nairobi Dar es Salaam Cape Town
Melbourne Auckland Madrid

and associated companies in
Berlin Ibadan

Oxford is a trade mark of Oxford University Press

Published in the United States
by Oxford University Press Inc., New York

British Library Cataloguing in Publication Data
Data available

Library of Congress Cataloging in Publication Data
Davies, P.L. (Paul Lyndon)
Labour legislation and public policy: a contemporary history/
Paul Davies and Mark Freedland.
(Clarendon law series)
Includes index.
1. Labor laws and legislation—Great Britain—History.
I. Freedland, M.R. (Mark Robert) II. Series.
KD3009.D385 1993 344.41'01—dc20 [344.1041] 92-43630
ISBN 0-19-876060-4
ISBN 0-19-876288-7 (pbk.)

1 3 5 7 9 10 8 6 4 2

Typeset by Best-set Typesetter Ltd., Hong Kong

Printed in Great Britain
on acid-free paper by
Biddles Ltd.
Guildford & King's Lynn

To

Leo, Emily, Megan, and Tessa

PREFACE

As we explain more fully in the Introduction, this volume in the Clarendon Law Series grew out of our dissatisfaction with the difficulties of teaching labour law according to the usual assumptions of undergraduate law teaching. By this we mean that the main task is seen to be that of expounding the current state of the law, with only limited analysis of how the law came to be in this state. There are, no doubt, many different possible approaches to an explanation of the current state of a particular legal area. In the case of labour law, however, it seemed to us that the subject lacked all coherence unless one had obtained a good grasp of the tumultuous history of the recent legislation in this area. Those who have lived through the evolution of the subject over the past thirty years have acquired this useful knowledge by accretion, but for students who were born only well after the development of modern labour law was under way, there seemed to us to exist no full-scale treatment of these matters. It is in this sense that we can claim to have written a book in line with the aims of the founders of the Clarendon series, which were that each book should introduce a particular area of law.

We hope that the result of our efforts may address a readership not confined to students of law. The origins of legislation concern not only lawyers but also students of politics, sociology, and economics. We have drawn heavily upon the writings of such scholars and we hope that in return we have said some things which may be of interest to them.

In writing a legislative history of the present era, the great temptation for the authors is to attempt to chronicle and evaluate events occurring as the work goes to press. This would lead to unreliable instant history; we have as far as possible drawn the line at the end of 1990, and in particular have not sought to analyse systematically the period after Mr Major succeeded Mrs Thatcher (as she then was) as Prime Minister in November 1990. We have, however, judged it useful to show where legislative provisions have been consolidated into the Trade Union and Labour Relations Act 1992 (TULRECA).

In the long process of attempting to qualify ourselves as writers of legislative history, we have drawn upon the resources of many libraries in Oxford, whose staffs have given us great help with unfailing cheerfulness. In particular we are grateful to the Bodleian Law Library, the library of the Institute of Economics and Statistics, the Social Studies Library, and the libraries of Balliol, Nuffield, and St John's Colleges.

We have also incurred in this process more than usually large intellectual debts to our colleagues and students. Among our colleagues, both inside and outside the ranks of labour law specialists, we have benefited especially from discussions with Steve Anderman, Hugh Collins, Colin Crouch, Simon Deakin, Linda Dickens, Bob Hepple, Bill McCarthy, Ross McKibbin, Ulrich Mueckenberger, Henry Phelps Brown, David Soskice, and Bill Wedderburn. A very special debt of gratitude is owed to Keith Ewing for commenting upon an almost final draft of the work as a whole; he is, however, no more culpable than any of those others for the multifarious theoretical errors which we expect will be attributed to us.

Our publishers have displayed their legendary courtesy and patience, especially in the person of Richard Hart. Our Faculty Office and our respective College Offices have been unstinting with help in typing, and latterly in helping to track and edit material on computer disks.

PAUL DAVIES and MARK FREEDLAND

Balliol College, Oxford and St John's College, Oxford

Ember Day, September 1992

CONTENTS

TABLE OF CASES

TABLE OF CASES

TABLE OF
LEGISLATION

(ii) UK DELEGATED LEGISLATION

(iii) INTERNATIONAL AND EUROPEAN COMMUNITY MEASURES

(a) Council of Europe

(b) European Community

ABBREVIATIONS

ACAS	Advisory, Conciliation, and Arbitration Service
ASLEF	Associated Society of Locomotive Engineers and Firemen
AUEF	Amalgamated Union of Engineering and Foundry Workers
AUEW	Amalgamated Union of Engineering Workers
BJIR	British Journal of Industrial Relations
CAC	Central Arbitration Committee
CBI	Confederation of British Industry
CIR	Commission on Industrial Relations
CML Rev.	Common Market Law Review
CO	Certification Officer
CRE	Commission for Racial Equality
CROTUM	Commissioner for the Rights of Trade Union Members
DEA	Department of Economic Affairs
DE Gaz.	Department of Employment Gazette
DEP	Department of Employment and Productivity
EA	Employment Act
EAT	Employment Appeal Tribunal
EEC	European Economic Community
EETPU	Electrical Electronic Telecommunications and Plumbing Union
EIRR	European Industrial Relations Review
EOC	Equal Opportunities Commission
EOR	Equal Opportunities Review
EPA	Employment Protection Act
EPCA	Employment Protection (Consolidation) Act
ERM	Exchange Rate Mechanism
ESU	Electricity Supply Union
ETU	Electrical Trades Union
GCHQ	Government Communications Headquarters
HSC	Health and Safety Commission
HSWA	Health and Safety at Work Act

ICR	Industrial Cases Reports
IDS	Incomes Data Services
IDT	Industrial Disputes Tribunal
ILJ	Industrial Law Journal
ILO	International Labour Organisation
Int. Lab. Rev.	International Labour Review
IRA	Industrial Relations Act
IRC	Independent Review Committee
IRLIB	Industrial Relations Legal Information Bulletin
IRLR	Industrial Relations Law Reports
IRRR	Industrial Relations Review and Report
ISTC	Iron and Steel Trades Confederation
IT	Industrial Tribunal
JCC	Joint Consultative Committee
JIC	Joint Industrial Council
LGHA	Local Government and Housing Act
MLNS	Ministry of Labour and National Service
MLR	Modern Law Review
MSC	Manpower Services Commission
NALGO	National Association of Local Government Officers
NAT	National Arbitration Tribunal
NBPI	National Board for Prices and Incomes
NCCI	National Council for Coloured Immigrants
NEDC	National Economic Development Council
NGA	National Graphical Association
NIRC	National Industrial Relations Court
NJAC	National Joint Advisory Council
NUM	National Union of Mineworkers
OJLS	Oxford Journal of Legal Studies
OPB	Occupational Pensions Board
PEP	Political and Economic Planning
PL	Public Law
PRP	Profit Related Pay
PSI	Policy Studies Institute
SI	Statutory Instrument
SJIC	Statutory Joint Industrial Council
SLADE	Society of Lithographic Artists, Designers, Engravers, and Process Workers

SOGAT	Society of Graphical and Allied Trades
SR&O	Statutory Rules and Orders
TDA	Trade Disputes Act
TEC	Training and Enterprise Council
TGWU	Transport and General Workers Union
TUA	Trade Union Act
TUC	Trades Union Congress
TULRA	Trade Union and Labour Relations Act
TULRECA	Trade Union and Labour Relations (Consolidation) Act
TVEI	Technical and Vocational Education Initiative
USSR	Union of Soviet Socialist Republics
YTS	Youth Training Scheme

INTRODUCTION

The purpose of this introduction is to explain why we have written this book on the contemporary history of labour legislation in Britain, and to say what we hope it may be able to offer to those who read it. Our starting-point was that we had come to feel dissatisfied with the results of presenting labour law in the way in which legal subjects are traditionally presented in textbooks, that is to say as a snapshot of the state of the law at the latest possible moment that the author, publisher, and printer of the book can between them contrive. We hasten to add that this was, on the one hand, a methodology which we had ourselves previously followed, and that, on the other hand, other authors had already on occasion successfully broken free of its constraints. Nevertheless, we perceived that our students were finding it increasingly difficult to arrive at their own snapshot of labour law; given the colossal rate of legislative change from the mid-1960s onwards, and the lack of continuity in labour law in recent years, they seemed to be finding the picture an impossibly kaleidoscopic one, and were accordingly becoming disenchanted with the subject. Moreover, this created the risk that their whole perspective upon the subject would be at variance with our own, with the resulting distortion of the framework of ideas we were seeking to impart to them. They, for example, would tend to form the view that the starting-point for all statutory individual employment law was the Employment Protection (Consolidation) Act 1978; we would find it difficult to convey the sense of the number of layers of historical development which were compressed into what was, for our students, a single instantaneous point of departure. Hence we embarked upon an initially unambitious project of narrating the legislative history of labour law in the post-war period. That period was chosen because we quickly came to the view that the period of active labour legislation from 1963 onwards could not satisfactorily be described without going back to the end of the Second World War, and finding our starting-point in the post-war resumption of civilian life and laws in industrial society.

We also took the view that it would be unwise to seek to operate as historians or as social scientists, for by doing so we would be attempting too much, and would quickly be exposed as amateurs. This would be true, for example, if we tried to analyse Cabinet papers—moreover, the thirty-year rule would make the main body of these unavailable, and there would be a lack of balance if we drew on them only for the first fifteen years of the period we would be looking at. This would also be true if we sought systematically to assess the impact, for example on the processes of industrial relations, of the legislation which we would be describing. We should need to do this sporadically, in order to understand and evaluate the judgments which the policy-makers themselves made about the impact of existing legislation when deciding about further legislation. But we would not presume to engage in continual analysis of the effects of legislation, if only because of the lack of primary empirical data available to us and our lack of competence to engage in the sort of statistical calculations upon which significant conclusions heavily depend. So we should be looking mainly at the policy developments leading up to and dictating the shape of labour legislation, and should be using policy documents and parliamentary debates as our main source of primary evidence.

Although there were those limitations upon what we could hope to achieve by concentrating upon legislative history, we nevertheless found that it was a methodology which opened up many interesting possibilities to us. Some of these are indicated in Bob Hepple's Introduction to *The Making of Labour Law in Europe*.[1] He begins by underlining the theme that labour law is part of a process, a theme which 'stands in opposition to conceptions of labour law as a relatively static and neutral set of rules and institutions which regulate employment'.[2] He goes on to cite, as one of the rationales for developing the comparative history of labour law in a number of European countries, the '"inner" social, economic and political relationship of parallel developments in different countries'.[3] That inner relationship is to be understood in terms of the variety of historical factors which

---

[1] B. Hepple, ed., *The Making of Labour Law in Europe: A Comparative Study of Nine Countries up to 1945* (London, 1986).
[2] Ibid. 1.
[3] Ibid.

shape the development of the system of labour law in each particular country.[4] Bob Hepple was making this point in the context of a comparative history of the growth of labour law in a number of European countries; we are hoping in this book to provide an account of that inner relationship in the UK which might be useful as the basis of comparative work by others; we are, moreover, taking as our starting-point the date of 1945, which is the point at which that comparative history stopped.

Thus we found it on the one hand necessary, but on the other hand illuminating, to try to understand the recent history of British labour legislation in terms of the social, economic, and political history of British industrial society during the period with which we were concerned. This meant that we would be engaged in inter-disciplinary work, and moreover that we would need to extend well beyond the discipline of industrial relations, the traditional focus of lawyers moving outside the confines of labour law. We would be concerned to some extent with sociology, to a greater extent with economics (especially labour market economics), but above all with the politics of industrial society, in particular of governments in relation to industrial society. (We would not, of course, be pioneers in this respect; the path-finding process had been carried out notably, as we shall see, by Otto Kahn-Freund, who had to all intents and purposes defined British collective labour law by means of the sociology of law, of which he was a past-master.) The duty to engage with those disciplines would present both stumbling-blocks and opportunities.

The main stumbling-block was that we would be open to the charge of identifying labour law as a political subject rather than a truly legal one. This was an accusation often levelled at those engaged in developing labour law, as an academic subject, out of the law of contract and tort in the 1960s. However, this very same linkage between labour law and politics also presented itself, properly understood, as the main opportunity which our chosen methodology had to offer. For the enterprise of writing about labour law and politics is made feasible if one realizes that political scientists can write in an acceptably detached way about politics, as their works (or, rather, the best of them) demonstrate.

[4] Ibid. 4.

Nor would we necessarily be in danger of seeking to outplay political scientists or economists on their own home grounds, if we confined ourselves to trying to discover what responses we should be making as labour lawyers to the ideas offered by their disciplines. Each of the disciplines has its own agenda, or at least a discourse about how its agenda should be defined. We would be concerned with defining the agenda of labour law, and with operating from within it.

Our aim in this book is, therefore, to analyse the development of labour legislation in Britain in the post-war period. The focus of our interest will be the policies adopted by successive governments towards labour law and we aim to provide a comprehensive analysis of the various legislative strategies that have been adopted or—often just as illuminating—rejected. We shall not be concerned systematically with what is perhaps regarded as the traditional task of the academic lawyer, namely the analysis and interpretation of case-law, though we shall naturally pay attention to the decisions of the judges where these influenced legislative policy. Our justification for this approach to labour law is the claim that legislation has been overwhelmingly the major source of new principles in labour law in the period in question and that, if a person wishes to obtain an understanding of the basic structures of that law, an examination of legislative policy is as necessary a task as—and certainly is a task prior to—a study of judicial policy. Yet studies of the legislative process in the labour law field are surprisingly uncommon. We do not think our view of the importance of legislative policy over judicial policy is weakened by the fact that in some cases, as with unfair dismissal legislation, the legislation has been in effect a partnership between Parliament and the courts, with Parliament declaring the principle that unfair dismissal should be unlawful and the courts developing the particular contours of unfairness; or that in other cases judicial development of the common law, as in the industrial conflict area, has sometimes prompted, or at least helped to crystallize, legislative action; or even that on occasion there is good reason for thinking that judicial interpretation of a particular piece of legislation has not accorded precisely with what the government that introduced the legislation intended. Despite these qualifications we would argue that, from the perspective of the early 1990s, labour law is predominantly a statutory subject, set, no doubt, in a common law context and subject to the (sometimes exaggerated) vagaries of judicial interpretation, and the main engine of its development has been legislative rather than judicial.

It also follows from what we said earlier that we wish to depart from what might be regarded as a more traditional approach not simply by placing more emphasis upon legislative, as opposed to judicial, policy but also by providing a historical account of the development of legislative policy up to the early 1990s rather than simply a snapshot of its current state. It is quite clear that the current legislative dominance of labour law is not the result of a single event but of a series of legislative enactments beginning, as we shall argue, in the early 1960s. Since that time there has been, on a conservative definition of what is important, a significant labour law statute on average every two years, though naturally there have been peaks and troughs in the incidence of legislative activity. This fact in itself would probably be enough to justify a historical treatment, as it is unlikely that, over a period of some thirty years, governments, with differing political priorities, would have adhered to a single policy or even a single range of policies. In fact, however, as is well known, the process of legislative development since 1960 has been anything but an example of the Whig view of history. It has been marked by sudden shifts, retreats, and branching-off in new directions. Some policies have been only half implemented in legislation before being abandoned for apparently more attractive options; other legislation has been half repealed as a consequence of the adoption of new strategies; and the result at any particular point in time has been a statutory framework expressive of a variety of different and often contradictory policies. Even the long period of relatively uniform labour law policy since 1979 has not (yet) produced a statutory framework explicable by reference solely to a small number of coherent principles.

There is obviously a substantial task of analysis of legislative policy to be undertaken, to try to explain this welter of statutory activity and its changing focus of concern. Yet there is more to be explained than that. The labour law of the 1950s was not a predominantly statutory subject; on the contrary, it was a predominantly common law subject upon which statute had impinged in only certain, albeit important, areas. The law relating, for example, to the individual employment relationship, to collective bargaining, and to internal trade union affairs was mainly common

law, whilst in many areas where statutes had been passed there
was no recent history of substantial legislative activity. Thus the
governing statutes in industrial conflict law dated back to the
early years of the twentieth century or even to the 1870s. Consequently, the process of legislative activity that began in the 1960s
must be seen, not as an attempt to change an already existing
comprehensive framework of statute law, but as one which involved the introduction of legislative regulation into areas of the
subject which governments had previously been content to leave,
wholly or largely, to regulation by the common law. We need to
try and explain, therefore, both why governments were content
to play a relatively non-interventionist role *vis-à-vis* labour law in
the 1950s and earlier and why this policy stance changed from the
1960s onwards. It was not a change that occurred all at once; it
occurred in different ways in respect of the different parts of
labour law; and, as we have already suggested, it occurred in
different ways at different times. Taken overall, however, the
cumulative effect of the process was really very considerable. The
labour law of the 1980s, and also that of the 1970s, would be
unrecognizable by those who knew only the labour law of the
1950s, and this was a change brought about almost entirely by
statute.

We do not propose to develop our argument about the
importance of statutory labour law merely by recounting the
contents of the major statutes that fall within our area of interest.
Statutes are an expression of government policy and it is the
underlying justifications for the statutory provisions that will be
our main focus of interest. What policy or policies was a particular statute designed to further? What reasons had the government in question for thinking that the adoption of a particular
policy was desirable? To what extent were the governments'
policy objectives shared by other sections of society, notably by
employers, trade unions, and workers? We shall seek to answer
these questions in the course of this book, taking as our subject-
matter legislative enactments designed to regulate both the
individual employment relationship and relations between
employers and collective organizations of workers. But we also
take the view that legislation is but one method available to
government for the implementation of policy. It may be the most
obvious method, perhaps even the most forceful method, but it

is only one method. There is, for example, a range of administrative actions government may take to achieve its policy objectives. We shall, therefore, also examine those situations where legislation was perceived as the appropriate method for implementing policy in employment matters and those where it was not, and we shall be alive to the issue of whether any tension might have developed between the policies being pursued by legislation and those being pursued by administrative or other action.

Before embarking on our legislative history of labour law in the post-war period, we wish to make one more preliminary point—a point which is in a certain sense a declaration of our objective in writing this history, and even a declaration of the objectives which we think labour law should pursue. By employing the method of legislative history, we shall be presenting the development of labour law as a political process, a product of the formulation and application of governmental economic and social policies in the sphere of industrial society. By doing so, we shall challenge the notion, implicit in much of the methodology of legal education, that law in general, or at least this particular branch of it, developed by the working-out of the principles of the common law. We shall not be guided, nor will we suggest that labour law was generally guided during this period, by a central notion of justice according to the common law (though we shall see that the common law, for instance of the contract of employment, retained an important influence). Does this mean that we shall be looking at law as politics rather than at law as justice? To some extent that will be the case; but we shall nevertheless be underlyingly concerned to see how ideals of social justice were defined, and how far they were realized, through labour legislation during the different phases of the post-war period. We shall discover powerful contrasts in this respect between the situation at the beginning of the post-war period and that prevailing at the beginning of the 1990s. That is why we shall start by setting the scene with a description of the strong set of ideals of social justice in industrial society which prevailed in the immediate post-war period, or at least in the thinking of those who sought to identify the role of labour law at that time. Those ideals were embodied, as we shall now see, in the idea of 'collective *laissez-faire*'.

1

COLLECTIVE
LAISSEZ-FAIRE

In this chapter we analyse the theory dominant in the early post-war period as to the appropriate government policy towards labour law. This theory is associated strongly with the writings of Otto Kahn-Freund, who in the 1950s sought to explain the relationship between the law and the system of industrial relations. His writings of the period were highly influential, on both a descriptive and a prescriptive level. Although his analysis deals with the relationship between the legal system as a whole—and not just statute law—and the industrial relations system, a major part of his task as he saw it was to explain both the paucity of statutory regulation of industrial relations and employment relationships and the reasons for the limited interventions that had occurred. We shall, therefore, as a starting-point for our own account, seek to provide a critical analysis of Kahn-Freund's position, emphasizing in particular his views about the role of statute law, and then move on to the task of making a preliminary assessment of the pressure which developed in the post-war period and which rendered his analysis untenable, even in his own eyes.[1]

1.1. KAHN-FREUND AND COLLECTIVE *LAISSEZ-FAIRE*

In 1953 Otto Kahn-Freund contributed an article to a book entitled *The System of Industrial Relations in Great Britain*.[2] The book was a collection of essays on the most important institutions which could be said to constitute the contemporary system of

---

[1] See the tantalizing hints in O. Kahn-Freund, *Labour Relations: Heritage and Adjustment* (Oxford, 1979), 88.
[2] O. Kahn-Freund, 'Legal Framework', in A. Flanders and H. Clegg, eds., *The System of Industrial Relations in Great Britain* (Oxford, 1954), ch. 2.

industrial relations, and Kahn-Freund's task was to consider the significance of law and legal institutions in this area. (Other chapters dealt with the trade unions, employers, collective bargaining, and joint consultation). Kahn-Freund's general conclusion was that the relationship between the law (and legal institutions) on the one hand, and the social institutions of industrial relations on the other hand, exhibited a 'characteristic peculiar to the British industrial scene',[3] as compared with similar relationships in, say, the United States, France, or Germany.[4] That characteristic he explained as follows: 'There is, perhaps, no major country in the world in which the law has played a less significant role in the shaping of [labour-management] relations that in Great Britain and in which today the law and the legal profession have less to do with labour relations.'[5] How then, the reader might have asked, was the world of work governed? The answer, as the other chapters in the book exemplified, was through mechanisms and procedures created, not by the state, but by employers, workers, and trade unions, notably, but not exclusively, through the institutions of collective bargaining. Thus the limited role played by the law did not mean that employment was an area unregulated by rules, but rather that those rules had a social rather than a legal character. More important, perhaps, was the fact that the law's 'abstention' from a major regulatory role meant that the participants in industrial relations played a much greater role in the regulation of their own activities than they would have done under a more interventionist legal framework.

British industrial relations have, in the main, developed by way of industrial autonomy. This notion of autonomy is fundamental and it is ... reflected in legislation and in administrative practice. It means that employers and employees have formulated their own codes of conduct and devised their own machinery for enforcing them ... within the sphere of autonomy, obligations and agreements, rights and duties are, generally speaking, not of a legal character.[6]

---

[3] Ibid. 45.
[4] Kahn-Freund did not, of course, assert that the relationship between the law and the system of industrial relations was the same in the United States, France, and Germany, but rather that none of these (different) relationships was similar to the one that obtained in Great Britain.
[5] Ibid. 44.
[6] Ibid.

Thus in Kahn-Freund's analysis the regulation of employment relations in the 1950s emerged, to a quite remarkable degree, as a matter of autonomous self-regulation. The role of the law was in consequence very much reduced in this area of social life. Direct regulation of relations between individual employees and their employers was predominantly not a matter for the law and legal institutions but for the social institutions of industrial relations, especially collective bargaining. This was self-regulation rather than legal regulation. But equally important, and indeed rather more emphasized in the writings of the time, was the notion that the system of social self-regulation should itself be largely free from legal regulation, i.e. the self-regulatory system should be 'autonomous' or free of state control. Thus in Kahn-Freund's analysis no large role was assigned to the law in the regulation of the collective bargaining system, any more than it was in the regulation of the individual employment relationship. Looking at it from the point of view of the state, one might say that the state had delegated the task of ordering working life to the social institutions created by employers and workers, whilst according to those social institutions a very substantial degree of freedom of action.

For labour lawyers an important consequence of the abstentionist stance of the state towards industrial relations was that the body of rules that comprised labour law in the 1950s was a small one. Even more important was the fact that many of the topics that were of primary importance to employers, employees, and trade unions were simply not within the purview of that body of legal rules at all. Certainly, a most effective way of describing the ambit of labour law in the 1950s is to explain what it did *not* cover, rather than to emphasize what was subject to legal regulation. That exercise we will carry out in Subsection (*b*) below. However, one cannot adequately analyse what Kahn-Freund himself described as the 'legal framework' of industrial relations simply in terms of the absence of legal regulation, even if that was its most significant feature. Two qualifications need to be made. First, there was what Kahn-Freund called 'the negative contribution of the law to the regulation of industrial relations',[7] by which he meant not those legal rules which had an adverse

---

[7] Ibid. 102.

impact upon industrial relations, but, on the contrary, those legal rules without which the functioning of the autonomous system of self-regulation would be impeded. These were the legal rules which did not regulate, restrict, or control the system of collective self-regulation, but rather permitted its free development. Since this was the one indispensable role for the law in the abstentionist system, we shall examine it first in Subsection (*a*) below.

There were to be found, however, in the labour law of the time, rules and institutions whose function could not be described as the negative one of clearing the ground for the operation of collective bargaining. Their function was, rather, the 'auxiliary' one of shaping the system of collective bargaining or the 'regulatory' one of shaping the content of the individual employment relationship (or sometimes both). These rules constitute the second qualification that needs to be made to the simple picture of the absence of laws. There were to be found relatively few such auxiliary or regulatory rules in the corpus of labour law in the 1950s, but, as will be readily appreciated, their existence on any scale posed a major theoretical problem for the abstentionist analysis of labour law. Was it consistent with an abstentionist policy towards industrial relations to use the law at all to support the system of collective bargaining or to regulate the individual employment relationship? If it was, how far could the law properly go in this direction? As we shall see, the answers given to these questions in the 1950s came under increasingly close scrutiny later on when the consensus behind the policy of abstention began to disappear and the issue began to be raised as to what precisely were the implications of the abstentionist analysis for the 'positive' use of law in the world of work. In Subsection (*c*) below we shall examine these issues as they appeared to Kahn-Freund in the 1950s.

(*a*) Negative Law

It was fundamental to Kahn-Freund's analysis of the relationship between the state and the industrial relations system that there should be a comprehensive framework of what he called 'negative' law in place. Negative law was law without which the autonomous functioning of the industrial relations system would be impeded. Its function was to remove legal obstacles to the smooth functioning of the social institutions of industrial self-governance. It may be wondered what the need for such negative law was in a legal system whose basic constitutional disposition is that activities not specifically prohibited or regulated by law may be freely carried out. In fact, however, the requirement for negative law arose from a failure of the common law to adjust itself to the needs of the system of collective self-regulation. The need, to be more precise, was not just for 'negative' law but for 'negative' statutes, to override, where necessary, the dispositions of the common law.

Such negative statutes existed in the 1950s in two main areas of labour law: in industrial conflict law and in trade union law. However, in both cases their function was the same: to protect the freedom of workers to combine and take concerted action, without which the social institutions of industrial relations could not, in Kahn-Freund's eyes, function properly. It was the essence of Kahn-Freund's view that the autonomous system of self-regulation in industrial relations should operate, on the workers' side, on a collective basis. This was because 'the individual employee or worker . . . has normally no social power, because it is only in the most exceptional cases that, as an individual, he has any bargaining power at all'.[8] Unless, therefore, workers could combine they would normally have no social power to counterbalance that of the employer, and in consequence the system of social regulation of employment relations would be wholly one-sided. In a striking phrase, used in another important essay written in the 1950s, Kahn-Freund characterized the social system of regulation which the law should encourage as one of 'collective *laissez-faire*', that is, 'allowing free play to the collective forces of society and [limiting] the intervention of the law to those marginal

---

[8] *Kahn-Freund's Labour and the Law* (3rd edn., London, 1983), 17. Kahn-Freund's writings of the 1950s usually assumed that organisation on the employer's side would be collective too, i.e. in employers' associations. This reflected, however, more the fact that collective bargaining on the employer's side was typically carried on through employers' associations at this time rather than the view that a corporate employer (in law an individual legal person) could be regarded as being without social power. Collective organization on the workers' side was a necessary condition for collective bargaining; on the employers' side, it was an adventitious feature, for the single corporate body was in itself a collectivity (of capital). See further, B. Bercusson, 'Workers, Corporate Enterprise and the Law', in R. Lewis, ed., *Labour Law in Britain* (Oxford, 1986), 134–7.

areas in which the disparity of these forces, that is, in our case, the forces of organized labour and of organized management, is so great as to prevent the successful operation of what is so very characteristically called negotiating machinery'.[9]

However, from the perspective of the common law a system of social regulation based upon the collective organizations of workers was a most difficult thing to accommodate.

Anyone who surveys the history and structure of labour law must become aware of an inherent tension between the social demands of the employment relationship and the spirit and possibilities of the common law. . . . This system of collective bargaining rests on a balance of the collective forces of management and organised labour . . . However, the common law knows nothing of a balance of collective forces. It is (and this is its strength and its weakness) inspired by a belief in the equality (real or fictitious) of individuals; it operates between individuals and not otherwise.[10]

Since, moreover, this fundamental disposition of the common law could not be extirpated by legislative action, there was a continuing risk that the common law would develop in ways that placed the collective organization of workers in jeopardy. What eventually came to pass, therefore, was the enactment of a series of negative statutes excluding from the field of labour relations a succession of doctrinal developments in the common law.

The *leitmotif* of the history of much of the British law of labour relations [has been] the clash between what the courts declared to be the principles of the common law, and what Parliament declared to be the principles of good social policy—in fact a clash of two policies . . .[11]

Nevertheless, from the standpoint of the 1950s, there was some reason for thinking that an equilibrium had been reached in what one Canadian authority had called 'a see-saw vendetta between the courts and the legislature'.[12] In the nineteenth century the

---

[9] O. Kahn-Freund, 'Labour Law', first published in M. Ginsberg, ed., *Law and Opinion in England in the 20th Century* (London, 1959), and reprinted in O. Kahn-Freund, *Selected Writings* (London, 1978), ch. 1. The citations in this book are from the latter source; the quotation in the text is at p. 8.

[10] *Labour and the Law*, 12.

[11] Ibid. 295.

[12] A. W. R. Carrothers, *Collective Bargaining in Canada* (Toronto, 1965), 57, quoted in Kahn-Freund, *Labour and the Law*, 295.

common law courts had developed the doctrine of restraint of trade so as to render both membership of a union, and unions as organizations, of doubtful legality; but the Trade Union Act 1871 had declared that the purposes of a trade union should not, by reason of being in restraint of trade, be unlawful so as to render either any member of the union liable to criminal prosecution (s. 2) or any agreement or trust of the union void or voidable (s. 3). These declarations had not been substantially undermined by subsequent common law developments. In the area of industrial conflict the law of criminal conspiracy had been effectively excluded from trade disputes by section 3 of the Conspiracy and Protection of Property Act 1875, and the multitude of criminal offences relating to picketing had been codified by s. 7 of the same Act. In this case, however, the effect of the substantial exclusion of the common law of crime from the area of industrial conflict had been to divert its creative potential into the civil common law. In the last quarter of the nineteenth century and the early years of the twentieth the courts had developed a number of heads of tortious liability—conspiracy, inducing breach of contract, interference with business—so as to render most forms of industrial action unlawful in civil law. As a government survey published in 1981 put it, 'it seemed that these new liabilities had put the law back almost to where it was before the 1870s. Though strike leaders could no longer be prosecuted for striking, they could be sued for an injunction or damages.'[13] This was especially so since the House of Lords had also held in the *Taff Vale* case[14] that, contrary to previous understanding of the law, a trade union, although an unincorporated association, could, if registered, be sued in its own name, *inter alia* in respect of torts committed by its officials, so that union funds were now at risk in legal actions.

Parliament responded with the Trade Disputes Act 1906, which reasserted in the sphere of the civil law the 'negative approach' of the 1870s legislation. The torts of conspiracy to injure, interference with business (if, indeed, that was a tort), and inducing breach of contracts of employment were excluded from the area of trade disputes. Peaceful picketing was declared to be lawful

[13] Trade Union Immunities, Cmnd. 8128 (1981), para. 46.
[14] *Taff Vale Railway* v. *Amalgamated Society of Railway Servants* [1901] AC 426 (HL).

(i.e. *vis-à-vis* both criminal and civil law). Trade unions were not to be capable of being sued in tort at all (with some exceptions). As important as the actual provisions of the 1906 Act were the subsequent indications that it had become generally accepted as setting the appropriate legal framework for industrial conflict law. At a legislative level the 1906 Act remained on the statute-book for seventy-five years (it was repealed by the Industrial Relations Act 1971), although, as we shall see, its policy was somewhat qualified between 1927 and 1946 by the Trade Disputes and Trade Unions Act 1927 and, more heavily, by wartime emergency legislation. Moreover, the policy of the Act seemed to have been accepted by the judiciary. Indeed, Kahn-Freund felt safe in saying that 'it is in connection with trade disputes that the retreat of the courts from the scene of industrial relations can be most clearly seen'.[15]

Thus, in the analysis of Kahn-Freund and other writers in the abstentionist tradition, the legislation of the 1870s and the Trade Disputes Act 1906 became the bedrock of the British system of labour law. Without these 'negative' statutes two important elements of the collective bargaining system—the freedom of employees to combine in trade unions and to apply collective sanctions against employers—would, in fact, have been subject to detailed regulation by the common law, to the point where self-regulation would have appeared to be a wholly one-sided system in the employer's favour. What is as important from our perspective, however, is that the policy of these Acts was *no more than* the exclusion of the common law. The common law doctrines having been excluded (at least, as it was thought), the legislature did not take in these Acts the further step of seeking to shape the way in which the collective bargaining system operated. But this point takes us on to the topic of the absence of statutory regulation, to which we now turn.

(b) *Absence of Statutory Regulation*

As we have seen, for Kahn-Freund the unique character of the relationship between the British state and the conduct of industrial relations consisted, on the one hand, in the state's reliance upon the system of collective bargaining to regulate the employ-

---

[15] Kahn-Freund, 'Labour Law', 21.

ment relationship and, on the other hand, in the fact that the collective bargaining system itself was free of significant legal regulation. In the UK, the state had adopted a posture of relying upon social institutions for the regulation of an important area of its citizens' lives, whilst in large measure abstaining from legal control of the actions of these social institutions.

We can best explain the operation of this policy in practice by looking at the main areas of regulation that one might expect to find in a comprehensive system of labour law and observing the very limited extent to which such regulation could be found in the British labour law of the 1950s. In principle, one can envisage the use of the law to encourage, support, and control the system of collective bargaining, for example, by encouraging the establishment of bargaining relationships and the observance of collective agreements and by controlling the weapons available to employers and trade unions in cases of industrial conflict. One can envisage the use of the law to regulate the operations of trade unions, considered not so much as parties to collective bargaining but as collective organizations of workers (the 'internal' dimension of trade union law). Finally, one can envisage the use of the law directly to regulate the relationship between the individual employee and his or her employer. How extensive, in fact, in the 1950s was British labour law when judged by the standards of a comprehensive system?

(i) *Collective Bargaining Law.* In spite of the state's reliance upon the collective bargaining system to regulate employment relations, the state in the 1950s took very few steps through the legal system actually to ensure that there was a bargaining system in place. In contrast with the Wagner Act of 1935 in the United States[16] or the post-war Canadian legislation[17] there was no general legal obligation upon employers in the UK to recognize and bargain with trade unions. It was true that the various nationalization statutes passed after the Second World War had imposed a legal obligation upon the new public corporations to establish bargaining and consultation machinery,[18] but this legislation was

---

[16] C. L. Tomlins, *The State and the Unions: Labour Relations, Law and the Organised Labour Movement in America, 1880–1960* (Cambridge, 1985), pt. II.

[17] American Bar Association, *The Labor Relations Law of Canada* (Washington, DC, 1977), 56–8.

[18] See below, ch. 2.2.

intended more to ratify existing practice in those already well-organized industries than to produce changes in bargaining practice. Certainly no special machinery was established, along any of the North American patterns, to adjudicate upon alleged breaches of the new statutory obligations. Nor did the legislation result from TUC or trade union pressure. Indeed, in the case of the Civil Aviation Act 1946 the TUC objected that such legislation would benefit only non-affiliated or breakaway unions,[19] an accurate enough perception of the industrial context in which such legislation was likely to be invoked, even if it was more than two decades before significant litigation occurred.[20]

Nor had English law followed a common continental European approach to the recognition problem, namely, the creation of a statutory works council. Patterns of works councils vary from country to country, but such a system typically involves their compulsory establishment in all but small firms, the election by the employees in question of representatives on to the council, and the placing of a legal obligation upon the employer to give information to the works council, to consult with it over certain matters of concern to the employees, and perhaps even to negotiate with it. Such a body could represent not only a way of compelling the employer to treat with his employees on a collective basis, but, more fundamentally, the primary expression of a philosophy that 'the factory or mine, office or workshop, [was] a community organised by legal principles'.[21]

Under this heading of the absence of legislation ensuring the existence of a bargaining system, one should also note that in the 1950s there was no legislative protection against the employer of employees' freedom of association. With the exception of government contractors[22] an employer was free to offer employment on the terms that the employee was not, and agreed not to become, a member of a union (the so-called 'yellow dog' contract), and, whether or not the employee had given such an

---

[19] Sir N. Chester, *The Nationalisation of British Industry, 1945–51* (London, 1975), 791.

[20] And then it mainly concerned the Post Office. See *Gallagher v. Post Office* [1970] 3 All ER 712 and *R. v. Post Office ex parte ASTMS* [1981] ICR 76.

[21] Kahn-Freund, 'Legal Framework', 49.

[22] Under cl. 4 of the Fair Wages Resolution 1946, 'The contractor shall recognise the freedom of his workpeople to be members of trade unions.' The wages provisions of the Resolution are discussed below in Subsect. (c)(i).

undertaking, an employer could lawfully dismiss an employee who joined a union or participated in its activities, provided only that notice to terminate the contract of employment in accordance with its terms was given to the employee. Thus the system of collective bargaining might be stymied at its very inception by the employer dismissing those of its employees who were recruited into membership of a union. Even if the employer did not, and most at this time did not,[23] employ such tactics, often the employer could effectively and without illegality deprive union membership of its substance by refusing to deal with the union chosen by the workforce. However, as we shall see when we come to look at auxiliary and regulatory legislation in Subsection (*c*), English law, whilst not imposing a direct duty to bargain, was not without legislation which, in design at least, aimed to encourage the growth of collective bargaining.

The second element that can be discerned in the policy of autonomy was that the state through legislation took few steps to ensure that any collective agreements which resulted from the bargaining process were observed. This policy could be subdivided into two elements. First, the collective agreement itself was, on the better view of the common law, not a legally enforceable contract as between the parties to it, and Parliament had passed no legislation designed to alter that view. Consequently, neither party could sue the other in contract for breach of the agreement. In particular, the employer (or employers' association) was not able to sue the union if the union called for industrial action over a dispute instead of taking that dispute through the procedure to be found in most collective agreements for the handling of such matters. 'Unconstitutional' action (i.e. action taken in breach of the disputes procedure) might be visited with social sanctions, but it did not attract legal obloquy. In a comparative context the UK was unusual in treating the collective agreement as not legally enforceable at collective level (although foreign systems differed in the consequences and significance that were attached to the characterization of the collective agreement as a contract). However that may be, the UK was marked by the absence of any debate about the extent of the legally enforceable

---

[23] For an example of a case involving an employer who did insist upon non-membership of trade unions on the part of its workforce, see *D. C. Thomson & Co. v. Deakin* [1952] Ch. 646. See below, p. 131.

'peace obligation' in the collective agreement. Elsewhere, it might be debated whether the peace obligation applied only to official union action or whether the union undertook also to attempt to control the actions of its members acting unofficially; whether the peace obligation was 'absolute' or 'relative', i.e. covered only disputes about matters settled by the collective agreement; whether, on the employers' side, the peace obligation applied only to lock-outs or also to attempts by employers unilaterally to alter conditions of work (the 'status quo' issue), and so on.[24] In the UK these matters were generally thought to be concluded by the simple statement that the collective agreement was not legally enforceable because the parties to it did not intend it to be. In Kahn-Freund's words, collective agreements 'are intended to yield "rights" and "duties", but not in the legal sense; they are intended, as it is sometimes put, to be "binding in honour" only, or (which amounts to very much the same thing) to be enforceable through social sanctions, but not through legal sanctions'.[25]

In those countries which regard collective agreements as legally enforceable that idea usually expresses itself in a second way, beyond the simple enforcement of the agreement as a contract between the collective parties. This second expression of the notion of legal enforceability involves treating those parts of the collective agreement which are intended to regulate the relationship between individual employee and employer (clauses about wages, hours, overtime rates, etc.) as automatically and compulsorily part of the individual contract of employment. In the UK the agreement between individual employee and employer was regarded at common law as legally enforceable (in contradistinction to the collective agreement), but the terms of any relevant collective agreement did not usually have any special legal status in respect of the individual contract of employment. No doubt the terms of the relevant collective agreement were usually incorporated into the individual contract of employment, but this result was dependent upon the will of the individual parties and not upon any law incorporating the collective terms whether the parties to the individual contract wished it or not. It

[24] G. Giugni, 'The Peace Obligation', in B. Aaron and K. W. Wedderburn, eds., *Industrial Conflict: A Comparative Legal Survey* (London, 1972), ch. 3.
[25] Kahn-Freund, 'Legal Framework', 57.

followed that where an employer (or, more likely, an employers' association) had concluded a collective agreement with trade unions, there was no legal guarantee that the employer (or any particular member of the employers' association) would automatically implement the collective agreement. Unless the employer had committed itself in the contract of employment to implement new terms and conditions as and when agreed at collective level, it would be free to consider on each occasion whether the new structure should be applied to its employees.[26]

Thus in the UK the incorporation process was not automatic, unless the parties to the individual contract chose to make it so. Nor was it (usually) compulsory, that is, the employer was free to agree with its employees that the terms of their contracts of employment should be altered so as to become less favourable than those stipulated in the collective agreement, even if the collective terms had at some earlier stage been incorporated into the individual contracts. Incorporation thus did not guarantee continued observance of the collective terms, because the common law placed the autonomy of the parties to the individual contract at the centre of its conceptual structure. During the depression of the inter-war period the lack of automatic and compulsory incorporation had caused severe problems for the national-level negotiating machinery in a number of industries, as we shall see in Section 1.2. Again, however, when we examine auxiliary and regulatory legislation we shall see that British law had developed by the 1950s a number of more limited instruments whereby in specific cases compulsory (and sometimes automatic) effect could be given to collective agreements at individual level.[27]

(ii) *The Law and Industrial Conflict.* The third area where a state interested in legal regulation of the collective bargaining system might have engaged in statutory regulation was that of dispute resolution. What role was the law to play if union and employer could not agree, say, upon the terms for a new collective agreement or about the correct way of resolving a grievance that had arisen on the shop floor? A state interested in such regulation might have intervened on either or both of two bases:

---

[26] See *Dudfield v. Ministry of Works* and *Faithful v. The Admiralty*, repr. in K. W. Wedderburn, *Cases and Materials on labour law* (Cambridge, 1967), 296–300.

[27] See below, Subsect. (c).

in order to resolve compulsorily the substantive matter in dispute between the parties or in order to regulate the weapons available to the parties in their struggle to resolve the dispute through their own social mechanisms. In the 1950s, the reader will not be surprised to learn, British governments made extensive use of neither mechanism.

The first approach would have involved some form of compulsory arbitration of the subject-matter of the dispute or, at a lesser level of intervention, the compulsory use of certain state-provided procedures (conciliation, mediation) designed to produce a settlement of the dispute. Compulsory arbitration was not unknown to British law, having been extensively used in both the First and Second World Wars. The remnants of the Second World War system were in fact still in force in the 1950s, the results of arbitration being, in effect, binding upon employers but not on unions or employees. As Kahn-Freund candidly admitted, the relevant law 'superimposes a scheme of compulsory arbitration upon the traditional voluntary system of British industrial relations',[28] which perhaps explains the repeal of the legislation in 1958. The removal of the vestiges of wartime compulsion did not, of course, suggest that the state should not offer on a voluntary basis facilities for conciliation, mediation, or arbitration to employers and unions which were in dispute. The state had in fact provided such facilities since the late nineteenth century, but neither party could be legally compelled to use them nor, without their consent, were the results of any arbitration legally binding upon the parties to the dispute.[29]

The second approach would involve legal restrictions on the social sanctions available to the disputing parties. We have already seen that the law had intervened in this area, but that intervention, notably the Trade Disputes Act 1906, was 'negative' law. Far from restricting the use of social sanctions, the Act was designed to clear away the common law obstacles to their free

[28] 'Legal Framework', 92.
[29] See K. W. Wedderburn and P. L. Davies, *Employment Grievances and Disputes Procedures in Britain* (Berkeley, Calif., 1969), pt. III. Governments could set up inquiries, notably 'Courts (*sic*) of Inquiry', into disputes without the parties' consent, in order to produce recommendations (not, of course, legally binding) for settlement of the underlying issues. Thus the mobilization of public opinion was the furthest the government could go by way of intervention without the consent of the disputing parties.

exercise. What is noteworthy in the present context is that the 1906 Act did not go beyond a policy of exclusion of the common law. Having excluded the common law, at least as it was then understood, from the area of trade disputes, the legislators of 1906 did not go on, as they might have done, to erect their own statutory structure of restrictions on the employment of social sanctions in trade disputes. The policy of the 1906 Act seemed to be that provided the social sanctions were peaceful, their use was not to be the subject of legal restriction. There were thus, in the 1906 Act, no statutory restrictions on secondary action, no requirement of a ballot before industrial action, no controls on peaceful picketing, and so on. Peaceful industrial action, it seemed, was not to be at risk of litigation, whether initiated by employer or government. Consequently peaceful industrial action was not to be the subject of injunctions, fines for contempt of court, sequestration of union assets, or any of the other remedies subsequently to become familiar in this field. Only a limited number of groups of employees—principally policemen, members of the armed forces, merchant seamen—were excluded from this legal regime, whilst the government had limited powers under the emergency powers legislation to take steps, notably the use of troops, to deal with the *consequences* of industrial disputes which caused serious inconvenience to the community, but without rendering the industrial action itself illegal.

(iii) *Internal Trade Union Law.* We may by now be thought to have established the proposition that the system of collective bargaining in the 1950s was very lightly regulated by legislation, despite the reliance placed upon it by the state for the governance of the employment relationship. This reluctance to legislate, however, extended beyond the establishment and functioning of the collective bargaining system itself to embrace trade unions considered not as bargaining partners but as organizations of workers.[30] Again, this policy was not perhaps the obvious one for governments to have adopted. Since workers depended for their protection under a collective bargaining system largely upon the efforts of their union on their behalf, the state might have legislated so as to ensure that workers could obtain access to and remain members of trade unions on fair conditions, that the

---

[30] The same general principles were applied to employers' associations.

union represented the various groups of its members fairly, or that the unions' internal procedures met some legislatively determined standard of democracy. In fact, however, the Trade Union Act 1871 followed a similar policy to that of the 1906 Act: the common law doctrine of restraint of trade was excluded but no legislative regulatory scheme was put in its place. The furthest the Act was prepared to go was in requiring unions to have rules about certain matters (whilst not specifying the content of these rules), and even this step was to a degree counterbalanced by section 4 of the Act which took out of the jurisdiction of the courts the 'direct' enforcement of certain other provisions in unions' rule-books (which, of course, at common law constituted a contract between the union and its members and among the members *inter se*).

The only substantial qualification to this policy in the period up to the 1950s was made by the Trade Union Act 1913, which, significantly, dealt not with a pure matter of industrial relations but with something that straddled the borderline between politics and industrial relations. That Act provided that 'political' expenditure by trade unions had to be made from a fund separate from the general funds of the union, that a political fund could be established only if a majority of the members of the union in a secret ballot approved of the proposal, that any individual member of the union was to be free not to contribute to the political fund, and that he or she was not to be discriminated against in other areas of union activity on account of the decision not to contribute to the political fund.

Finally on the theme of the lack of regulation of the social structures of industrial relations, one should note that the self-regulation vouchsafed by the law to trade unions extended also to the forms of union security (i.e. mechanisms for retaining members) that they might establish. In particular, the 'closed shop' (i.e. the situation in which union membership was *de facto* or *de jure* a condition of employment in a particular workplace) was not subject to special legal controls. The general freedom of the union to employ peaceful economic sanctions in pursuit of its objectives extended to industrial action to establish or maintain a closed shop,[31] and the employer was as free to terminate the

---

[31] *Reynolds v. Shipping Federation* [1924] 1 Ch. 28; *Crofter Hand Woven Harris Tweed v. Veitch* [1942] AC 435.

employment of an employee for non-membership of a union as to dismiss for any other reason.

(iv) *Regulation of the Individual Employment Relationship.* We have now looked at the lightness of the legal regulation of the collective bargaining process and of the organizations that engaged in it. There is one final area of exiguous statutory regulation that we must note. In the 1950s the lack of legal regulation in this area was not often emphasized, but it was in fact an important area and the lack of legal regulation was as much a consequence of the system of autonomous self-regulation as was the lack of legal regulation of the collective bargaining system. We refer to the individual employment relationship itself, which was, under the system of collective *laissez-faire*, to be regulated by social rather than legal institutions. In the light of later developments the degree of legislative abstention at this time is striking. To be sure, the common law conceptualized the relationship between employee and employer as a contractual one, but the fictitious equality which the common law assumed as the basis of this contract meant that the contract did not regulate, but rather articulated, the inevitable subordination of employee to employer. As for statutory regulation, that was most marked by its absence. The termination of the employment relationship, later to be a subject of acute legislative attention mainly, but not exclusively, through unfair dismissal legislation, was at this time a matter essentially for the parties to the contract. This meant for most employees, employed on contracts of indefinite duration, that the employer could lawfully terminate the employment for any reason (or no reason) upon giving the relevant (and usually short) period of notice.[32] The dominance of contractual principles applied equally to the terms of the employment (no equal pay or maternity legislation, for example)[33] and the formation of the relationship (no laws against sexual or racial discrimination).[34]

[32] Hence the legal ease with which the employer, if it chose, could enforce the closed shop.

[33] The Truck Acts and the health and safety legislation were, of course, exceptions. See below, Subsect. (c)(ii).

[34] Some preference in job-seeking was given to those returning from war service (Reinstatement in Civil Employment Act 1944—see below, p. 62) and to the disabled (Disabled Persons (Employment) Acts 1944 and 1958). See below, p. 62.

All this was perfectly understandable as things were viewed in the 1950s, for the low level of protection afforded to the individual employee by the common law principles was to be redressed through the norms supplied by collective bargaining.

The government's reluctance to use legislation directly to regulate the individual employment relationship caused Britain many difficulties over the issue of the ratification of International Labour Organization Conventions. The ILO was founded in 1919, in the aftermath of the First World War, and was 'largely the creation of British civil servants and trade unionists'.[35] Nevertheless, from the beginning this difficulty emerged, at least where the Convention in question fell outside the traditionally legally regulated area of health and safety or the conditions of employment of women and young persons.[36] Thus three Conventions, adopted at the ILO's first session in Washington in 1919 and relating to the minimum age for the admission of children to industrial employment and to night work by women and young persons, were quickly ratified by the UK and translated into domestic legislation by the Employment of Women, Young Persons, and Children Act 1920.[37] On the other hand, the ILO's very first convention, laying down maximum working hours in industry of 48 per week and 8 per day, although signed by the UK at the time, was never ratified, let alone translated into domestic legislation. The proposal to do so gave rise to continuing debate between government, employers, and trade unions in the inter-war period, the employers being, perhaps naturally, implacably opposed, but even the trade unions found it difficult to formulate legislative proposals that took sufficient account of the variety of patterns of working to be found in practice.[38] As

[35] R. Lowe, 'Hours of Labour: Negotiating Industrial Legislation in Britain, 1919–1939' (1982) 35 *Economic History Review* at 260.

[36] See below, p. 34.

[37] The Conventions were Nos. 4 (Night Work (Women) Convention), 5 (Minimum Age (Industry) Convention), and 6 (Night Work of Young Persons (Industry) Convention). When the first of these was revised in 1934 by Convention 41 (Night Work (Women) Convention (Revised)), legislation again followed, almost as speedily: see the Hours of Employment (Conventions) Act 1936.

[38] Lowe, 'Hours of Labour', *passim*. This issue was to re-emerge in the 1980s in the context of proposed European Community legislation on hours of work. See B. Hepple, *Working Time*, Employment Paper 3, Institute of Public Policy Research (London, 1990), and below, p. 591.

we shall see, an equivalent debate was conducted over British ratification of the Equal Remuneration Convention of 1951 in the post-Second World War period.[39]

(c) Auxiliary and Regulatory Law

We have now identified the two essential elements in Kahn-Freund's analysis of British labour law in the 1950s by virtue of which that law could justifiably be said to express a policy of abstention from regulation of the social institutions of industrial relations, whilst at the same time the state's overall policy towards the regulation of work relations was to rely upon that task being performed by these largely unregulated social institutions. Those elements were, as we have seen, the *presence* of a pretty comprehensive framework of negative statutory law, whereby the common law doctrines that would impede the free development of the social institutions of industrial relations were excluded from this field, and the *absence* of a regulatory legal code governing the collective bargaining system, the operations of trade unions, or, indeed, the individual employment relationship itself.

However, as we have also hinted, it was clear that the corpus of British statutory labour law in the 1950s, small though it might be in comparison with, say, that of the North American countries, France, or Germany, did extend beyond the fundamental negative principles that we have already described. How did these statutes fit into Kahn-Freund's analysis in the 1950s? He might have said that they were in principle inconsistent with his analysis, the remnants of different and earlier policies which were no longer the dominant ones pursued by British governments towards the regulation of industrial relations. After all, as he put it in his 1959 essay, there was currently a 'tendency towards non-intervention'[40] on the part of the legislature and the courts in respect of industrial relations, not that such a policy had always been followed. Yet the burden of Kahn-Freund's analysis was that these positive statutes were in fact consistent (or, at least, not inconsistent) with a policy of abstention or collective *laissez-faire*, and we therefore need to examine them in this light. They fall into two groups: those statutes aimed at influencing the collective bargaining process as well as at regulating the individual

[39] See below, p. 212.
[40] Kahn-Freund, 'Labour Law', 11.

employment relationship, and those having only the second objective.

(i) *Auxiliary Legislation.* In the first group Kahn-Freund placed the Wages Councils legislation, the Fair Wages Resolution (not, of course, strictly a statute), and certain analogous fair wages provisions in statutes, and what subsequently became section 8 of the Terms and Conditions of Employment Act 1959 but was earlier in the decade the 'issue procedure' of Order 1376.[41] All three instruments had in common that they might result in a legal obligation being imposed upon an employer to observe terms and conditions of employment for his employees that were at least as favourable as those specified in the relevant legal instrument, so that here, contrary to what one would expect under the policy of collective *laissez-faire*, the pressures upon an employer to offer terms of employment of a certain standard were legal rather than (or as well as) social ones. Furthermore, these three instruments were, in Kahn-Freund's eyes, designed in addition to support the bargaining process, in the case of Wages Councils by encouraging recognition of trade unions by employers, in the case of the other two instruments by requiring observance of terms and conditions of employment laid down in collective agreements. 'The law', he said, 'seeks to stimulate collective bargaining and the application of collective agreements by indirect inducements in preference to direct compulsion, and, where this fails, to provide substitute standards enforceable by legal sanctions.'[42] Thus, use of the law to support the collective bargaining system was not to be excluded under the policy of abstention, but where was the line between direct and indirect support to be drawn?

It is, of course, clear that where a government relies upon collective bargaining to regulate employment relations, it might determine that it was sensible policy to use the law to support and encourage the development of such bargaining or to regulate individual employment relations in those cases where, for one reason or another, the process of social regulation proved ineffective. However, as we have seen, it was Kahn-Freund's analysis that the characteristic peculiar to the policy of the British

[41] Before that a somewhat analogous obligation was contained in art. 5 of Order 1305 (SR&O 1940, No. 1305).
[42] Kahn-Freund, 'Legal Framework', 65.

state was that it both relied upon collective bargaining for the regulation of employment relations and by and large abstained from regulation of the bargaining system itself. For the state to engage in the encouragement by legislation of collective bargaining and the provision of legal substitutes for collective standards where the latter were ineffective might not necessarily cast doubt upon the state's *preference* for regulation through voluntary, collective organization of workers and employers, but it would raise a question of whether the state's attitude towards the bargaining system could any longer correctly be described as one of *laissez-faire*.

It has to be said that Kahn-Freund at this time offered no precise theoretical answer to this question. It seemed to him to be enough to dispose of the issue that the state preferred collective regulation to legal regulation. It was clear, he said, that statutory interventions were regarded as 'a second best' so that 'all British labour legislation is, in a sense, a gloss or a footnote to collective bargaining'.[43] But, of course, a theory of the 'second best' did not necessarily exclude a much more extensive framework of positive labour law than existed in the 1950s. The theory of the second best was, after all, later avowed by the Royal Commission on Trade Unions and Employers' Associations (of which Kahn-Freund was a member). In its Report in 1968 it said: 'We consider it to be of importance that employers and employees should be given improved facilities for the speedy and informal settlement of such disputes as may arise between them. The best way of achieving this end is to stimulate the growth of collective bargaining.'[44] Yet in order to protect those not covered by collective bargaining the Commission went on to recommend the introduction of labour tribunals and the establishment of a statutory unfair dismissal jurisdiction, which recommendations led to a fundamental extension of the regulatory role of the law in respect of both the individual employment relationship and, indirectly, the voluntary dispute resolution procedures that were operated in industry and commerce.[45] The Commission also recommended a statutory recognition tribunal, with powers to order compulsory

[43] Ibid. 66.

[44] Report of the Royal Commission on Trade Unions and Employers' Associations, Cmnd. 3623 (1968), para. 568.

[45] W. Daniel and E. Stilgoe, *The Impact of the Employment Protection Laws* (PSI 577, London, 1978), 74–5.

arbitration, to deal with employers who failed to recognize trade unions in appropriate circumstances, even though it took the view that 'non-intervention [by the law] should continue to be normal policy'.[46] Indeed, as we shall see, in the 1970s the whole question of how much support could be given by the legal system to the social institutions of industrial relations without the law abandoning its abstentionist characteristics became part of a lively debate.

We may suspect that in the 1950s this issue did not appear to Kahn-Freund to be a very exciting one because those legal measures—Wages Councils, fair wages provisions, and section 8 of the 1959 Act—which could be said to have the 'auxiliary' aim of supporting and encouraging collective bargaining and of regulating the employment relationship in the absence of effective collectively agreed standards, although potentially important, were in the social and economic conditions of the 1950s in practice of very little significance. Moreover, there was little pressure from unions, employers, or government to alter that situation.

Let us look at the system of Wages Councils in terms of its actual and potential effectiveness. Under the Trade Boards Act 1918, implementing the recommendations of the Whitley Committee,[47] the Minister had power to establish a Trade Board (as Wages Councils were originally called) in any industry where there was no effective voluntary bargaining machinery for the regulation of wages (and, later, other terms and conditions of employment). The 'second best' role of the Wages Council was emphasized by the fact that a council could not be established where adequate voluntary machinery did exist, and the council could be abolished by the Minister once such machinery was established. However, the council also had the auxiliary role of encouraging the recognition of trade unions by employers, for, as the Minister introducing the 1918 Bill put it, Wages Councils were viewed as 'a temporary expedient facilitating organization within the industry, so that, in the course of time, the workers or the employers will not have need of the statutory regulations'.[48]

---

[46] Report, Cmnd. 3623, paras. 253–6, 273–4, 751–2.

[47] The Whitley Committee produced five reports. Of particular relevance to Trade Boards is the second: Committee on Relations between Employers and Employed (Whitley Committee), *Second Report on Joint Standing Industrial Councils*, Cd. 9002 (1918). See further below, Sect. 1.2.

[48] Quoted in F. J. Bayliss, *British Wages Councils* (Oxford, 1962), 14.

Until that desirable position was reached, however, the council, which consisted of employer, trade union, and independent members, all appointed by the government, was to perform the regulatory role of determining minimum terms and conditions of employment for the industry in question. Once embodied in an order by the Minister the council's decision became legally enforceable, in the sense that the terms were compulsorily and automatically incorporated into the contracts of employment of workers in the industry, and the employer also committed a criminal offence if it did not observe the terms of the order.

Under the stimulus of later legislation, notably the Catering Wages Act 1943 and the Wages Councils Acts 1945 and 1948, the system of councils had expanded, so that by the early 1950s there were sixty-five councils, covering $2\frac{1}{2}$ million workers or 12 per cent of the workforce.[49] A considerable effort was expended by the Ministry of Labour in servicing the councils, and the annual reports from the period of both the Ministry and the TUC devote significant space to their activities. Yet the Donovan Commission concluded in 1968 that the councils had done 'little to fulfil the aim of extending voluntary collective bargaining',[50] or to raise the relative levels of wages of low-paid employees in particular industries, or to change the relative position of industries that were as a whole low-paying. Perhaps this should not surprise us. If, as seemed likely, it was the inability of unions to recruit and retain members in the wages councils industries that was the main barrier to their obtaining recognition from employers, it was wholly unclear why the deliberations at national level of union and employer representatives on a Wages Council should be thought likely to ameliorate that situation. Again, the British experience with wages-setting by statutory bodies, namely that they tended to follow rather than lead the wage levels set in the voluntary sector of the economy, even though there was no provision in the relevant legislation that mandated this result, seems to be one shared quite generally by countries which have such machineries.[51]

---

[49] These figures do not included agricultural workers, who were covered by a similar system established initially under the Corn Production Act 1917.

[50] Report, Cmnd. 3623, para. 234.

[51] G. Starr, 'Minimum Wage Fixing: International Experience with Alternative Roles' (1981) 120 *Int. Lab. Rev.* 545.

Nevertheless, our present concern is to argue that, given the size of the Wages Council sector in the 1950s, one's view of the abstentionst nature of the British system of labour law might well have been very different had the legislation in fact led to the creation of effective bargaining machinery in the sixty-odd Wages Councils industries, or had the wages determinations of the councils been the leaders rather than the laggards in the pay rounds. In the former case, the collective bargaining system might have appeared much more dependent upon statutory support than we are accustomed to viewing it at this time, whilst in the latter case the statutory system of wage determination would have appeared as a real challenge to the effectiveness of the voluntary system. That neither situation obtained made the legislation easier to reconcile with the abstentionist theory of labour law, but did not explain how the legislature had come to adopt such interventionist, if unsuccessful, legislation.

A similar picture of ineffectiveness can be painted of the Fair Wages Resolution and the 'issue' procedure under Order 1376. The former was an instruction from the House of Commons that the government, when contracting for goods and services, should insert into its contracts a clause requiring its suppliers to observe certain levels of terms and conditions of employment *vis-à-vis* the workers they employed. The practice was also widely followed by local authorities, nationalized industries, and the public services. The Resolution thus regulated individual contracts of employment, albeit that the legal obligation stemmed from the commercial contract between government department and supplier and was backed by essentially administrative sanctions (removal from the list of acceptable government contractors), rather than from a legal duty owed directly to the employees or their trade union. The original resolution of 1891 had its origins, like the Wages Councils, in a desire to combat 'sweating', that is, industries where wages were below subsistence level, hours of work were excessive, and working conditions insanitary. It was thought inappropriate that public bodies should benefit from such conditions when obtaining their supplies. In the Fair Wages Resolution of 1946, however, the instrument had acquired in addition a clear auxiliary role, not the encouragement of recognition, as was the case with the Wages Councils, but the enforcement of collectively agreed standards. The 'fair' standard was defined by reference to collectively agreed standards, that is, primarily those agreed at national or district level in an industry through voluntary negotiation or arbitration machinery 'to which the parties are organisations of employers and trade unions representative respectively of substantial proportions of the employers and workers engaged in the trade or industry in the district'. In the absence of such collectively agreed standards, contractors were to observe 'the general level of wages, hours and conditions observed by others whose general circumstances in the trade or industry in which the contractor is engaged are similar.'[52]

The definition of fairness by reference to national or district level multi-employer agreements was echoed in clause 2(*a*) of Order 1376 (although that Order contained no equivalent to the 'general level' part of the definition). Order 1376 applied generally. If an employers' organization or trade union, which habitually took part in collective bargaining in the trade or industry in question, thought that the 'recognised terms and conditions of employment' (the shorthand way of referring to the national or district agreements) were not being observed by a particular employer, it could get that issue referred to the Industrial Disputes Tribunal. If that Tribunal agreed with the contention, it would make an order that the employer observe the recognized terms, and that order had the effect of compulsorily embodying the recognized terms in the contracts of employment of that employer's workers. Like the compulsory arbitration provision mentioned earlier, the 'issue' procedure was a remnant of the wartime regulation of the collective bargaining system. Strikes were prohibited at that time, and the enforcement of recognized terms through legal machinery was a substitute for the social sanctions which had been removed.[53]

Thus, although of rather different origins and operating in rather different ways, by the 1950s both the Fair Wages Resolution and Order 1376 could be used to give legal enforceability to the code of terms and conditions of employment contained in national or district collective agreements. Neither instrument, it was true, operated automatically to achieve this result. The Fair Wages Resolution, indeed, technically left the contract of employment

---

[52] Fair Wages Resolution 1946, cl. 1(*a*) and (*b*). For a history of the Resolutions see B. Bercusson, *Fair Wages Resolutions* (London, 1978).

[53] See below, Subsect. 2.3(*b*)(i).

untouched, whilst Order 1376 produced a change in the contracts of employment only once the IDT had made an award.[54] Nevertheless, both were potentially powerful legal mechanisms for ensuring that employers observed the terms of the relevant collective agreements. Yet neither was extensively used. The Industrial Court, the body to which disputes over fair wages clauses were referred, never dealt with more than half a dozen cases per annum in the 1950s, and in the eight years of its existence (1951–9) the IDT dealt with only about 300 issue cases.[55] The truth of the matter was that non-observance by members of employers' associations or by non-federated employers of collective agreements concluded by these associations at national or district level was not a problem in the years of full employment that followed the Second World War. The pressures of the labour market ensured, generally, that the terms of these agreements were respected. Indeed, as we shall see, these pressures led to the development in many industries of a supplementary tier of single-employer bargaining at establishment level, so that the multi-employer agreements at national or district level became no more than the basis for further negotiations. Again, however, for present purposes the argument is that, had multi-employer national- and district-level collective agreements been the main source of the norms supposed to regulate individual contracts of employment and had there been a substantial proplem of non-compliance by individual employers with the collective agreements negotiated by the employers' federations, it is difficult to believe that much greater use of the Resolution and Order 1376 would not have been made in the 1950s. In those circumstances the characterization of the British system of collective bargaining as one unregulated by law would have been much more debatable. In this hypothetical situation the observance in practice of the results of collective bargaining would have been attributable to the operation of legal mechanisms as well as to trade union or labour market pressures. Ironically, such circumstances had to some degree existed during the depression of the inter-war period, but neither the Resolution nor Order 1376 had been available at

---

[54] *Simpson* v. *Kodak Ltd.* [1948] 2 KB 184; *Hulland* v. *Saunders & Son* [1945] KB 78.

[55] Wedderburn and Davies, *Employment Grievances*, 158; Royal Commission on Trade Unions and Employers' Associations, Research Paper 8 (1968), 33.

that time to deal with the problem.[56] In the post-war situation of full employment, the relevant mechanisms were available but, by and large, were not needed. As anachronistic devices to deal with a social and economic problem that had largely disappeared, they provided in terms of impact at a practical level little challenge to the abstentionist theory, even if the theoretical problems they posed were never satisfactorily resolved.

It is, perhaps, fair to conclude that, as far as collective labour law was concerned, abstentionism appeared to be established in relation to legal support for the development of collective bargaining, because, in the social and economic conditions of the time, the legislation designed to address that matter was highly ineffective. However, it could not be argued that Parliament had failed to legislate at all in this area, and the question therefore might well re-emerge as to what legal support should be provided for collective bargaining if, say, the social institutions of bargaining should fail to keep pace with changes in the composition of the workforce. On the collective side, then, the pure doctrine of abstentionism seemed most clearly to operate in relation to the law of industrial conflict, where, with the repeal of the wartime restrictions discussed in the next chapter, the peaceful deployment of economic sanctions in trade disputes was virtually unregulated by the law. Indeed, for many at this time and later the crucial test for the policy of collective *laissez-faire* was whether the legislation effectively excluded the common law liabilities tending to render industrial action tortious.

(ii) *Regulatory Legislation.* It was mentioned at the beginning of Section 1.1(c) that the positive elements of British labour law, as it existed in the 1950s, included not merely the mechanisms we have been considering in the previous paragraphs (which had both auxiliary and regulatory objectives), but a second group of rules whose purposes were simply regulatory. That is, this second group of laws aimed to regulate the individual employment relationship without, however, having any very obvious additional auxiliary functions by way of encouraging or supporting the collective bargaining system. The two most important examples

[56] The predecessor of Order 1376 was not introduced until the Second World War, and the Fair Wages Resolution was amended so as explicitly to adopt collectively agreed standards of fairness only in 1946.

of such legislation were the health and safety laws[57] and the social security system. Both were of long standing. The earliest Factories Acts dated back to the first half of the nineteenth century, whilst the system of social (or national) insurance had its modern origins in the period before the First World War (though the system had not been placed on a comprehensive basis until the legislation of the period immediately after the Second World War, which implemented William Beveridge's recommendations made in his report, *Social Insurance and Allied Services* (1942)).[58]

These were not the only examples, however, of regulatory legislation that were extant in the 1950s. One could point also to the Truck Acts (which regulated the form of payment of and deductions from wages) and laws restricting the hours of work of women and young people.[59] How was one to explain the regulation of these matters by law rather than by collective agreements? It was not possible to brush aside this legislation as ineffective (not even in the case of the Truck Acts). On the contrary, it was clear that, in the case of health and safety and social insurance, the legislation had occupied the space that might have been available for social regulation through collective bargaining or unilateral trade union provision. A historical explanation might have been given for the centrality of health and safety legislation, for legislation in this field preceded the growth of the modern system of collective bargaining.

Kahn-Freund, however, regarded such legislation as a mere 'supplement to collective bargaining. Standards of health, safety and welfare, or of hours of work of women and juveniles and similar matters, do not, on the whole, lend themselves well to

[57] Notably the Factories Act 1937 and the Mines and Quarries Act 1954.

[58] See below, Subsect. 2.1(*b*).

[59] See the Employment of Women, Young Persons, and Children Act 1920, Children and Young Persons Act 1933, Hours of Employment (Conventions) Act 1936, Employment of Women and Young Persons Act 1936, Young Persons (Employment) Act 1938, as well as the relevant provisions of the Factories Act 1937 and the Mines and Quarries Act 1954. In some 'special' industries the hours of work of adult males were controlled. This was the case with mining (under the Coal Mines Regulation Act 1908), railways (under the Railway Regulation Act 1893), drivers of motor vehicles (under the Road Traffic Act 1930), certain pottery workers (by virtue of a Special Order made under s. 60 of the Factories Act 1937), workers in the baking industry (under the Bakery Industry (Hours of Work) Act 1938, replaced by a similarly named Act in 1954), and shop assistants (under the Shops Act 1950).

collective bargaining, and—exceptions apart—they are much better enforced by inspectors than by union representatives.'[60] One may suspect an element of rationalization in this proposition,[61] but, however that may be, of greater importance to us is the potential significance of the notion of the 'desirable use of legislation to fill gaps left by collective bargaining'.[62] Once this concept became linked with the fact that, even in the flourishing British system of collective bargaining, a substantial proportion of the workforce was not covered by collective agreements, the way would be open for a considerable extension of regulatory legislation. As we have already seen, this argument was subsequently deployed by the Royal Commission on Trade Unions as part of its justification for introducing legislation on unfair dismissal. Moreover, it was not only in the uncovered sectors of the economy that such regulatory legislation might be seen as having a role to play. In industries subject to collective bargaining it was not impossible to conceive of a situation in which legislation laid down minimum standards for all employees upon which collective bargaining then elaborated. That the TUC might not be opposed to such a role for the law was perhaps indicated by its support for more regulatory laws in the immediate post-war period. In 1946, for example, the General Council called for legislation to implement the 40-hour week (for all workers, not just women and juveniles), to provide two weeks' holiday with pay for all workers, and to protect workers asked to engage in double day-shift working.[63] None of these proposals came to fruition (and the matters were in fact dealt with through collective bargaining and general labour market pressures), but they perhaps indicated the width of the potential scope for 'gap-filling' laws, once 'gap-filling' came to be seen more broadly than simply topics which the collective bargaining system did not touch upon at all.

[60] Kahn-Freund, 'Labour Law', 28. Cf. Professor Wedderburn's remark: 'Expediency not theory drew the boundaries of what we have come to regard as the ground natural to employment legislation' ('Labour Law and Labour Relations in Britain' (1972))10 BJIR 270, 271.

[61] The Report of the Committee on Safety and Health at Work, Cmnd. 5034 (1972), later concluded: 'Our present system encourages rather too much reliance on state regulation, and rather too little on personal responsibility and voluntary, self-generating effort. This imbalance must be redressed. A start should be made by reducing the sheer weight of the legislation' (para. 28).

[62] Kahn-Freund, 'Labour Law', 25.

[63] TUC, *Annual Report 1946*, 183–93.

It may be fair to conclude, then, that the abstentionist analysis contained certain ambiguous elements. The Legislative support for collective bargaining was seen as acceptable provided it operated by way of 'indirect inducement' rather than 'direct compulsion', but the borderline between these two ideas was not explored in any detail. Direct legal regulation of the employment relationship was not seen as giving rise to theoretical problems provided it was confined to matters which collective bargaining could not easily regulate, but again the analysis of which matters were appropriately regulated by collective bargaining and which by legislation was not pursued at any length. We have suggested that these two limitations in the analysis may be explained by reference to the ineffectiveness of the auxiliary legislation and the limited scope of the regulatory laws in the 1950s. They may deprive the abstentionist analysis of some of its prescriptive force (as we suggest happened in the 1960s and 1970s), but they do not detract from the accuracy of the abstentionist description of British labour law as it stood in the 1950s. Industrial relations were conducted at that time largely through a system of autonomous self-government, in the regulation of which statutes played little part, but that factual statement disguises the extent to which British labour law even then contained impulses of a more interventionist kind and the difficulty of placing those impulses in an exact theoretical framework.

1.2. GOVERNMENTAL LEGISLATIVE AND ADMINISTRATIVE POLICY, 1916–1948

Before turning to a preliminary analysis of the challenges that the policy of collective *laissez-faire* was to face in the post-war period, it is worth looking at two further linked matters which are relevant to Kahn-Freund's theories. First, it is sometimes suggested, though not by Kahn-Freund himself, that the policy of abstention was confined to the state's attitude towards the use of legislation to regulate industrial society and that similar restraint was not exercised in relation to the use of non-legislative forms of governmental action. In other words, abstentionism did not characterize the overall policy of the state but rather its policy towards the use of one very important method of implementing its policies. In particular, it is sometimes suggested that the state was in general prepared to use administrative measures to promote the development of collective bargaining, and especially the recognition of trade unions by employers, whilst refraining from imposing a general legal obligation upon employers to engage in collective bargaining.

Second, Kahn-Freund's analysis was essentially a static or 'snapshot' view of labour law as it appeared to him in the 1950s. However, he did not argue that abstentionism was a novel doctrine of British labour law. Although, as we shall see in Chapter 2, abstentionism had to be re-created after the adoption of highly interventionist measures during the Second World War, its essential legislative foundations dated back to the beginning of the century, to the Trade Disputes Act 1906, setting out the framework of negative industrial conflict law, and to the Industrial Courts Act 1919, in which the government rejected the principle of compulsory arbitration and provided only facilities on a voluntary basis for the settlement of disputes by conciliation, mediation, and arbitration. Equally, much of the legislation whose relationship to abstentionism was difficult to define with exactitude, dated from this period, notably the Trade Boards Act 1918. It is thus necessary to examine briefly governmental administative and legislative policy during the inter-war period. Our conclusion, in brief, is that the hypothesis of a divorce between the administrative and legislative policies pursued by successive governments is not made out, but that, on the other hand, a sense of the essential fragility of abstentionism as an overall policy on part of government emerges: governments may have wished to abstain, but often found they could not.

The view that government was committed to the promotion of collective bargaining by non-legal measures is often based on the reports of the Whitley Committee, established in 1916, and especially upon its First Interim Report, which recommended 'the establishment for each industry of an organisation representative of employers and workpeople, to have as its object the regular consideration of matters affecting the progress and well being of the trade from the point of view of all those engaged in it . . .'.[64]

___

[64] Interim Report on Joint Standing Industrial Councils, Cd. 8606 (1917), para. 5.

This slightly obscure call for the development of national-level collective bargaining on an industry-by-industry basis 'constituted', said Henry Clay, 'a public and official recognition of trade unionism and collective bargaining as the basis of industrial relations'; 'collective bargaining . . . was authoritatively pronounced normal and necessary.'[65] The importance of such an endorsement of collective bargaining should not be underestimated. It meant that government would at least view the spread of collective bargaining in a benign light and would not seek to undermine its development. For example, the Ministry of Labour's commitment to collective bargaining led it to oppose, largely successfully, proposals from employers and the right wing of the Conservative Party wholly to recast British labour law in the wake of the unions' defeat in the General Strike of 1926.[66] However, that Act did expose to criminal and civil liability the organizers of sympathetic industrial action and of action designed to put pressure on the goverment, as well as those who engaged in large-scale picketing. Moreover, endorsement of collective bargaining did not mean that the government would necessarily take active steps to secure the spread of the practice.

Nevertheless, after some hesitation,[67] the government of the day did accept the Committee's report and the view that this committed the government to positive action to promote industry-wide collective bargaining through the joint industrial councils recommended by the Committee as its preferred model. The time was a good one for the trade unions to press their case. The government needed the co-operation of the trade unions to run a successful war effort—indeed, the Ministry of Labour was created in 1916 with a trade unionist at its head—and the Whitley Committee had been established in the context of a perceived need on the part of government to bolster official trade unionism against unofficial, militant, even revolutionary shop stewards' movements that wartime conditions had created. So government acted, but it is to be noted that legislative and administrative policy went hand in hand. The Committee's preference was for wage-setting machinery to be established on a voluntary basis,

---

[65] H. Clay, *The Problem of Industrial Relations* (London, 1929), 154 and 177.

[66] R. Lowe, *Adjusting to Democracy* (Oxford, 1986), 108.

[67] R. Charles, *The Development of Industrial Relations in Britain 1911–1939* (London, 1973), 110–16.

but in trades where organization was not sufficient to sustain voluntary machinery, trade boards should be used. So having secured an extension of the trade boards legislation,[68] the Ministry of Labour set enthusiastically about the task of selling the new gospel to employers, who, perhaps not surprisingly, were not wholly convinced by it. Nevertheless, twenty JICs were formed in 1918; thirty-two in 1919; sixteen in 1920; and six in 1921.[69] As Charles comments, 'especially effective was the free use of the threat of the possible establishment of a trade board if a Council was not set up.'[70] In addition, twelve trade boards were in fact established in badly organized trades in 1919 and twenty-three in 1920; by the end of 1921 the total number of trade boards was sixty-three, as compared with thirteen before the War.

Although the impact of the JIC model in the private sector was somewhat patchy—it was rejected by employers in mining and engineering, for example, and the bargaining arrangements set up in other industries often incorporated substantial variations on the Whitley model[71]—nevertheless, this was a period in which government, through the newly created Ministry of Labour, devoted considerable legislative and administrative efforts to the promotion of national-level collective bargaining. It was, however, a very short period of activism. It came to an abrupt end during 1921 when post-war depression set in, destroying both the unofficial shop stewards' movement and with it a good deal of the political rationale for the government's promotion of official trade unionism. The Ministry ceased to promote JICs and the Cabinet forbade the creation of further trade boards. The staff in the industrial relations division of the Ministry was reduced from 115 to 20 under pressure from the Treasury to control public expenditure; the Geddes Report on public expenditure in 1921–2 even contemplated the abolition of the Ministry of Labour; and the Cave Committee on the Trade Boards recommended the reversal of the 1918 Trade Boards Act, a recommendation implemented in effect by administrative action within the Ministry.[72]

[68] See above, p. 29.

[69] Charles, *Development of Industrial Relations*, 124–5.

[70] Ibid. 140.

[71] Ibid. chs. 6–12. In two industries special legislation was passed, establishing variants of the Whitley model. See the Mining Industries Act 1920 and the Railway Act 1921.

[72] Charles, *Development of Industrial Relations*, 204; Lowe, *Adjusting to Democracy*, 100.

The depression had a debilitating effect upon national-level collective bargaining, but the Ministry successfully resisted proposals to make the decisions of JICs legally enforceable, except in the limited circumstances of the cotton industry through the Cotton Manufacturing (Temporary Provisions) Act 1934.[73] Some JICs collapsed and others became ineffective, although the Whitley model had become well enough established that it remained a significant feature of bargaining in many industries until national-level bargaining itself underwent a secular decline in the period after the Second World War. As Lowe remarks, the Ministry's record in industrial relations in the inter-war period, once the initial flurry of enthusiasm was past, was one of 'failure actively to promote constructive reform'.[74]

In one area of employment, however, the Whitley Committee's First Interim Report had a sustained impact. This was in the public sector of employment, where 'for the first time the government as a major employer was compelled work out its own labour policy'.[75] Although government departments were initially among the most reluctant of employers to accept the Whitley Report, in the event they decided to do so, since government could hardly promote Whitleyism in the private sector, if it was unwilling to apply it to its own employees. In fact, the public sector became a bastion of Whitleyism, partly because, in the absence of established bargaining arrangements, Whitleyism was applied in a rather pure form in this area of employment, and partly because the public sector was sheltered from the worst effects of the inter-war recession. Moreover, as the public sector expanded in the period after the Second World War, Whitleyism also grew, especially in the National Health Service, and, as we have seen, a legal requirement of union recognition, though not necessarily through a JIC, was imposed upon the nationalized industries.[76] In consequence of governmental support for collective bargaining, union density (i.e. the percentage of potential union members who had actually joined a trade union) in the

[73] Charles, *Development of Industrial Relations*, ch. 13; Lowe, *Adjusting to Democracy*, 116–19. See also F. Tillyard and W. A. Robson, 'The Enforcement of the Collective Bargain in the UK' (Mar. 1938) 48 *Economic Journal*, at 20–1. Only two orders were ever made under the 1934 Act: Ministry of Labour and National Service, *Industrial Relations Handbook* (2nd edn. 1953), 160.

[74] Ibid. 130.

[75] Charles, *Development of Industrial Relations*, 120.

[76] Above, p. 16.

public sector reached and remained at a high level. In 1948, when overall union density was 45.2 per cent, density in central government was 52.9 per cent, in local government and education 69.4 per cent, and in posts and telecommunications (then a government department) 87.3 per cent.[77] However, although government was prepared to give a lead in respect of the machinery for setting terms and condition of employment, there were limits on its willingness to be a model employer as far as substantive terms and conditions were concerned. Thus in 1936 the Treasury and the Ministry firmly rebutted a TUC request that government show the way forward by reducing the working week of civil servants to 40 hours.[78]

In the period immediately before, during, and after the Second World War state activism returned, and for similar reasons to those which had motivated the government in the earlier period. Both legislative and administrative efforts were again bent towards the promotion of union recognition, especially at national level. The possibility of legislation on union recognition was considered by the TUC and the Ministry of Labour, but eventually rejected in 1943 as too difficult to draft. Nevertheless, the Minister was willing to appoint (non-binding) Courts of Inquiry into recognition disputes, and these invariably found in favour of the unions' claim or some version of it; fifty-six JICs were revived or newly established between 1939 and 1946; and the trade board (now Wages Councils) system was expanded by the enactment of the Catering Wages Act 1943 and the Wages Councils Act 1945. The wartime compulsory arbitration machinery[79] put some pressure on employers to deal with trade unions, whilst in the immediate post-war period the Fair Wages Resolution was strengthened by the introduction of a clause requiring government contractors to recognise the freedom of their employees to be members of a union (though the clause did not require recognition of the union), and the government ratified ILO Conventions 87 and 98 on freedom of association and collective

[77] G. S. Bain and R. Price, 'Union Growth: Dimensions, Determinants and Destiny', in G. S. Bain, ed., *Industrial Relations in Britain* (Oxford, 1983), tables 1.1 and 1.5. During the period of operation of the Trade Disputes and Trade Unions Act (i.e. 1927–46), however, civil servants were not permitted to join unions affiliated to the TUC.

[78] Lowe, *Adjusting to Democracy*, 120.

[79] See below, p. 80.

bargaining (but did not introduce any consequent legislation).[80] By the end of the 1940s, however, the quiescent pattern of inter-war behaviour on the part of the government had reasserted itself.

1.3. ABSTENTIONISM AND GOVERNMENT POLICY IN THE POST-WAR PERIOD

In the first section of this chapter we examined Kahn-Freund's analysis of the state of English labour law as it appeared to him in the early 1950s. We saw that his abstentionist analysis was very largely supported at a descriptive level, but that prescriptively the labour law system even of that time contained elements whose full theoretical reconciliation with a thoroughgoing abstentionist viewpoint was difficult to achieve. In the second section we supplemented our examination with a more historically based account of governmental policy in the first half of the century, at least so far as it pertained to the recognition of trade unions by employers for the purposes of collective bargaining. What tentative conclusions can be drawn from the discussion so far and what implications did they have for the post-war development of British labour law?

It seems, first, to be clear that there was no great divergence between governmental legislative and administrative action. From government's point of view these were tools to be employed to further government policy and, perhaps not surprisingly, in periods of state activism both tended to be employed and in periods of quietism, neither was. Second, the preference on the part of government for regulation of industrial relations via voluntary bargaining machinery emerges very strongly. This theme is given pride of place in the first edition of the Ministry of Labour and National Service's *Industrial Relations Handbook*, published in 1944. The Preface to the Handbook states the Ministry's position as follows:

It is important to recognize that the main responsibility for the regulation of wages and conditions of employment rests with the joint voluntary machinery established by employers' organisations and trade

[80] G. S. Bain, *The Growth of White-Collar Unionism* (Oxford, 1970), 155–8 and 175–6.

unions. Collective bargaining between employers and workpeople has for many years been recognised in this country as the method best adapted to the needs of industry, and to the demands of the national character, in the settlement of wages and conditions of employment. Although collective bargaining has thus become established as an integral part of the industrial system it has discharged its important function so smoothly and so unobtrusively that the extent of its influence is apt to be underestimated.

As to the government's attitude towards collective bargaining, 'since the 1870s the Government has recognised "collective bargaining" as the normal means of settling wages and working conditions and more recently has actively encouraged the establishment of joint agreed machinery of negotiation and consultation in industry.' Nevertheless, 'the central fact in the growth of industrial relations in this country has been the growth of voluntary organizations; the legislation is secondary. It is for these reasons that the Handbook gives first place to the development of joint negotiation between employers and employed.'[81]

Third, however, the thesis of state abstention from regulation of the sphere of employment and industrial relations emerges in much less clear-cut a manner than one might expect. Two periods of active state promotion of collective bargaining can be identified in the first half of the twentieth century. Indeed, given that the preferred model of bargaining was at national level on an industry-by-industry basis, rather than enterprise- or establishment-level bargaining, it may not be fanciful to see the trade boards and, later, wages councils legislation as the first British example of statutory recognition machinery, in design at least, if not always in terms of achievement. Of course, these periods of activism were brief and were associated with the abnormal conditions of mobilization for the two World Wars. However, it may be too narrow an explanation to view these as wartime emergency measures—after all, the first period of activism came largely after the First World War had ended. A broader view would be that government was unlikely to be happy—no matter how much in principle it thought such a stance to be correct—to leave the regulation of collective and individual employment relations entirely in the hands of employers and

---

[81] Ministry of Labour, *Industrial Relations Handbook* (3rd edn. 1961), 3 and 4.

trade unions, in situations where the government's view was that the voluntary system was failing to achieve—or, worse, was actually hindering the attainment of—goals to which government attached high priority.

Voluntarism was, of course, itself such a goal, but not necessarily and in all circumstances an overriding goal. Thus, governmental promotion of Whitleyism, which had district committee and works council components as well, though these never came to anything, was motivated by a desire that official unionism should be seen to offer an effective alternative to the militant unofficial shop-steward movement, and was thus an indication that the government was not indifferent to the aims and modalities of the voluntary system. The interesting question is, perhaps, not about whether the government would ever seek to regulate the voluntary system, but about what it would regard as a sufficient reason for attempting such regulation. For example, in the late 1920s and 1930s, as we have seen, the government refused to use legislation to prop up the tottering national bargaining system. In the absence of a militant shop-floor challenge, the government seemed now relatively indifferent to the fate of the official bargaining machinery, since it took the view that the competitiveness of British goods would be enhanced by allowing wages to drift downwards, and it required a governmental need for trade union co-operation in the Second World War to produce a change in the government's attitude.

Although we have looked at changes in governmental policy in the inter-war period mainly in relation to the promotion of union recognition, there was evidence that the other elements of abstentionism could come under challenge. Thus we saw that modifications were made to the 1906 trade dispute laws by the Trade Disputes and Trade Unions Act 1927, and these would probably have been more extensive had the defeat of the unions in the General Strike not been so complete. In the early period, when the government was promoting Whitleyism against unofficial trade unionism, it was also taking steps to modify trade dispute law: the police were deprived of the legal freedom to strike by the Police Act 1919; existing prohibitions in the gas and electricity industries on striking in breach of contract were extended to electricity supply by the Electricity Act 1919; and general powers to deal with emergency disputes were enacted in the Emergency Powers Act 1920, a direct response to the threat of industrial action from the 'triple Alliance' of railway, mining, and transport unions. Finally, the promotion of union recognition in the Second World War was accompanied by restrictions of an extensive kind upon participation in industrial action. So abstention might be the policy the government preferred, but it was a policy and not an accident. Like any other policy, it might be changed if it was thought by the government not to be working. What, however, in the post-war period might lead the government to such a conclusion?

The history of the inter-war period might be taken to suggest that simply to demonstrate that there were deficiencies in the operation of the bargaining system from the unions' or workers' point of view would not by itself be enough to induce governmental intervention. Undoubtedly, such deficiencies could be pointed to, both in relation to the scope of union membership and the range of matters bargained over. Outside government service the percentage of white-collar workers who were unionized was low. In 1967 it was estimated that overall only 30 per cent of white-collar workers were unionized (and in private manufacturing industry the percentage was as low as 10), whilst 50 per cent of manual workers were unionized, and it was thought that the figures for white-collar workers had not changed since 1948.[82] Consequently, the coverage of collective bargaining for white-collar workers was correspondingly less. Given the changing composition of the workforce in favour of white-collar and against manual work, these statistics became a cause of concern in the 1960s for the Royal Commission on Trade Unions and Employers' Associations.[83] Equally startling was the disparity between the rates of trade union membership for men and women: in 1951 56 per cent of male workers were members of trade unions, but only 27 per cent of females.[84] It took much longer, however, even perhaps until the 1980s, for the significance of this fact to come home to trade unions. Only then did the steady post-war growth of part-time (and largely female) workers impinge upon unions' recruitment and bargaining strategies in a major way.

[82] Royal Commission on Trade Unions and Employers' Associations, Research Paper 6 (1967), 28–9.
[83] Report of the Royal Commission on Trade Unions and Employers' Associations, Cmnd. 3623 (1968), paras. 213–24, 253–6.
[84] Ministry of Labour, *Industrial Relations Handbook* (3rd edn., 1961), 11.

The subject-matter coverage of collective bargaining could also be shown up as rather limited. At the outset of our period the system of collective bargaining was predominantly based upon national-level machinery, as the 1944 *Handbook* suggests by its reference to voluntary machinery established by 'employers' organizations' and trade unions. Multi-employer bargaining was notorious for the limited range of its substantive concerns: often only the length of the standard working week and wage rates (including overtime and shift premia), together with holiday entitlement.[85] Even after the post-war development of single-employer bargaining (with its much wider range of substantive concerns), collective bargaining still by and large confined itself to the area of terms and conditions of employment. There was no general penetration by collective bargaining into managerial decisions relevant to the employment prospects of the company—which would be, indeed, a very wide range of managerial decisions. It might be asked, however, whether even the most refined and sophisticated system of bargaining over terms and conditions of employment was adequate if employees had no input into managerial decisions which affected the issue of whether there were to be any jobs to the occupants of which the collectively agreed terms could be applied. If this were thought to be an inadequacy in current collective bargaining, the question would then arise of whether collective bargaining could effectively be expanded to cover these new subject-matters or whether such a fundamental attack upon managerial prerogatives could be achieved only by means of legally required mechanisms.

Thus we can see that, in the post-war period, various questions could be raised about the continuing effectiveness of voluntary collective bargaining and about the possible role of the law in redressing any perceived inadequacies in the voluntary system. So far, however, the problems we have discussed all concerned the ability of the system to achieve the goals it had set for itself, and that by itself, inter-war history suggested, might not be enough to produce governmental intervention. What might be needed in addition was a perception by government that the

---

[85] In 1966 Marsh referred to the 'tendency in the British system for the parties to rely for their relationships upon mere frameworks of substantive rules and to improvise their detailed joint regulation upon procedural handling of grievances': Royal Commission on Trade Unions and Employers' Associations, Research Paper 2.1 (London, 1966), 17.

deficiencies in the voluntary system were impeding the government's achievement of policies which, willy-nilly, it had come to accept as enshrining its responsibilities. What were the relevant policies that emerged in the post-war period and in which ways did they challenge the policy of abstention towards industrial society on the part of the state? We suggest there were two such broad categories of policy.

(a) Citizenship and Individual Rights

It was inherent in the voluntary system that not every employee in every workplace would be covered by collective bargaining. Some employers would always successfully resist the pressures for union recognition. In other cases recognition might mean little in practice because of the employer's attitude to bargaining, the inadequate resources of the union, the lack of membership among the workforce, or some combination of these factors. As we have said, this problem is inherent in a policy of reliance by the state upon the efforts of independent social groups, especially as English employers, if never so bitterly hostile to unionism as many American employers had been, could not be relied upon to be natural supporters of the principle of collectivizing employment relations. Has any collective bargaining system in a free society ever achieved 100 per cent coverage of the workforce at a uniform level of protection? Being inherent in the voluntary system, the problem was also not a new one in the post-war period. On the contrary, with the post-war growth of collective bargaining and, eventually, of union membership, the problem could be thought to have become *less* pressing than it had been during the depression of the 1930s. And yet the issue of whether the state should guarantee a level of protection to the individual employee, primarily, but not exclusively, the employee in the non- or weakly-unionized establishment, was one of the major debates in labour law in the post-war period. Acceptance of the argument that at least partial guarantees should be provided by the state led to a substantial intervention by the law into direct regulation of the employment relationship.

Why should this development have occurred? No doubt an important background factor was the decline of belief in the virtues of freedom of contract. So long as that doctrine held sway, there would be a reluctance on the part of the state to regulate the individual contract of employment, on the one hand, whilst, on the other, regulation of the individual relationship via a collective contracting process would be more acceptable. It is perhaps significant that the Webbs, writing at the turn of the century, represented collective bargaining as 'exactly what the words imply: a collective equivalent and alternative to individual bargaining [which enabled workers] to secure better terms by controlling competition among themselves'.[86] Although this view has been criticized by modern writers as inadequate,[87] it was a natural one to present in a society still strongly influenced by notions of freedom of contract. However, at the very moment the Webbs were writing, freedom of contract was losing its hold on English political thought. As Atiyah has put it: 'Gladstonian liberalism gave way to Asquithian liberalism, and with it there came an increasing concern for the under-privileged and the poor, an increasing willingness to enact paternalistic legislation, an increasing acceptance of the redistributive nature of much social legislation.'[88] For him, it is 'plain that the late 1880s virtually saw the end of freedom of contract as a political slogan, capable of swaying opinion to any great degree'.[89]

And yet the impact of the decline of freedom of contract upon the system of collective *laissez-faire* was relatively modest up until the outbreak of the Second World War, the main examples being the trade boards' legislation and the Fair Wages Resolutions,[90] and developments outside labour law proper in the adjacent fields of workmen's compensation and the beginning of a social security system in the period before the First World War. As Fox has suggested, this situation may have resulted from the view that the one-sided nature of the contract at the individual level was legitimated by the institution of collective bargaining.

In so far as trade unionism appeared to offer redress of that inequality between master and man which some were now prepared to acknowledge, collective bargaining could be held as providing legitimation for a

[86] A. Flanders' description of the Webbs' view in *Management and Unions* (London, 1970), 215. Flanders was commenting on S. and B. Webb, *Industrial Democracy* (London, 1902).
[87] Flanders, *Management and Unions*, 216–66.
[88] P. Atiyah, *The Rise and Fall of Freedom of Contract* (Oxford, 1979), 583.
[89] Ibid. 587.
[90] See above, Sect. 1.2.

system characterized by extreme division of function, mobility of resources, and free contract. Labour might be a commodity, but given collective bargaining it sold its services under fair regulative procedures which removed what had admittedly been a genuine grievance.[91]

However this may be, the negative factor of the collapse of belief in freedom of contract in the last decades of the nineteenth century was not enough to produce extensive state intervention directly to regulate the employment relationship. That had to await the post-war growth of what Selznick has referred to as an enlarged notion of citizenship. Citizenship was now conceived as going beyond notions such as the right to vote and the freedom to stand for public office, to embrace '(1) new expectations of what public government should do, including the opportunities it should create for individual betterment and self-esteem; (2) the notion that "full citizenship" means effective participation in an entire opportunity structure, social and economic, as well as in the formal political process; and (3) the recognition that private relationships decisively affect the achievement of full citizenship'.[92]

Obviously, a very great deal of what the state was now expected to do in order to achieve the goals of an enlarged concept of citizenship was to take place outside the realm of labour law, a point to which we shall turn in a moment. Expanded state activity in the areas of education, housing, and health care would be obvious examples, and one can see such activity in Britain in the immediate post-war period. At this time the Education Act 1944 was passed, a National Health Service was established, and there were the great housing drives of the 1950s. Even within the general area of what in European law is usually referred to as social policy, the impact of the new ideas was felt in the area of social security law (with the post-war plans, inspired by Beveridge,[93] to generalize and centralize the social insurance system) before it reached labour law proper. Yet the notion of an enlarged citizenship did eventually reach labour law and challenge the older ideals of collective *laissez-faire*. One can detect

---

[91] A. Fox, *Beyond Contract: Work, Power and Trust Relations* (London, 1974), 205.
[92] P. Selznick, *Law, Society and Industrial Justice* (New York, 1969), 249.
[93] See Social Insurance and Allied Services, Cmnd. 6404 (1942).

echoes of the idea of 'effective participation in an entire opportunity structure' in the debates on industrial democracy, for
example, but we suggest that the major, direct impact of the
notion of citizenship upon labour law was not the result of a new
emphasis upon participation. Rather, the ideas which seem to
have had the most substantial impact upon the positive law
were those of protection against arbitrary treatment, on the one
hand, and of equality or, in its usual legal formulation, of non-
discrimination, on the other, together with some extension of the
notion of non-discrimination into the area of equal opportunities.
The two ideas overlap to a large degree at a conceptual level,
although in terms of policy formation in post-war Britain they
tended to have rather separate sources of support, the great
monument to the former concept being the unfair dismissal
legislation and to the latter the laws against sexual and racial
discrimination.

As our use of a quotation from the American sociologist of
law, Selznick, suggests, these strains towards a broader idea of
citizenship were part of a general movement in Western industrialized societies in our period. Thus Eliane Vogel-Polsky,
analysing the law on termination of the contract of employment
in Europe in the period up to 1945, concludes that 'the basic and
important principle that termination of employment must be
motivated by a fair reason . . . in the period of our study . . . had
not been generally accepted.'[94] Looking at the post-war period,
also on a comparative basis, Bob Hepple can say, however, that
'the German Protection against Dismissals Act 1950, introducing
the concept of "sociably unjustified" dismissals, was an influential
post-war landmark, but most of the legislation dates from the
1960s and was strongly encouraged by the ILO Recommendation
no. 119 of 1963', so that 'the great majority of countries today
have explicit legislative requirements that dismissals must be for
justified reasons'.[95] Again in relation to discrimination legislation,
Leslie Scarman, writing in 1974, saw the challenge to English law
from 'the Human Rights movement' at that time almost entirely
in terms of the embodiment of human rights values in interna-

---

[94] In B. Hepple, ed., *The Making of Labour Law in Europe* (London, 1986),
192.
[95] In R. Blanpain, ed., *Comparative Labour Law and Industrial Relations* (3rd
edn., Deventer, The Netherlands, 1987), 497.

tional instruments to which the UK was a party—international instruments predominantly of the post-war period.[96]

A further dimension of this development has been the penetration of principles of public law into the private area. Thus Selznick, from whose study we have quoted, set out to answer the question: 'can we justify, within the framework of legal theory, the application to private organizations of principles hitherto restricted to public government?' The argument for so doing was that administrative law was essentially the law for controlling the exercise of power within bureaucracies, and administrative law therefore 'should address itself to the similar institutions of the private sector',[97] so that the rule of law could be introduced into an otherwise inadequately regulated sphere. Similarly, in respect of laws against discrimination, T. Ramm has emphasized, even in relation to countries with long-standing constitutional prohibitions upon discrimination, that the crucial issue for 'modern antidiscriminatory law' was 'how the step was taken from the prohibition of legal discrimination within the field of public law to state intervention in order to avoid social discrimination'.[98]

For this study, however, the most significant issue concerns the challenges posed by these intellectual and doctrinal developments for the theory of collective *laissez-faire* as, in Kahn-Freund's words, the 'characteristic peculiar to the British industrial scene'.[99] In essence the problem for the voluntary system lay in the notion that individuals had a right to be protected against arbitrary or discriminatory treatment. This protection did not necessarily have to be conferred by statute law—Selznick's definition of law was certainly broad enough to encompass rules derived from collective agreements—but a general right to protection on an individual basis certainly set a standard of achievement which the voluntary system found it hard to meet. This was

---

[96] L. Scarman, *English Law: The New Dimension* (London, 1974), 14. He referred especially to the European Convention on Human Rights of 1950, the UN's Declaration of Human Rights of 1948, and the Declaration of Philadelphia of 1946, restating the objectives of the ILO.

[97] Selznick, *Law, Society and Industrial Justice*, 243–4. See also the stimulating essay by Hugh Collins, 'Against Abstentionism in Labour Law', in J. Eekelaar and J. Bell, eds., *Oxford Essays in Jurisprudence*, 3rd ser. (Oxford, 1987), 79.

[98] In F. Schmidt, ed., *Discrimination in Employment* (Stockholm, 1978), 36.

[99] Above, p. 9.

so both because the voluntary system found it difficult to provide comprehensive protection, but also because the protection of the collective agreement often lay within the control of the parties (employers and unions) to that agreement, and so it did not confer an *entitlement* to protection upon the individual employee.[100] As we shall see later on, in the UK, after fierce argument, the case was accepted in the late 1960s for individual statutory protection against unfair dismissal, and so statutory rules appeared alongside the norms of collective bargaining as, so to speak, competitors in the task of regulating the individual employment relationship. By the same token the UK took a step away from collective *laissez-faire* and towards the legal position of those states which had traditionally engaged in direct statutory regulation of the employment relationship and for whom the new developments posed less of a problem of adjustment.

It may be said that to describe the new statutory rules as competitors is to go too far. Cannot individual employment law, in Professor Wedderburn's phrase, be seen as creating a 'floor of rights',[101] upon which the voluntary system could freely build in those situations where the trade unions' bargaining power or employer policies permitted it? Although the notion of a floor of rights gives us a valuable perspective upon these laws, difficult issues of the relationship between the legal rights of the individual and the operations of the voluntary collective structures were bound to arise, as we shall see. For example, the argument for individual protection against arbitrary and discriminatory treatment applied as strongly to trade unions as to managerial bureaucracies, perhaps even more strongly if the democratic rationale for collective bargaining were taken seriously.[102] But if this were accepted as a rationale for legislative action, the law would be regulating the internal affairs of the workers' collective

---

[100] This issue has been much discussed in the legally regulated bargaining system of the USA. See e.g. C. Summers, 'Individual Rights in Collective Agreements and Arbitration' (1962) 37 NYU Law. Rev. 362. For an English discussion in the context of exemption of voluntary procedures from the unfair dismissal legislation, see S. D. Anderman, *Voluntary Dismissal Procedures and the Industrial Relations Act* (PEP Broadsheet 1538; London, 1972), 68–74.

[101] K. W. Wedderburn, *The Worker and the Law* (3rd edn., Harmondsworth, 1986), 6.

[102] See P. Elias and K. Ewing, *Trade Union Democracy, Members' Rights and the Law* (London, 1987), ch. 8.

bargaining representative, and so be involved in the operation of the voluntary collective machinery. Again, how was the law to approach the questions of the fairness of the dismissal of strikers or of those who refused to join a union, or of the expulsion from a union of a non-striker? All these became deeply controversial issues in the post-war period, as we shall see; all we need note here is their undoubtedly collective dimension and their potential impact upon the operation of the voluntary machinery.[103]

The challenge of individual employment law to the collective structures was, however, potentially even greater. In the case of unfair dismissal legislation, the argument for statutory protection was that the voluntary machinery was providing an inadequate level of protection, but at least the voluntary machinery and the statute were engaged on broadly the same task. In the case of laws against discrimination, this was not obviously the case. Ramm has put the point in the following way:[104]

Let us begin with the distinction between the two labour law systems based upon 'self-help' and 'state-intervention'. Evidently self-help does not work satisfactorily as a means of solving the discrimination questions, if we observe the small importance of collective agreements in this field. The explanation is simple: if discrimination has expatiated upon the population then the representatives of the trade unions, the works councils and the shop stewards normally are just the mirror of the population. They cannot be better or more enlightened than the workers on whom they are dependent for their election. They might even be more involved in prejudice than the employer who, as a single person because of his position, may sometimes 'make an exception' for individual reasons while members of a group support each other in their prejudices. Social protection of discriminatees by the institutions of self-help therefore meets the natural barriers of a democratic system: the interests, opinions and prejudices of the majority. These institutions are insufficient for the protection of minorities. We may therefore say that antidiscriminatory law is the domain of state intervention.

Although the argument might be thought to be overstated, to the extent that it is true it suggests that regulation of the collective structures is not an incidental but an integral part of providing

---

[103] For an extended discussion see K. W. Wedderburn, 'Discrimination in the Right to Organise and the Right to be a Non-Unionist', in Schmidt, ed., *Discrimination in Employment*.

[104] In Schmidt, ed., *Discrimination in Employment*, 518.

protection against discriminatory acts. From this perspective, collective agreements and legislative rules are not partners in an attack upon discrimination, as in the case of unfair dismissal, but rather the collective machinery becomes one of a number of objects of statutory regulation in the name of equality. To the extent that this is so, both dimensions of the theory of collective *laissez-faire* come under pressure: the freedom of operation of the collective parties as much as the absence of state regulation of the individual employment relationship.

A related, equally important, point is that anti-discrimination legislation provides an example of the agenda for labour law no longer being set by the concerns of the industrial parties. On the contrary, it was the introduction of legislation that eventually spurred the parties to collective agreements to take these issues more seriously. We make this point, not by way of criticism of the bargainers, but to show how the proper scope of labour law was perceived to be limited so long as its sole task was seen to lie in the definition of the correct relationship between government and legal institutions, on the one hand, and the institutions of collective self-regulation on the other. The identification of additional tasks for labour law in relation to the interests of individual employees enabled the legislator to tap a major new source of legitimacy for the legal system in the employment field. In terms of the number of cases handled, legislation against unfair dismissal was the most important development, but in terms of the developing autonomy of the legal system from the precepts of collective *laissez-faire*, the anti-discrimination legislation can claim to have been the more significant.

(b) Economic Citizenship and Collective Bargaining

The development of the idea that individuals should have rights to protection against arbitrary and discriminatory conduct, which were not dependent either upon the existence of an effective collective agreement or upon the willingness of the union to process the claim where such an agreement did exist, provided, therefore, a potentially far-reaching challenge to the structures and ideals of collective *laissez-faire*. This development was also the most obvious way in which broader ideas of citizenship posed new challenges to the structure of post-war labour law. However, we would wish to argue that there was another aspect of the broader notion of citizenship that Selznick identified which we must also take into account because of the challenges it posed to collective *laissez-faire*. These challenges were at first sight more indirect than those we have discussed in the previous pages, but in the end they probably had a more profound impact upon the structure of labour law.

We would suggest that in the post-war period an important element of the 'new expectations of what public government should do, including the opportunities it should create for individual betterment and self-esteem' was public demand, and governmental acceptance, that the state take responsibility for the availability of jobs for those who wished to work. This principle was expressed in the famous White Paper of 1944 in which the government undertook to maintain 'a high and stable level' of employment.[105] At first sight this new political commitment posed no challenge to the structures and policies of collective *laissez-faire* because, following the strategy of Keynes, the governmental mechanisms for ensuring full employment came to be seen as lying in the adoption of appropriate macro-enonomic measures by the Treasury rather than in the extension into peacetime of the extensive labour market controls that the Ministry of Labour had acquired during the War.

Nevertheless, the arrival of full employment did pose profound indirect challenges to collective *laissez-faire*. The state always ran some risks in relying upon the voluntary system to settle terms and conditions of employment. One obvious risk arose from the fact that, in the absence of compulsory arbitration, unions depended for their success in collective bargaining upon their ability to make a credible threat of industrial action. To be sure, in order to enable that threat to be deployed without, in most cases, industrial action being called for, the bargaining parties had developed sophisticated negotiating procedures, which were supplemented by the state through the provision of conciliation and arbitration services on a non-compulsory basis. In other words, the principle of autonomy prevailed in relation to dispute settlement as much as in other aspects of collective relations, but it might be speculated that this policy would come under pressure, if full employment led to much higher levels of industrial conflict

---

[105] See below, ch. 2.3.

because, on the one hand, full employment reduced the costs to employees of industrial action and, on the other, it raised their expectations as to the benefits the bargaining system ought to produce for them. If, moreover, the employees' expectations as to the benefits to be derived from the bargaining system expressed themselves significantly in terms of wage increases, another risk for the state might materialize, this time from the government's lack of influence in a voluntary system over the outcomes of bargaining. Indeed, as we shall see, it was the inflationary consequences of free collective bargaining in a situation of full employment that worried the government's advisors in the immediate post-war period more than the frictional harms from industrial conflict.

Thus it is possible to perceive, at least with hindsight, that governments might be tempted to counterbalance the advantages produced by full employment for workers and trade unions in the voluntary systems with legal restrictions of one sort or another upon the freedom of action of the collective parties, so as to restore an equilibrium thought to have obtained before the advent of full employment. However, the potential of the indirect challenge of full employment to collective *laissez-faire* went further than that, far-reaching though such a development might be. As governments in the post-war period came to be judged electorally more and more on their performance in managing the domestic economy, and as it came to be perceived that many of the strains produced by full employment could be managed more easily in an economy that produced steady economic growth, so governments might demand that the system of industrial relations make a positive contribution to the achievement of growth targets. Active manpower and labour market policies of one sort or another might then be contemplated which would provide yet another layer of challenge to the ideas of collective *laissez-faire*.

Indeed, at this point we reach perhaps a general issue of profound significance. It is important to recall that at the outset of our period the British state's relationship with the industrial relations system was a strong, but not unique, example of the state's general relations with the British economy. Fox has suggested that the state's relationship with the industrial relations system at this time reflected 'the long persistence of the limited state, which allowed the pace of much, though not all, social and legislative change to be set by "voluntary" (that is, non-state) associations, groups or movements, either acting by themselves or bringing pressure to bear upon governments'.[106] Writing in a more critical vein, Andrew Shonfield, in an influential book published in 1965, *Modern Capitalism: The Changing Balance of Public and Private Power*, attacked the traditional view whereby 'anything which smacked of a restless or over-energetic state, with ideas of guiding the nation on the basis of a long view of its collective economic interest, was instinctively the object of suspicion'.[107] He naturally included within his attack the system of collective *laissez-faire* in industrial relations (see, in particular, his powerful Note of Reservation to the Royal Commission's Report[108]), but that attack ranged generally over successive governments' economic and industrial policies and, in particular, their failure to plan effectively the public and, even more interesting, the private sectors of the economy. As such attacks upon the 'limited state' bore fruit in the post-war period, the abstentionist stance of the law in particular and of the government in general towards industrial relations was called increasingly into question. Could government accept political responsibility for the success of the economy whilst leaving the pace of industrial change to be determined by others?

We have thus identified three main themes which we shall explore in the remainder of this book. The first is whether changes in the economy and in society were occurring such that the achievement by the voluntary system of its traditional goals was becoming less possible without legislative support. The second is how the voluntary system and the state responded to the new demands that were articulated in the post-war period, especially in relation to employee participation in decision-making and in relation to individual protection against arbitrary and discriminatory treatment and, indeed, the promotion of equality of opportunity. The third is how governments viewed the operation of the voluntary system in the new situation of full

---

[106] A. Fox, *History and Heritage: The Social Origins of the British Industrial Relations System*, (London, 1985), 373.

[107] At p. 88. See also more recently D. Marquand, *The Unprincipled Society* (London, 1988), ch. 1.

[108] Cmnd. 3623 (1968), at 288.

employment and the greater electoral emphasis on sustained economic growth. We are far from saying that each post-war government gave equal attention to each of these themes; and we are certainly far from saying that the policies developed by post-war governments in response to the problems, as they identified them, were similar. On the contrary, those policies ranged from doing almost nothing (on the grounds that the present system might not be ideal but reforming it would make it worse), through attempts of various sorts to reform and supplement the collective bargaining system, to policies whose aim was to downgrade collective settlement of terms and conditions of employment in favour of alternative mechanisms. The only common theme of the post-war policies seems to have been that, as time passed, the policies adopted by successive governments tended to become more radical. That, however, is to take us beyond the scope of this chapter. All we need note here is that each of the developments we have identified posed a powerful set of problems for traditional collective *laissez-faire*; cumulatively, they destroyed it.

The problems posed were particularly difficult for the traditional system to respond to where they resulted from a process of reasoning and criticism that had its basis ouside the assumptions and conventions of the collective bargaining system itself. However, whether the starting-point for questioning the autonomy of the collective bargaining system was an internal or an external one, there is no doubt that the cumulative effect of the criticisms was to destroy collective *laissez-faire* within a remarkably short time after Kahn-Freund, with acclaim from employees, unions, and government, had written its eulogium. In the succeeding chapters we shall chronicle that process, and attempt also to answer the difficult question of how one analyses the structure of legal rules that has replaced the traditional framework of labour law.

2

FULL EMPLOYMENT
AND THE POST-WAR
CONSENSUS, 1945 – 1951

We begin our analysis of the post-war development of British
labour law by looking at the immediate aftermath of the Second
World War. It is in many ways a period that confirms the significance of collective *laissez-faire* as the central feature of
government's relations with industrial society. One of the two
outstanding features of this period from our point of view is that
the enormous apparatus of state intervention into the operation
of the labour market and into the conduct of collective bargaining
that had been built up during the war was dismantled after
hostilities had ceased. That apparatus was not used, as some
might have hoped, as a basis for a new and permanent recasting
of the role of the law in regulating the conduct of industrial
society. To be sure, that state apparatus was so extensive and the
change from a wartime to a peacetime economy so far-reaching
that the wartime controls could not be done away with at a stroke
when peace was achieved. The Ministry of Labour made some
use of its labour market controls throughout the 1940s, and the
removal of the prohibitions on striking did not occur until 1951.
Nevertheless, the tendency towards the dismantling of the wartime regime was clear, and when Kahn-Freund came to analyse
the British system in the early 1950s in terms of collective *laissez-
faire*, he was able to regard the wartime structures as belonging
to a chapter of history that was by then more or less closed.[1]

Hence it is conventional wisdom to regard the wartime legisla-

[1] The main feature of the wartime system continuing into the 1950s was the
system of compulsory arbitration, but now without the concomitant prohibitions
on striking. See above, p. 21 and below, Subsect. 2.3(*b*)(i). The extent of the
government's labour market powers during the war is well described in Ministry
of Labour and National Service, *Report for the Years 1939–1946*, Cmd. 7225
(1947), chs. 1 and 7–11.

tion as a temporary intrusion of interventionist mechanisms into a system of labour law and labour relations that was able eventually to reject these foreign bodies. The temporary and emergency character of the wartime legislation is emphasized by its having been made largely by means of orders under the Emergency Powers (Defence) Acts 1939 and 1940. We do not dispute this view, but it is important to note that the wartime experience (if not the legislation itself) produced one fundamental change which was of lasting significance to governments in the post-war period in their attitudes towards the voluntary system of collective bargaining. This was the arrival, both as a fact and as a policy objective of government, of full employment. As we indicated in the previous chapter, full employment posed a number of potential challenges to the ideals of collective *laissez-faire*, especially that dimension of it which counselled non-intervention by the government in the operation of the voluntary bargaining machinery, and we shall examine in this chapter the emergence of those challenges in the immediate post-war years. Before turning to that task (the main one of this chapter), however, we should note what influence in the years 1945 to 1951 was exercised by the other pressures which we have identified as operating on the doctrine of collective *laissez-faire* in the post-war period.

2.1. INDIVIDUAL RIGHTS

(a) Labour Law

The idea that the state should guarantee to individual employees legal protection against arbitrary and discriminatory treatment had little impact upon labour law in this period. This was to be a development of the 1960s and later. Nevertheless, we should note briefly two legislative developments of a general character and one confined to the public sector which suggested that it was not impossible to generate pressures for governmental action that would trench upon the general philosophy of leaving individual contracts to be regulated through collective bargaining.

The two general developments had their political origins in a desire to do justice for those who had contributed to the war effort but who in consequence might find re-entry into the civilian labour market difficult. These two Acts were in fact early examples of what we might now call 'positive discrimination' in favour of what was seen as a disadvantaged group. The Reinstatement in Civil Employment Act 1944, in the event relatively little used in the circumstances of full employment which prevailed, required employers to take former employees back into their previous employments upon the ending of their war service 'at the first opportunity (if any) at which it is reasonable and practicable for the former employer so to do'[2] and to employ them for at least twenty-six weeks in that capacity;[3] that is, the Act created a system of hiring preferences in respect of former employees who had been away on war service. The tripartite Reinstatement Committees, to which disputes were referred, had the power to order the employer to offer employment to an applicant (as well as a power to order compernsation), and failure to comply with this order was a criminal offence on the part of the employer.[4] It is interesting that, in the wartime context, and in contrast with later developments, it was thought unobjectionable to use criminal sanctions to support reinstatement orders.

The second general Act, of the same year, was the Disabled Persons (Employment) Act 1944. Although applying to disabled persons generally, it seems clear that the political support for the measure in Parliament derived largely from a desire to help those disabled in war service. This category of the disabled, contrary to the government's initial proposals and as a result of back-bench pressure, was given a preference over other disabled persons in access to vocational training and industrial rehabilitation facilities.[5] As far as employment was concerned, the Act made it a criminal offence for an employer to take into employment, or to offer to employ, a person other than a disabled person so long as the employer had in its employment fewer disabled persons than were required by the quota fixed for it by the Ministry of Labour.[6] Similar provisions applied to dismissals, except for 'reasonable cause'.

[2] S. 1(2).
[3] S. 4(1).
[4] S. 11.
[5] S. 16. See also HC Deb., vol. 396, cols. 106-15 (18 Jan. 1944).
[6] S. 9(2) and (5). In 1946 the quota was fixed at 3% for employers employing 20 or more workers. Unlike the Reinstatement Act, the Disabled Persons Act did not aim to deal with a purely transitional problem, and yet it seems that the

The TUC displayed no objections of principle to the legislation and even envisaged a somewhat wider role for individual employment laws when it pressed, unsuccessfully, in 1946 for legislation to implement the 40-hour week and to provide two weeks' holiday with pay to all workers.[7] (These ends were in fact secured quite quickly by collective bargaining.[8]) Indeed, in one specific and now largely forgotten area the TUC had a signal victory in the 1940s in extending individual employment rights. In the Civil Service in the early nineteenth century, when Civil Service jobs—or offices—were in some real sense regarded as the property of their holders, it became the practice to compensate employees who were deprived of their jobs as a result of legislation. In the 1880s the principle was extended to local government, and in the early twentieth century to job losses caused by the statutory reorganizations of the railway and electricity industries. What practice would be followed in the extensive nationalization programme envisaged by the post-war government? The government, arguing that compensation in conditions of full employment was anachronistic, wished to confine it to the services in which it had traditionally been paid, but under TUC pressure was forced to concede it to all workers in all the industries that were nationalized and to embrace cases of 'worsening of position' (e.g. demotion) as well as job loss as compensable events. Compared with contemporary private industry practice (which did not recognise redundancy as a compensable event at all) or even with the later (1965) general statutory scheme, which provided for lump-sum compensation, the 'Crombie Code' for compensation upon nationalization was generous. The essence of the compensation was continuing compensation until retirement age (with compensation on a lower basis thereafter until death), based upon one-sixtieth of the loss for each year of service plus an additional one-sixtieth for each year over the age of 45 (subject

pressure behind the scheme was reduced once the wartime disabled had been accomodated. By the late 1980s only 24 per cent of employers met the quota requirement, about 25 per cent of employers had never heard of the quota requirement, and use of criminal sanctions seemed minimal: Department of Employment, *Consultative Document on Employment and Training for People with Disabilities* (1990), 36–8, 105. It might be said that non-intervention thus reasserted itself at the level of enforcement of this piece of legislation.

[7] TUC, *Annual Report 1946* (London), 183–6.

[8] Ministry of Labour and National Service, *Industrial Relations Handbook* (2nd edn., 1953), 166.

to a maximum of two-thirds of the total loss), with only relatively limited opportunities for government to review the compensation after two years had passed.[9] The Crombie Code was thus a genuine attempt, at least for the older or long-serving employee, to provide permanent income replacement in a way that the general unemployment benefit scheme never did (because it was essentially a short-term scheme) even when it was expanded and supplemented by a redundancy payments scheme in the 1960s. Two further, and perhaps contrasting, reflections are suggested by this account of the Crombie Code. The first is that it indicated how, behind an essentially common set of legal rules, public sector employees were thought by both unions and employers to be entitled to rather greater protection against the vicissitudes of working life than were the general run of private sector employees. The second is that TUC pressure for the Crombie scheme suggested that, should government wish to expand general individual employment rights in this way (as it did in the 1960s), it would not meet with any strong opposition from the trade unions, even if collective *laissez-faire* were thereby and to that extent qualified.

(b) Social Security Law

We have seen that within the area of labour law proper the development of individual legal rights made little headway in this period. This was in sharp contrast with what was happening in the adjacent field of what we would today call social security law, then more commonly, and significantly, referred to as the area of 'social insurance'. There developments flowed from a government inquiry and report, *Social Insurance and Allied Services*[10] of

[9] For a detailed account of the TUC pressure on the government see Sir N. Chester, *The Nationalisation of British Industry, 1945–51* (London, 1975), 747–82. The Crombie code was first embodied in the Local Government (Compensation) Regulations 1948 (SI 1948, No. 1458), but was applied under all the nationalization statutes. There is a parallel here with developments in US law. Selznick (*Law, Society and Industrial Justice* (New York, 1969) 222 ff.) notes 'how regulation of employment may emerge as an incident of other [governmental] commitments', citing the Interstate Commerce Commission's power, from 1933 onwards, to protect employees' acquired rights when railroads were merged. Such 'indirect' regulation avoided a head-on challenge to the bargainers' autonomy.

[10] Cmd. 6404. This report is the one generally referred to as 'the' Beveridge report. In fact, of greater interest to us is his later study of full employment (below, p. 72). The later study was a private one, in part because Beveridge had

1942, which was conducted by William Beveridge. Our interest is not in the details of this report, but in the implications it had for other areas of government policy. In fact, the 1942 Report, in so far as it concerned itself with the welfare state narrowly conceived, was a relatively modest document. First, the principle of income support in times of unavailability of or for work was widely recognized in pre-war Britain, but through a 'complex of disconnected administrative organs',[11] which Beveridge wished to systematize and generalize. The National Health Service was the principal novel addition that resulted from the Beveridge Report and that, of course, was a concept much influenced also by the thoughts and actions of Aneurin Bevan, the post-war Minister of Health.[12] Second, Beveridge insisted, wherever possible, upon the principle of social (or compulsory) insurance as the method of financing benefits and proposed keeping payments from general tax revenues to a minimum. This again emphasized continuities with existing practice.

Although social insurance was a relatively modest and, indeed, already widely accepted principle, it was for Beveridge 'one part only of a comprehensive policy of social progress'. In his famous words: 'Social insurance fully developed may provide income security; it is an attack upon Want. But Want is one only of five giants on the road of reconstruction and in some ways the easiest to attack. The others are Disease, Ignorance, Squalor and Idleness.'[13] On can see, thus, why Beveridge was keen to extend his activities into the field of full employment (to deal with Idleness), and how a full account of the working-out of his ideas would have to include the Education Act 1944 and the Town and Country Planning Act 1947, as well as the 1944 White Paper, the National Health Service and the National Insurance and National Assistance Acts. This we have no space to do here, but we do need to ask what influence the overarching idea which could be said to underlie these various distinct pieces of legislation had upon the doctrine of collective *laissez-faire* in relation to labour

campaigned so hard to secure acceptance of his earlier report by the somewhat reluctant members of the wartime coalition government that the Prime Minister would not countenance another official inquiry by him: J. Harris, *William Beveridge: A Biography* (Oxford, 1977), 434–5.

[11] Ibid., para. 3.

[12] J. Campbell, *Nye Bevan* (London, 1987), ch. 12.

[13] Cmd. 6406, para. 8.

law. That idea can be said to be that the state should take active steps to guarantee its citizens not merely a minimum level of income no matter what the vicissitudes of life but also a minimum standard of quality of life in terms of access to medical care, education, and housing. It was an idea, and this is its importance to us, which was not by any means Beveridge's unique property but was quite generally advanced at the time by progressive forces in society, and it was an idea which, being dependent upon state activism, was the very antithesis of collective *laissez-faire*, that is of leaving the pace and direction of economic and social change to employers and trade unions.

It is perhaps for this reason that the TUC's Annual Reports of this period keep the discussion of social insurance, on the one hand, and of collective bargaining and full employment, on the other, in separate boxes. Whilst warmly welcoming Beveridge's 1942 Report as likely to improve the lives of trade unionists in general, the TUC attached greater importance to collective bargaining and full employment issues, which, of course, were the daily concerns of trade unions in the way that the state social security system was not. In the short and medium term this dichotomy proved sustainable, albeit at the cost of conceding to the state areas in which collective bargaining, or some analogous form of trade union action, might have developed. Thus British collective agreements never developed the richness of provision of North American agreements on matters such as medical, sickness, accident, or life insurance or pension benefits, even though Beveridge saw his proposals as providing a minimum upon which workers, either individually or collectively, might want to inprove.[14] In this area the UK followed the common European pattern in which the state became the leading player in the provision of income support to the sick, the unemployed, and the retired, although occupational sick pay and, especially, retirement schemes were present throughout the post-war period and, as we shall see in a later chapter, some attempt was made in the 1980s to redraw the boundaries between state and occupational provision in favour of giving more weight to the latter.

It might be thought that there was a symbiotic (rather than an antagonistic) relationship between the state-provided (and highly

[14] Ibid., para. 9.

bureaucratic) system of social insurance for those out of work and the autonomous system of collective bargaining for the fixing of terms and conditions for those in work. This was no doubt largely true so long as the state's obligations were perceived in terms of income support, although the early presence of occupational sick pay and pension schemes should warn us against taking too firm a view about the scope of collective bargaining being confined to protecting the interests of those in work. Equally, however, this working example of state activism in the area adjacent to collective bargaining could be seen to challenge, as much as to confirm, the system of collective *laissez-faire*, especially when the ideas of state guarantees of non-discriminatory treatment of those in work (touched on in the previous chapter) began to develop in the 1960s.

In 1945, however, all this was in the future, and there was in the 1940s no extension of individual employment rights which matched the rights created in the social security field. On the contrary, the view that the rights of individual workers were to be derived from collective bargaining rather than legislation continued to hold sway.

2.2. COLLECTIVE BARGAINING AND INDUSTRIAL DEMOCRACY

We remarked in the previous chapter that a source of pressure on collective *laissez-faire* in the post-war period was concern on the part of the state that, in one way or another, the coverage of collective bargaining was inadequate. Again in the immediate post-war period, as with the issue of individual rights, such concerns were rather muted. On the contrary, the collective bargaining system was thought to have made a major contribution to the war effort and it therefore shared the public esteem which, by and large, was accorded to the successful wartime machineries. There was, however, one particular and important context in which new questions were being posed about collective bagaining. This context was the nationalization of a number of major industries, notably in the utilities and transport fields. What was striking about the answers to these new questions, however, were the efforts made by those involved to get the old answers to continue to do duty.

The general question that was raised for trade unions by the nationalization programme was whether, in industries that were now to be run, as it was sometimes put, in the public interest rather than for private profit, unions would or should be prepared to take a wider role in their managment. This would involve trade unions having an influence over a wider range of issues than terms and conditions of employment, and perhaps exercising that influence through mechanisms other than collective bargaining. Such a role would give trade unions greater rights in relation to managerial planning and strategy, but also no doubt greater responsibilities. From an early stage it was apparent, however, that the TUC and the union movement generally were prepared to take only the most cautious steps in this direction, as the TUC's *Interim Report on Post-war Reconstruction*[15] made clear.

First, it was proposed, and government seems to have had no other plans, that the model for the conduct of the nationalized industries should be the public corporation, a body analogous to the private sector company, but with the members of the board appointed by the relevant Minister (who would be responsible to Parliament for general policy) rather than by the shareholders.[16] This ruled out, of course, any direct accountability of the board members (or even some of them) to the workers employed in the industry, let alone any election by the workers of directors to the board of the nationalised corporation. This stance was justified by the need to select board members 'on the basis of their competence and ability to administer the industry efficiently in the public interest'.[17] The rationale for selection was thus technocratic, not democratic; the interest to be served the public interest not that of the workers. The TUC did concede that, although technical and administrative competence was the touchstone for selection, 'experience gained "on the job" and in collective organization of the workpeople may well be regarded as an important factor in selection'.[18] This led to one of the few conflicts between government and TUC on this matter. The

[15] TUC, *Annual Report 1944*, app. D.
[16] Chester, *Nationalisation*, 383–7.
[17] TUC, *Annual Report 1944*, para. 38.
[18] Ibid. para. 94.

government was happy to include provisions in the nationalization statutes, as in s. 2(3) of the Coal Industry Nationalization
Act 1946, that the members of the board should be appointed
'from amongst persons . . . having had experience of, and having
shown capacity in, industrial, commercial or financial matters,
applied science, administration or the organization of workers'.
However, it was not prepared to and did not accept a statutory
obligation to consult the TUC before making board appointments
of people experienced in the organization of workers, and it was
a constant complaint of the TUC in the later 1940s that the
government had not in fact appointed enough such persons to the
boards of the nationalized industries.[19] However, this disagreement between TUC and government may be thought to be minor
in comparison with the agreement between them that those
appointed 'should surrender any position held in, or any formal
responsibility to, the Trade Union'.[20] The aim of this proposal
was to ensure that 'trade unions shall maintain their complete
independence',[21] that is, the trade unions' freedom of action in
collective bargaining should in no way be compromised by participation in the general management of the nationalized industry.
In spite of moves by some unions influenced by syndicalist ideas,
notably the Union of Post Office Workers, to branch out in new
directions, this stance was overwhelmingly endorsed by affiliated
organizations.

It was consistent with this rejection of innovation at board
level, in order to preserve freedom of action in collective bargaining, that the form of collective bargaining in the nationalized
industries should also imitate that in the private sector. Although,
upon government rather than TUC initiative, the nationalized
industries boards were placed, as in s. 46 of the Coal Industry
Nationalization Act 1946, under an obligation to set up collective
bargaining machinery, this was regarded more as a statement of
'good employer' policy than as a legal obligation that might bite,
and there was no attempt to require specialized bargaining
machinery for these industries. There was no attempt, for
example, to insist upon compulsory arbitration provisions as part

[19] Chester, *Nationalisation*, 466-78; TUC, *Annual Reports 1946*, 218; *1949*,
211.
[20] TUC, *Annual Report 1944*, para. 104.
[21] Ibid., para. 99.

of the bargaining machinery, or to extend the criminal prohibition upon strikes in breach of contract which applied to gas,
water, and electricity industries under an Act of 1875[22] to all
nationalized industries, even though most nationalized industries
were monopolies upon which the public depended. The underlying
view, shared by both government and trade unions, was that the
same labour law and collective bargaining regime should apply to
both nationalized and private-sector employers. For government
this meant in particular that wage-bargaining was a matter for the
board and the trade unions and not for the relevant Minister.
But—harbinger of many future such problems—during the wage
freeze of 1948 to 1950 the government found it impossible to
adhere to this strategy. 'During this period any major wage claim
was likely to reach the Cabinet or its committees.'[23] The line
between government as government and government as employer
was not so easy to draw, even when the public corporation was
the formal employer of the workforce.

The only real claim to innovation in industrial relations in the
nationalized industries can be found in the field of joint consultation, though even here the nationalized industries were
explicitly building on the wartime experience with joint production
committees.[24] The nationalization Acts imposed upon the boards
the duty to consult with the relevant trade unions with a view to
establishing permanent consultation machinery in respect of
safety, health, and welfare issues, 'the organization and conduct
of the operations' in which the employees were employed, and
'other matters of mutual interest to the Board and such persons
arising out of the exercise and performance by the Board of their
functions'.[25] This form of participation was acceptable to the
TUC since the machinery was under the control of the unions,
did not embrace the matters that were central to collective bargaining (wages, hours, etc.) and did not commit the unions to the
decisions reached. On the other hand, it was a very limited form
of participation, and there were inevitably grumbles from particular unions in the late 1940s and the early 1950s that joint
consultation gave them little influence over managerial decisions.

---

[22] Conspiracy and Protection of Property Act 1875, s. 4.
[23] Chester, *Nationalisation*, 813 ff.
[24] P. Inman, *Labour in the Munitions Industries* (London, 1957), 379–91.
[25] See e.g. the Coal Industry Nationalisation Act 1946, S. 46(1)(6).

In its review of the nationalized industries for the 1953 Congress the General Council decided to make its view explicit:

Joint consultative machinery is essentially advisory as distinct from executive in scope. In the last resort, and after full discussion with their employees, the responsibility for policy decisions must rest on the Boards concerned. This limitation, which is inherent in the policy of Congress, must be recognised and accepted, and joint consultative machinery must not be expected to give executive power to workers' representatives. In instances where too much has been hoped for the results have been disappointment and frustration and, what is perhaps even more important, subsequently the machinery has not been used adequately for its intended purpose.[26]

This paragraph from the General Council's report stands as an eloquent statement of the limited ambitions that the TUC entertained in respect of industrial relations in the nationalized industries. Releasing the nationalized industries from the shackles of private ownership might make it easier for trade unions to protect their members' interests through collective bargaining, but the basic structure of employer and trade union relations in the nationalized industries was not expected to diverge significantly from that in the private sector.

2.3   FULL EMPLOYMENT AND COLLECTIVE LAISSEZ-FAIRE

We now turn to the topic of full employment which, we have suggested, was the development of this period which had the greatest, albeit indirect, impact upon collective *laissez-faire*. Full employment during the war and in the post-war period was in stark contrast with the situation that obtained during most of the inter-war period. After 1920 the level of unemployment in Great Britain fell below 10 per cent in only one year (1927), and the average level was 14 per cent. The phenomenon was not evenly spread either across industries or the different regions of the country. Industries dependent upon foreign markets were particularly badly hit (unemployment in ship-building was 63 per cent in 1932, and it was over 40 per cent in jute and steel-rolling), whilst those catering directly for the domestic market fared much

---

[26] TUC, *Annual Report 1953*, 115.

better (in tramways and buses unemployment was generally about the 3 per cent level). The unevenness of the industrial incidence of unemployment affected also its geographical dispersion, with northern England, Scotland, and Wales particularly badly hit. In spite of these variations, it is fair to conclude that the 'dark clouds [of unemployment] hung persistently over the country in the inter-war years'.[27]

By the end of the first year of the war, however, involuntary unemployment had virtually disappeared; on the contrary, the problem became one of an acute shortage of manpower. As everyone expected, the end of the war produced an economic boom, but, unlike the aftermath of the First World War, the boom was sustained really until the middle 1960s, and so unemployment continued at a low level. Between 1946 and 1952 it was at a general level of less than 2 per cent, and during this period there were always more vacancies than persons unemployed.[28] Although this general picture was not inconsistent with geographical pockets of high unemployment, the situation continued to be one in which involuntary unemployment, certainly involuntary long-term unemployment, was virtually excised.

However, the war was significant not merely for the arrival of full employment—and on what increasingly looked like a long-term basis—but also for the public policy commitment to maintain that situation. That commitment can be associated with two documents in particular, namely the White Paper, *Employment Policy*,[29] published in May 1944, and William Beveridge's private study, *Full Employment in a Free Society*, published later in the same year. Beveridge's study had in fact been completed before the White Paper was published, and it was partly in order to head off the public support that it was anticipated his study would arouse that the coalition government decided to publish its own proposals beforehand. In its famous first sentence the White Paper stated: 'The Government accepts as one of their primary aims and responsibilities the maintenance of a high and stable level of employment after the war', although the document

[27] H. M. D. Parker, *Manpower: A Study of War-Time Policy and Administration* (London, 1957), 23–6.
[28] A. Cairncross, *Years of Recovery: British Economic Policy, 1945–51* (London, 1985), 23.
[29] Cmd. 6527, 1944.

carefully refrained from stating how it defined a 'high' level of employment. Beveridge was less reticent. Full employment meant there should always be more jobs than unemployed persons, and the available jobs should be at such wages, at such places, and of such types as to be attractive to the unemployed. In statistical terms Beveridge thought this would produce an unemployment level of about 3 per cent, consisting of the unemployable and the frictionally unemployed.[30]

Although it is far from clear that post-war full employment was the result of British government policy, as opposed to a worldwide economic boom, it does seem fair to conclude that the acceptance by government that it was possible for it to take deliberate steps to maintain full employment and that unemployment was not an unavoidable consequence of the trade cycle amounted to 'a revolution in economic policy'.[31] Two particular consequences followed. The first was that, until the 1980s, governments became very sensitive to upward changes in the levels of unemployment and sought quickly to take policy initiatives that would reduce those levels. Second, and more immediately important to us, because full employment became, not merely a fact, but also a policy objective, there was more discussion, both in government and in public, than might otherwise have occurred about the likely impact of this development upon other areas of government policy, and in particular upon the government's *laissez-faire* attitudes towards the industrial relations system.

It was recognized by all the participants in the debate about full employment that this change in the economic context was capable of posing new challenges to the government's traditional policy of abstention in respect of labour law. That policy had been suspended in any event during the wartime emergency. The question could now be asked whether the arrival of full employment might not bring about a permanent move away from collective *laissez-faire*. At an early stage some, including even Bveridge himself, seem to have thought that continuance in some form of the wartime controls would be necessary to ensure full employment. That situation would have meant a major qualification to

[30] W. H. Beveridge, *Full Employment in a Free Society* (London, 1944), 18.
[31] Cairncross, *Years of Recovery*, 15.

the policy of collective *laissez-faire*. However, by the time he produced *Full Employment in a Free Society* he had been convinced by his economist advisers that this was not necessary. As he now put it, it was possible to have full employment 'by socialisation of demand without socialisation of production'.[32] By the end of the decade it had been accepted that regulation of demand in the economy by the Treasury rather than controls over the supply of labour, operated by the MLNS, would be the main method of ensuring full employment (and equally that the Treasury rather than the MLNS would be the dominant economic department of state). To this extent the threat to collective *laissez-faire*, posed by full employment, receded.

Although the techniques for ensuring full employment eventually came to be seen as located in the area of economic policy rather than in the law, so that legislation was not perceived as a major instrument for maintaining the situation of full employment, it could be expected that the voluntary collective bargaining system might operate very differently in a period of full employment as compared with the inter-war period of high unemployment. It was difficult to predict the nature and extent of these changes, but the possibility could at least be foreseen that these might be significant and that they might either undermine the effectiveness of the voluntary system or bring that system into conflict with the government's policy objectives. The problem was identified, although from a very particular standpoint, by *The Times* in a leader of 23 January 1943. Its view was that 'unemployment is not a mere accidental blemish in a private-enterprise economy. On the contrary, it is part of the essential mechanism of the system, and has a definite function to fulfil.' It identified the function as being to 'maintain the authority of master over man' and to 'preserve the value of money'. One did not need to share the view that a private-enterprise economy could operate only on the basis of high unemployment in order to perceive that the maintenance of full employment would not involve a change in an isolated aspect of the economy but would rather bring about a fundamental shift in the context in which the voluntary system of industrial relations operated, the consequences of which needed careful thought. The aspects of the

[32] Harris, *William Beveridge*, 436.

voluntary system which were thought at the time most likely to come under pressure as a result of full employment were the level of wage settlements, procedures for settling disputes, and issues about the efficient use of labour. We shall examine each in turn.

(a) Wages Policy

The most widespread debate at the time concerned the question of whether, in order to avoid an unacceptably high level of price inflation, a policy of full employment would need to be accompanied by the formulation of a wages policy, either by government or by the TUC, or at least by the exercise of considerable restraint on the part of bargainers in respect of wage settlements. The White Paper, *Employment Policy*, opened the debate cautiously. Having argued that the maintenance of full employment depended upon government action to maintain the level of demand in the economy, it continued:

Action taken by Government to maintain expenditure will be fruitless unless wages and prices are kept reasonably stable. This is of vital importance and must be clearly understood by all sections of the public. If we are to operate with success a policy for maintaining a high and stable level of employment, it will be essential that employers and workers should exercise moderation in wage matters so that increased expenditure at the onset of depression may go to increase the volume of employment.[33]

Later on that White Paper added: 'The principle of stability does mean . . . that increases in the general level of wage rates must be related to increased productivity due to increased efficiency and effort.'[34]

(i) *A New Role for the TUC.* The discussion of the potentially inflationary consequences of full employment in the White Paper is relatively undeveloped—although enough is said to bring home the central importance the government attached to the point— because there was considerable disagreement amongst Civil Servants as to the long-term compatibility of high levels of employment and price and wage stability and about the likely behaviour of trade unions in conditions of full employment.[35]

[33] *Employment Policy*, Cmd. 6527 (1944), para. 49.
[34] Ibid. para. 50.
[35] Cairncross, *Years of Recovery*, 15.

In Beveridge's study, a private venture, a more detailed consideration of the issues can be found and solutions are proposed. He began from the argument against full employment put forward by *The Times* (of 23 January 1943):

If free wage bargaining as we have known it hitherto is continued in conditions of full employment there would be a continuous upward pressure upon money wage rates. This phenomenon also exists at the present-time and is also kept within bounds by the appeal of patriotism. In peace-time the vicious spiral of wages and prices might become chronic.

Beveridge thought this was an argument that deserved 'careful consideration'. Unlike some, he was not perturbed at the thought that in a tight labour market the share of the national product going to labour as a whole might increase; indeed, such a result was desirable. What, for him, was a problem was the fragmented nature of even industry-level collective bargaining under the system of industrial self-government, where each group bargained on its own account, without having any way of taking into consideration the impact of its settlements upon workers in other industries or companies. Beveridge accepted that there was a 'real danger' that 'irresponsible sectional wage bargaining' might lead to inflationary developments which would bestow no benefits upon the working class but which would endanger the very policy of full employment. There was, he conceded, 'no inherent mechanism in our present system' which could prevent such a development. Beveridge offered a twofold solution. First, the TUC should devote its attention 'to the problem of achieving a unified wage policy which ensures that the demands of individual unions will be judged by reference to the economic situation as a whole'. Second, in future wages ought to be determined 'by reason' and 'not simply by the bargaining power of particular groups of men'. To achieve this result, collective agreements in each industry should contain arbitration clauses whereby the parties agreed to accept the decision of an arbitrator if they themselves could not agree.[36]

Thus the solution to the problem of the coexistence of full employment and low levels of inflation offered by Beveridge was

[36] Beveridge, *Full Employment*, 198—201.

a corporatist one. The government would formulate its economic policy so as to achieve the goal of full employment so much desired by trade unions, but trade unions for their part must restrain the full exercise of their industrial power. This latter aspect of the arrangement might involve individual unions in restrictions *vis-à-vis* both the employers with whom they bargained and the TUC, whose authority over the bargaining activities of affiliated unions would be much increased. But if the arrangement proposed was corporatist—favourable governmental economic policies balanced by restraint on the use by trade unions of industrial power—it was corporatism in the voluntarist mode. The state, let alone the law, was to play no part in compelling the TUC to create its 'unified wage policy' or in requiring individual bargainers to adopt compulsory arbitration. Throughout his study Beveridge showed a general concern to meet the criticism that might be levelled at him that the measures needed to ensure full employment might be thought to interfere unduly with traditional British liberties. Consequently, he was keen to insist that 'so long as freedom of collective bargaining is maintained, the primary responsibility of preventing a full employment policy from coming to grief in a vicious spiral of wages and prices will rest on those who conduct bargaining on behalf of labour. The more explicitly that responsibility is stated, the greater can be the confidence that it will be accepted.'[37] The role of the state in this particular matter was to be confined to creating conditions favourable to the adoption of a wages policy, notably by ensuring stability of prices.

(ii) *Wartime Arrangements.* To what extent was this ideal realized, indeed to what extent was it a realizable ideal, in this period? The foundations for such a policy had to some degree been developed during wartime, in the sense that very close trade union and government relationships had been established. Thus it was realistic to expect that the TUC and the union leaderships generally would exercise, and indeed had already been exercising, a moderating influence over wage claims. These close relations between trade unions and government were in very sharp contrast with how these matters had been conducted in the pre-war period.

[37] Ibid., 200.

After the defeat of the unions in the General Strike of 1926, and the enactment of the restrictive Trade Disputes and Trade Unions Act 1927, the TUC and the government had dealt with each other very much on an arm's length basis.

The policy of government intervention by consent in industrial relations in the Second World War was symbolized above all by the appointment by Churchill of Ernest Bevin, formerly general secretary of the Transport and General Workers' Union, as Minister of Labour and National Service. The impact of this appointment was heightened by the fact that the MLNS was not, as its successor is today, one of a number of second-rank departments of government, but, because of the centrality of manpower to the war effort and the Ministry's role in allocating manpower to the forces and the essential industries, 'the principal department of state'.[38] In consequence, it is not surprising, but is nevertheless highly significant, that Bevin became a member of the small War Cabinet, which had effective conduct of the war. Moreover, Bevin's appointment was not a purely symbolic measure. He insisted that the draconian measures taken to control labour in wartime should be adopted only if supported by trade unions and employers, and so he ensured that substantive consultation took place with these groups before proposals were put to the War Cabinet; and employers and trade unions were heavily involved in the administration of the measures that were eventually adopted. The main forum for consultation was the National Joint Advisory Committee of the MLNS, which had been set up in October 1939, with fifteen employers and fifteen TUC representatives. In fact, during the War, consultation tended to be with the smaller (seven plus seven) Joint Consultative Committee of the NJAC, but, in any event, the principle of proceeding by consent was firmly entrenched in the Ministry's wartime activities.[39]

Bevin's policy was to ensure not only that the main outlines of the new legal framework were agreed with the trade union movement , but also that the specific orders were made only after

[38] K. Middlemas, *Power, Competition and the State, Volume I: Britain in Search of a Balance, 1940–61* (Basingstoke, 1986), 20.

[39] D. Barnes and E. Reid, 'A New Relationship: Trade Unions in the Second World War', in B. Pimlott and C. Cook, eds., *Trade Unions in British Politics* (London, 1982), 155.

consultation with the General Council of the TUC and, if appropriate, with individual unions. But the method of proceeding by consensus generated through consultation was applied quite generally and was by no means confined to labour market regulation. As Pelling has put it, under Churchill and Bevin

the trade union leadership was heavily committed to the Government's policy at every level. Union officials served on innumerable committees for the encouragement of production, for the operation of rationing schemes, and for a wide range of other purposes. The annual reports of the TUC General Council began to read like the records of some special government department responsible for coordinating policy in the social and industrial spheres.[40]

Thus trade union influence extended beyond mobilization issues to cover government policy on general industrial relations matters, and even beyond that to embrace policy formulation in related areas which might be thought directly to affect war production, for instance, rationing of food and consumer supplies, price levels for necessities, and protection of the civilian population.

From our point of view, the continuation of co-operative relations after the war is as important as the circumstances of their genesis. At one level, it is perhaps not surprising that these arrangements should have continued. They were now part of what was regarded as a very successful status quo. From their point of view, the unions had acquired considerable political influence and public prestige from their close involvement in the war effort, whilst the government had been able to achieve the levels of mobilisation it required. Moreover, those closely involved in and with government were aware that the economic problems the country would face after the war were as daunting as, if of a rather different nature from, those involved in running the war. It was natural to try to deploy the mechanisms that had helped so successfully with the one crisis to tackle the second. Finally, the basis for a further period of partnership seemed to be in existence, with the election in 1945 of a Labour government committed to consolidating and extending the economic and social gains made by the labour movement during the war. And, indeed, there developed what was in many respects a very successful partner-

[40] H. Pelling, *A History of British Trade Unionism* (3rd edn., Harmondsworth, 1976), 215.

ship between the leading politicians in government and the most influential members of the General Council of the TUC in the period under review.[41]

However, it was one thing for the TUC and the union leaderships to exercise restraint in formulating wage claims, and another thing for them to agree to a formal, public incomes policy. Such a step would be a direct challenge to free collective bargaining, a concept which the unions held dear; would give the TUC greater power over its constituent unions than they had traditionally been willing to grant it; and might lead trade union members to view their unions, not as representing their interests, but as imposing a govenmental policy upon them. Within government, too, there was no unanimity over the issue. The contingency planners of the 1930s had discussed whether a wages policy would be needed in wartime. The Treasury had argued strongly in favour of a wages policy, whilst the Ministry of Labour argued the voluntarist corner.

If prices were held in check, representatives of employers and workers could be trusted, through the joint negotiating machinery which had brought the two sides closer together, to observe a realistic restraint in dealing with demands for higher wages; whereas any attempt to impose external control would lead to industrial unrest, which would both weaken morale and disrupt the whole economy of the country.[42]

The debate continued with renewed intensity after the outbreak of war, especially at meetings of the NJAC. Even Bevin flirted briefly with the idea of a wages policy. At an early meeting of the JCC Bevin put forward for comment two proposals for taking wages out of controversy during the war period. The first, which treated all industries alike, involved freezing wage rates at their present level and permitting increases only when a responsible independent tribunal recommended an increase, which would apply across the whole economy. The second was a more decentralized approach, which involved no public articulation of a wages policy. Instead there should be compulsory arbitration (coupled with a prohibition on industrial action) if in a particular industry the negotiating machinery failed to produce a settle-

---

[41] V. L. Allen, *Trade Unions and Government* (London, 1960), 287–91.
[42] Parker, *Manpower*, 424.

ment. The second proposal was directed more obviously at taking wages out of controversy by ensuring industrial peace rather than by controlling the level of wage increases, although the compulsory arbitration body would no doubt be sensitive to the government's view on what was economically justified. Not surprisingly, perhaps, the JCC (i.e. both employers and unions) rejected the first proposal and opted instead for the second, and that decision was quickly embodied in the Conditions of Employment and National Arbitration Order 1940, which made striking illegal (in most cases) and provided for compulsory arbitration of matters unsettled by the voluntary bargaining machinery. We shall discuss the 1940 order in greater detail in the next section, but here we should note this early example of a fundamental change in labour law being brought about by government's view of the need to control inflation (even if the particular legal change effected did not specifically control wage rates).[43]

Although the supporters of a wages policy within government continued to argue that it was illogical in wartime to treat the determination of wages as a private matter between employer and workers in which the government had no interest so long as there was no stoppage of work, the Ministry of Labour's policy prevailed: 'wages policy was now to be developed by a combination of faith and good works—faith in the moderating influence of trade unions, and action to control the cost of living,'[44] In pursuit of a policy of creating conditions favourable to wage restraint by trade unions the Chancellor of the Exchequer announced in his budget speech in April 1941 that, by subsidizing necessities, he aimed to keep the cost-of-living index within the range 125 to 130 (it was at 126 in January 1941) in the expectation that wage rates would also be stabilized. This policy was embodied in the White Paper, *Price Stabilisation and Industrial Policy*,[45] the first of what was to become a long series of White Papers dealing with these matters in modern Britain.

---

[43] Ibid. 425–6; W. K. Hancock and M. Gowing, *The British War Economy* (London, 1949), 333. The latter authors refer to Bevin's proposal 'that wages should be stabilized at existing levels' as 'this unsuccessful attempt at radical change'. The proposal for arbitration on a dispute-by-dispute basis was presented as the alternative method of controlling inflation if an overall policy proved unacceptable.

[44] Parker, *Manpower*, 428.

[45] Cmd. 6294 (1941).

(ii) *Post-War Arrangement and the Wages Freeze.* Fears of inflation did not end with the war. Because of the export drive (itself needed because of the sale of overseas assets and the build up of overseas debt that had occurred during the war), the domestic situation of increased purchasing power chasing few consumer goods continued to obtain. Indeed, the situation was exacerbated by a change in the terms of trade against the UK between 1945 and 1951, as world demand pushed up the price of imports. In fact, in the immediate post-war years the policy of 'faith and good works' continued largely unchanged—that is, reliance upon the voluntary restraint of bargainers to control wage increases, whilst the government took action to control prices. In particular—and this was a remarkable testament to the TUC's desire to co-operate with the post-war Labour government—the system of wartime compulsory arbitration with its prohibition upon striking was continued under the Supplies and Services (Transitional Powers) Act 1945, even though the Emergency Powers (Defence) Act 1940, under which it had originally been set up, had expired. Although the TUC's consent to this extension was conditional upon the TUC or employers' organizations being able to request the cancellation of the provisions at any time, it was a significant act of co-operation by the TUC, given the opposition within some parts of the trade union movement to the compulsory arbitration machinery.[46]

Equally, however, the wartime debates over whether government should itself adopt a wages policy continued amongst Civil Servants and in Cabinet and its committees, with ideas, such as for a National Wages Commission, which were to bear fruit in the early 1960s, being propounded. In the immediate post-war years the views of the Ministry of Labour continued to prevail. Wage restraint was advocated by government to the NJAC and by the NJAC to individual trade unions and employers' associations, but the responsibility for formulating claims and agreeing settlements was left entirely to the bargainers. When the government tried to inject more bite into this process by getting the NJAC to endorse a White Paper[47] on the subject, the draft was

[46] TUC, *Annual Report 1946*, 175–7.
[47] *Statement on the Economic Considerations Affecting Relations between Employers and Workers*, Cmd. 7018 (1947).

amended by the union representatives on the NJAC so as to
remove virtually all reference to wage restraint.[48]

Within fifteen months, however, the General Council's attitude
had undergone a volte-face under, as was to happen in later
years, the joint impact of economic crisis and a belief that government had at last screwed itself up to intervene in wage-bargaining
if the TUC did not take upon itself that task. The economic crisis
was that produced in the late summer of 1947 by the government's
decision, under American pressure, prematurely to restore convertibility to the pound, that is, to allow holders of sterling freely
to convert their pounds into other currencies, especially dollars.
Given the worldwide shortage of dollars, the result, perhaps not
surprisingly, was a massive drain on Britain's dollar reserves and
thus a severe threat to Britain's ability to make the necessary
imports from the dollar area. Convertibility was quickly suspended,
but only after enormous damage had been done.

As far as wages were concerned, the crisis led the government
to publish another White Paper, *Statement on Personal Incomes,
Costs and Prices*,[49] issued, significantly, by the Prime Minister
and without prior consultation with the NJAC. Whilst reiterating
the general principle that it was not desirable for government to
interfere directly with the incomes of individuals except through
direct taxation, the White Paper laid down two principles for
bargainers to observe. The first was that there should be the
'strictest adherence' to the terms of national- and district-level
collective agreements and that individual employers should not
pay above these collectively agreed rates. Departure by individual employers from the terms of collective agreements 'will
inevitably constitute a grave danger to the stability of the system
of collective bargaining and may well lead to competitive bargaining, and thus to general but unjustifiable increases in wages and

---

[48] The nature of the debates over the draft of the White Paper can be gauged
from the comments in the General Council's Report to the TUC that the draft
had been 'subjected to considerable amendment' and that 'it was made clear to
the Minister and the Government that the approval of the General Council to
this . . . White Paper was on the definite understanding that unions would
continue to be free to submit wage applications as formerly where this was found
to be necessary' (TUC, *Annual Report 1947*, 219).
[49] Cmd. 7321 (1948).

salaries and to serious inflation . . .'.[50] This was an early recognition of the problems associated with what later became known as 'wage drift' and the breakdown of the 'official' system of collective bargaining in many industries, which was later to be analysed by the Royal Commission.

Of more immediate importance, however, was the second principle that there was in 'present circumstances no justification for any general increase in individual money incomes', including wages. A specific exception to the general principle was recognized in the national interest, namely, the need 'to man up a particular undermanned industry', but other specific exceptions should be considered only on their 'national merits'[51] and certainly not in order to restore traditional differentials or parities between different groups of workers. On its face, the 1948 White Paper was no more than an appeal by the government to bargainers (except that the government committed itself to follow the principles in the negotiations for which it was directly responsible and said that in settling controlled prices, etc. it might not take account of wage settlements that departed from the principles).[52] However, at a special meeting in February 1948 the General Council endorsed the White Paper and accepted that its principles should be applied to wage claims, thus departing in the clearest fashion from its 1947 position and coming closer to the position advocated by Beveridge. In March the General Council presented its policy to a meeting of the executives of affiliated unions (1,550 delegates representing 155 unions), which endorsed the policy by 5,421,000 votes to 2,032,000 (each union having one vote for each of its members).[53]

What caused the General Council to change its mind? A fundamental factor was clearly that the TUC accepted the government's analysis of the gravity of the economic situation. Unless the balance of payment problems were resolved, there would have to be cuts in imports of food and raw materials which would

[50] Ibid., para. 7.
[51] Ibid.
[52] Ibid., paras. 9 and 10. This was an early example of the government finding it impossible to keep its role as employer separate from its general economic policy objectives, thus creating the risk that any incomes policy will be particularly strictly applied in the public sector.
[53] TUC, *Annual Report 1948*, 289–91.

involve 'stringent austerity and considerable unemployment',[54] both of which would hurt trade unionists above all. Since the TUC accepted the analysis, it was difficult for it to resist the argument that it should play its part in resolving the problem. Second, the TUC was convinced that the government would impose statutory controls if the TUC did not accept the White Paper, probably via a central arbitral body with compulsory powers over wage claims.[55] Consequently, having somewhat extended the list of exceptions to the general principle of no increase in wages and having seen the government take firm action over price increases, the General Council endorsed the government's policy, even though, about the same time, the government gave notice that it no longer regarded its financial commitment to food subsidies as open-ended. The General Council's acceptance of what was in effect—although the TUC fiercely resisted the terminology—a wage freeze was a strong indication of the close relations and the high degree of co-operation that existed between government and TUC leaders at this time. According to Middlemas, 'the TUC responded more loyally than anyone in Cabinet had forecast when the freeze was first discussed.'[56]

The success of the policy, at least in the short term, was also a tribute to the influence of the TUC leadership over the actions of individual trade unions. From June 1945 to March 1948 wage rates increased at about 9 per cent per annum; for the eighteen months after March 1948 the rate of increase was 2.8 per cent per annum, and it was a mere 1 per cent for the next twelve months. Meanwhile, prices increased at a rate of 3.3 per cent per annum for the first eighteen months and at 2 per cent for the year thereafter, so that real wages were stationary or falling during the period of the freeze.[57] But in the longer term the freeze proved unsustainable. Following an unwise attempt on the part of the

---

[54] Ibid., app. A, para. 3. In the *Annual Report 1949*, app. C, para. 52, the General Council put its understanding of the position as follows: 'trade unions have it within their power to wreck the full employment policy, and to defeat their other efforts to maintain and improve living standards if they prosecute wage demands inconsistent with the effort to achieve economic stability and to enhance the real purchasing power of wages.'

[55] Middlemas, *Power, Competition and the State*, 156.

[56] Ibid. 157.

[57] Cairncross, *Years of Recovery*, 405-6.

General Council to tighten the policy after the government devalued the pound against the dollar by a large margin in September 1949, the conference of union executives approved the new policy by a majority of only 657,000. The General Council could see the writing on the wall, and in its report to the 1950 Congress it asserted the need for 'more flexibility within the policy of wage-restraint', and stressed the importance of the traditional policy of relying on 'the good sense and reasonableness of individual trade unions'.[58]

In spite of this furious backtracking by the General Council, it was faced at the 1950 Congress with a resolution, moved by a delegate from the Electrical Trade Union, which 'declared' that 'wage increases can be met without resulting in increased prices, for example by reducing profits' and which called upon the General Council 'to abandon any further policy of wage restraint and at the same time urges the government to introduce statutory control of profits'. In spite of the opposition of Arthur Deakin, general secretary of the Transport and General Workers' Union and a strong supporter of the government, who described the policy contained in the resolution as one 'of smash and grab', the resolution was narrowly passed.[59] Thus came to an end TUC support for a government policy of wage restraint, though, fortunately from the government's point of view, the arrival of Marshall Aid had relieved the immediate pressures on the balance of payments.

It would be wrong, however, to put down the defeat of wage restraint simply to the attempt to strengthen it which the General Council had made in 1950. After all, it was the whole policy that was rejected, not just its extension. It is clear that unions were under pressure from their members to end wage restraint, which had curtailed increases in their living standards and had perhaps even reduced them. As we have noted above, restraint in making wage increases, whether imposed by government, 'recommended' by the General Council, or adopted voluntarily by bargainers, is bound to cause dissatisfaction amongst trade union members when labour markets are tight, and unions, as democratic institutions, cannot ignore such grassroots pressures indefinitely. In this

---

[58] Ibid. 265 and 269.
[59] Ibid. 467–73.

respect, the period 1948 to 1950 was no different from the period 1940 to 1948, except that the restraint took the particularly acute form of a 'wage freeze', which was likely to generate membership discontent more quickly, and the need to win the war could no longer be prayed in aid to encourage the sacrifice of self-interest.

In terms of an analysis of government policy, at first sight the interesting fact appears to be that a government which had survived the war by relying upon voluntary restraint by bargainers, felt it necessary to formulate and impose (albeit not by law) upon the trade unions a wages policy in peacetime. This view, however, perhaps reflects the general failing at the time to appreciate how enfeebled by the war the British economy had become. As Cairncross has put it, 'the underlying weakness of the British economy was concealed in the euphoria of victory.'[60] Few appreciated that the British economy was in a state more akin to that of the liberated European countries than to that of the US economy. The questions then, that the 1948 to 1950 freeze raised were whether a government-imposed wages policy was just a temporary expedient needed during reconstruction and whether, in more normal times, full employment and price stability would prove to be compatible goals. These, however, were questions for a later period.

(b) The Settlement of Disputes

(i) *Order 1305.* We have already noted Beveridge's view that 'in the new conditions of full employment wages ought to be determined by reason, in the light of all the facts and with some regard to general equities and not simply by the bargaining power of particular groups of men.'[61] It was perhaps ambiguous whether he took this view because he saw it primarily as a way of discouraging leap-frogging wage-claims, that would lead to inflation, or in order to discourage unacceptably high levels of industrial conflict. As we have also seen, a similar ambiguity lay behind the introduction and continuance after the war of the Conditions of Employment and National Arbitration Order 1940 (Order

---

[60] *Years of Recovery*, 11.
[61] *Full Employment*, 200.

1305).[62] What is more important from our point of view, however, is that neither the TUC nor the government seems to have
viewed the 1940 Order as representing the introduction of a
permanent new principle along the lines Beveridge advocated.
The 1940 Order was a temporary measure, introduced to deal
with the war-time emergency and continued to ease the transition
to a peacetime economy, but only for so long as the TUC and the
employers' associations were prepared to tolerate it.

The long-term policy was more accurately represented by the
repeal in 1946 of the Trade Disputes and Trade Unions Act 1927,
which had withdrawn the 1906 Act's immunities against the law
of torts in respect of, and had made it a criminal offence to
organize strikes unless the strike was aimed at furthering a trade
dispute in the industry in which the strikers were employed and
provided it was not aimed at 'coercing' the government or inflict-
ing hardship on the community. This provision was directed fairly
specifically at the events which had occurred in the General
Strike itself, when the TUC had organized other unions to support
the miners' claim that government subsidies to the industry
should be continued so that wages did not have to be reduced.
The same was true of the further provision which deprived trade
unions of the power to discipline members who refused to take
part in a strike declared illegal by the Act, and which rendered
picketing unlawful (both criminally and tortiously) if it took place
at or near the picketed person's residence or if it involved large
numbers of pickets who engaged in intimidation, obstruction, or
a breach of the peace.

---

[62] SR&O 1940, No. 1305. See O. Kahn-Freund, 'Collective Agreements under
War Legislation' (1943) 6 MLR 112. Order 1305 also introduced what later
became the 'issue' procedure of Order 1376 (see above, p. 27). Because striking
was forbidden, trade unions were deprived of their primary weapon not only
where the employer would not agree the terms of a new collective agreement but
also where, an employers' association having voluntarily agreed such terms, the
individual employer refused to implement them. Part III of Order 1305
introduced the concept of 'recognized terms and conditions of employment' (see
above, p. 32) which all employers in the trade or industry were obliged, under
criminal sanction, to observe (or to observe terms and conditions not less
favourable). If a question arose as to whether a particular employer was observing
the recognized terms and conditions, it could be referred to the NAT by the
Minister in the same way as a dispute under art. 2. Any award of the NAT
became a compulsorily implied term in the contracts of the relevant employees,
the term being that the employee's terms and conditions 'shall . . . be in
accordance with the award' (art. 5(4)).

Given the temporary nature of the 1940 Order, it seems sensible to deal with it briefly and to concentrate on those aspects of it which were subsequently thought to hold lessons for legislative policy towards the industrial conflict. These lessons were primarily learned in the area of enforcement. The ban imposed on striking by the 1940 Order was a conditional one, the condition being that the Ministry of Labour take steps to settle the underlying dispute, normally by referring it to the National Arbitration Tribunal. Any award of the NAT was binding upon the parties, both in the sense that it became a compulsorily implied term in the contracts of employment of the employees to whom it related and in the sense that, of course, the ban on striking continued to operate, so that employees could not take industrial action so as to obtain directly from the employer an improvement on the NAT's award.

The prohibition on striking had three features which are worth remarking upon in the light of subsequent experience. The first was that the prohibition was confined to striking and did not extend to other forms of industrial action, such as going slow, working-to-rule, or banning overtime, which could be highly disruptive. Perhaps it was desired to produce an apparent equivalence with the extent of the prohibition on employers, which extended only to the lock-out and did not embrace, for example, the unilateral imposition of changes in working practices.[63] Second, like other breaches of the emergency laws, striking was sanctioned by criminal,[64] not civil, penalties, but this can be seen as reflecting the gravamen of the offence, which was impeding the war effort rather than harming the employer. Finally, the illegal act was striking, not organizing a strike, which was the action the common law torts normally caught. It may have been thought that, given the political commitment on the part of the TUC which lay behind Order 1305, the organization of strikes did not need to be penalized.[65]

During the War some 109 prosecutions were initiated under

---

[63] Art. 4.

[64] Defence Regulation 92.

[65] Towards the end of the war even Bevin became convinced that politically inspired, unofficial strikes were the cause of problems in the engineering and coal industries. Consequently, he secured the introduction of a new Defence Regulation, 1AA, which made it an offence to instigate strikes amongst workers engaged in the essential services. However, no prosecution was ever commenced under Reg. 1AA.

Article 4, all but two against strikers, and some 6,281 workers were prosecuted. Seventy-two of the 107 prosecutions of strikers took place in Scotland, where prosecution policy was in the hands of the Lord Advocate.[66] Thus in England and Wales, where the Minister of Labour was generally able to control prosecutions, only thirty-nine prosecutions were brought in the whole war period. Bevin was aware that extensive use of the Order might expose its weakness if large numbers of workers chose to defy it, and he therefore initiated prosecutions 'only where he could count on the support of those elements among the workpeople that had a respect for constitutional procedure, and where he was satisfied that the purposes of the strikers was mischievous'.[67] The wisdom of this policy was demonstrated by the fiasco of the prosecution of the miners at Betteshanger Colliery in Kent in 1941, where about 1,000 men were prosecuted for going on strike against an arbitrator's award. Significantly, this prosecution was insisted upon the by the Secretary for Mines (a former miners' leader) rather than by the Minister of Labour. The prosecutions resulted in three local union officials being gaoled (one for two months, two for one month each) and nearly 1,000 men being fined.[68] Quite apart from the fact that the mechanics of prosecution could not operate without the co-operation of the strikers—the union instructed its members to plead guilty and agreed to accept a decision on a few test cases—the imprisonment of the officials did not end the strike. On the contrary, negotiations, which eventually gave the strikers what they wanted, had to be conducted with the officials in gaol and, even then, the miners would not resume work until their leaders were released (which happened after some eleven days). The problem of the fines, which remained unpaid, was solved by the government advising the court not to enforce them.[69] This history not only suggested the difficulty of prosecuting large numbers of workers who believed in the justice of their cause but also implied that the

[66] Ministry of Labour and National Service, *Report for the Years 1939–46*, Cmnd. 7225 (1947), 282.

[67] Parker, *Manpower*, 467.

[68] Thus, although the offence was striking, the organizers of the strike were sentenced more severely than those who merely participated in it.

[69] For an account of the Betteshanger prosecutions, on which we have drawn heavily, see the Report of the Royal Commission on Trade Unions and Employers' Associations, Cmnd. 3623 (1968), app. 6 (Sir Harold Emmerson).

prosecution of strike leaders might not prove to be more feasible in such circumstances—that is, that confining the illegality to strike organizers would not necessarily solve the problem. As we shall see, this was a lesson that had to be learnt again in the early 1970s.

The impact of Order 1305 upon the incidence of disputes is difficult to gauge. During the war the numbers of strikes, of workers involved, and of days lost all increased compared with the 1930s, but the percentage of strikes that were short (less than one week) increased to nearly 90 per cent.[70] This suggests strikes were a way of expressing pent-up workshop grievances, which would not be surprising given the exigencies of wartime production. This does not mean Order 1305 had no impact—without it, strike levels might have been higher—but one careful study has concluded that 'it may well be doubted whether the number of stoppages would have been appreciably greater, if the Minister of Labour in the crisis of 1940 had not decided to declare strikes illegal.'[71]

However that may be, we have seen that the government asked for and secured TUC agreement to the extension of Order 1305 into peacetime, in order to help deal with the economic problems facing the country when the war ended. The Ministry of Labour, aware of the fragility of the consent upon which Order 1305 rested after 1945, was even more cautious about initiating prosecutions than it had been in wartime. It was not until late 1950 that the Attorney-General insisted on prosecuting ten unofficial leaders of a gas strike amongst workers of the North Thames Gas Board, and in early 1951 he proceeded in the same way against seven unofficial dockers' leaders. These actions of the Attorney-General destroyed what was left of the TUC's support for the restrictions on striking contained in Order 1305, and it exercised its right to have the Order reviewed.[72] The TUC's aim was not, however, the simple removal of Order 1305 as a whole, for 'unions which, for sections of their membership, have not yet achieved a proper recognition have been able to

---

[70] Inman, *Labour in the Munitions Industries*, 392–6.

[71] Parker, *Manpower*, 470.

[72] TUC, *Annual Report 1951*, 232–3. For more detail on the course of these two disputes, see Justin Davis Smith, *The Attlee and Churchill Administrations and Industrial Unrest, 1945–1955* (London, 1990), 21–3 and 26–31.

take employers, unwilling to negotiate, before the Tribunal and obtain awards which are legally enforceable'.[73] The TUC wished to keep those aspects of Order 1305 which helped union recognition, whilst having the restrictions on industrial action removed. One of the last acts of the Labour government was to replace Order 1305 with the Industrial Disputes Order 1951, which gave effect to the TUC's wishes. The Minister might refer disputes reported to him to an Industrial Disputes Tribunal (in effect, the NAT under another name) whose awards were compulsory implied terms in the contracts of employment of the relevant workers, but the restrictions on striking had been removed.[74] Like Order 1305, Order 1376 was made under the emergency laws and was subject to review at any time if either employers or unions requested it, but in the Parliamentary debates on the new Order the Minister expressed the hope that review would not be necessary and that the Order would 'provide a piece of machinery suitable for our peacetime requirements'.[75]

It may be thought that the experience with Order 1305, both in war and peace, had demonstrated the difficulties of using legal sanctions against individuals, whether leaders or not, who engaged in strike action in the pursuit of industrial grievances which they felt to be just. Not only had it been difficult for government to secure the continued support of the trade unions for such measures (at a time when the TUC's attitude towards government was generally co-operative), but there was considerable reason to doubt the efficacy of these sanctions when applied in practice. The ultimate failure to sustain the restrictions on industrial action also meant that Beveridge's vision whereby 'in the new conditions of full employment wages ought to be determined by reason, in the light of all the facts and with some regard to general equities and not simply by the bargaining power of particular groups of men'[76] had failed to be realized. Not only, as

[73] Ibid. 232.

[74] SI 1951, No. 1376. Besides abandoning the prohibition on strikes and lockouts, the drafters of Order 1376 omitted generally the criminal sanctions that had underpinned Order 1305 (see para. 12(3)). Consequently, observance of recognized terms and conditions by employers became an obligation supported only by the civil law and coming into effect as an implied term only when the IDT made an award.

[75] Ministry of Labour and National Service, *Industrial Relations Handbook* (2nd edn., 1953), 138.

[76] See above, Subsection 2.3(*b*)(ii).

we have already observed, did the TUC refuse to develop a wages policy, but the system of compulsory arbitration, although continued by Order 1376, was no longer protected against industrial action designed to settle the dispute outside the arbitration machinery or against employers' decisions to pay more than the IDT had awarded. The system of compulsory arbitration after 1951 might help the weakly organized, but did nothing to restrain the labour market power of the strong.

(ii) *Emergency Powers.* Thus, by the early 1950s, the system whereby the threat of prosecution was held over individual and normally unofficial strikers had had to be abandoned because it no longer carried the support of the union movement. It was lack of union support rather than lack of governmental concern with unofficial strikes that led to this development. The government's worry about unofficial disputes continued to be a lively one throughout the period after 1945, as is illustrated by the use made of its emergency powers. These were another way in which the government intervened very directly in unofficial disputes, but not by prosecuting strikers but rather by using the state's resources to ameliorate the consequences of industrial action (and so, incidentally, to reduce the strikers' bargaining power). Such action was taken under the Emergency Powers laws of which, apart from the royal prerogative, there were two sources. The first was the Emergency Powers Act 1920, passed against the opposition of the Labour Party in the face of impending joint industrial action by the 'Triple Alliance' of miners, railwaymen, and dockers. This authorized the King to declare a state of emergency if any event 'by interfering with the supply and distribution of food, water, fuel or light, or with the means of locomotion [threatened] to deprive the community, or any substantial proportion of the community, of the essentials of life'.[77] Once an emergency had been declared the government had power to issue regulations of the broadest nature (subject to Parliamentary ratification), but it could not impose industrial conscription or make striking or peacefully persuading others to strike an offence. Second, under the Defence (Armed Forces) Regulations 1939, Regulation 6,[78] made under the Emergency

[77] Emergency Powers Act 1920, s. 1(1).
[78] SR&O 1939, No. 1304.

Powers (Defence) Act 1939, the government could make temporary use of services personnel on 'urgent [civilian] work of national importance'. Like Order 1305, Regulation 6 was continued after the war on a piecemeal basis, but, unlike Order 1305, it was ultimately given permanent form in the Emergency Powers Act 1964.

Regulation 6 was originally intended to deal with anticipated wartime manpower shortages (although troops were used during one industrial dispute in 1942), but after the war the Labour government used troops in this way remarkably freely. Between 1945 and 1979 troops were used in twenty-three industrial disputes, but eleven of these happened in the years 1945 to 1951. At times considerable numbers of troops were deployed, 21,000 in the dock strike of 1945, for example. In addition, on two occasions states of emergency were declared, in both cases in dock strikes. Strikes in the docks were particularly likely to attract the use of troops (they were called out in 1945, 1947, 1948, 1949, and 1950); strikes by meat-handlers caused troops to be used on three occasions; and strikes by gas and electricity workers caused the government to resort to the use of troops on one occasion each.[79] Jeffery and Hennessy have commented: 'The fact that most of the major strikes during the Attlee administration directly impeded food supplies goes a long way towards explaining the government's consistently tough attitude and the regular use of service labour.'[80] But the fact that the government used troops so freely and with so little dissent within the Cabinet shows how far at this time unofficial strikes put those involved outside the pale so far as government and trade union leaders were concerned.[81] An important element in the close co-operation between TUC and government was that union leaderships should not countenance unofficial action; if they could not prevent it

[79] For the statistics in this paragraph see C. J. Whelan, 'Military Intervention in Industrial Disputes' (1979) 8 ILJ 222–5 and K. Jeffery and P. Hennessy, *States of Emergency* (1983), 143 ff.

[80] Ibid. 171.

[81] 'The readiness of the union leadership to accept the deployment of troops was due in large measure to the unofficial nature of the disputes. Union leaders were as anxious as the government to stamp out unofficial organizations and reaffirm union discipline' (Justin Davis Smith, *Attle and Churchill Administrations*, 50). The fact that 'unofficial' tended to be equated with 'Communist' only added to official opposition in the heated atmosphere of the late 1940s: ibid., ch. 6.

themselves, they should not stand in the way of government's dealing with its consequences.

Thus, the period 1939 to 1951 illustrates well the tensions created for traditional policies for handling industrial disputes by the arrival of full employment. On the one hand, full employment much increased the bargaining strength of workgroups, and this led government to propose the extraordinary step of criminalizing the most obvious expression of that new bargaining strength, in order to control inflation and ensure continuity of production. On the other hand, the strength of the tradition of 'negative' law, designed to confer legality upon all peaceful economic sanctions available to workers in industrial disputes, asserted itself in the government's repeal of the 1927 Act in 1946, the relatively limited use made of Order 1305, and in the ultimate demise of the criminal restrictions on industrial action in 1951. In the period of national consensus that obtained during the War and in the course of post-war reconstruction the government was able to keep unofficial action within acceptable bounds by patriotic appeal, the threat (rather than the use) of the criminal law, and vigorous use of its emergency powers in the unofficial disputes that seriously threatened economic recovery. By the end of this period the traditional policy had reasserted itself pretty strongly, but it remained to be seen whether that policy would be sustainable as the national consensus over social priorities weakened and the official union leaderships began to pay more attention to the challenge from below of the shop stewards' movement and to attach a lower priority to close co-operation with the government.

(c) *The Efficient Use of Labour*

Both Beveridge in his report on *Full Employment in a Free Society* and the authors of the White Paper, *Employment Policy* saw full employment as having implications for the mobility of labour, in both a geographical and an occupational sense. As the latter put it, 'in an expanding economy workers must be ready and able to move freely between one occupation and another.'[82] However, neither document envisaged a high level of compulsion upon individual workers to make such changes. In particular, the

[82] Cmd. 6527 (1944), para. 31.

continuation into peacetime of the war system of direction of labour was not regarded as a real possibility, a point which the TUC was concerned to emphasize, in case there was any doubt about it, in its reply to this aspect of Sir William Beveridge's questionnaire.[83] As we have seen, labour market controls were quickly relaxed after the war ended, although Essential Work Orders continued to operate in relation to agriculture and coal-mining until 1950 and control of engagement was reintroduced in a limited form after the fuel crisis in 1947 and was continued, again, until 1950. Beveridge was concerned to assert the principle 'that if there is a demand for labour at fair wages, men who are unemployed for any substantial period should be prepared to take that work and not to hold out indefinitely for work in their own trade or place'.[84] As we have seen, however, he was sensitive to the charge that his scheme for full employment would infringe unduly upon individual liberties, and so he made it clear that he envisaged this principle being enforced, not by criminal penalties, but by deprivation of unemployment benefit. This way of proceeding in fact found expression in s. 13(2) of the National Insurance Act 1946—disqualification for a period of up to six weeks—upon which the General Council commented that 'no doubt some individuals will feel aggrieved if they are for any reason deprived of benefits from a fund to which they have contributed, but if it were made clear that benefits would not be payable in those circumstances, the withholding of benefit would not be a serious reflection on a free society.'[85]

In fact, as far as geographical mobility was concerned, the government in its post-war policy placed more emphasis upon mobility of industry than mobility of labour. Taking work to the worker was in general regarded as an easier and more effective policy to implement than taking workers to the work—which, indeed, in the absence of legal powers to direct labour or gross disparities in regional living standards, was probably correct. Under the Distribution of Industry Acts 1945 and 1950 the government had powers to subsidize the establishment of industrial undertakings in development areas, whilst under the

---

[83] TUC, *Annual Report 1944*, app. D, 'Answer to Sir William Beveridge's Questionnaire', paras. 13–15.

[84] Beveridge, *Full Employment a Free Society*, 173.

[85] TUC, *Annual Report 1944*, app. A, para. 19.

Town and Country Planning Act 1947 industrial development in non-development areas could be controlled. Between them these Acts gave the government 'a powerful influence on the location of industry in the post-war years',[86] although it is not clear that government action had much impact upon the overall pattern of regional unemployment rates.

Rather more attention was focused on the obstacles that might face workers who were prepared to be occupationally mobile. Both Beveridge and the White Paper referred unfavourably to workgroup demarcation practices, a point to which the TUC seemed alive, for it observed that 'trade unions may well be expected not to impede the achievement of full employment by the rigid maintenance of demarcation practices which were themselves designed to ensure the continuity of employment of their own members during periods of industrial insecurity.'[87] Indeed, to the extent that demarcation practices were the result of the British movement's overlapping and competing structure of trade unions, the TUC itself towards the end of the War took steps to deal with the problem by setting up its own inquiry into trade union structure. This inquiry produced a long report but little in the way of concrete recommendations. It accepted that inter-union competition was a major problem, but also thought that a basic alteration of trade union structure was impossible, so that it was reduced to proposals to encourage amalgamations between trade unions and various forms of inter-union co-operation.[88] In spite of this failure of the voluntary initiative, the government showed no inclination to take legislative steps to address the issue and indeed resisted Opposition attempts to bring restrictive labour practices within the scope of the Monopolies and Restrictive Practices (Inquiry and Control) Act 1948.[89]

Indeed, despite the relative failure of the TUC inquiry into trade union structure, it could be argued that voluntary action had succeeded in dealing with other aspects of the problem. During the War various relaxations of customary working arrangements had been negotiated between employers and trade unions

---

[86] Cairncross, *Years of Recovery*, 317.

[87] Cmd. 6527, para. 18.

[88] TUC, *Annual Report 1944*, app. A: Interim Report on Trade Union Structure and Closer Unity.

[89] See the proviso to sections 3(2) and 4(2) of the Act.

(notably for the employment of unskilled women on jobs previously done by male craftsmen), and employers and employees
had often co-operated effectively at plant level on joint production committees. The Restoration of Pre-War Trade Practices
Act 1942 gave a legislative guarantee of the reinstatement of
these practices once the War ended, but, as part of its participation in the post-war rebuilding, the TUC periodically agreed that
the Minister should refrain from appointing a day on which the
War had ended for the purposes of the 1942 Act, so that the
legal obligation to restore did not bite. In the end the Act was
not brought into effect until 1952, by which time the TUC had
further agreed that changes in customary practices that had
occurred after the real end of the War should not be caught by
the Act at all.[90] Although the General Council's co-operation in
this respect was in some sense misleading, because in a strong
labour market workers could usually obtain through collective
bargaining the restoration of the practices which they regarded as
important, it did help 'to maintain the sense of urgency in solving
production problems'.[91]

However, the White Paper did not identify union and workgroup opposition as the only obstacles to occupational mobility.
It stressed the importance of training and the role of government
employment exchanges in securing for employees the necessary
skills to equip them to perform the jobs for which there was
demand and in drawing the availability of these jobs to the
attention of the unemployed. The perspective of the White Paper,
and of later government action, was—perhaps not surprisingly in
the context—in terms of training the unemployed so as to fit
them for jobs. Following the precepts of collective *laissez-faire*,
the need to train and update the skills of those in employment
was not generally regarded as a matter for government action.
Thus the Employment and Training Act 1948, in part anyway a
consolidating measure, made important changes in the Youth
Employment Services (i.e. in the process of moving from school
to work) but 'had little effect on vocational training in industry
and commerce'.[92] It was not until the 1960s that the legitimacy

---

[90] See TUC, *Annual Reports 1946*, 180; *1948*, 216; and *1950*, 211, and the
Restoration of Pre-War Trade Practices Act 1950.
[91] Allen, *Trade Unions and Government*, 267.
[92] P. J. C. Perry, *The Evolution of British Manpower Policy* (London, 1976),
51

of an important government role in updating the skills of the employed was recognized.

Thus it seems legitimate to conclude that, although it was widely recognized that full employment would require employers to make efficient use of their workers and would deprive workers of many of the traditional justifications for restrictions on occupational mobility, the policy of collective *laissez-faire* was relatively little modified in this area. The government was perceived as having a responsibility for bringing jobs to the attention of job seekers, but work practices and the training of the employed were seen as a matter for employers and trade unions to deal with in collective bargaining and at their own pace.

2.4. CONCLUSION

In the period 1945 to 1951 the great wartime apparatus of state intervention into the operation of the labour market and the collective bargaining system was steadily dismantled, as the traditional values of collective *laissez-faire* reasserted themselves. On the other hand, outside the area of labour law proper a development had occurred which raised some profound questions about those traditional values. Those concerned with the new full-employment policies were well aware of these issues. Among the most willing to spell out some answers was William Beveridge, perhaps because his intellectual and political affiliations lay not so much with the trade union movement as with those who advocated a more active role for the state bureaucracies as a way of solving social problems. Yet his proposals for a permanent, formal, voluntary incomes policy, run by the TUC, never came to pass; instead what one had was some fairly extensive, behind-the-scenes manipulation: by the TUC of bargainers' objectives and by the government of the price levels. Even his complementary proposal for the settlement of disputes by compulsory arbitration, adopted in wartime, had been rejected by the time the end of the decade was reached.

Why should this have been? There was no doubt about the attachment shown by the TUC, trade unions, and union members to the notion of 'free' collective bargaining. Interventionist though the TUC might be in relation, say, to nationalization and planning of the private sector of the economy, it was firmly wedded to the notion of autonomy and the virtues of limited state control in so far as collective bargaining was concerned.[93] Once the war was over, neither employers nor the state seemed willing to challenge this set of attitudes on the part of the union movement, except in moments of extreme crisis, as in 1948. This was not necessarily a pusillanimous attitude on the part of the state. A direct challenge to free collective bargaining would, at one and the same time, have alienated the unions and deprived the government of the assistance that was proving essential in the fight against inflation and for greater exports. Government could not be sure that what it would have to rely upon in the absence of trade union co-operation would be more effective. This was a co-operation based upon wartime experience, derived from an analysis shared with government of the broad nature of the economic problems facing Britain, and nourished by the trade unions' approval of the general direction of the economic and social policies being pursued by the Labour government, above all the maintenance of full employment. Thus the development that cast the longest shadow over the government's long-term commitment to collective *laissez-faire* also gave it the strongest claim to the trade unions' support in dealing with the adverse consequences of that situation as government perceived them. As we have remarked before, the degree of corporatism involved in the policy of co-operation with government over matters such as wage increases and compulsory arbitration sat oddly with a full-blown policy of collective *laissez-faire*. The quesstion for later decades was whether co-operation and the collective *laissez-faire* system would prove to be compatible and, if not, how the inflation and industrial conflict issues would be dealt with.

[93] Employers were, by and large, as much opposed in their particular areas to intervention by the state as were trade unions. See their opposition to the establishment of development councils under the Industrial Organization and Development Act 1947: TUC, *Annual Reports 1948*, 240–2; *1949*, 236–9; *1950*, 242–3; *1951*, 266–7.

3

THE EASY DECADE, 1951–1961

3.1. INTRODUCTION

It is not necessary to spend time at this point giving a detailed account of the relationship between the legal and industrial relations systems in the 1950s, for that task was discharged in Chapter 1, when we described and analysed Kahn-Freund's theory of collective *laissez-faire*. It was in the early 1950s that Kahn-Freund's original writing on this subject took place and, indeed, the first half of the decade can claim to have been the high-water mark of post-war abstentionism. As we saw in the last chapter, by the fall in 1951 of the second, post-war Labour government, the wage freeze of 1948 had collapsed, and in its final year the government was operating without a wages policy, whilst the wartime restrictions on striking had eventually been repealed. All that was left of the wartime emergency legislation in this respect was the system of compulsory, unilateral arbitration (but without any accompanying prohibitions on strikes and lock-outs) and the system of legal enforcement of recognized terms and conditions of employment (both contained in Order 1376). Finally, the various corporatist initiatives which some people had advocated had failed to develop and become institutionalized to any significant degree in the immediate post-war period, although a live, if declining, tradition of co-operation between government and trade unions continued into the 1950s.

The Conservative government elected in 1951—Conservative governments were continuously in power from then until 1964—apparently saw no need to change this situation. Indeed, if anything the abstentionist stance of the law was reinforced by the repeal of Order 1376 in 1958, although legal enforcement of recognized terms and conditions of employment was continued under the provisions of section 8 of the Terms and Conditions of Employment Act 1959. The 1950s were not, it is true, years entirely bereft of labour legislation, but it fell largely within the established, 'exceptional' categories of labour law. Thus, there was some updating and expansion of the regulatory health and safety laws through the Mines and Quarries Act 1954, the Agriculture (Safety, Health, and Welfare Provisions) Act 1956, and the Factories Act 1959 (consolidated in 1961), whilst hours of work were controlled in the baking industry by the Baking Industry (Hours of Work) Act 1954 (replacing a previous Act of 1938). The auxiliary Wages Councils legislation was updated in the Terms and Conditions of Employment Act 1959, and then the whole law relating to Wages Councils was consolidated in the Wages Councils Act 1959.[1]

The most surprising of these pieces of legislation was, perhaps, the Baking Industry Act of 1954, regulating as it did the hours of work of even adult male workers.[2] In one sense, however, it represented a defeat for the trade unions, which had campaigned since the middle of the nineteenth century for the prohibition of night work in bakeries. The 1954 Act regulated, but did not prohibit, such night work, mainly by providing that an employer could not insist upon continuous night work on the part of any particular employee, but only upon such work for up to half the weeks worked in any calendar year. Nevertheless, it is a tribute to the Conservative government's commitment to good relations with the trade union movement in the early 1950s that such legislation was passed at all, for it might have taken the view that the matter was capable of being dealt with by the Wages Councils that existed in the industry.[3] Instead, the government decided to implement the recommendations of the Rees Committee,[4]

[1] This consolidation left s. 8 of the Terms and Conditions of Employment Act 1959, dealing with the enforcement of recognized terms and conditions of employment, as the sole effective part of that Act in force at the end of the year in which the statute had been enacted!

[2] Hence, of course, its repeal in the deregulatory 1980s by the Sex Discrimination Act 1986. See below, ch. 10.4(c).

[3] Wages Councils had been established in 1938 (one for England and Wales and one for Scotland) and consequently, as provided in that Act, the Baking Industry (Hours of Work) Act 1938, the predecessor of the 1954 Act, had never come into force.

[4] Report of the Committee on Night Baking, Cmd. 8378, 1951 (Chairman: Sir Frederick Rees).

established by the previous Labour government with the support of both sides of the industry. In good voluntarist fashion the legislation departed from the recommendations of the jointly supported committee only 'where after careful discussion between the parties, an agreed basis for departure from these recommendations has been reached'.[5] Even so, the government clearly felt some uneasiness about legislating for terms and conditions of employment of the type normally dealt with by collective bargaining and, in an interesting section designed to prevent the legislation from freezing voluntary initiatives, it was provided that the Minister could by order disapply the Act to any bakery workers covered by an agreement between 'one or more organisations representing employers in the industry and one or more trade unions representing bakery workers' which dealt with the issue of night work.[6]

As for the more traditional health and safety legislation, not only was it even less adventurous than the 1954 Act, but the government showed few signs of urgency about the legislative process. Thus one of the major post-war developments in health and safety was the extension of systematic coverage beyond the traditional areas of factories and mines. This was recommended in the report of the Gowers Committee[7] on health and safety in non-industrial employments as early as 1949. However, only with the 1956 Agriculture Act were the Committee's recommendations in relation to agriculture fully implemented, whilst the recommendations relating to offices had to await the Offices Act 1960, a private member's bill passed against government opposi-

---

[5] HC Deb., vol. 552, col. 1466 (25 Jan. 1954). This meant that both trade unions and employers each failed to obtain one major modification to the Committee's proposals which they wanted but to which the other side would not agree: ibid., cols. 1466–7. The Rees Committee's report was thus treated by the government as a form of voluntary arbitration.

[6] S. 9. The section was designed particularly with the Scottish industry in mind, where organisation was more advanced and an agreement regulating night work was in existence. In England and Wales it was hoped that s. 9 'will have the effect of stimulating progress towards an effective system of organisation and joint negotiations in the industry'; HC Deb., vol. 522, col. 1465 (25 Jan. 1954).

[7] Report of a Committee of Enquiry into Health, Welfare and Safety in Non-Industrial Employment, Cmd. 7664, 1949 (Chairman: Sir Ernest Gowers). The Committee made recommendations in respect of shops and offices; hotels and restaurants; indoor and outdoor entertainment; rail and road transport; agriculture; fishing and shipping; and domestic work. (The Committee also carried out a separate inquiry into the hours of employment of juveniles.)

tion, and other industries were not dealt with until the 1960s.[8] On this declining scale of innovation last place must be accorded to the Wages Councils provisions of the Terms and Conditions of Employment Act 1959, the main purpose of which was to convert the four Catering Wages Boards, set up under the Catering Wages Act 1943, into Wages Councils. This was a metamorphosis which 'was barely noticeable, since the powers of councils differ little from those of boards'.[9]

Thus the pattern of very limited legislative activity and, in its place, of broad reliance upon collective bargaining, so brilliantly analysed by Kahn-Freund, seemed well and truly established in the 1950s. The policy of abstention was applied, as we have already noted, even to the question of whether a trade union should be recognized for the purposes of collective bargaining. Thus, throughout the 1950s—and indeed earlier—there festered a dispute between a number of TUC-affiliated unions, on the one hand, and the clearing banks and certain insurance companies, on the other, about the latter's policy of dealing with their employees only through non-affiliated staff associations. At the end of the decade the issue was referred by the TUC to the International Labour Organization, on the grounds that the employers' policy infringed the ILO's conventions, which had been ratified by the UK, on freedom of association and collective bargaining. The ILO requested the UK government to hold an impartial inquiry into the complaints—though this availed the unions little, for Lord Cameron rejected the complaints and handled the unions' case pretty roughly.[10] The interesting thing, however, is that no domestic legal procedure was available for handling the dispute, and Lord Cameron's at best quasi-judicial enterprise was set up by the government only after an international body had intervened, even though it could clearly have

---

[8] The provisions of the Offices Act 1960 were later incorporated in the government's Offices, Shops, and Railways Premises Act 1963. The government did not show any greater urgency in dealing with the Committee's recommendations on the hours of employment of juveniles or with its interim report on the Closing Hours of Shops (Cmd. 7105 (1947)), neither of which resulted in legislation in our period. (The Shops Act 1950 was a purely consolidating measure.) An interesting Parliamentary debate on the government's inaction over the Gowers Reports occurred in 1957 (HC Deb., vol. 572, cols. 34–166 (25 June 1957)), in which the government partly blamed the inability of employers and unions to agree on the issues: ibid., cols. 56–7.
[9] F. Bayliss, *British Wages Councils* (Oxford, 1962), 86.

acted on its own initiative to set up a non-binding inquiry at any stage.

What, it may be wondered, had become of the problems associated with full employment and economic management which so preoccupied the previous Labour governments? Unemployment continued at this time at a low level: in the years 1951 to 1961 (inclusive) the average level of unemployment was 1.7 per cent, and in no single year did it exceed 2.3 per cent. This was not the accidental effect of Conservative government policy. As early as 1947 the Conservative Party had reaffirmed in its *Industrial Charter* its commitment to the full employment policy laid down in the 1944 White Paper, a document issued, after all, not by a Labour government but by the wartime Coalition in which the Conservatives had been the major partner. The 1947 document reaffirmed, moreover, that control of demand in the economy would be the main instrument for ensuring full employment:

The Conservative Party stands by the Coalition White Paper and would in some respects go further to ensure that the demand for goods and services is always maintained at a level which will offer jobs to all who are willing to work. We believe such a policy can succeed, provided that both sides of industry have confidence in each other and in the government's leadership.[11]

Indeed, the general thrust of the Conservative government's domestic policy in the early 1950s was to affirm its acceptance of the changes brought about by the post-war Labour governments in respect of the welfare state (including the National Health Service) and the mixed economy. Again these were both areas where the Labour governments had to a significant degree been implementing wartime and even pre-war proposals for change produced by independent bodies. It is true that both the road

[10] Report of the Inquiry by the Honourable Lord Cameron, DSC, QC, into the Complaint made by the National Union of Bank Employees on 12th March 1962 to the Committee on Freedom of Association of the International Labour Organisation, Cmd. 2202 (1963).

[11] Conservative and Unionist Central Office, *The Industrial Charter* (London, 1947), 16. 'We should use to the full the Government's powers of taxation. Although the Budget must be balanced over a period, it is not necessary or desirable to balance it exactly each year. . . . It is when there is considerable unemployment that a deficit is legitimate.'

haulage and the iron and steel industries were denationalized, but these were probably the two most controversial of the previous government's nationalization measures—and also the ones where the Labour government itself had had its greatest doubts.[12] For the rest, the nationalized sector was left intact. On the other hand, if the welfare state, the mixed economy, and full employment (and the accompanying Keynesian revolution in economic policy) were confirmed as objectives of central government, the Conservative governments of the 1950s had no plans for any further significant advances in these directions. The Conservative Party's slogan in the early 1950s was 'Set the People Free", which translated into practice meant that the wartime controls still existing in 1951 were quickly dismantled—although that process was in any event well under way in the late 1940s—and that the domestic changes of the period 1945 to 1951 were to be consolidated but not extended.[13]

3.2. FULL EMPLOYMENT, ECONOMIC GROWTH, AND INFLATION

(a) In General

However, our purpose in this chapter is not to provide a general account of the Conservative government's economic and social policies. In terms of the analysis presented in the previous two chapters, the crucial fact is that the governments of the 1950s continued the full employment policies of their predecessors and that the continuing economic boom amongst the industrialized countries meant that world economic conditions were propitious for the success of such policies. How then, to pose the question again, did the governments of this period cope with the problem of reconciling full employment with stable prices? As we have pointed out before, the increased bargaining strength that full employment brought to trade unions would not necessarily lead to inflation. If the increase in money wages did not exceed the

---

[12] Kenneth O. Morgan, *Labour in Power, 1945-1951* (Oxford, 1984), 107-8, 110-21.
[13] P. Oppenheimer, 'Muddling Through: The Economy, 1951-1964', in V. Bogdanor and R. Skidelsky, eds., *The Age of Affluence, 1951-1964* (London, 1970), 154-5.

level of national economic growth, then inflation would not be inevitable (although it might well be that wage earners were increasing their share of the national income if, for example, other forms of income were not able to keep pace with the increases in wages). In other words, in a successful economy the aspirations among wage earners that full employment would eventually generate could more easily be satisfied without adverse economic consequences.

From one perspective, the performance of the British economy in this period was in fact highly successful. Between 1950 and 1964 productivity (measured in terms of national income per person) increased by 2.2 per cent per annum,[14] an increase 'faster than in any other period of comparable length in the twentieth century'.[15] The figure of 2.2 per cent may seem low, but an increase even at this level compounded over a number of years can have a very significant effect and was the basis for Conservative claims at this time that the country's standard of living would double over twenty-five years, a remarkable thing to those who had known the inter-war depression. Certainly, there was in this period a large increase in levels of private consumption (especially of cars, televisions, and other consumer durables) and also in public consumption (especially in education and, to a lesser extent, health care), whilst levels of welfare benefits, especially retirement pensions, were improved.[16] These facts provided the basis for the Conservatives' appeal to the electorate and their claim, 'you've never had it so good.' Writing about the industrial relations system in particular, Colin Crouch has made a similar point, whilst showing up the contrast with the earlier period of 1945 to 1951:

Seen from the perspective of 1945 the main safeguards of order in the post-war world would be institutional and consensual: a national system of bargaining under a centralised trade union leadership which broadly accepted the priorities of government and industry as a result of the needs of post-war recovery, the urgency of post-war reconstruction and their links with the new party of government. Gradually all these items were reduced in significance . . . As these elements declined, so prosperity

[14] Ibid. 147.
[15] M. Pinto-Duschinsky, 'Bread and Circuses: The Conservative Party in Office, 1951–64', in Bogdanor and Skidelsky, eds., *Age of Affluence*, 55.
[16] Ibid. 55–6.

rose in significance as a major basis of cohesion. The shift was gradual, always relative, but eventually of considerable importance in its
implications.[17]

However, there were two flaws in this strategy whereby the
possible difficulties for stable prices caused by full employment
were absorbed by economic growth. The first was that continuous
economic growth was by no means a unique British achievement.
All the advanced, industrialized countries benefited. Indeed, with
the exception of the USA, all Britain's major economic competitors did much better in this respect. The French rate of
growth was nearly twice the British; the Italian rather more than
twice; the German rate was over two-and-a-half times the British
rate; and the Japanese did even better.[18] In other words, from an
international perspective the period was one of relative *failure* on
the part of the British economy. However, realization of these
facts did not really influence policy-making in Britain until the
very end of the 1950s; we shall consider in the next chapter the
implications for collective *laissez-faire* of the policies that were
then adopted.

The second problem was that the rate of economic growth in
Britain was not continuous. This was the period of 'stop–go',
that is, of alternatively deflating and reflating demand in the
economy. There were two such cycles in the 1950s and another in
the period to 1964. It proved impossible for the government to
run the economy at a continuously high level of domestic demand
without exports falling off and imports being sucked in, which
led, in an era of fixed exchange rates, to balance of payments
problems and foreign exchange crises. To correct these, the level
of demand in the economy was reduced, but that led, of course,
to a slowdown in, or even a cessation of, economic growth, and
to rising unemployment. To correct these consequences, the
economy would be reflated, and so on. There is no doubt that
the British balance of payments problem in the 1950s had its
structural dimension: notably the low level of the reserves as
compared with the level of overseas sterling liabilities (both
consequences of the need to finance the Second World War). In

[17] C. Crouch, *The Politics of Industrial Relations* (2nd edn., London, 1982),
32–3.
[18] Pinto-Duschinsky, 'Bread and Circuses', 57.

1951 the UK reserves were £800 million whilst the overseas liabilities stood at £3,500 million.[19] The situation was exacerbated by the high levels of British military expenditures overseas. Slowly and haltingly during the 1950s and 1960s these structural problems were addressed, but, perhaps not surprisingly, governments also looked for more immediate causes and remedies for the periodic balance of payments crises.

Following this line of enquiry, it became clear that retail prices were increasing at a faster rate than economic productivity (3.25 per cent per annum between 1952 and 1964). Unlike in the 1940s, when inflation was largely the result of an increase in the price of imports, in the 1950s, after the end of the Korean War, the terms of trade moved in Britain's favour. The causes of inflation in the 1950s were thus largely domestic, and in fact 'the inflationary process basically took the form of a wage–wage and price–wage spiral.'[20] The increase in money wages in this period was on average 6 per cent per annum, not a high increase by later standards, but a level that comfortably exceeded the growth of output per head. Thus we see that the problem of reconciling full employment and stable prices, which policy-makers had been debating since the War, did not in fact evaporate with the advent of economic growth (at least at the levels obtained in Britain in the 1950s), though growth no doubt ameliorated the problem. Before looking at the specific policy instruments that governments in the 1950s adopted to address the problem as thus defined, we ought to look at a second factor, in addition to economic growth, that reduced the size of the problem from government's point of view.

This second factor was the degree of moderation over wage claims that the TUC continued to exercise, at least in the first half of the 1950s. We have seen that the influence exercised by the General Council was a central element of governments' wages policies throughout the 1940s, and the election of a Conservative government in 1951 did not immediately bring a change in the TUC's position. From the TUC's point of view, the most important of the post-war changes was undoubtedly the commitment by government to full employment, and the

---

[19] Oppenheimer, 'Muddling Through', 124.
[20] Ibid. 139.

Conservative government's ready reaffirmation of that policy provided a good basis for continued cooperation between government and TUC. Moreover, the welfare state appeared safe in the government's hands and, even if further nationalization was not on the cards, it was not clear how enthusiastic the General Council really was for further measures of this sort. It may be that the General Council's attitude towards nationalization had been tempered by its appreciation that, contrary to its previous expectations, nationalization had not been necessary to ensure full employment under post-war economic conditions.[21] Furthermore, at the outset of our period the TUC largely shared the government's analysis of the economic situation. In its 1952 report to Congress the General Council put forward the view that the British balance of payments situation was precarious; increasing exports must be a priority if full employment was to be preserved, but 'substantial wage increases are bound to raise costs'; a number of steps needed to be taken to deal with the problem, but one of them was to control the price of exports, a factor 'largely within our control—and to some extent within the control of the Trade Union Movement'.[22] This fairly explicit call for moderation in wage claims was accompanied by the assertion that there should be no interference by government in the traditional methods of wage settlement via collective bargaining, but it was clear that the General Council saw full employment as being at risk if the bargaining strength of workers was fully deployed.

Such calls for moderation in wage claims were a regular part of General Council reports in the first part of the 1950s. Thereafter, they cease to appear, partly because of the arrival of a new generation of more radical trade union leaders, partly because full employment increasingly came to be taken for granted, partly because the Conservative governments could offer little to supplement full employment as an additional attraction for TUC loyalty, and partly because their domestic policies began to be

[21] TUC, *Annual Report 1953*, app. A, para. 15. See also para. 13: 'It would not be true today to say that public opinion is strongly prepared for the transfer of further industries to public ownership. Any proposals for the extension of this form of public control must therefore grow logically and demonstrably out of the experience of nationalization already gained, and out of the needs of the community.'

[22] 'The Trade Unions and the Economic Situation', paras. 27-8, repr. in TUC, *Annual Report 1952*, at p. 285.

seen as working against the interests of TUC members, for example by the elimination of food subsidies whilst reducing taxation on the well-off or by imposing the first 'stop' in the middle 1950s and so increasing unemployment. Nevertheless, throughout the 1950s there is no evidence of the General Council positively encouraging wage militancy, something for which the government was grateful.[23]

(b) Anti-Inflation Measures

Looking at the matter schematically, one can see that there were three broad policy choices before governments which wished to deal with the dilemma of full employment and stable prices. The first was to tolerate the resulting level of inflation; the second to move away from the commitment to full employment; and the third was to bring to bear on the bargaining process novel forms of constraint which might be thought in some degree to replace the previous constraint of high unemployment.[24] It is the third category that is the most interesting in our perspective. This is not simply because the first two policy options involve an—at least implicit—admission that full employment and stable prices cannot be reconciled, but also because the third category is likely to involve governmental administrative or legislative action designed to control the bargaining process. In fact, the third category contains a rather wide range of possible specific policies, ranging from general exhortation to the most precise of criminal prohibitions.

The Conservative governments of the 1950s took policy initiatives under each of the three headings described in the previous paragraph. The initiatives were, however, in all cases rather modest, partly, no doubt, because economic growth kept the problem of inflation within bounds most of the time and partly for fear that such policies would alienate the General Council, whose moderating influence was thought to be helping to keep level of wage claims in check. The policy of tolerating inflation meant, as we have seen, that retail prices rose at an average of 3.25 per cent per annum in this period, a level that was regarded

[23] R. Flanagan, D. Soskice, and L. Ulman, *Unionism, Economic Stabilization and Incomes Policies: European Experience* (Washington, DC, 1983), 377.
[24] C. Crouch, *Class Conflict and the Industrial Relations Crisis* (London, 1977), 196.

in many circles as tolerable. However, the level was not constant. The gross domestic product (GDP) deflater rose to 6.2 per cent in 1956 and was above 4 per cent in each of the succeeding two years.[25] This illustrates the risk from the government's point of view in using inflation as the safety valve, namely, that in the long run the situation is unlikely to prove stable—since increased prices are likely to prompt a higher level of wage claims—and may quickly get out of hand. Certainly, as we shall see, when higher rates of inflation coincided with balance of payments crises, even the governments of the 1950s were induced to take further steps.

The second policy option was to move away from the commitment to full employment. As we have seen, the Conservative government of the early 1950s in fact confirmed their commitment to full employment, and unemployment remained at very low levels throughout the decade. So this policy option cannot be said to have been taken up. Nevertheless, it is significant that the 1956 White Paper, *The Economic Implications of Full Employment*,[26] for the first time in the post-war period questioned the priority to be attached to full employment as an object of government policy, if it could not be reconciled with stable prices. The first paragraph of the White Paper stated:

Full employment has brought with it one problem to which we have not yet found a satisfactory solution: yet, unless we do find the solution, it will be more difficult to achieve a further advance in living standards, and full employment itself may be threatened. The problem is that of continually rising prices.

Later on the White Paper put the following dilemma:

It may seem that the country can make a choice—albeit a painful one—between full employment and continually rising prices, or price stability secured with some danger to the level of employment that might otherwise be achieved. But soon looms up the grim danger that the first of these apparent alternatives will turn out to have been no alternative at all, because we may fail to secure sufficient imports to maintain full employment and our present standard of living.[27]

[25] Flanagan, Soskice, and Ulman, *Unionism*, 368.
[26] Cmd. 9725.
[27] Ibid., para. 26 .

Having thus, so to speak, put down a marker that the government's commitment to full employment was not unconditional, the White Paper placed its main emphasis in its proposals for solving the dilemma between full employment and stable prices upon continuing self-restraint in the making of wage claims and in the fixing of incomes in general and upon greater and more efficient investment and greater co-operation by workers in the introduction of new methods of working, so as to increase the levels of industrial productivity. In other words, the White Paper's preferred policy was to strengthen the operation of the two forces which we have already analysed as keeping the problem of inflation within limits: economic growth and moderation on the part of the bargainers.[28] With the White Paper we have also clearly arrived at an example of the third category of policy options, namely, the government bringing to bear upon the bargaining process a form of constraint derived from its own powers. The constraint chosen was, of course, the mildest one that lay at the government's disposal and one that had been frequently used by governments since the early 1940s, namely, exhortation of those engaged in bargaining to exercise self-restraint—in their own best interests. In its penultimate paragraphs the authors of the White Paper, having noted that wages in Britain 'are fixed by free negotiation between employers and workpeople, within a system of collective bargaining', went on to suggest that governmental acceptance of that system might depend upon self-restraint.

But the satisfactory operation of this whole system depends upon everyone involved being fully aware of the issues at stake, and upon their acceptance of the full duties of citizenship which this realisation places upon them. If they always place sectional interest before the nation's welfare, economic stability will be endangered and the possibilities of future expansion impaired, possibly to the extent of jeopardising those very sectional interests which they seek to protect.

Having thus hinted at more active forms of intervention, the White Paper ended by putting the emphasis on rational, voluntary action.

[28] The resignation of Peter Thorneycroft, the then Chancellor, in Jan. 1958 was essentially because of his willingness to tolerate higher unemployment, if that was the price to be paid for bringing inflation down, and the rest of the Cabinet's unwillingness to do so.

We all want full employment and we all want stable prices. But we have not yet succeeded in combining the two. . . . The Government does not believe there is any inevitable conflict between the two objectives. We can achieve them both if certain conditions are fulfilled; and it has been the aim of this White Paper to state what these conditions are, in the belief that greater awareness of the nature of the problem will contribute to finding a solution for it.

Information, argument, and exhortation were indeed major weapons in the 1950s in what the government perceived as its struggle to reconcile stable prices and full employment. They may seem, from the perspective of the 1980s, feeble enough devices, but they nevertheless contributed to a growing divergence between the government's and the TUC's way of viewing the country's economic difficulties. The TUC, for example, refused to circulate the 1956 White Paper to its affiliated unions on the grounds that 'the White Paper could not adequately be considered in its self-imposed isolation from broader issues of economic policy, including Government's responsibility for maintaining a favourable climate for price stability'.[29] However, government intervention in the bargaining process was not confined to exhortation but went on to embrace, at various points in the decade, a variety of administrative actions and, indeed, one legislative act.

We have noted that when the Conservative government came to power, its predecessor's wage freeze had collapsed. The new government did not propose a new income policy, perhaps because, as a free market party, it did not view such interventions in the labour market with favour. In any case, the experience of 1948 to 1950 did not encourage such interventions, and the conventional wisdom of the time was that centralized wages policies, in the decentralized British industrial relations system, were beyond the power of the government or the TUC to operate.[30] But at a meeting of the NJAC in May 1952 the Chancellor of the Exchequer did call for wage increases to be moderated in view of their inflationary effect. The Minister of Labour and National Service then sought to implement this

[29] TUC, *Annual Report 1956*, 265.
[30] See e.g. C. W. Guillebaud, 'Problems of Wages Policy', in Ministry of Labour and National Service, *The Worker in Industry* (Centenary Lectures, 1951); B. C. Roberts, *National Wages Policy in War and Peace* (London, 1958), Preface.

policy in one particular sector. Under the Wages Council legislation, decisions of the councils about wage increases did not
(except in agriculture) automatically acquire legal effect, but
rather had to be turned into Wages Orders by the Minister. As
part of this process the Minister had the power to refer back (but
not amend) proposals to the council in question for reconsideration. The Minister's powers of reference back were apparently
unlimited.

The issue of whether the Minister should use his powers of
reference back to support wages policy had arisen in 1948 in the
context of the wage freeze, but had not been pushed to the point
of a public dispute between Government and TUC. In late 1951
and early 1952 the new Conservative Minister referred back
wages proposals from the Brush and Broom and the Paper Bag
Wages Councils on the grounds that they included a cost-of-living
sliding-scale provision. The Minister thought 'it was undesirable
under present economic conditions to fix statutory minimum
wages at an undetermined level varying with the cost of living'.[31]
The proposals were later approved when resubmitted without
the sliding-scale provisions. However, in July 1952 the Minister
confirmed that he was referring back wages proposals from
twelve councils 'so that they could be reconsidered in the light of
the statement on wages policy made by the Chancellor of the
Exchequer to the National Joint Advisory Council on May 15'.[32]
This led to vigorous TUC protests to the Prime Minister and
the Minister of Labour, who rather rapidly backed down. The
Minister refused to withdraw the reference back, but intimated
that the councils' proposals would be immediately approved
when resubmitted, which they duly were in unamended form.[33]
The episode thus shows the government casting about for indirect
ways of supporting wages policy, but not being disposed to risk a
major confrontation with the TUC over the issue.[34] The episode
also shows the degree to which the General Council was attached

[31] TUC, *Annual Report 1952*, 291.
[32] Ibid. 292–3.
[33] Ibid. 294.
[34] By the end of the decade the government had become less sensitive over this
issue. Thus Selwyn Lloyd's 'pay pause' (see below, p. 117), announced in July
1961, was applied to Wages Councils by virtue of the Minister simply postponing
the implementation date of the wages order (for up to 6 months). TUC protests
this time did not cause a change of mind: TUC, *Annual Report 1962*, 246.

to the principle of non-interference by government in wage-setting and to restraint being an autonomous activity, even when, as we have seen, it shared the government's general economic analysis of the need for wage restraint.

As the middle of the decade approached, and with it balance of payments problems, the government, finding that simple exhortation was inadequate for its purposes, began to develop two supplementary, but rather inconsistent, policies. One was to attack trade unions as the cause of the country's economic problems—a significant change from the earlier, eulogistic analyses of trade unions and collective bargaining—and to encourage employers to stand up to trade union wage demands. The 1956 White Paper, analysed earlier, was widely seen by employers as expressing this policy. When, however, in 1957 employers in the shipbuilding and engineering industries decided to put into practice the policy of treating inflation as a more important threat to the economy than industrial action, the government quickly backed down in the face of national strikes in those industries. The employers, feeling badly let down, were encouraged to settle.[35]

The other policy was to attempt to support the government's calls for wage moderation by praying in aid independent and authoritative economic analysis pointing in the same direction. In 1954 the reports of Courts of Inquiry into disputes in the engineering and shipbuilding industries had proposed that there be an 'authoritative and impartial' inquiry into the economic problems surrounding wage claims, a suggestion rejected by the General Council, who thought that 'whatever needed to be said to the Trade Union Movement on the present economic situation could most appropriately be said by themselves'.[36] After the failure of the policy of standing firm and the sterling crisis of 1956, however, the government moved to implement the idea by establishing a Council on Prices, Productivity, and Incomes,

[35] For an account of this episode see H. A. Clegg and R. Adams, *The Employers' Challenge* (Oxford, 1957). For the government to be seen to encourage industrial conflict was a sharp contrast with the policy pursued earlier in the decade of placing the highest priority on industrial peace, a policy associated above all with Sir Walter Monckton (Minister of Labour and National Service, Oct. 1951 to Dec. 1955). On Monckton, see Justin Davis Smith, *The Attlee and Churchill Administrations and Industrial Unrest, 1945–1955* (London, 1990), ch. 7.

[36] TUC, *Annual Report 1954*, 290.

under the Chairmanship of Lord Cohen. The Council was to be independent of government, and negotiators and arbitrators were under no legal obligation to take account of its views, but it would have the function of defining the national economic interest, so that negotiators and arbitrators would be able to take account of its views. The General Council reluctantly agreed to give evidence to the Council—a reluctance derived from the 1956 TUC's rejection of all forms of wage restraint—but when its first reports (1958) tended in the direction of increasing unemployment in order to eliminate inflation, the TUC deplored its views and refused to co-operate any further in the Council's activities. The Council issued three further reports in the period to 1961, but they probably had little influence.[37]

Thus by the middle of our period the policy of simple exhortation had been supplemented by three further devices: referring back of wages councils orders, encouraging employers to stand firm against wage claims, and setting up a body to provide an authoritative and non-governmental view of the national economic interest. None of these devices was particularly successful nor, indeed, were they pursued with any intensity by government. In the later 1950s, during the good period of a 'stop–go' cycle, government continued to be concerned about the issue but produced no new policy initiatives. However, when sterling came under serious pressure in early 1961, the Treasury revived arguments for a general incomes policy and this time won the argument against the Ministry of Labour, which continued to argue against interference by government in collective bargaining. Thus a decade after the Conservatives came to power, rejecting the general wages policy of their predecessors, they were forced to resort to such an incomes policy. The policy announced by Mr Selwyn Lloyd in July 1961, like its predecessor of 1948, was a non-statutory policy. However, it had two significant differences from its predecessor. First, it was imposed by government without prior consultation with the unions. This was an indication of how far co-operative relations between government and trade unions had deteriorated in the 1950s and of how the government now regarded it as politically sustainable to risk a confrontation with the TUC. Second, although the policy announced by Selwyn

[37] Crouch, *Class Conflict*, 71–4, 201–4.

Lloyd was initially a wage freeze—or 'pay pause', as it was called—it was intended that the pause should be only a first stage in a permanent incomes policy. Wages policy was to be no longer something just for economic crises, but a part of the standing mechanisms for the management of the economy.[38]

How was the non-statutory pause to be implemented, if it did not have trade union support? The answer was that it was simply imposed[39] by government in the public sector, including the nationalized industries, whilst in the private sector the government, reverting to its policy of the mid-1950s, encouraged employers to follow suit. In the Wages Council sector the policy was implemented by the Minister approving the proposals submitted but postponing their implementation for up to six months. The pause was relatively successful from the government's point of view, and in February 1962 they announced the next stage of the policy (a 'guiding light' for wage increases of 2 per cent) in the White Paper, *Incomes Policy: The Next Step*.[40] The fate of this first attempt at a permanent incomes policy will be considered in Chapter 4.

However, before leaving the topic of governmental policy towards inflation, we ought to note one legislative action that resulted from the government's policies. This was not legislation to impose a wages policy—that stage was not reached until the 1960s—but rather the repeal of legislation which, although having some other objective as its main purpose, was thought by government to have inflationary consequences. The repeal of Order 1376 in 1958 was perhaps the first example of what was in the 1980s to become a common form of government action. The ostensible reason for the repeal of the system of compulsory unilateral arbitration was the employers' request that this should happen because workgroups (after the repeal of the criminal prohibitions on striking in 1951) did not always accept the IDT awards. In fact, the evidence for this view was rather thin, and it

[38] D. Barnes and E. Reid, *Governments and Trade Unions* (London, 1980), 35.

[39] The 'pause' gave rise to some interesting legal issues as to whether wage increases agreed collectively before the announcement of the pause, but not implemented, had been incorporated into individual contracts of employment. See *Dudfield* v. *Ministry of Works. The Times* (24 Jan. 1964), and *Faithful* v. *The Admiralty*, ibid., both repr. in K. W. Wedderburn, *Cases and Materials on Labour Law* (Cambridge, 1967), 296–300.

[40] Cmnd. 1626.

seems that both employers and, especially, government took the view that there was another, stronger objection to Order 1376, namely, that the arbitration machinery operated in an inflationary manner.[41] In any event, as we have noted, Order 1376 was repealed, with only the enforcement of recognized terms and conditions being carried over to s. 8 of the Terms and Conditions of Employment Act 1959.

(c) Civil Service Pay and Equal Pay

Thus it seems fair to conclude that in this period, and especially from the mid-1950s onwards, governments were concerned at the rate of increase of money wages, but found it difficult to define and adhere to a single policy, or set of policies, which would address the issue. But it would be wrong to assume that governmental wages policy was solely concerned with the potential inflationary consequences of pay settlements in this period. At least in relation to its own employees, and those in the public sector more generally, who constituted a significant part of the national workforce, two further policies can be discerned, relating to comparability and equal pay.

At least since the 1930s Civil Service pay had been fixed mainly on the basis of comparability (under the 'Tomlin formula' of 1931). In 1955 a Royal Commission on the Civil Service (the Priestley Commission) reported.[42] This was a somewhat ill-named commission, since its terms of reference were confined to examining conditions of service, especially pay, whilst broader issues of recruitment, training, promotion, grading structure, and efficiency of performance were excluded. It received evidence, moreover, almost exclusively from government departments and the Civil Service unions; no attempt was made to secure evidence of the 'public interest', except as presented by the organizations of Civil Service employers and employees. Not surprisingly, perhaps, the Commission confirmed the comparability principle and, indeed, strengthened it, by proposing the establishment of a Civil Service body independent of both the Treasury and the Civil Service unions to assemble and analyse information about comparable jobs outside the civil service. (Existing practice was

[41] J. W. Durcan, W. E. J. McCarthy, and G. P. Redman, *Strikes in Post-War Britain* (London, 1983), 366.
[42] Cmd. 9613.

for both unions and the Treasury to produce at the bargaining
table what they respectively regarded as compelling comparisons).
Bargaining could then take place on the basis of the independently
verified evidence thus produced.

The Commission made full play with the virtues of comparability. It enabled the government to say that it treated its
employees fairly, because it paid what comparable employers
paid for comparable work, but this principle could also be justified
vis-à-vis the taxpayer. More important, perhaps, the principle
operated so as to take wage determination in the Civil Service
out of politics, protecting civil servants from political pressure.[43]
Moreover, although the Commission made less of this point, it
could be said that it reduced the chances of industrial conflict
between the government and its employees by providing an
agreed, quasi-objective basis for settling pay levels. What is
interesting from our point of view, however, is that the government accepted and implemented the Priestly Commission's
Report without demur, by setting up the Civil Service Pay
Research Unit, even though the whole principle of comparability
gave the government less control over its pay bill than it might
have wished and even though, if pay settlements in the private
sector were thought to be inflationary, the principle could be
viewed as an instrument for spreading inflation into the public
sector. It was not until the 1980s, however, that these disadvantages of the comparability principle came to be seen by
government as outweighing the undoubted advantages that the
consensual, reactive policy advocated by Priestley engendered.[44]

It was part of the Priestley philosophy of pay determination in
the Civil Service that pay should not be set by government, in

[43] Ibid. 25.

[44] See the Report of the Inquiry into Civil Service Pay, Cmnd. 8590 (1982)
(below, ch. 10.2(d)), which recommended that 'comparisons . . . should have a
much less decisive influence than in the past' (para. 367, point 4). The operation
of the Pay Research Unit and the criticisms of the comparison system are
described in chs. 3 and 4 of the Report. Comparability was publicly endorsed in
the mid-1950s also in relation to fixing the remuneration of doctors and dentists
(for whom a Review Body was established) and, in the nationalized industries,
the remuneration of railwaymen and London busmen. The arrangements for the
latter two groups were condemned in the 1960s by the National Board for Prices
and Incomes as inconsistent with the then incomes policy and abandoned. See H.
Clegg, *The Changing System of Industrial Relations in Great Britain* (Oxford,
1979), 111–12.

relation to its own employees, 'with the intention of giving a lead on such matters to the country as a whole or in order to further a political or social objective'.[45] Yet in respect of equal pay that can be argued to be precisely what government did in the 1950s. The campaign by and on behalf of women for equal pay was, of course, a long-standing one—the TUC passed its first resolution in favour of the principle in 1888—and the establishment of equal pay proved extremely difficult to achieve in practice. The greater employment of women in the First World War looked likely to change social attitudes, and a Report of the War Cabinet Committee recommended in 1919 that equal pay should be introduced into the Civil Service.[46] In the inter-war period, however, this recommendation was not acted upon; indeed, the position of women in employment worsened as the bar on the employment or continued employment of married women was applied more rigorously in the Civil Service,[47] as in other public and private sector employments. The depression was not a propitious time for social advance and, indeed, the marriage bar was often an overt attempt to switch part of the burden of unemployment from the shoulders of young males to married females.[48]

The Second World War again produced sentiment in favour of equal pay, partly because the crucial role of women in the civilian

[45] Cmd. 9613, para. 99. The government should simply follow the private sector, i.e. it should be a 'good' but not a 'model' employer. On the other hand, the Priestley Commission rejected the 'market clearing' principle for setting Civil Service pay, i.e. that it should be set simply at the levels necessary to recruit and retain the required numbers of employees of the relevant abilities, because 'the State is under a categorical obligation to remunerate its employees fairly' (para. 90). It was precisely this principle, rejected by Priestley, that was advocated in the 1982 Report: Cmnd. 8590, para. 367, point 1.

[46] Report of the War Cabinet Committee on Women in Industry, Cmd. 135 (1918), para. 223. The Committee was in favour of equal pay generally and not just in the Civil Service. 'We desire to accept the principle involved by the general formula [of equal pay for equal work] insofar as it is intended to prevent reduction of men's wages by the competition of women with lower standards and less organization' (para. 211).

[47] Civil Service National Whitley Council Committee, The Marriage Bar in the Civil Service, Cmd. 6886 (1946), para. 7.

[48] See Price v. Rhondda UDC [1923] Ch. 372. In this case the Education Committee of the local authority decided to terminate the engagement of all married women teachers 'having regard to the large number of certified teachers who would complete their course of training in the month of July without any prospect of securing employment'. The decision survived a legal challenge to its validity.

workforce was seen to strengthen their moral claim to equal pay and partly because the greater employment of women created a desire on the part of male workers to protect themselves from undercutting. Thus the typical substitution agreement concluded between employers and trade unions in wartime not only confined the employment of women on 'men's work' to the period when male workers were not available but also required the women to receive the full male rate for the job 'if they are able to undertake it without additional assistance or supervision'.[49] The purpose of the latter provision was more to protect men's than to advance women's interests. Like the First, the Second World War also produced a government committee to consider the question: in 1944 the coalition government established a Royal Commission on equal pay.[50] This, however, had the most limited terms of reference. It was not asked to recommend in favour or against the principle, but to examine the 'social, economic and financial implications' of the claim. The principle was framed in terms of 'equal pay for equal work', but, as was usual at the time, this was conceived, as we should see it today, largely in terms of equal pay for 'like work' rather than for work for equal value, and certainly did not embrace a study of fair differentials between different jobs.

Perhaps not surprisingly, the Royal Commission's Report in 1946 did little to add to the campaign for equal pay, which in many ways had already achieved its greatest success of the 1940s

[49] TUC, *Annual Report 1945*, para. 30. Legislative provision was made to this end during the First World War: Munitions of War Act 1915, Sched. 2, para. 5.

[50] Report of the Royal Commission on Equal Pay, Cmd. 6937, 1946 (Chairman: Asquith LJ).

[51] In the committee debates on what became the Education Act 1944, Mrs Cazalet Keir secured the acceptance of an amendment which prohibited the body responsible for fixing teachers' remuneration (the Burnham Committee) from differentiating between teachers on grounds of sex (HC Deb., vol. 398, cols. 1356–91 (28 Mar. 1994)). However, the Prime Minister later made the removal of this amendment a matter of confidence in the coalition government (ibid., cols. 1452–7, 1654), but the episode clearly put pressure on the government to establish the Royal Commission (HC Deb., vol. 399, col. 1709 (9 May 1944)). The government's refusal to give the Royal Commission the power to make recommendations was both an indication of the coalition government's reluctance to act on the issue and a classic example of the importance of terms of reference in controlling the results of official committees. See generally H. L. Smith, 'The Problem of "Equal Pay for Equal Work" in Great Britain during World War II' (1981) 53 *Journal of Modern History* 652.

in 1944.[51] In the economic crises of the immediate post-war period the Labour government proved as unwilling as governments after the First World War to add to employers' labour costs. In 1948 the TUC, which had given spirited evidence to the Royal Commission in favour of equal pay, accepted 'that in the present economic situation the General Council should not press for immediate and comprehensive implementation of the principle'.[52] This time, however, unlike thirty years earlier, the economic crisis led, not to depression and unemployment, but to labour scarcity and the relative prosperity of the 1950s. This climate proved more favourable and the equal pay campaigns,[53] within and outside the union movement, revived. The TUC did not envisage at this time the use of legislation to achieve equal pay, but rather its implementation in the public sector by government administrative action and in the private sector through collective bargaining. In January 1955 a major part of the campaign for the public sector was achieved when the government agreed through the Civil Service National Whitley Council to the introduction of equal pay (for like work) in the non-industrial Civil Service—but the achievement of equal pay was to be phased in through seven annual instalments of special pay increases for women civil servants. No doubt with government approval, similar developments took place in local government, the nationalized industries, and the health service.[54] Thus by the early 1960s the main groups of women workers not to have achieved equal pay (for like work) were manual workers and workers, whether manual or white-collar, in private industry and commerce. As we shall see, however, the tackling of that bastion of inequality was ultimately seen to require the use of legislation.

[52] TUC, *Annual Report 1949*, 252.

[53] A. Potter, 'The Equal Pay Campaign Committee: A Case-Study of a Pressure Group' (1957) 5 *Political Studies* 49.

[54] C. A. Larsen, 'Equal Pay for Women in the UK' (1971) 103 *Int. Lab. Rev.* 1. Under labour market pressures the marriage bar seems to have dissolved rather earlier. It was removed in the Home Civil Service in 1946 (see HC Deb., vol. 426, cols. 381–8 (25 July 1946) and vol. 427, cols. 794–6 (15 Oct. 1946)). This decision 'was probably dictated as much by the necessities of the national manpower situation as by the views of the Government on equality of the sexes': H. Keast, 'Married Women in Established Employment' (1947–8) 2 *Industrial Law Review* at 162. Cf. Education (Scotland) Act 1945, s. 51. See also H. L. Smith, 'The Womanpower Problem in Britain during the Second World War' (1984) 27 *Historical Journal* 925.

Two general reflections are prompted by this history of equal pay. First, although legislation was not needed to secure it in the public sector, its implementation in this sector was nevertheless a challenge to collective *laissez-faire*, in the sense that the reasons for the reform were not primarily pressures from the collective bargainers in this area, but rather pressures from outside the industrial relations system. The public sector unions did play a major part in the reform effort after 1951, but the longer and more influential input came from the feminist Equal Pay Campaign Committee,[55] which was chaired throughout its existence by female Conservative MPs. Equally, the Conservative government's commitment to and actual introduction of equal pay in the Civil Service seems to have owed more to calculations of electoral advantage against the Labour Party (which had refused to implement equal pay when it was in office) than to difficulties in recruiting female civil servants. In other words, this reform was prompted more by considerations relevant to the state as a government than as employer. Perhaps most significant is the fact that it was the Ministry of Labour, that guardian of collective *laissez-faire*, which opposed (successfully) the Treasury's proposal that equal pay be extended to industrial, as well as non-industrial, civil servants, seemingly on the grounds that such an extension would generate industrial unrest in the private sector.[56]

The second reflection is that government's response to both the equal pay and the comparability issues shows the way in which public sector employees were thought to be entitled to 'fair' treatment from their employer and not just to the treatment dictated by the labour market. 'Fair' treatment was not always pure benefit to the employee: it might mean, for example, a harsher application of the government's current incomes policy than was the case in the private sector, even if it also meant a stronger claim to equal pay. More fundamentally, this situation demonstrated a difficulty with the application of collective *laissez-faire* in the public sector. In relation to the private sector, the government could set the abstentionist legal framework and then leave (other) employers and the trade unions to proceed with the

---

[55] Potter, 'The Equal Pay Campaign Committee'.

[56] See H. L. Smith, 'The Politics of Conservative Reform: The Equal Pay for Equal Work Issue, 1945–1955' (1992) 35 *Historical Journal* 401, on which this paragraph draws heavily.

bargaining, subject to the constraints of the labour and product markets. In the public sector the government both set the rules and then either conducted or controlled the bargaining. In these circumstances, it is perhaps not surprising that the state's roles as government and as employer could not always be kept entirely separate, especially as the function of government was not traditionally conceived as a market-based activity.

3.3. INDUSTRIAL CONFLICT

We have seen that, after the impact of full employment on price stability, the second most debated issue was the relationship between full employment and the settlement of industrial disputes. Beveridge's hopes for the development of a system of dispute settlement other than by 'a trial of strength' were disappointed, and once the Trade Disputes and Trade Unions Act 1927 and Order 1305 had been repealed, the policy of the Trade Disputes Act 1906 was fully restored, namely, that peaceful resort to economic sanctions in the settlement of industrial disputes should be lawful, both in criminal and civil law. There seems, however, to have been no close correlation between these changes in the law relating to industrial disputes and variations in the strike statistics. As we have seen, the number of strikes, especially the number of short strikes, increased during the war, although striking was an offence and some attempts were made to enforce the law. In the period 1946 to 1952, however, despite the repeal of the 1927 Act in 1946 and the non-enforcement of the criminal restrictions on strikes, strike activity fell to a historically low level and the trend of strike activity was downwards. On average there were some 525 strikes per year in this period, involving some 228,000 workers and the loss of some 1.3 million working days.[57] Thus strikes in general were not a main topic of concern for the post-war Labour governments, although, as we have seen, strikes in certain specific industries, notably the docks, did cause the government difficulties, which were often alleviated by the deployment of troops.[58]

[57] Durcan, McCarthy, and Redman, *Strikes*, 26.
[58] Above, ch. 2.3(*b*)(ii).

From the latter part of 1953 onwards, however, the downward trend in strikes was reversed. Durcan, McCarthy, and Redman[59] have isolated two different strands in this development. The first was an increase in the number of strikes, usually of a short duration. In fact the average over the years 1953 to 1959 was no higher than in the period 1946 to 1952, but the worrying feature of the statistics from the government's point of view was that the trend was now clearly upwards: there were, for example, 439 strikes in 1953 but 786 in 1959. The second feature was 'the reappearance of the "set piece strike" in both token and total forms—i.e. industry-wide stoppages conducted with the support and approval of the trade unions concerned'.[60] These strikes had a big impact upon the statistics, not for the number of strikes, but for the number of workers involved (551,200 per annum on average in this period) and the number of working days lost (3.4 million). The weakness of the unions after the General Strike and the unions' commitment to Order 1305 after 1940 meant that large official stoppages had not been part of the British industrial relations scene for two decades—Durcan, McCarthy, and Redman identify the last 'set piece' strike before the one-day stoppage by engineering workers in December 1953 as having been that by textile workers in 1933.

What were the causes of this reversal of the previous trend? It seems clear that governmental attempts to impose wage restraint helped to precipitate most of the major stoppages in the 1950s, so that it is wrong to put government concern with inflation and with levels of industrial conflict in entirely separate boxes. As we have seen, in 1956 and 1957 the Government for a while seemed willing to tolerate a higher level of industrial conflict if that produced a lower level of wage increases. The shipbuilding and engineering disputes of 1957 by themselves involved 800,000 workers and led to the loss of 6 million working days. The shift in the focus of government concern from industrial peace, even at a high cost in terms of wage increases, the policy of the first half of the 1950s, to an equal concern with inflation was also reflected in the declining readiness with which the government was prepared to offer its conciliation services. For example, in the busmen's

[59] Durcan, McCarthy, and Redman, *Strikes*, 58.
[60] Ibid.

dispute of 1958 the government withheld the conciliation services, as an indication of its resolution.[61] Indeed, Durcan, McCarthy, and Redman detect[62] a general decline in the 1950s in the government's willingness to intervene in industrial disputes and suggest this contributed to the increasing levels of strike activity. What is clear is that the government's well-publicized withholding of its conciliation services in some prominent disputes, together with the abolition of the quasi-independent post within the Ministry of Chief Industrial Commissioner, fed trade union suspicions of the impartiality of government-sponsored conciliation and arbitration and contributed to the ultimate hiving-off of these services from the Ministry in the early 1970s.

As for the increase in the number of small, short, unofficial stoppages arising from shop-floor issues, that was related to the development of workplace trade union organization and bargaining. As we have seen, this process can be identified as having begun during the war and was closely linked with the advent of full employment and increased bargaining strength for workers, not just through the official trade union structures at national or regional level, but within the enterprise itself and especially at shop-floor level. Precisely why the development of shop-floor bargaining should have led to higher levels of strikes and why that higher level of strike activity should show itself at this time particularly in certain industries, notably the metal trades, were questions to which the Royal Commission on Trade Unions and Employers' Associations was to devote considerable attention in the 1960s, and we shall return to the subject in a later chapter.

Our focus of interest, however, is in knowing what legislative or administrative action on the part of government was prompted by the upward trend in strikes. As with inflation, the activities of the government *vis-à-vis* strikes were modest in this period, and perhaps for rather similar reasons. Although the trend was upwards, this was a development from a historically low base and was not perceived by government as presenting a major threat to the economy. Indeed, to the extent that governmental anti-inflation policies at times relied upon strengthening employer resistance to wage demands, higher levels of industrial con-

[61] Ibid. 374.
[62] Ibid. 392.

flict may have been regarded as a desirable, or at any rate an inevitable, consequence of these policies. In so far as action was seen to be required, the government relied mainly, following the voluntarist tradition, upon employers and, especially, trade unions to take it. Thus in 1955, after some major disputes in the docks and on the railways, the General Council met with the Prime Minister. The latter expressed his concern about the impact on the economy of the stoppages, but

so far as the Cabinet was concerned . . . it had not discussed, nor had it in mind, the possibility of additional legislation relating to strikes or industrial disputes. The Prime Minister said he was convinced that the best course to follow was to leave the two sides of industry to work out their problems and to continue to make available the machinery of the Ministry of Labour for help in reaching agreed settlements. Other suggestions had been made in and around Parliament of a general inquiry into the industrial problems by a committee of one kind or another . . . [but] he could see very great difficulties about the terms of reference and the composition of such a committee and the government itself was not greatly enamoured of the suggestion.[63]

Indeed, the TUC showed itself willing to take what action it could and to discharge its responsibilities as it saw them. Thus the disputes that were the subject of the 1955 meeting with the Prime Minister had all had an element of inter-union conflict in them, and the General Council proposed to broaden its powers under Rule 11 of the Rules and Standing Orders of Congress to intervene in industrial disputes. Rule 11 confined powers of intervention to situations where a dispute was likely to involve other workers represented by a TUC union beyond those involved in the dispute with the employer. However, as it stood, the General Council could intervene only once negotiations between the direct parties to the dispute had broken down, and so Rule 11 was amended to allow intervention when a breakdown seemed likely.[64] Again, in 1960 the General Council reported to Congress on a review it had undertaken of disputes and workshop representation. The review indicated clearly the considerable reservations union leaders in general had about the growth of workplace representation by shop stewards, especially the

---

[63] TUC, *Annual Report 1955*, 139–40.
[64] Ibid. 140–1.

practice of forming joint committees of shop stewards from a number of different unions. Joint committees of shop stewards formed at national, industry, or even enterprise level were roundly condemned as a challenge to the authority of established unions. Even at establishment (or plant) level, the traditional and most widespread area of operation for shop stewards, joint committees were assessed with caution. Some joint arrangements at establishment level had been 'harmful' because 'joint stewards' bodies have concluded agreements inconsistent with union policies: in these cases the joint character of the stewards' body has been used as an excuse for not referring the matters to the proper channels in the union concerned'.[65] Stewards who took action, including industrial action, contrary to the advice of their unions should be disciplined, for example by the withdrawal of their credentials as stewards. In spite of some spirited opposition at Congress to the tenor of this report, it was approved.[66]

However, although the Conservative governments of the 1950s did not feel it appropriate to address the problem of strikes by altering the law relating to industrial conflict, as time went by it became clear that by no means all the influential parts of the Conservative Party accepted that this was the correct approach. In 1958 the Inns of Court Conservative and Unionist Society published a document, *A Giant's Strength*, which articulated an analysis of labour law based upon a view of trade unions as 'overmighty subjects'. The document was well publicized and, although it seems not to have had an immediate impact upon government policy, it did set down a marker for the future. As far as industrial conflict was concerned, the authors addressed themselves to the issues of both unofficial and official strikes, and proposed radical changes in the law. Persons acting in the course of unofficial disputes should lose all statutory protections against

---

[65] TUC, *Annual Report 1960*, 124 ff.

[66] Ibid. 346–54. TUC disquiet at the activities of unofficial groups of workers had earlier been reflected when Order 1376 replaced Order 1305. The former provided access to the arbitration machinery only for disputes reported (on behalf of workers) by a trade union which 'habitually takes part in the settlement' of terms and conditions of employment in the industry through voluntary machinery or which 'represents a substantial proportion of . . . workers . . . in the trade or industry'. The latter had allowed disputes to be reported 'by or on behalf of either party'. The change was designed to exclude unofficial groups from access to the arbitration machinery.

the common law torts (so that the organization of unofficial action would normally become unlawful at civil law), whilst trade unions and those acting in the course of official strikes would retain the statutory immunities only on conditions. These conditions involved the registration of the union with the Registrar of Friendly Societies and the requirements that any strike should have been 'preceded by an inquiry by an independent tribunal into the facts and issues of the dispute and [that] a period of fourteen days has elapsed between the date of the publication of the report of that tribunal and the calling of the strike'.[67]

The tone of the 1958 document was markedly different from that of the Conservative Party's previous major statement on industrial relations, the *Industrial Charter* of 1947. That document had accepted in principle the repeal in 1946 of the Trade Disputes and Trade Unions Act 1927, threatening that the issues of the closed shop, the political levy, and the political activities of civil servants might have to be looked at afresh by a future Conservative government, but not singling out the repeal of the industrial conflict provisions of the 1927 Act for adverse comment.[68] More generally, the authors of the 1947 document had 'desired to state quite clearly that the official policy of the Conservative Party is in favour of trade unions' and 'that the Conservative Party attaches the highest importance to the part to be played by the unions in guiding the national economy'.[69] The switch of emphasis to an analysis of trade unions as overmighty subjects threatening the interests of both the public and individual workers was an indication of how far the view of trade unions held by at least some elements of the Conservative Party had changed in the course of a decade.

Another straw in the wind could be found outside the immediate circles of party politics. The judiciary, as ever pursuing their own somewhat idiosyncratic agenda, began to give notice in the

[67] Inns of Court Conservative and Unionist Society, *A Giant's Strength* (London, 1958), 54 and see generally pp. 14–24.

[68] Conservative and Unionist Central Office, *The Industrial Charter* (London, 1947), 22. Although the Charter promised 'that legislation should be introduced to resolve these three features of the Trade Disputes Act', the Conservative governments of the 1950s did not in fact do so. On the general issue of repeal of the 1927 Act the document stated that 'we do not intend to indulge in a game of political tit for tat.'

[69] Ibid. 21.

1950s that the structure of immunities against the common law torts, conferred upon those acting in contemplation or furtherance of a trade dispute by the Trade Disputes Act 1906, might not be completely secure, despite the apparently ringing endorsement of the policy of judicial abstention in this area provided by the House of Lords in the *Crofter* case in 1942.[70] In 1952 the Court of Appeal in *D. C. Thomson & Co. Ltd.* v. *Deakin*,[71] confining the policy of *Crofter* to the tort of conspiracy, developed the tort of inducing breach of commercial contracts, notably the indirect form of that tort, in such a way as to threaten the legality of secondary industrial action. Since the 1906 Act gave protection only in relation to the tort of inducing breaches of contracts of employment, this was a potentially serious breach in the principle that the peaceful infliction of economic sanctions in furtherance of a trade dispute should not give rise to legal liability. However, the full force of that decision was muted because the court found that on the facts the tort had not been committed by those threatening the secondary action, and for the rest of the decade employers seemed little interested in exploiting the possibilities for injunctive relief that the decision had created. Once again, it was only in the following decade that the House of Lords in *Stratford* v. *Lindley*[72] demonstrated beyond a doubt the potential of this head of tortious liability and, more significantly, placed the whole issue of industrial conflict law back on the political agenda by its decision in *Rookes* v. *Barnard*,[73] which created or at least significantly developed another head of tortious liability, that of intimidation.

3.4. OTHER AREAS AND CONCLUSION

We have concentrated on the areas of wages policy and industrial conflict because these seemed to be the main areas of governmental concern in the 1950s. In spite of the misgivings felt by governments in these areas, we have sought to stress how relatively limited were the moves away from collective *laissez-faire*

---

[70] [1942] AC 435.
[71] [1952] 1 Ch. 646.
[72] [1965] AC 269.
[73] [1964] AC 1129, and see below, p. 240.

that actually occurred at this time, although indications that something more bold was in contemplation could easily be found. The very qualified nature of the moves away from *laissez-faire* can, no doubt, be explained by a lack of conviction on the government's part that, on the one hand, the problems it faced were of crisis proportions or, on the other, that the advantages of moving away from the established policy of the state towards industrial relations would clearly outweigh the disadvantages of abandoning collective *laissez-faire*, unsatisfactory though that policy in some ways might be turning out to be.

The same theme can be detected running through the issues to which in this period the government attached less importance. For example, employers outside and backbenchers in Parliament grumbled from time to time about restrictive working practices. Although the Conservative Party, when in opposition in 1948, had urged such a course of action upon the then government, it refused when in government itself to take the opportunity offered by the passing of the Restrictive Trade Practices Act 1956 to submit workers' restrictive practices to legislative control.[74] Instead, the government now expressed the view that 'whatever restrictions may be exercised on the workers' side are not a matter for legislation but for joint consultation within industry',[75] and took the time-honoured step of referring the issue to the NJAC. Three years later the NJAC produced a report, after a survey of largely private manufacturing industry, and this concluded that the vast majority of industries either had no problem with the efficient use of manpower or had machinery to deal with any such problems, and so, in the voluntarist tradition, there was no need for government intervention.[76]

The classical voluntarist approach on the part of the government was also on display in respect of its handling of an early piece of 'deregulation' of the employment relationship. By virtue

---

[74] See the exclusion contained in s. 7(4) of the 1956 Act, and cf. the contrary proposal of the authors of *A Giant's Strength* to submit labour restrictive practices to judicial scrutiny (at pp. 31 ff.).

[75] TUC, *Annual Report 1957*, 134.

[76] TUC, *Annual Report 1959*, 132. It is particularly significant that the existence of voluntary machinery to deal with the problem (as opposed to the non-existence of the problem) was regarded as a good reason for non-intervention by the government.

of the provisions of s. 3 of the Truck Act 1831, that the employer must pay a workman 'in the current coin of this realm and not otherwise . . . the entire amount of the wages earned by or payable to him', employers were to their increasing irritation often unable to pay their manual employees[77] by cheque (or money or postal order) or by bank transfer. In 1957 a private member's Bill proposed to make such payments lawful, if the workman so agreed, the agreement to be unilaterally revocable with seven days' notice. The Minister consulted the NJAC, where the TUC's advice against the change prevailed: 'it was appreciated that workers in small concerns or in tied cottages might be in a poor position to exercise free choice.'[78] The relevant clause was dropped from the Bill. However, backbenchers kept up the pressure with further Bills in subsequent years, and in 1959 the NJAC agreed that the Minister should set up a separate inquiry[79] into the general question of reforming the Truck Acts (which were agreed to contain many anomalies), but that in any event the principle of legal payment by cheque etc. or bank transfer at the employee's request should be introduced. This was done by the Payment of Wages Act 1960, which scrupulously preserved the need for the workman's request (and his right to change his mind).[80]

Thus a minor piece of modernization, probably not in itself enough in most cases to enable an employer to switch entirely to a non-cash payments system, came about as a result of non-governmental pressure and only after the government had been

[77] The definition of 'workman' confined the operation of the Truck Acts largely to manual workers: Truck Amendment Act 1887, s. 2 and the Employers and Workman Act 1875, s. 10.

[78] TUC, *Annual Report 1957*, 136.

[79] The Report of the Committee on the Truck Acts (Ministry of Labour, 1961) dealt primarily with the issues of fines for bad workmanship and deductions for stock losses and so on. The Committee wished to have a modernized code to cover these matters, but its rather complex proposals did not receive universal approval and were not implemented. See Note (1962) 25 MLR 215. One interesting proposal, however, was that disputes about whether a deduction or fine was fair and reasonable should go, not to the ordinary courts, but to new tribunals constituted on a tripartite basis: Report, p. 19.

[80] S. 6(7): 'Nothing in this Act shall operate so as to enable an employed person to be required, by the terms or conditions of his employment or otherwise, to make such a request . . . or to refrain from cancelling such a request.'

able to obtain the acquiescence of the union movement in the proposals.[81] Nor was it governmental pressure that produced significant change in the law relating to internal trade union affairs, but rather the courts. In *Bonsor* v. *Musicians Union*[82] (1956) the House of Lords, perhaps foreshadowing the more active role it was to play in labour law in the 1960s, markedly improved the remedies available to a member expelled from a union in breach of its rules by holding that the member was entitled to damages, as well as to an injunction or a declaration. It had previously been doubted whether a member could obtain damages against an unincorporated association, as trade unions were, but the House of Lords in *Bonsor* effectively dealt with the problem, albeit on grounds that, doctrinally, were not entirely persuasive.[83] Since Mr Bonsor had been expelled from a union which operated a quite widespread closed shop and so he had to a large degree lost his livelihood as well as his union membership, the House of Lords' decision could be described as 'a useful blow in favour of individual' freedom',[84] and it was eagerly seized upon by advocates of the 'overmighty subject' analysis of trade unions.[85] From our point of view what is interesting, however, is that government seemed content to let whatever changes in the law were thought necessary in this area be decided by the courts and saw no need for it itself to take the initiative.

However, in spite of the clear reluctance of government in this period to legislate without union and employer consent, there were signs that this policy was under pressure. In the *Industrial*

---

[81] The backbench pressure and the dealings on the NJAC were recounted by the Minister of Labour (Edward Heath) when making the Second Reading speech: HC Deb., vol. 616, cols. 385-9 (28 Jan. 1960). For later developments see below, p. 562.

[82] [1956] AC 104. Another harbinger of judicial developments was the decision of Harman J. in *Huntley* v. *Thornton* [1957] 1 WLR 321, where he interpreted both the common law of conspiracy and the Trade Disputes Act 1906 so as to make liable local officials of a trade union who had taken steps against a member who refused to take part in industrial action. The officials had in effect secured the plaintiff's expulsion from the union and made it very difficult for him to obtain employment in the area.

[83] See Lord Wedderburn, 'The Bonsor Affair—A Postscript' (1957) 20 MLR 105.

[84] Lloyd, Note (1956) 19 MLR 121 at 134.

[85] Lloyd, Note (1954) 17 MLR 360 at 364; C. Grunfeld, 'Trade Unions and the Individual: A Study of Recent Developments in England' (1958) *Journal of Public Law* 289.

Charter the Conservative Party had shown itself attracted by the idea that more effective use of labour would be achieved if employees were guaranteed 'security of employment', and that legislation might have some role in providing such guarantees.[86] This idea did not entirely fade away when the Conservatives came to power, for in 1956 the Minister of Labour consulted the General Council of the TUC about the idea that a Resolution of the House of Commons should be passed putting the House's support behind the principles that employees should be given by their employers written statements of the main terms of employment, and should be entitled to minimum periods of notice, varying with length of service, for lawful termination of their contracts, to have a procedure followed before employment was terminated, and to be informed in advance about changes in organization and production likely to result in loss of employment. This rather half-hearted attempt by government to take the initiative in the manpower field with a species of quasi-legislation was straightforwardly rejected by the TUC: 'The General Council gave their view . . . that there was nothing new in these principles all of which are operative within industry and that nothing of material value would accrue from a resolution of the House of Commons on the lines suggested.'[87] However, as we shall see in the next chapter, the idea that the functioning of the labour market could be improved by legislative intervention did not go away, but rather achieved considerable support from both political parties in the first half of the 1960s.

Thus both in the central areas of wage settlement and industrial conflict and in more marginal areas the government's approach was similar. On the one hand, the system of collective *laissez-faire* was not operating entirely satisfactorily from the government's point of view; on the other, it was not clear that the problems merited a radical break from the prevailing doctrines, given the difficulties such a break would probably entail. It was a delicate balance, but one which was beginning to tilt towards intervention as the decade progressed. The problems of inflation and the levels of unofficial action were tending to increase, whilst government and TUC were drifting into a more adversarial rela-

---

[86] p. 29.
[87] TUC, *Annual Report 1957*, 134.

tionship. Governmental eulogizing of trade unions and collective bargaining was being replaced by a more critical theme, whilst even more sceptical analyses of trade unions and collective bargaining were being heard in policy-making circles adjacent to government. If these trends continued, it was likely that the 1960s would see the first significant steps by government away from collective *laissez-faire*.

4

MODERNIZATION AND EXPERIMENTS WITH PLANNING, 1961–1969

4.1. INTRODUCTION

During the 1950s, and especially in its latter half, considerable dissatisfaction began to emerge amongst policy-makers about both the level of performance being achieved by the British economy and the government's methods of economic management. As we have already seen, the performance of the economy in the 1950s seemed to permit analysis from two different perspectives, which yielded two very different sets of conclusions. Comparison with British economic performance in the immediately preceding decades seemed to suggest that the growth rates achieved in the 1950s made that decade one of unparalleled economic success; comparison with the growth rates achieved by competitor countries in the 1950s suggested the period was one of significant, relative economic decline, on a par with what Britain had experienced, especially *vis-à-vis* Germany, in the years before the First World War. Both lines of analysis were, no doubt, correct as far as they went, but, as the decade progressed, the latter began to impress itself more upon government, as the greater success of other countries became manifest. However, the problem was seen to be not merely that Britain's rate of economic growth was relatively low, but also that it was uneven. The 'stop–go' cycle of economic management, which governments had used in pursuit of the apparently competing goals of full employment, low inflation, and a balance of payments equilibrium, itself came to be seen as a cause of the relatively low growth rate, because, it was said, 'stop–go' deprived industrialists of the confidence necessary for the making of large-scale and long-term investments.

The increasing perception of the domestic economy as unsuccessful, coupled no doubt at some deeper level with the obvious decline in Britain's world role, as evidenced in particular by the Suez débâcle, eventually shook the governing élites out of their complacency with the 1950s ways of doing things. In particular, a more active role for the state in the field of economic management became an accepted part of conventional wisdom. It is impossible to date precisely when this change of heart occurred, but the conversion of the Conservative government under Mr Macmillan to the need to 'modernize' the economy (which occurred during 1961) is a convenient starting-point. What, however, did 'modernization' mean? It is important to grasp, first, what it did *not* mean. It did not mean the abandonment, or even the qualification, of the three main pillars of government economic and social policy which had been erected in the period 1944 to 1950: full employment, a comprehensive welfare state, and a mixed economy. Nor did modernization mean the abandonment, or even the qualification, of Keynesian demand management as the primary method of achieving full employment. What modernization did mean, however, was that Keynesian demand management (necessary to maintain full employment) was to be supplemented by governmental intervention on the supply side of the economy, in order to increase economic efficiency and growth. Keynes himself had tended to assume that, provided government regulated the level of demand in the economy, the market could be left to regulate other matters. In the 1960s development of the Keynesian position, demand management came to be seen to need supplementation by governmental guidance of the supply side of the market. Applied to the labour market, for example, this view might mean that it was not enough (though it was indispensable) for government to ensure that demand was at a sufficient level in the economy for employers to have available job opportunities for all employees seeking work. It was also a responsibility of government to ensure that there was available to employers a sufficient number of appropriately skilled and trained workers, at an appropriate 'price'. In Marquand's terms, if the 1950s had been a period of 'arms-length' Keynesianism, the early 1960s ushered in the period of 'hands-on' Keynesianism, which lasted until the eclipse of Keynesian policies in the late 1970s.[1]

However, whereas 'arms-length' Keynesianism (i.e. governmental intervention confined to the use of macro-economic instruments to regulate levels of demand in the economy) can be seen as a relatively coherent single set of policies, the supplementary supply-side interventions came in a great variety of different forms in the decade and a half after 1961. As Marquand puts it, 'governments followed a bewildering variety of policies with a bewildering variety of instruments—often undoing, in one mood, what they had laboriously and painfully done in another.'[2] It will be our task in this and the succeeding two chapters to trace to some degree the twists and turns of supply-side policy, whilst bearing in mind that our primary focus of concern is the implications of these developments for the role of labour law, rather than an analysis of governmental economic management for its own sake.

At this stage, however, two very general points need to be stressed. The first is that the initial phase of 'modernization' received a remarkable degree of bipartisan support. The period we are discussing straddles the Conservative administrations of Mr Macmillan and Sir Alec Douglas Home and the Labour administrations of Mr Wilson, and yet, as we shall see, the policy continuities in our areas of interest are more remarkable than the discontinuities. In other words, the party-political consensus over full employment, the welfare state, the mixed economy, and demand management extended initially to the concept of modernization as well. This is the opposite of what one might expect from Marquand's description of a 'bewildering variety of policies'.

But, for reasons that we shall touch on, the modernization policies were manifestly not successful in raising Britain's rate of economic growth and, if anything, the British economy was to be less successful in the 1960s than it had been in the 1950s. This failure led in time to the ever-more-frantic search for effective methods of intervention, which Marquand hints at. More fundamentally, the failure of the supply-side policies of the 1960s

---

[1] D. Marquand, *The Unprincipled Society* (London, 1988), 43–5.
[2] Ibid. 46.

ultimately threatened the consensus about the value of supply-side interventions and even about the feasibility of the governmental commitments to full employment, the welfare state, and the mixed economy. These forces did not have a significant impact until the late 1970s, but non-consensus policies, naturally of differing types, did begin to make headway in both the Conservative and Labour parties in the 1960s and were given, as we shall see, some outlet in the governmental policies of the early 1970s. These developments lay, however, largely outside the immediate period under review.

The second general point is of more immediate importance to the role of labour law. We have seen that in the period of 'arms-length' Keynesianism, labour law played a very limited role. Full employment, in so far as it depended upon governmental policy, was to be achieved through macro-economic measures implemented primarily by the Treasury, whilst neither the welfare state nor the mixed economy were seen in the 1950s as making immediate demands upon labour law. It is true that in the 1950s governments took some tentative initiatives in relation to labour policy as they attempted to grapple with the consequences of running a successful economy at a high level of employment, but these had the appearance of imposed, *ad hoc* initiatives. What modernization (and supply-side policies generally) implied was that government would in the future undertake intervention on a continuing basis in the economy in order to ensure that it achieved the greatest possible level of growth. Interventions on the supply-side would become part of the normal procedures of economic management, not signs of a pathological state. Clearly such interventions might be aimed at only some areas of the economy, but, given the perceived need to increase the efficiency of utilization of economic resources, it was probable that the labour market and the industrial relations system would be important foci of governmental attention. Equally, whilst governmental intervention might take a number of forms, it was likely that sustained intervention at a serious level would express itself in legislation. There were, then, good reasons to suppose at the beginning of the 1960s that modernization would lead to new tasks for labour legislation. That, indeed, came about and it is, we will argue, possible to date the onset of the decline of collective *laissez-faire* to the early 1960s.

So far, we have talked about modernization only in the most general terms. What, specifically, was it taken to mean in the first half of the 1960s? There are three main themes running through governmental policy in this period, as far as it related to labour policy. The first was a renewed interest in economic planning, not, however, the 'command' style planning that had characterized the war period and which had been rapidly dismantled in the five years after the war, but rather 'indicative' planning,[3] much influenced by contemporary French policies. Such planning embraced the whole economy and was not specifically aimed at the labour market—indeed, its prime focus of concern was probably businesses' investment decisions—but it did provide an essential background for the more specific labour market policies. The second theme was incomes policy. As we saw in the last chapter, Selwyn Lloyd introduced his 'pay pause' in 1961, and for most of the rest of the decade governments operated an incomes policy of one sort or another, with a greater or lesser degree of effectiveness. Planned growth of the economy was aimed to make control of the price of labour more acceptable.

The third theme was intervention in the functioning of the labour market so as to promote both mobility of labour and the general level of skill in the workforce. There was also a fourth theme, the reform of industrial relations, which government began to approach gingerly from the early 1960s onwards, but which did not lead to legislative proposals until the end of the decade, after a Royal Commission had reported. The reform of industrial relations was perceived by governments as a 'hot potato' and their expectations that the issue would be difficult to handle were more than fully met when, first, a Labour government produced proposals for legislation at the end of the 1960s, and, second, a Conservative government actually enacted (rather different) legislation in 1971. This theme, however, will be taken

---

[3] 'An indicative plan is neither a statement of what the government intends to happen (because its power to make things happen is limited) nor simply a forecast of what it expects to happen (for that would hardly be a plan) but something between the two. It is an ambitious but realistic indication of what might be achieved—in terms of the overall growth rate, the level of employment, the balance of payments, increases in private and public consumption and so on—provided that appropriate courses of action are followed both by the government itself and by private firms and individuals' (M. Stewart, *The Jekyll and Hyde Years: Politics and Economic Policy Since 1964* (London, 1977), 47–8).

up in a future chapter. We begin here with the themes of job mobility and industrial training, and then move on to consider incomes policies.

4.2. PLANNING AND LABOUR MOBILITY

At an institutional level indicative planning was associated in our period with two bodies in particular. The first was the National Economic Development Council, established by the Conservative government in 1962. Its objects were 'to examine the economic performance of the nation with particular concern for plans for the future', to consider the obstacles to quicker growth, and to 'seek agreement upon ways... to increase the rate of sound growth'.[4] It was conceived as a tripartite body, that is, it contained representatives of goverment, employers, and trade unions. The TUC, which was at loggerheads with the government at the time over incomes policy, was cautious about joining the NEDC, but eventually did so because of the attractions the General Council saw in getting the system of economic planning on its feet and in having some influence over governmental policy in this respect.[5] The General Council drew a sharp distinction between NEDC and the National Incomes Commission, which the government also established in 1962 as an impartial body to consider the National interest in wage claims. With this body the General Council refused to co-operate.[6] Although the TUC appreciated that the NEDC would have no executive functions but would rather be a meeting-place for the tripartite discussion of economic policy, that was thought to be an attractive enough initiative to secure TUC participation. When a Labour government was elected in 1964, the government commitment to indicative planning was strengthened with the creation of a government department to oversee the planning process. This was the Department of Economic Affairs (DEA), which produced in 1965, in co-operation with the NEDC, the National Plan.

[4] NEDC, *Conditions Favourable to Faster Growth* (London, 1963), Introduction.
[5] TUC, *Annual Report 1962*, 254.
[6] Ibid. 468–71.

Given the purposes of economic planning, as envisaged at this time, it is not surprising that both the NEDC and the DEA concentrated heavily upon the question of economic growth. Early in 1963 the NEDC adopted a 'growth objective' of 4 per cent per annum for the years 1961 to 1966,[7] whilst the National Plan aimed at 25 per cent growth between 1964 and 1970.[8] Both the NEDC in its various publications (notably *Conditions Favourable to Faster Growth* (1963)) and the National Plan itself then devoted considerable attention to specifying the wide range of economic decisions, to be taken by government, employers, and trade unions, that would need to be co-ordinated if these objectives were to be achieved. Our concern is with the areas where planning of this type was seen to require a new role for labour law and, as we have already indicated, this was above all in the areas of labour mobility and incomes policy. In this section we deal with the former topic.

Both the NEDC and, even more, the National Plan anticipated that the labour market would continue to be tight and that the manpower resources needed to meet the higher growth rates could be provided only if the activity rate[9] among the population, especially among the unemployed in the less prosperous regions, among married women, and among older workers, could be raised. The issue of activity rates is not of central concern to us, however, because increasing them was not seen as requiring changes in labour law; indeed, it was observed that the rise in the activity rate among married women 'has taken place through changes in social habits and in response to the demand for labour, without any special measures being taken to encourage it'.[10] Two other manpower problems, however, were perceived as demanding new governmental initiatives. The first was 'movements of work people from declining industries to expanding industries and from less productive firms to more productive firms;'[11] the former type of movement was expected to be 'large'

---

[7] NEDC, *Growth of the UK Economy, 1961–1966* (London, 1963), Foreword.

[8] The National Plan, Cmnd. 2754 (1965), Foreword.

[9] i.e. the proportion of any relevant group which was in employment. The phrase does not in this context refer to any measure of the effort expended by people when at work.

[10] NEDC, *Growth*, 21.

[11] NEDC, *Conditions*, 10.

and the latter 'substantial'.[12] In other words, whereas tempting
into employment people presently unemployed or not seeking
work was not thought to require important governmental action,
encouraging those in employment to change employers was.
The second manpower area where governmental action was
thought to be required was that of training to meet skilled labour
shortages which 'have prevailed in this country throughout the
post-war period',[13] and which were likely to be exacerbated by
policies of higher economic growth. Thus, mobility of labour was
perceived as a problem not only in geographical terms but also in
occupational ones.

What, then, were the initiatives taken by governments in
our period to address these problems? Looking back from the
standpoint of the late sixties, four statutes stand out in particular,
although a range of administrative measures[14] can also be
attributed to the desire to improve labour mobility. The four[15]
statutes in question are the Contracts of Employment Act 1963,
the Industrial Training Act 1964. the Redundancy Payments Act
1965, and parts of the National Insurance Act 1966. The 1963 Act
conferred two new statutory rights upon individual employees.
The first was an indefeasible statutory right to a minimum period
of notice to terminate the contract of employment (or to pay in
lieu of notice if the employer offered this and the employee
accepted it), provided, of course, the employee had not engaged
in conduct justifying summary dismissal. The minimum periods
varied with length of service and were set at one week after six
months' employment, two weeks after two years, and four weeks
after five years.[16] The common law, of course, implies into

[12] The National Plan, 10.

[13] NEDC, *Growth*, 24.

[14] e.g. putting more resources into the Government Training Centres (NEDC,
Conditions, 7) or into the Youth Employment Service and the already existing
scheme which provided allowances to workers moving from one area to another
(National Plan, 39). The obstacles to mobility presented by occupational pension
schemes, however, were not tackled until the major reforms in this area in the
1980s. See below, p. 570.

[15] One might add the selective employment tax legislation of 1966, but this
seems to have been something of an afterthought. See below, p. 152.

[16] The periods of notice required of employees to terminate their contracts
were originally proposed to be the same, but, after protest from the TUC, they
were reduced to a single minimum requirement of one week. This was a proposal
whose main significance was in relation to the legality of strikes.

the contract a right to a reasonable period of notice, but the common-law-implied term, unlike the statute, is subject to contrary agreement between employer and employee: that is, in practice, to the employer specifying in the terms of its job offer short periods of notice. The second right conferred upon employees by the 1963 Act was for those without written contracts to be given written particulars by the employer of at least the most important terms of their oral contracts. This part of the 1963 Act was more concerned with avoiding disputes than with giving employees rights upon termination that would reduce their opposition to job transfers.

The 1964 Act empowered the government to establish Industrial Training Boards on an industry-by-industry basis. The purpose of a board was to be the promotion of training by employers in the industry in question and, to that end, a range of functions was conferred upon them. The crucial power that the boards had, however, was to impose a levy upon all employers in the industry to finance training, and to make grants to employers which carried out training to the standard specified by the board.

The 1965 Act provided that employees dismissed on grounds of redundancy should be entitled to receive a lump-sum payment from their employer, calculated on the basis, normally, of a week's pay for each year of service.[17] A proportion[18] of any payment was to be rebated to employers by government from the Redundancy Fund, which was itself financed by a payroll levy on all employers. Although the concept was to prove productive of a considerable case-law,[19] the core of the idea of 'redundancy' was

---

[17] The payment was increased to $1\frac{1}{2}$ weeks' pay for years of service after the age of 40 and reduced to $\frac{1}{2}$ week's pay for years of service between 18 and 21. Years of service below the age of 18 did not count. This is still the basis of payment.

[18] The original scheme was that the employer bore the cost of one-third of a week's pay, whether the employee was under or over 50. By the Redundancy Rebates Act 1969 the employer's share was increased to one-half *of the redundancy payment*. Besides reducing the financial strain on the Redundancy Fund, this change was intended to create a disincentive to employers to select for redundancy employees over the age of 40, who, at this time, accounted for some two-thirds of redundancy dismissals: S. Mukherjee, *Through No Fault of Their Own* (London, 1973), 74–8. The rebate was reduced further in subsequent years, abolished for all but small firms by the Wages Act 1986, and completely eliminated by the Employment Act 1989.

[19] P. Davies and M. Freedland, *Labour Law: Text and Materials* (2nd edn., London 1984), 530–52.

that the employer had ceased to have a business need for the job that the employee in question had been doing and had accordingly decided to dismiss[20] the employee.

Finally, the 1966 Act marked a break with the Beveridge principle of equal rights in the field of social security, which, in the case of unemployment benefit, had meant the payment of equal contributions by all employees within the scheme and an entitlement to equal levels of unemployment benefit. Inevitably, contributions had had to be set at a level which the lower paid would not find too burdensome, but the consequence was that the benefits replaced only a relatively small proportion of the wages lost by an unemployed worker who had been in receipt of average or above-average earnings. The 1966 Act introduced the principle of relating benefits to previous earnings, in exchange for a linking of contributions in the same way.[21]

These were the four main statutes presented to Parliament by governments in the name of modernization in general and encouraging mobility of labour in particular. We shall analyse them a little more deeply under four headings: the decline of voluntarism; the extent of the political consensus; the relationship between mobility of labour, industrial justice, and work-group attitudes; and methods for resolving disputes under the new Acts.

(a) The Decline of Voluntarism

A striking feature of the four Acts was the extent to which the Ministry of Labour (and government more generally including, of course, the Ministry of Pensions and National Insurance in the case of the 1966 Act) took the initiative in securing their enactment. The contrast with the enactment of the Payment of Wages Act, described in the previous chapter,[22] is stark. There,

[20] Any offer of suitable alternative employment by the employer to the employee, which was unreasonably refused, deprived the employee of his entitlement to a payment.

[21] The same principle was applied to sickness and widows' benefit, but it is clear that the desire to relate unemployment benefit to earnings was the driving-force behind these changes. The earnings-related supplement to unemployment and the other short-term benefits was abolished by the Social Security (No. 2) Act 1980, though the principle of relating contributions to earnings was retained.

[22] Above, ch. 3.4. Equally, although the government was prepared to say publicly in the mid-1950s that written contracts of employment, minimum periods of notice increasing with length of service, and advance warning of redundancies were all good ideas, it backed off from even the mild interventionism implied by a

government, following the precepts of voluntarism, was unwilling to legislate except at the joint initiative of the TUC and the employers' associations, and its hand was forced only by back-bench pressure. Now the Ministry itself took up the lead, a change associated very much with the appointment in July 1960 of John Hare as Minister, of whom his successor said that 'he brought a striking new sense of purpose to the activities of the Ministry of Labour.'[23] This is not to say that the TUC and the employers opposed the legislation that was eventually introduced. They were, by and large, content with it; certainly, they did not see it as threatening their vital interests as, for example, the proposals for restricting the freedom to take industrial action, on the one hand, or to introduce workers onto the boards of private-sector companies, on the other, were later to be perceived. But it is to say that government, committed to modernization, now had its own reasons for wishing to legislate, and it set about securing the degree of employer and trade union consent needed for successful legislation, without being prepared to regard itself as necessarily restricted to whatever joint initiative the industrial parties could develop. Indeed, there is little evidence of generalized pressure from industry for any of the four Acts. On the contrary, the TUC complained that the government had not consulted through the NJAC in respect of the 1963 Act 'both prior to the Government's decision to proceed by legislation and during the preparation of the Bill',[24] and it was clearly lukewarm about the introduction of the statutory redundancy payments scheme.[25]

However, government was not making a constitutional point, namely, that it had the authority to introduce legislation into Parliament whether or not the TUC and the employers' organ-

proposal to embody them in a Resolution of the House of Commons when the TUC objected: TUC, *Annual Report 1957*, 134.

[23] HC Deb., vol. 684, col. 1001 (Mr Godber). Writing in 1962 Michael Shanks, a leading advocate of modernization, especially in his book *The Stagnant Society* (1st edn., Harmondsworth, 1962), attacked the Ministry of Labour as 'too reticent up to now in championing the cause of sanity and progress, too concerned with patching up the fabric and hiding contentious issues under the carpet—in a word too *immobiliste*', but he acknowledged too the pressures on the Ministry to change: M. Shanks, 'Public Policy and the Ministry of Labour', in B. C. Roberts, ed., *Industrial Relations: Contemporary Problems and Perspectives* (London, 1962), 285.

[24] TUC, *Annual Report 1963*, 143–4.

[25] TUC, *Annual Report 1963*, 138–40; *Annual Report 1964*, 142–3.

izations agreed with the proposals to legislate. Rather, the government's seizing of the initiative reflected a worry on government's part about the pace and direction of change in the industrial relations system under the principle of industrial autonomy. Government now wished to increase the pace of change and direct it into certain channels, and in setting out the justifications for its legislative interventions it was inevitable that it would to some degree be seen to be critical of collective *laissez-faire*. Introducing the 1963 Act the Minister of Labour (John Hare) said in the Second Reading debate in the House of Commons:

Voluntary methods are fine, but they are fine only if they are effective. Some progress has been made . . . on a voluntary basis in recent years, but not nearly enough . . . A legalistic approach carries no one very far, but it has its uses especially when the spontaneous approaches of unions and employers are crowned with only patchy success.[26]

This attitude was shared by the Opposition. Speaking in 1963 in the Second Reading debate on the Industrial Training Bill, Mr Gunter (later to become Minister of Labour in the Labour government elected in 1964) said in remarks that foreshadowed his own future proposals on redundancy payments and that neatly expressed the bi-partisan approach to these matters:

There will inevitably be greater intervention by the State in industry . . . It is inevitable, in the technical revolution that is about us and with the monolithic structures in industry that are being created, that we and the party opposite will have to accept State intervention if the national needs are to be met. This Bill is the background and it is in considering further measures that might deal with severance pay and redundancy that I again say to the Minister that he will have to do the job for them [employers and unions] because he will never get agreement there.[27]

When it comes to the redundancy payments legislation in 1965, the notion of lump-sum payments based on years of service that was adopted in the Act was taken from existing industrial practice. The justification for legislation, however, was that the existing practice was not sufficiently developed, either in terms of workers covered by schemes (only about a quarter of the working population) or in terms of the payments made (the average was

---

[26] HC Deb., vol. 671, col. 1505 (14 Feb. 1963).
[27] HC Deb., vol. 684, col. 1017 (20 Nov. 1963).

half a week's pay for each year of service). A purely voluntary approach would have laid the main emphasis upon encouraging the parties to improve existing practice, especially as the Minister admitted that schemes had recently been improving in both coverage and benefits, but the government was now in too much of a hurry for such a policy.[28]

The government's decreasing willingness to be completely tied to the principles of voluntarism can be illustrated particularly clearly in respect of industrial training. As recently as 1957 the National Joint Advisory Council had examined the adequacy of industrial training arrangements, and in the 'Carr Report'[29] had recommended that the government confine itself to the expansion of facilities for technical education and that responsibility for industrial training and apprenticeship should continue to rest firmly with industry. By 1962 the results of this policy were perceived to be inadequate: 'At its best, the standard of training in this country is high; unfortunately this is by no means universal. Much is barely adequate and some definitely unsatisfactory.'[30] The White Paper which preceded the 1964 Act attributed this result above all to the following theory, in effect a version of the 'free rider' argument.

A serious weakness in our present arrangements is that the amount and quality of industrial training are left to the uncoordinated decisions of a large number of individual firms. These may lack the necessary economic incentive to invest in training people, who, once trained, may leave them for other jobs. While the benefits of training are shared by all, the cost is borne only by those firms which decide to undertake training themselves.[31]

The government was determined to qualify the voluntary principle to the extent necessary to overcome this problem. Thus, although industry control of training remained the principle in the sense that boards were set up on an industry-by-industry basis

---

[28] For earlier, exhortatory efforts in the voluntarist mode by the Ministry of Labour, see: *Positive Employment Policies* (1958) and *Security and Change* (1961).

[29] NJAC, *Training for Skill* (1957). For an account of the overthrow of the Carr Report and the elaboration of interventionist ideas, see S. Terry Page, *The Industrial Training Act and After* (London, 1967), chs. 1–5.

[30] *Industrial Training: Government Proposals*, Cmnd. 1892 (1962), para. 3.

[31] Ibid., para. 5.

and employers and trade union representatives dominated the boards, the fact that the boards were under a duty to promote training and to levy employers to that end[32] meant that the Act aimed to generalize best practice on training and to eliminate the 'free rider' disincentive to training in a way that the industry-wide voluntary machineries had not been able to achieve.

(b) Political Consensus

The four Acts we have been dealing with can be said to be the result of consensus in two ways. The first we have already touched upon, namely, that employers and trade unions accepted and, in some respects, welcomed these legislative initiatives, even if the government was the main engine of reform. The second form of consensus was consensus in party-political terms. Two of the Acts (those of 1963 and 1964) were passed by Conservative governments and the other two by Labour governments, and in no case did the then Opposition divide the House at the end of the Second Reading debates. All four seem to have been regarded from the beginning as part of a single package aimed at increasing labour mobility. The analysis of the role of legislation in this respect developed by the NEDC in its early years when the Conservative government was in power did not differ very much from that to be found in the Labour government's National Plan. Thus in *Conditions Favourable to Faster Growth* (1963)[33] the NEDC discussed two main ways of dealing with 'the financial loss which often accompanies job displacement', namely, earnings-related unemployment benefits and lump-sum redundancy payments, upon which the subsequent Labour government legislated. Again, the National Plan's proposals[34] for increasing skill levels in industry relied heavily upon a rapid establishment of industrial training boards under the previous government's Industrial Training Act.

In the Parliamentary debates on the four Acts the particular proposals under consideration were invariably presented as part of a larger package of measures, the composition of which, however, was broadly similar under governments of both political parties. Thus, the Contracts of Employment Bill was but 'one

---

[32] Industrial Training Act 1964, ss. 2, 4–5.
[33] pp. 12–13.
[34] pp. 41–2.

step in the Government's policy to meet this problem of security', and needed to be seen in context with 'already published proposals for improving arrangements for apprenticeship and other industrial training' and with the government's intention 'to improve arrangements for dealing with redundancy'.[35] Introducing the Redundancy Payments Bill, the Labour Minister acknowledged that 'the previous Government had for some time been discussing with industry the possibility of legislation on this matter', and again argued that redundancy payments legislation was part only of 'a broader policy', which included 'further changes in National Insurance benefits which will have an important bearing on labour mobility'.[36] This is not to say that the eventual legislative package existed in a clear-cut way as early as 1962. Clearly, the details (some very important) of the Acts needed to be settled and were sometimes controversial; there was some debate as to priorities, especially as between redundancy payments and earnings-related national insurance benefits;[37] and it seems that initially government was not convinced that improving the coverage of redundancy payments schemes would require legislation.[38]

What does emerge, however, from a consideration of the origins of the four Acts is a clear sense that all governments in the period 1961 to 1966 shared a sense of the importance of legislative initiatives to encourage mobility of labour and a view of which instruments were likely to operate most effectively to achieve the required levels of mobility. In other words, the cross-party consensus on the rather passive relationship between the state and the industrial relations system, which had been a central feature of the 1950s, survived into the first phase of a more active role for the state. It is significant that none of the four statutes we have been discussing suffered any substantial change of principle before the 1980s, and that the Contracts of Employment Act 1963 and the Redundancy Payments Act 1965 are still today part of the corpus of our labour law.[39] It seems worth stressing this

[35] HC Deb., vol. 671, col. 1504 (14 Feb. 1963) (Mr Hare).
[36] HC Deb., vol. 711, col. 33–4 (26 Apr. 1965).
[37] Ibid., cols. 54–69.
[38] See the documents cited in n. 28 above.
[39] For the Redundancy Rebates Act 1969 see n. 18 above. The principles contained in the Contracts of Employment Act 1963 were strengthened by the Industrial Relations Act 1971, ss. 19–21 (later consolidated in the Contracts of

point if only because, as we shall see, further state intervention, beyond the area of labour mobility, did prove destructive of consensus, both as between Conservative and Labour parties and as between government and the trade union movement.

There is one exception to this picture of a group of measures emerging in the early 1960s, which was likely to be enacted whichever government was in power. This was the adoption of the Selective Employment Tax in 1966.[40] This pay-roll tax was intended to restrain consumption, but it also had labour mobility objectives because labour employed in the services industries generated a higher level of taxation than that employed in manufacturing industry. As the Minister of Labour, who, significantly, introduced the Second Reading debate on the Selective Employment Payments Bill, said: 'In the longer term it has the additional aim of making more manpower available for manufacturing industry by encouraging economy in the use of labour in the services.'[41] This tax seems not to have resulted from proposals by the NEDC or the DEA but from the Chancellor's taxation adviser. Significantly, the Opposition did divide the House at the end of the Second Reading over this proposal and the tax itself did not survive beyond 1972, when a Conservative government repealed it upon the introduction of Value Added Tax.[42]

(c) Labour Mobility, Industrial Justice, and Workgroup Attitudes

So far, we have presented the legislative measures of 1963 to 1966 as unambiguously aimed at promoting mobility of labour, in both geographical and occupational terms. We submit that this is clearly the perspective that emerges from the NEDC documents and the National Plan. The National Plan, for example, put together industrial training, redundancy payments, and earnings-related benefits under the heading of 'an active labour market

---

Employment Act 1972 and, after further amendment, in the Employment Protection (Consolidation) Act 1978, pts. I and IV). There was, however, a significant change to the powers of the industrial training boards when the Employment and Training Act 1973 introduced a levy/exemption system. See further below, chs. 7.3(b) and 10.5.

[40] Finance Act 1966, s. 44; Selective Employment Payments Act 1966.

[41] HC Deb., vol. 730, col. 933.

[42] Finance Act 1972, s. 122. VAT did not have the mobility aims of SET.

policy' and stated that they, and the associated administrative measures, 'should encourage a wholesale attack on "overmanning" in industry'.[43] Yet there were hints at the time of a rather different, and even contradictory, perspective on two of the Acts, namely the Contracts of Employment Act 1963 and the Redundancy Payments Act 1965. As we have already noted, Mr Hare presented the 1963 Bill as 'a part of the Government's plans to provide greater security for workers',[44] and even Mr Gunter, who was careful to avoid the claim that the 1964 Bill increased security of employment, nevertheless quoted with approval a *Times* leader, which said: 'a man has some rights in his job just as an employer holds rights in his property.'[45] The perspective of 'job security' and 'property in the job' has with time developed a greater hold upon the thought-processes of labour lawyers, partly because of the conventional view of the boundaries of the subject and partly because of the legislative developments in the 1970s in the field of individual employment law.

As to the former, academic labour lawyers have traditionally regarded social security as a separate topic from labour law, whilst industrial training lives in an underworld, largely unrecongnized except occasionally by administrative lawyers. There has thus been some reluctance to view the four Acts as coming together to promote a single set of governmental objectives. However, the difficulty is not simply in seeing that the government was at the time engaged in a process of reordering the pieces of the jigsaw puzzle in the name of promoting mobility of labour. There is also the problem that this rationale was not sustained into the 1970s, when the four Acts came to be regarded as having rather discrete objectives and the Redundancy Payments Act, in particular, was largely assimilated to the industrial justice goals of the unfair dismissal legislation. There seem to have been two explanations for this development. On the negative side, as we shall see, the National Plan, to which promotion of labour mobility was closely linked, collapsed after the crisis measures taken by the government in 1966. Thereafter, the labour market began to be characterized by unemployment (rather than full employment) and, in any event, the government

[43] National Plan, 11.
[44] HC Deb., vol. 671, col. 1503 (14 Feb. 1963).
[45] HC Deb., vol. 711, col. 35 (26 Apr. 1965).

became more concerned with balance of payments problems than economic growth. Thus the government's own commitment to the use of legislation to promote labour mobility was rather short-lived. Although the legislation that had been enacted was not repealed, it began to lose its coherence at a policy level.

On the positive side, the industrial justice argument in favour of providing greater security of employment for workers gathered momentum throughout the 1960s, as we shall see in the next chapter, and resulted in legislation against unfair dismissal in 1971. That legislation came so to dominate individual employment law, and especially the workings of the industrial tribunals, that its rationale came to infect earlier legislation, especially the Redundancy Payments Act, disputes about which were also adjudicated upon by the industrial tribunals. This development was symbolized by the consolidation of the 1963 and 1965 Acts along with the individual employment legislation of the 1970s in the Employment Protection (Consolidation) Act 1978.

We have sought to argue that the 'security of employment' view of these four Acts is unhistorical, but the point is stronger than that. It is, after all, not unknown for legislation introduced for one purpose to be continued in existence to achieve another; indeed, as we shall see, something like this did in fact happen to the Redundancy Payments Act. We would wish to argue, however, that at a conceptual level the security of employment rationale for the 1963 and 1965 Acts is incoherent. To put the matter at its simplest, how can legislation which confers entitlements on employees only once the decision to dismiss them has been taken, and which gives the employee, individually or collectively, no control over the decision to dismiss, be said to promote in any substantial way security of employment or property in the job? It is important to stress here that the Redundancy Payments Act created, as its title says, only an entitlement to a money payment. The legislation which now requires employees individually or recognized unions to be consulted was a product entirely of the 1970s. Indeed, the 1965 Act was concerned to protect the prerogative of the employer in deciding whether to declare employees redundant, when to do it, and whom to select. The Act itself provided (in section 4) that an employee who resigned upon receipt of his redundancy notice, rather than working it out, might forfeit the whole or part of the redundancy payment; and the courts soon held that an employee who resigned after receipt of a 'warning' from the employer that there might be redundancies was not dismissed at all and so had no right to a payment.[46] There is a clear contrast here with the unfair dismissal legislation, whose whole rationale is to permit judicial scrutiny of the reasons for dismissal in order to assess their adequacy, with the implication that an inadequately motivated dismissal is one that ought not to have taken place (even if the consequent remedy is not always, or even usually, reinstatement).

However, even if the argument in the previous paragraph is accepted, to the effect that employment protection seems a poor rationale for the 1963 and 1965 Acts, it may be argued that labour mobility provides no better an explanation. How, one might ask, is the employer placed in a position where it is easier for it to shed unwanted labour, by legislation which increases the employer's legal liabilities upon termination? Before the 1963 and 1965 Acts were passed, the procedures and consequences of termination were controlled by the contract of employment alone. After 1965 the employer must give the minimum periods of notice required by the 1963 Act and pay a lump sum to many redundant employees, only part of which was rebated by the government. These may not be major disincentives to employers to dismiss, but how exactly do they *promote* mobility of labour? The point was one made at the time by some of those who wished to give priority to earnings-related national insurance benefits over lump-sum redundancy payments, and it is well worth addressing.

The answer to the question lies in a contrast between the legal rules governing the termination of employment, on the one hand, and the factual situation and the industrial relations practices obtaining in industry, on the other hand. Clearly the 1963 and

---

[46] *Morton Sundour Fabrics* v. *Shaw* [1967] ITR 84 (DC): 'the employee has the perfectly secure right if he thinks fit to wait until his contract is determined, to take his redundancy payment and then see what he can do in regard to obtaining other employment. If he does . . . choose to leave his existing employment before the last minute in order to look for a new job before the rush of others competing with him comes, then that is up to him.' For a trenchant critique of the 1965 Act from a job protection point of view, see R. H. Fryer, 'The Myths of the Redundancy Payments Act' (1973) 2 ILJ 1.

1965 Acts tended to make the exercise of the employer's legal freedom to terminate the contract of employment financially more onerous, but the government's objective was to tackle the strong resistance to redundancy dismissals on the part of workers and trade unions that in fact prevailed in industry, which made the employer's exercise of its legal freedom often illusory. In other words, the strategy of the legislation was, by enhancing the employee's financial entitlements upon a redundancy dismissal, to make it more likely that the employee would accept the fact of the termination of his or her employment. This argument was clearly put by Mr Gunter when defending in 1965 the government's decision to give priority to lump-sum redundancy payments (whose amount did not vary according to the length of any period of unemployment) as against earnings-related benefits (although he said the government intended to introduce the latter as well).

It is also, I think, fair to say that if our object is to encourage mobility of labour *by reducing resistance to change*, then redundancy pay based on length of service bears more directly on the problem in some ways than improvements in unemployment benefit. It offers substantial compensation to those workers who have most to lose through change of job and who will, therefore, naturally be most opposed to change.

Unemployment benefit, on the other hand, is a uniform payment spread over a much wider range of workers—those with short service as well as long service, and those losing their jobs for a wide variety of reasons besides the economic and technological change with which we are specially concerned in the context of labour mobility.

I do not want to suggest that wage-related unemployment benefit has no bearing on mobility of labour. It has, but it is quite wrong to suggest that, in meeting our economic problems, wage-related benefit comes first and redundancy pay comes nowhere. In the Government's view, both are necessary, and the scheme which we are considering today is just as desirable on economic grounds as it is on social grounds.[47]

The government's view of the nature of the prevailing resistance to redundancy deserves some further elucidation. First, it was seen as a resistance which had its impact not simply at the point when redundancy dismissals were proposed, but also in creating a general unwillingness to accept efficient methods of working. As the NEDC put it:

[47] HC Deb., vol. 711, col. 37 (26 Apr. 1965).

Redundancy has a far greater significance for economic growth, how-ever, than the actual number of workpeople directly affected by the contraction of particular firms or industries would suggest. The fear of redundancy acts as a brake on industrial expansion, whether it causes strikes, restrictions, or resistance to change.[48]

The second point is that the resistance was seen as collective in nature, in particular as a resistance to change on the part of workgroups, rather than as an attribute of individual employees. This provides a major part of the explanation of the considerable resources expended in statutory redundancy payments. In the six years after the introduction of the Act some £380 million was spent on redundancy payments, whilst in the same period only £100 million was spent on adult re-training and the public em-ployment services. In 1968 some 164,000 workers received on average £130 each (about ten weeks' earnings) or about £60 million in total in redundancy payments, whilst only £12 million was spent on training some 10,000 people in Government Training Centres.[49] These figures caused an OECD Committee of Experts, in an inquiry into manpower policy in the UK published in 1970, to ask:

Is it socially equitable and economically rational to give most of the money used to alleviate the readjustment of redundant workers to a great number of persons without any very direct connection with the actual cost which the dismissal has caused the individual, but only very limited sums and incentives to a very limited number of persons for covering expenditure on actual costs and efforts for finding new em-ployment, such as following a training course, seeking work in distant areas, or actually moving house?[50]

Certainly the balance of expenditures seemed to be struck differently in Germany and France.

The answer to the experts' questions shows the links between this piece of individual employment law and the general indus-trial relations system, in particular collective resistance to change; for example, insistence upon the maintenance of working prac-tices that resulted in overmanning, refusal to co-operate with

---

[48] NEDC, *Growth*, 24.
[49] Mukherjee, *Through no Fault*, 17; OECD, *Manpower Policy in the UK* (Paris 1970), para. 13.7.
[50] Ibid.

management in the introduction of new machines and methods, or the taking of industrial action over proposals by management to declare redundancies. The Act offered financial inducements in order to undermine collective resistance or, as the OECD experts put it, 'the reasons which had led to the adoption of the present system derive from the wish to improve industrial relations so that there would be less friction when structural changes resulting from improved technology, methods of production, changes in demand etc. took place.'[51] The law might be framed in terms of individual rights, but it was aimed at a social issue that was collective in nature, and it was a measure of government's perception of the strength of workgroup resistance to the more efficient utilization of labour that it chose to devote such large resources to overcoming the resistance. If the Acts of 1963 and 1965 are usually seen as marking the beginnings of individual employment law, they could as well be seen as the first legislative attempts by post-war governments to influence the operation of collective industrial relations.

If the rationale for the Redundancy Payments Act is accepted as being to overcome resistance to redundancy dismissals and to the adoption of more efficient working practices, then we submit that a clear distinction emerges between the policy thrust of the 1965 Act and of unfair dismissal legislation. The behavioural assumption underlying the legislation of 1963 and 1965 was that by giving employees legal entitlements to money payments upon the termination of their employment, they would be less likely to resist that termination and be more willing to undertake the risks involved in looking for another job. Thus, in many ways, the legislation of this period, and especially the Redundancy Payments Act 1965, was designed to operate in exactly the opposite way to unfair dismissal legislation. The latter was designed to make dismissal less likely; the former to make it easier for management to secure termination. The two types of legislation are directed at really rather different sorts of issue. The essence of the idea of 'redundancy' was that the employer no longer had a need for any employee to fulfil the functions the dismissed employee had fulfilled. The payment to the employee of a redundancy payment might encourage him or her to accept that

[51] Ibid., para. 13.8.

fact and depart to utilize his or her talents in another occupation that needed them. In dismissing an unwanted employee and freeing talents for use elsewhere, the employer was acting in part in the public interest and, far from incurring odium for doing so, should be to some degree reimbursed from a central Redundancy Fund for the payment made to the departing employee. The amount of the lump-sum redundancy payment itself was geared, not to the amount of time the dismissed employee was likely to remain out of work, but to the degree of resistance to dismissal the employee was likely to show, a rough-and-ready index of which was taken to be the length of service with the employer. If the redundant employee obtained a new job the next day, the right to a redundancy payment was in no way reduced (except in certain cases of new employment with the same or an associated employer). A finding of unfair dismissal, on the other hand, would imply that the employee ought not to have been dismissed (or not dismissed in that particular way), the burden of any compensation payable would normally fall on the dismissing employer, and the main element in the compensation would be the amount of income lost as a result of the dismissal. It would not, therefore, have been inconsistent for the government to have introduced at the same time both redundancy payments and unfair dismissal legislation. The significant fact for our purposes is that in the 1960s redundancy payments legislation was given priority over unfair dismissal legislation. We would suggest that the government's commitment to labour mobility in the early 1960s explains one of the minor curiosities of modern British labour law, namely that the redundancy payments legislation preceded by some six years the general protection against arbitrary dismissal.

(d) Practical Impact

In the light of the above analysis of the 1965 Act as being designed to alter workgroup attitudes towards redundancy dismissals, it is worth concluding this section by asking whether the Act achieved the goals the government set for it. It seems to be the case that the traditional policy of most trade unions,[52] which was, reflecting workgroup attitudes, to express opposition

[52] Mukherjee, *Through No Fault*, 35.

in principle to redundancies, underwent a change in the latter half of the 1960s, in the sense that union officials were now prepared to negotiate with management over redundancy issues. How far this was due to the effect of the Act upon individual worker's attitudes and how far to economic changes is not clear. After 1966 economic growth slowed down, and many redundancies were due, not to organizational or technical changes introduced by management, but to a decline in demand for the employer's product. In such a situation a refusal to negotiate over redundancies was a much less viable position for a trade union to take. Collective bargaining over redundancy issues spread, but even in the late 1970s an ILO study reported, at least in the private sector, an unwillingness to bargain over redundancies in advance of their occurring.[53] An *ex ante* agreement might imply for unions too explicit an acceptance of the principle of redundancies (and for management, a fettering of their freedom), even though a prior agreement provides greater opportunities to deal with all the matters that a comprehensive agreement should cover, such as measures to keep dismissals to a minimum, selection of employees to be dismissed, assistance in finding alternative employment, as well as the size of the redundancy payments. There is also some evidence that the Act, at least initially, caused employees to be less ready to take industrial action over redundancy issues, though it is unclear whether it led to any greater general co-operativeness on the part of workers over the introduction of new methods and machinery.[54]

Precise evidence of the effectiveness of any particular piece of labour legislation is always difficult to obtain, but, as indicated above, in the case of the 1965 Act there is the additional complication of the change in the economic climate after 1966. The Act was conceived of in order to deal mainly with technological redundancy, whereas in a worsening economic situation much redundancy was caused by lack of demand. This development threw doubt on the rationale of the Act. Some argued that there was no longer any need to persuade employees to accept redundancy. Where lack of demand was the cause, both man-

[53] E. Yemin, ed., *Workforce Reductions in Undertakings* (Geneva, 1982), 123.
[54] Durcan, McCarthy, and Redman, *Strikes in Post-War Britain* (Oxford, 1983), 385-7.

agement and workers would see redundancies as inevitable. The 1965 Act should therefore be repealed and situations of unfairness dealt with under the unfair dismissal legislation. This view gained some ground in the early 1970s and can be seen being given judicial approval as recently as 1980.[55] The alternative view was that, if redundancy was no longer to be seen as a desirable contribution to economic growth, but rather as the unfortunate effect of economic failure, then the correct response was to supplement the redundancy payments legislation with laws controlling the redundancy decision itself. Meanwhile, redundancy payments could be justified as a useful supplement to unemployment benefit, especially for those facing the prospect of long spells of unemployment. As we shall see, the latter view prevailed, with redundancy handling laws being introduced in 1975, whilst the parties to collective agreements in the 1970s spent much time negotiating voluntary additions to the statutory payments. In 1981 it was reported that 40 per cent of employees with two or more years of service received voluntary as well as statutory payments, and that the voluntary payments increased the total sum paid by nearly 150 per cent.[56]

(e) Dispute Settlement and the Industrial Tribunals

Our discussion so far has concentrated on the substance of the four Acts, but there is also an important procedural, or rather dispute-resolution, issue to be looked at. At least at a theoretical level, an inevitable corollary of the affirmative answer to the question of whether labour law was going to play an expanded role in the 1960s was the question of whether the new role for substantive labour law would lead to the creation of new forms of adjudicative machinery for the settlement of disputes arising under the Acts. This procedural issue was also answered in the affirmative by the establishment of the industrial tribunals, which were (and still are) locally based bodies constituted on a tripartite basis, with a professionally qualified lawyer as chairman and two lay side-members, one broadly representative of the interests of employers and the other of employees. There are three points worth making about the origins and operation of the industrial tribunals in the 1960s.

[55] *O'Hare* v. *Rotaprint Ltd.* [1980] ICR 94 (EAT: Kilner Brown J.).
[56] A. Anderson, 'Redundancy Provisions' (1981) 89 *Employment Gazette* 350.

The first is that those who established the tribunals clearly perceived that the statutes we have been discussing had a common thrust and wished to provide, as far as was necessary, a common adjudicative mechanism. Thus the tribunals were in fact established under the Industrial Training Act 1964, to handle disputes about levies under that Act, but it was clear that it was anticipated at the time that disputes under the Redundancy Payments legislation, too, would be given to the tribunals. In the 1965 Act the opportunity was also taken to amend the provisions of the 1963 Act, concerning written particulars. Failure to provide these had been treated as a minor criminal offence by the 1963 Act. The 1965 Act abolished the criminal sanction and instead enabled a reference to be made to an industrial tribunal to determine what the correct particulars were.[57] Finally, disputes about industry classifications under the Selective Employment Tax legislation were given to industrial tribunals. In fact, in only two cases were bodies other than industrial tribunals used to adjudicate upon disputes under the statutes we have discussed in this chapter, and in both cases the reason seems to have been the view that the necessary adjudicative machinery was already in existence. This was clearly the case with the earnings-related benefits under the National Insurance Act 1966, since social security law had long had its own specialized system of tribunals and it would have been odd to give disputes about earnings-related unemployment benefits to the industrial tribunals whilst retaining, say, disputes about earnings-related sickness benefits or flat-rate unemployment benefits for the social security tribunals. Equally, it seems to have been thought that disputes about statutory rights in the period of notice should go to the ordinary courts, since they already had jurisdiction over the contractual rights arising in such circumstances.

This last decision, although perhaps defensible at the time, looked increasingly odd once the tribunals acquired in 1971 the power to adjudicate upon the adequacy of the employer's reasons for dismissal. Indeed, in the 1970s it became common to regard the tribunals as the British version of labour courts, at least in the sphere of relations between individual employer and employee, and from this perspective the 1960s jurisdictions of the tribunals

[57] Redundancy Payments Act 1965, s. 38.

did have a distinctly heterogenous look. In fact, the tribunals' association above all in the 1960s with the policy of promoting labour mobility meant that they were only marginal instruments of labour law in the first six years of their existence, although they themselves had larger ambitions from an early stage. It needed the establishment of the unfair dismissal jurisdiction in 1971 to drag the tribunals into the centre of labour law, and this development happened to coincide with the abolition of selective employment tax (in 1972) and with changes in the industrial training system which reduced the significance of the levy and hence of levy appeals (in 1973). One respected practitioner has noted that before 1971, 'industrial tribunals were often concerned . . . with adjudicating in cases of disputes between private citizens and the State on the exercise of certain aspects of the State's functions', whereas after 1971 employer and employee disputes were seen as the main focus of the tribunals' work.[58]

The second point about the tribunals is that their creation was not the result of any serious public or Parliamentary debate. The White Papers and NEDC documents that preceded the various Acts we have discussed in this chapter did not address the issue of adjudicative mechanisms. Rather, the momentum for this development seems to have been located almost entirely within the Ministry of Labour, where senior civil servants, contemplating the initiatives in labour mobility which were developing in the early 1960s, came to the conclusion that the establishment of a single set of tribunals, to which disputes under the new legislation could be referred, would be the best course of action.[59] Indeed, the first public flotation of the idea of industrial tribunals seems not to have been located in the *travaux préparatoires* for the Acts we have been discussing, but in the Report of the Committee on the Truck Acts, published by the Ministry of Labour in 1961, which recommended the creation of local tribunals 'each composed of an independent chairman, an employer's and a worker's representative',[60] to deal with grievances arising under the proposed (but not implemented) reform of the truck legislation put forward by the Committee.

[58] R. M. Greenhalgh, *Industrial Tribunals* (London, 1973), 10.
[59] Lord Wedderburn, R. Lewis, and J. Clark, *Labour Law and Industrial Relations: Building on Kahn-Freund* (Oxford, 1983), 173–8.
[60] Ministry of Labour, *Report of the Committee on the Truck Acts* (1961), 19.

The third point is, perhaps, a consequence of the second. One may hazard the guess that the bureaucratic origin of the tribunals played a large part in the relatively modest virtues which were claimed for them by government. Speaking in the debates on the Redundancy Payments Bill, the then Minister of Labour said that the tribunals 'will be organised so as to be easy of access to workers and employers, and to provide a speedy means of settling disputes with less formality and expense than might be entailed if disputes were to go to the courts'.[61] This is a classic formulation of the argument for tribunals, whether in labour law or elsewhere, as being 'court substitutes'.[62] The crucial thing is what is *not* claimed for the tribunals. In particular, it is not claimed that the tribunals' methods of handling disputes will be significantly different from those of the ordinary courts, except in the limited areas of access, speed, and formality of procedure. Indeed, in the case of the industrial tribunals, the underlying persistence of the ordinary courts' model for deciding disputes is emphasized by the failure of Parliament to amend the usual precise and technical language of British statutes in the case of statutes to be interpreted by the tribunals; by the adoption in the tribunals' procedural regulations of an accusatorial (rather than inquisitional) model for the presentation of evidence and argument at hearings;[63] and by making the decisions of the tribunals appealable on a point of law to the ordinary courts—in the period under discussion to a Divisional Court of the Queen's Bench. No wonder that from the begining a rather sterile debate about the 'legalism' of the tribunals has raged, and not simply in academic circles. However, subsequent tinkerings with the system, notably the introduction of a conciliation stage before hearing and of initial appeals to a specialist division of the High Court (both in 1971), have done little to ameliorate the structural strait-jacket within which the tribunals must operate.

4.3. INCOMES POLICY

The 1960s were the decade when incomes policy became central to governmental management of the economy and serious

---

[61] HC Deb., vol. 711, col. 46 (26 Apr. 1965).
[62] B. Abel-Smith and R. Stevens, *In Search of Justice* (London, 1968), 218–24.
[63] See R. Munday, 'Tribunal Lore: Legalism in the Industrial Tribunals' (1981), 10 ILJ 146; Justice, *Industrial Tribunals* (1987).

attempts were made—in the event unsuccessful—to develop a permanent institutional and policy framework for the conduct of incomes policy. We have already noted previous attempts by governments to employ wages policies, notably the Labour government's freeze of 1948 to 1950 and the Conservative government's encouragement of employers to stand firm against wage claims in the middle 1950s, but these were temporary expedients. The aim now was to fashion incomes policies that could be a permanent tool of economic management. In governments' eyes, the attraction of the permanent incomes policy (the substantive content of which would, no doubt, vary from time to time) was that it seemed to offer an escape from 'stop–go', that is, it promised to enable government to maintain a high level of demand in the economy, whilst preventing that demand from leading to high levels of wage settlements, which would both render British exports uncompetitive and suck in imports, and thus create a balance of payments problem. Incomes policy, in the new orthodoxy, was to be the substitute for the deflationary policies that had been used in the 1950s to escape from the balance of payments constraint. As Derek Robinson put it:

Unlike demand management policies which seek to influence wage and price decisions by changing the level or pressure of economic forces, prices and incomes policy seeks to influence the outcome of decisions without changing the level of pressure of demand.[64]

Incomes policy was thus a typical supplementary, supply-side policy of the 1960s, for the hope was that it would enable government to reduce inflation and prevent balance of payments problems by controlling the rate of increase in the price of labour rather than by restricting the level of demand. Indeed, at the time, incomes policy was a much more important policy for the labour market and the bargainers in the industrial relations system than were the policies for labour mobility discussed in the previous section, although the latter in the event bequeathed more to the substantive legal framework that obtained in the 1970s and 1980s.

There were really two attempts at a permanent incomes policy in the 1960s. The first commenced with Selwyn Lloyd's 'pay pause' of 1961, which was presented as a temporary expedient

[64] D. Robinson, 'Labour Market Policies', in W. Beckerman, ed., *The Labour Government's Economic Record, 1964–1970* (London, 1972), 303.

but also as the precursor to a long-term policy. This policy was initiated in the White Paper, *Incomes Policy: The Next Step*,[65] which announced a 'guiding light' for wage increase of 2 to $2\frac{1}{2}$ per cent. In fact, within months the government had abandoned its long-term policy in the face of actual or threatened industrial action by doctors, postmen, nurses, and railwaymen, and the National Incomes Commission, an independent body established 'to provide impartial and authoritative advice on certain matters relating to incomes',[66] issued a few reports but had virtually no discernible impact upon the course of events.[67] We shall therefore concentrate in this section upon the second attempt at a permanent incomes policy, which was publicly signalled by the signature on 16 December 1964 of a Joint Statement of Intent on Productivity, Prices, and Incomes[68] by representatives of government, management, and unions and which lasted, in one form or another, for the rest of the decade.

In spite of the greater commitment to pursuit of incomes policy shown by the Labour government in comparison with its Conservative predecessor, it was hardly a successful initiative. In terms of the impact of the policy in restraining growth of incomes, Clegg has summarized the position as follows:

Apart from the second half of 1966 reality did not accord with policy, nor come near it. During 1965 and the first half of 1966, when the norm was $3–3\frac{1}{2}$ per cent, weekly earnings were rising abour 8 per cent a year. During 1967, with a zero norm, or no norm, and all the increases requiring exceptional justification, the increase was about 6 per cent. In 1968 and 1969, with a ceiling of $3\frac{1}{2}$ per cent, the rate of growth returned to the 1965 level. Judged by these figures the whole policy was a colossal failure.[69]

However, our concern is not with the failure as such of incomes policies to achieve the set degree of restraint of earnings, but rather with the lessons that can be learned from that failure in respect of governmental intervention in the operation of the collective bargaining system in general and the role of the law in

[65] Cmnd. 1626 (Feb. 1962).

[66] National Incomes Commission, Cmnd. 1844 (Nov. 1962), para. 1.

[67] D. Barnes and E. Reid, *Governments and Trade Unions* (London, 1980), 35–7.

[68] This is reproduced as Appendix A in Joan Mitchell, *The National Board for Prices and Incomes* (London, 1972).

[69] H. Clegg, *How to Run an Incomes Policy* (London, 1971), 13.

that process in particular. Two features of the history of incomes policies from 1964 onwards call for further analysis. The first is that, as the Joint Statement indicated, and in contrast to the immediately preceding policy of the Conservative government, the incomes policy began life in 1964 with the agreement of the union movement, albeit perhaps grudgingly given in some quarters. Yet by the end of the 1960s relations between the government and the unions had reached, largely because of incomes policy, a point lower than at any time since the General Strike and the 1927 Act, and this at a time when the Labour Party was in power. The contrast with the period 1945 to 1951, when co-operation and consensus between government and unions was the predominant feature of their relationship, could not have been stronger. Why had this breakdown of relations occurred and what lessons did it suggest about the methods and costs of governmental intervention in collective bargaining? Linked with this is the role of statute. Unlike previous incomes policies, the policy of 1964 to 1970 was given some degree of statutory backing, which varied in its intensity during the course of the policy. Prices and Incomes Acts were passed by Parliament in 1966, 1967, and 1968. How did they fit into the general machinery for operating the incomes policies? Before addressing these questions, it is worth sketching the outlines of the policy as it developed.

(a) The Structure of Incomes Policy, 1964–1970

The government quickly followed the Joint Statement of Intent, which was a very general document, with two White Papers, the *Machinery of Prices and Incomes Policy*[70] (February 1965) and *Prices and Incomes Policy*[71] (April 1965). Since the aim at this stage was to have a wholly voluntary policy, the crucial documents were White Papers, rather than Acts of Parliament, and even after the intervention of statute, the substance of the incomes policies continued to be embodied in White Papers, whilst the legislation was confined to issues of implementation and enforcement of the policies. The first of the two early White Papers stipulated that the formulation of prices and incomes

[70] Cmnd. 2577.
[71] Cmnd. 2639.

policy would be a matter for government departments and the NEDC because 'an agreed policy for prices and incomes requires that representatives of the Government, Management and Unions should be closely associated with the general review'.[72] However, as far as implementation of the policy was concerned, and adjudication upon particular cases, a National Board for Prices and Incomes was established by Royal warrant, consisting of 'an independent chairman, a number of independent members, a businessman and a trade unionist'.[73] Cases could be referred to the NBPI by, and only by, the government. Since, however, the NBPI was expected to carry out a thorough investigation of cases referred to it, it had the capacity to consider only a small fraction of the wage claims and settlements that were made. Consequently, in practical terms the policy was implemented to a large degree by the officials in the Ministry of Labour who decided whether to let a particular claim or settlement through (perhaps after some negotiation with the parties) or to refer it to the NBPI.

The second White Paper set out the pay norm of 3 to $3\frac{1}{2}$ per cent. The norm was to be an average of all pay settlements so that increases above the norm 'will need to be balanced by lower than average increases to other groups if the increase in wages and salaries over the economy as a whole is to be kept within the norm'.[74] In this context the White Paper set out the four circumstances in which, exceptionally, increases above the norm should be allowed.[75]

As already indicated, these two White Papers envisaged a purely voluntary policy, that is, non-compliance with any aspect of it would attract no legal sanctions, civil or criminal. However, the *Machinery* White Paper did warn that the government

[72] Cmnd. 2577, para. 2.

[73] Ibid., para. 7.

[74] Cmnd. 2639, para. 14.

[75] Ibid., para. 15. (i) 'where the employees concerned, for example, by accepting more exacting work or a major change in working practices, make a direct contribution towards increasing productivity in the particular firm or industry'; (ii) 'where it is essential in the national interest to secure a change in the distribution of manpower'; (iii) 'where there is a general recognition that existing wage and salary levels are too low to maintain a reasonable standard of living'; and (iv) 'where there is widespread recognition that the pay of a certain group of workers has fallen seriously out of line with the level of remuneration for similar work and needs in the national interest to be improved'.

would resort to 'other methods' if 'they were convinced that the voluntary method had failed'.[76] As early as August 1965, that is, before the voluntary policy could be said to have been really tested, the government announced statutory backing for the voluntary policy in what was to become Part II of the Prices and Incomes Act 1966. This part contained an 'early warning' and a 'standstill' procedure. The former procedure enabled the government to make an order requiring all or any category of pay claim to be notified to the appropriate government department within seven days of being made, and similar powers were available in respect of awards and settlements. Employers and trade unions failing to comply with the notification provisions were liable on summary conviction to a fine not exceeding £50. If an award or settlement was referred to the board for scrutiny (whether it was one requiring notification or not), the government could require the award not to be implemented until the board had reported (provided that the board reported within three months). This was the standstill procedure, for breach of which a fine of £100 or, on indictment, £500 could be imposed upon the employer if it implemented the agreement during the standstill period, or upon a trade union or any other person if they took any action to induce an employer to pay during the standstill period.

However, before the Bill could be enacted the government came under pressure to take further deflationary measures, and an important part of them was a pay freeze for six months, to be followed by six months of 'severe restraint'. The freeze, announced in the White Paper, *Prices and Incomes Standstill*,[77] was more or less what it said, whereas in the second six-month period, announced in the White Paper, *Prices and Incomes Standstill: Period of Severe Restraint*,[78] there was in effect a zero norm for increases in pay, with increases being allowed in 'exceptional' cases, essentially those stated in the 1965 White Paper but expressed even more restrictively. However, in this case the substantive policy was at least partly embodied in legislation, in Part IV of the Prices and Incomes Bill which was then before Parliament. Part IV, which was to lapse automatically

[76] Cmnd. 2577, para. 18.
[77] Cmnd. 3073 (July 1966).
[78] Cmnd. 3150 (Nov. 1966).

twelve months after its being brought into force, enabled the government, by order, to prohibit an employer from paying remuneration at a higher rate than that applicable on 20 July 1966, or on the date preceding the making of the order, unless the government gave its consent to a higher rate. This principle enabled the government to implement both six-month phases of the policy (i.e. both the freeze and the 'severe restraint' policy) without changing the legislation. Similar criminal sanctions were applied to trade unions and others as under Part II of the Act.

From June 1967 the government continued its policy that there was no general entitlement to increases in pay and that increases should be made only in 'exceptional' cases.[79] These exceptional cases were to be assessed by reference to the criteria set out in the 1965 White Paper, but without the restrictive interpretation put upon them by the *Severe Restraint* White Paper. Moreover, the policy no longer had the backing of Part IV of the 1966 Act, which lapsed, according to its terms, on 11 August 1967. In the middle of 1968 the policy was revised again,[80] so as to institute a $3\frac{1}{2}$ per cent norm for the period until the end of 1969, with exceptional cases again defined as in the 1965 White Paper. Priority was given to the productivity criterion for exceptional treatment (productivity now including reorganization of wage and salary structures), whilst the other three criteria were somewhat devalued. The final White Paper, *Productivity, Prices and Incomes Policy after 1969*,[81] substituted a range of $2\frac{1}{2}$ to $4\frac{1}{2}$ per cent for the norm of $3\frac{1}{2}$ per cent and permitted a rather wider range of exceptional factors to be taken into account, including equal pay for women, upon which the government had decided to legislate.

In spite of the lapsing of Part IV of the 1966 Act in August 1967, the policy did not lose its statutory support entirely. After August 1967, however, the statutory support was procedural rather than substantive. The government implemented Part II for the first time, but not before amending it in the 1967 Act so as to give itself power to extend an existing standstill period or impose one for the first time in a case where the board reported

[79] *Prices and Incomes Policy after 30th June 1967*, Cmnd. 3235 (Mar. 1967).

[80] *Productivity, Prices and Incomes Policy in 1968 and 1969*, Cmnd. 3590 (Apr. 1968).

[81] Cmnd. 4237 (Dec. 1969).

adversely upon a settlement that had been referred to it. Such a standstill period would normally expire some three months after the adverse report. These extended standstill provisions were stated to expire automatically on 12 August 1968, but they were re-enacted by the 1968 Act until the end of 1969, and, indeed, extended so as to apply, in the normal case, for up to eight months after an adverse report. At the end of 1969 the provisions of the 1968 Act were not re-enacted, but Part II of the 1966 Act in its original form was implemented by order for a further and final year.

(b) Incomes Policy and Corporatism

As we have already noted, the incomes policy of 1964 to 1970 began with the support of both the TUC and the central employers' associations. The support of the employers was perhaps not surprising, though individual employers were later to find some aspects of the policy irksome, but the TUC had always sought to defend the autonomy of the collective bargaining institutions, from which perspective incomes policy, if it could be permitted at all, was acceptable only as a temporary expedient to deal with a particular crisis. Only two years previously the TUC had spurned the Conservative government's attempts to establish a long-term incomes policy. Why was the Labour government's policy, at least initially, acceptable?

There was a strong, rationalist argument in favour of incomes policy that it was in the unions' own best interests to adhere to one. Without an incomes policy, it was said, much of the increase in money wages achieved in collective bargaining was dissipated in subsequent price increases, which made British goods and services less competitive in world markets. If, on the other hand, wage increases in general could be restrained within the limit suggested by the overall growth of the economy, then increases in wages restricted in this way should not impose an upward pressure on prices. It was argued that unions would not lose by such a policy, because although the increase in money wages would be less, the increase in real wages would be the same. More important, it was further argued that unions and their members would gain from such a policy, because the removal of this pressure on prices would enable the British economy to export more and import less, in short to grow faster, and this would facilitate a higher level of real wage growth than would have been the case without an incomes policy. In short, in exchange for restraint in the short term, unions and their members would benefit in the medium term.

This argument was pushed hard by the advocates of planning in the early 1960s, especially by the staff of NEDC,[82] but, although it appealed to some unions, it was not enough to attract TUC support as a whole for incomes policy. The Labour government policy, and the National Plan of which it was part, offered essentially the same rationale for incomes policy, but went further in what it offered to trade unions in exchange for adherence to an incomes policy. The National Plan, like the NEDC documents, argued that 'price stability requires that the growth of money incomes should keep in line with growth in real output',[83] and that 'the objective' of a successful incomes policy was 'a higher rate of increase of real income per head'.[84] However, the National Plan went beyond the previous government's policies in apparently offering a firmer control of prices and of incomes other than earned incomes. There must be, it was said, 'a comprehensive policy covering prices and money incomes of all kinds'.[85] The TUC leaders knew from wartime experience that restraint by bargainers was much easier to achieve in a situation of relative price stability, and the National Plan seemed much firmer on this point than, say, the previous government's White Paper, *Incomes Policy: The Next Step*. The Labour government's policy was thus from the beginning a *prices* and incomes policy and not just an incomes policy.

However, more important to the TUC than the extension of the policy to embrace prices was the proposal that trade unions be included in the development of the prices and incomes policy and indeed the National Plan more generally. The unions were not to stand outside the process of policy formation, accepting incomes restraint because it would lead to higher growth, but were to be involved in, and thus have a chance to influence, that process. From the unions' point of view it was thus of the utmost importance that the National Plan had been developed in 'close

---

[82] NEDC, *Conditions*, paras. 200-15.
[83] *National Plan*, 65.
[84] Ibid. 66.
[85] Ibid.

association' with the tripartite NEDC, and that under the Plan the NEDC 'will review the general movements of productivity, prices and incomes of all kinds at regular intervals', and that these reviews 'will also be concerned with the way in which the distribution of the national income ... is developing under the impact of a prices and incomes policy'.[86] Unions were thus to be involved in the social (or distributional) aspects of planning as well as the economic (or wealth-creating) ones.

It is this last element of the agreement arrived at between government and TUC in 1964 and 1965 that also makes it worthwhile to examine the applicability of the notion of 'corporatism' to the agreement. We use 'corporatism' to describe forms of state intervention in the economy which rely upon the use of apparently private associations to control the behaviour of the members of those associations. In thorough-going forms of corporatism the 'private' associations may become wholly the creatures of the state, as in some forms of Fascism, but it is possible to apply the term 'corporatism' to situations where the associations maintain their independence of government, but negotiate with it as to the extent to, and the terms on, which they will co-operate in facilitating the state's goals. Such 'bargained' or 'voluntary' corporatism, as Crouch[87] calls it, is conceptually distinct from collective *laissez-faire*, which, by insistence upon the rigid separation of politics and the economy, places itself firmly in the liberal camp. Nevertheless, when one looks at the actual behaviour of trade unions, one can discern a tension, as the Webbs long ago pointed out, between the 'method of collective bargaining' and the 'method of legal enactment'.[88] In other words, one can see trade unions as uncertain whether their objectives would be furthered more effectively by putting the main emphasis on striking deals with employers (here the doctrine of collective *laissez-faire* maximized the unions' freedom of action) or on persuading government to enact legislation or to take administrative action, that is, to intervene in the economy. The twentieth century is usually presented as the period when unions unequivocally adopted the method of collective bargaining

[86] Ibid. 67.
[87] C. Crouch, *Class Conflict and the Industrial Relations Crisis* (London, 1977), 33 ff.
[88] S. and B. Webb, *Industrial Democracy* (London, 1920).

in preference to the method of legal enactment, although we would argue that the latter tradition was never entirely submerged, whilst the corporatist features of the wartime arrangements are surely clear to all. In any event, it seems plausible to present the incomes policy of 1964 and 1965 as one in which the government persuaded the trade unions to surrender a certain freedom of action in bargaining in exchange for a greater influence over the government's social and economic policies, at least as these related to wages and the distribution of income. If untrammelled collective bargaining was thought to pose difficulties for government in a period of full employment, then a government which did not wish to abandon full employment would perhaps have to secure restraint in bargaining by expanding the political role of the TUC. Equally, for the TUC as an organization (if not always for individual affiliated unions), the attractions of bargained corporatism were easy to see, for it would enhance the authority and prestige of the TUC, and carry with it the promise of some sort of resuscitation of its wartime role.

However, this tentative step towards a new (or revived) form of relationship between government and TUC, and the trade unions in general, did not lead to the mapping-out of a new path. Almost before the new structure was put in place, it was destroyed, although the idea which underlay it survived to be elaborated in the 1970s in the shape of the 'Social Contract'. In part, the experiment collapsed because it did not bring quick results in restraining incomes. We have already noted Clegg's comment that 'during 1965 and the first half of 1966, when the norm was $3–3\frac{1}{2}$ per cent, weekly earnings were rising by 8 per cent a year.'[89] This was largely because an agreement with the TUC was not the same thing as an agreement with individual affiliated unions, given the lack of authority of the TUC over the bargaining policies of its member unions. Still less was an agreement with the TUC an agreement with individual bargainers, especially in those industries where shop-floor bargaining was well developed. To put the matter another way, one defect in the proposed corporatist strategy might be said to be the absence of an effective, central trade union authority. Yet

[89] Above, p. 166.

the National Plan had foreseen this problem and so it is not clear that it can alone explain the rapid demise of the policy. As the Plan put it, the policy 'needs to be accepted by all organizations and individuals concerned with prices and incomes decisions' and, as such, 'the Government recognize that a revolution in traditional practices and habits of thought cannot be accomplished overnight'.[90]

A more fundamental obstacle in the way of the new relationship was the unexpectedly large balance of payments deficit which, the incoming Labour government found upon entry into office, was projected for 1964 and 1965, and the methods the government chose for dealing with it.[91] In essence the government chose to right the balance of payments by deflationary policies which would have been largely familiar to governments of the 1950s. It chose initially not to devalue the pound, one of the most controversial economic decisions of the 1964 to 1970 government. Whilst it would be wrong to present devaluation as a complete alternative to deflation, it can be argued that early devaluation would have permitted a more rapid and less painful adjustment. In fact, the government sought to solve the problem by deflation at home and borrowings abroad to shore up Britain's dwindling reserves. Foreign creditors, concerned with the repayment of their loans, demanded tough domestic policies, including restrictive incomes policies, and thus reinforced the deflationary stance the government had initially adopted. Whether the government should have devalued the pound immediately upon taking office we need not decide.[92] What is clear is that the deflationary policies, applied first in the middle of 1965 and then again in July 1966 (when the wages freeze was applied), destroyed the whole context in which wage restraint had been sold to the TUC—namely, as part of a policy of planned economic growth. The economic-rationalist argument for wage restraint may not have been enough to convince the TUC to

[90] *National Plan*, 68.
[91] *The Economic Situation: A Statement by Her Majesty's Government* (Oct. 1964), para. 4.
[92] For an evaluation of the policy choices see Beckerman, ed., *The Labour Government's Economic Record*, Introduction and ch. 1: Stewart, *Jekyll and Hyde Years*, ch. 4; L. Panitch, *Social Democracy and Industrial Militancy* (Cambridge, 1976), chs. 4 and 5. The bitter irony, of course, is that the government was eventually forced to devalue, in Nov. 1967.

accept an incomes policy, but the chances of continued TUC co-operation certainly became slim once the prospects for growth dimmed. As Michael Stewart has written:

It is difficult to imagine a more complete *volte-face* in policy than that represented by the July measures . . . Now the Labour Government had introduced the biggest deflationary package ever, and had imposed a compulsory freeze on all wages and prices. The consequence was bound to be rising unemployment, stagnant output, and the complete abandonment of the National Plan[93]

From 1966 onwards incomes policy ceased to be presentable as part of a policy for economic growth. Rather, it was a policy for managing economic crisis, rather on the lines of the 'freeze' of 1948 to 1950. On this basis, it proved possible to obtain the endorsement of both the General Council and of Congress for the six-month standstill, but there was no basis for securing agreement on a long-term policy, as had been envisaged in the early 1960s. Increasingly, the TUC and the government drifted apart. The TUC attacked in particular the continued use by government of legislation to support its incomes policy and the restrictiveness of the government's substantive criteria governing wage increases. The TUC began to operate its own, more relaxed policy and to abandon all responsibility for the government's policy. Partly because of the gravity of the economic situation and partly because of the TUC's withdrawal from an active role in wage restraint, the government proved rather unreceptive to the TUC's attempts to influence policy-making and, in particular, to raise distributional questions. In 1967, for example, the government agreed to set up an inter-departmental working party of civil servants on the question of a national minimum wage. That committee's rather negative conclusions were commended by the Secretary of State as 'essential reading' and 'the basis for a more informed discussion', but no action followed.[94] Clearly, the basis for any 'bargained corporatism' had disappeared. On the contrary, by the end of the 1960s relations between government and TUC had reached a very low point and the TUC and the

[93] *Jekyll and Hyde Years*, 73.
[94] Department of Employment and Productivity, *A National Minimum Wage* (1969), p. iii. This was despite the fact that the 1969 White Paper declared the improvement of the position of the low paid to be one of three aims of incomes policy: Cmnd. 4237, para. 11.

unions were reasserting in militant fashion the illegitimacy of governmental 'interference' in wage-setting.

(c) Incomes Policy and the Law

Differing views have been expressed about the significance of the Prices and Incomes Acts 1966 to 1968 for labour law. Professor Kahn-Freund, writing in 1968, called them 'the deepest inroad ever made into . . . the freedom of collective bargaining in Britain',[95] and a commentator upon the 1966 Act termed it 'without doubt, the most important legislation affecting trade unions since [the Trade Disputes Act] 1906'.[96] On the other hand, Professor Wedderburn has argued that incomes policy legislation should be kept to a large degree in a separate category from labour law. 'There was between 1948 and 1979 a dichotomy in government policies: anti-wage-inflation policy on the one hand, and traditional labour law, or I.R., policy on the other.' In consequence, 'as the incomes policy statute drew near traditional labour law it was repulsed by a countervailing magnetic field.'[97] How should one evaluate these competing views?

The basis for Kahn-Freund's view is clear enough in the light of his analysis of the traditional relationship between the law and the institutions of collective bargaining. That traditional role gave the law only minor auxiliary functions, and the general abstention of the law from a regulatory role was represented above all by the refusal of the collective bargaining parties to treat collective agreements as legally enforceable contracts and the failure of government to provide legal mechanisms which could be used to compel employers to recognize and bargain with trade unions. Now government was injecting into that 'abstentionist' framework statutory provisions which, in certain cases at least, made it a criminal offence for an employer to implement a freely agreed bargain (something not imposed even during the Second World War) and a criminal offence for a trade union or any other person to take any action whose object was to persuade an employer to implement the agreement.[98] Indeed, in relation to

---

[95] O. Kahn-Freund, *Labour Law: Old Traditions and New Developments* (Oxford, 1968), 19.

[96] N. Lewis, Note (1967) 30 MLR 67.

[97] Lord Wedderburn, 'Labour Law Now: A Hold and a Nudge' (1984) 13 ILJ at 77 and 74.

[98] See e.g. Prices and Incomes Act 1966, s. 16(1) and (4).

the six-month 'freeze' in 1966, it was thought necessary to give employers express protection in some cases against actions for breach of contract by their employees,[99] so that the non-implementation of a collectively agreed increase was, by the Act, made immune from civil legal sanction, whilst implementation became a criminal offence. The use of the law in this way to control the outcomes of collective bargaining would be regarded as a strong form of state intervention in any industrial relations system that relied upon collective bargaining to set terms and conditions of employment; in the abstentionist British system it was, indeed, a novel departure for the law.

The arguments in favour of the contrary view are threefold, relating to the sanctions, usage, and permanence of the legislation. As we have seen, the positive requirements of the Acts were enforced by criminal sanctions, and considerable pains were taken to ensure that non-compliance with the Acts did not attract civil sanctions (or, indeed, criminal sanctions other than those specified in the Act). Thus section 16(5) of the 1966 Act provided that 'this section shall not give rise to any criminal or tortious liability for conspiracy or any other liability in tort', and the definition of 'trade dispute' in the 1906 Act was widened to include disputes between employers and workers 'connected with' the restrictions imposed by the Acts.[100] The policy was clearly that the regime of sanctions laid down in the Acts should be self-contained and wholly within the control of government[101] (hence the need to exclude tort liabilies that might be invoked by employers or other non-government parties). Given that the development of the substance of the policy was controlled by government and that only government could make references to the NBPI, this exclusiveness at the level of sanctions is comprehensible. Only by excluding, as a matter of definition, legislation enforced by criminal sanctions from the ambit of labour law, however, does this policy seem to cast doubt upon Kahn-Freund's analysis, and such definitional exclusion seems to ignore the traditional role of criminal sanctions where payment of wages is concerned, e.g. under the Wages Council Acts, or where

---

[99] Ibid. s. 30.

[100] Prices and Incomes Act 1966, s. 17.

[101] S. 22 provided that proceedings under the Act could be instituted in England and Wales only by or with the consent of the Attorney-General.

control of individual terms and conditions of employment is at issue, e.g. under the Baking Industry (Houses of Work) Act 1954.[102]

The second argument relates to the extent of the use that was made of the statutory powers, which was indeed modest. Fourteen orders were made in relation to incomes under part IV of the 1966 Act. In thirteen cases notices were issued under part II of the 1966 Act requiring a settlement not to be implemented until the board had reported, and in four of these cases orders were made under the 1967 or 1968 Acts imposing a delay after the board had made an adverse report.[103] This is certainly a modest rate of use, but it is possible to see why this was so and why there was a greater rate of use of the prohibitory provisions of part IV of the 1966 Act (which was in force, of course, for only one year) than of the mere delaying powers of part II and the 1967 and 1968 Acts. This apparent paradox can be explained if it is remembered that the freeze was endorsed by both the General Council and Congress and so the government could, on the basis of this general support, relatively freely use the law against particular employers and trade unions which sought to evade the policy. In 1967, however, Congress passed a resolution to the effect that 'the Prices and Incomes Acts have been detrimental to the best interests of the trade unionists and calls for their repeal'.[104] The government was astute enough to appreciate that, with union support for an incomes policy crumbling, the law could not be used on a widespread scale to make up for that lack of support, but rather that the lack of general support for incomes policy would reduce the number of situations in which the law could be used effectively. Clegg has summarized the position as follows:

The experience of both periods shows that the law can play a part in reinforcing an incomes policy; that, although governments are naturally reluctant to use powers of this kind, they can on occasion bring themselves to do so; and that trade unions have some respect for the law. However, there is a *contrast* between the two periods in the effect of the law. In the period of the standstill the policy was rigorously enforced.

---

[102] See e.g. the Wages Councils Act 1959, s. 12(2); Baking Industry (Hours of Work) Act 1954, s. 7.

[103] See Mitchell, *National Board*, apps. D1 and D2.

[104] TUC, *Annual Report 1967*, 633.

The use of the law in a few cases demonstrated the government's determination to make the policy work and to give everyone the same treatment. The consequence was to strengthen public confidence in the government and the policy. By the time that the law was used against the busmen and the builders the policy was already crumbling. The government now picked out for exemplary treatment one or two among the many instances in which the policy was being flouted. This might have been more effective if they had picked out the worst offenders. But they carefully chose those cases where a strike would not have been very damaging to the economy.[105]

However, the difficulties of enforcement of laws are by no means confined to the criminal law, as the experience with the tort-based 'unfair industrial practices' under the Industrial Relations Act 1971 was later to demonstrate or, with different results, the direct experience with the common law torts in the 1980s.[106] At least the restraint shown by government in respect of the Prices and Incomes Acts meant there was no outright defiance of the orders made under them.

The third feature of the Acts was their expressed lack of permanence. Even part II of the 1966 Act needed to be renewed by Order in Council at twelve-monthly intervals, whilst part IV and the 1967 and 1968 Acts were all stated to expire automatically at the end of a fixed period (twelve months in the cases of part IV and the 1967 Act and nearly seventeen months in the case of the 1968 Act).[107] Thus, even if the government had not wanted in 1968 to extend the standstill period but only to keep the provisions of the 1967 Act alive, it would still have had to pass a new Act of Parliament. Consequently, the argument for viewing the Acts as an insignificant episode is not so much that they were not part of labour law, but rather that they were only a temporary part, and, moreover, were perceived by the government as temporary. There was, in other words, a distinction between incomes policy, which government wished to establish on a permanent basis, and the legislation which, apart perhaps from part II of the 1966 Act, was perceived as a temporary expedient. But to put the matter this way may be to miss the true

[105] Clegg, *How to Run an Incomes Policy*, 56.
[106] See below, Subsect. 7.2 (*b*) and Sect. 9.6.
[107] See Prices and Incomes Acts 1966, s. 25(1); 1967, s. 6(3); and 1968, s. 13(4).

significance of incomes policy and the supporting legislation. Whether or not supported by legislation, incomes policy was a major departure in terms of governmental policy from the doctrine of collective *laissez-faire*. What could be further from respecting the autonomy of the parties to collective agreements than controlling their wage settlements, even if on a voluntary basis? If collective *laissez-faire* could be abandoned in one area, was it vulnerable elsewhere? Moreover, the use of the law to support the freeze could be taken to demonstrate that there was a role for the law in enforcing interventionist policies, provided that those policies were underpinned by a general consent among government, unions, and employers. Finally, there *was* a continuity in government's mind between prices and incomes legislation and other types of labour law, even if it existed only at the level of impressing foreign creditors by 'doing something about the trade union problem'. As Barnes and Reid have put it, by the end of the 1960s the government faced a problem, with the need to maintain the confidence of foreign creditors, on the one hand, and an increasingly ineffective incomes policy on the other, which was perceived as threatening the government's chances of re-election.

The government was in a dilemma. By March 1969 it thought it had found the solution: to relax on incomes policy but retain foreign confidence by dealing directly with industrial relations and 'the trade union problem'. It had, in any event, to produce a policy on these crises, since the Donovan Report had been published in June 1968.[108]

4.4. CONCLUSION

We have seen that at the beginning of the 1960s a significant development occurred in the policy of economic management in Britain, with the supplementation of macro-level demand-management policies by a variety of supply-side interventions. We have sought to demonstrate that this was also a significant development for governmental labour policy. The policy of 'abstention' or of 'collective *laissez-faire*' in respect of the labour market and the industrial relations system was, through this

---

[108] Barnes and Reid, *Governments*, 105.

change, made a conditional one. That is to say that abstention became, at least over time, less and less a principled commitment and more and more a starting point or a presumption, capable of being overturned in a specific area by a convincing argument that some particular piece of intervention would promote the government's economic goals.

Naturally, there was no simple, overnight abandonment of collective *laissez-faire*. It was too strongly entrenched and valued a doctrine for that to occur. [109] However, we shall seek to show in the following chapters that by, say, 1975 (by which time a Conservative government had enacted the Industrial Relations Act 1971 and a Labour government the Employment Protection Act 1975), the framework of abstentionism had ceased to be an applicable one for analysing British labour law. What we have sought to demonstrate in this chapter is the beginnings of that process of collapse and, in that respect, the interesting issues can be seen to be the questions of which areas of intervention commended themselves to government and, of especial interest to us, which forms of intervention were thought likely to be effectively implemented by or with the aid of legislation (as opposed to other modes of governmental intervention).

From this point of view the two areas of intervention we have discussed in this chapter—mobility of labour and incomes policy—are something of a contrast. The mobility policy was, from the beginning, envisaged as having legislation as its central technique for implementation (even if various administrative measures were also associated with it); in relation to incomes policy, legislation was to some degree forced upon an unwilling government by external pressures as a late and temporary addition to what was envisaged originally as a voluntary policy. It is not difficult to see why legislation should have been assigned, at least initially, such contrasting roles in the two areas. The use of law to control the outcomes of collective bargaining was a very direct challenge to the philosophy of collective *laissez-faire* and to the long-entrenched freedom of employers and trade unions to reach whatever settlements they judged best suited their private

[109] Nor do we wish to argue that changes in the policy of economic management were the sole causes of the downfall of abstentionism (see Chapter 5 on industrial justice and the individual worker), still less that there was a consensus over what should replace collective *laissez-faire*.

interests. The use of the law to inject a limitation upon that freedom in the name of public policy (as defined by government) was bound to be highly controversial. It is not surprising, therefore, that government placed a consensual corporatism, rather than legal enforcement, at the centre of its incomes policy. Nor is it surprising that, although driven in the event to greater legislative backing for its policies, government refrained from trying to use the law as a substitute for consensus rather than as a reinforcement of it.

The legislation in the area of labour mobility, by contrast, represented very much less of a challenge to the autonomous collective institutions. It was difficult for trade unions to become very exercised about the Contracts of Employment Act 1963 and the Redundancy Payments Act 1965 in so far as they conferred information and monetary rights upon individual employees.[110] Even if it was said that the aim, and to some extent the effect, of the 1965 Act was to undermine collective resistance to changes in working practices, the defenders of the Act could say that it did nothing more than generalize schemes already developing on a voluntary basis. By the same token, employers' arguments that the Act limited their prerogatives seemed less convincing. As to the National Insurance Act 1966, that operated wholly within an area which, at least since Beveridge, was regarded as a governmental responsibility and outside the area of collective bargaining. The most radical Act, it could be argued, was the Industrial Training Act 1964, which imposed a new statutory structure, the industrial training board, upon the voluntary machinery. However, regrettable though it was, training had traditionally been regarded as a marginal issue in collective bargaining, so the new structures, dominated in any event by employers' and employees' representatives, did not threaten voluntary institutions, except possibly the system of apprenticeships. Rather, it was the absence of such institutions that made the case for governmental intervention. It was to be expected, therefore, that the mobility legislation would be less controversial and make a more lasting contribution to the emerging new structure of British labour law than did the Prices and Incomes Acts.

---

[110] The mild anti-unofficial-strike ambitions of the 1963 Act were, of course, another matter. See below, p. 239.

However, there was one respect in which both the prices and incomes and the mobility legislations suffered a common fate. The destruction of the National Plan by the 'July measures' of 1966 removed, as we have seen, the basis for the consensus between government and the union movement over incomes policy. The policy limped on for a while as a measure of crisis management, but its long-term fate was sealed in 1966. New incomes policies had to await the building of a new consensus in the 1970s. Equally, the deflationary measures introduced in 1966 removed the basis of the tight labour market projections which had provided the impetus for the mobility legislation. Indeed, some authorities[111] have identified the beginning of the government's slow abandonment of its commitment to full employment with the decisions taken in 1966. What, then, can be said to have been the long-term significance of the legislative measures we have discussed in this chapter?

Certainly a coherent concept of legislation promoting mobility of labour failed to take root in our labour law. The statutes we have discussed under this heading went their separate ways, finding new and separate rationales for their continued existence. The Industrial Training Act was the first of a bewildering variety of governmental measures designed to upgrade levels of skill in the workforce. It soon became appreciated that there was a good argument for improving levels of industrial training even if, overall, there was a surplus supply of labour and, in the 1980s, training came to be perceived as a partial antidote to *un*employment. The National Insurance Act soon came to be seen as part of measures later taken to upgrade the benefits provided by the welfare state: for instance, in respect of pensions, a major concern of the 1970s. The Contracts of Employment Act 1963 and the Redundancy Payments Act 1965 became absorbed, as we have suggested, into the growing corpus of legislation dealing with employment protection. These statutes thus made a significant contribution to the new framework of labour law, even if not quite in the way their proponents envisaged in the early 1960s. Even the temporary Prices and Incomes Acts, we would suggest, had a profound significance. At an obvious level, lessons

[111] Report of the Select Committee of the House of Lords on Unemployment, HL 142 (1982), para. 5.10.

were drawn from them which were applied in the prices and incomes legislation of the 1970s. At a less obvious level, the relative ease with which the Labour government in the late 1960s moved from controlling the outcomes of bargaining to proposals for legislation controlling the methods of bargaining (notably the use of the strike weapon) suggests that the Acts of 1966 to 1968 (and the policies associated with them) broke a fundamental inhibition on governmental intervention into the functioning of the autonomous institutions of collective bargaining. We shall attempt to develop the various themes identified in this paragraph in the next two chapters.

5

INDUSTRIAL JUSTICE AND THE INDIVIDUAL WORKER, 1968–1974

5.1. THE TRADITIONAL LAW AND A NEW PRINCIPLE

In our initial discussion of the concept of collective *laissez-faire*, we noted that there were 'exceptional' circumstances in which the law was used, rather than collective bargaining, to protect the interests of individual workers.[1] Indeed, these exceptional situations were of long standing, pre-dating in many cases the development of an effective collective bargaining system, which could carry the weight of state reliance upon it to protect individual interests, which the theory of collective *laissez-faire* entailed. We referred, in particular, to the legislation on health and safety at work, to that controlling the hours of work of women and young people, to the Truck Acts, and to the Wages Councils legislation. The law having staked out an early claim to predominance in these fields, it continued, even after the articulation of abstentionist theories on the part of the state *vis-à-vis* industrial relations, to maintain its position. We discussed in an earlier chapter developments in this field in the 1950s;[2] it is now necessary to analyse further developments in the 1960s and early 1970s. Once that has been accomplished, we wish to spend the major part of this chapter in charting the development of what we see as a new principle supporting the enactment of individual employment legislation.

As far as the traditional law is concerned, the major develop-

[1] Above, ch. 1.1(*c*).
[2] Above, ch. 3.1.

ments took place in the field of health and safety at work. As we have seen, the long campaign to get the recommendations of the Gowers Committee of 1949, for the extension of significant statutory health and safety protection beyond the early bastions of factories and mines, culminated in the enactment of the Offices, Shops, and Railway Premises Act 1963, though that Act fell somewhat short of what the Committee had recommended.[3] Very soon, however, the Ministry of Labour returned to the principle of comprehensive legislation and in 1967 issued proposals for legislation to replace both the 1963 Act and the Factories Act 1961.[4] Following the leisurely tradition in these matters, tripartite discussions ensued until in 1970 the Secretary of State set up an outside inquiry under Lord Robens. That took two years to produce a report,[5] and legislation based upon the report reached the statute-book in what was record time in this area in the shape of the Health and Safety at Work Act 1974.

The main aims of the legislation[6] were to simplify and generalize the law by having a set of principles applicable to all workplaces; to unify the administration of the legislation under an independent statutory body; to place greater responsibility for safety upon management and workers and, thus, relatively less responsibility upon the inspectorate; and to give significant attention to the protection of self-employed workers and members of the public. Although the Act had some ambitions to move away from the stereotyped pattern of immensely detailed regulations enforced primarily by an inspectorate, overall the Act confirmed the centrality of legislation in the health and safety field. From our point of view, there were two features of the Act which will call for more discussion in future chapters. The first was the devolvement of responsibility for administering the legislation from the Department of Employment to an independent, statutory body, the Health and Safety Commission, upon which both sides of industry were represented.[7] The second was the introduction of statutory mechanisms to encourage greater

[3] Above, ch. 3.1. See also TUC, *Annual Report 1963*, para. 113.
[4] TUC, *Annual Report 1968*, para. 114.
[5] Safety and Health at Work, Report of the Committee 1970–2, Cmnd. 5034 (1972).
[6] See Department of Employment *Gazette*, June 1973, p. 549 and July 1973, p. 649.
[7] See below, p. 409.

involvement by workers' representatives in maintaining safety standards in the form of statutory safety representatives and safety committees.[8]

Elsewhere in the traditional field, developments were fewer. We noted in an earlier chapter the greater flexibility brought to the truck legislation by the Payment of Wages Act 1960.[9] However, the employer's freedom to pay wages other than in cash depended upon the consent of the individual worker, and the employers continued to argue that this was an insuperable obstacle to a general switch to non-cash payments systems. The matter was referred to the NJAC in 1968, and that body eventually reported in 1972.[10] It said that 'the committee's consideration of the evidence as a whole does not lead to the conclusion that the present legislation is the main impediment to the more widespread introduction of non-cash forms of payment and there is no reason therefore to believe that a change in the law would greatly accelerate the changeover.'[11] Thus the employers' position was rejected and that of the TUC broadly endorsed, so that nothing in the way of legislative change emerged from this initiative, any more than it had from the broader review of the Truck Acts a decade earlier.[12]

What is interesting about this episode, however, is that, unlike in the health and safety field, the pressures for legislative change were, in 1980s' terminology, deregulatory. This was even more true of the unsuccessful initiatives in the field of hours of work. Arising out of discussions on shift-working, the general issue of the legislation controlling the hours of work of women and young people was referred to an NJAC committee in 1966, which reported in 1969.[13] Employers and union representatives on the committee differed as to the continuing need to restrict by legislation the hours of work of women (except at night), though

[8] See below, ch. 8.3(*c*).

[9] Above, ch. 3.4.

[10] Department of Employment, *Methods of Payments of Wages*, Report by a Committee of the National Joint Advisory Council (1972).

[11] Ibid. 42.

[12] Above, ch. 3.4. Equally, the TUC made equally little headway with its related campaign for the law to require all workers to be supplied with itemized pay slips, the absence of which was said to be a particular problem in agriculture. See e.g. TUC, *Annual Report 1966*, para. 63.

[13] Department of Employment and Productivity, *Hours of Employment of Women and Young Persons Employed in Factories* (1969).

they were in agreement that some restrictions were needed in respect of young people.[14] What was remarkable was the Department of Employment and Productivity's response to this NJAC report. It circulated a discussion document proposing to remove all the restrictions on the hours of employment of women (including night work) and, in addition, to repeal certain provisions of the Shops Act 1950 relating to hours of employment (which applied to both men and women) and of the Baking Industry (Hours of Work) Act 1954 (which applied to men only). Finally, the legislation relating to young people should be simplified and its requirements reduced.[15] The reaction of the TUC to this document from a Minister in a Labour government can be easily imagined—it was, the General Council said, 'unacceptable'[16]—and in fact not even the ensuing Conservative government took up the proposals. However, as an indication of the Department's unwillingness by the late 1960s to be bound by the framework for discussion agreed between employers and unions, even on a central issue of terms and conditions of employment, and as a pointer to developments in the 1980s, the Department's 1969 document was a significant one.

Similar deregulatory tendencies can be found in this period in the final area of 'exceptional' labour law, the Wages Councils. Here the pressures towards deregulation did lead to some legislative changes—albeit minor ones by the standards of the 1980s—probably because the pressures emanated to some degree from both employers and trade unions. After the Wages Councils Act 1945[17] the system grew to its peak in the early 1950s, with over sixty councils in operation, and it was then left largely undisturbed until it was examined by the Donovan Commission in the second half of the 1960s.[18] The Commission was rather critical of the councils, on the grounds that they seemed to have made little progress over the decades in achieving what were said to be their two main objectives: improving the position of the low paid and encouraging the growth of collective bargaining. The relative position of workers in the Wages Councils industries seemed not to have changed very much, whilst the maintenance of the status quo, the Commission thought, could be as much

[14] Ibid. 29–31.
[15] TUC, *Annual Report 1969*, para. 74.
[16] Ibid.

attributable to labour market pressures arising from full employment as to the activities of the councils. As to the encouragement of collective bargaining, rather few councils had ever been abolished, and some unions even argued the traditional voluntarist point that the councils operated to discourage employees from joining trade unions because they took the view that their terms and conditions of employment depended upon the councils' decisions rather than the activities of the union.

The Labour government, in its White Paper[19] reacting to the Commission's Report, stated that the Commission had 'pointed out that the Wages Council system has impeded the growth of voluntary collective bargaining and strong trade unionism in many of the industries covered by it', and it proposed consultations as to the steps to be taken to remedy this situation. The implicit policy was carried through into the succeeding Conservative government's Industrial Relations Act 1971, which made it easier to abolish councils by removing the precondition that adequate voluntary machinery must actually exist—and be likely to continue to exist—before the Secretary of State abolished a council. Instead, the main criterion became whether the council was 'any longer necessary for the purpose of maintaining a reasonable standard of remuneration'.[20] Thus, if labour market pressures were likely to sustain wages, the council could be abolished to give the unions a free run at organizing the industry. A further change was made by the Employment Protection Act 1975, which introduced Statutory Joint Industrial Councils as a half-way house between a full Wages Council and voluntary collective bargaining. There were no independent members on an SJIC, but its decisions were to be enforceable by the wages inspectorate.[21] Thus the Wages Councils were under pressure in this period, which we have described as deregulatory. However, the arguments were mounted from the traditional, voluntary, collectivist standpoint and had thus a very different

---

[17] Above, ch. 1.1(c)(i). On the minor changes of the late 1950s, see above, p. 104.

[18] Report of the Royal Commission on Trade Unions and Employers' Associations, Cmnd. 3623 (1968), paras. 225–34, 257–66.

[19] *In Place of Strife*, Cmnd. 3888 (1969), para. 63.

[20] Industrial Relations Act 1971, sched. 8.

[21] Employment Protection Act 1975, ss. 90–3 and sched. 8. No SJIC was ever created.

basis from the deregulation arguments against the Wages Councils that were to be deployed with such drastic effects in the 1980s.

In general, then, the traditional legislative interventions to protect the interests of individual employees were under retreat in this period. The exception was the health and safety legislation, but even here, greater emphasis was placed by the 1974 Act upon voluntarist mechanisms at the level of the enforcement of the legislation. However, these changes, actual or proposed, tended to enhance, rather than undermine, the theory of collective *laissez-faire*, for what was proposed when legislative protection of the individual was removed was the substitution of the protections of collective bargaining. Nevertheless, viewed as a whole, this period did add to the challenges to collective *laissez-faire*, because, as the traditional legislative interventions came to be questioned, at the same time a new principle emerged for enacting legislation protecting the interests of individual employees, which was to have a profound effect upon policy-makers' views of the tasks it was proper to assign to labour law.

The legislation we have discussed so far was motivated mainly by a concern to protect the employee's health and personal security. This was true, not only of the health and safety legislation proper, but also of the legislative restrictions on hours and even the minimum wage legislation, which grew out of a concern for conditions of work in the 'sweated trades', even if the legislation subsequently acquired an auxiliary role in encouraging the growth of collective bargaining.[22] The new principle was rather different. We can take as a starting-point for analysis Kahn-Freund's remark in his 1954 essay that:

It is essential to realize that English law, contrary to most of the legal systems of the European Continent, knows nothing or little of the factory or mine, office or workshop, as a community organized by legal principles. The legal constitution of that community, if one may use that term, is still that of an absolute monarchy to the rule of which its members have submitted by contract.[23]

The inability of the individual contract of employment to capture either the group or collective aspect of most work situations or

---

[22] The truck legislation does not fit this pattern, of course: it aimed at controlling forms of unconscionability.

[23] 'Legal Framework' in A. Flanders and H. A. Clegg, eds., *The System of Industrial Relations in Great Britain* (Oxford, 1954), 49.

even, very accurately, the long-term nature of many employment relationships, with the constant *de facto* redefinition of the obligations of employer and employee, did not need to be laboured. For Kahn-Freund the gap between the law and social reality was to be filled, in this as in so many other respects, by the institutions of collective labour relations, here notably by shop stewards and shop stewards' committees, with whom the employer would bargain and consult where the employees were well organized, whether the law required this or not. So the powers of the absolute monarch were to be tamed by voluntary organization among the subjects.

In the 1960s, however, the question began to be asked whether the law did not have a role to play in reducing the degree of arbitrariness in the exercise of authority in the employment sphere. If the 'rule of law' was to make its presence felt in the workplace, could purely social mechanisms be relied upon to achieve that end? To adopt Selznick's language, one could ask whether freedom of association was enough to guarantee freedom in associations (meaning by 'association' any large organization and not just, or even mainly, trade unions).[24] It has been argued that the theorists (and presumably also the practitioners) of the abstentionist stance of law *vis-à-vis* industrial relations simply failed to realize the importance of controlling the misuse of 'bureaucratic' power, because their theories of collective bargaining were rooted in inequalities of power in the labour market.[25] In other words, in the criticized theories the role of collective bargaining was limited to defining the terms upon which employment was to be offered by employers and did not extend further to embrace the exercise of power by employer over employee after employment had commenced.

In the light of the comments made by Kahn-Freund in the essay quoted above, this position is perhaps difficult to sustain. The point was put even more clearly by Allan Flanders, one of the leading theorists in the abstentionist tradition, in an essay written in 1968:

[24] P. Selznick, *Law, Society and Industrial Justice* (New York, 1969), which remains the leading theoretical work in this area.

[25] H. Collins, 'Against Abstentionism in Labour law', in J. Eekelaar and J. Bell, eds., *Oxford Essays in Jurisprudence*, 3rd ser. (Oxford, 1987), 79.

Moreover, these wider and more enduring social consequences of collective bargaining are not limited to defining rights of employees with respect to their remuneration by regulating the price of work. The rules in collective agreements may also regulate such matters as dismissal, discipline, promotion or training, which cannot by any stretch of the imagination be included under price. What is more, because they are rules defining rights (and obligations) they are a means of preventing favouritism, nepotism, victimization and arbitrary discrimination of any sort. Thus one great accomplishment of collective bargaining has been its promotion of the 'rule of law' in employment relations. Far from being a change in the method of marketing labour, it has to be regarded as an institution freeing labour from being too much at the mercy of the market. Any evaluation of it which disregards this accomplishment cannot be taken seriously.[26]

Nevertheless, the question could still be asked whether collective bargaining was, or was capable of creating, an adequate realization of the principle of the rule of law in the workplace. What about workers employed in enterprises where there was no, or no adequate, collective organization? Even where effective collective bargaining was established, did it adequately protect the interests of all groups of workers, including women and minority groups, and, if not, was it capable of providing such protection? Was it even possible that the arbitrary exercise of power was not uniquely associated with employers, but could be found, on occasion, in the joint institutions of management and labour or even in trade union organizations alone? As we shall see, all these questions began to be addressed in the period we are considering.

Why these questions began to emerge in policy-making circles at this particular time is a large question which we have touched upon in Chapter 1. One may note, however, intellectual tendencies, such as the extension of the traditional concern with the exercise of arbitrary power by the state as against its citizens to embrace similar concern at the exercise of power within large-scale, often multi-national, but private organizations.[27] One may note the post-war extension of the welfare state towards comprehensive coverage of those not in work.[28] That system was

[26] A. Flanders, *Management and Unions* (London, 1970), 225.
[27] Selznick, *Law, Society and Industrial Justice*, chs. 2 and 7.
[28] Above, pp. 64–7.

devoted mainly to income support and health care, but it was not a very much bigger step to ask what the state's responsibilities were in ensuring fair treatment for those in work. One may note the emergence in the 1960s of a newly revitalized women's movement and effective campaigns against racial discrimination and for civil rights, both in the UK and in other countries.[29] Above all, perhaps, one should recall the general challenge to established authority in the late 1960s, encapsulated by, but by no means confined to, the events in Paris in 1968.[30] These challenges raised in an acute form the question of how the authority of organizations (state and non-state) over individuals was to be legitimated. A part, if only a small part, of the answer to that question was to be found in greater safeguards against the abuse of organizational power. In this chapter, therefore, we shall examine how these influences were reflected in British labour legislation which, as ever, had to address these challenges from the particular starting-point of the voluntarist tradition.

5.2. UNFAIR DISMISSAL

In the previous chapter we argued that the Redundancy Payments Act 1965 (and, indeed, the Contracts of Employment Act 1963) were very largely justified in governments' eyes by the contribution they made to the encouragement of labour mobility, and that they were not significantly underpinned by a rationale of securing the worker's continued employment in a particular job. However, the 1965 Act did take the crucial step of attaching to the employment relationship by legislation what were regarded at the time as fairly substantial entitlements in favour of the employee upon the termination of employment by the employer, and, moreover, entitlements which (in contrast to the 1963 Act) had no counterpart in the common law of the contract of employment. It was therefore natural and not surprising that attempts were quickly made—and we have seen that references were made to this process in the debates on the 1965 Act[31]—to

[29] Below, Sects. 5.3 and 5.4.
[30] See C. Crouch and A. Pizzorno, eds., *The Resurgence of Class Conflict in Western Europe since 1968* (2 vols.; London, 1978).
[31] Above, ch. 4.2(c).

extend the pattern of legislative intervention to embrace a more obvious concept of 'employment protection' in the shape of a legislative control over arbitrary, unjust, or, as they eventually became known, unfair dismissals.

An important catalyst for this development was the adoption in 1963 by the International Labour Organisation (of which the UK was a member) of Recommendation 119 concerning Termination of Employment at the Initiative of the Employer. Of course, UK membership of the ILO did not necessarily mean that Recommendation 119 would lead to British legislation on the topic. Even in the case of ILO Conventions a member state is not obliged to ratify them so as to make them binding upon it in international law, and the post-war period contained many examples of ILO Conventions which the UK had not ratified, e.g. No. 100 of 1951 on Equal Remuneration for Men and Women Workers for Work of Equal Value, or No. 103 of 1954 concerning Maternity Protection. The compelling force of a Recommendation was, of course, even less than that of a Convention. Nevertheless, the adoption of a Recommendation by the ILO did require the UK as a member state to give 'consideration with a view to effect being given to it by national legislation or otherwise',[32] and so the UK government had to formulate a view on the issue.

Moreover, although we shall argue that the decision to legislate on the topic of unfair dismissal was taken largely for domestic reasons, the ILO Recommendation clearly had a strong influence on the formulation of the statutory right not to be unfairly dismissed that was eventually enacted. The central tenet of Recommendation 119 was that 'termination of employment should not take place unless there is a valid reason for such termination connected with the capacity or conduct of the worker or based on the operational requirements of the undertaking, establishment or service.'[33] Thus the reason had to be both a valid one and one connected with the specified matters. One can see these requirements, somewhat expanded, running through what is now section 57 of the Employment Protection (Consolidation) Act 1978: the reason for the dismissal must fall within

[32] Art. 19(6) of the Constitution of the ILO.
[33] Art. 2(1).

one or more of the categories specified in the section, and it
must be a sufficient reason to justify the sanction of dismissal.
Moreover, Recommendation 119 also contained a supplementary
principle, whereby certain grounds for dismissal were specified as
invalid reasons. Again, the ultimate British legislation also made
use of this approach (e.g. by specifying union membership as
an unfair reason for dismissal), though its list of automatically
unfair dismissals was rather shorter than that contained in the
Recommendation.[34]

We propose to analyse the development of British unfair
dismissal legislation under a number of headings.

(a) Voluntarism and the Development of a Consensus in Favour of Legislation

As was its wont, the government gave rapid consideration to the
question of what its attitude should be towards the new ILO
instrument that had just been adopted. In 1964 it announced that
it accepted the Recommendation. However, this acceptance did
not automatically mean that legislation would follow. We have
already noted that the UK's obligation as a member of the ILO
was to give consideration to implementing the Recommendation
'by national legislation or otherwise', whilst article 1 of Recommendation 119 specifically stated that 'effect may be given to this
Recommendation through national laws or regulations, collective
agreements, works rules, arbitration awards, or court decisions or
in such other manner consistent with national practice as may be
appropriate under national conditions.' Since one of the best
known and most effective systems of protection against arbitrary
dismissal was the grievance arbitration system established in the
USA, not by the governmental authorities, but under the terms
of particular collective agreements, such flexibility in methods
of implementation was to be expected in the international
instrument. However, this also meant that, even after UK
acceptance of the Recommendation, the potential role, if any, for

[34] Art. 3 of Recommendation 119 specified, in addition to trade union
membership or activities, acting as a workers' representative, filing a complaint
against an employer or participating in legal proceedings against it, and race,
colour, sex, marital status, religion, political opinion, national extraction, and
social origin.

legislation in implementing unfair dismissal protection in this country remained to be argued out.

As might have been expected, the government's method of proceeding was to refer the matter to the NJAC, which, in early 1965, set up a subcommittee, which two years later produced a report, *Dismissal Procedures*. The debate within the committee and outside it came to focus in effect on the requirement in article 4 of Recommendation 119 that 'a worker who feels his employment has been unjustifiably terminated should be entitled . . . to appeal . . . against that termination . . . to a body established under a collective agreement or to a neutral body such as a court, an arbitrator, an arbitration committee or a similar body.' It was perceived that the common law, even as supplemented by the 1963 Act, afforded the employee little opportunity to make such an appeal. In what was regarded as the typical case of a worker employed on a contract of indefinite duration, the contract could be terminated lawfully on relatively short notice without the employer's reason for the termination being in any way relevant to the legality of the termination. Summary termination certainly would be unlawful at common law unless it was for conduct amounting to a serious breach of contract by the employee, and here the court could scrutinize the employer's reason and assess its validity against the standard of serious breach. But even so, the employee's remedy was likely to be simply the amount of wages the employee would have earned during the period of notice had the employer terminated the contract lawfully upon notice rather than summarily without good reason. Reinstatement was thought not to be available in 'the ordinary case of master and servant'. Consequently, only the uncommon case of an employee employed for a fixed term was thought to give rise to a substantial claim at common law, and even then the remedy would sound only in damages and be subject to the duty to mitigate.[35] Although in the 1980s this might have been regarded as a somewhat overly pessimistic statement of the potential common law claims of the dismissed employee,[36]

[35] Ministry of Labour, *Dismissal Procedures*, Report of a Committee of the National Joint Advisory Council (1967), para. 11–13.

[36] See H. Carty, 'Dismissed Employees; The Search for a More Effective Range of Remedies' (1989) 52 MLR 449; K. Ewing, 'Job Security and the Contract of Employment' (1989) 18 ILJ 217.

there was little sign of these later developments in the 1960s. Indeed, one may suspect that an essential spur to the common law developments of the 1980s was the introduction of statutory protection against unfair dismissal in 1971.

However, the crucial issue in the debate about whether legislation should be introduced was not whether the common law provided adequate remedies—it was universally agreed not to do so—but whether voluntary disputes procedures, agreed between employers and trade unions, and operating perhaps across a whole industry ('external' procedures) or perhaps within a particular plant or company ('internal' procedures), provided adequate redress for dismissed employees or could be adapted speedily so as to do so. The NJAC subcommittee devoted considerable attention to this point and came out in favour of the traditional, voluntarist response: inadequate though the current voluntary procedures might be, the best solution to the problem of unfair dismissal lay in their reform and extension, especially the reform and extension of internal procedures, which were 'simple, inexpensive and quick'.[37] The subcommittee took this view even though, outside the public sector and large firms in the private sector, internal procedures were thought to be unusual. No more than 20 per cent of firms in the private sector were thought to have adequate internal procedures, so that 'a very large number of firms, including the vast majority of smaller firms, . . . have no formal dismissal procedure'.[38]

The alternative strategy was to supplement the encouragement of the reform and extension of voluntary procedures with the introduction of a statutory protection against unfair dismissal. This the subcommittee rejected on the main ground that 'it could lessen the incentive to develop satisfactory voluntary procedures . . . where these do not already exist'.[39] That the subcommittee may have guessed that its defence of voluntarist solutions was not shared by many other important groups in industrial relations, at least in a situation where voluntary procedures had responded so little to a clear need, was perhaps indicated by the committee's recommendation that the Secretary of State keep the question of the introduction of statutory

---

[37] Ministry of Labour, *Dismissal Procedures*, para. 180.
[38] Ibid., paras. 19 and 72.
[39] Ibid., para. 170.

machinery under review[40]—a clear incentive to employers and unions to take action—and by the analysis in the subcommittee's report of the sort of statutory procedure it thought appropriate, if such were eventually introduced.[41] If the subcommittee did entertain such thoughts about the lack of appeal of a purely voluntarist solution, then it was right to do so. The General Council's Report to Congress in 1967 welcomed the encouragement of voluntary procedures, but said that 'legislation should be introduced which would provide workpeople with the right of appeal against dismissal and the opportunity to receive compensation in cases where dismissal is found to be unjustified.'[42] The Conservative Party's document, *Fair Deal at Work* (1968), recommended the introduction of legislation,[43] as did the Labour government's White Paper, *In Place of Strife* (1969), which commented that 'while it is desirable that voluntary procedures relating to dismissal should be improved and extended, the development of such procedures is much too slow.'[44] Legislative proposals on unfair dismissal were contained in Part IV of the Industrial Relations Bill, introduced in 1970 by the Labour government but not enacted because of the fall of that government, and similar (but not identical) provisions reached the statute-book as part of the succeeding Conservative government's Industrial Relations Act 1971.[45]

If one ignores those areas where the newly created individual right not to be unfairly dismissed intersected with collective structures and activities, especially the relationship with the closed shop, where the law underwent amazing gyrations, and concentrates instead on the purely individual aspects, one can say that the political consensus that speedily built up over the need for such legislation survived its enactment for the period of the 1970s. Thus Schedule 1 to the Trade Union and Labour Relations Act 1974 continued in existence the unfair dismissal provisions of the 1971 Act with only minor amendments; relatively slight further changes were made by the Employment Protection Act

[40] Ibid., para. 175.
[41] Ibid. pt. III(c).
[42] TUC, *Annual Report 1967*, 160.
[43] Conservative Political Centre, *Fair Deal at Work* (London, 1968), 42–3.
[44] *In Place of Strife*, Cmnd. 3888 (1969), para. 103.
[45] Ss. 22–32, 106, 118–19.

1975; and the unfair dismissal provisions, consolidated in the Employment Protection (Consolidation) Act 1978, survived the 1980s remarkably little altered. However, as we shall see in a later chapter,[46] the 1980s did see government acceptance of an argument of principle against unfair dismissal legislation, namely, that it discouraged employers from taking on labour and so contributed to unemployment; but even so, the right not to be unfairly dismissed seems to have been thought to be too well entrenched to invite a frontal assault. The substantive formulation of the right was left largely untouched, but the conditions for access to that right became more stringent, notably as a result of the extension of the qualifying period of service and of the encouragement of forms of employment not falling within the legislative protection established in 1971. It is significant that the updating Convention (No. 158) and Recommendation (No. 166) on Termination of Employment at the Initiative of the Employer, adopted by the ILO in 1982, were this time rejected by the UK government.[47] Nevertheless, the unfair dismissal legislation, introduced in 1971, can claim to have been both a highly significant and a durable addition to the corpus of British labour law.

It may be wondered why the walls of the voluntarist citadel fell so quickly in this respect at the sound of the legislative trumpets. There seem to have been two reasons motivating statutory intervention, one of a collective, the other of an individual nature. The collective argument was put pithily in *Fair Deal at Work*:

Britain is one of the few countries where dismissals . . . are a frequent cause of strike action. . . . It seems reasonable to link this with the fact that Britain is one of only seven out of sixty-two countries covered in an ILO study where dismissal procedures are not regulated by statute.[48]

Although this was a pretty crude piece of comparative argument, the basic argument was endorsed, in somewhat more cautious terms, by the Donovan Commission. Having pointed out that in the period 1964–6 there were on average 276 unofficial strikes over the employment, suspension, or dismissal of individual employees, the Commission commented:

---

[46] Below, ch. 10.3(*b*).
[47] See B. Napier, 'Dismissals: The New ILO Standards' (1983) 12 ILJ 17.
[48] p. 42.

It can be argued that the right to secure a speedy and impartial decision on the justification for a dismissal might have averted many of these stoppages, though some cases would no doubt still have occurred where workers were taking spontaneous action to try to prevent a dismissal being given effect.[49]

Whether the enactment of unfair dismissal legislation in fact had an impact on the level of industrial action over such issues is disputed among the industrial relations experts. Dickens *et al.* conclude: 'From the available evidence, with the reservations expressed above, it appears that the introduction of statutory protection has not reduced the level of strikes over dismissal.'[50] Durcan, McCarthy, and Redman, on the other hand, are more optimistic: 'In summary, both the number of stoppages and the amount of time lost over alleged unfair dismissals fell in the four years following the implementation of the Act. The reductions in strike activity were not especially large but it was not expected that the provisions would have much impact in strongly organised workplaces.'[51] What is clear is that no informed person expected the new legal procedures wholly to replace industrial action over dismissal issues. This was not merely because, as we shall see, industrial action might provide a quicker and more effective remedy (notably reinstatement of the unfairly dismissed employee), but also because, in some cases, the dismissal was perceived by the workgroup as raising, not a purely individual issue, but a collective one, to which collective action might be seen as a more appropriate response. This could occur, not only in relation to the obvious cases, say of dismissal of a shop steward, but in relation to almost any dismissal. A dismissal for misconduct might arise out of a context of employer introduction of new technology which the employees were refusing to operate. It was not possible to say, a priori, which dismissals would be regarded by fellow workers as raising a collective issue over which they were prepared to take industrial action, but that possibility was often there. Certainly no attempt was made in

---

[49] Report of the Royal Commission on Trade Unions and Employers Associations, Cmnd. 3623 (1968), para. 528.

[50] L. Dickens *et al.*, *Dismissed* (Oxford, 1985), 225.

[51] J. W. Durcan, W. E. J. McCarthy, and G. P. Redman, *Strikes in Post-War Britain* (1983), 389.

1971 to link the availability of the new legal procedure with a statutory prohibition on strikes over dismissals.[52]

The other, individual, argument in favour of unfair dismissal legislation was, perhaps, a more obvious one. As the Donovan Commission put it:

> In practice there is usually no comparison between the consequences for an employer if an employee terminates the contract of employment and those which will ensue for an employee if he is dismissed. In reality people build much of their lives around their jobs. Their incomes and prospects for the future are inevitably founded in the expectation that their jobs will continue. For workers in many situations dismissal is a disaster. For some workers it may make inevitable the breaking up of a community and the uprooting of homes and families. Others, and particularly older workers, may be faced with the greatest difficulty in getting work at all. The statutory provision for redundancy goes some way to recognise what is really at stake for an employee when his job is involved, but it is no less at stake if he is being dismissed for alleged incompetence or for misconduct than if he is being dismissed for redundancy. To this it is no answer that good employers will dismiss employees only if they have no alternative. Not all employers are good employers. Even if the employer's intentions are good, is it certain that his subordinates' intentions are always also good? And even when all concerned in management act in good faith, are they always necessarily right? Should their view of the case automatically prevail over the employee's?[53]

This argument loses nothing of its force by the reflection that it could have been put forward as strongly in favour of legislative intervention twenty or even fifty years earlier—indeed, perhaps even more strongly given the post-war developments in the coverage of collective bargaining. What that reflection does serve to do, however, is to remind us that what was new in the 1960s was not the availability of an argument in favour of individual statutory protection against unfair dismissal, but the willingness in governmental circles to act upon the argument. This may be explained, partly by reference to the supplementary collective argument in favour of legislation, but also, and perhaps prin-

---

[52] Contrast the provisions of s. 9 of the Employment Act 1990, relating to the dismissal of unofficial strikers, which deprives them of both industrial and statutory protections (now TULRECA 1992, ss. 223 and 237).

[53] Cmnd. 3623, para. 526.

cipally, by a general move at this time towards conferring legal protections upon individual employees, which this chapter chronicles and analyses. Moreover, despite the inadequacies and imperfections of the unfair dismissal legislation introduced in 1971, it is difficult not to conclude that it made a significant contribution to the ability of employees, and their representatives, to resist and to challenge arbitrary termination of employment by employers.

Although we have argued that the voluntarist approach of the NJAC subcommittee on the issue of unfair dismissal legislation was pretty widely rejected, it would be wrong to suppose that voluntarist arguments were not treated with respect. In particular, the Donovan Commission felt able to recommend in favour of legislation in part because it regarded the 'main argument' the NJAC put forward against legislation (namely, that it would hinder the development of voluntary procedures) as erroneous.

. . . if employers know that employees have a right to challenge dismissal in a statutory tribunal then there is a clear incentive for them to see that dismissals are carried out under a proper and orderly procedure, so as to ensure both that as many cases as possible are settled satisfactorily without recourse to an outside appeal and that in those cases where appeal is made it can be shown that the dismissal was fair and justified.[54]

On this point the Commission seems to have been right, for 'there is no doubt that, since the statutory provisions were enacted, there has been a great increase in the incidence of formal procedures in this area.'[55] This occurred, not only because of the availability of a legal challenge to dismissals, but also because of the emphasis on procedural correctness over dismissal issues in the Industrial Relations Code of Practice, issued under the 1971 Act, and in the early decisions of the National Industrial Relations Court (NIRC),[56] and also because of the general climate of procedural reform in the post-Donovan period.[57]

Indeed, an important element of the Donovan strategy was that appropriate voluntary procedures might be exempted

[54] Ibid., para. 533.
[55] Dickens *et al.*, *Dismissed*, 232.
[56] D. Jackson, *Unfair Dismissal* (Cambridge, 1975), 22–5.
[57] Department of Employment, *The Reform of Collective Bargaining at Plant and Company Level*, Manpower Paper no. 5 (1971).

entirely from the legislation and provide an exclusive avenue of redress for those covered by them. Such a provision was included in the subsequent legislation, but only one procedure has been so exempted.[58] This seems to have been because some of the criteria for exemption went beyond what dismissal procedures normally contained. The procedure must be jointly agreed with a trade union (many dismissal procedures are laid down unilaterally by management), must provide adequate remedies for those unfairly dismissed (which is usually taken to mean that compensation must be a possible remedy under the procedure, which it rarely is), and it must provide for a decision to be made by an independent body where the parties to the procedure cannot agree over a case (which not all procedures do). As important, perhaps, in explaining the absence of exemption applications, is that management could usually obtain from a procedure the advantages mentioned by the Commission without carrying through the reforms needed to obtain exemption. However, it seems reasonable to conclude that the introduction of statutory unfair dismissal protection had the effect of encouraging the growth of voluntary dismissal procedures, though not necessarily jointly agreed ones and not necessarily procedures in the statutory model needed for exemption. Depending upon one's view of what would have happened to voluntary procedures had the NJAC's prescription been adopted, one might argue that it was wrong to see the choice as one between voluntary protection and statutory protection, but that it should be seen, rather, as one between the introduction of statutory protection, which stimulated voluntary reform, and continuation of the situation in which low levels of both voluntary and legal protection obtained.

(b) Unfair Dismissal and the Industrial Tribunals

It is not our purpose to give a general account of the structure of the unfair dismissal legislation, still less to analyse subsequent judicial interpretation of the law, but we do wish to say something about what seem to us the two main features of the legislation enacted in 1971: the decision to give dispute settlement under the new provisions to the industrial tribunals and the continuing

[58] Industrial Relations Act 1971, ss. 31–2, now Employment Protection (Consolidation) Act 1978, ss. 65–6; P. Davies and M. Freedland, *Labour Law: Text and Materials* (2nd edn. London, 1984), 264–5.

equivocation about the centrality of reinstatement as a remedy for unfair dismissal, so that compensation became in the event the primary remedy for unfair dismissal.

As to the former, we noted in the previous chapter that the conferment of this jurisdiction upon the tribunals brought them very much centre stage as far as individual employment law was concerned. Unfair dismissal cases both led to a great increase in the number of disputes handled by the tribunals and became the single most important source of litigation before them. In 1977 there were nearly 50,000 applications to industrial tribunals (by no means all led, of course, to hearings), as compared to 11,600 in 1970, and over three-quarters of the 1977 applications concerned unfair dismissal.[59] In the light of developments in the 1980s it is interesting to note that the unfair dismissal case-load took some time to build up: even in 1974 there were only about 15,000 unfair dismissal applications. The leap to over 40,000 unfair dismissal applications in 1976 seems to have been the result of the reduction of the qualifying period of continuous service with an employer, needed to bring a claim, from two years (as laid down in the 1971 Act) to one year in September 1974 (by TULRA 1974) and then in 1975 to six months, where it remained until the 1980s. This was an expected development, since the two-year period had been fixed in 1971 for administrative reasons (to avoid the tribunals being flooded with claims) rather than for reasons of principle. As the Department's Consultative Document on the Industrial Relations Bill put it:

Initially, because of limitations on the rate at which the ITs can be expanded for their additional functions, this right would have to be limited to employees with two or more years' service in their employment; but the intention would be to extend the right to other employees later.[60]

As we also noted in the last chapter, the rise of the unfair dismissal case-load and the decline of the selective employment tax and industrial training levy cases caused the tribunals to cast off their ambiguous image as, in part, administrative tribunals dealing with disputes between citizen and the state, and become

---

[59] Davies and Freedland, *Labour Law* (1st edn. 1979), 731–3.
[60] Department of Employment and Productivity, *Industrial Relations Bill: Consultative Document* (1970), para. 53.

full-blooded labour courts (at least in the individual area). The Donovan Commission proposed to underline this change of emphasis by a change of name (from 'industrial' to 'labour' tribunals—a proposal not in fact implemented) and, more important, by conferring upon tribunals jurisdiction to deal with all disputes 'arising between employers and employees from their contracts of employment or from any statutory claims they may have against each other in their capacity as employer and employee'.[61] Although a power to confer a contractual jurisdiction on the industrial tribunals was included in the 1971 Act (and has appeared in subsequent legislation), it was not exercised, initially for fear that the tribunals would not be able to cope with the case-load,[62] and later because of an objection from the TUC that such a jurisdiction 'would necessarily involve interpretation of collective agreements',[63] that is, where they had been incorporated into the individual contract of employment. Although the feeling that the courts should be kept out of collective matters was very strong in the mid-1970s, this particular objection came to lack force as it became apparent that the tribunals would necessarily have to interpret provisions of collective agreements imcorporated into individual contracts under their unfair dismissal jurisdiction—for instance, in claims of 'constructive' dismissal. Nevertheless, in the late 1980s this issue was still a matter of controversy and the tribunals still lacked a straightforward contractual jurisdiction.[64]

Although the unfair dismissal jurisdiction was a new and important one, there seems to have developed an easy and rapid consensus that this jurisdiction should be conferred upon the industrial tribunals. Only the NJAC sub-committee pressed the idea that 'it may be that a new and rather different body is needed.'[65] The Donovan Commission[66] clearly saw the disadvantages of creating fragmented jurisdictions, and government quickly acquiesced in its proposals. The NJAC sub-committee gave two specific reasons for not using the industrial tribunals:

---

[61] Cmnd. 3623, para. 572–3.

[62] *Industrial Relations Bill: Consultative Document*, paras. 61–3.

[63] TUC, *Annual Report 1969*, 169—a view repeated in later Reports.

[64] Note in (1989) 97 *Employment Gazette* 345. The provisions of the Wages Act 1986 on deductions from wages had already covered some of the ground, probably unintentionally. See *Delaney* v. *Staples* [1992] IRLR 191 (HL).

[65] Cmnd. 3623, para. 151.

[66] Ibid., para. 572.

that it would enable non-legally-qualified chairs to be appointed and enable a conciliation stage to be built into the system of handling disputes. The first proposal the Commission found unattractive, whilst the second, it thought, could be grafted on to the tribunal system.[67] Conciliation was indeed introduced into the tribunals' procedures in 1971, albeit conciliation carried out by officers of the Department of Employment (later of the Advisory, Conciliation, and Arbitration Service) rather than by the tribunal itself, as Donovan had envisaged, and it proved to be a valuable addition. Some two-thirds of applications to industrial tribunals are disposed of without a hearing and, although it is not easy to say how many settlements are the result wholly or mainly of conciliation officers' efforts and how many consist of the conciliation officer rubber-stamping an agreement reached by the parties themselves (or, more likely, their representatives), the conciliation officers clearly play a vital role in the processing of (now) all claims before industrial tribunals.[68]

Although there was a general assumption that the industrial tribunals should take the unfair dismissal jurisdiction, the idea, expressed by the NJAC, that some more appropriate dispute-settlement body could and should be found has continued to attract supporters. From early days the tribunals were criticized for 'legalism' (or sometimes for 'excessive legalism', suggesting that some degree of 'legalism' was acceptable), but these debates generated more heat than light.[69] This was partly because of a failure to define what was meant by 'legalism', and partly because of critics' penchant for concentrating upon the characteristics of the personnel who constituted the tribunals rather than upon the structural constraints within which the tribunals had to operate (for example, the fact that the development of the law to be applied by the tribunals was ultimately controlled by the appellate courts). On the other hand, more radical proposals for structural changes, usually based upon some notion of importing an arbitration element into dispute settlements over individual issues,[70] failed to have an impact upon policy-makers. Indeed, as

---

[67] Ibid., paras. 582 and 584.

[68] Dickens, et al., Dismissed, ch. 6.

[69] See R. Munday, 'Tribunal Lore: Legalism and the Industrial Tribunals' (1981) 10 ILJ 146.

[70] Dickens et al., Dismissed, ch. 9; H. Collins, 'Capitalist Discipline and Corporatist Law' (1982) 11 ILJ 78, 170.

we shall see, in the 1980s even well-reasoned proposals[71] for change within the existing structure had little effect as the emphasis switched to discouraging 'undeserving' applicants from wasting management's time over 'hopeless' claims.

(c) Remedies and the Problem of Reinstatement

It was apparent to all involved in the discussion of the new unfair dismissal jurisdiction that the tribunals should have the power to award compensation to unfairly dismissed workers, although it took some time for the pattern of the compensatory provisions to be settled. The Labour government's Industrial Relations Bill[72] was clearly influenced by the backward-looking method of assessment employed by the Redundancy Payments Act. It was proposed that the 'basic amount' of compensation should be two-thirds of eight weeks' pay plus two-thirds of a week's pay for each year of service up to a maximum of twenty years, though there was a power to adjust this amount upwards or downwards in certain defined circumstance. The advantage of this approach was, as with the 1965 Act itself, that the unfairly dismissed applicant had a virtual guarantee of a significant monetary award. The drafters of the 1971 Act, however, seem to have taken the view that unfair dismissal was a species of statutory tort and that the appropriate way of measuring compensation was not by reference to past service but by reference to the loss flowing from the employer's wrongful act. Thus the 1971 Act adopted the formula, which appears with but slight changes in the current law, that the compensation should be 'such amount as the . . . tribunal considers just and equitable in all the circumstances, having regard to the loss sustained by the aggrieved party in consequence of the matters to which the complaint relates, in so far as the loss was attributable to action taken by or on behalf of the party in default'.[73]

Into such a formula it was perhaps natural to build a duty to mitigate loss (which had not been present in the Labour government's bill), and there was present also a notion of contributory fault (which had, in fact, been part of the Labour proposals). Finally, a limit was placed on the maximum amount

---

[71] See e.g. Justice, *Industrial Tribunals* (London, 1987).
[72] Bill 164, Session 1969/70, cls. 40–2.
[73] Industrial Relations Act 1971, s. 116(1).

of compensation of two years' pay or £4,160 (whichever was the lesser),[74] the latter being two years' pay at average earnings. All these have remained features of the compensatory provisions for unfair dismissal, except that in 1975 the first alternative way of expressing the limit on compensation was abolished.[75] It is interesting to reflect that had the £4,160 limit been increased in line with the increase in earnings, it would by 1988 have been in the region of £25,000 as compared with the actual limit at that time of £8,500. However, the notion of a 'basic amount' resurfaced in the 1975 reforms in the guise of a 'basic award', which was now to supplement rather than to replace the compensatory award. The basic award was calculated in essence in the same way as a redundancy payment and was in part an endorsement and supplementation of the principle developed by the NIRC under the 1971 Act that a head of compensation for unfairly dismissed workers should be loss of statutory redundancy protection, conventionally set at 50 per cent of the redundancy payment that would have been due had the dismissal been on grounds of redundancy.[76]

The controversial question, however, was not the remedy of compensation, but that of reinstatement. Was reinstatement (or re-engagement) to be made available to the tribunals as a remedy; what would be the priority as between reinstatement and compensation; and how would a reinstatement order be enforced? As the Donovan Commission recognized, an effective reinstatement order was the clearest possible vindication of the unfairly dismissed employee's entitlements; on the other hand, the Commission seems to have entertained doubts about reinstatement being effective unless the remedy was accepted on a voluntary basis. It therefore proposed as 'more in accord with reality' that compensation should be the primary relief, with the compensation order lapsing if both employer and employee opted for reinstatement.[77] A strong campaign was waged by supporters of the new legislative proposals to reverse this position,[78] and at one stage the Labour government seems to have

[74] S. 118(1).
[75] Employment Protection Act 1975, sched. 16, pt. III, para. 17.
[76] M. Freedland, Note (1975) 39 MLR 571–3.
[77] Cmnd. 3623, paras. 551–2.
[78] See esp. G. de N. Clark, *Remedies for Unjust Dismissal* (PEP Broadsheet 518; London, 1970).

been persuaded to give reinstatement a much higher profile. This was to be done both by making it a remedy the tribunal should order (rather than one the parties to the litigation could opt for) and by enabling an employee not reinstated after a tribunal order to this effect 'to ask the tribunal to refer his case to the Industrial Board. The Industrial Board would have power to impose upon the employer a countinuing financial penalty for each day for which the order is defied.'[79]

When the Labour government's bill was published, the priority of the reinstatement remedy was preserved, in the shape of an obligation upon the tribunal to order reinstatement where the employee wished to be reinstated and the tribunal thought it an appropriate case for reinstatement, but the sanction behind the reinstatement order had been reduced to an additional award of compensation (up to six months' pay) to be awarded by the tribunal in cases of non-compliance.[80] A similar, but weaker, scheme was contained in the 1971 Act,[81] but the 1975 reforms brought in a set of provisions closer to those of the 1970 Bill, which provisions continue as part of the current law. The crucial point, however, is that the 1970 Bill, 1971 Act, and 1975 reforms all protected the freedom of the employer to buy its way out of an award of reinstatement upon payment of a relatively modest additional lump sum. It was thought inappropriate to confer the contempt powers of the High Court (or even the county courts) upon the industrial tribunals. However, in practice discussion over the years has concentrated upon the small number of reinstatement (or re-engagement) orders made by tribunals (in spite of provisions contained in the 1975 reforms requiring tribunals to explain to successful applicants the availability of the reinstatement order) rather than upon the limited sanctions behind such orders. In 1987/8, for example, only 3 per cent of successful applicants were awarded reinstatement by tribunals. Dispute rages over whether this result is due to non-implementation by tribunals of the 1975 reforms through a traditional common law aversion to specific performance, or to the un-

[79] Quoted in TUC, *Annual Report 1969*, 163.

[80] Bill 164, Session 1969/70, cls. 37–9 and 52.

[81] IRA 1971, s. 106. Re-engagement was a possible remedy under the Act, but it was given no particular priority over compensation, which in fact became the standard remedy.

willingness of employees, after the trauma of a tribunal hearing, to be reinstated.[82] At this point, of course, the specific discussion of remedies merges with the wider discussion of the nature of decision-marking by tribunals, an issue we do not wish to develop further in this book.

5.3. EQUAL PAY ACT 1970

(a) Introduction

In terms of effecting legal protection against arbitrary treatment in employment the unfair dismissal legislation was the most important development of this period, because the types of unfair treatment with which it was capable of dealing were broadly conceived. However, the unfair dismissal provisions of the 1971 Act were not the first legislative effort in this direction. Legal protection against some types of arbitrary treatment in employment had already been introduced by the Race Relations Act 1968 and the Equal Pay Act 1970. Pursuing our somewhat counter-chronological approach to the fair treatment provisions of this period, we shall look first at the 1970 and then at the 1968 Act.

As speakers at TUC congresses throughout the 1960s never failed to recall, the TUC had passed as early as 1888 a resolution in favour of the proposition that 'it is desirable in the interest both of men and women that in trades where women do the same work as men they shall receive the same payment', and on that basis the claim for equal pay as between men and women could be said to be 'the oldest wage claim of the trade union movement'.[83] We saw in an earlier chapter[84] that, after the Second World War and during the 1950s, trade unions and women's organizations operating relatively independently of the labour movement had been able to secure the appointment of a Royal Commission on equal pay and, later, through negotiation, the achievement, in stages, of equal pay (at least for 'like work') for non-manual workers in the civil and public services. However, when in 1960 the General Council surveyed affiliated unions'

---

[82] See Dickens *et al.*, *Dismissed*, 111–22.
[83] TUC, *Annual Report 1968*, 455 (Miss J. O'Connell, DATA).
[84] above, pp. 121–5.

subsequent progress in this area, it was forced to state that 'most of the unions reported failure in their attempts to secure equal pay for industrial workers'.[85]

The significant change at this time from our point of view, however, is that, in the context of greater willingness on the part of government to use legislation to promote labour mobility, the TUC was now prepared to press more vigorously for governmental action to help achieve selected TUC objectives. In the case of equal pay, the TUC's main demand of government was that it ratify ILO Convention 100 of 1951, which provided that 'each member shall, by means appropriate to the methods in operation for determining rates of remuneration, promote and, insofar as is consistent with such methods, ensure the application to all workers of the principle of equal remuneretion for men and women workers for work of equal value.'[86] Besides its broad definition of equality, which will be discussed further below, this Convention was perhaps attractive to the TUC because, whilst committing government to action to promote equal pay, it did not insist that the means used be necessarily or primarily legislative. Nevertheless, as early as 1961 the General Council did recognize that 'as a last resort, this [i.e. ratification] might mean that legislation would have to be introduced to enforce equal pay in industries where employers were not willing to introduce it by collective bargaining.'[87]

In fact, governments throughout the 1960s (Labour as well as Conservative) took the view that the TUC's demand put the cart before the horse, and that the UK should stick to its traditional policy of not ratifying any particular ILO Convention unless it was thought that British practice was already broadly in conformity with it.[88] So from government's point of view the question became, not whether Convention 100 should immediately be ratified, but what, if anything, government should do to bring about a situation in which ratification became possible. The Conservative administrations of the early 1960s were unwilling to

[85] TUC, *Annual Report 1961*, para. 330.
[86] ILO Convention 100 concerning Equal Remuneration for Men and Women Workers for Work of Equal Value, 1951, art. 2(1). There was a similar provision in art. 4(3) of the European Social Charter of 1961, which article the UK government also refused to ratify: TUC, *Annual Report 1963*, para. 72.
[87] TUC, *Annual Report 1961*, para. 330.
[88] TUC, *Annual Report 1962*, para. 319; *Annual Report 1966*, para. 67.

undertake any commitment in this direction. The crucial change occurred when, in its 1964 election manifesto, the Labour Party, in the context of its proposed National Plan, put forward the notion of a seven-point 'Charter of Rights for all employees', one of the heads of which was 'the right to equal pay for equal work'.[89] For the rest of the decade the Ministry of Labour, CBI, and TUC engaged in desultory talks as to how this commitment should be implemented (including the question of the role of law in the process of implementation), with the government asserting, on the one hand, its acceptance of the principle of equal pay and, on the other, its view that in the context of economic crisis and the resulting statutory incomes policy, the timing was not appropriate for a move that would inevitably increase employers' labour costs.[90] These tensions were not resolved until the end of the decade when Barbara Castle, as Minister at the now renamed Department of Employment and Productivity, turned to equal pay and secured the passing of the Equal Pay Act 1970 as a means of repairing the fissures that had opened up in relations between the Labour Government and the union movement over incomes policy and the government's proposals for reform of collective labour law, as proposed in the White Paper, *In Place of Strife*.[91]

(b) The 1970 Act, Inflation, and Pay Structures

Although the government concluded in the late 1960s that the balance of political advantage lay with implementation of the commitment to equal pay rather than with further procrastination, this did not mean that the government's concern with its potential impact upon the rate of wage inflation had vanished. Nor did the government's decision to proceed via legislation mean it was not aware of the potential pitfalls for legislation in this area. In particular, the government was aware that, if claims to equal pay as between men and women could be used to

[89] E. W. S. Craig, *British General Election Manifestos 1900–1974* (London, 1975), 260. The pledge was repeated in 1966: ibid. 302.
[90] TUC, *Annual Report 1968*, para. 65.
[91] See above, ch. 4.3 on incomes policy and below, ch. 6.3 on *In Place of Strife*. It seems that by this stage the Conservative Party had come out in favour of legislation too, for the Opposition did not divide the House at the end of the Second Reading debate on the Equal Pay Bill, and it criticized the Government Bill for not going far enough: HC Deb., vol. 795, col. 932 (9 Feb. 1970).

challenge on a general basis inequities and anomalies in pay structures, the legislation might have a destabilizing effect upon industrial relations and add to the causes of unofficial strikes which the government was committed to reducing. The government thus became committed to a policy of restricting the scope of the legislation. Inflationary concerns were most evident in the discussions over the phasing-in period, the government proposing initially seven years (the period used in the Civil Service in the 1950s) and the TUC counter-claiming with two.[92] The legislation settled on five, so that the 1970 Act came into force only at the end of 1975.[93] However, both the inflation and industrial conflict concerns left permanent marks upon the legislation, and in three areas in particular the government decided to pull back from a full-scale implementation of the principle of equal pay. These areas have remained controversial, especially in terms of their relationship to the UK's obligations under article 119 of the Treaty of Rome.

The first area concerns the application of the Act to collective agreements. Although collective agreements in the UK are not normally legally binding, the government did not therefore conclude that it need apply the Act only to contracts of employment, into which the terms of the relevant collective agreement might have been incorporated. Instead, section 3 of the 1970 Act provided a procedure whereby an allegedly discriminatory collective agreement (or non-collectively-bargained pay structure) could be referred to the Industrial Court for amendment, if one of the parties to it or the Secretary of State decided to make a reference. This was an apparently bold provision which brought the law into play in controlling the content of collective agreements. However, this apparent boldness was qualified by two provisions. First, the Industrial Court could act only upon provisions in the collective agreement or pay structure applying on their face only to men or only to women. If the agreement were *ex facie* discriminatory (e.g. men's rate x; women's rate $70\%x$), then the Industrial Court had jurisdiction; if the agreement was

[92] TUC, *Annual Report 1969*, para. 71.

[93] Equal Pay Act 1970, s. 9(1). Ss. 9(2) and (3) provided that the Secretary of State might make an order coming into effect on 31 Dec. 1973, which would have required employers to pay at least 90 per cent of equal pay from that date, but this power was never exercised.

facially neutral (e.g. Grade I workers x; grade II workers 70%x), it had no jurisdiction, even if all Grade I workers were in fact male, and all Grade II workers were in fact female.

The second qualifying provision in Section 3 concerned the Industrial Court's powers if the agreement was found to be *ex facie* discriminatory. The situation the legislature seems to have had in mind was the one not uncommon at the time in which an industry-wide collective agreement laid down several rates for male workers (say a skilled, semi-skilled, and an unskilled rate) and then a separate rate for women workers which was lower than any of the male rates. The Industrial Court had power to amend the female rate (and, thus, affect any individual contract into which the collective agreement was incorporated), but only by bringing the female rate up to the lowest of the male rates. Although the raising of women-only rates in collective agreements (and, pretty soon, their disappearance) had a significant impact upon women's pay in the years immediately after 1975,[94] this was an obviously rather inadequate way of implementing equality for those women workers who were other than unskilled. Although the provisions of subsection (4) of section 3, which produced this result, were highly obscure and not well understood in the Parliamentary debates, which in consequence tended to irrelevance, fear of legal intervention, even by an arbitration body, into the mysteries of collective agreements seems to lie behind the Minister's comment that, 'Insofar as the Industrial Court has any role, it must be strictly defined by statute; and that is what subsection (4) seeks to do. It severely limits the extent of the amendment that the Industrial Court can initiate.'[95]

As things turned out, and as was probably intended, the main form of enforcement of the 1970 Act was by way of complaint by

---

[94] M. Snell, P. Glucklich, and M. Povall, *Equal Pay and Opportunities* (Research Paper 20, Dept. of Employment, 1981), 65.

[95] HC Deb., vol. 795, col. 264 (9 Feb. 1970). In fact, the Central Arbitration Committee. which succeeded to the functions of the Industrial Court in 1975, made a brave attempt to overcome both sets of limitations on s. 3, but was eventually slapped down by the Divisional Court in *R* v. *CAC ex parte Hy-Mac Ltd.* [1979] IRLR 461. See Davies [1980] CLP 165. S. 3 itself was repealed by the Sex Discrimination Act 1986 and replaced by something even less effective (see s. 6 and sched. pt. II), ironically as a result of a finding by the ECJ that the Sex Discrimination Act 1975 did not comply with Directive 76/207, on the grounds that the 1975 Act contained no equivalent to s. 3 of the 1970 Act: Case 165/82, *Commission* v. *UK* [1984] ICR 192.

individual employees to an industrial tribunal. In contrast with the collective procedure described above, in which the Industrial Court, within the limits of its jurisdiction, could look at the collective agreement or pay structure as a whole, the individual procedure required the complainant to indentify a particular person of the opposite sex with whom the applicant was doing equal work but who was receiving more favourable terms and conditions of employment. The crucial questions thus became how the law defined equal work and what restrictions, if any, it put on the choice of comparator by the applicant, beyond the requirement that the comparator be of the opposite sex. On the latter point the law was in fact very restrictive, for it required (and still requires) that normally the comparator be employed at the same *establishment* as the applicant (even in the case of large organizations based on more than one site) by the same or an associated employer.[96] The purpose of this restriction seems to have been to reduce the possibility of equal pay claims being made across (rather than within) the boundaries of existing pay structures, and thus to reduce the potential of the Act to disrupt established relativities. This policy is perhaps revealed by the exception to the rule: comparison could be made with employees at other establishments (employed by the same or an associated employer) provided 'common terms and conditions of employment' were observed at the two establishments. Thus the applicant could go outside the establishment if, but only if, those responsible for setting the pay structure had already brought the other establishment within it.[97]

The most contentious item in the legislation, however, was the definition of equality. The issue was conceived as located on a spectrum, at one end of which was the broad definition of equality contained in ILO Convention 100 (equal pay for work of equal value, so that jobs of very different content could be held to be of equal value in terms of the demands put upon their occupants),

---

[96] Equal Pay Act 1970, s. 1(5).

[97] 'There may be perfectly good geographical or historical reasons why a single employer should operate essentially different employment regimes at different establishments. In such cases the limitation imposed by section 1(6) will operate to defeat claims under Section 1 as between men and women at the different establishments', *per* Lord Bridge in *Leverton* v. *Clwyd CC* [1989] ICR 33, 60, where, however, comparison was allowed because the terms and conditions of the applicant and the comparator were governed by the same collective agreement.

whilst at the other end of the spectrum was what was seen as the narrow definition of equal pay contained in article 119 of the Treaty of Rome, namely, 'equal pay for equal work'.[98] It is, of course, highly ironic, in the light of subsequent EEC developments, that the formulation of equality in article 119 was seen at this time as the narrow one of equal pay only where the jobs being compared were the same or similar in content, but this perception of the scope of artice 119 was widespread at this time, and not just in the UK.[99] The TUC pressed the government to adopt what it saw as the ILO model, but the government resisted and embodied in the 1970 Act no more than a slightly expanded version of the model based on the then current interpretation of article 119. Equal pay was required where the jobs performed by the applicant and the comparator were 'of the same or a broadly similar nature' or, where this was not the case, where they had been rated as equivalent in an evaluation exercise.[100] The crucial lacuna was that in the case of dissimilar jobs, the tribunal could neither compel an evaluation exercise to be conducted or conduct its own, so that, again, those industrial parties responsible for determining the criteria upon which the pay structure was based could also determine whether a 'work rated as equivalent' claim was to be made available to potential applicants in equal pay cases. If the industrial parties chose to use criteria that amounted to an evaluation of jobs, an equal pay claim might lie; if they did not, their freedom to utilize different criteria was not challengeable under the Act. It was not until the 1980s that this gap in the legislation was closed, it being a further ironical aspect of the

[98] The UK was not, of course, a member of the European Community at this time, but the provisions of art. 119 were well known from the begining in policy-making circles: TUC, *Annual Report 1962*, para. 319.

[99] Thus, Treu has described the European Commission's own interpretation of art. 119 in the early 1960s as follows: 'The official interpretation of [art. 119] confirmed the narrow scope of the equal pay principle as referring only to the same work or work substantially similar', T. Treu, 'Equal Pay and Comparable Work: A View from Europe' (1986) 8 *Comparative Labor Law Journal* 1, at 7. Treu also points out that even the meaning given to Convention 100 by the TUC was not universally accepted. Some argued that 'equal value' meant 'equal economic value', so that 'women's work could be paid less than similar men's work on the ground it had less "economic value".'

[100] Equal Pay Act 1970, s. 1(2)(*a*) and (*b*). Before the Equal Pay Act 1970 came into force it was amended in various ways that need not concern us by the Sex Discrimination Act 1975. The references to s. 1 of the 1970 Act are as amended by the 1975 Act.

view taken of article 119 in the late 1960s that this extension of the UK legislation resulted from a finding by the European Court of Justice that, in this respect, British law did not comply with the Treaty requirements.[101]

(c) The 1970 Act: Effectiveness and Equal Opportunities

Thus the 1970 Act constituted a limited attack upon the problem of unequal pay. The government was as much concerned with protecting existing bargaining structures and minimizing the inflationary consequences of equality as with legislating for equal pay. Nevertheless, within its limited substantive structure, it was intended that the Act should be effective. The Industrial Court's amendments to a collective agreement or pay structure would alter the provisions of contracts of employment concluded by reference to the agreement or structure, and such amendments might be backdated to the time when the reference was made to the Court.[102] An industrial tribunal which found in favour of an applicant could award back pay for up to two years, as well as making provision for equal pay in the future.[103] Although the individual woman applicant had no standing to invoke the collective procedure, but would have to persuade the relevant union or employer or the Secretary of State to do so, the complaint to the industrial tribunal was, at least formally, wholly within her control—a considerable contrast, as we shall see, with the enforcement provisions of the Race Relations Act 1968.[104] No doubt in practice a woman applicant to a tribunal would find her task much easier if she were supported by her trade union and male colleagues, but these were hardly matters Parliament could legislate for. What, of course, the government might have done was create an administrative agency whose job was to support applicants to tribunals, but the Equal Opportunities Commission

---

[101] The expansion of the meaning of art. 119 occurred in two stages, both after 1970: Directive 75/117, issued in order to make art. 119 more concrete, referred to equal pay 'for the same work or for work to which equal value is attributed', and the ECJ in Case 61/81, *Commission* v. *UK* [1982] ICR 578, 598, interpreted those words as meaning that 'a worker must be able to claim before an appropriate authority that this work has the same value as other work'. The equal value basis of comparison was then introduced into British law by the Equal Pay (Amendment) Regulations 1983 (SI 1794). See below, ch. 10.4(b).

[102] Equal Pay Act 1970, s. 3(2) and (3).

[103] Ibid. ss. 1(1) and 2(5).

[104] Below, Subsect. 4(c).

was not set up until the Sex Discrimination Act was enacted in 1975. There was an example of an administrative agency operating in the enforcement process at this time, namely the Race Relations Board under the Race Relations Act, but, as we shall see,[105] that body had exclusive control over complaints. As between having no administrative agency and one which deprived the applicant of control over her grievance, the former was probably the better choice.

The picture of a limited but, within those limitations, relatively effective Act is perhaps borne out by the statistics on the impact of the legislation when it eventually came into force at the end of 1975. In 1970 the hourly earnings of women were 58 per cent of those of men; by 1977 this had risen to 68 per cent, after which no further progress was made.[106] The Act produced a significant, one-off improvement in women's pay, but seemed unlikely either to have eliminated all discrimination in pay as between men and women or, as drafted, to be capable of so doing.[107]

With hindsight, however, it is possible to see that the 1970 Act was limited in other important ways which were unconnected with inflation or the integrity of bargaining structures. Although the 1970 Act was wider than its name suggests, because it applied to all contractual terms and conditions of employment and not just to pay, it was far from being legislation for equal opportunities in general. Discrimination against women in access to employment, to promotion, and to training, for example, was not included. Coverage of these matters was effected only with the Sex Discrimination Act 1975. Within the wider women's movement the relationship between equal pay and equal opportunities was well appreciated (suppose employers reacted to the higher cost of female labour by refusing to employ women), but at the TUC Congresses in the 1960s the accent was firmly on equality of pay. ILO Convention 100 was much debated; Convention 111 of 1958 relating to discrimination in general in employment received only passing mentions. The UK was, of course, by no means unusual in addressing the problem of equal pay before that of equal opportunity. The same sequence, as we

---

[105] Below, Subsect. 4(c).

[106] A. Zabalza and Z. Tzannatos, *Women and Equal Pay* (Cambridge, 1985), 2.

[107] Ibid. 11–16.

have noted, is found at the ILO, in European Community law,[108] and, perhaps most interesting, in the USA.[109] There might be a number of explanations for this development, but one factor may be that the equal pay claim, made on behalf of workers in employment, fitted more neatly the contours of collective bargaining and trade union activity, so that legal support for it was easier for the industrial relations parties to accept. The affinities of the equal pay legislation with existing laws laying down minimum wages—in the shape of Wages Councils legislation, fair wages provisions, and section 8 of the Terms and Conditions of Employment Act 1958—may also have helped to present the equal pay claim as a more natural form of labour law than general equal opportunities legislation. In any event, in the debates on the Equal Pay Bill the government resisted efforts to broaden it so as to embrace equal opportunities, and the TUC began to push for equal opportunities legislation only in 1973.[110]

5.4. RACE RELATIONS ACT 1968

(a) The Origins of the Act

The Race Relations Act 1968 achieved the enormously important objective of introducing the principle of non-discrimination on grounds of race into the field of employment. It was not the first Race Relations Act: a Race Relations Act had been passed in 1965, but that was confined to discrimination in public places and to the introduction of an offence of incitement to racial hatred, although that Act had also created the Race Relations Board and its network of local committees. Indeed, the 1968 Act can claim to be the first piece of post-war legislation to have inserted the

---

[108] The provision for equal pay is to be found in art. 119 of the Treaty of Rome, concluded in 1957; the Community addressed the issue of equal opportunities only with Directive 76/207. See below, p. 583.

[109] The temporal gap between the two sets of provisions was much shorter in the USA but, nevertheless, the two issues were addressed in significantly different sorts of legislation: equal pay by way of amendment in 1963 to the minimum wage legislation (the Fair Labor Standards Act 1938) and sex discrimination generally in Title VII of the Civil Rights Act 1964.

[110] P. L. Davies, 'EEC Legislation, UK Legislative Policy and Industrial Relations', in C. McCrudden, ed., Women, Employment and European Equality Law (London, 1987), 36.

notion of fair treatment for individuals into the field of employment, preceding as it did both the equal pay and unfair dismissal provisions. In this respect, the significance of the Act was not greatly reduced by the fact that it was confined to rendering unlawful only what we should now term 'direct' discrimination. It defined discrimination as occurring where 'a person . . . on the ground of colour, race or ethnic or national origins . . . treats that other [person] . . . less favourably than he treats or would treat other persons'.[111] The crucial step of extending the definition of discrimination to embrace acts having discriminatory effects, even where the relevant act was not done 'on the ground of' race ('indirect' discrimination), was not taken until the mid-1970s. Nevertheless, the introduction of even a limited principle of non-discrimination, backed by legal sanctions (again, as we shall see, of a rather limited type), represented a theoretical departure of great significance for 1960s labour law.

However, to focus attention simply on the novelty of the legal principle at the heart of the 1968 Act would fail to capture the full importance of the Act. This is because the 1968 Act resulted from the impact upon the labour law and industrial relations systems of policy concerns and pressures which were very largely, as far as these systems were concerned, exogenous. Unlike the issues of unfair dismissal and equal pay, which had long been defined by the parties to industrial relations and by the Ministry of Labour as problems to be dealt with in collective negotiations—even if the role of the law in their resolution was still a subject of debate—racial discrimination had not been so perceived. This was the situation, not, of course, because employer's and workers' organizations had adopted policies in favour of racial discrimination,[112] but because, as in most sections of society, before the publication in 1967 of the highly influential report by Political and Economic Planning, *Racial Discrimination*,[113] it was not thought that racial discrimination was a significant social problem. This report, commissioned by the Race Relations Board and the National Committee for Commonwealth

---

[111] Race Relations Act 1968, s. 1(1).

[112] The TUC had resolved as early as 1955 that 'This congress condemns all manifestations of racial discrimination or colour prejudice whether by Government, employers or workers', TUC, *Annual Report 1955*, 456.

[113] London, 1967.

Immigrants, argued, however, on the basis of empirical investigation, that there was 'substantial discrimination against coloured immigrants in the main aspects studied—employment, housing and the provision of services', and that 'discrimination in employment [was] the biggest single criticism in immigrants' spontaneous criticisms of life in Britain, and it [was] the area in which the greatest number of individual claims of discrimination were made'.[114] However, given that the PEP report appeared rather late in the process of policy formation on the 1968 Act, most of the running was in fact made by pressure groups supportive of the immigrants' case, notably the Campaign Against Racial Discrimination, and a number of well-placed individuals, largely from the legal and academic worlds.[115]

Even so, it is doubtful whether these pressures would have resulted in legislation had not the Labour government elected in 1964 undergone a change of heart on the related issue of immigration control. After all, a number of Bills against racial discrimination had been introduced by back-benchers (notably Mr Fenner Brockway) throughout the 1950s and early 1960s without attracting government support.[116] What changed at this point was the linking of the issues of immigration control and racial discrimination. From shortly after the end of the War, coloured immigrants had been attracted to Britain by the tight labour market conditions of the 1950s, and some employers, indeed, had carried out recruitment campaigns to encourage such immigration. As a result, the number of coloured people in Britain rose from about 100,000 in 1950 to about 1 million by the mid-1960s.[117] As the immigrants were overwhelmingly from the colonies or Commonwealth countries and were thus British subjects, their entry into Britain was not controlled. By the end of the 1950s, however, the Conservative government began to respond to what it perceived as pressures from the white population for immigration control, and in 1962 it introduced the principle of control with the Commonwealth Immigrants Act of that year.

---

[114] Ibid. 8.
[115] See A. Lester and G. Bindman, *Race and the Law* (Harmondsworth, 1972), 110–12.
[116] Ibid. 108–9.
[117] W. Daniel, *Racial Discrimination in England* (Harmondsworth, 1968), 9.

That Act was fiercely opposed by the Labour Opposition, but within a year the party had changed its stance.[118] When elected to government in 1964 the Labour administration not only kept the 1962 Act on the statute-book, but tightened up the administration of it in 1965, and added new legislative controls in the shape of the Commonwealth Immigrants Act 1968 (prompted by a feared exodus of Asians from Kenya). As a means of salvaging something from this pretty inglorious episode, protection of immigrants already in the country was linked with controlling the admission of new settlers. As Mr Roy Hattersley put it at the time: 'Without integration, limitation is inexcusable; without limitation, integration is impossible.'[119] This new policy showed itself clearly in the 1965 White Paper, *Immigration from the Commonwealth*,[120] part II of which proposed to exercise the powers under the 1962 Act more vigorously, whilst part III proposed various measures to promote integration. Although part III did not in terms envisage race relations legislation going beyond the 1965 Act, it did indicate the existence of a political climate which the then Home Secretary, Mr Roy Jenkins, was able skilfully to exploit so as to get the 1968 Act passed.[121] As Rose has put it:

From being an aspect of this country's relationship with the world outside, this matter had become a wholly internal problem, and one of regulation: control at entry and control of the situation resulting from entry, preservation of the Queen's Peace, prevention of discrimination and incitement to racial hatred, and the averting of inter-racial conflict.[122]

(b) The Race Relations Act and Voluntarism

Thus the government's concern with racial discrimination in employment was part of a wider concern with discrimination against immigrants in society (though employment was regarded as the most important single area of discrimination, since it was largely the prospect of relatively well-paid jobs that had drawn the

---

[118] S. Patterson, *Immigration and Race Relation in Britain, 1960–67* (London, 1969), 19 and 43.
[119] Quoted in N. Deakin *et al.*, *Colour, Citizenship and British Society* (London, 1970), 106.
[120] Cmnd. 2739.
[121] For an account of Mr Jenkins's policies, see E. J. B. Rose, *Colour and Citizenship* (London, 1969), chs. 26 and 27.
[122] Ibid. 230.

immigrants to this country[123]) and, beyond that, it was part of an overall policy relating to immigration. What were the challenges that this policy presented to the traditional abstentionist or voluntarist character of labour law? There are three points to make. First, since the concern was discrimination in general against immigrants, the lead department and minister in relation to the 1968 Act were the Home Office and the Home Secretary, though the Ministry of Labour was, of course, consulted on the employment aspects. The Home Office was likely to be less impressed by the claims of employers and trade unions to autonomy from legislative controls than the Ministry. Second, the legislation in relation to employment was designed to deal with an issue which was not only one the industrial relations parties had failed to identify as a problem, but also one which could be seen as in part generated by the industrial relations system. That is to say, whereas issues such as unfair dismissal and equal pay could be seen as arising out of conflicts of interest between or among the established groups within the industrial relations system, recial discrimination could be presented as the 'insiders' ganging up to exclude the newly arrived outsiders. Such an analysis was unduly simplistic. Was it right to regard women as 'insiders' in the industrial relations system? Was it correct to see coloured people as uniformly excluded from participation in the industrial relations system? Nevertheless, there was enough evidence of unacceptable industrial practices to give the accusation an element of truth. Some, not many, collective agreements did contain explicit clauses discriminating against foreign or coloured workers.[124] More important, actual industrial relations practice, especially in relation to recruitment, was shown to be capable of giving rise to direct discrimination. Rose summarized the position as follows:

The one fact that stands out above all others is that, throughout the field of employment, discrimination is widespread and pervasive. It manifests itself in recruitment, training, promotion and a host of other ways.

[123] The 1968 Act applied, in addition to employment (ss. 3 and 4), to housing and business premises (s. 5) and to the provision to the public of goods, facilities, and services, including credit, insurance, education, entertainment, and travel (s. 2).
[124] B. A. Hepple, *Race, Jobs and the Law in Britain* (1st edn. Harmondsworth, 1968), app. II.

This discrimination is not a result of any centrally inspired policy of government, unions or employers' organizations, but is determined by decisions at local level . . . The role in which British industry has cast the coloured worker is that of spare man or reserve—to be used only when necessary.[125]

In spite of this explicit exoneration of the formal institutions, the overall picture was necessarily one that put the TUC and CBI on the defensive and in poor position to assert the values of industrial autonomy.

Finally, if legislation against discrimination in employment must be placed in its broader context from the government's point of view, the same is true for the TUC. For the TUC that context was the campaign it was waging in and around the Donovan Commission for the preservation of the traditional stance of abstention on the part of labour law. We shall discuss that campaign more fully in the next chapter, but in so far as the acceptance of legislation against discrimination in employment opened the way for legal control of other aspects of industrial relations, the TUC would necessarily be worried. That this was a serious risk was demonstrated by the second report commissioned by the Race Relations Board and the NCCI on the appropriate shape of anti-discrimination legislation.[126] That report, the Street Report, having noted 'the tradition in our industrial relations of leaving the law as little sphere of operation as possible', nevertheless went on to state:

We discern a trend towards increased legal intervention in industrial relations: the Redundancy Payments Act 1965 and the Industrial Training Act 1963 [sic] are important examples. Our proposals are not inconsistent with these recent legislative developments.[127]

Such tendencies to treat labour law as an undifferentiated mass would naturally cause deep concern at the TUC, which was at this time responding to proposals to regulate strikes and trade unions by legal means.

In this context it is important to remember that it was proposed—and in fact legislated—that discrimination should be

---

[125] *Colour and Citizenship*, 325.
[126] H. Street, G. Howe, and G. Bindman, *Report on Anti-Discrimination Legislation* (London, 1967).
[127] Ibid. 73.

prohibited not only by employers but also by trade unions,[128] in relation to admission, benefits, and expulsion. In this respect also the 1968 Act was a new departure from what had been enacted earlier in the decade, when obligations had been laid mainly on employers.[129] The deep water in which the unions could thus find themselves swimming is well demonstrated by the exchange between Professor Wedderburn and members of the Donovan Commission when Professor Wedderburn gave oral evidence to the Commission. He found himself having to defend his support for legislation against racial discrimination in employment in the context of his equally strong view that the law had little part to play in regulating collective labour relations.[130]

In any event, the initial responses of the TUC,[131] in which it was joined, for rather different reasons, by the CBI,[132] was to oppose the principle of legislation, a position which received 'the tacit sympathy of the Ministry of Labour'.[133] After the publication of the PEP report, that stance of total opposition changed to one of acceptance that legislation might have a residual role to play, coupled with an insistence that the primary responsibility for complaints of racial discrimination should rest with the voluntary procedures in industry. Where such voluntary machinery did exist, the TUC thought it should be the exclusive method of dealing with complaints.[134] In the event the drafters of the 1968 Act did not accept even this, but they made a very considerable concession to the voluntarist argument by accepting that, where appropriate machinery existed, it should have the initial responsibility for handling complaints. Much greater deference to the

[128] Race Relations Act 1968, s. 4.

[129] Sometimes also on individual employees (e.g. Contracts of Employment Act 1963, s. 1(2)—minimun period notice for termination), but not on trade unions.

[130] Royal Commission on Trade Unions and Employers' Associations, Minutes of Evidence 31, qq. 4880–98.

[131] Though not of all trade unionists. Jack Jones, then Acting Assistant General Secretary of the TGWU, was prepared to support legislation: Rose, *Colour and Citizenship*, 530.

[132] The CBI presumably objected to legislative restrictions on managerial freedom, for it was no longer, as its evidence to the Donovan Commission made clear, a whole-hearted supporter of abstention by the law from industrial relations. In any event, in respect of the 1968 Act, it 'for tactical reasons preferred to leave the initiative to the TUC': Rose, *Colour and Citizenship*, 529.

[133] Ibid. 532.

[134] Ibid. 535–7.

voluntary machinery was thus shown in the 1968 Act than in the subsequent unfair dismissal legislation.

The procedure for the handling of employment and trade union claims, contained in schedule 2 of the Act, was broadly as follows. Complaints would be handled initially by the Secretary of State for Employment and Productivity, who would refer the complaint to suitable voluntary industrial machinery, if such existed. If it did not, the complaint would be referred immediately to the Race Relations Board for investigation by it or one of its local committees. The voluntary machinery had an initial period of four weeks (which could be extended) to settle the complaint. In the case of a failure of the voluntary machinery to produce a settlement within the time permitted, the matter would be referred to the Board. There might also be an appeal to the Board by an aggrieved party where the voluntary machinery did produce a decision, for instance, that there had been no discrimination. Thus the voluntary machinery operated subject to ultimate review by the Race Relations Board, but it did obtain the right to a first attempt to settle the issue.

In spite of the TUC and CBI's defence of voluntary machinery, however, experience with it was disappointing. No special machinery seems ever to have been set up to deal with complaints against trade unions as such, the issue being partly overtaken by proposals, discussed in the next section, to provide general remedies in favour of individuals who claimed to have been unfairly treated by trade unions.[135] In respect of employment complaints, by 1970 forty-three industries had established machinery which met the Department's criteria for approval.[136] These industries employed about 7 million workers, but this left 16 million workers uncovered by voluntary machinery, including those in engineering. The machineries were nearly all industry-wide, external procedures, partly because the Department's criteria required investigation to be carried out by persons independent of the workplace where the alleged act of discrimination took place. The voluntary machineries that were estab-

[135] J. C. McCrudden, 'Discrimination against Minority Groups in Employment' (unpublished D.Phil. thesis, Oxford, 1981), 172–3.
[136] (1970) 78 *Employment and Productivity Gazette* 100. The Department's criteria for approval are discussed in Lester and Bindman, *Race and the Law*, 317–19.

lished managed to dispose of 60 per cent of the 1,000 complaints referred to them in the period 1968 to 1976, but findings of discrimination were made in only twenty cases.[137]

(c) Administrative Agencies, Conciliation, and Remedies

As ever in labour law, the question of sanctions proved to be a sensitive one in respect of the 1968 Act, especially as the legitimacy of using the law at all in this field was, as we have seen, the subject of a lively debate at the time. Here the Street Report was important and it, in turn, was much influenced by the types of enforcement machinery in discrimination cases which were to be found in North America. (The authors of the report visited both the USA and Canada.) The committee recommended the adoption in the UK of the US-style administrative agency for the enforcement of the legislation and saw in the Race Relations Board the makings of such an agency. The advantages that the committee saw in this approach were the emphasis placed upon conciliation as the way of dealing with complaints, so that 'the primary aim is not to seek out and punish discriminators [but] . . . to create that climate of opinion which will obviate discrimination . . . enforcement is conceived as a last resort, to be used only when conciliation is found impossible.' On the other hand, the conciliation process would have some force behind it because the administrative agency 'investigates complaints, it initiates independent investigations, it decides whether discrimination appears to have occurred, it endeavours to conciliate, it holds hearings where conciliation has failed in order to determine whether illegality is proved, it prescibes remedial measures to be taken against a transgressor and it superintends the compliance with its orders'.[138]

As translated into legislation in 1968, however, the aspect of these proposals which said that enforcement should be a last resort was given greater prominence than the aspect which suggested a powerful role for the Race Relations Board. The ability of the Board (or its local committees) to achieve effective, conciliated settlements was diminished by the failure to give it adequate investigative powers. Neither was the Board given its

---

[137] McCrudden, 'Discrimination', 177.
[138] Street Report, 90–1.

own enforcement powers. Rather, it had to institute proceedings before one of a number of selected county or sheriff courts, whose powers to award damages or issue injunctions were rather limited. The heads of damage did not include injury to feelings and the injunctive power was limited to negative injunctions, restraining the repetition of past acts of discrimination, and did not embrace mandatory injunctions requiring steps to be taken to reform discriminatory practices.[139] Interestingly, the proposal that the enforcement body in the employment sphere should be the industrial tribunals was rejected by the government, apparently on the grounds that enforcement in such a difficult area might be a task that overstretched the authority of these newly created bodies.[140]

Perhaps the most significant aspect of the remedial provisions of the 1968 Act, however, was its exclusion of the individual from direct access to the courts. Unlike the individual complaining of unfair dismissal or unequal pay, the complainant in a race relations case had to channel his or her complaint through the Board (or its local committee or the relevant voluntary machinery). Even if these machineries failed to produce a settlement, the decision on taking proceedings in the courts lay exclusively in the hands of the Board, to whom indeed any award of damages was made, although the Board had to account to the individual for the money received.[141] This procedure had two consequences. First, the resources of the Board were overwhelmingly deployed in the handling of individual complaints, so that it had very little opportunity to initiate independent investigations into situations which suggested that deep-seated patterns of discrimination had become established. Yet pattern-centred inquiries would probably have done more to reduce overall levels of discrimination in society than purely individual investigations. Second, from the point of view of the individual, the remedies against discrimination appeared rather ineffective. Especially in the employment field, where the voluntary machinery, if established, operated first, the procedures were cumbersome and slow, whilst the monopoly of the Board deprived the individual of control over the handling of the grievance. In fact. before 1975

[139] Race Relations Act 1968, ss. 19–22.
[140] Hepple, *Race, Jobs and the Law in Britian* (2nd edn. 1970), 214–15.
[141] 1968 Act, ss. 15, 19(1), 22(3).

only one employment case had reached the courts.[142] There is, therefore, much to be said for the view that, although the Race Relations Act 1968 represented, as we have argued, an enormously important theoretical departure in labour law, its significance was overwhelmingly confined to the law 'in the books' and did not extend to anything like the same degree to the law as it operated in practice. This perhaps explains why the general debate about the proper role of labour law was conducted by many people at this time as if the 1968 Act had not been passed.

5.5 INDIVIDUAL RIGHTS AGAINST TRADE UNIONS

We have so far discussed arbitrary treatment against individual workers mainly in terms of arbitrary treatment by employers, although we have noted that sometimes the unfair treatment could be attributed to the joint institutions of management and labour (e.g. discriminatory collective agreements) or to trade unions or workgroups alone. It is now necessary to consider directly the situation of unfair actions by trade unions. The argument in favour of legislative protection against unfair action by trade unions was made strongly by Otto Kahn-Freund in an article published in 1970,[143] in which he supported the proposals of the Donovan Commission,[144] of which he had been a member, for legislative attention to this problem. Like the Donovan Commission,[145] he drew a parallel with the proposals for legislation against unfair dismissal: 'Resistance to social legislation on the pretext of freedom of property or of management rights has the musty smell of the mid-nineteenth century. So has the resistance to the legal protection of the individual against the

---

[142] McCrudden, *'Discrimination'*, 251.

[143] 'Trade Unions, the Law and Society' (1970) 33 MLR 241 (the Gaitskell Memorial Lecture of 1970), also printed in O. Kahn-Freund, *Selected Writings* (London, 1978), to which page references are given here.

[144] Report of the Royal Commission on Trade Unions and Employers' Associations, Cmnd. 3623 (1968), ch. 11.

[145] Ch. 11 of the Commission Report (ibid.) followed ch. 9 on unfair dismissal and ch. 10 on labour tribunals, and began with the sentence: 'In this further chapter concerning safeguards of individual workers we turn to consider their relationship with trade unions.'

abuse of organizational power on the pretext of unfettered autonomy.'[146] For Kahn-Freund, the organizational power of trade unions, and thus the case for legislation, was not confined to situations where the union helped to operate a closed shop,[147] though the effects of arbitrary exclusion or expulsion of an individual by a trade union would be the greatest in this context. Since trade unions normally operated to represent the interests of all the workers of a particular class at a particular workplace, and since union membership was 'often a condition for a reasonable social existence even where there is no closed shop',[148] legislative protection should not be so confined either. Kahn-Freund was not asserting that abuse of power by trade unions was widespread; indeed, the Donovan Commission[149] had concluded, on the basis of empirical enquiries, that it was not; but this was 'no answer' to the proposals for legislation, any more than the fact that 'most employers are conscientious' was an answer to proposals for unfair dismissal legislation.[150]

What, then, was needed? The largest gap in the existing law seemed to relate to those excluded from trade union membership, since the common law had made little progress in recognizing and protecting the legitimate interests of applicants for trade union membership.[151] In respect of expulsions (and unfair discipline generally) the contract of membership gave the trade unionist greater protection at common law than the contract of employment gave him or her in the capacity of employee, but even here the member's power to challenge substantive unfairness was not fully guaranteed by the common law.[152] Thus,

---

[146] Kahn-Freund, *Selected Writings*, 130.

[147] The Donovan Commission's report was ambiguous as to how far it proposed legal protection for individuals at the point of admission if there was no closed shop in operation: see Cmnd. 3623, paras. 619–31.

[148] Kahn-Freund, *Selected Writings*, 130.

[149] Cmnd. 3623, para. 622.

[150] Kahn-Freund, *Selected Writings*, 129.

[151] The traditionally non-interventionist stance of the common law had been qualified by the then recent decision of the Court of Appeal in *Nagle v. Fielden* [1966] 2 QB 633. Although clearly part of a judicial trend which we have identified as beginning in the late 1950s (above, p. 134) to extend the common law controls over the internal aspects of trade unions, it was (and still is) unclear what was the precise ambit of this decision.

[152] The grounds for discipline and expulsion had to be found in the contract of membership itself, so that there was no equivalent to termination on notice, and the principles of natural justice applied at common law, so as to ensure some

in Kahn-Freund's view, a case could be made for providing a legislative basis for challenging arbitrary actions by trade unions at the stage of both admission and expulsion. It is interesting, in the light of the discussion in the previous section, that Kahn-Freund, in arguing for the feasibility of legislation, made frequent reference to the fact that limited legislation of this type was already in place in the shape of Section 4 of the Race Relations Act 1968.[153]

However, Kahn-Freund was concerned to recognize not only the worker's entitlements to obtain and retain membership of a union, but also rights arising during membership, which he categorized as rights to 'equal representation' and to 'equal participation'.[154] Equal representation referred to the union's obligation to represent all sections of its membership fairly in the bargaining process—what is referred to in the USA as the union's 'duty of fair representation'—and equal participation to members' rights to take part in the democratic procedures provided for in the union's constitution. He was, thus, staking out a claim for a fairly extensive role to be played by the law in protecting individual rights, both in access to and retention of membership and in the exercise of rights arising from membership. The proposals went far beyond what the common law and the Trade Union Act 1871 then provided.[155]

The main counter-argument to this set of legislative proposals —and one of which Kahn-Freund was himself well aware—was that the enactment of individual membership rights would, by design or effect, undermine the ability of the union to act collectively. As Professor Wedderburn put it: 'Individuals must be protected . . . by the law against unfair treatment by employers or

degree of procedural fairness. Here again the common law was on the move, with the suggestion in *Edwards* v. *SOGAT* [1971] Ch. 354 (CA) that the courts had some ill-defined power to control the content of union rules in the name of a 'right to work'.

[153] Kahn-Freund, *Selected Writings*, 132, 139, 148.

[154] Ibid. 147 ff.

[155] For present purposes the relevant policy was that contained in s. 14 and sched. 1 of the 1871 Act, viz. that a union must have rules covering a specified range of matters, but it was up to each union to define the content of its rules. Nevertheless, the Donovan Commission (para. 625) found that union rule-books 'generally fall far short of reaching a satisfactory standard' in terms of clarity, and advocated that they be redrafted and more closely supervised by the proposed Registrar of Trade Unions. This was one of the motivations behind sched. 4 of the Industrial Relations Act 1971. See below, p. 300.

unions. But the duty of a labour law system is *first* to the individuals in the collective majority; and only *second*—not to be forgotten, but *second*—to individuals who wish to opt out of collective labour relations.'[156] Kahn-Freund was particularly concerned to draw a clear line between the protection of individual interests and the undermining of collective structures and modes of action. This can be seen in the relationship between his proposals and the issues of the closed shop and union democracy. As to the former, his proposals for controlling arbitrary exclusion or expulsion by trade unions operated so as to protect what one might call 'willing unionists'. People who, whether in a closed shop situation or not, wished to become or remain members of a union, might seek the protection of the proposed new laws, but such laws would do nothing to protect those who wished not to join or to remain members of a union. As far as the closed shop was concerned, Kahn-Freund accepted the Commission's recommendation that it should not be prohibited, and that the only remedy for unwilling unionists that should be provided was for people who were non-members when the closed shop was introduced, and, even then, the remedy should lie in the law of unfair dismissal against the employer.[157] Accordingly, we shall not discuss the 'right to dissociate' further in this chapter.[158]

As to union democracy, Kahn-Freund made a clear distinction between using the law 'to ensure that union constitutions comply with certain standards of democracy' and the law 'guaranteeing to members such democratic rights as the union constitutions give them'. It was to the latter, 'more modest' end that his proposals were directed.[159] The law should not be used to impose patterns of democracy upon trade unions, but only to guarantee equally to all members such democratic procedures as the union had chosen to adopt. Kahn-Freund's arguments were thus directed firmly at the protection of individuals' membership rights rather than at ensuring the accountability of the union to the members as a whole.[160] In some ways this is surprising. Kahn-Freund accepted the view, common among industrial relations theorists, that

[156] K. W. Wedderburn, 'Labour Law and Labour Relations in Britain' (1972) 10 BJIR 270, 290 (the Lerner Memorial Lecture of 1972).

[157] Cmnd. 3623, paras. 598–608.

[158] But see below, ch. 7.2(*a*)(v).

[159] Kahn-Freund, *Selected Writings*, 149–50.

[160] For an elaboration of the distinction between the 'job regulation' and the 'industrial democracy' approaches to trade union government, see P. Elias and K.

one, if not the, main justification for the system of collective bargaining was its democratic potential. It was a very effective form of industrial democracy because it gave the workers a role through their representatives in the setting of terms and conditions of employment. The democratic potential of collective bargaining, however, was unlikely to be realized unless the unions that did the bargaining were responsive to the wishes of their members. Whilst well aware of the force of this argument, Kahn-Freund thought that to prescibe patterns of democratic decision-making for trade unions ran the risk of promoting within a trade union 'a permanent fight between groups based on external political allegiances', and this would weaken its effectiveness as 'a fighting organization' on behalf of its members. When legislative proposals for control of the internal affairs of trade unions led to such a risk, then the matter became one, in Kahn-Freund's view, 'which the law should severely leave alone'.[161]

Finally, one may note a relationship between individual rights and collective freedoms which Kahn-Freund did not much stress in his 1970 lecture, but which did prove subsequently to be of importance. This was the relationship between legal control of arbitrary discipline imposed by trade unions and the union's freedom to discipline those who failed to take part in industrial action. As we shall see, the legislators of the 1971 Act were unable to resist the temptation to use controls upon unions' internal disciplinary procedures to support controls upon unions' external actions by way of organizing industrial action, and in the 1980s this policy was to be developed in a major way.[162]

As we have noted already, the Donovan Commission made proposals for legal controls upon arbitrary exclusion or expulsion by trade unions, but went less far in ensuring equal representation and equal participation than Kahn-Freund would have desired.[163] The White Paper, *In Place of Strife*,[164] followed Donovan, but the 1971 Act laid down a code of 'guiding prin-

Ewing, *Trade Union Democracy, Members' Rights and the Law* (London, 1987), ch. 8.

[161] *Selected Writings*, 149–50. See also O. Kahm-Freund, *Labour and the Law* (1st edn. London, 1972), 210, 222.

[162] See below, ch. 7.2(*a*)(viii) and 9.7(*a*).

[163] The Donovan Commission devoted substantial attention only to union elections: see paras. 632–47.

[164] Cmnd. 3888 (1969), paras. 114–18.

ciples' to govern the internal aspects of trade unions (whether registered or not), which was presented as a 'bill of rights' for workers *vis-à-vis* trade unions.[165] Complaints by individuals of breach of the guiding principles lay to the industrial tribunals (which could award compensation on broadly the same basis as in unfair dismissal cases) or directly to the National Industrial Relations Court, which also had powers to order injunctive relief.[166] Either way, the Act had not followed the Donovan recommendation that internal trade union cases be referred to a special independent body, consisting of a lawyer chair and two trade unionists.[167]

The guiding principles made it unlawful 'by way of arbitrary or unreasonable discrimination' to exclude appropriately qualified applicants from membership[168] or to subject members to 'unfair or unreasonable' disciplinary action.[169] Disciplinary action was also subject to procedural rules which went beyond the requirements of natural justice.[170] The equal participation argument was recognized in principles prohibiting 'arbitrary or unreasonable discrimination' against a member standing as a candidate for office, voting in elections, or taking part in union meetings, whilst voting in ballots was required to be secret and every member was to be given the opportunity of voting in a ballot 'without interference or constraint'.[171] In the equal participation principles the line between individual protection and collective control was well observed, since, for example, the Act did not purport to tell (at least unregistered) unions when they had to hold a ballot, but only how to conduct one if the union decided to hold one. The same cannot be said, however, of the controls on unfair discipline. Here the union was straightforwardly prohibited from disciplining any member who refused to take part in industrial action that amouted to an unfair industrial practice, either on the member's part or the union's.[172] As Kahn-Freund commented at the time, 'we see how thin is the line which separates the protec-

---

[165] Industrial Relations Act 1971, s. 65. For the special position of registered unions, see below, ch. 7.2(*a*)(viii).
[166] Industrial Relations Act 1971, ss. 101, 107, 109, 118.
[167] Cmnd. 3623, paras. 658–69.
[168] S. 65(2).   [169] S. 65(7).   [170] S. 65(8).
[171] S. 65(4)–(6). The equal representation argument seems not to have carried any weight with the legislators.
[172] S. 65(7)(*a*), (*b*), and (*c*).

tion of the individual from what may come close to a disruption of the organization.'[173]

It might have been thought that this provision, providing as it did a neuralgic point of contact between internal trade union law and the law of industrial conflict, would have given rise to considerable litigation. In fact, the guiding principles in general did not give rise to much litigation, the most celebrated case being the bizarre litigation brought by Mr Goad,[174] which led to the AUEW being fined for contempt by the NIRC at a time when the government was trying to open negotiations with the trade union movement on incomes policy, much to the government's embarrassment. Since, however, the union chose not to appear before the NIRC, the strength of the union's claim, that Mr Goad had not been allowed to attend union meetings because he was not a member of the union, was never properly tested. After the return of a Labour government in 1974, it was determined, as we shall see, to return to the position of legislative *laissez-faire* on members' rights that had prevailed before 1971, and, in spite of Opposition success in delaying this move in 1974, that position was reached in 1976.[175]

5.6. CONCLUSION

Between 1968 and 1971 four quite separate pieces of legislation promoting the goal of industrial justice were passed, two by a Labour government (the Race Relations Act 1968 and the Equal Pay Act 1970) and two by a Conservative government (the unfair dismissal and members' rights provisions of the Industrial Relations Act 1971). As with the 'modernization' statutes in the first half of the decade, there was a considerable measure of party political consensus on these measures, in the sense that the need for legislation, if not its precise form, was accepted by both political parties. The one exception to that statement was the Race Relations Act 1968, which was the piece of legislation upon which pressures from outside the world of work came most

---

[173] Kahn-Freund, *Selected Writings*, 193.
[174] *Goad* v. *AUEW* [1972] ICR 429; (No. 2) [1973] ICR 42; (No. 3) [1973] ICR 108.
[175] See below, ch. 8.2.

strongly to bear. There was also a considerable (if lesser) degree of agreement between government and TUC that some form of legislation was necessary in these areas, agreement which embraced the areas of unfair dismissal and equal pay if not, at least initially, those of race relations and members' rights.

With the exception of members' rights legislation, the new provisions proved to be enduring. In the case of members' rights, the Conservative government of 1971 proved unable, or unwilling, to identify and confine itself to a distinct rationale for legislation which related to the protection of the individual against arbitrary treatment. The temptation to use such legislation to add to the legal controls over unions' resort to industrial action was too strong, so that these provisions were caught up in the general disapprobation which the anti-strike provisions of the 1971 Act earned themselves, as we shall see in the next chapter. So they were repealed in mid-1974, and when they returned to the statute-book in the 1980s, they were again fatally linked with the goal of containing industrial action. By way of sharp contrast, the other three sets of legislation have not only become permanent features of our labour law, but were elaborated in the 1970s: the unfair dismissal legislation was upgraded by the Employment Protection Act 1975; in the same year the Equal Pay Act was complemented by a Sex Discrimination Act; and in the following year the 1968 Act was replaced by a much more sophisticated Race Relations Act. Moreover, these pieces of legislation survived the 1980s and were even—with the help of European Community labour law—expanded during that decade. We shall examine all this in later chapters. What we need to note here is the rapid, initial protection by legislation of notions of industrial justice, an idea whose time had clearly arrived.

6

THE END OF
AGREEMENT:
COLLECTIVE LABOUR
LAW, 1964–1970

6.1. THE SEARCH FOR ORDER AND THE DONOVAN DEBATE, 1964–1968

(a) Introduction: Collective Labour Law and the Challenge to Governmental Power

In Chapter 4, we saw how the Labour Governments of 1964 and 1965 sought to modernize the economy; and how that initiative became subverted into a series of increasingly desperate manœuvres to control wage inflation. What began in 1964 as a great exercise in identifying and implementing positive economic and industrial strategies had by 1968 become a search for short-term defensive tactics to protect incomes policies dependent on coercion as the consensus necessary to sustain them proved increasingly lacking. For a number of reasons, which are of great interest and concern to us in this narrative, the Labour government responded to this set of problems by making plans for significant changes in the structure of labour legislation, plans published in the White Paper *In Place of Strife* in January 1969. Those proposals were to prove abortive, but the political struggle which they produced did much to weaken the Labour government and led to the election, in 1970, of a Conservative government pledged to introduce its own legislation to reform industrial relations—enacted in due course as the Industrial Relations Act 1971. The purpose of this chapter is to try to explain these closely interconnected events, and to show how fundamentally they changed the collective *laissez-faire* assumptions upon which post-war labour legislation had down till then been based. We saw in the previous chapter how the individual dimension of collective *laissez-faire* was challenged around this period—that is to say, the abstention from regulating the individual employment relationship, the voluntarist approach to which was embodied in the law of the individual contract of employment. In this chapter, we are concerned with the contemporary, but quite distinct, move towards regulating collective bargaining, collective dispute resolution, and the behaviour of trade unions. We shall see in the course of the chapter how far these two impulses away from collective *laissez-faire* reinforced each other.

When the Labour government came into power in 1964, the initiatives upon which it embarked by way of modernizing the economy did not include any systematic plans to restructure existing collective labour legislation—it was the pressure of events which impelled them in that direction. The new government was not even minded to achieve a measure of collective regulation in the course of providing new rights for individual workers, as the previous, Conservative, government had attempted to do in the Contracts of Employment Act 1963, by making the new rights to statutory notice periods contingent upon refraining from industrial action in breach of the contract of employment.[1] On the contrary, it was intended to continue the structure of collective *laissez-faire*. Government would continue, in the shape of the Ministry of Labour, to intervene only in its traditional role of mediator and conciliator between employers and the workforce. This would be a function separate from the interventionist task which the new Department of Economic Affairs would perform for the industrial economy on a larger plane. The maintenance of voluntarism in the sphere of industrial relations became increasingly difficult, of course, in the face of a rapid growth of industrial action, especially unofficial industrial

---

[1] Contracts of Employment Act 1963, sched. I, para. 7. The rule that industrial action in breach of the contract of employment broke continuity of service was intended to penalize unofficial industrial action. When *dicta* in *Rookes* v. *Barnard* [1964] AC 1129 and *Stratford* v. *Lindley* [1965] AC 269 indicated that official industrial action was normally equally in breach, it was judged appropriate by the Labour government, in the Redundancy Payments Act 1965, to reduce the penal provision to a mere stipulation that the time spent on industrial action would not itself count towards the period of continuous service—see now EPCA 1978, sched. 13, para. 15.

action,[2] and an even faster growth in the perception that this was a problem over which the government had to assert control.[3] Moreover, as we shall shortly explain in greater detail, the abstentionist legal framework of the Trade Disputes Act 1906 was reinterpreted from 1963 onwards under the guidance of a judicial House of Lords which felt impelled to contain the growing use of trade union industrial power, especially against dissentient workers and employers who were not party to the industrial disputes in which that power was deployed. This new judicial interventionism stemmed from the landmark decision of the House of Lords in the case of *Rookes* v. *Barnard* in 1963.[4] The strategic debate which, as we shall see, had been precipitated by *Rookes* v. *Barnard* was relegated to the forum of a Royal Commission on Trade Unions and Employers' Associations, rather than being allowed into the area of open dialectic between the Labour government and the trade union movement. Moreover, even as the government moved into the phase of statutorily backed incomes policy from 1966 onwards, it was convenient for all concerned to proceed as if incomes policy and industrial relations, with their respective bodies of legislation, existed in two quite distinct spheres, to be kept apart on both theoretical and pragmatic grounds, so that the ephemerality of the intrusion upon free collective bargaining would be kept in full view.

Nevertheless, by 1968 the convenient separation of these two areas of operation was tending to break down, and the two lines of governmental policy were inexorably collapsed into each other under severe economic and political pressures. Not only did the 'strike problem' seem to be defying attempts to control it, but it also seemed to be undermining the government's attempts to improve the state of the economy. A Labour government expected, and was expected by public opinion, to be able to command fraternal support from the trade union movement not only at TUC level for its income policies and modernization strategies, but also at single union and shop-floor level for its claims to be able to run industrial society efficiently and success-

---

[2] See E. Wigham, *Strikes and the Government, 1893–1981* (London, 1982), 135 ff.

[3] See e.g. D. Barnes and E. Reid, *Governments and Trade Unions: The British Experience, 1964–79* (London, 1980), 68.

[4] [1964] AC 1129.

fully. Harold Wilson was considerably influenced towards a restructuring of labour legislation by the intractability of the unions, and its visible contribution to the series of economic crises which he faced from 1965 onwards. This was especially true of the official strike of the National Union of Seamen in May 1966 which led up to the introduction of statutory incomes policy, and produced his famous attack on 'this tightly knit group of politically motivated men'—the militants in the NUS who were, as he perceived it, endangering the security of the industry and the economic welfare of the nation.[5] He experienced a similar reaction to the dock strikes of October 1967, which were a protest against the Government's implementation of the Devlin Report's recommendations for the ending of casual work in the docks, and contributed to a crisis of confidence in the government which culminated in the devaluation of the pound by 14.3 per cent in November 1967.

Both the seamen's strike and the dock strike could have been regarded straightforwardly as examples of resistance by large and powerful trade unions to the economic policies of the government. But Harold Wilson's characterization of the former as the work of a small group of politically motivated men indicates that a somewhat different frame of reference was being used. This was a period in which a public perception intensified of an industrial relations problem consisting of the inability of trade unions to control or channel into constructive form the shop-floor militancy which was causing more and more unofficial wild-cat strikes, and hence delay in delivery of orders which was fundamentally weakening the manufacturing economy and destroying foreign confidence in British exports. Harold Wilson had launched an initiative in 1965 to address this problem in the motor industry, where it was perhaps at its most intense and most damaging. A conference convened from the two sides of the industry failed, however, to produce agreement for any fundamental overhaul of the system of industrial relations in the industry, and gave rise only to a tactical 'trouble-shooting' operation in the shape of a Motor Industry Joint Labour Council, with Jack Scamp as its independent chairman and chief trouble-shooter.[6] By 1968 both

[5] See E. Wigham, *Strikes and the Government, 1893–1981*, 138.
[6] See Barnes and Reid, *Governments and Trade Unions*, 68.

his credit, and that of the Prime Minister himself, as physicians to the 'British disease' of chaotic industrial relations, were exhausted.

An important feature of the industrial relations background to these events was the rapid growth of shop-steward organization and shop-floor collective bargaining conducted by shop stewards, especially in the engineering industry. The development of shop-steward organization was significant from the 1950s until the end of the 1970s; the number of shop stewards was estimated at 90,000 in 1961, and at 175,000 in 1968, which indicates that the 1960s were a particularly important phase in this respect.[7] Michael Terry describes the model of shop steward behaviour at this time as having four main features.[8] These were the close identification of shop stewards with the workgroups they represented, the autonomy of shop stewards from trade union organization, the lack of management control systems over informal shop-steward bargaining with foremen, and the extent of shop-steward influence over the processes of shop-floor wage-bargaining. All these features contributed, in this analysis, to a close association between a perceived high level of shop-steward bargaining power and a perceived high level of unofficial and unconstitutional forms of industrial action.

In order to understand the significance of these developments and the reasons for the choices that were made in response to them, especially by governments, it is necessary to realize they eventually produced a crisis of truly constitutional proportions. A crisis can be said to have become a constitutional one when the government feels itself and is felt to be fundamentally incapable of dealing with the demands which its society makes of it, and when by way of response a reordering of the basic power relationships in society is sought by means of changed normative patterns. Nothing less than this was at stake in the long upheaval in the relations between the trade union movement and the government which occurred from the mid-1960s onwards. Admittedly this is to adopt a very wide definition of the constitution; but there is good reason to do so when discussing the

[7] See M. Terry, 'Shop Steward Development and Managerial Strategies', ch. 3 of G. Sayers Bain, ed., *Industrial Relations in Britain* (Oxford, 1983), at 67–8.

[8] M. Terry, 'Shop Steward Development', at 71–7: 'Shop Steward Activity and Organisation: Before Donovan'.

politics of industrial society and labour law at this period. We proceed to develop this argument more fully.

The Labour government in the mid-1960s, while responsive to the crisis in collective industrial relations, was reluctant to acknowledge its underlying significance; that would be to admit that the two branches of the labour movement—the Labour Party and the trade union movement—had failed to make good their claim to provide the natural form of government for industrial and civil society. As we shall see, the difficulty of this admission was to blind Harold Wilson and Barbara Castle to the impossibility of the demands which they were to make of the trade union movement in their White Paper proposals; it generated a false optimism about what the TUC could deliver or even undertake to deliver to a Labour government. When the Government in 1969 proposed to use the law to intervene in industrial relations, the response was a challenge by the TUC to the legitimacy of governmental power in industrial society. The succeeding Conservative government was to experience this challenge in response to its Industrial Relations Act. The result of attempted governmental and legislative intervention was thus to elevate the crisis to constitutional proportions. Before that point was reached, however, there had been a major effort to resolve or at least deflect the crisis by means of a Royal Commission; we turn to the events leading up to the Report of that Commission, known as the Donovan Commission after Lord Donovan, its Chairman.

(b) *The Reasons for Setting up the Donovan Commission*

As we have seen, the Conservative governments of the 1950s and early 1960s had had their own reasons for cultivating good relations with the trade unions and therefore not exploiting popular fears of trade unions as a threat to industrial stability. Among the more right-wing of Conservative political sections no such reticence was felt. It was the lawyers who were to the fore in giving expression to these shades of opinion. Thus in 1958 the Inns of Court Conservative and Unionist Society produced a study emotively titled *A Giant's Strength*, but even more interestingly sub-titled, *Some Thoughts on the Constitutional and Legal Position of Trade Unions in England*. It amounted to an argument that the nation could no longer sustain the amount of freedom of collective action accorded by labour law to trade unions, a freedom which, it was argued, was being used to oppress both individual worker and the public at large. There is an explicit demand for a new normative order:

> The time has come when not humanity alone but our very existence demands justice in industry. Justice between master and man, between employer and union, between a union and its members and, perhaps above all, justice to the public. To obtain these things, it may be necessary to question the validity of certain assumptions that have come to be very nearly articles of faith to trade unionists.[9]

The assumptions in question seem to be (1) the freedom to engage in big economically damaging strikes, especially for reasons not concerned with immediate terms and conditions of work, (2) the freedom to engage in restrictive practices and inter-union rivalries, and (3) the freedom to run closed shops and so victimize individual workers.[10] This analysis of the problem of trade union power closely follows and is influenced by existing legal categories such as the doctrine of restraint of trade.[11]

The fierce, if rather unspecific, liberal individualism of *A Giant's Strength* reflected the political outlook upon industrial society of many lawyers, not least the judiciary. It was in this sub-culture that the power of trade unions was most readily perceived as a challenge to the whole political and constitutional ordering of society. This helps to explain why the Law Lords who decided *Rookes* v. *Barnard* and *Stratford* v. *Lindley* felt free to, indeed impelled to, deal such heavy blows to the body of the political settlement expressed in the law of trade dispute and trade union immunities. They were animated by a sense of outrage born of the perception that Mr Rookes—like Mr Bonsor[12]—was the victim of oppression which only a fundamentally defective constitution could fail to remedy. The case of *Rookes* v. *Barnard*[13] was the labour law *cause célèbre* of the 1960s in which the House of Lords encroached upon the assumption, crucial to the whole structure of collective *laissez-faire*, that the Trade Disputes Act

---

[9] *A Giant's Strength*, 13. Cf. also above, p. 129.
[10] Ibid. 15–16.
[11] For a near-contemporary account of the relevant aspects of the doctrine, see C. Grunfeld, *Modern Trade Union Law* (London, 1966), 64–70.
[12] See above, p. 134 for discussion of *Bonsor* v. *Musicians' Union* [1956] AC 104.
[13] [1964] AC 1129.

1906 had been intended to exclude economic tort law from the whole field of industrial disputes and should be construed accordingly. The plaintiff had been a draughtsman employed by BOAC; his complaint was that trade union officials had procured his dismissal for his refusal to belong to the draughtsmen's trade union, by the threat of industrial action. The House of Lords broke through the trade dispute provisions of Section 3 of the 1906 Act by holding that these facts amounted to the tort of intimidation, that the threat to strike amounted to the threat of breach of contract which constituted the requisite unlawful means for that tort, and that this tort was outside the protective scope of Section 3. The technicalities of that decision, and of the subsequent decision of the House of Lords in *Stratford* v. *Lindley*,[14] where further possibilities of economic tort liabilities outside the protection of Section 3 were developed in relation to secondary boycotting, need not detain us at this stage. The important point is that the Law Lords felt so strongly that the policy embodied in Section 3 was unduly protective of certain kinds of trade union industrial action that they were willing to develop the common law and to use statutory construction to achieve radical new policy outcomes.

Even before *Stratford* v. *Lindley* followed it up, the decision of the House of Lords in *Rookes* v. *Barnard* had imparted a critical momentum to the pressure on the government to respond to the perceived crisis in industrial relations. The TUC pressed the Conservative government, then in power, for legislation to reverse the decision, offering in return to accept a Royal Commission to look into the whole state of industrial relations and labour law; but the government wanted the inquiry to take place before any legislation was passed.[15] The Labour Government which took office in 1964 was readier to accede to the idea of legislation to restore the trade dispute immunities pending the results of an inquiry. Hence the appointment of the Royal Commission, to be chaired by Lord Donovan, on 2 February 1965 was followed by the publication of the Trade Disputes Bill, which would reverse the immediate effects of the two House of Lords decisions, on the next day.[16] As far as the TUC was concerned,

---

[14] [1965] AC 209.
[15] Barnes and Reid, *Governments and Trade Unions*, 42–3.
[16] Ibid. 67.

the 1965 Bill was the price they demanded for agreeing to the setting-up of the Commission.

In this instance, as in many cases where the judiciary enter the constitutional arena, their decisions threatened to upset an applecart, and were taken with little enough regard for the delicately stacked state of the apples or the difficulty of putting them back in place. This rather cavalier quality is both a strength and a weakness. Those who wished to tread more cautiously were nevertheless all too conscious of widespread concern with the perceived instability of industrial society, and this was recognized in the width of the terms of reference with which the Donovan Commission was set up to review the state of industrial society in 1965. In the measured but eloquent language of its civil servants, the Ministry of Labour identified the fundamental issues starkly enough in the Covering Note which introduced its written evidence to the Commission:

The Commission is required by its terms of reference to consider 'the role of trade unions and employers' associations in promoting the interests of their members and in accelerating the social and economic advance of the nation.' It is obvious that the trade unions have a cardinal role in promoting the interests of their members. It is not self-evident that they have an obligation to play a part in accelerating the social and economic advance of the nation, and there is certainly scope for argument about the priorities between the two and the way in which possible conflict between the roles can be reconciled.[17]

The careful language does not wholly conceal the sense that the existing normative order of industrial society—and therefore indirectly of civil society as a whole—was inadequately defined in relation to the demands being made upon it. There was a crisis which had been sharpened and focused by the decisions of the House of Lords, but it was by no means solely attributable to their intervention. The Donovan Commission was now asked to do nothing less than discover by rational inquiry what was the right normative order for industrial society for the future.

(c) *The Evidence to the Donovan Commission*

The setting-up of the Donovan Commission thus provided a focus for a search for a new normative order for British industrial society. The impulse to search was there before the Commission

[17] Royal Commission on Trade Unions and Employers' Associations, *Written Evidence of the Ministry of Labour* (London, 1965), para. 4.

was set up; indeed, the setting-up of the Commission was a response to it. But the search was institutionalized, and therefore intensified, by the existence of the Commission and by its elaborate processes of gathering written and oral evidence and arranging for the preparation of research papers. The result is that we have an invaluable picture of how the problems were perceived, and what solutions were proposed, by representatives of most of the interest groups in industrial society. Of course, neither they nor the Commission itself had the same role in this search process as the government itself. The interest groups were lobbying for their preferred solutions. The Commission was in search of solutions which would command assent among its own members, hoping that the representativeness of its own composition and the exhaustiveness of its enquiries would endow those solutions with sufficient moral authority to guarantee their implementation. As a paradigm of the policy-making process, that is altogether too Utopian; we shall see that the governments to whom the Donovan prescriptions were addressed operated according to quite different paradigms in deciding what new normative orders to try to introduce. This is not necessarily to imply that they were more cynical or less far-sighted than the Donovan Commission, but merely that their role was an essentially different—and more difficult—one. For them, the crisis in industrial society amounted to a constitutional one, whereas the discourse of the Donovan Commission tended for the most part to be contained within a frame of reference of industrial relations.

Within the latter framework, the troubles in industrial society, although very serious, did not seem quite so apocalyptic as they did to governments. Nevertheless, it was within the more contained framework of the Commission's deliberations that the options for the succeeding decade were identified, so it is there one looks to see the new agenda being formulated. The written and oral evidence given to the Commission contained a large number of formulations going right across the political spectrum. The significant variables, which shaped the different normative orders that were contended for, can be identified as follows:

1. the political outlook of those making the proposals;
2. their perceptions of the dimensions and nature of the disorder within industrial society; and

3. their perceptions of the role and utility of the law and the legal process in industrial society.

There was at that time, and has continued to be, an acute set of difficulties for all but the most dogmatic formulators of policies for industrial society in relating the first two variables to the third one. The political taxonomy of the evidence to and conclusions of the Donovan Commission has been carried out almost definitively by Colin Crouch, and we shall depend in part on his classifications.[18] For our particular purpose, it is useful also to examine the new normative orders, which were in contention, with particular emphasis on the third variable. That is to say, we are particularly concerned with the legal outcomes which were associated with the different policy orientations. That emphasis produces some interesting results.

Of all the new normative orders which were canvassed during the Donovan debate, the one which was most prominent was that based on legal enforcement of collective agreements. It was a central feature of the CBI's proposals,[19] and of the Conservative Party's policy document, *Fair Deal at Work*. Many of those giving evidence to the Commission, and indeed the Commission itself, regarded the prevailing doctrine, which characterized collective agreements as not intended to create legal relations, as having become profoundly controversial. In particular, it was widely thought that the reversal of the doctrine by legislation would place a legal obligation upon unions to control unofficial strike action, by making them responsible for securing observance by the workforce of the undertakings in collective agreements that industrial action would not take place in violation of the dispute resolution procedures contained in those agreements. There would, in other words, be legal sanctions to make unions use their authority over their members to control 'unconstitutional' industrial action.

This terminology was significant; coming from the vocabulary of collective bargaining, it shows how the participants in that process regarded themselves as creating their own normative,

---

[18] See ch. 8 of C. Crouch, *Class Conflict and the Industrial Relations Crisis* (London, 1977).

[19] See Royal Commission on Trade Unions and Employers' Associations, *Selected Written Evidence Submitted to the Royal Commission* (London, 1968), Written Evidence of the CBI, paras. 172–5.

or constitutional, order for industrial society. It was that normative order which the advocates of legal enforcement wished to
strengthen and re-activate. Colin Crouch argues[20] that the move
to make it legally enforceable represented a kind of private
corporatism: corporatist in its aim of harnessing trade unions
to the service of a particular policy objective, private in that
the objective concerned was determined by bargaining between
private interest groups. One could argue that it was therefore
a contractual normative order. That characterization, however,
understates the procedural dimension of the collective bargaining
process. Otto Kahn-Freund had pointed to the 'dynamic' as
opposed to the 'static' quality of collective bargaining processes.[21]
By this, he meant that those processes consisted of a continuous
interplay of conflicting interests rather than a striking of discrete
treaties at particular moments. This both emphasized their procedural dimension,[22] and by the same token indicated how little
those processes fitted a simple contractual model. This was
illustrated by the fact that the distinction between 'disputes of
interest' and 'disputes of right', which was clearly embodied in
the more contractual American collective bargaining practice,
simply could not be distilled out of British collective bargaining
procedures.[23] The advocates of legal enforcement, on the other
hand, committed themselves to insisting that these loose procedural norms could be understood and operated as tight contractual ones. The Donovan Commission, although undoubtedly
attracted by the idea of collective promise-keeping as a governing
principle for industrial society, ultimately accepted that the
translation of this normative order into legal contractual terms
was over-ambitious and therefore destructive.[24]

[20] Crouch, *Class Conflict*, 147-8.
[21] O. Kahn-Freund, 'Intergroup Conflicts and their Settlement', (1954) 5
British Journal of Sociology 193, esp. 202 ff. (repr. in Kahn-Freund, *Selected
Writings* (London, 1980), 41 ff.).
[22] See A. Marsh, *Royal Commission Research Paper 2*, pt. 1 (London, 1966),
paras. 67-74, 'The Preference for Procedural over Substantive Rules'. The
'dynamic' characterization applies rather better to the shop-steward bargaining
which Arthur Marsh had primarily in mind than to the national-level bargaining
which Otto Kahn-Freund had been describing in 1954.
[23] See Marsh, *Royal Commission Research Paper 2*, para. 66.
[24] Report of the Royal Commission on Trade Unions and Employers'
Associations, Cmnd. 3623 (1968), paras. 500-19. The Commission had great
difficulty in accepting this; their chairman was finally persuaded to do so by the

During the Donovan debate, the next most favoured candidate for a new normative system which would provide an ordering of industrial society was that based on the registration, and Registrar-administered control, of trade unions. Under the existing legal regime as created by the Trade Union Act 1871, unions were expected, though not ultimately forced, to register with the Registrar of Friendly Societies; registration involved only the most exiguous of controls over the unions concerned, and those were of an accounting–administrative, rather than a democracy-ensuring, character. Many of those who gave evidence believed that it would be desirable to have a substantially more interventionist system of registration and continuing control by the Registrar. Any such proposal tended to be statist in that it would emphasize the subjection of the union to the immediate or ultimate control of the state, and generally tended to be corporatist in that it would see the purpose of registration as maximizing the obligation of the trade union to conduct itself in such a way as to implement or further the goals of the state in industrial society, however they were defined. But the further characterization of registration proposals depends on the particular system of control which it was proposed to use registration to implement. A strongly statist use of registration would consist of making it compulsory; but in that case de-registration by the Registrar would place a trade union out of compliance with the registration requirement and would therefore urgently raise the question of whether the state should apply sanctions to trade unions which continued to function though unregistered.

This difficulty was seen as a creating a preference for making registration voluntary, but associating with it a set of protections for the trade union in the exercise of its trade union functions, protections which it can only dispense with at a normally unacceptable cost; for example, the CBI proposed[25] that trade union and trade dispute immunity in tort should be limited to registered trade unions and their authorized officials. That was an essentially corporatist proposal in the sense that trade unions

argument that legal sanctions against unions and their officials could be effectively defied, as they had been in the Betteshanger Colliery incident during the Second World War—see his addendum to the Report and above, p. 90.

[25] See Royal Commission, *Selected Evidence*, Written Evidence of the CBI, para. 179.

would thereby be placed under pressure to align their corporate functioning to goals prescribed for them by the public policy of the state. Those goals were identified by the conditions attached to acquiring and maintaining registered status. At the time of the Donovan debate, the conditions which were proposed tended to be designed to ensure that the democratic rights of individual members were protected, and were not susceptible to the sort of extremist gerrymandering revealed by the ETU ballot-rigging scandal.[26] Although partly driven by a libertarian impulse, such proposals shaded off into more obviously corporatist colours at the point where they concerned themselves with ensuring that unions would take decisions about industrial action which were responsive to the public interest in minimizing industrial disruption. This identifies an ambiguity underlying not just proposals for trade union registration, but also a wider range of proposals directed towards maximizing 'trade union democracy'.

Analysis of the evidence to the Donovan Commission by concentrating on the legal solutions which were proposed for the problems of industrial society suggests that two further normative orders were being put forward, albeit in a rather inchoate form. The first was one which would reintroduce to industrial society the controlling principles of the common law, above all those derived in one way or another from the basic idea of the illegality of most trade union activity under the doctrine of restraint of trade. The suggestion of a complete or even nearly complete return to common law rules would have seemed at that time too extreme a departure from existing approaches to merit serious discussion; but in the evidence, particularly, of some groupings of lawyers, there are perceptible tendencies towards that end.[27] The climate of discussion did not favour naked market liberalism, either at the rhetorical or at the practical level; but it did permit suggestions to be advanced that there should be a major attack upon restrictive practices in industrial society; that trade union and trade dispute immunities should be subject to major qualifications; and that the principles of individual libertarianism for which the common law had shown such potential should be

---

[26] See C. H. Rolph, *All Those in Favour: The ETU Trial* (London, 1962).

[27] Cf. the evidence given by the Inns of Court Conservative and Unionist Society: Royal Commission, *Minutes of Evidence 35* (London, 1967). The Society had produced the document *A Giant's Strength* in 1958.

further developed, for example to control abuse of trade union power where there was a closed shop.

A sharply contrasting, though perhaps equally loosely defined, new normative order to emerge from the Donovan debate was one whose distinguishing feature was the creation of new legal rights in industrial society, both individual and collective rights, whose existence would so define and clarify work relationships as to minimize disputes, whether between employers and workers, employers and unions, or unions amongst themselves. As we have seen, the view that there was much to be gained from legislating along these lines was fairly popular in both the main political parties at the time, and had provided the impulse for the Contracts of Employment Act 1963. The extent and direction of further proposals depended very much, of course, upon the political orientation of the particular proposers. Nevertheless, the evidence reflects a widespread perception that this approach could usefully give rise to individual rights not to be unfairly dismissed, and to enjoy freedom of association, and rights on the part of trade unions to be recognized by employers for collective bargaining purposes. The granting of the latter right to the union or grouping of unions best suited to represent the workgroup in question was seen as a method of reducing inter-union competition and friction, which were seen by many as a powerful counter-productive force in industrial society. Proposals of this kind reflect the tendency to juridify industrial relations and individual employment relationships; that tendency cuts across classifications of political approaches to industrial society such as 'corporatist' or 'liberal collectivist'. For example, the creation of a statutory trade union recognition procedure may be corporatist to the extent that it is envisaged as a way of impressing a sense of its responsibilities to the state upon the union so recognized; but that corporatism in implied and indirect rather than express and direct. Such a statutory procedure may be thought of as 'liberal collectivist' in the sense that it supports trade unions in their capacity as collective bargaining agents; but it cannot claim to be voluntarist in as far as it seeks to restrain collective bargaining with any representatives other than those of the union or unions to which the process accords recognition.

There is one final normative order to emerge from the evidence to the Donovan Commission which it is useful to identify by reference to its institutional source rather than by reference to the type of legal mechanism which it proposed; that is to say, it is useful to identify the normative order which the Trades Union Congress sought or was prepared to agree to. Colin Crouch argues that the TUC basically took the position which he defined as liberal collectivism with union emphasis; but that, as he puts it, the TUC coupled this with an acceptance of some degree of accommodation either to state intervention or to a managerial interpretation of the Compromise.[28] Thus the TUC was willing for the government to be, in a general way, active in securing the reform of industrial relations and in seeking more ordered workplace industrial relations; but it was not ready for greater legal regulation of the central areas of collective activity. This was true even in relation to types of legal regulation which favoured or supported trade unions—in particular, the TUC was opposed to a legal right of trade union recognition, probably because of the difficulties of superimposing legal regulation upon the TUC's system of dealing with inter-union disputes about recognition under the Bridlington principles.[29] The TUC was much more firmly opposed to legal intervention to enforce the procedural aspects of collective agreements,[30] or to exert greater control over relations between trade unions and their members.[31] The TUC was, on the other hand, less demanding of the full rigours of legal abstentionism than was the most effective exponent to the Royal Commission of the pure abstentionist position, namely Professor Wedderburn.[32] This in a sense was natural; the whole position of the TUC, like the normative order it proposed to the Commission, was an essentially defensive one. The TUC wished to maintain the framework of collective *laissez-faire* and corporatism as far as was possible in the post-*Rookes* v. *Barnard* era; it was becoming aware that this was something it could no longer simply demand as a matter of course. In so far as the TUC

[28] Crouch, *Class Conflict*, 156–7.

[29] Cf. Royal Commission, *Selected Evidence*, TUC Written Evidence, paras. 304–9; and as to the Bridlington principles, see P. Davies and M. Freedland, *Labour Law: Text and Materials* (2nd edn. London, 1984), 611 ff., and P. Kalis, 'The Adjudication of Inter-Union Membership Disputes', (1977) 6 ILJ 19.

[30] Royal Commission, *Selected Evidence*, TUC Written Evidence, paras. 338–41.

[31] Cf. ibid., paras. 466–9.

[32] Royal Commission, *Minutes of Evidence 31* (London, 1966).

had an existing model for the normative order it put forward, it was the Swedish one;[33] but in Britain the corporatist relationship between the TUC and the government was so much less institutionalized than in Sweden, and in any case under such strain because of the economic crises of the mid-1960s, that it was hard to make this model the basis for a convincing normative order. Neither the TUC itself nor the individual trade unions which gave evidence to the Commission did succeed in creating that conviction.

Hence the Donovan debate concluded with the initiative having been effectively taken by the institutions of the Right and the advocates of tighter legal regulation of industrial relations. This probably reflected the political development of industrial society at that period. It did not, as we shall see, reflect the balance within the Donovan Commission itself, which had its own complex internal politics,[34] but which in the end, as Middlemas has put it, 'tried to find a framework of reference in the reality of trade unions' existence in contemporary society'.[35] To devise a normative order which would protect that reality, the Commission had to look beyond the proposals put forward by the institutions which contributed to the Donovan debate. Hence it was that the main intellectual influence upon the Commission, and the main source of the evaluations on which it relied, was not the evidence of the institutions but the evidence and research papers coming from the Oxford group of industrial relations specialists—the real winners, in the short term, of the Donovan debate.[36] In the next section, we consider the Report itself, which was the immediate (though not the ultimate) outcome of that debate.

[33] K. Middlemas, *Power, Competition and the State*, ii (1990) 227.
[34] See H. Clegg, 'Otto Kahn-Freund and British Industrial Relations', in Lord Wedderburn, R. Lewis, and J. Clark, *Labour Law and Industrial Relations: Building on Kahn-Freund* (Oxford, 1983), 16–23. Clegg describes the experience of the members of the Commission in terms of an 'awakening' to the changes which had occurred and were occurring in shop-floor industrial relations, and to the need for (voluntary) reform thereof.
[35] Middlemas, *Power*, ii. 227.
[36] Cf. ibid. 227 and 229; Clegg, 'Otto Kahn-Freund', 17. The group consisted of Hugh Clegg, who was a member of the Commission and responsible for its central descriptive analysis of the state of industrial relations in Britain; William McCarthy, who was the Commission's research director; Allan Flanders, who submitted crucially influential evidence; and Alan Fox, John Hughes, and Arthur

6.2. THE DONOVAN REPORT

The Report of the Royal Commission on Trade Unions and Employers' Associations[37] published in May 1968 was the first comprehensive governmental response within our period to the problems of disorderly and inefficient industrial relations, or, in the perception of many, the excessive and disruptive power of organized labour; and also to the question whether the law should be deployed to order industrial relations and to limit the power of organized labour. It may seem surprising to describe a Royal Commission as a governmental activity, for Royal Commissions are less used and acknowledged as a way of taking governmental decisions today than twenty-five years ago. That is itself a measure of the polarization of the process of government that has occurred within those twenty-five years. In the 1960s, the formulation of a response to these particular problems and questions was seen as an exercise in maintaining and extending a political consensus about the role of the law in industrial relations. That consensus might be under strain, but it seemed realistic to suppose that it could be preserved and strengthened by subjecting it to the overhaul of a Royal Commission chaired by a Law Lord, representing the two sides of industry, containing academic experts, and afforced by the great and the good. The resulting Report was, as we shall see, succeeded by a series of political developments which took the policy of the state down paths very different from those mapped out by the Report. Nevertheless, the Report commanded a moral, intellectual, and political authority which made it, in its own way, as significant a state activity as the White Papers, Bills, Acts, and Codes of Practice which we shall have to consider later on. So it is worth trying to look at it in the round.

A simple account of the Donovan Commission Report would describe it as a thorough-going defence of collective *laissez-faire*—a rejection of the idea of an enlarged role for the law in

Marsh, who submitted important research papers. Associated with the group was Otto Kahn-Freund, at that time initiating the study of labour law at Oxford and, as a member of the Commission, a most important intellectual ally of the group and intermediary between them and his fellow-lawyer, Lord Donovan, the Chairman of the Commission.

[37] Cmnd. 3623.

industrial relations. It was, indeed, the thesis of the Report that the system of collective bargaining could, if reformed in the ways suggested in the Report, provide the basis for a socially adequate system of industrial relations which would not need to be regulated by legal sanctions. It was indeed the majority verdict of the Commission that there should not, in the immediate future at least, be the sort of imposition of legal constraints upon industrial action that many people were demanding—for example, by making collective agreements legally enforceable against industrial action in breach of agreed procedures. But it would be wrong to conclude from this account that the Report was either a straightforward defence of the existing system of collective bargaining, or a straightforward defence of the abstention of the law from industrial relations. The Report was far from being a mere rearguard action in favour of a fatally weakened status quo. Its approach was much more sophisticated than that.

The first evidence of this highly sophisticated approach is to be found in the way that the Commission defines its own role and the problem which it intends to address. The Report begins by identifying the Commission as the latest in a succession of committees 'to be appointed to inquire into questions affecting industrial relations in the last hundred years'.[38] These consisted of four Royal Commissions,[39] and the Whitley Committee, whose five reports had contributed so significantly to the evolution of collective *laissez-faire*.[40] The stage is at once set for the Commission to play the part of inspector-general of industrial relations and guardian of collective *laissez-faire*. Indeed, the Commission goes on overtly to assume this role, defining its primary task as the examination of industrial relations (rather than as that of evaluating the case for legal sanctions).[41]

When it comes to an introductory survey of the role of the state in those industrial relations, the very first words assert the voluntarist tradition: 'Until recent times it was a distinctive feature of our system of industrial relations that the state remained aloof

[38] Ibid., para. 1.
[39] Those of 1867, 1874, 1891, and 1903.
[40] The Committee on Relations between Employers and Employed under the Chairmanship of J. H. Whitley, MP was appointed in 1916 and produced five reports from 1917–18. See above, p. 38.
[41] Cmnd. 3623, para. 23.

from the process of collective bargaining in private industry'.[42] Indeed, in a key paragraph of astonishing significance,[43] the Commission defines its whole task as that of addressing what it sees as the recent legislative challenge to voluntarism. This paragraph begins, 'Certain recent Acts of Parliament, however, have made a new departure from the general principle of non-intervention.' A catalogue of upstart Acts is given with an item for each of the years from 1963 to 1968[44] (and 'further legislation on prices and incomes now under consideration'). Thus violation of collective *laissez-faire* is depicted as a new annual ritual; and moreover as the very starting point for the work of the Commission:

It may fairly be said *therefore* [emphasis added] that as a Royal Commission we have been sitting at a time when the basic principles of our system of industrial relations are in question. Should they be restored, revised or replaced? In order to set out the reasoning by which we have arrived at our own answers to these questions, we now turn to a more detailed examination of the system and its working.

Thus issue is joined even with existing erosions of collective *laissez-faire*, let alone with proposals for further legal sanctions. Since, however, some of the existing departures from collective *laissez-faire* will turn out on examination to have been desirable and beneficial, there is in this the basis of a case for further limited legislative advance.

It is not only at the presentational level, moreover, that the strategy of the Report was an extremely sophisticated one. The same subtlety is at work in the devising of the central part of the Report, namely the analysis of the system of industrial relations in chapter 3 and the prescription for the reform of collective bargaining in chapter 4. Let us take chapter 3 first. The identification of remediable shortcomings in the system of industrial relations was the very essence of the case for maintaining the voluntarist approach, for without this there could be no convincing resistance to the demand for legal sanctions. The Donovan Report's analysis was that the remediable problems flowed from the fact that

---

[42] Ibid., para. 39.
[43] Ibid., para. 45.
[44] Contracts of Employment Act 1963, Industrial Training Act 1964, Redundancy Payments Act 1965, Prices and Incomes Acts 1966 and 1967.

Britain has two systems of industrial relations. The one is the formal system embodied in the official institutions. The other is the informal system created by the actual behaviour of trade unions and employers' associations, of managers, shop stewards and workers.[45]

The remediable problems are ultimately attributed to the tension between the formal and informal systems:

What is of crucial importance is that the practices of the formal system have become increasingly empty, while the practices of the informal system have come to exert an ever greater influence on the conduct of industrial relations throughout the country; that the two systems conflict; and that the informal system cannot be forced to comply with the formal system.[46]

This analysis in terms of *tension between two systems* displays a polite reticence; for what the chapter has really done is to display the near-fatal weaknesses of each of the two systems as well as of their combination.

That analysis has since been so fully accepted that it is easy to lose sight of its originality—or of the severity of the challenge which it presented to the orthodoxies of industrial relations. The whole tradition of collective *laissez-faire* revolved around the official institutions of industry-wide collective bargaining, which are here characterized as an almost empty shell, purporting to lay down rates of pay which were far below the average earnings actually received by reason of the operation of the informal system of bargaining,[47] or purporting to lay down common procedures for dispute resolution, which were in practice largely pre-empted by 'the transfer of authority in industrial relations to the factory and the workshop'.[48] Moreover, each of the pillars of the traditional structure is in its own way found to be hollow and crumbling. Employers' associations are seen to display 'an unquestioning commitment to maintain the formal system of industrial relations'.[49] The management of many firms has 'no effective personnel policy to control methods of negotiation and pay structures, and perhaps no conception of it'.[50] Trade unions, for their part, 'have been as guilty as employers' associations and

---

[45] Cmnd. 3623, para. 46.   [46] Ibid., para. 154.
[47] Ibid., para. 57.   [48] Ibid., para. 61.
[49] Ibid., para. 82.   [50] Ibid., paras. 94, 95.

managers of sustaining the facade of industry-wide bargaining'.[51]
Nor does the system of workplace bargaining—the second system
in the Donovan analysis—escape unscathed. It is seen as fragmented because conducted in such a way that different groups get
different concessions at different times.[52] It is seen as informal
because of the predominance of unwritten understandings and of
custom and practice.[53] And it is seen as largely out of the control
of trade unions and employers' associations.[54] In many situations,
moreover, shop stewards and workgroups so far fail to exercise
effective control over wage-bargaining that 'industrial relations
can border on anarchy'.[55] The Donovan Commission was, as we
shall see, to be thought to have offered inadequate solutions; but
they certainly made sure that they could not be accused of complacency in the way they described existing industrial relations in
the private manufacturing sector.

Just as the chapter 3 descriptive analysis turns out to be different in nature from what the simple account of the Report
might suggest, so also does the chapter 4 prescription for the
reform of collective bargaining. The simple account of chapter
4 might depict it as making proposals which were radical in
industrial relations terms while being reactionary in legal terms—
as advocating revolutionary changes in patterns of industrial
relations while insisting on the maintenance of the abstentionist
status quo so far as the law is concerned. There is an argument
for precisely the opposite view. The direction of reform advocated by the Commission was that of the development of
plant- and company-level bargaining. By operating at a level
between industry-wide bargaining and workshop bargaining,
plant- and company-level agreements could hope to combine real
effectiveness with order and rationality.[56] This was certainly
radical to the extent that it involved the abandonment of that
industry-wide system of bargaining which had for so long—at
least since the days of the Whitley Reports—been regarded as an
ideal for industrial relations. But to recognize that the future lay
with single-employer collective bargaining was to do little more
than bow to a process of change that was already well under way,
and which was to continue of its own volition without the inter-

[51] Ibid., para. 111.   [52] Ibid., para. 67.
[53] Ibid., para. 68.   [54] Ibid., para. 66.
[55] Ibid., para. 109.   [56] Ibid., paras. 162 ff.

vention of external policy-makers. The Commission was much influenced by the constructiveness of some examples of single-employer productivity agreements, especially those which Esso had entered into for its Fawley oil refinery.[57] But the trend towards single-employer,—that is, plant- or company level bargaining—was not confined to that sort of rather idealistic productivity bargaining, and was indeed to continue even when productivity bargaining became discredited as an ideal. So the Donovan prescription cut less against the grain of existing industrial relations than might at first appear.

On the other hand, chapter 4 is far more positive about the role of the law in industrial relations than it is often given credit for being. It is true that the chapter develops an underlying argument for preferring reform of collective bargaining to the use of legal sanctions in industrial relations. But the law may have an important effect on industrial relations without necessarily consisting in coercive sanctions; and the role of the state need not be defined solely in terms of civil remedies or criminal penalties. It is significant that in their statement of their reformist goal, the Commission state the voluntarist reservation in terms of excluding the *courts* rather than in terms of excluding the law in general:

What is needed first of all is a change in the nature of British collective bargaining, and a more orderly method for workers and their representatives to exercise their influence in the factory; and for this to be accomplished, if possible, without destroying the British tradition of keeping industrial relations out of the courts.[58]

It is evidence of their positive preparedness for a greater role for the law in this, that the Commission go straight on to say,

As a first step to accomplish this [emphasis added] a statute, which might be called the Industrial Relations Act, should lay an obligation on companies of a certain size to register collective agreements with the Department of Employment and Productivity.[59]

The registration of collective agreements is not an obviously significant step in itself; but the Commission had taken a decisive

[57] See A. Flanders' Written Evidence (Royal Commission, *Selected Evidence*, esp. p. 579), and his book, *The Fawley Productivity Agreements* (London, 1965).
[58] Cmnd. 3623, para. 190.
[59] Ibid., para. 191.

step towards a legal framework for industrial relations. Again, the proposal to have a continuing Industrial Relations Commission,[60] and for its operation to be subject to a declared set of guiding principles,[61] was the starting-point for a very important extension of the role of the state in industrial relations. Although governments in the ensuing years were to disregard the caution that the Donovan Report urged upon them about the use of legal sanctions, they could certainly claim to find support in the Report for the idea of a legal matrix for industrial relations, and for passing an Act to set up that matrix.

Wherever governments were subsequently going to take the ideas set out in chapters 3 and 4, the Commission saw those ideas as setting out a strategy which enabled them to deal with the whole range of issues that they had been called upon to discuss. It becomes clear as one goes through the rest of the Report that a fragile consensus within the Commission was built upon a foundation of those two chapters. In the later chapters, the whole notion is worked out of a reformist role for the law and the state combined with an abstention from collective legal sanctions. In the process, most of the agenda is established for the discussion of labour law which is to ebb and flow for the following decade. Thus in chapter 5, a programme is set out—as a related exercise to the reform of collective bargaining—for the extension of collective bargaining by means of, firstly, new legislative protection for freedom of association, secondly, legislation to give power to the Industrial Relations Commission to adjudicate upon disputes about trade union recognition, including inter-union disputes, and thirdly, by legislative change to encourage the abolition of Wages Councils and their replacement by voluntary collective bargaining machinery. There is even, strange though it seems today, a proposal for legislation placing on all arbitrators an obligation to take account of incomes policy in their awards—a striking illustration of the lengths to which the Commission was prepared to go in creating *by legislation* a favourable context, as they saw it, for restructured collective bargaining.

The way in which the reformist strategy was used to counter the arguments for collective legal sanctions is very well illustrated

---

[60] Ibid., para. 198.
[61] Ibid., para. 203.

by chapter 6 of the Report which, under the head of 'The Efficient Use of Manpower', advocates its programme for the reform of collective bargaining as the best response to the problem of restrictive labour practices, and as a preferable approach to that of setting up a Restrictive Labour Practices Tribunal as the engineering employers had urged in their evidence to the Commission. The idea of applying legal sanctions to trade union restrictive practices was a popular one at the time; it was, after all, the heyday of the Restrictive Practices Court in the commercial sphere, and it is perhaps an indication of the influence of the conceptual framework that the Donovan Report set up that this subsequently had little or no place on the agenda for legal regulation of industrial relations. The suggestions for collective legal sanctions with which the Report deals in the succeeding two chapters (chapter 7 on strikes and other industrial action, and chapter 8 on legal enforcement of collective agreements) were going to remain very firmly on the agenda for subsequent discussion, and it is here that the reformist consensus is most under strain from the pressure within and outside the Commission for the introduction of collective legal sanctions. The essence of chapter 7 is a descriptive analysis of patterns of industrial action, which is really an extension of the analysis of patterns of collective bargaining in chapter 3. The argument of this analysis is that small-scale unofficial industrial action is far more of a problem, both in its incidence and in its disruptive effects, than large-scale official trade union industrial action. That argument leads on to two conclusions; the first is that large-scale official strikes were not such a problem or such a threat as to necessitate or justify the introduction of government-imposed compulsory cooling-off periods on the model of the Taft–Hartley Act in the United States, or compulsory strike ballots. The second is that the larger problem of unofficial industrial action is mainly caused by the inadequacy of procedures to resolve workplace and individual disputes and grievances; and that the problem, thus understood, can best be dealt with by the reform of collective bargaining as already proposed, and by the enhanced use of legal machinery to resolve individual disputes that is proposed later in the Report.

The Commission had by these means prepared the ground for the central resolution in the Report of the conflict between voluntarism and the use of collective legal sanctions. This occurs in chapter 8 on the enforcement of collective agreements, which we know was drafted by Kahn-Freund.[62] The suggestion for legal enforcement of procedure agreements was at the time the most popular proposed way of introducing collective legal sanctions. The failure legally to enforce collectively agreed peace obligations was widely seen as the most significant contrast between the British legal regime for industrial relations and that of other comparable countries, and as linked with the large number of unofficial and especially of unconstitutional strikes which the Report identified as a problem peculiar to Britain.[63] That meant that the voluntarist approach was most vulnerable at that particular point. The approach was sustained (though only at the cost of specific dissent by two members of the Commission)[64] by the combination of two arguments. The first was that to introduce legal enforcement in advance of the process of reform of collective bargaining would merely aggravate the very problems for which legal enforcement was advanced as a solution, namely the inefficiency of existing dispute resolution procedures. The second argument was that in any event legal sanctions would be ineffective and impracticable, whether they sought to penalize unions for failing to control unofficial activity or whether they sought to penalize individual workers, for example, by the supposedly 'automatic' sanction of loss of rights based on continuity of service where service was interrupted by unconstitutional industrial action. The second argument, sustained in the Report by a special Appendix providing evidence of the impracticability of legal sanctions even in the conditions of World War II,[65] was clearly necessary for those for whom the first argument was insufficient; Lord Donovan makes it clear in his Addendum to the Report that it was on this ground alone that he accepted the conclusion of chapter 8; and there is evidence that it was only Kahn-Freund's convincing of Donovan by means of that

[62] See Clegg, 'Otto Kahn-Freund', 20.

[63] Cmnd. 3623, para. 501.

[64] Ibid., para. 519 (Lord Robens and Sir George Pollock).

[65] Cmnd. 3623, app. 6: Written Evidence of Sir Harold Emmerson, Chief Industrial Commissioner of the Ministry of Labour 1942–4, on Mass Prosecution in Wartime. The incident to which this evidence referred is described above at p. 90.

argument that made possible a consensus within the Commission on this crucial point.[66]

This was not, however, a simple victory for old-fashioned voluntarism. If Kahn-Freund had provided the key to a consensus within the Commission about abstention from collective legal sanctions, he had also ensured that there would be an enhanced role for the law in the way that he thought it useful. As we have already seen, an enhanced role for the law was a crucial element in the programme for the reform of collective bargaining set out in chapter 4, which underpins the argument of chapter 8. The Report reminds us of this at the outset of chapter 8:[67]

In Chapter IV, we recommended that an Industrial Relations Act should be passed under which certain collective agreements would be registered with the Department of Employment and Productivity. To this extent, therefore, we have already accepted the view that legislative measures are required for the purpose of the reform we have in mind.

It would be a mistake to regard this as mere defensive rhetoric for a simple voluntarist position; it is a reminder that there is a credo underlying the Report which distinguished between collective legal sanctions and the role of the law in general, and which, while rejecting the first, positively develops the second. Thus, where chapter 8 goes on to contemplate future legislation for selective enforcement of procedure agreements once the reform of collective bargaining has taken place,[68] many have regarded this as evidence of a negotiated settlement within the Commission—as a sop from the voluntarists to those wishing for immediate legal enforcement of collective agreements. We suggest that it was the expression of a new view of the role of the law, which shaped the Report at a more profound level than that of political bargaining, and which was to exert an influence in the succeeding years also at that more profound level.

It is this new view of the role of the law which explains why the Report next goes on to recommend, in chapter 9, the introduction of unfair dismissal legislation, and in chapter 10 the setting up of labour tribunals which will be a much extended and elaborated version of the existing industrial tribunals. We have

---

[66] Clegg, 'Otto Kahn-Freund', 20. See above, p. 249.
[67] Cmnd. 3623, para. 459.
[68] Cmnd. 3623, para. 518.

said a good deal about this in the previous chapter; suffice it to say here that this is part of the grand strategy; it is much more than a mere taking of the opportunity to deal with individual employment law as a side issue. We may explain in the same way the fact that the Report should next turn in chapter 11 to the question of safeguards for the individual in relation to trade unions; and that it should, under this head, while rejecting the possibility of prohibiting the closed shop, propose a new legal framework for the relationship between the trade union and the individual worker or individual trade union member, under which both categories of person are to be given rights of complaint to an independent review body to be attached to a Registrar of Trade Unions, which would make legally enforceable awards. This new view of the role of the law also explains why the discussion of particular changes to the existing body of traditional labour law can be relegated to a concluding chapter (chapter 14), and presented as largely an exercise in simplification and stream-lining, as a sort of administrative overhaul of an archaic body of law. Indeed, the Report overtly identifies this exercise as a sort of extension of the work of the Law Commission in this particular area.[69] One result of this presentation is that the one major victory for the protagonists of increased legal sanctions, namely the majority recommendation for the restriction of trade dispute immunity from liability for inducing breach of contract to registered trade unions and those acting on their behalf,[70] seems isolated from the rest of the Report and to that extent has less of an impact. That is not to say that this proposal lacked influence; we shall see that it had considerable influence. But it impinged little upon the voluntarist and reformist message of the Report itself.

We find the same contrast between tactics and strategies if we look at the rest of the qualifications to the Report which were made by those members of the Commission who wished for collective legal sanctions. The two Supplementary Notes

[69] Ibid., para. 756.
[70] Ibid., para. 800. It is interesting that the majority seem to have proceeded upon a false premiss, namely that, 'in order to avoid a breach of their contracts, most employees will need to do no more than give a week's notice of their intention to cease work'—a view even by that time rather dubious, though temporarily sustained by the decision of the Court of Appeal in *Morgan* v. *Fry* [1968] 2 QB 710.

appended by no less than four members of the Commission[71] confined themselves to tactical points; in particular, to the proposal that the Industrial Relations Commission should have power to de-register trade unions for breach of their own rules or breach of registered procedure agreements. This would have the effect of exposing the de-registered unions and those acting on their behalf to the loss of trade dispute immunity, which, as we have just seen, was the majority proposal of the legal sanctionists in the tail end of the Report itself. This was an essentially tactical attempt to mount legal sanctions on the back of the reformist strategy of the Report as a whole.

It was only one of the partial dissenters, Mr Andrew Shonfield, who attacked the strategy of the Report as a whole and proposed a different strategy. The crucial point of his attack was stated in the first two sentences of his Note of Reservation:

The main Report addresses itself to the immediate situation in British industrial relations and proposes a number of remedies which I heartily support. But it barely concerns itself with the long-term problem of accommodating bodies with the kind of concentrated power which is possessed by trade unions to the changing future needs of an advanced industrial society.[72]

His alternative strategy moved beyond the confines of existing labour law, just as the Report itself had done. Instead of seeking merely to engraft legal sanctions upon the Report's proposals for reform of collective bargaining, he proposed a new framework in which reform would be integrally linked with legal regulation of a far more exacting kind than that contemplated in the Report itself. Thus his version of the Industrial Relations Commission would have a judicial arm which would apply hard adjudication to problems such as that of inter-union competition or, for that matter, refusal by employers to bargain in good faith with representative unions. Again, he favoured a presumption of legal enforceability of collective agreements not simply because it offered the best point at which to breach the defences of voluntarism against legal sanctions, but rather as a way of

---

[71] Lord Tangley, Lord Robens, Sir George Pollock, and Mr John Thomson. These would have been regarded as the most clearly right-wing members of the Commission.

[72] Cmnd. 3623, Note of Reservation by Mr Andrew Shonfield, p. 288, para. 1.

creating a general atmosphere of greater legal obligation and regulation. His Note of Reservation, more or less alone of the partial dissents and qualifications, is on the same strategic plane as the Report as a whole, as is implicitly acknowledged by the particular weight that was accorded to it in the reception of the Report.

It was now for governments to work out what to make of the Report, or how to respond to the problems which the Report addressed. As we shall see, successive governments felt impelled to move away from the voluntarism which had prevailed within the Commission but did not seem to answer the political necessities as perceived by those in government. But even if they were now to move away from the voluntarism which the Commission had sought to re-validate and sustain, the Report had created a new context in which they were to do so. Before the Commission did its work, the options for change had seemed to lie within the confines of traditional labour law, perhaps as modified by the importation of some particular patterns of law from, say, Sweden or the USA. Now the debate would be whether to move to a completely new relationship between industrial relations and the law; and if so, was it to be fundamentally reformist, or fundamentally regulatory; or could it aspire to be both at once?

6.3. IN PLACE OF STRIFE

The Donovan Commission Report had thus set up an ideological framework for the future development of industrial relations and labour law. It had argued that the pressures for change in these normative systems could best be contained and channelled by a process of government-led reform in which the law and the institutions of the state would support and encourage an essentially voluntary and voluntarist development of more efficient patterns of work, management, and dispute resolution in industrial society. The test of the political viability of this approach —indeed, the demonstration of its lack of viability in the short term at least—was to come very soon after the Report was published. The political pressures upon the Labour government to secure a more effective control of the economy as a whole and of the 'strike problem' in particular, which had led to the setting-up of the Donovan Commission in 1965, had increased very greatly during the years in which the Commission was taking evidence and deliberating. The Labour government's response to the industrial relations aspects of this complex of political and economic problem was expressed in a White Paper, produced in January 1969, entitled *In Place of Strife: A Policy for Industrial Relations*.[73] The process of producing the White Paper, and its reception by the trade union movement, led to an intense crisis for the Labour government.[74] As these events formed a crucial transition in the development of labour legislation away from the policy of collective *laissez-faire*, we need to examine both their causes and their legal ramifications in some detail, although, as we shall see, the proposals themselves were abortive in the sense that they never gave rise to enacted legislation.

By 1968, the government's management of the economy, and the work of the Department of Economic Affairs were in disarray, and it was decided to transfer responsibility for prices and incomes policy to an aggrandized Ministry of Labour with the title of Department of Employment and Productivity and with Barbara Castle as Minister. One important effect was to import into the structure of the former Ministry of Labour a body of civil servants whose priorities and expertise lay within the sphere of controlling inflation, and who had some time since rejected—if they had ever accepted—the aversion to collective labour legislation which had hitherto been so important a part of the ethos of the Ministry of Labour. This linking together of the two aspects of governmental management of industrial society—incomes policy and industrial relations—was in one sense no more than a recognition of the way that the Government had been forced by events to assume an all-encompassing responsibility to direct and control the labour economy. But the two areas of activity were still regarded as distinct; the Donovan Commission, which reported in May 1968, reflected that distinction by identifying incomes policy as generally separate from its concerns. Barbara Castle, for much of her first year as Secretary of State for Employment and Productivity, was concerned, as Peter Jenkins

---

[73] Cmnd. 3888.
[74] The whole episode is ably chronicled by Peter Jenkins in his near-contemporary account, *The Battle of Downing Street* (London, 1970).

put it, 'to convert the unpopular and over-rigid prices and incomes policy into a true instrument of socialist planning'.[75]

It was in the course of this exercise, and perhaps because of the frustrations it produced, that she was persuaded of the need to reform industrial relations by reconstructing labour legislation. To quote Peter Jenkins again,

[S]he came to the conclusion that no prices and incomes policy was likely to get very far, no Social Democratic Society was likely to be constructed, until something radical was done to reform the structures and attitudes of the British Trade Unions.[76]

This was the starting-point of the strategy which was embodied in the White Paper, *In Place of Strife*. The detailed agenda for the formulation of these proposals had been set by the Donovan Commission Report; but the White Paper proposals took up an interventionist stance where the Donovan Report had been regarded as advocating a non-interventionist continuation of collective *laissez-faire*.

The White Paper proposals were to a significant extent, and no doubt deliberately, aligned to follow the structure of the Donovan Commission Report. Having set out the need for extended state intervention and involvement in industrial relations[77]—which as we have seen the Donovan Report itself had fully recognized—the White Paper went on to adopt the Donovan Commission's analysis of the current state of industrial relations, and of their deficiencies.[78] The White Paper went on to pursue many of the Report's suggestions for the reform, extension, and support of collective bargaining. There was to be a continuing Commission on Industrial Relations, and an Industrial Relations Act to place the operation on a statutory footing, just as the Report had suggested.[79] There was to be a system of registration of collective agreements with statutory backing from the Industrial Relations Act, as the Report had recommended.[80] Collective agreements were to be subjected to a presumption against legal enforceability, rebuttable by express written provision, as the Report had

<hr>

[75] Ibid. 8.
[76] Ibid. 9.
[77] *In Place of Strife*, paras. 5–9.
[78] Ibid., paras. 10–27.
[79] Ibid., paras. 33–8; Cmnd. 3623, paras. 188–91, 198–201.
[80] *In Place of Strife*, paras. 39–41; Cmnd. 3623, paras. 191–7.

recommended.[81] The Commission on Industrial Relations was to be given powers to deal with refusal by an employer to recognize any trade union, much in the way that the Report had recommended (on the suggestion of Allan Flanders).[82] The White Paper had a proposal to extend the legal protection of individual workers by means of legislation against unfair dismissal, to be administered by an enlarged system of industrial tribunals, just as the Report had recommended.[83] Thus far, the White Paper could claim to be putting the wisdom of the Donovan Report into practice.

However, although the White Paper followed much of what the Report had initiated, it also took a significantly different direction. The White Paper not only sketched out an interventionist role for the government in industrial relations,[84] but also proposed to arm the government with coercive powers backed up by legal sanctions for three purposes. These were: (1) to enforce the recommendations of the new Commission for Industrial Relations in recognition disputes;[85] (2) to enable the government to secure a 'conciliation pause' in relation to unconstitutional strikes or strikes not preceded by adequate joint discussions;[86] and finally, (3) to require unions to hold a ballot on the question of strike action when the support of those involved might be in doubt.[87] It was these proposals that incurred the wrath of the trade union movement, and which represented a crucial break on the government's part with the voluntarist approach to industrial relations. It is this re-definition of the role of the law and the state that makes the White Paper a central development, even though the legal changes which it proposed did not come about.

This fundamental shift of direction can be explained at different levels. The policies embodied in the White Paper can be seen as largely the brainchild of Mrs Barbara Castle, then

[81] *In Place of Strife*, paras. 42–6; Cmnd. 3623, paras. 500–9.
[82] *In Place of Strife*, paras. 56–9; Cmnd. 3623, paras. 253–6. (The White Paper proposed an indirect sanction of imposed arbitration; the Report had come out against 'penalties' for refusal to carry out recommendations about recognition: *In Place of Strife*, para. 58; Cmnd. 3623, para. 256).
[83] *In Place of Strife*, paras. 103–4; Cmnd, 3623, paras. 544–50.
[84] *In Place of Strife*, paras. 5–9.
[85] Ibid., para. 60.
[86] Ibid., paras. 93–6.
[87] Ibid., paras. 97–8.

Secretary of State for Employment and Productivity;[88] or they can be seen as the result of the political process by which the Ministry of Labour had been entrusted with the enlarged function of keeping control of the industrial economy, as its new name betokened. Another kind of explanation might consist in seeing the government as reacting to particular manifestations of the 'strike problem'; it is said, for example, that the proposal for compulsory strike ballots was a suggestion from Harold Wilson and that he was activated by concern over a national engineering strike that had been threatened in October 1968.[89] These, however, are really pointers towards the underlying fact that the 'strike problem' and the perceived disorders and inefficiencies of the industrial economy placed the government under great pressure to depart from the voluntarist approach. Collective *laissez-faire* was no longer thought by the government to be an available strategy, as the Donovan Commission had regarded it. This epitomizes the way in which the problems of government brought about a re-definition of roles; and it is indicative of the magnitude of those pressures that it was a Labour government that first decided to adopt a policy which included legal sanctions in response to them.

The outcome of the White Paper proposals is a matter of central significance to the whole history of labour legislation in the period with which this book is concerned. In the months immediately following the publication of the White Paper, the proposals seemed to have commanded some degree of acceptance or at least acquiescence in the trade union movement; but the level of controversy about legal sanctions against industrial action was greatly heightened by the litigation in which the Ford Motor Company sought to enforce its procedure agreement against the AUEF and the TGWU. The legal outcome was a decision in favour of the presumption of unenforceability of collective agreements;[90] the political outcome was a renewed determination

---

[88] Her diaries provide support: entry for 15 Nov. 1968: 'I had decided to hold a long discussion weekend to clear my ideas about the Donovan Report . . . [A] consensus emerged that we rejected the concept of "collective *laissez-faire*" and were in favour of state intervention in industrial relations. The questions to decide were: intervention for what and by what means.' Barbara Castle, *The Castle Diaries 1964-1970* (London, 1984), 549.

[89] Jenkins, *Battle of Downing Street*, 33-4.

[90] *Ford Motor Co. Ltd.* v. *AUEF* [1969] 2 QB 303.

on the part of the unions to resist legal sanctions, and on the part of the government to press ahead with the implementation of the White Paper proposals as the industrial relations situation came to seem incapable of being stabilized by any other means.

By April 1969, Harold Wilson, the Prime Minister, was persuaded that the right way to reinforce his own authority within the Labour Party, and the position of the Labour government in the face of growing hostility towards it from the trade unions, was to bring forward interim industrial relations legislation which would implement the essential core—which meant the most coercive parts—of the White Paper proposals. This was how the decision came about to bring forward a 'short Industrial Relations Bill' to be followed by a long Bill implementing the whole of the White Paper at such later time as would be politically convenient. Most significantly, this decision was announced in Parliament by Roy Jenkins as Chancellor of the Exchequer in his Budget speech;[91] it would seem that he was anxious to convince the representatives of the International Monetary Fund then visiting London that he was involved in active steps to repair the economic difficulties associated with the failure of the government's incomes policies.[92] This was followed by Barbara Castle's announcement that the short Bill would contain five measures:

(a) establishing the statutory right of every worker to belong to a trade union;

(b) empowering the Government to order an employer to implement a recommendation for trade union recognition made by the CIR;

(c) enabling the Government to impose settlements in inter-union disputes where voluntary agreement could not be reached;

(d) enabling the Government to impose a twenty-eight day conciliation pause upon unconstitutional industrial action and;

(e) narrowing the trade dispute disqualification from unemployment benefit.[93]

Items (c) and (d) were proposals which could involve penal sanctions against trade unions or their members; hence the

[91] HC Deb., 5th ser., vol. 781, col. 1006 (15 Apr. 1969).
[92] Jenkins, *Battle of Downing Street*, 93-4.
[93] HC Deb., 5th ser., vol. 781, cols. 1181 ff. (16 Apr. 1969).

division between the government and the trade union movement was focused and intensified.

In May 1969 the TUC produced counter-proposals in the shape of a policy document entitled *Industrial Relations: Programme for Action*, which offered TUC intervention in inter-union disputes or unconstitutional industrial action instead of legislative penal sanctions. These counter-proposals were overwhelmingly supported by a Special TUC Congress held at Croydon in June 1969. Later that month, the government reached an agreement with the TUC whereby in return for a 'solemn and binding undertaking' by the TUC to strengthen its own capacity to intervene against inter-union or unconstitutional industrial action by its member unions, the government agreed not to pursue the 'penal clauses' of the Short Bill. The government would in due course—in April 1970, with a General Election pending—produce an Industrial Relations Bill to 'give effect, with modifications, to certain of the proposals for legislation in the White Paper "In Place of Strife" ' ; this would be neither the 'Short Bill' nor the 'Long Bill', but rather the Bill with the penal clauses altogether dropped; it was clear that the impetus behind the White Paper *In Place of Strife* had been altogether deflected.

The position of the Labour government was very seriously weakened by this defeat at the hands of the trade union movement. In terms of its implications for the development of labour legislation, it was a climactic event. So far from securing the future of collective *laissez-faire*, it marked an important stage on the road away from it. Henceforth, and for years to come, the issue would be not whether to have legislative regulation of collective bargaining and industrial relations, but what form of legislative regulation to seek. Edward Heath as Leader of the Opposition was able to claim that the Labour government was powerless against the trade unions. The Conservative Party capitalized upon this weakness by making a prominent commitment to succeed in passing industrial relations legislation in despite of the trade unions where the Labour government had failed to do so. The Conservative Party had a detailed set of proposals ready for this purpose; in the closing stages of the policy debate stimulated by the Donovan Commission—and in an attempt to pre-empt the voluntarist conclusions of the Donovan Report—they had produced a policy document entitled *Fair Deal at Work*, which had contained detailed proposals for an Industrial

Relations Act—much more interventionist in character than the Donovan Report would recommend—indeed similar in many respects to the proposals later advanced in the White Paper *In Place of Strife* itself.

In June 1970, Edward Heath and the Conservative Party secured victory in a General Election. They took the view that their industrial relations policy, prominent in their manifesto, had contributed to that victory—that they had been elected in part because the electorate thought that they could govern the trade unions who had seemed to prevail over the Labour government. Edward Heath was fully committed to introducing legislation to implement the policy document *Fair Deal at Work*, and his new government would quickly bring forward its own Industrial Relations Bill to achieve that purpose. In July 1970, Peter Jenkins drew his conclusions about the battle over the *In Place of Strife* proposals, and about the prospects for the incoming government, in a passage of such prophetic power that it is useful to quote from it even with more than twenty years' hindsight:

Now a Conservative Government will soon be in confrontation with the trade unions. It could be the making or breaking of Edward Heath; not only will it be a trial of strength, a test of governmental authority; the outcome will also help to determine the success or failure of the Heath Government in achieving an acceptable rate of increasing prosperity, the pre-condition of electoral success.... It is by no means certain that the proposals of the Conservative Government for reforming industrial relations—in essence the creation of a legal framework for the conduct of collective bargaining and in practice not dissimilar from what the Labour Government attempted—will either serve to reduce the economic damage caused by strikes or to promote greater industrial efficiency and less inflationary wage settlements.[94]

This passage shows perceptively enough how and why the Conservative government of 1970 to 1974 would overtake the Labour government in moving away from the policies of collective *laissez-faire*. In the next chapter we shall examine this process, starting with the enactment and outcome of the Industrial Relations Act of 1971, the main legislative instrument by which it was attempted to make that move.

---

[94] Jenkins, *Battle of Downing Street*, 170.

7

THE FAILED
REVOLUTION:
COLLECTIVE LABOUR
LAW, 1970–1974

7.1. INTRODUCTION: THE WATERSHED YEARS

In any historical description of post-war labour law or industrial relations and employment policy, it is all too obvious to think of 1979 as the single most important turning-point or watershed, as the point at which collective *laissez-faire* underwent its final demise, and at which the whole relationship between the state and industrial society changed into its modern or current form. A convincing case can, however, be made out for locating that watershed not at the end of the 1970s but in the opening years of that decade—in fact, in the period of Conservative government from 1970 to 1974 when Edward Heath was the Prime Minister. There are different ways in which that case can be presented. We can say that between 1945 and 1970, the formative experiences which shaped labour law and employment policy were those of the inter-war years and of the Second World War itself; after 1974, the historical base-line moves forward, and policy choices tend to be made by way of reaction to the events and political decisions of the period 1970 to 1974. We shall see that this was as true for the Labour governments of 1974 to 1979 as for the post-1979 Conservative governments. We can say that, so far as labour law itself was concerned, in 1971 the whole post-war voluntarist legal structure, indeed the whole post-1871 peacetime legal structure, was both formally and substantively replaced by the Industrial Relations Act, and was not subsequently reconstituted in its previous form although the Act was repealed in 1974. We could therefore say that collective *laissez-faire*, and the particular set of legal and corporatist dispositions which it involved or depended upon, were abandoned between 1970 and 1974. These are the developments we shall consider in the course of this chapter, but before we do so in detail it is worth pursuing slightly further the questions of why these were watershed years, and what interplay of circumstances and policies made them so.

We saw in Chapter 4 how Harold Wilson's Labour governments of 1964 and 1966 responded to the deepening crisis of the British economy by seeking ways to modernize that economy, and that the attempts to do so resulted in important changes to the structure of labour law, especially though not solely in the field of individual employment law. The responses of Edward Heath's Conservative government, and their choices as to how to seek to modernize the economy, were crucially different, with even more momentous consequences for the development of labour law. The presence of economic crisis required governments to address questions which had been much less sharply posed in the easier conditions of, for example, the 1950s. Governments now had to take much harder decisions than before as to how far they could maintain the commitments which were integral to the post-war settlement of industrial society—above all, the commitments to full employment, to free collective bargaining, and to the welfare state—and as to their priorities between these commitments in so far as they could not maintain all of them fully. They had to decide how far to become or remain interventionist or *dirigiste* in pursuing these goals and reconciling them with the control of inflation, of public expenditure, and of the balance of payments. In the end, they had to estimate where, among these choices, the greatest political risks lay, and how those risks could best be minimized or most safely be taken. Edward Heath's government faced great problems, adopted radical strategies, and was confronted by the high-risk nature of those strategies, especially in the field of labour law.

It is important to identify the underlying differences between these strategies and those of the preceding governments. We have, after all, thus far been more aware of similarities than of differences. Edward Heath was, for example, more or less as concerned as his predecessor to maintain full employment and the welfare state, and had to be equally concerned with controlling inflation. The experiment in legislative reform of industrial relations, which his party's election manifesto promised, did not seem totally dissimilar from the *In Place of Strife* proposals. These similarities are, however, to some extent misleading. For whereas Harold Wilson's government had sought to achieve modernization by planning and intervention, Edward Heath's aim was to achieve it by a progressive disengagement of the state from the management of the industrial economy, and by the fostering of an enterprise economy which would power and support itself. The state would provide technical expertise to this end, and would by its own example set the style of managerial efficiency; but it would modernize by liberation rather than by command. This was the essence of Edward Heath's self-proclaimed 'Quiet Revolution'; it prefigured much that was to happen in the 1980s.

The crucial feature of this programme, from the point of view of the development of labour law, is that Edward Heath regarded the legislative regulation of collective bargaining and of industrial relations as an essential concomitant of this otherwise neo-liberal programme. This explains the strength and centrality of the manifesto commitment to a comprehensive Industrial Relations Bill. Where Harold Wilson's government had hoped on the whole to retain a voluntarist system of labour law in a planned economy (though they had experienced considerable difficulty in fitting incomes policy into this strategy), Edward Heath had the diametrically opposite intentions of securing legally regulated collective industrial relations in the framework of a self-regulating industrial economy and a free labour market. This was conceived of as a radical strategy, but as a low-risk one; Edward Heath was optimistic that it would provide a sound basis for taking the UK into the European Economic Community with a competitive economy, that success would thereafter breed success, and that the legal regulation of industrial relations would be seen to have justified itself, and would become uncontroversial.

That this grand design dramatically failed to work is in no small part due to the troubles over the Industrial Relations Act, the enactment and implementation of which irreparably damaged relations between the government and the trade union movement. From early 1972 onwards, the government, faced with unacceptably rapid inflation and unwilling to take the political risks of letting unemployment rise to pre-war levels, felt itself forced, not only to make the famous 'U-turn' away from non-intervention in industry, but also to seek a renewed set of corporatist strategies involving the trade unions as well as employers. But for all their offers to 'put the Industrial Relations Act on ice', they were to discover that the Act would stand firmly as an obstacle in the middle of the corporatist path for the remainder of their term of office. The supposedly low-risk strategy turned out to be a high-risk one, which could not be rescued despite all the interventions designed to secure positive control over the labour economy in the final two years of this ill-fated government.

Although therefore the instrument of an unsuccessful strategy, the Industrial Relations Act nevertheless brought about the most profound changes in the state of labour law and of the relations between governments, employers, and trade unions. Not only did it mark an apparently irreversible move away from collective *laissez-faire*, but it also powerfully demonstrated the interdependence of government policies in the areas of labour law, employment, and the control of inflation. This was truly a watershed, to the extent that all the subsequent history of labour legislation has had those developments as its main starting-point. In this chapter, we therefore concentrate initially upon the Industrial Relations Act itself, but go on to relate that discussion to other kinds of legislation and measures directed at controlling the labour economy in the period from 1970 to 1974.

7.2. LEGISLATING FOR INDUSTRIAL RELATIONS, 1971-1974

The Industrial Relations Act was, as we have seen, to a very great extent the carrying into execution of strategies identified in the policy document of 1968, *Fair Deal at Work*.[1] In retrospect, it is clear that this was the first of a series of such documents in which political parties recognized that their own credibility as parties of government depended upon convincing the electorate that they could acquire and retain control over industrial society. *Fair Deal at Work* embodied the conclusion that this could only

---

[1] See above, p. 248.

or best be achieved by a great increase in legal intervention; it is essentially a programme for the juridification of power relationships in industrial society. While acknowledging that 'success or failure in this field depends principally on human behaviour, not the law',[2] the authors of *Fair Deal at Work* stress that 'We have seen our main task as being to concentrate on those problems which we believe can be alleviated by direct government action through legislation and other means.'[3]

The doctrine which was thus evident in 'Fair Deal at Work' and fully carried through to the 1971 Act proclaimed that if only the legal structuring of industrial society was sufficiently extensive and systematic, it would bring about orderly and responsible conduct. The success of labour law systems in countries such as Sweden and, in a certain sense, the USA was thought to be due to those qualities, which were encapsulated in the idea of 'comprehensiveness'. The document's conclusions about the lessons to be learned from other labour law systems are summed up under the heading of 'Benefits of comprehensive legislation',[4] and Mr Carr's Foreword (he being Shadow Spokesman on Labour at that time, and Secretary of State for Employment from 1970 onwards) speaks of the gains to be expected from 'comprehensive modernisation along the lines proposed'. By November 1970, introducing the Consultative Document on the Industrial Relations Bill, he went so far as to say that: 'every other industrial country but Britain has already found both in theory and in practice that a comprehensive system of industrial law is useful and, indeed, necessary.'[5]

This commitment to legislative 'comprehensiveness' had very significant effects. It helps to explain some internal inconsistencies within the 1971 legislation—those, for instance, which led Clark and Wedderburn to suggest that 'the Act . . . might be the work of two "phantom" draftsmen':[6]

The first may be thought of as a civil servant or 'organization man' concerned mainly to bring 'order' and a tidy structure into collective

---

[2] *Fair Deal at Work*, 10.
[3] Ibid. 11.
[4] Ibid. 17.
[5] HC Deb., 5th ser. vol. 807, col. 633 (26 Nov. 1970).
[6] In Lord Wedderburn, R. Lewis, and J. Clark, eds., *Labour Law and Industrial Relations: Building on Kahn-Freund* (Oxford, 1983), 135.

industrial relations. The second is quite different, a Conservative lawyer imbued above all else with doctrines of individual rights, often without regard to the shop floor problems of collective bargaining.[7]

The second, individualist, tendency was the longer-standing one; it was deeply-rooted in the political thought, or at least the political impulses, of the Conservative Party; it certainly shaped the mid-1950s policy document, *A Giant's Strength*, which we encountered earlier.[8] The first of the two tendencies to which Wedderburn and Clark refer was in fact a later development; it was superimposed upon the earlier one, a stratum of juridification, a set of responses to the perceived disorders in industrial society—and above all to the perception that if the Conservative Party was to re-establish its 1950s position as the party of government, it must have and be seen to have a way of imposing order upon industrial relations. The friction between these two layers of policy was an example of a frequently occurring dilemma, for governments aspiring to some form of liberal democracy, as to how to balance individual rights with 'law and order'.

In fact, so much did this dilemma become common to governments of both parties that one can see at least the period of 1968–79 as one in which governments sought to combine a framework for order in industrial society with a process for upholding individual rights and expectations. If that was a problem common to successive governments, it was one which was singular to government and did not concern the parties to industrial relations to nearly the same extent. The Labour Government's White Paper, *In Place of Strife*, by seeking to address this problem, brought itself into sharp conflict with the trade union movement. Although the Conservative government's proposals for addressing the same complex of problems, in their Industrial Relations Bill, did not involve a corresponding outright conflict with employers, they certainly did diverge significantly from employers' perceptions as to what changes should be made, as expressed through the CBI. Michael Moran shows very effectively how marked this divergence was, in relation, for example, to the relative power and importance to be accorded to

---

[7] Ibid., quoting from Wedderburn in 'Labour Law and Labour Relations in Britain' (1972) 10 BJIR 270, 282.

[8] See above, pp. 129 and 143.

the National Industrial Relations Court (favoured by the government) and the Registrar of Trade Unions (favoured by the CBI because it could have a more discretionary role).[9]

This divergence between the situation of the government and that of the 'social partners'—in this instance, the employers—is highly significant. For the makers of the policies underlying the 1971 Act were motivated by considerations about the legitimation of the government in times of economic crisis, which were more fundamental and less pragmatic than the considerations which shaped employers' ideas about labour law reform. Employers, for the most part, were more concerned to salvage the better aspects of their existing industrial relations with trade unions and their own workforces. The government's more underlyingly radical intentions meant that its proposals would be less concerned to preserve any aspects of the existing culture and custom of industrial society. The whole presentation of the new proposals was overtly fundamentalist in its style and tone; that is partly why the trade union movement perceived the proposals as such a direct challenge to their own legitimacy. Hence they regarded the detailed proposals as anathema, though many of those proposals, taken one by one, seem favourable to the trade unions, at least by comparison with much of the labour legislation of the 1980s. Thus it came to seem ironical that an Act which the trade union movement regarded as systematically hostile to it could begin with the following commitment:

Section 1(1). The provisions of this Act shall have effect for the purpose of promoting good industrial relations in accordance with the following general principles, that is to say,—(a) the principle of collective bargaining freely conducted on behalf of workers and employers and with due regard to the general interests of the community.

But it was not really ironical for the trade union movement to feel threatened by an Act even beginning in that way, if the detailed provisions sought significantly to control the freedom to organize and take industrial action. Many of the Act's provisions did have that effect, and a number of different kinds of control were introduced. In the event, because the trade union movement challenged the whole strategy of the Industrial Relations

---

[9] The Registrar could in their view have been a 'Robens figure': Michael Moran, *The Politics of Industrial Relations*, (London, 1980), 79.

Act by means of a concerted refusal on the part of trade unions to be registered under the Act,[10] the controls on industrial action operated very differently from the way they were meant to, and a section of the Act which was meant to be marginal—section 96, which dealt with inducing breach of contract other than by registered unions—became pivotal. Meanwhile, the controls upon industrial action to which the powers of the legislation attached most importance were in various ways marginalized. So it is more than usually important not to infer the intentions of the legislators from the outcomes of their legislation. We shall look in detail first at the scheme which the legislators had in mind, and then at the rather different story of the Act in operation.

(a) The Industrial Relations Act 1971 and the Control of Industrial Relations

(i) Unofficial Industrial Action and the Idea of Comprehensiveness. The framers of the Industrial Relations Act 1971 had a central concern with the control of industrial relations. Securing some degree of control over industrial relations was perceived by the government as crucial to its political credibility and survival: the government had been elected on the promise that it could succeed in this respect where the Labour government had failed; it had come into office with a well-developed set of proposals for this purpose, based on the 1968 policy document, *Fair Deal at Work*. The framers of the Act, in approaching the task they had set themselves of asserting control over industrial relations by means of legislation, were influenced by many different ideas and proposals for change; but they seem in the end to have been guided by two overriding perceptions which shaped the instruments of control they sought to create. Both of these perceptions are expressed in the Second Reading speech with which Mr Robert Carr as Secretary of State for Employment introduced the Industrial Relations Bill in 1970. He put the first perception thus:

When one looks at industrial relations in Britain compared with other industrial countries, two outstanding features distinguish them. The first is that we are the only industrial country of any size which does not

[10] See Moran, *Politics of Industrial Relations*, p. 124 ff. (ch. 8, 'The Politics of Defiance').

already have a comprehensive system of industrial relations law. The types of systems vary considerably from one country to another, but every other industrial country but Britain has already found both in theory and in practice that a comprehensive system of industrial laws is useful and, indeed, necessary.[11]

This commitment to comprehensiveness—to a fundamental juridification of industrial relations—had major consequences for the formulations of the ways in which industrial action would be controlled. Firstly, it meant that the Government thought it necessary completely to replace the existing legislation about industrial action, that is to say, the trade union and trade dispute immunities contained in the Trade Disputes Acts 1906 and 1965. Secondly, it meant that it was regarded as appropriate to take a large number of measures to control industrial action; to legislate 'comprehensively' was to enact all those policies which had been identified as likely to contribute to the effective control of industrial action by law—perhaps with insufficient attention to their consistency with each other, or their cumulative effect. Thirdly, the commitment to 'comprehensiveness' involved an attempt to construct an industrial relations system which would be structured by a legal framework. The ambition of remodelling the industrial relations system—which may be implicit in any programme of controlling industrial action by legal means—was explicit, obvious, and prominent in the Industrial Relations Act. This legal framework was part of a larger economic framework for which Edward Heath had identified the following ambitions in *Fair Deal at Work*:

Such a framework would be able to withstand the pressures which have defeated previous attempts at an economic breakthrough: the critical balance of payments position, the difficulty of reconciling the concepts of full employment and free collective bargaining, the menace of rising prices and the inflationary scramble that ensues.[12]

The second perception which crucially shaped the provisions of the Industrial Relations Act in relation to the control of industrial relations was about the nature of the strike problem. The perception was that it was the unofficial 'wildcat' strikes typical in

[11] HC Deb., 5th ser. vol. 807, col. 633 (26 Nov. 1970).
[12] *Fair Deal at Work*, Preface.

private sector manufacturing industry that were at the heart of the problem. As Robert Carr put it:

The second outstanding feature [after the lack of a comprehensive system of industrial system of industrial relations law] which distinguishes industrial relations in Britain is that the overwhelming majority of our strikes are unofficial and/or unconstitutional. As the Donovan Commission said in paragraph 501 of its Report, 'The problem is peculiar to this country.' The typical British strike can still be small in scale and only last a few days. . . . Every time that there is a strike, there is disruption not only in the factory where it occurs but also in the factories of that company's customers and suppliers. These indirect effects are not recorded in the strike figures. Moreover, the typical British strike occurs at unpredictable times and often with little or no notice. There can be little doubt that, in a modern economy with highly capitalised production methods and a high degree of interdependence between one company and another, stability is increasingly important, and the frequent and unpredictable interruptions in production from which we suffer are particularly damaging.[13]

One of the ironies of the 1971 Act is that the 'strike problem', as it presented itself to government, was re-defining itself rapidly at the very time at which the Act was introduced; henceforth, the large-scale, official, public-sector disputes would have the greatest impact.[14] But the 1971 Act was undoubtedly based on a model of industrial relations in which unofficial sporadic shop-floor strike action was seen as the key problem.

The framers of the Industrial Relations Act therefore sought to control industrial action by putting in place a comprehensive legal framework for industrial relations in which the power to take industrial action would be effectively confined to trade unions 'acting responsibly' in their conduct of industrial relations. In order to achieve this, it was seen as necessary considerably to restrict the existing system of trade union and trade dispute immunities; it was felt that the existing immunities amounted to special privileges which created false assumptions about the legitimacy of industrial action. These problems were centred upon the immunity of trade unions and upon the definition of a

[13] HC Deb., 5th ser. vol. 807, cols. 633–4.
[14] See J. W. Durcan, W. E. J. McCarthy, and G. P. Redman, *Strikes in Post-War Britain: A Study of Stoppages of Work due to Industrial Disputes, 1946–73* (London, 1983), 168–71.

'trade dispute'. Thus it had been said in *Fair Deal at Work*, under the heading of 'Legal Definition of Industrial Disputes', that:

We believe this nettle should be grasped. We see no justification for granting special legal protection to combinations of employers or work people who induce, or take part in, certain types of dispute which, in modern conditions, we regard as neither necessary to support legitimate claims nor desirable in the national interest.[15]

In October 1970 Robert Carr told a delegation of TUC leaders, meeting with him to discuss the Consultative Document on the Industrial Relations Bill, that the Government's proposals rested on eight pillars which were irremovable. Many if not all of them related in some way to the control of industrial action; among them was the restriction of existing legal immunities possessed by the unions.[16]

(ii) Restricting Immunities.   This restriction of existing immunities was achieved in rather a complex way which both reflected the aim of the Act to create a whole new legal framework for industrial relations, and contributed to the unworkability of the Act in practice. The Trade Disputes Acts 1906 and 1965 were repealed outright.[17] This meant that trade unions were not in any sense protected defendants at common law; and that all immunities for unions or anybody engaging in industrial action depended wholly on the 1971 Act. The Act adopted a new concept—that of the 'industrial dispute'—which was more narrowly defined than 'trade dispute' had been,[18] particularly in that it no longer included disputes between workers and workers because it was felt that inter-union disputes should be excluded. Not only did the Act adopt a new concept—that of the industrial dispute—in place of the old concept of trade dispute, but it also accorded a new function to the concept. Action which was not 'in contemplation or furtherance of an industrial dispute' was totally exposed to liability at common law—without the former immunity accorded to trade unions by section 4 of the 1906 Act. In the thinking of those who formulated the Act, industrial action out-

---

[15] *Fair Deal at Work*, 30.
[16] Moran, *Politics of Industrial Relations*, 88.
[17] Industrial Relations Act 1971, s. 169 and sched. 9.
[18] Ibid., s. 167(1) 'industrial dispute', (5).

side the industrial dispute formula was so clearly not part of any legitimate industrial relations process that it was appropriate for it simply to be subject to full ordinary tort liability in the common law courts.

That was not, however, where the framers of the Act saw the main controls upon industrial action as lying. For industrial action *within* the industrial dispute formula no longer enjoyed the civil immunity previously accorded to industrial action within the trade dispute formula. Admittedly such action was the subject of immunity from common law tort liability, corresponding closely to the old trade dispute immunity.[19] But it was exposed to potential liability for a large number of 'unfair industrial practices' which were the functional equivalent of economic torts, and which were justiciable by the new National Industrial Relations Court which the Act set up to adjudicate upon them.[20] Some of these unfair industrial relations practices corresponded fairly closely with the common law torts;[21] in particular, section 96 set up an unfair industrial practice of inducement of or threat to induce breach of contract which was not unlike the common law tort; but the immunity accorded to trade unions in respect of section 96 was—in the event crucially—confined to those trade unions who were registered under the 1971 Act. So the proposal which had been contained in *Fair Deal at Work* and which had, perhaps surprisingly, won a majority in the Donovan Commission, to confine trade unions' immunity to registered unions, was in 1971 implemented in this rather intricate way.

In the event, the effect of section 96 was to expose trade unions to liability for inducing breach of both commercial and employment contracts, because most trade unions refused to be registered under the Act. This was not the intended effect, for the framers of the legislation had assumed that most if not all trade unions would be registered; they had intended section 96 to be unavailable against registered trade unions as the legitimate bearers of the power to organize industrial action, and to be a sanction against the usurping of that power by persons or *ad hoc* associations who were not in the view of the legislators the legitimate bearers of that power—that is to say, shop stewards

[19] Ibid., s. 132.
[20] Ibid., ss. 99, 101–5, 112.
[21] Ibid., ss. 96–8.

or committees of shop stewards organizing unofficial industrial action. The fact that section 96 was never intended to involve trade unions in a draconian analogue of common law tort liability is borne out by the absence of provisions about the organic or vicarious liability of trade unions under section 96 for the acts of their officials—which was in the event to open up a vast area of controversy.

There are positive as well as negative reasons for thinking that section 96 was not as central to the strategy of the Industrial Relations Act for controlling industrial action as it was, in the event, to appear. The framers of the Act had more radical objectives than would have been expressed in a simple re-invention of the common law of economic tort in the new guise of unfair industrial practices. They wanted to control industrial action by channelling it into the hands of 'responsible' trade unions operating within a framework of orderly, legally structured industrial relations procedures. The unfair industrial practices were designed to give effect to these heavily *dirigiste* objectives; they were, above all, directed against the sort of unofficial and 'unconstitutional' industrial action which the government thought was at the heart of the 'strike problem'. This necessitated the creation of a background of unfair industrial practice liabilities which echoed the common law economic torts, but these were subordinate in importance to other measures to which we now turn our attention.

(iii) Enforcing Collective Agreements.   In the perceptions of the framers of the 1971 Act, the central provisions for the control of industrial action were those concerned with the structure of collective bargaining. In their concept of the Act, perhaps the single most important set of unfair industrial practices was that contained in section 36, which dealt with breach of the collective agreement. If this was to be an operative provision in practice, it depended upon the presumption of legal enforceability of collective agreements imposed by section 34. In the event, just as the action of trade unions in refusing to be registered brought section 96 into unintended prominence, so the actions of employers in generally agreeing to the inclusion of express non-enforceability clauses in their collective agreements made section 36 almost a dead letter; this was, equally, a major deflection of the orienta-

tion of the legislation as a whole. Had the provisions of section 36 been a live issue, their application must surely have been intensely controversial, for the unfair industrial practices which were specified included not only breaking a legally enforceable collective agreement, but also failing to take all reasonably practicable steps to prevent any breach of the agreement by members of or by anybody acting or purporting to act on behalf of an organization party to the agreement.[22] It was in this way that the framers of the Act sought to address the problem of the unofficial unconstitutional strike; the primary standard of legitimacy of industrial action was to be that it should not be in violation of procedures contained in legally binding collective agreements, and registered trade unions were to be at once the sole bearers of power to organize such action and the agency responsible for policing the observance of agreements by their members and shop stewards.

This targeting of control of industrial action upon securing observance of legally binding procedure agreements is central to the whole strategy of the 1971 Act, and puts it in contrast with the quite differently and less specifically targeted controls upon industrial action provided by the common law of economic tort and of the contract of employment. It is fully consistent with this strategy that the framers of the 1971 Act were quite prepared, in section 147 of the Act which dealt with the effect of strike notice, to reverse by statute the common law rule (established by dicta in *Rookes* v. *Barnard*[23] and *Stratford* v. *Lindley*[24]) that strike notice normally amounted to repudiation of the contracts of employment and the strike itself to breach of the contracts of employment,[25] with this crucial proviso, that industrial action was not be regarded as other than in breach of the contract of employment where it was contrary to a no-strike obligation in the contract of employment—which would typically be incorporated in that contract by reference to the procedural provisions of a collective agreement.

The section 36 unfair industrial practices were closely bound up

[22] Ibid., s. 36(2).
[23] Donovan LJ in the Court of Appeal, [1963] 1 QB 623, 682–3; Lord Devlin in the House of Lords, [1964] AC 1129, 1204.
[24] Lord Denning MR in the Court of Appeal, [1965] AC 269, 285.
[25] Industrial Relations Act 1971, s. 147(1)(2), implementing a version of the decision of the Court of Appeal in *Morgan* v. *Fry* [1968] 2 QB 710.

with the aim of reforming collective bargaining in the direction of encouraging the development of legally binding procedure agreements which would create no-strike obligations. This close link between control of industrial action and restructuring of collective bargaining was intended to be further strengthened by another set of provisions, which proved in the event to be a dead-letter, namely the provisions of sections 37–43 of the Act, entitled 'remedial action where procedure agreement non-existent or defective'. These curious provisions sought to give concrete legal effect to the work of the Commission on Industrial Relations in investigating and reporting on procedural arrangements at plant and company level with a view to securing the adoption of better procedures and the achievement of more orderly industrial relations. These provisions enabled the Secretary of State for Employment or either party to an existing collective bargaining process to apply to the National Industrial Relations Court for a reference to the CIR to assess the defectiveness of existing procedural arrangements and recommend remedial action.[26] This was to lead in the first instance to action by the CIR to promote the voluntary adoption by the parties of adequate legally enforceable procedural agreements;[27] but if that did not succeed, the CIR was to make a report to the Industrial Court[28] and an employer or trade union, party to the original reference to the CIR, could apply to the NIRC on the basis of that report for an order directing that the recommended procedural provisions should 'have effect as a legally enforceable contract, as if a contract, consisting of those provisions, had been made between those parties'.[29] This elaborate process for the imposition of procedures fictitiously deemed to be procedure agreements would, if operated, have created no-strike obligations enforceable via the unfair industrial practices created by section 36; the restructuring of industrial relations procedures and the control of industrial action would have been mutually reinforcing.

(*vi*) *Statutory Recognition Procedure.* The aim of relating the control of industrial action to the restructuring of industrial relations also underlay one of the most important sets of pro-

---

[26] Industrial Relations Act, s. 37.
[27] Ibid., s. 39.
[28] Ibid., s. 40.
[29] Ibid., s. 41.

visions in the Act, namely sections 44–50, which dealt with the recognition of trade unions as sole bargaining agents for specified workgroups. The policy document *Fair Deal at Work* had identified non-recognition of a trade union by the employer as one of the causes of industrial disputes which it wished to address by legislation;[30] and had gone on to identify the fact that 'in many cases the nub of the problem lies in an inter-union dispute: where the employer recognises one or several unions but not a particular one which is claiming representation'.[31] Inter-union disputes were to be excluded from the new legal definition of 'industrial dispute'; but the policy document acknowledged that the practical problem would remain, and also the point of principle that:

It is just as wrong for an employer to refuse to recognise a union which can claim reasonable representation in his establishment as it is for a union without reasonable representation to try to force its way to the bargaining table by threats of strike action on the part of a few key personnel who belong to it.[32]

The Industrial Relations Act set up a statutory procedure to address this problem which was quite closely modelled on the National Labour Relations Board statutory procedure in the USA. It enabled a registered union or grouping of registered unions to apply to the Industrial Court for a reference to the Commission on Industrial Relations as to the suitability of recognizing that union or group as the sole bargaining agent for a specified collective bargaining unit.[33] Upon a favourable report from the CIR, there could be an application to the Industrial Court for a ballot of the workers in the bargaining unit concerned; and upon approval of the recommendation by a simple majority of workers voting, the Industrial Court would make an order for the recognition of the sole bargaining agent.[34] This would place the employer under an obligation, analogous to the 'good-faith bargaining' obligation of the Wagner Act, 'to take all such action by way of or with a view to carrying on collective bargaining as might reasonably be expected to be taken by an

---

[30] *Fair Deal at Work*, 41.
[31] Ibid. 44.   [32] Ibid.
[33] Industrial Relations Act, ss. 45, 46.
[34] Ibid., ss. 48–50.

employer ready and willing to carry on such collective bargaining'
and would make it an unfair industrial practice for him to fail
to do so[35] or to bargain with any other trade union.[36] The
employer's failure to carry out his recognition obligations to
engage in collective bargaining was subject to the sanction of an
order of the Industrial Court for reference of the trade union's
claim to the Industrial Arbitration Board.[37] The registered trade
union thus having been given access to a statutorily protected
role in a legally structured industrial relations system, it was seen
as appropriate to impose a set of controls upon industrial action
violating the constraints of that system. Section 55 made it an
unfair industrial practice to take or threaten industrial action to
induce an employer not to engage in collective bargaining with a
sole bargaining agent or to induce a bargain with a rival union.

(v) *The Closed Shop.*   Just as the provisions of the Industrial
Relations Act 1971 with regard to trade union recognition
represent an attempt to combine the legal restructuring of
industrial relations with the legal control of industrial action, so
also do its provisions concerned with the closed shop. In the eyes
of Conservative Party policy-makers, the closed shop was a
powerful contributor to unacceptable patterns of industrial
relations and unacceptable uses of trade union industrial power.
This is well illustrated by the following, very revealing, passage in
the 1958 document, *A Giant's Strength*:

So far we have discussed the strike for better wages and conditions, and
have argued that in a free economy it is socially and economically
justified. But as we said at the start of this chapter, strikes vary widely in
character and not all strikes fall into this category. We turn, therefore, to
discuss some of the strikes which fall outside it. Empire-building strike.
First there is the strike, not directly for better pay or conditions, but
against other unions. Such are the strikes to resolve whether a certain
job shall be done by the members of one union or another; or to break
a rival union, whether one already in existence or one newly formed as
a splinter of the other; or to establish a new union or an old union in a
new place or a new grade. Closely allied is the strike to establish a closed
shop. The strike is thus an instrument of trade union empire-building.[38]

[35] Ibid., s. 55(1)(b).
[36] Ibid., s. 55(1)(a).
[37] Ibid., s. 105(5).
[38] *A Giant's Strength*, 24–5.

In the policy document, *Fair Deal at Work*, the concerns expressed in *A Giant's Strength* have been elaborated into a programme for legal restructuring of the closed shop. It was proposed that:

strikes called, or threatened, with the predominant purpose either of forcing non-unionists to join a union or of obtaining the dismissal of non-unionists should not be protected as lawful 'trade disputes'.[39]

But a distinction was drawn between the pre-entry closed shop, and the post-entry closed shop or 'union shop', on the ground that the latter had a less undermining effect upon managerial authority and efficiency:

[S]ince trade unions—and in many trades, local branches or chapels— often make their own working rules, this situation [in which, in a pre-entry closed shop, the union has a powerful say in the recruitment of labour] can mean that production methods, job-allocation and general conditions of work are controlled more by employees than by management. This can also happen in a 'union shop', but here the pressures on management are less powerful because it retains greater authority in the engagement of labour.[40]

Fair Deal at Work therefore went on to make proposals which would allow post-entry or 'union shop' agreements to function, subject to a number of safeguards for individual workers. The safeguards included the adoption of the model of the 'agency shop' agreement extensively found in the USA whereby conscientious objectors to union membership would have the alternative of paying an amount equal to the minimum union dues into some agreed fund:

This might normally be, as in the United States, to the appropriate union itself on the clear understanding that this did not constitute membership or invest the union with any other rights in relation to the employee concerned. Alternatively, in exceptional cases, opportunity should be given to subscribe this amount to a charity.[41]

Such a 'union shop agreement' had to have the support of a majority of employees in a secret ballot.

This plan for legal restructuring of the closed shop was im-

---

[39] *Fair Deal at Work*, 27.
[40] Ibid. 24.
[41] Ibid. 26.

plemented in the Industrial Relations Act. Section 7 rendered pre-entry closed-shop agreements void. Section 5 conferred upon workers, on the one hand the right to belong to a trade union of their choice and to take part in its activities and on the other hand what the framers of the Act regarded as the 'equal right to choose not to belong to a trade union'.[42] This was, in aim at least, an important instrument of legal restructuring, firstly because the positive rights of freedom of association, which it provided, arose only in relation to registered trade unions; and secondly because its right of freedom to disassociate, which arose in relation to any trade union, registered or not, was qualified by exemptions for certain types of post-entry agreements by which the framers of the Act sought to bring about restructuring in conformity with its approved models. There had originally been intended to be just one legally approved model, that of the agency shop agreement, for which provision was made by sections 11–15. In the event, the government responded to pressure from trade unions, representing in particular actors and merchant seamen, to the effect that the continuance of effective collective bargaining and trade union representation in those occupations depended upon more extensive exemption for post-entry closed shops. Amendments were permitted which, enacted in sections 17–18, provided for the Secretary of State for Employment to confer authorization upon 'approved closed shop agreements', subject to stringent conditions of joint application by employers and trade unions and balloted approval by the workforce concerned by at least a simple majority of those eligible to vote or a two-thirds majority of those voting.[43] So in its final form the Industrial Relations Act put forward two models for union security arrangements; its own preferred model of the agency shop with the alternative of paying the equivalent of a membership subscription without belonging to the union, and the approved closed shop which did not have to offer that alternative. The former model was scarcely adopted in practice.

Again, as with the trade union recognition provisions, the Act sought to combine legal restructuring of industrial relations with

[42] DEP Press Notice, 3 Dec. 1970, p. 1. The presentation by Robert Carr on Second Reading was rather confused on this point: HC Deb., 5th ser., vol. 808, col. 965 (14 Dec. 1970).

[43] Industrial Relations Act 1971, s. 17 and sched. I.

legal control of industrial action, and to make that restructuring and that control reinforce each other. Instead of the simple exclusion of industrial action in support of the closed shop from the ambit of trade dispute immunity (as favoured in *Fair Deal at Work*), the Act identified as unfair industrial practices the organizing or threatening of industrial action challenging its restructured closed shop arrangements in a number of specific ways. These included the key provisions of section 33, which dealt with industrial action for the purpose of placing pressure on an employer to infringe the rights of workers under section 5,[44] and section 16, headed 'pressure to anticipate result of ballot', which dealt with industrial action inducing an employer to enter into an agency shop agreement after an application had been made to the Industrial Court under section 11 for a ballot to approve an agency shop. As with the provisions for linking control of industrial action to the making of legally enforceable collective agreements, these provisions too were rendered largely inoperative by the preference of employers to acquiesce in the continuance of existing closed-shop practices; but the way in which the Act was designed to link re-structuring of those practices with control of industrial action in support of the closed shop remains highly significant to the extensive subsequent history of measures directed at the closed shop and industrial action associated with it.

(*vi*) *Secondary and Sympathetic Industrial Action.*   In a number of the areas we have so far considered, the Industrial Relations Act sought to align provisions for restructuring industrial relations with provisions for controlling industrial action. In one area at least, the attempt was made to accomplish the restructuring directly by means of the control of industrial action: this was in relation to secondary or sympathetic industrial action. The Conservative Party had for a long time been concerned about this type or method of industrial action. The policy document *A Giant's Strength* addressed the question whether sympathetic and secondary strikes should be regarded in the same way as political or general strikes. The document concluded that political strikes should clearly be pronounced to be illegal, but that while the

---

[44] Ibid., s. 5(3).

power to strike sympathetically was 'almost certainly unnecessary', it should nevertheless be dealt with by the mandatory conciliation procedures that the authors were proposing for strikes generally, rather than by special provisions.[45] By the time of *Fair Deal at Work*, the concern had became more acute, and led to the view that the definition of a trade dispute should be narrowed so as to exclude 'Sympathetic strikes or lock-outs and the practice of blacking the goods or services of a different employer who is not in dispute with his employees'.[46]

The framers of the Industrial Relations Act, as we have seen, chose the method at various points of leaving certain types of industrial action within the concept of 'industrial dispute' but designating them as unfair industrial practices and thus subject to sanctions administered by the Industrial Court. The Consultative Document on the Industrial Relations Bill had accordingly proposed that:

The following kinds of 'secondary' industrial action would be unfair industrial actions. First, to threaten or induce industrial action in support of any such action which is itself unfair (for any of the reasons given elsewhere in this document). Secondly, even where the original industrial action was not unfair, the Government intends that it should be unfair for anyone to threaten or induce industrial action to persuade any other person not to enter into or perform a commercial contract, unless that person is himself participating in, or directly interested in or supporting any party to the industrial dispute which gave rise to the original industrial action.[47]

These proposals were substantially implemented in sections 97 (industrial action in support of unfair industrial practice) and 98 (industrial action against extraneous parties). As with a number of the Act's provisions, these were largely neglected in practice because employers and trade unions did not act in the way the legislators had intended or predicted. By refusing to be registered under the Act, most trade unions made themselves vulnerable to section 96, which had not been intended to be available against them; the more specific controls upon industrial action contained in sections 97 and 98 were therefore scarcely relied upon. They

---

[45] *A Giant's Strength*, 26–7.
[46] *Fair Deal at Work*, 30.
[47] Consultative Document, para. 71.

nevertheless foreshadow a controversy about the legitimacy of sympathetic and secondary industrial action which was to continue in one form or another through the 1970s and 1980s.

(*vii*) *Emergency Procedures.* Thus far, the provisions of the Industrial Relations Act we have considered have this in common, that, having where necessary made provision for the restructuring of the relevant industrial relations systems, they relied on civil proceedings, normally by employers, as the method of implementing their controls upon industrial action. The experience of major industrial disputes in the 1960s, especially the 1966 seamen's strike and the 1967 dock strikes, persuaded Conservative Party policy-makers (and for that matter Labour Party policy-makers too) that industrial action posed problems of control for governments which could not be sufficiently resolved by the reform of industrial relations procedures, whether imposed by law or not, or by the reintroduction of civil sanctions. Such measures would not touch a national strike which was official trade union action, not in breach of collectively agreed procedures, but which was nevertheless unacceptably damaging, so far as the government was concerned, to the economy or the life of the community. By 1968, the policy document *Fair Deal at Work* embodied the conclusions that the powers of the Ministry of Labour to appoint a Court of Inquiry were not sufficiently coercive, while the statutory powers to declare a State of Emergency to safeguard essential supplies and services were too circumscribed by being available only in circumstances which were too extreme.[48] Hence there was felt to be a need for new powers of governmental intervention to control industrial action.

The authors of *Fair Deal at Work* were clearly much influenced by the system in force in the USA by which, under the Taft–Hartley Act, the President could, if he considered that a dispute might 'imperil national health or safety', appoint a fact-finding Board of Inquiry and then instruct the Attorney-General to secure an 80-day injunction to stop a strike or lockout, after 60 days of which the National Labour Relations Board would if necessary put the employer's latest offer to a ballot of employees. *Fair Deal at Work* concluded that 'a record of success in

[48] *Fair Deal at Work*, 37, 40; and see above, p. 93.

nearly three out of four cases provides a powerful argument in favour of the system . . . It would be less extreme, and therefore more useable, than the ultimate action of declaring a state of emergency.'[49]

In the Industrial Relations Act itself, these proposals were implemented in the form of two distinct sets of emergency procedures or powers conferred upon the Secretary of State for Employment, capable of being used cumulatively in relation to one dispute; they were so used, as we shall see later, with results rather unsatisfactory to the Government, in relation to the ASLEF industrial action on the railways in 1972. The first power, contained in sections 138 and 141, was for the Secretary of State to apply to the Industrial Court for an order for discontinuing or deferring industrial action for up to 60 days. The conditions for such a 'cooling-off' order were *inter alia* that industrial action had begun or was threatened which was likely gravely to injure the national economy, imperil national security, create a serious risk of public disorder, endanger the lives of a substantial number of people, or expose them to a serious risk of disease or injury.[50]

The second set of powers, contained in sections 141 to 145, enabled the Secretary of State for Employment to apply to the Industrial Court for an order requiring a ballot relating to industrial action where he was satisfied either that there were emergency circumstances as defined in section 138 or that there was a threat to the livelihood of a substantial number of workers in the particular industry, and in either case that there was reasonable doubt whether the industrial action had the support of the workers involved, and whether they had had adequate opportunity to express their wishes.[51] It was for the Industrial Court to define the area to be covered by the ballot, the question to be put, the period allowed for its conduct, and the provisions for determining the workers eligible to vote.[52] The use of this second procedure in the ASLEF dispute resulted in a substantial majority voting in favour of industrial action, which was rather a rebuff to the government and indicated to later Conservative governments that it was inadvisable to provide for or rely upon

[49] Ibid., 40.
[50] Industrial Relations Act 1971, s. 138(2).
[51] Ibid., s. 141(1), (2).
[52] Ibid., s. 142(1)–(4).

direct legal intervention using executive powers in industrial disputes. These subsequent developments made the Emergency Procedures part of the Industrial Relations Act seem rather isolated; it is nevertheless the case that, for the framers of the legislation themselves, this was a significant and integral part of the grand design for controlling industrial action.

(*viii*) *Trade Union Registration and Guiding Principles.* The emergency procedures concentrated upon the direct control of industrial action rather than the restructuring of industrial relations. No doubt they reflected the view that industrial action in major disputes should be avoided or at least preceded by full conciliation measures and by a secret ballot to ensure majority support within the union for the industrial action concerned. But they reflect an acceptance that it was appropriate to impose these requirements only by way of reserve powers to control particular instances of major industrial action rather than by way of systematic reconstruction. By contrast, another, centrally important, set of provisions of the Industrial Relations Act can be seen as aiming to control industrial action entirely indirectly by means of legal restructuring of industrial relations, rather than by means of direct controls upon particular instances of industrial action; these are the provisions for the registration and conduct of trade unions in part IV of the Act. We have seen that an important part of the programme for the legal control of industrial action which the Act was intended to implement consisted in effectively confining the power to organize and authorize industrial action to registered trade unions, and that section 96 was the main provision directed specifically to that aim. The underlying purpose of section 96 was to confine the power of industrial action to trade unions 'acting responsibly in the public interest', and part IV of the Act contained the mechanisms intended to ensure that trade unions would act responsibly in the public interest as a condition of obtaining and maintaining registered status.

The interconnection between trade union registration and the control of industrial action was made very clear in Robert Carr's presentation of the Consultative Document on the Industrial Relations Bill to the House of Commons, when he said:

There will be clear statutory confirmation for registered unions of their full rights and protection in calling and carrying on fair industrial action.

What we are asking from the trade unions in return are, above all, two things. First we are asking them to accept registration. Trade unions are voluntary associations of free members, and so they will remain. They ought to be able to make their own rules and so they shall. But they are not just horticultural societies or angling clubs. They are major institutions claiming and exercising, and rightly claiming and exercising, great influence in our economy and society. Surely it is fair and right that any voluntary association which claims to do that should be prepared to accept some authority of approval to make sure that its rules include certain basic standards in the public interest and in the interest of its members, and some supervision to make sure that those basic rules are observed. . . .

Secondly, we ask trade unions to accept that some kinds of industrial action are unfair to the community at large and that they must therefore accept liability for the harm which they do to other people against whom they direct such unfair actions.[53]

There is scope for debate about how far the requirements for obtaining and maintaining registration as a trade union were themselves directed at the control of industrial action. Part IV of the Act laid down guiding principles for the conduct of trade unions[54] and made it a condition of maintaining registration that the rules of the union be consistent with those principles, by setting up a procedure for the cancellation of registration by the Industrial Court at the instance of the Registrar of Trade Unions if the rules remained defective in this respect.[55] The guiding principles were laid down by section 65: they dealt with the position of individual workers in relation to the union, covering applications for and termination of membership, the rights to nominate for, seek, and hold office, to vote without constraint, to take part in meetings, and to institute proceedings and give evidence before a court or tribunal; the secrecy of ballots; and disciplinary proceedings. They made various requirements that the trade union should act fairly and reasonably towards the individual member or applicant, avoid arbitrary discrimination, and implement the procedural principles of natural justice. Although apparently largely concerned with the protection of the individual worker against oppressive behaviour by the trade

---

[53] HC Deb., 5th ser., vol. 807, cols. 644–5 (26 Nov. 1970).
[54] Industrial Relations Act 1971, s. 65.
[55] Ibid., ss. 75–6.

unions, the guiding principles are nevertheless also significantly concerned with the use by the union of its industrial action powers; thus the control upon unfair or unreasonable disciplinary action by the trade union, contained in section 65, was particularly defined to include disciplinary action on the ground of the member's refusal or failure to take part in industrial action which would constitute or involve an unfair industrial practice on the part of the member or the union.[56] A registered union was, under the provisions of part IV of the Act, susceptible to complaint by an individual member, ex-member, or applicant, to the Registrar of an unfair industrial practice consisting of violating the guiding principles in relation to that person; the Registrar had powers to investigate such a complaint and ultimately present it to the Industrial Court.[57] So registration involved a specific control by the Registrar over trade union discipline relating to refusal to take part in industrial action.

Moreover, part IV of the Act also involved the scrutiny of the rules of registered trade unions to ensure that they were and remained in compliance with the Rules Requirements of schedule IV of the Act.[58] The Rules Requirements were in general directed towards ensuring that the rules made provisions to deal with a number of matters concerned with the union's constitution and management, its members, and its property and finances. So these Rules Requirements seem to be largely concerned with the sound and constitutional administration of the union and the protection of the interests of individual members or applicants. But again, as with the Guiding Principles, there are indications of a special concern with the control of industrial action; thus, it was specifically required that:

'The rules must specify any body by which, and any official by whom, instructions may be given to members of the organisation on its behalf for any kind of industrial action, and the circumstances in which any such instructions may be so given.[59]

This requirement was crucial to the aim of making sure that the registered trade union would be the sole bearer of the power to

[56] Ibid., s. 65(7).
[57] Ibid., ss. 81–3.
[58] Ibid., ss. 75(1)(c), 77(1).
[59] Ibid., sched. IV, para. 10.

take industrial action, and would be accountable for the exercise of that power other than 'responsibly in the public interest'. So although it is by no means the case that the provisions of part IV of the Act were engineered entirely to this aim, nevertheless the control of industrial action was a significant concern of this part of the legislation also. Moreover, as in many other parts of the 1971 Act, the aim was to increase that control by means of a legal restructuring of industrial relations practices; in this case, the practice of the internal government of the trade unions themselves, and their relations with individual members and other workers. Having at a number of points in this discussion of the provisions of the Act observed that the Act in practice would seem very different from the Act in theory, we go on to look in some detail at the outcomes of this legislation.

(b) The Industrial Relations Act in Operation: The Problems of Comprehensiveness

The period of operation of the Industrial Relations Act was a short one. Technically on the Statute Book for just under three years from 1971 until its repeal by the Trade Union and Labour Relations Act in 1974, its period of full operation was, apart from the unfair dismissal provisions, even shorter. Some of its provisions did not come into force until 1972[60] and many were effectively a dead-letter by the end of that year, the Act having been 'put on ice'[61] to try to reduce the confrontation between the government and the trade union movement to which it had by then extensively contributed. Short though it was, the period of the operation of the Industrial Relations Act was fraught with consequences for the development of labour legislation in the rest of the 1970s and the 1980s. In very different ways, the Labour governments of 1974 to 1979 and Conservative Governments from 1979 onwards shaped their labour legislation according to their perceptions of the lessons to be learnt from this period. Those perceptions were fundamentally divergent, save in agreeing that the operation of the Act had been a great failure from

---

[60] See, for an account of the interesting confusion about whether the Emergency Procedures of the Act were in force in time for the 1972 Miners' Dispute (in which they were not actually used), B. Weekes et al. Industrial Relations and the Limits of Law (Oxford, 1975), 227.

[61] As to the meaning and significance of this, see later in this subsection.

the point of view of the government, a failure which had on no account to be repeated. The problems which gave rise to that agreement can best be understood as the problems of comprehensiveness.

We have already seen how the framers of the Act deliberately embarked upon a comprehensive programme of legal reform of industrial relations, and put forward that comprehensiveness both as a distinctive feature of the programme and as the one most likely to ensure its overall success in getting industrial action under control and in creating an acceptable system of industrial relations. In the event, it was that very comprehensiveness which made the Act an ultimately unstoppable engine of discord and confrontation between the government and the trade union movement. This was true in a number of different ways which we need to consider in turn. The first of the problems of comprehensiveness reaches back into the process of formulating the Industrial Relations Bill and its passage through Parliament, but also extends forward into the period of operation of the Act; it is the way in which the comprehensiveness of the Act elevated the legal reform of industrial relations on to a constitutional plane, thereby greatly raising political investment in the success of the Act. In 1968 the Conservative Party in opposition decided, perhaps in order to sustain and improve its own morale, to publish its plan for the comprehensive legal reform of industrial relations in time to pre-empt the Donovan Report, in the hope of thereby gaining a commanding position as the outcome of the Donovan Debate was determined. This ensured that *Fair Deal at Work* had the role of a manifesto for the next election. In 1970, Edward Heath was moved by the Labour government's crisis over its *In Place of Strife* proposals to seek an electoral mandate to implement *Fair Deal at Work* as a way of restoring the constitutional authority of government over the trade union movement, and he assumed that the election victory was to be interpreted as conferring that mandate. For these reasons, the Industrial Relations Bill was presented in 1970 very much as a ready-made package, and the integrity of the package was identified as a matter of constitutional significance.

The comprehensiveness and integrality[62] of the *Fair Deal at*

---

[62] In the perceptions of its authors; for discussion of other perceptions that it lacked internal consistency, see later in this subsection.

Work framework of law for industrial relations, which made its enactment seem to Edward Heath a matter of high constitutional significance,[63] also dictated, as we have seen,[64] a fairly peremptory approach to consultation with trade unions, and for that matter employers, about the details of the proposed legislation. This amounted to more than mere impatience with the delays and complexities of tripartism and corporatist consensus politics. It reflected Edward Heath's perception that the Conservative government could and should govern in the interests of the community as a whole, and that it was of the essence of the comprehensive legal framework for industrial relations that it was not arrived at by consulting the sectional preferences of trade unions or employers.[65] For Edward Heath, the fate of the Labour government's *In Place of Strife* proposals demonstrated both the unwisdom and the impropriety of proceeding in the latter way. Given this view, it was fully explicable that Robert Carr should bring the process of consultation with the TUC about the Bill to an abrupt conclusion before it ever got under way by announcing that the proposals had eight pillars which were irremovable.[66]

All this had profound consequences for the Industrial Relations Act when it came into operation. In the first instance, it shaped events during the passage of the Bill through Parliament. The trade union movement, feeling comprehensively threatened by the content of the Bill and comprehensively rebuffed by the unwillingness of the Government to negotiate its terms, embarked upon an equally comprehensive programme of resistance to the Bill.[67] As the trade union campaign against the Bill became increasingly militant, it tended to split into two

[63] Michael Young says that Mr Heath's 'high-minded and governmental style of opposition meant that he came to power over-armed with policies'(*Contemporary Record*, 3/2(Nov. 1989), 24).

[64] See above, Sect. 7.1.

[65] Michael Yong, *Contemporary Record*, 3/2, 24. Geoffrey Goodman expressed the same view more trenchantly: 'In 1970, Heath promised a break with post-war consensus politics . . . It was all very Thatcherite' (*Contemporary Reecord*, 4: 1 (Sept. 1990), 36).

[66] See above, Subsect. 7.2(*a*).

[67] Perhaps the best account of this, and the most cogent exposition of its significance, is to be found in Moran, *Politics of Industrial Relations*, (London, 1977) ch. 5, 'The Politics of Consultation', ch. 7, 'The Campaigns Against the Bill', and ch. 8, 'The Politics of Defiance'.

levels. At one level, there was mass protest and unofficial strike action;[68] at another level, the TUC became the co-ordinating force in a campaign which, in Michael Moran's argument, matched the constitutional concerns of Edward Heath and and Robert Carr with a countervailing and rather effective constitutionalism of its own.[69] Thus, while Heath and Carr argued that the trade union movement was usurping or denying the legitimate functions of government, the TUC for its part depicted the Bill as a broad challenge to the constitution of industrial society and thus civil society as a whole, which justified a demand for the return of a Labour government committed to the root and branch repeal of the Act, and constitutional resistance in between times.

The result was that as the Act began to come into force during 1971, the TUC was well placed to lead the search for a constitutional basis for resistance to it.[70] The comprehensiveness of the Act turned out to have included provision of an Achilles' heel, for the whole elaborate structure was erected on the assumption that trade unions would feel obliged to be registered under the Act.[71] The Industrial Relations Act, once derailed by this form of constitutional sabotage, was an engine lurching out of control over decidedly rough terrain. The problems caused by the trade union campaign of de-registration,[72] and the way that de-registration threw the comprehensiveness of the Act into

[68] See D. Barnes and E. Reid, *Governments and Trade Unions: The British Experience, 1964–79* (London, 1980), 140, 'The language was violent: the slogan was "kill the Bill".'

[69] Moran, *Politics of Industrial Relations*, 125: 'The key to the TUC campaign against the Bill [was] its adherence to a strategy of constitutionalism.' Moran goes on to identify three shades of trade union constitutionalism: (1) the extreme constitutionalists such as Frank Chapple who thought the law must be obeyed in all events; (2) the moderate constitutionalists, the overwhelming majority, who thought passive resistance to the Act was in order; and (3) the qualified constitutionalists such as Hugh Scanlon who thought that in general the law must be obeyed but that the 1971 Act and its courts were an exception.

[70] Ibid., 'the campaign against the Bill merged imperceptibly into resistance to the Act.'

[71] Above, pp. 298–9.

[72] Moran (*Politics of Industrial Relations*, 123) notes how the Bill was amended, when the government saw that the TUC would pursue a non-registration strategy and realized how destructive it would be, to create the Provisional Register containing all unions registered under the 1871 Act and thereby put the onus on those unions to de-register. 'This single amendment came close to destroying the campaign of opposition to the Act.'

reverse, were graphically demonstrated in the course of 1972. Michael Moran offers the metaphor of the spider's web to describe how the unions felt they would be completely entangled by Act once they registered.[73] The events of 1972 were to show that once the trade unions de-registered, the Act became a spider's web in which unions, shop stewards, employers, courts, and the government itself eventually became entrapped.

The central events of 1972, so far as the operation of the Industrial Relations Act was concerned, were the industrial disputes on the railways (the ASLEF dispute) and at the docks; the latter dispute was critical in terms of trade union liability and trade union registration. The industrial dispute in the docks was about containerization—the new practice of loading ships' cargoes into steel containers which were in turn placed into purpose-built container ships. Containerization enabled the work of loading and unloading to be carried out anywhere inland and thus threatened the employment of dock workers. Not for the last time in the period which this book covers, the combination of labour saving based on new technology and a re-allocation of the remaining work to a different group of workers produced a bitter industrial dispute in which the law played a major part.[74] The dockers were especially opposed to the operation of companies which carried on the business of collecting part-loads from consignors and loading them into containers outside the dock area without using dock labour,[75] and unofficial committees of shop stewards at the docks, belonging to the Transport and General Workers Union, organized industrial action consisting of blacking [76] the lorries of road haulage firms in Liverpool and Hull and picketing container depots and cold-storage depots in the Greater London area.

In the legally-structured world of industrial relations that the framers of the Industrial Relations Act had been confident of creating, the well-oiled mechanisms of the grand design would

[73] Ibid., 128.
[74] The main parallel is the developments in the newspaper industry in the early and middle 1980s: see below, pp. 198–9.
[75] So-called 'groupage business'. See P. L. Davies, 'In Search of Jobs and Defendants' (1973) 36 MLR 78 at 79.
[76] i.e., in this instance, denying the lorries passage into the docks without evidence of an agreement between the haulage company and the joint shop stewards committee: Davies, 'In Search of Jobs', at 79.

have gone to work on this situation. Legally enforceable procedure agreements would have been in place to ensure an orderly
resolution of the underlying dispute.[77] Section 96 of the Act
would have been properly available as a sanction against the
organizing of industrial action by unofficial shop stewards
committees, but not against the TGWU as a registered union.
The TGWU would have been liable under section 36 for failure
to police industrial action in breach of a procedure agreement;
but the registration process would have ensured that the union
had rules clearly determining where authority lay to organize
industrial action for which it was responsible.[78] The TGWU
having de-registered (and there being no procedure agreements
between it and the container operators), the reality was dramatically different. The liabilities both of the union and of the shop
stewards and their joint committees fell out quite differently
from what had been intended. We have already seen[79] that, in
essence, the unintended outcome was that those affected by the
industrial action had an unrestricted opportunity to sue the trade
union or the shop stewards for the unfair industrial practice of
inducing breach of contract in contemplation or furtherance of
an industrial dispute under section 96 of the Act.[80] In order to
understand the many ironies and intricacies of that situation,
we need to consider another of the problems caused by the
comprehensiveness of the 1971 Act.

One of the ways in which the Industrial Relations Act sought
to establish a comprehensive legal framework for industrial
relations was by creating a set of purpose-built institutions to
administer it, all dedicated to the purposes of the legislation.
These included the Registrar of Trade Unions, and the Commission on Industrial Relations;[81] but the institutional centre-

[77] The judgment of the President of the Industrial Court in *Craddock Bros.* v.
TGWU shows, revealingly, that he clearly had such a hypothesis in mind; [1972]
ICR 302, esp. 305 B–D.

[78] See above, p. 300.

[79] See above, pp. 286–7.

[80] The point is that while the framers of the Act fully intended s. 96 to be
available against unregistered unions, they calculated that this would in practice
force trade unions to register. Moran (*Politics of Industrial Relations*, 138)
reminds us that 'in the Summer of 1972 it still looked as if [the government] could
win the battle over registration.'

[81] First set up by Royal Warrant in 1969, but placed on a statutory footing by
ss. 120–1 of the 1971 Act.

piece was undoubtedly the National Industrial Relations Court, of which Sir John Donaldson was made the President. The Industrial Court was to consist of judges drawn from the High Court and Court of Appeal, and lay members with special knowledge or experience of industrial relations.[82] Section 1 of the Industrial Relations Act laid down a series of principles 'for the purpose of promoting good industrial relations', and it was something of a constitutional innovation for the Industrial Court, like the Department of Employment and the CIR, to be required to regard those as guiding principles in the performance of their functions under the Act,[83] as it was for Highway Code status to be accorded to a Code of Industrial Relations Practice laid down and revised as necessary by the Department of Employment.[84] There has been discussion in recent years as to whether juridification—the intensification of legal regulation—is a universal trend in labour law.[85] Even those who contend that juridification is a universal trend in labour law would accept that the lining-up of a set of committed national institutions, including a committed court, to administer a comprehensive legal framework amounts to an unusually advanced and ambitious expression of that universal trend. Placed under the supervision of a President with a strong overt commitment to ensuring its effectiveness,[86] the National Industrial Relations Court rapidly became the focus of a continuing confrontation between the government and the trade union movement.

The industrial action in the docks provided a series of specific occasions for that confrontation, in the course of which attitudes hardened on the part of all the principal actors. The President's intention to make his court, and the Act itself, effective was manifested as soon as a container firm in St Helens, due to

[82] Industrial Relations Act 1971, s. 100. In practice one High Court judge would sit with one representative of employers and one trade unionist.

[86] Ibid., s. 1(2).

[84] Ibid., ss. 2-4.

[85] The thesis was advanced by Spiros Simitis. See J. Clark, 'The Juridification of Industrial Relations' (1985) 14 ILJ 69 and below, ch. 8.5.

[86] See e.g. Sir John Donaldson's Presidential Statement on the Opening of the Court in Dec. 1971 ([1972] ICR 1). In retrospect, it is highly significant that the President said, 'The use of the word "court" is entirely accurate but at the same time may convey a misleading impression . . . It may be misleading in that, in the context of industrial relations, traditional court attitudes and procedures are inappropriate' (at p. 2).

become a household name in labour law, proceeded against the
TGWU under section 96 of the Act in respect of the organizing
of the blacking of its lorries by TGWU shop stewards at the
Mersey Docks.[87] Because the TGWU had de-registered,[88] and
because the union did not appear and was not represented by
reason of its unwillingness to submit to the jurisdiction of the
court,[89] the NIRC immediately granted interim relief on the
footing that the union was in breach of section 96, with no
discussion of what the basis was for holding the union liable for
the actions of its shop stewards. In May 1972 the TGWU, having
been fined successively £5,000 and £50,000, appeared before the
court and argued the substantive issue of its liability for the
actions of the Merseyside dockers' shop stewards. The Industrial
Court held that the union was liable on the basis simply that the
shop stewards were the authorized agents of the union for a
general class of trade union tasks. The message to union was a
trenchant one:

The law is plain. The union is accountable if its officers, officials,
representatives or shop stewards do their union work in breach of the
law. It is for the union to see that they do not break the law.[90]

The Industrial Court was here, in effect, writing section 36 into
section 96 as a response to the trade union campaign of de-
registration. It was a creative view of the NIRC's role as a court
dedicated to the purpose of the 1971 Act.[91]

[87] The complaint was made on 22 Mar. 1972. See *Heatons Transport Ltd.* v.
TGWU [1972] ICR 285.

[88] Sir John Donaldson, P.: 'It would be otherwise, of course, if it were
registered.' Ibid. at 288 H.

[89] Sir John Donaldson, P.: 'If we have misappreciated the facts and are making
an order which, if all the facts were known, should not have been made, it would
be a matter of regret to this court. But we are not unmindful of the fact that an
opportunity has been given to TGWU to appear here and explain where we are
wrong. They have chosen not to do so . . .'. Ibid. at 289 D–E.

[90] Sir John Donaldson, P. in *Heatons Transport Ltd.* v. *TGWU* [1972] ICR 308
at 326 A–B. The indication was that the union would have to withdraw the shop
stewards' credentials. Ibid. at 326 C–D.

[91] The President's judgment is notably egocentric on behalf of the Court and
the Act: 'The National Industrial Relations Court is a court, but a court with a
difference. [. . .] The Industrial Court is more than a court of law; it is a court of
industrial common sense. [. . .] Usually, courts have to be guided solely by the
words of the Act of Parliament and their general knowledge of the reasons which
led Parliament to pass it. However, in the case of the Industrial Relations Act

In a crucial reversal, widely seen as a blow to the government, the Court of Appeal overturned the decision of the NIRC, holding the TGWU not liable for the actions of the shop stewards on the grounds that the shop steward has a dual role, as representative both of his own work group and the trade union, and that the shop stewards were here acting as representatives of their workgroups, outside the scope of their authority as representatives of the union. For Lord Denning MR, this was ground that the common law courts had long since traversed, leaving clear common law principles behind them.[92] He indicated in his judgment that he was unhappy with an approach in which this clear common law was subordinated to statutory policies about trade union registration:

If this trade union had been registered under the Act, it would undoubtedly have gone clear. Its rules would have provided expressly—as, in my opinion, these do impliedly—that the shop stewards have no authority to call for industrial action on their own initiative. If registered, the shop stewards would be guilty of unfair industrial practices but the union would not: see Section 96(1)(a). Why then should the union be mulcted in heavy fines and large compensation simply because it was not registered?[93]

Lord Denning went on to hint that he regarded the contrary decision of the NIRC as one unduly influenced by political considerations.[94]

The Industrial Court, in its determination that neither its own authority nor the policy of the 1971 Act should be flouted, immediately turned its attention to enforcing the Act against individual shop stewards' leaders. Relief for breach of section 96 had been obtained against three of them by workers at the Chobham Farm cold storage depot in East London, which was being picketed on behalf of the London Joint Shop Stewards'

1971, Parliament has gone out of its way to help us by setting out guiding principles.' Ibid. at 316 B–C, H to 317 A.

[92] '[T]he case is, to my mind, not governed by the decision of the House of Lords in *Taff Vale Railway Co* v. *Amalgamated Society of Railway Servants* but by the later decision in *Denaby and Cadeby Main Collieries, Ltd.* v. *Yorkshire Miners Association*.' [1972] ICR 308 at 324 B–C.

[93] Ibid. at 344 D–E.

[94] Ibid. at 344 F–G. Lord Denning has since written of the NIRC: 'No wonder it was regarded with hatred by those whom it affected. No wonder they moved heaven and earth to do away with it.' *The Closing Chapter* (1983), 165.

Committee.[95] The three shop stewards' leaders were now committed to prison for contempt of court, the President of the NIRC saying that 'The conduct of these men, as it appears at present, has gone far beyond anything which could be appropriately disposed of by the imposition of a fine.'[96] The Court of Appeal set aside the committal orders on the grounds that the evidence of breach of the Court's earlier order had been insufficient, and reminded the NIRC that the grounds for depriving contemnors of their liberty must be as strictly proved in the NIRC as in the High Court. Within four weeks, however, the NIRC was to commit five shop stewards' leaders to Pentonville Prison for organizing picketing at another London cold storage depot, this time at the instance of the company that owned the cold store.[97]

The consequences for the future development of labour law were extensive. The Industrial Court, in its zeal to ensure its own effectiveness and that of its parent Act, had been less than cautious about the dangers of allowing the shop stewards' leaders to establish themselves as martyrs for their cause. Given their enthusiasm for this role, it had required rather dubious expedients, a contrived extension of the normal role of the Official Solicitor, to bring about the appeal against their first committal to prison.[98] Meanwhile, extensive industrial action had been initiated or threatened by reason of these individual imprisonments. The embarrassment to the government and to the judicial system caused by the second committal, that of the 'Pentonville Five', was resolved by means no less ingenious. These consisted in a shift of emphasis from the liability of individuals under the Act to the liability of trade unions, a shift which came about as follows. The House of Lords gave a much expedited and, unusually for that time, a single unanimous judgment on the appeal in the *Heatons* case, holding that the TGWU was, con-

---

[95] See *Churchman* v. *Joint Shop Stewards Committee* [1972] ICR 222. The plaintiff employees had formed a 'Manual Staff Association' for the company at which they worked, London (East) ICD Ltd. The NIRC's order was made against three shop-stewards' leaders and against the Joint Shop Stewards' Committee.

[96] Ibid. at 225 A–B.

[97] See *Midland Cold Storage* v. *Turner* [1972] ICR 230.

[98] There is a nice question how far this took place at the instigation of the Master of the Rolls himself. Cf. his contemporary statement in open court, [1972] ICR 229 G to 230 D.

trary to the view of the Court of Appeal, liable for the actions of the Merseyside dockers' shop stewards. The House of Lords rejected the Court of Appeal's theory of the dual role of shop stewards, and put forward a countervailing one in which shop stewards might have, and in this case did have, an implied authority to take[99] industrial action on behalf of their union, an authority acquired by upward delegation from the membership of the union at large and therefore not dependent upon a downward delegation from the official leadership of the union.

Moreover, the House of Lords held that as soon as the NIRC, having been entitled to conclude from the evidence that the union was guilty of an unfair industrial practice under section 96 through its shop stewards, had issued orders restraining the union, 'the union became responsible for taking all possible steps to stop the blacking, including the unequivocal withdrawal of the shop stewards' authority and, if necessary, disciplinary action'.[100] This was an implementation of the policy of the Act to the extent that it reproduced the notion of union responsibility contained in Section 36; but the framers of the Act had articulated that notion only in the specific context of enforcement of legally binding collective agreements rather than in relation to the more open-ended liability created by section 96; and the framers of the Act had not purported to establish a sweeping theory of trade union implied authority or vicarious liability as the House of Lords had now done.[101]

The Industrial Court re-defined its goals in light of the House of Lords' decision in the *Heatons* case, evolving new approaches to section 96 which were no less purposive than its former ones, but rather more sophisticated. The House of Lords' judgment was used, as seems to have been intended,[102] as a reason for the NIRC to grant an application from the Official Solicitor for the release of the Pentonville Five on the basis that:

---

[99] This is the word used in the House of Lords' Summary of its Opinion: [1972] ICR 308 at 405 H to 406 A. It was really their authority to *organize* industrial action which was at issue.

[100] Ibid. at 406 A–C.

[101] For the difficulties and uncertainties left by the House of Lords exposition, see esp. Davies, 'In Search of Jobs', at 81–4, where it is argued that the House of Lords to an undue extent assimilated the relationship of union and shop steward to that of master and servant.

[102] Lord Denning is fairly explicit about this in *The Closing Chapter*, 175–6.

The Lords' judgment makes it clear that the primary method of enforcement contemplated by the Industrial Relations Act is against the funds of organizations rather than against individuals.[103]

This argument was more expedient than cogent, but the NIRC did thereafter remain intent on systematically preferring remedies against unions[104] to remedies against individuals. Moreover, the NIRC sought to extend the union liability recognized in *Heatons*—unwarrantably it may be argued—so that it became a liability for the acts of members, whether or not they were shop stewards;[105] at the same time, the NIRC started to use these extended powers against unions in a way which paid more heed to whether the union could, and had made genuine efforts to, control the actions which were thus placing them in jeopardy.[106] It has been shown, indeed, that the NIRC was involved, after the débâcle of the docks dispute, in trying to legitimate itself as a specialist industrial court by attempting to develop its injunction procedure so as to try to bring about a resolution of the underlying dispute which had produced the application for injunctive relief.[107]

This development, significant though it might have been in other circumstances in the development of the debate about whether specialist labour courts are a good idea, was largely obscured by the hostility with which the NIRC came to be viewed, a hostility generated by the comprehensiveness of its parent Act and the overt zeal of the court in prosecuting its policies.[108] The situation was reached in which large employers were generally unwilling to apply to the Court for injunctions (and ready to declare collective agreements not legally enforce-

---

[103] Sir John Donaldson, P., *The Times*, 28 July 1972.
[104] See Wedderburn, 'Will NIRC Expand Vicarious Liability?' (1973) 36 MLR 226 at 229 n. 13.
[105] *Howitt Transport Ltd.* v. *TGWU* [1973] ICR 1. See Wedderburn 'Will NIRC Expand Vicarious Liability?', *passim*.
[106] See e.g. the *Howitt Transport* case itself, and *Davenports C.B. & Brewery (Holdings) Ltd.* v. *TGWU* [1973] ICR 632; *Seaboard World Airlines Inc.* v. *TGWU* [1973] ICR 458.
[107] S. D. Anderman and P. L. Davies, 'Injunction Procedure in Labour Disputes II' (1974) 2 ILJ 30 at 36–45. The cases most in point are *Shipside (Ruthin) Ltd.* v. *TGWU* [1973] ICR 503 and *Horizon Holidays Ltd.* v. *ASTMS* [1973] IRLR 22.
[108] The President of the Court was later to come close to acknowledging this: 'Using hindsight, it would have been better if the court had been set up under a

able to pre-empt that possibility).[109] Some of the small employers who were inclined to seek injunctions started to apply to the High Court, because its orders were more likely to be respected by unions and shop stewards;[110] and the confrontational effects of the continuing pursuit in the NIRC of the Engineering Union by one determined small employer[111] were so great that the union's fines were eventually paid by anonymous donors thought to have the interests of the business community in mind.[112]

The capacity of the Industrial Relations Act, once in operation, to embroil the institutions administering it in confrontation, and frustrate their efforts to manage the unions by its sheer over-ambitiousness, was further demonstrated by the use of emergency procedures in the rail dispute of April–June 1972. The government in proposing the emergency procedures had been, as we have seen,[113] motivated by a curiously optimistic view of the success of the Taft–Hartley Act's cooling-off provisions and of their transferability to the environment of UK industrial relations. They had been surprisingly impervious to the evidence that it was the proposals for similar procedures in the Labour Government's White Paper *In Place of Strife* that had most alienated the trade union movement from that whole set of proposals.[114] But whereas the emergency procedures had been quite central to the Labour government's proposals, they were relatively marginal in the Conservative government's scheme— attractive mainly because they seemed to make a neat continuity in the grand juridified legal framework between the rationalized structures of collective bargaining the Act was to produce and the

separate Act—an Administration of Justice (Labour Court) Act. This would have made it clear that the court was one thing and the law which it administered was quite another.' Sir John Donaldson P., 'The Role of Labour Courts' (1975) 4 ILJ 63 at n. 3.

[109] Cf. Weekes *et al.*, *Limits of Law*, 210–13 (General Attitudes to the Strike Law).

[110] As e.g. in *Midland Cold Storage Ltd.* v. *Steer* [1972] ICR 435. The High Court, in that case and in others, was on the whole unwilling to be drawn into the industrial dispute area while the Act was in force, a position which the Court of Appeal reinforced—see Anderman and Davies, 'Injunction Procdeure in Labour Disputes II', at n. 57.

[111] The company was Con-Mech (Engineers) Ltd.; the litigation is chronicled by N. Lewis in 'Con-Mech: Showdown for the NIRC' (1975) 4 ILJ 201 ff.

[112] See Moran, *Politics of Industrial Relations*, 145–6.

[113] See above, p. 296.

[114] See above, ch. 6.3.

existing government powers of appointing a Court or Committee of Inquiry or declaring a State of Emergency.[115] There seems to have been a real prediction that the emergency procedures would probably not need to be invoked in practice.[116] In the event, the government's voluntary incomes policy was under much greater pressure by mid-1972 than the government had allowed for, especially following the miners' victory in their industrial action of 1972.[117] In the midst of the difficulties over the Industrial Relations Act and the dockers' shop stewards, Maurice Macmillan as the new Secretary of State for Employment took the step of invoking the Act's emergency procedures—first a cooling-off period and then a compulsory strike ballot—to try to secure an acceptable settlement of the union ASLEF's pay claim against British Rail.[118]

The attempt was a failure, in that no settlement occurred in the cooling-off period, and the compulsory ballot produced such a majority vote in favour of the industrial action that the union's position was strengthened and they soon won a high pay settlement. As Moran put it:

[T]he Government had suffered an important defeat; the final settlement was well above what it had hoped, and its first attempt to use the Act had been a humiliating failure. It established an impression that the Act was accident prone.[119]

[115] M. Moran, *Politics of Industrial Relations*, observes that these provisions were 'peripheral to the legislation in the sense that they operated quite independently of the heart of the Act which concerned registration' (p. 139).

[116] R. W. Rideout, 'When is a Rule not a Rule' (1973) 36 MLR 73: 'As late as March 1972, one suspects that few experts in this field would have been prepared to predict the use of the emergency procedures . . . for at least a further twelve months.'

[117] A valuable narrative of the strikes against the policy of 'de-escalation' can be found in E. Wigham's *Strikes and the Government 1893–1981* (London, 1982), 165–9: 'The Conservative Government's incomes policy was ultimately even more destructive than its industrial relations law' (p. 165).

[118] Barnes and Reid, *Governments and Trade Unions*, comment at pp. 160–1, 'The provision in the Act, conceived to operate in a situation where industrial relations were unaffected by government policies on wages, was being used as a device for supporting what remained of the government wages policy.'

[119] *Politics of Industrial Relations*, 139. So also M. Holmes, *Political Pressure and Economic Policy: British Government, 1970–1974* (London, 1982), 26: 'Ministers considered the settlement to be a major political defeat as it was thought to be particularly inflationary. But the settlement was not in itself the defeat; that lay in the extension of the dispute and its escalation to a degree that would have been highly unlikely in the Act's absence.'

The episode—the sole occasion on which the emergency procedures were invoked—is recalled for the government's ill-judged commitment to a model of industrial relations behaviour which assumed that an apathetic rank-and-file membership was being misrepresented by a more militant union leadership; and for Lord Denning's exposition of an essentially unitary theory of the employee's implied obligations under his contract of employment, which identified the railwaymen's work-to-rule as being in breach of contract, and hence 'irregular industrial action short of a strike' such as to fulfil the statutory conditions of availability of the emergency procedures.[120]

These are important aspects of the Act's attempted juridification of governmental handling of major industrial disputes; they have somewhat obscured the effects, prominent at the time, which this episode had on the standing of the NIRC itself. The framers of the Act had sought to legitimate the emergency procedures by making their imposition an act done by the NIRC at the instance of the Secretary of State for Employment rather than by the government itself. In the event, the NIRC, being thus required to conduct a sort of public-law judicial review of the Secretary of State's application for use of the emergency procedure, was markedly executive-minded in its scrutiny of those applications,[121] in a way which served to reinforce the notion that the NIRC had and saw itself as having the function of implementing the Governmental policies embodied in the Industrial Relations Act.[122] In implementing this part of the Act, the Department of Employment was tending to lose, and the Industrial Court was failing to gain, credibility as an independent arbiter in the industrial relations system.

[120] *Secretary of State for Employment* v. *ASLEF (No. 2)* [1972] ICR 19.

[121] The NIRC's formulation of the scope for scrutiny was subtly more limited than that of the Court of Appeal: contrast Sir John Donaldson at [1972] ICR 19, 31 E–F with Lord Denning MR at [1972] ICR F–H on the question of whether the Court was satisfied that it 'appeared' to the Secretary of State that there were reasons for doubting whether the members of the union wanted the industrial action.

[122] See e.g. A. Jones, *The New Inflation* (1973), 140–1: 'In requiring the Industrial Relations Court to "rubber-stamp" the Minister's view that a "cooling-off" period was desirable, the Act went far towards making the Court an arm of Government, not part of the independent arm of the judiciary.' An expert in public law would be unlikely to make quite so harsh an assessment; but it is significant that this was the view of a highly placed public figure, which was not untypical: see Weekes *et al.*, *Limits of Law*, 214.

In other areas of the Industrial Relations Act's operation, it also occurred that the NIRC was beset by problems caused by the comprehensiveness of the Act, the way the provisions of the Act interlocked with each other, the success of the trade union campaign of resistance, and the Court's own reputation as a creature of the Act. The area of trade union recognition provides an example. As we have seen, the fact that only registered unions could invoke the statutory recognition procedure[123] or be made sole bargaining agents meant that the whole procedure threatened to become a means whereby non-TUC unions or staff associations could steal a march on their TUC rivals. The NIRC used its powers as a filter on referrals of recognition issues to the CIR as a means of minimizing the disruption of existing bargaining structures by break-away unions[124] or professional associations.[125] Although one of the major commentaries on the working of the Act gave the NIRC due credit for this,[126] it could simply be regarded as another form of over-interventionism by the NIRC.[127] The Court of Appeal and the House of Lords eventually clipped the wings of the NIRC in this respect,[128] having no doubt become uneasy about the way that the overt intrusiveness of that court into the politics of industrial relations was casting doubt upon the detachment of the courts as a whole.

Another area of operation of the Industrial Relations Act well illustrates its capacity, and that of the NIRC, to fall foul of industrial relations systems by trying to implement an over-juridified model of them. That area concerns the individual right, conferred by section 5 of the Act, not to be discriminated

---

[123] See above, p. 290.

[124] See e.g. *ESU* v. *CEGB* [1972] ICR 418 (which concerned the claim of the Electricity Supply Union to represent manual workers at the Ferrybridge C power station).

[125] See e.g. *UKAPE* v. *Rolls Royce & Associates* [1972] ICR 162 (UKAPE was a professional association of engineers).

[126] A. W. J. Thomson and S. R. Engleman, *The Industrial Relations Act: A Review and Analysis* (1975), 79–84.

[127] See Weekes *et al.*, Limits of Law, 153: 'The function which the NIRC at first developed for itself was in the end declared to have exceeded its proper boundaries and generally served to increase the time and expense spent in attempts to obtain recognition.'

[128] *TSA* v. *Post Office* [1974] ICR 97 (CA) [1974] ICR 658 (HL). The Telecommunications Staff Association was a break-away from the Union of Post Office Workers, challenging its recognition for telephonists.

against by the employer by reason of membership of or participation in the activity of a registered trade union or by reason of being unwilling to belong to a trade union whether registered or not.[129] Again, we have seen earlier that this was one of the many provisions whose effect was fundamentally diverted from its intended course by the trade union campaign of nonregistration. As with the statutory recognition provisions, this raised the possibility that an unrecognized but registered breakaway union or professional association could use the legal process to gain an advantage over an unregistered rival union which was recognized by the employer, by getting an individual member to claim discrimination contrary to section 5 where the employer accorded union facilities to the recognized union which were denied to the unrecognized one.

This strategy was pursued by the Telecommunications Staff Association in its battle to win recognition, in place of the Union of Post Office Workers, in respect of telephonists. Essentially the battle for parity in respect of all union facilities falling short of negotiating rights was won in the Court of Appeal and in the House of Lords.[130] The NIRC had taken the contrary view, maintaining that the inequality of facilities amounted to discrimination against the union rather than the discrimination against the individual member against which section 5 was directed.[131] As with the case law on trade union recognition, the NIRC had earned itself such a generally unfavourable reputation that such decisions were apt to be written off as further instances of over-legalism on its part. The NIRC was perhaps given insufficient credit for trying to preserve existing collective bargaining structures,[132] by contrast in this instance with the readiness of the Court of Appeal to cast the break-away union as David challenging Goliath in the shape of the big recognized union.[133]

---

[129] See above, p. 293.
[130] *Post Office* v. *Crouch* [1973] ICR 366 (CA); *Post Office* v. *UPW* [1974] ICR 378 (HL).
[131] [1972] ICR 174 *sub. nom. Post Office* v. *Ravyts*. Cf. also *King* v. *PO and UPW* [1973] ICR 120 (NIRC).
[132] Cf. Weekes *et al.* 296–8. Thomson and Engleman, *The Industrial Relations Act*, 63 do note that the NIRC had the 'statutory purpose' of constraining the rights of individuals where their successful exercise was likely to promote conflict.
[133] [1973] ICR 366 at 374 X–Y (Lord Denning MR—who but he?).

There were, moreover, at least two situations in which the NIRC itself, in applying section 5, moved away from its original concern to protect existing industrial relations systems and thereby minimize the conflict which section 5 could generate. One was in relation to representation in grievance procedures: the Ferrybridge C Power Station episode provides a good illustration. A registered union which pursued its recognition contest indirectly via section 5 as well as directly via the statutory recognition provisions[134] was the Electricity Supply Union, which had targeted itself upon the Ferrybridge C Power Station. Members of the ESU invoked section 5 against a rule that only members of one of the recognized unions were eligible for election to the works committee as union representatives. The NIRC held that this was not a violation of section 5, and has, once again, received more criticism for the over-sophistication of its legal reasoning[135] than credit for its efforts to preserve existing bargaining structures. Sir John Donaldson, however, embarked on an exercise of reviewing the whole set of procedures in operation at Ferrybridge C power station, in order to suggest to the parties to the National Joint Industrial Council how they might amend their procedures to make them safe from section 5 claims in all respects. The Industrial Court suggested that the grievance procedure be amended so that the trade union representative of an individual in the grievance procedures would no longer have to be chosen from one of the recognized unions.[136]

Other judges in the NIRC were, perhaps, less prone than Sir John Donaldson to take zeal for the Act's objectives to the lengths of re-drafting existing procedure agreements by way of 'constructive suggestion'[137] (in the absence of an application under the section 37 procedure for this purpose). But other judges would be ready to seize on the suggestion that the free choice of union representative in a grievance procedure was self-evidently required by section 5, and it was so held in a later

[134] See above, p. 290.
[135] Even from the often more generous Thomson and Engleman, *The Industrial Relations Act*, 63, where the argument used is said to be 'semantic'.
[136] *CEGB* v. *Coleman* [1973] ICR 230 at 239.
[137] Ibid. at 239: 'The principal object of this court is to promote better industrial relations. No one who has the same object at heart should object to being asked to consider constructive suggestions for the improvement of the agreed procedure.'

case,[138] despite the argument that this would in substance be to give the professional engineers association UKAPE indirectly some of the negotiating rights which ought to be allocated directly by the statutory recognition procedure or not at all. The NIRC responded to this argument that:

If the UKAPE representative abused the occasion [i.e. the grievance interview about an individual's salary] and tried to turn the interview into an attempt to start collective bargaining, the employer's remedy is to terminate the interview.[139]

Employers were as apt as unions to conclude that an Industrial Court prepared to deploy such arguments was less than fully in tune with existing industrial relations procedures.

This divergence, between the objectives pursued by the Act in operation and the preference of the great majority of employers to maintain existing industrial relations practices, is perhaps at its most evident in relation to the impact of that Act upon the closed shop. Section 5 of the Act, as well as providing a patent opportunity for the pursuit of inter-union rivalries as we have seen above, also provided individual workers with an opportunity to challenge the various practices whereby employers assisted unions in maintaining a closed shop.[140] So also did section 33 in relation to closed shop dismissals, with its complex combination of a provision estopping the employer from pleading industrial action pressure in justification of a dismissal and a provision enabling the employer to complain against the union in respect of that industrial action pressure as an unfair industrial practice.[141] On the whole, the NIRC understood how disruptively these provisions could operate where an individual worker sought to challenge a closed shop arrangement in which the employer acquiesced, especially when the main TUC unions had, by de-registering, disqualified themselves from running statutory approved closed shops or agency shops. Thus at certain crucial points the NIRC held that it was not practicable to award

---

[138] *Howle* v. *GEC Power Engineering Ltd.* [1974] ICR 13.
[139] Ibid. at 20 F (Sir Hugh Griffiths).
[140] The number of such claims was not large. Weekes *et al.* record that there were only 325 section 5 applications down to 1 July 1973—of which an unknown smaller number related to closed shops—at a time when over 4 m. were employed in closed shops (*Limits of Law*, 55–6).
[141] See above, p. 294.

reinstatement or re-engagement to workers dismissed for refusing to belong to a trade union.[142]

However, such was the comprehensiveness and complexity of the legislative pattern created by the 1971 Act, that the non-union worker could use it to play off the NIRC against the Court of Appeal in a curious contest of jurisdiction, and ultimately of perceptions about industrial relations practices. In 1973 the owners of a fleet of tugs in the Port of London sued the TGWU in the High Court in tort in respect of their threat of industrial action if a non-member was allowed to work. The decision to sue reflected the fact that the employers, although sympathetic to the closed shop, could not secure the permission of the Dock Labour Board to dismiss the non-unionist in question. The Court of Appeal held, provocatively, that the Industrial Relations Act 1971 had allocated this issue to the common law and the High Court, rather than the NIRC and the law of unfair industrial practices.[143] This was because the 1971 Act had excluded disputes between workmen and workmen from the ambit of industrial disputes;[144] the Court of Appeal classified this dispute as one between the non-member and the union. Having thus asserted jurisdiction, the Court of Appeal refused an interlocutory injunction, Lord Denning MR indicating that the Dock Labour Board should permit the dismissal of the trouble-maker.[145] Later in 1973, the NIRC reclaimed jurisdiction in closed-shop cases, retorting to the Court of Appeal that 'too ready an acceptance of the view that Cory's case covers all disputes which may have begun between workmen and workmen will greatly cut down the protection given to workmen by section 33.'[146]

The stage was thus set for the working out of the almost ludicrously intricate proceedings concerning Joseph Langston, a car welder at Chryslers' plant at Ryton near Coventry. He sought to establish a right to work in defiance of the AUEW closed shop at Ryton. Early in 1973, the NIRC had ruled that he could not complain of a section 33 unfair industrial relations practice on the

---

[142] *Coleman* v. *Magnet Joinery Ltd.* [1974] ICR 25; *Langston* v. *AUEW* (No. 2) [1974] ICR 510.
[143] *Cory Lighterage Ltd.* v. *TGWU* [1973] ICR 339.
[144] See above, p. 285.
[145] [1973] ICR 339 at 359 B–E.
[146] *Coleman* v. *Magnet Joinery Ltd.* [1974] ICR 25 at 29 G–H (Sir Hugh Griffiths).

part of the AUEW, because the right of complaint under the relevant provision of section 33 was confined to the employer.[147] The Court of Appeal, appearing (at least so far as Lord Denning MR was concerned) to view Langston as an individual being denied justice, set itself to discovering remedies for Mr Langston where the NIRC had failed to do so. Thus the Court of Appeal, showing the dispute could be classified as an industrial dispute despite their own earlier reasoning in the *Cory* case, suggested that the plaintiff could found a case against the union on section 96 of the Act, and provided him with the makings of an implied contractual right to be provided with work to do, as the basis of the section 96 claim.[148] The Industrial Court took up this suggestion, and upheld the view that the AUEW would be committing a section 96 unfair industrial practice by threatening industrial action if Mr Langston were allowed to come to work at the Ryton factory.[149] The Industrial Court sought to avoid placing Chryslers in a difficult position, by refusing to make a recommendation for re-engagement against them;[150] but this was a sterile ingenuity in so far as it sought to drive a wedge between the employer and the union, since, in Michael Moran's words, 'of those who had initially favoured a legislative solution to the problems of industrial relations, none were more disillusioned by the experience of the Act in its twilight days than the large employers who dominate the economy and their chief spokesman, the CBI.'[151]

The upshot of all this was that the closed shop came to be seen as a patent example of the capacity of industrial relations systems to resist legal reform which did not command the support of employers. In 1975 the authors of the Warwick study on the effects of the 1971 Act commented that:

The closed shop, then, has proved such a stable and sturdy institution that, as the *Langston* and some other cases show, in the end even the law had to bend to the inevitable. The main reason was that the employers defended it almost as tenaciously as did workers . . . Their success must raise doubts about the ability of the law to protect indi-

[147] *Langston* v. *AUEW* [1973] ICR 211.
[148] *Langston* v. *AUEW* [1974] ICR 180.
[149] *Langston* v. *AUEW* (No. 2) [1974] ICR 510.
[150] Ibid. at 523–4.
[151] *Politics of Industrial Relations*, 145.

vidual rights in the field of employment, unless these rights are seem to command wide support or serve the interests of the parties to collective bargaining.[152]

This could be regarded as a sort of epitaph for the 1971 Act as a whole. The government's decision in August 1972 to 'put the Act on ice' was certainly influenced by the realization of how reluctant employers were to operate its provisions.[153] Successive governments turned out to have their own reasons for drawing rather different lessons from the failure of the 1971 Act to achieve its purposes. The tensions and contradictions which it created by the over-ambitiousness of its attempt to juridify the industrial relations system were to prove extremely difficult to resolve, especially as there was no practical possibility of reconstructing the *status quo ante* either in legal or in industrial relations terms.

Should we conclude from all this that the Industrial Relations Act failed to achieve its aims because of its unwieldiness and the internal contradictions of its elaborate structures? The authors of the Warwick survey felt that we should; they emphasized the inconsistencies between measures designed to reinforce collective bargaining and the position of trade unions in collective bargaining on the one hand, such as the statutory recognition procedures, and, on the other hand, measures tending to undermine trade unions, such as those restricting the closed shop.[154] They were concerned about the confusion between amplifying the voice of a supposedly moderate rank-and-file trade union membership by imposing strike ballots on the one hand, while on the other hand requiring trade unions to police legally binding collective agreements against a militant unofficial activism among trade union members.[155] They felt that when managements, unions, and workers colluded in maintaining closed shops and non-legally-enforceable collective agreements, those social

---

[152] Weekes *et al.*, *Limits of Law*, 63.

[153] Holmes, *Political Pressure*, 31. 'Putting the Act on ice' amounted to an executive decision not to enforce the Act; it was never clear how far and by what means it involved discouraging employers from enforcing it.

[154] Weekes, *et al.*, *Limits of Law*, 220–2.

[155] Ibid. 223–6, esp. at p. 223 where they say, 'The confusion of aims, and in particular the orbit of fear created by the Act's provisions against industrial action, has been widely accepted as a reason for the Act's failure to reform industrial relations.'

partners were reacting against these very contradictions and confusions.

While agreeing with much of this, we would place our emphasis slightly differently in explaining the failure of the 1971 Act to achieve its aims. In any advanced industrial democratic society—certainly in the UK—most governments are likely to be under pressure to control and moderate the industrial power of the workforce and the trade unions. Most governments are likely to feel a tension and an uncertainty as to how far to achieve this control by, on the one hand, coercion and arming employers with sanctions and, on the other hand, encouraging and supporting trade unions to act as the responsible representatives and regulators of the workforce. The framers of the Industrial Relations Act thought they could achieve both these kinds of control by means of comprehensive juridification. That does not necessarily indicate confusion on their part; but it turned out to be a considerable misconception of what was acceptable to trade unions, the workforce, and in consequence most employers. That, in the end, was what the Donovan Commission had warned would be the case. The Labour government had discovered much the same thing with its *In Place of Strife* proposals. However, no government would now feel that a return to collective *laissez-faire* would reassure the electorate of its ability to govern industrial society. So new experiments with the use of the law would have to be tried.

(c) *Control of Industrial Action by Legislation: The Role of Unfair Dismissal Law and Social Security Law*

Before we turn to look at a wider range of measures designed to control the labour economy during the period of the Industrial Relations Act, two off-shoots of our discussion of the Act itself need to be considered, both in different senses concerned with the control of industrial action—for both unfair dismissal law and social security law were regarded as having an important role in this respect. We have seen in a previous chapter that one of the reasons for the adoption of unfair dismissal law by the Industrial Relations Act 1971 was that it was regarded as a way of minimizing industrial disputes relating to individual dismissals.[156]

---

[156] See above, pp. 200–1.

Thus in the 1968 policy document *Fair Deal at Work*, the recommendation to introduce a law of unfair dismissal is made in the context of a discussion of what to do about industrial disputes, and is stated to be made 'both on grounds of principle and as a means of removing a major cause of industrial disputes'.[157] Given that the framers of the Industrial Relations Act thus saw unfair dismissal law as broadly relevant to the control of industrial action, they nevertheless had to take policy decisions about the relationship between unfair dismissal law and the control of industrial action in two specific dimensions:

1. How far should industrial action over dismissal issues be restricted by reference to the fact that unfair dismissal law would now provide an alternative or preferred method of dispute resolution?
2. How far should unfair dismissal law relate to dismissals by way of or in response to industrial action?

The decisions taken in those two dimensions indicate that the legislators did have in mind a fairly tight instrumental relationship between unfair dismissal law and the control of industrial action, and one, moreover, which linked up with the Act's other main strategies for controlling industrial action and restructuring industrial relations.

So far as control of industrial action relating to dismissals was concerned, the policy was not to seek to restrict industrial action which was aimed at protesting against dismissals, or seeking to achieve reinstatement, even if the action was taken without first exhausting the industrial tribunal procedure for unfair dismissals. Probably the framers of the legislation would have regarded that as an over-ambitious programme which would place the statutory process under too much strain—though it is interesting that the Industrial Court tried at one stage to implement a very similar policy by purposive use of section 96 of the Act.[158] The policy of the Act itself was the different one of seeking to control industrial action aimed at *bringing about* an unfair dismissal. It was sought to implement this policy by section 33, which dealt with pressure on employers to infringe rights of workers and, as

[157] *Fair Deal at Work*, 43.
[158] *Shipside (Ruthin) Ltd.* v. *TGWU* [1973] ICR 503.

we have seen earlier,[159] was intended to reinforce the Act's attempted restructuring of closed shop arrangements—the point being that pressure exerted by industrial action, or the threat of industrial action, upon an employer to effect an unfair dismissal would normally consist of pressure to dismiss a worker for refusal to belong to a trade union.

So far as the availability of unfair dismissal law in relation to dismissals occurring by way of or in response to industrial action is concerned, the legislators claimed that their purpose was simply that of ensuring the neutrality of unfair dismissal law in relation to industrial action: but it is arguable that the Act's unfair dismissal provisions did in fact relate to industrial action in a more purposive way than the neutrality explanation admits, having the particular aim of preserving the employer's sanction of dismissal in relation to industrial action. The neutrality justification was put by the Lord Chancellor in debate in the House of Lords on what was to become section 26 of the Act, the section dealing with dismissal in connection with a strike or other industrial action:

The basic situation here is that we are trying to apply the unfair dismissal provisions of the Bill to a strike situation. As in the case of a lockout—because strikes and lockouts are part of the field of collective action in the struggle for power—so far as unfair dismissal is concerned we try to be neutral. It does not mean that we encourage strikes or lockouts, but that we try to be neutral in applying unfair dismissal provisions both to the employers in the case of a lockout and employees in the case of a strike.[160]

That neutrality justification applies fairly straightforwardly to the treatment of dismissal in connection with a lockout by section 25 of the Act, where the solution adopted was in effect to make such dismissals not unfair if, but only if, the employee was offered re-engagement as from the date of resumption of work.

On the other hand, in relation to dismissals for which the reason was that the employee was currently taking part in a strike or other industrial action, section 26 provided that such dismissals should not be regarded as unfair save in the much narrower range of circumstances that there was selective re-engagement of those

[159] See above, p. 294.
[160] HL Deb., 5th ser., vol. 318, col. 1483 (13 May 1971).

taking part in the industrial action, and that the reason for which the particular employee was not offered re-engagement consisted in his exercise or intended exercise of his rights under section 5 of the Act to belong to a (registered) trade union or take part in its activities, or to refuse to belong to a trade union. This narrow confinement of unfair dismissal law to a particular reason for selective non-re-engagement of those taking part in industrial action suggests that the framers of the Act were specially concerned to preserve the employer's sanction of dismissal in response to industrial action in all cases save where such a dismissal would have cut across structures set up by other parts of the Act. This is borne out by the fact the legislators were at pains to declare, in relation to the provision of section 147 of that Act (which, as we have seen, relieved strikes, if preceded by due notice, of their character of breach of the contract of employment), that:

(4) Nothing in subsection (2) of this section shall be taken to exclude or restrict any right which an employer would have apart from that subsection to dismiss (with or without notice) an employee who takes part in a strike).

The existence of an intention carefully to preserve the employer's sanction of dismissal is further borne out by the fact that in the Bill as originally presented, the claim in respect of selective non-re-engagement was further confined, so far as taking part in the activities of a (registered) trade union was concerned, to activities before the industrial action in question had begun. This laid the proposers of the Bill open to the accusation that they were prepared to countenance victimization of activist shop stewards, and the Lord Chancellor's elaboration of the neutrality rationale may seem a little strained at this point:

Of course, the ordinary result of a strike, and what usually happens, is that the strike is followed by a resumption of work by all those who went on strike, and almost always there is a non-victimization clause as part of the terms of resumption.[161]

However, it is extremely interesting to note that the preceding Labour government's Industrial Relations Bill, which the Conservative Industrial Relations Bill followed closely so far as the drafting of the unfair dismissal provisions was concerned,

---

[161] Ibid., col. 1484.

contained a closely similar provision with regard to dismissal in connection with a strike, even including the restriction to trade union activity before the strike began.[162] So perhaps we should conclude that victimization was really not seen as a sufficient risk to justify bringing the unfair dismissal process into the arena of industrial action—or that the preservation of the employer's sanction of dismissal in relation to industrial action was a matter of cross-party consensus at that time. We shall see that this was an issue to which governments would have to return, or to which they would choose to return, on more than one subsequent occasion.

Finally, we should note that a discussion of the measures controlling or seeking to control industrial action during this period should not be wholly confined to the Industrial Relations Act 1971. That would obscure the importance of a measure whose long-term impact was very considerable, namely sections 1 and 2 of the Social Security Act 1971. The Industrial Relations Act was in a real sense fighting the battles of the 1960s with weapons designed in the 1960s. That is to say, it concentrated on the industrial relations problems with which the Donovan Commission had been most concerned, namely, those of un-official or unconstitutional strike action in the private manu-facturing sector of the labour economy. It aimed to address those problems by the quintessentially late-1960s approach of finding legal mechanisms to make unions shoulder the responsibility of minimizing the damage inflicted by those patterns of industrial relations behaviour.

Even while the legislative Titanic which was the Industrial Relations Act 1971 was on the slipway, another initiative was being launched in these sections of the Social Security Act 1971. It had different designers—Sir Keith Joseph as Secretary of State for Social Services introduced it in the House of Commons—and new lines of design, of which a good deal more would be seen in the 1980s. These provisions were a response, perhaps to an extent unrealized even by their designers, to a new pattern of industrial action; and they reflected a new set of attitudes about the appropriate kind of response for governments to make. The

---

[162] Cl. 47 of Bill 164 of the 1969/70 Session, presented to the House of Commons on 29 May 1970.

new pattern of dispute was one of large, official, primarily public-sector disputes which were in effect if not in intention a challenge to government economic policies, and which were very costly in terms of working days lost.[163] The new pattern of response was one in which the post-war assumptions about the neutrality of the state—especially as a provider of social security—in relation to industrial disputes began to be challenged and eroded. One of the first things the Conservative government had set in hand after the election was a review of the arrangements for the payment of supplementary benefits to the dependants of those involved in trade disputes.[164] It was discovered that the proportion of strikers receiving supplementary benefits for dependants had increased dramatically as the result of two very large strikes—at the Post Office and at Fords.[165] The Social Security Act 1971 accordingly enacted that any personal resources of a claimant, such as tax refunds or strike pay, should now count against such supplementary benefits to a much greater extent than before.[166] It was also discovered that strikers were now relying on supplementary benefits to dependants rather than subs from employers in the period after a return to work because the former were neither repayable nor taxable.[167] Those supplementary benefits were accordingly made repayable.[168] At this stage, the reduction of supplementary benefit to strikers was confined to the curbing of what were viewed as positive abuses.[169] The next Conservative government was to return to the question with more vigorous aims in 1980.

7.3. CONTROLLING THE LABOUR ECONOMY, 1970-1974

(a) Responses to Inflation

It is all too easy, when considering the development of employment law in the period under discussion, to confine all one's

---

[163] See Durcan, McCarthy, and Redman, *Strikes in Post-War Britain*, 168-71 ('Main Features of the Strike Pattern, 1969-1973' and app. 2, 'Political Stoppages, 1969-73'.

[164] See HC Deb., 5th ser., vol. 816, col. 31 (Sir Keith Joseph, Secretary of State for Social Services).

[165] Ibid., col. 54.

[166] S. 1(4), which reduced the disregard of resources from £4.35 to £1.

[167] HC Deb. 5th ser., vol. 816, col. 58.

[168] Social Security Act 1971, s. 2.

[169] HC Deb. 5th ser., vol. 816, col. 53.

attention to the measures that attempted to impose a legal framework upon industrial relations in order to remedy their disorder and inefficiency. There were a number of other developments outside that area of activity which had a great impact on the whole shape of employment law. Some of these can be seen as responses to the growing pressure of inflation, which tended very much to be perceived of as wage-led inflation in this period. The most obvious form of response to inflation in the area of employment law is the imposition of incomes policy, and we shall be concerned in this section to examine what was done in that direction during this period. But there are a number of other policy developments which were responses to the concern with inflation in a less direct sense, or which were crucially influenced by that concern. Indeed, part of the motivation for the Industrial Relations Act itself was the notion that the rationalization of industrial relations would assist in the control of inflation, and it was undoubtedly the hope of the Conservative government when it came to power in 1970 that a prominently interventionist policy on industrial relations would create a context in which a formal incomes policy would be unnecessary. We shall see that the history of government of industrial society in the ensuing four years was dominated by the dashing of that expectation.

During the period of the Conservative government from 1970 to 1974, there was a retreat from voluntarism in the direction of incomes policy which was as significant for employment law in some ways as the counter-voluntarism of the Industrial Relations Act itself. The abandonment of voluntarism in this area was the more noticeable because the government began with a proclaimed intention so to manage the economy and industrial relations as to obviate the need for formal incomes policy. But from November 1970 it emerged that they were running a policy of restraining public sector wage increases. This was known as the 'n minus 1 policy', because it aimed to ensure that each pay settlement should be for a slightly smaller increase than the one before.[170] By July 1971, moreover, the government was pursuing a policy of actively reflating the economy to try to control a

---

[170] See M. Holmes, *Political Pressure and Economic Policy: British Government 1970–1974* (London, 1982), ch. 4, 'The "n minus 1" Experiment and the Reaction to Rising Unemployment'.

sharp rise in unemployment, and was finding that wage inflation was becoming ever more of a problem. In the early months of 1972, the '*n* minus 1' policy was revealed as ineffective by Lord Wilberforce's settlement of the miners' strike for a 21 per cent wage increase. By July 1972, the government was engaged in tripartite talks with employers and unions to try to achieve an effective prices and incomes policy and was prepared to 'put the Industrial Relations Act on ice' in order to achieve this.

By November 1972, having failed in this aim, the government found it necessary to impose a statutory incomes policy, of which Stage 1 was a 90-day freeze on prices and incomes.[171] This was given legal force by the Counter-Inflation (Temporary Provisions) Act 1972. In March 1973, a more elaborate prolongation of statutory prices and incomes policy occurred (Stage 2). It was implemented in legal terms by the Counter-Inflation Act 1973, which provided for the making of a Price and Pay Code, which was duly issued[172] and which set a pay norm limiting pay increases to £1 per week per person plus 4 per cent of the existing wage bill including overtime. The flat-rate element tended to help low-paid workers; but this compression of differentials brought its own problems. The Code was to be administered by a Prices Board and a Pay Board set up by the Act.[173] The Pay Board had a remit to maintain a tighter hold on wage settlements with less flexibility than the National Board for Prices and Incomes had enjoyed under the Labour government's incomes policy. In November 1973, as the maintaining of strict control grew ever more difficult, Stage 3 was introduced, which allowed a looser pay norm of 7 per cent or £2.25 per week, and which made some exceptions, such as an 'unsocial hours' exception, perhaps representing an unsuccessful attempt to accommodate the miners, who were again threatening to strike. Stage 3 was still in force when the government fell in 1974, its defeat being largely attributable to the miners' second strike, which this time successfully challenged even a statutory incomes policy.[174] So an initially voluntarist approach was transformed by

---

[171] Ibid., ch. 5, 'The "Heath Dilemma" and the Drift to Incomes Policy'.

[172] Counter-Inflation (Price and Pay Code) Order 1973, SI 1973, No. 658.

[173] S. 1.

[174] See Holmes, *Political Pressure and Economic Policy*, ch. 7, 'Stage III, the Miners' Strike and the February 1974 Election'.

the pressure of wage inflation into an interventionism upon which the government was forced to stake its political survival—only to lose that gamble.

In the years after 1974, incomes policies assumed sufficiently different forms to make the sort of tight legally backed norms that existed from 1972 to 1974 seem rather unfamiliar. Nevertheless, we have recounted the incomes policy developments of those years in a little detail, because it is useful to remind oneself of the impact that such legal regulation, viewed as an aspect of employment law, can have.[175] Formal and statutory incomes policies had a considerable impact on patterns of collective bargaining and of industrial conflict in this period. Superficially, they appear simply to constrain collective bargaining during their currency, and to bottle up industrial conflict so that it breaks out with renewed or increased vigour upon their expiry; but their effects, properly understood, are more pervasive and complex than that. They seem slightly to have added momentum to the tendency for private-sector collective bargaining to become more concentrated on single-employer plant- or company-level bargaining, as compared with national-level bargaining. For example, the Stage 2 pay norm, taking as it did the wages total of the whole of a company's workforce as a starting-point, encouraged a sort of 'kitty bargaining', allowing manœuvring within the compass of the single employing enterprise which could best be carried out in plant- or company-level bargaining.

In the public sector, incomes policies brought about even more fundamental changes, and did much to bring about a new sort of public sector employment relationship both at individual and collective levels. The fact that the government sought to achieve incomes policy goals by pressure on the public sector—especially, but not solely, during the voluntary phase when the 'n minus 1' policy was in force—tended to undermine a consensus about pay levels that had been successfully maintained both in the Civil Service and elsewhere in the public sector. As the government figured increasingly in public sector collective bargaining as the cost-conscious employer or stringent paymaster, so the pattern of industrial conflict tended to shift from one dominated by the

---

[175] What follows is much influenced by Hugh Clegg's analysis in ch. 9 of *The Changing System of Industrial Relations in Great Britain* (Oxford, 1979).

wild-cat or unofficial industrial action associated with fragmented bargaining in the private sector to one in which the set-piece public sector official strike loomed very large. So much was this the case that public sector earnings moved up considerably in proportion to private sector earnings during the period.[176] But this was not without much strain on the traditionally moderate and accommodating collective stance about pay which had prevailed in much of the public sector. The new tension was to do much to shape the development of labour law in the next decade, not least by bringing trade unions into a virtually bipartite strategic collective bargaining relationship with the government even more obviously then before. Within the period under consideration, that strategic bargaining relationship broke down so completely under the political pressures associated with inflation that the government broke out of the relationship with an unsuccessful appeal to the electorate to vindicate its managerial authority. It was left to the succeeding labour government to attempt to reconstruct that relationship on a more favourable basis. The consequences for labour law, as we shall see, were profound ones.

Finally, so far as responses to inflation during the 1970–4 period are concerned, it is important to realize that, even though the government abandoned a voluntarist stance towards incomes policy, not all its responses to wage inflation were in the direction of restricting compensation for inflation. Just as, for the Labour government, the growing pressure of inflation had lent an impetus to the protection of women's pay in the Equal Pay Act, so certain measures of the Conservative government aimed to protect the workforce or sections of it against the erosion of living standards by inflation. We have already noted that for example, in Stage 3 of their statutory incomes policy the government—rashly in the event—felt able to permit wage increases to compensate for inflation when a threshold level (set at 7 per cent p.a.) was reached. There was also one measure of great significance designed to protect public service workers—in their retired capacity as pensioners—from inflation; it was the Pensions (Increase) Act 1971. Governments had hitherto for more than fifty years responded to the erosion by inflation of the value of

[176] Ibid. 373.

public service pensions by a series of *ad hoc* Pensions Increase Acts each making a particular increase. In 1971 they moved to a systematic continuing programme of relating public service pensions to the cost-of-living index, and consolidated the base for this operation by restoring all pensions in the course of payment in April 1969 to their original purchasing power when they had started to be paid. In doing this, they were consolidating and upgrading a tradition of viewing the financial security of retired public service employees as a responsibility of central and local government in their capacity as employers.[177] No doubt it was significant that the Government was at this time embarked upon the '*n* minus 1' policy of restraining public sector pay increases. At all events, this measure contributed considerably to a divergence of the legal regime for public service workers from that of private sector workers,[178] which, as we shall see, was to become profoundly controversial in the 1980s.

(b) Responses to Unemployment

We have in earlier sections traced the moves away from voluntarism during this period in the areas of industrial relations and of incomes policy. There was a parallel counter-voluntarist development in relation to the control of the labour market; it was a response to rapidly rising unemployment. As we have indicated earlier, the period down to 1968 is to be regarded as voluntarist in relation to the labour market only in a special sense. Successive governments had been committed to maintaining full employment since 1944; but they had been able to rely on Keynesian management of the economy to sustain full

[177] Thus David Howell, Parliamentary Secretary to the Civil Service Department, introducing the Bill on Second Reading:—'A good pension system is one of the compensations of public service.' HC Deb. 5th ser., vol. 818, col. 250 (25 May 1971).

[178] It is to be noted that the Social Security Act 1973 (associated with Sir Keith Joseph, then Secretary of State for Social Services, and implementing the proposals contained in the White Paper, *Strategy for Pensions* (Cmnd. 4755, 1971)) was partly designed to encourage the development of occupational pension schemes in the private sector, and set up the Occupational Pensions Board to control their operation. But this was more designed to channel some of the responsibility for social security provision for the retired workforce towards private sector employers; the protection accorded to the pension expectations of private sector workers by that Act was in no way comparable with that conferred upon public service workers by the Pensions (Increase) Act 1971.

employment without the necessity for any very direct management of the labour market. As we saw in an earlier chapter, the
Labour government in the period 1964–8 could still regard itself
as in the business of industrial modernization rather than in the
business of labour market regulation. This atmosphere persisted
in that part of the Labour government's term of office which fell
within the period under consideration in the previous chapter.
Thus although by 1969 the government found it necessary to bring
forward the Redundancy Rebates Act 1969 to reduce the rebates
paid from the Redundancy Fund to employers making statutory
payments to their redundant workers under the 1965 Act—in
order to reduce the deficit into which the Fund had fallen—that
measure could still be presented as a cost of the programme of
industrial modernization, rather than as a response to rising
unemployment.[179] Moreover, Edward Heath's incoming Conservative government consciously espoused a new voluntarism in
relation to the private sector economy, and hence the labour
market. There was a deliberate design of leaving the economy
free to manifest what was thought to be its capacity, if left
untrammelled, to grow and permit effective competition with
the Continental European countries with which it was sought
to associate the UK economy by means of EEC membership
(achieved in 1972). There was even a preparedness to risk
economic reflation to stimulate this development.[180] So in 1970 or
even in 1971 there was a fairly thorough-going governmental
voluntarism towards the labour market.

This position changed drastically from 1971 onwards in response
to rapidly rising unemployment, which passed the politically
critical total of 1 million in January 1972. It is argued that the
control of unemployment overtook the control of inflation as the
primary objective of economic policy by July 1971.[181] That is an
extreme view; but in the area of labour market control we can
certainly detect a radical shift at that time towards intervention
designed to remedy unemployment. Industrial and regional

[179] See the presentation of the Bill by Roy Hattersley as Under-Secretary of
State for Employment and Productivity: HC Deb., 5th ser., vol. 776, cols. 1555 ff.
(30 Jan. 1969).
[180] These developments and their relevance to the labour market are very well
chronicled by Holmes, *Political Pressure and Economic Policy*, esp. in ch. 3, 'The
U-turn over Industry Policy'.
[181] Ibid. 65, quoting J. Bruce-Gardyne.

policy provides the sharpest example. At the beginning of 1971, the government brought forward a bill, which was to become the Industry Act 1971, which had the aim and effect of dismantling much of the apparatus of active industry policy set up by the previous Labour government. Thus the Act repealed the legislation which had set up the Industrial Reorganization Corporation in 1966 and wound up the corporation; it also terminated the powers by which the government had been enabled to involve itself in industrial investment schemes under the Industrial Expansion Act 1968. The presentation of the bill indicated the view that the government had regarded and continued to regard the 1966 and 1968 measures as conducing towards an excessive and arbitrary distribution of public funds to industry.[182] But by mid-1972, having felt impelled to abandon the policy of not rescuing industrial 'lame ducks', in relation first to Rolls Royce and then to Upper Clyde Shipbuilders, the government was in the position of proposing a new Industry Bill which was enacted as the Industry Act 1972, which implemented a policy set forth in a White Paper on Regional and Industry Policy in March 1972[183] of providing a wide range of support for the regeneration of industry with special assistance to depressed regions of the country. We shall return in later chapters to the consideration of the impact on collective bargaining and on the labour market of the particular industry and regional policies adopted by successive governments from this time onwards; suffice it at this stage to point to the way in which political concern with unemployment brought a new wave of interventionist governmental action in this area.

If we turn from the area of industrial and regional policy to that of labour supply management (in the sense of provision of training and relating the available workforce to job opportunities—the area comprised under the head of 'employment and training' in administrative terminology), we find that, without the abrupt reversal away from voluntarism that there was in industrial and regional policy, there was nevertheless a highly significant increase in governmental interventionism while the

[182] See the speech on Second Reading of John Davies as Secretary of State for Industry and President of the Board of Trade: HC Deb., 5th ser., vol. 810, cols. 347 ff. (26 Jan. 1971).
[183] *Industrial and Regional Development*, Cmnd. 4942.

Conservative government was in office, which must be seen as a consequence of the political pressures exerted by rising unemployment. This was, initially at least, a matter of initiatives coming from the Department of Employment (whereas industry and regional policy were within the province of the Department of Trade and Industry). In April 1972, the former Department introduced (under powers conferred by the Employment and Training Act 1948) a new Employment Transfer Scheme which was an upstaged and elaborated version of the Resettlement Transfer Scheme under which the governmental assisted labour mobility policy had been implemented (with varying degrees of intensity) since 1948. It was hoped by this new measure of assistance to double the number of unemployed workers transferring to full-time employment in new areas, with conditions favouring the movement of workers from assisted areas.[184] The importance of this sort of government assistance as an aspect of the management of redundancy has continually been underestimated; but an even more important new expansion of governmental activity was soon to occur. This consisted of the radical restructuring of the whole institutional framework of governmental employment and training activity which was accomplished by the Employment and Training Act 1973. That Act marked a decisive increase in the level of governmental regulation of the labour market and contributed greatly to a growing countervoluntarism in employment law for this period seen as a whole; we need to examine it in some detail.

The Employment and Training Act 1973 shows very clearly what the main themes were of the labour legislation—apart from the Industrial Relations Act and the individual employment legislation which we have already considered—of Edward Heath's Conservative government of 1970 to 1974. There were two main measures in the 1973 Act;[185] firstly, sections 1-4 remodelled the governmental machinery concerned with services to help people to obtain employment and with arrangements for

[184] Assisted Labour Mobility Policy has, for this sort of reason, been viewed as an aspect of regional policy: see P. B. Beaumont, ch. 3 of D. Maclennan and J. B. Parr, eds., *Regional Policy, Past Experience and New Directions* (Oxford, 1979).
[185] S. 5 also created the important power of the Secretary of State for Employment to make temporary employment subsidies; see below, p. 603.

training for employment, by setting up the Manpower Services Commission as an overseeing body to deal with these concerns, and the Employment Service Agency and Training Services Agency as the two executive agencies to carry out the activities themselves. Secondly, section 6 and schedule II of the Act modified the Industrial Training Act 1964 so that where originally the Industrial Training Boards, set up under the 1964 Act, were financed by a system of compulsory levies upon employers with the possibility of grants back to the employers, there would now be provision for schemes of exemption for the appropriate employers from the industrial training levies. These two measures of institutional reform represented between them a very important initiative towards a new legal basis for governmental management of the labour economy. The Act tells us significant things about the interplay between voluntarism, governmental managerialism, and tripartism in the development of labour legislation under the 1970–4 Conservative administration.

The modification to the financing of Industrial Training Boards was an essentially voluntarist development; it was meant to relieve some employers of the compulsion to pay the industrial training levy, on the assumption that it was acceptable for them to take their own decisions about arrangements for and allocation of resources to training. Sarah Vickerstaff has argued that the operation of the Industrial Training Act 1964 had produced a situation in which, in her words,

By the early 1970s there were at least three policy options being discussed . . . The view of the trade unions (and many educational lobbies) that there should be more training, more government finance and greater central co-ordination. The view of larger industrial capital that the existing arrangements were basically all right, and, lastly, the opinion of small industrial capital that there should be less government interference and an end to the levy.[186]

The change to the levy/exemption system in the 1973 Act was a choice in favour of the small firms' preferred option; Vickerstaff goes on to show how the small firms gained ground in the early 1970s, with a recommendation in favour of exemption of small

---

[186] S. Vickerstaff, *The Post-War Development of Industrial Training Policy: A Case Study in the Contradictions of Corporatism* (European University Institute, 1983), 11–12 (Paper to 1983 Summer School on Comparative European Politics).

firms from the training levy (with the possibility of their opting in to the levy/grant system if they so chose) in the Report of the Bolton Committee of Inquiry on Small Firms in 1971;[187] so that:

In February 1971 the Secretary of State [for Employment] said he was looking to the ITBs to exempt more small firms from the levy in future and in the same month he revealed plans to wind up the Hairdressing and Allied Services Training Board on the grounds that small firms characterised the industry.[188]

This voluntarism led by the short-term financial strategies of small firms[189] foreshadows the de-regulation policies of the early 1980s; we shall see that this particular policy was taken considerably further by the Employment and Training Act 1981.

In the 1980s, that kind of voluntarism—which was individual rather than collective *laissez-faire*—was to become more dominant. In the Employment and Training Act 1973 it was one of several strands in the policy formulation. Another very important one was the new governmental managerialism associated with Edward Heath's 'Quiet Revolution' of the first couple of years of his 1970–4 administration. The impact of the 'Quiet Revolution' upon labour legislation and employment policy was a subtle but important one which deserves some of our attention, if only because it prefigures, to a remarkable extent, many of the attitudes, policies, and policy measures of 1980s governments. Martin Holmes describes the objectives of the 'Quiet Revolution' in these terms:

What the 'Quiet Revolution' sought to reverse was the steady progression towards a collectivist economy dominated by state regulation. The 'Quiet Revolution' approach was not only about reversing the trends towards collectivism, important though that was; it was also concerned with the modernisation of the U.K. economy and the reinvigoration of industry and enterprise that were essential if the U.K. were to face a European future from a position of industrial strength rather than

[187] Cmnd. 4811, paras. 14.22–4.
[188] Vickerstaff, *Post-War Development*, 14–15. The Hairdressing ITB was not at that stage wound up.
[189] Ibid. 13–14 shows how the CBI took an equivocal stance between this extreme voluntarism of its small firms and the greater enthusiasm of its larger (and on the whole more influential) member enterprises for state-co-ordinated corporate investment in training.

weakness, a policy to which Mr Heath was personally dedicated more than any other that had been worked out in Opposition.[190]

There were significant tensions within this set of policy objectives; but it did at least seem to suggest a coherent programme for improving the quality of management of governmental activities. The final plan for the execution of this design was published in October 1970 as a White Paper, *The Reorganization of Central Government*.[191] One of the areas of governmental activity upon which this programme was concentrated was the Employment Service of the Department of Employment, which dealt with the work of local employment offices (consisting both of helping people find jobs and administering unemployment benefit). By December 1971, the government, in a document entitled 'People and Jobs', announced that the Employment Service should be 'modernised and more closely geared to the requirements of its customers'. Among the ways of achieving this were to be:

Creating a new management framework so that the Employment Service becomes a self-managing unit—a 'Departmental Agency'—within the Department of Employment;
Administratively and physically separating employment and unemployment benefit work;
Analysing and reappraising the work of employment staff giving advisory interviews, to ensure better-trained staff equipped to advise workers about jobs and to meet employers' needs;
Introducing experiments to develop the role of employment offices in providing local labour market intelligence.[192]

By the end of 1972, a further policy document entitled *Into Action—Plan for a Modern Employment Service* announced that the Employment Service Agency had been established as a self-managing unit within the Department of Employment, and that an Action Plan had been prepared with this stated aim:

The objective of the modernisation is to give the customer the employment service he needs, when he needs it, in the way he needs it. For only by being wholly orientated towards its customers' needs will the service attain its declared aim.

[190] Holmes, *Political Pressure and Economic Policy*, 11.
[191] Cmmd. 4506.
[192] *DE Gazette*, Dec. 1971, p. 1097.

The Action Plan included these items on Management Control:

Quantified national objectives for the Employment Service to be set for 1973 and a system of accountable management to monitor performance of agreed plans, allowing for further delegation of authority and responsibility, to be developed.

Early in 1973, the Department of Employment proposed in a White Paper[193] to take the further step of moving the Employment Service Agency out of the Department and making it a wholly separate agency, to be the responsibility of a newly created Manpower Services Commission; the proposals were carried out by the 1973 Act. This was all significantly similar to the aims and methods of the Initiative for Efficiency in Government of the 1980s, which, as we shall see in due course, had an important impact on the labour legislation policy of that period.[194]

In a slightly different way, the setting-up of the Training Services Agency by the 1973 Act, again under the control of the Manpower Services Commission, was also a product of the 'Quiet Revolution'. The plan to set up a National Training Agency as 'a hived-off body outside the Civil Service' was set out in a policy document issued by the Department of Employment in 1972.[195] But the setting-up of the Training Services Agency, as it was named in the 1973 Act, and the 1972 plan represented the 'Quiet Revolution' in other ways than by merely hiving-off and streamlining the training functions of the Department of Employment. On the one hand, the *laissez-faire* element in the 'Quiet Revolution' was present in the proposal, described earlier, to modify the levy/grant system in relation to the Industrial Training Boards. On the other hand, the broad aim of 'promoting a technological, managerial man looking to a European commitment to aid the regeneration of competition in industry and personal initiative in the wealth creating process'[196] was seen, in the 1972 plan, as requiring a general intensification of governmental activity in the training field, with three particular aims:

---

[193] *Employment and Training: Government Proposals*, Cmnd. 3250, Mar. 1973.
[194] See below, pp. 628–34.
[195] *Training for the Future: A Plan for Discussion*, paras. 153–4.
[196] Holmes, *Political Pressure and Economic Policy*, 11.

(i) to maintain adequate machinery for the setting of agreed standards for training for particular occupations;

(ii) to stimulate firms to use up-to-date methods to train to these standards;

(iii) to develop machinery which can ensure an adequate supply of trained workers in key occupations if individual firms do not do this themselves.[197]

In pursuit of the third aim, the existing Vocational Training Scheme under which 16,650 people were trained in 1970 was to be expanded into the Training Opportunities Scheme which was intended to train 60,000 to 70,000 people a year by 1975.[198] Here we see the 'Quiet Revolution' transformed into a statist and even welfare-oriented aspect; as we shall see, the transformations of the 1980s, though from very similar starting-points, were to be in the opposite direction.

In planning a massive increase in its provision of training, the government was influenced not just by the ideals of the 'Quiet Revolution', but also by its difficulties in dealing with mounting unemployment and inflation, which by 1972 were forcing it into the famous 'U-turns' in the fields of industry policy and incomes policy.[199] We can explain in terms of that general policy development the presence of tripartism in the Employment and Training Act 1973, which is chiefly to be found in the last of its main measures not yet discussed, namely, the setting-up of the Manpower Commission itself. This was not an integral part of the plans so far discussed; it was announced as a distinct proposal by Maurice Macmillan as the new Secretary of State for Employment in a House of Commons Statement in November 1972.[200] To such an extent was this a separate initiative that it was felt necessary to explain in the government's action plan for the employment service that 'The implementation of the programme will not be immediately affected by the government's decisions, announced on November 22, 1972, to set up a Manpower Services Commission.'[201]

There was, certainly, a sound functional case to be made for an

---

[197] *Training for the Future*, para. 10.
[198] Ibid., para. 146.
[199] See Holmes, *Political Pressure and Economic Policy*, chs. 3–5, *passim*.
[200] HC Deb., 5th ser., vol. 840, cols. 1293 ff. (22 Nov. 1972).
[201] *Into Action: Plan for a Modern Employment Service*, 3.

overseeing body to co-ordinate the work of the two proposed new executive agencies for employment services and training services; but the decision to set up the Manpower Services Commission was not arrived at solely on those grounds. In his November 1972 statement, Maurice Macmillan said that:

I must retain general responsibility for manpower policy, but I am proposing to set up a Manpower Services Commission representative of employers, trade unions and other interests which would have direct responsibility to me for the employment and training services. The TUC and CBI agree with this proposal . . . The important point here is that this is a new relationship. It is not a wholly hived-off body over which the Government have no control. It is a body for which the Department is responsible to Parliament.[202]

This marked shift towards tripartism has to be seen in the context of a general move in a corporatist direction which occurred in the course of 1972, and which really amounted to an attempt by the government to arrive at an understanding with the trade union movement that they would be accorded greater influence in the management of the economy in return for wage restraint— what would under a later government be described as a 'Social Contract'.[203] During 1972, Edward Heath was, indeed, to attempt to formalize such an understanding by holding talks with the leadership of the trade union movement.[204] These talks had, however, reached an impasse by November 1972 so far as wage restraint was concerned.[205] The limited significance of the measures actually taken towards tripartism, such as the setting-up of the Manpower Services Commission, is perceptively assessed by Colin Crouch as follows:

---

[202] HC Deb., 5th ser., vol. 840, cols. 1293, 1295.

[203] See below, p. 354 ff.

[204] Holmes describes the development thus: '[B]y the summer of 1972 Mr Heath's commitment to a joint programme for curbing wage and price increases was a strong personal one. It is widely believed, with much justification, that Mr Heath had been impressed by the way that the German Chancellor, Herr Brandt, regularly consulted on a permanent basis the leading trade unionists in Germany on all matters vital to the German economy—the prosperity of which, in comparison to Britain was, and had been for some years, plainly evident. The discovery of an equivalent group in Britain was a task that Mr Heath set himself with great dedication in the summer of 1972' (*Political Pressure and Economic Policy*, 78).

[205] Ibid. 84.

The attempt at involving union leaders and major employers in tripartite relationships is a less risky strategy for governments [than industrial relations law reform]. The object is to secure a commitment to restraint in exchange for a share in economic policy—though the latter may well mean little more than presenting the unions with the government's view of likely developments in the economy and hoping to persuade them to accept that view and the priorities which flow from it. Understandings of this kind were important in the war years and immediately afterwards, but . . . the very special priorities of that period could not have been permanent. Attempts at reconstructing something similar have not been very successful unless they remain at the level of uncontroversial or long-term policy—in which case they are not very effective in tempting the unions into a commitment to restraint. These policies cost little but gain little. To move further means involving the unions in a more tangible share in decisions, which may actually mean conceding power, and this is no longer safe, uncontroversial politics. A prime example were [sic] the talks between Edward Heath and the unions in 1972. The Prime Minister said he would take the CBI and the TUC into policy making across the whole range of government decisions, in exchange for which he expected a commitment to wage and price restraint. The unions took him at his word and made policy demands across a wide front. The Ministers decided that this was an attempt to interfere in the government's prerogative to make policy, and the talks failed to result in agreement.[206]

The shaping effect of the 'Quiet Revolution' and of Edward Heath's exercise in tripartism upon the Employment and Training Act 1973 had one interesting parallel elsewhere in the employment law field, consisting in the establishment of the Health and Safety Commission by the Health and Safety at Work etc. Act 1974. The setting-up of the Robens Committee, whose Report[207] gave rise to that Act, had been the work of Barbara Castle as Secretary of State for Employment and Productivity in June 1972. The presenting of the Bill which was enacted in 1974 fell to Michael Foot as Secretary of State for Employment in the new Labour government which took office in March 1974. But in the meantime the Conservative government had developed the legislation proposed by the Robens Report—had indeed taken as far as its First Reading a version of the Bill very close to the one

---

[206] C. Crouch, *The Politics of Industrial Relations* (2nd edn. 1982), 150–1.
[207] *Safety and Health at Work: Report of the Committee, 1970–72*, Cmnd. 5034 (July 1972).

eventually enacted. The proposal in the Robens Report for a new health and safety authority fitted in well with their plans for reorganization and rationalization of governmental activities, and by May 1973 they announced their intention of implementing the main recommendations of the Report. Interestingly, their proposed legislation had a more specifically tripartist element than the Committee itself had suggested. The Robens Report had suggested that the Authority for Safety and Health at Work should have a Managing Board whose part-time directors 'should include people with experience in the field of industrial management, in the trade union field, and in the medical, educational and local authority sphere'.[208] The government, however, preferred to follow its own directly tripartite model:

The Government agree that there should be an independent statutory authority in this sector and the legislation will establish it. A suitable structure for the new authority could be broadly on the lines of the Manpower Services Commission and its agencies which are to be established under the Employment and Training Bill.

The one significant change to the Conservative Bill made by the incoming Labour government consisted in amending[209] the provisions of section 2 of the Act so as to require the employer to consult solely with the representatives of recognised trade unions over health and safety matters. We shall consider other such provisions in the next chapter; the change to one-channel consultation in the Labour government's legislation is one initial indication of a contrast between Edward Heath's experiments with tripartism and the 'Social Contract' policies of the succeeding government.

There were other measures during this period which had a bearing upon the development of employment law. Foremost among those, of course, were the 1972 Treaty of Brussels effecting British accession to membership of the EEC and the European Communities Act 1972, whose consequences we shall consider in later chapters. There were provisions in the Finance Act 1971 to control evasion of income tax and social security liabilities by the use of labour-only sub-contracting in the construction industry. A private member's bill which received government support was

---

[208] Cmnd. 5034, paras. 117–18.
[209] By EPA 1975, s. 116.

enacted as the Employment Agencies Act 1973, which subjected employment agencies to a regime of legal control designed to prevent financial abuse of agency workers and the employer clients of such agencies. But the central phenomena in employment law in this period were undoubtedly those responses we have examined in detail to the political pressures upon governments flowing from the disorders of industrial relations, from wage inflation, and from rising unemployment. In the concluding section of this chapter, we shall consider how these responses interacted with each other, and what was the significance of that interaction for the overall state of labour law and policy.

7.4. CONCLUSION: FROM CONSENSUS TO POLARIZATION

The titles of this chapter and of the previous one depicted the period from 1964 to 1974 as one of the breakdown of consensus about collective labour law and policy. The fact of that breakdown in consensus is hardly in doubt: whereas in the General Election of 1964 the state of labour law and of industrial relations was scarcely an issue between the political parties, by 1974 two governments had fallen with the failure of their policies in this area as a major source of weakness, and with the opposition in each case making much of its own rival policy prescription. It is more difficult to identify the exact nature of that breakdown in consensus; between which adversaries had polarization occurred, and where and how extensive was their area of contention? This section of the chapter attempts an assessment constructed around those questions. In the introduction to the previous chapter, we saw how the issues seemed to present themselves in constitutional terms; how was industrial society (or perhaps even civil society as a whole) to be governed, and by whom? In the latest section, we saw how there was a dominating and continually growing concern with controlling inflation on the one hand and unemployment on the other. What should we conclude from these different emphases or explanations?

The first main conclusion to be drawn from the events surveyed in these two chapters is that the central breakdown of consensus, and the main axis along which polarization occurred, was between governments and trade unions. The crucial confrontations of this period were between the government on the one hand, whether as the overall regulator of the labour economy or as the employer in the public sector, and the trade union movement on the other, whether in the form of the TUC, of the leaders of individual large and powerful unions, or of the locally organized forces of trade union or shop-floor militancy. This may appear to be too obvious to be worth stating; but it is precisely because we accept this as an obvious or inevitable feature of industrial society in the late 1960s and early 1970s that we are apt to neglect other dimensions of the situation. Thus we tend, perhaps, to have paid insufficient attention to the other two sides of the triangle—that is to say, to relations between governments and employers, and between trade unions and employers. We may have indicated in passing that employers got on surprisingly well, in all the circumstances, with a Labour government in the 1960s, and with the trade unions during the period of the Industrial Relations Act; but we have not explored those theses at all fully, because the leading protagonists seemed to be governments and trade unions at odds with each other.

There are, therefore, dangers in concentrating too heavily upon the polarization between trade unions on the one hand and governments on the other; but that concentration does nevertheless offer some important insights into the events of the period. It helps, for example, to explain why the Report of the Donovan Commission failed to provide a renewal of the post-war settlement of industrial society in the way that it aimed to do. For although the debate which preceded the Report, and the Report itself, were to a significant extent concerned with the relations between governments and trade unions—certainly with the role of the state in relation to trade unions—the government was not a leading protagonist in the debate, and, perhaps in consequence of that, was not heavily committed to accepting or implementing the Report itself. If the Labour government spoke in the Donovan debate, it was in the measured and cautious tones of the civil servants from the Ministry; the politicians, after all, had set up the Commission not least in order to distance themselves from this particular hubbub. When the Conservative Party made its contribution to the Donovan debate, in *Fair Deal at Work*, it was thinking more as a party of opposition than as a party of government; this was something they themselves perhaps insufficiently appreciated when later transmuting that policy document so directly into the Industrial Relations Act. In short, the government was not a key player in the making of the Donovan Report; yet it was very much the key player in the subsequent political conflicts which the Report had sought to pre-empt by rational inquiry and constructive planning.

If the Government and the trade unions were the central protagonists in the de-consensualization of industrial society, what was the area which became contentious? Our second conclusion was that the area of contention was largely defined by and around government, and that governments on the whole sought to impose their own definitions of the area of contention. It was during this period that it became apparent that the political economy of post-war Britain would place governments under continual pressure. Governments would face a continuing crisis of poor economic performance threatening to create both high inflation and high unemployment. The government would be held accountable for that crisis, and would be expected to gain and maintain control over industrial society so as to avert the crisis. Their difficulty in doing so would tend to transform the crisis into a quasi-constitutional one, casting doubt upon the governability of industrial society. So the general area of contention was neither primarily economic nor primarily political; it was an area created by the interaction of economic and political pressures upon government itself. It was, as we have seen, the area of tension created by the commitment to maintaining full employment while seeking to control inflation (and to avoid an adverse balance of payments) in an international market in which Britain competed on increasingly unfavourable terms. Fundamentally, the problem was that the Donovan Report did not come up with a solution to the strike problem, so far as government was concerned. Government did not believe that bargaining reform led by employers and trade unions sufficiently addressed the problem. It was at that point that collective *laissez-faire* ceased to be acceptable to any government; the whole debate turned to the question of what to put in the place of collective *laissez-faire* at the collective level of labour law, just as the move away from abstentionism at the individual level was by now under way.

In that situation, governments at this period (and for that matter at other times, but notably at this one) tended to impose, or at least attempt to impose, their own definitions upon the area in contention. They seemed to prefer a political or constitutional definition of the area to an economic one. An economic definition of the crisis referred to a set of problems which were visibly intractable ones, and which governments were accordingly reluctant to acknowledge; otherwise they would be seen to be vainly trying to fend off an underlying and apparently irreversible economic decline. If, on the other hand, the problems of industrial society were defined in political or constitutional terms, this would imply a more reversible encroachment upon the legitimate functions of government itself by usurpers pursuing sectional interests. Sometimes the casting of the trade unions in that role might be a mere rhetorical device. At other times, it might verge on the disingenuous; Harold Wilson's reference to the 'tightly-knit band of politically motivated men' may be a case in point. At a deeper level, however, it was a natural response for governments to make to the recurring crisis by which they were confronted. Translated into the context of labour law, it was the basis of a trend towards the juridification of industrial relations which may not have been a manifestation of a 'universal' trend,[210] but which at least transcended the division between Government and Opposition from 1968 to 1974.

This brings us to the question of what determined the choice of policies within the area of contention thus established, and to our third main conclusion from the events described in this chapter. This conclusion is that in this period governments, faced with these severe problems in the management of industrial society, sought to address them by procedural solutions but tended to be driven towards attempting substantive solutions instead. Procedural solutions consisted of efforts to make the labour economy function more efficiently by reforming the processes and institutions of industrial relations. The Donovan Commission Report, the *In Place of Strife* proposals, and the Industrial Relations Act 1971 represented three widely differing attempts at procedural solutions. Substantive solutions, on the other hand, consisted in measures directly bearing upon the outcomes of collective bargaining or more generally upon the *results* of the

---

[210] For discussion of juridification as a supposedly universal trend in labour law, see below, pp. 410–17.

working of the labour market. The obvious example of substantive solutions at this period consists of formal incomes policies (though, as we shall argue in a moment, incomes policies may themselves sometimes be procedural in character); but measures to control unemployment by subsidizing employment and training also deserve consideration for inclusion in the category of substantive solutions.

For much of the 1960s, and certainly in the later 1960s and early 1970s, governments preferred both to define the problems of industrial society in procedural terms, as we have already observed, and to offer procedural solutions to them. This preference was reflected, indeed, in the early incomes policy measures of the Labour governments of the 1960s; in particular, the Prices and Incomes Board saw the solutions to the problems of wage inflation in procedural terms. The PIB therefore concentrated on the reform of pay-bargaining and the encouragement of productivity bargaining. As is often the case, the manner of defining the problems was closely linked with the way in which it was hoped to address them. Thus the creation of the Department of Employment and Productivity in 1968 and the formulation of the *In Place of Strife* proposals showed that kind of linkage at work; industrial relations reform was being promoted in the hope of taking the pressure off incomes policy measures. At the beginning of the 1970s, Edward Heath concentrated upon the legislative reform of industrial relations with the clear intention of achieving a procedural equilibrium in industrial society which would make substantive incomes policy measures unnecessary.

Our final conclusion about the events of this period was that these choices on the part of government (though the terminology of 'choice' may exaggerate the scope for manœuvre which the governments in question possessed) proved difficult to sustain and aggravated the very problems they attempted to address. On the one hand, the problems tended to present themselves in economic terms, however much government might prefer a political definition of them. Governments seemed driven by events towards attempting to control substantive outcomes, most notably when Mr Heath's government made its 'U-turns' towards incomes policy and interventionist industrial policy from 1972 onwards. On the other hand, the trade union movement seemed at least as hostile to procedural intervention as to substantive intervention, as governments found to their heavy cost in relation to the *In Place of Strife* proposals and the Industrial Relations Act.

Governments seemed to underestimate the extent to which the autonomy of the trade union movement was expressed, at least in the perceptions of those within it, in procedural terms—in the custom and practice of the processes of collective bargaining and industrial relations. They also probably overestimated the enthusiasm of employers for moving away from that status quo, or rather for being moved away from that status quo by means of labour legislation. In the course of bringing forward and attempting to operate the Industrial Relations Act, the government was learning that discarding collective *laissez-faire* and using the law in industrial relations was more difficult than anticipated, just as their predecessors had made the same discovery when they produced the White Paper, *In Place of Strife*. It involved the abandonment of a century-old peace-time tradition defining the relationship between government and industrial society; the government failed to grasp the extent of the task it was thus setting itself. Both Harold Wilson and Barbara Castle, and then later Edward Heath, wholly underestimated the resistance to law which would arise; they were testing the extent of submission to law in industrial society, and finding it wanting. They regarded the application of law to industrial relations as a matter of technicality, of finding the most efficient way of regulating. They did not accept that, in terms of the perceptions of many of those affected, they were challenging a way of life. In the next chapter, we shall see how a new government sought and ultimately failed to restore the consensus which had thus broken down fairly comprehensively by 1974.

8

THE SOCIAL CONTRACT, 1974–1979

8.1. INTRODUCTION

When in early 1974 a General Election resulted in the return of Mr Wilson as the head of a (minority) Labour government, it was the signal for a profound change in the structure of our labour law. The Industrial Relations Act, against which the union movement had struggled long and hard, was removed from the statute-book: as subsection 1 of section 1 of the Trade Union and Labour Relations Act 1974 baldly declared, 'the Industrial Relations Act 1971 is hereby repealed.' But the Act had to say more than that. The erroneous view was taken by some that the repeal of an Act which had itself repealed earlier Acts caused those earlier Acts automatically to revive. Since this was not so, it was necessary for Parliament to re-enact the relevant provisions of the Trade Union Acts 1871–6 and of the Trade Disputes Acts 1906 and 1965. Otherwise, trade unions and workers would have had, upon repeal of the 1971 Act, no protection against the common law doctrines of restraint of trade, inducing breach of contract, conspiracy, intimidation, and so on. Since judicial interpretation of the earlier Acts had revealed various defects in their construction and since the common law itself had moved on from what it had been understood to be when these Acts were passed, the opportunity was taken in the 1974 Act (and the amending Act of 1976) to update the statutory protections rather than to re-enact them *verbatim*.

As we shall see, this process of, in Lord Scarman's words[1] in a case in 1979, putting 'the law . . . back to what Parliament had intended when it enacted the Act of 1906—but stronger and clearer than it was then', was extremely contentious in Parliament.

[1] *NWL Ltd* v. *Woods* [1979] ICR 867, 886.

The minority Labour government in 1974 was unable to push the whole of its policy through Parliament. That was achieved only in 1976 with the enactment of the Trade Union and Labour Relations (Amendment) Act, after a second election in 1974 had secured for the government a narrow overall majority and the government had threatened to use the Parliament Act to overcome opposition in the House of Lords. As we shall also see, the legislation, once enacted, received a most hostile reception from the Court of Appeal. Although the House of Lords ultimately reasserted the primacy of the Parliamentary policy, as against judicial policy-making, by the time this was done a Conservative government had been returned in the General Election of 1979. Thus it can be argued that the government's policy of restoring to trade unions and workers the full legal freedom to engage in peaceful industrial action in pursuit of industrial grievances was never wholly achieved, because of, first, Parliamentary, and then judicial opposition. Nevertheless, from the moment that the bulk of the Trade Union and Labour Relations Act came into force on 16 September 1974, the framework of law governing industrial action became much more favourable to trade unions and workers than that in operation under the 1971 Act.

However, in terms of the development of trade union attitudes towards the role of the law in industrial relations, perhaps more important than the attempt to restore the *status quo ante* in relation to industrial conflict law were the legislative changes made in respect of collective bargaining law and individual employment law. Here the aim was by no means to restore the pre-1971 position. On the contrary, in these areas some of the legislative initiatives of the 1971 Act were adopted and others were remoulded, and some entirely new ones made their appearance. Already in the Trade Union and Labour Relations Act 1974 the beginnings of the process were revealed. After section 1(1) had repealed the Industrial Relations Act 1971, section 1(2) provided: 'Nevertheless, Schedule 1 to this Act shall have effect for re-enacting ... the under-mentioned provisions of that Act', and the most important re-enactment that followed was of the unfair dismissal provisions of the 1971 Act. However, it was the Employment Protection Act of 1975 that cemented the process. Further individual rights were placed by that Act upon the statute-book—notably in the areas of guaranteed pay, maternity rights, and redundancy—whilst the remedies for unfair dismissal were upgraded and employment rights were made more secure where the employer was insolvent; trade union members and representatives acquired rights to time off for various purposes and were given greater protection against discrimination on grounds of their union membership; and finally, the institution of collective bargaining was given a boost by the introduction of compulsory consultation by employers with trade unions in certain circumstances, by the re-introduction of a modified statutory recognition procedure, and by the establishment of a much improved legal mechanism for 'extending' the results of collective bargaining to non-federated or underpaying employers.

The recognition and extension procedures were to prove quite contentious in operation and will be examined, along with the other parts of the 1975 Act, in due course. The purpose of this examination will not be, however, to elucidate the details of the legal provisions, but rather to ask what light they throw upon the role played by the law in regulating industrial relations after 1974 and upon trade union attitudes towards the law in this role. It is sometimes said that in the 1960s (and earlier) the attitude of the unions was that the law should be 'kept out' of industrial relations. Its sole legitimate function was to provide the immunities against the common law doctrines that would otherwise impede the processes of collective bargaining, but, that done, the function of regulating the employment relationship was a task for collective bargaining. 'Negative' law, as exemplified by the Acts of 1871, 1906, and 1965, was acceptable and, indeed, necessary, but beyond that it was dangerous for the trade union movement to go, for what the state gave, the state could take away. If that was the trade union attitude of the 1960s—and it may be doubted whether it was ever quite as crude and dogmatic as the above account suggests—it had undergone a significant change by 1974. When sending its proposals for inclusion in the Employment Protection Bill to the Secretary of State for Employment in October 1974, the General Council of the TUC stated that, although 'the General Council consider that statute law can only play a subordinate part in the conduct of industrial relations' and 'the main method is voluntary negotiations between employers and unions', nevertheless 'legislation should ensure that all workers have certain minimum rights and should encourage the development of voluntary collective bargaining and supplement it where necessary.'[2]

It is, then, fair to conclude that the legislation of this period 'envisaged a shift away from *laissez-faire* voluntarism towards legislative intervention',[3] a conclusion that is only strengthened if one takes into account, as one must, the proposals for employee representation on the boards of large companies, which were much discussed during this period, although never enacted. But the interesting point is not just that the legislation of 1974–6 resulted in 'more law', nor even whether there is, now, a persistent trend towards 'more law' in our industrial relations system. One must know what *sort* of law was introduced. What were its purposes? Since the aim was clearly not to supplant collective bargaining by legal regulation of the employment relationship, one can ask how the authors of the legislation envisaged the boundary-line between the two. At what point does the legislative stipulation of 'minimum rights' for all workers (whether unionized or not) and the 'encouragement' of collective bargaining through legal mechanisms challenge the fundamental tenets of the doctrine of collective *laissez-faire*? Having defined the strategy of the legislators, one must move on to ask about the success of the strategy once it was implemented. What factors might explain the degree of success achieved (or the lack of it)? Finally, and irrespective of the goals of the legislation, one may enquire about consequences that were perhaps not intended or even foreseen. Did the legislative interventions of this period help towards the 'incorporation' of trade unions into the state apparatus or towards the 'juridification' or 'judicialization' of the conduct of industrial relations? Some attempt will be made to deal with these questions in later segments of this chapter.

(a) The Social Contract and the Influence of the TUC

Any full analysis of legislative goals requires some analysis of the background to the formation of labour law policy by the government of this period. This was the era of the 'Social Contract', a

---

[2] TUC, *Annual Report 1974*, 74.

[3] J. Clark and Lord Wedderburn, 'Modern Labour Law: Problems, Functions and Policies', in Lord Wedderburn, R. Lewis, and J. Clark, eds., *Labour Law and Industrial Relations: Building on Kahn-Freund* (1983), 196.

'contract' between, on the one hand, the TUC and the trade union movement as a whole and, on the other, first the Labour Party in opposition and then the Labour government. The nature of the 'contract' is sometimes presented as one whereby the government enacted the labour legislation favourable to the trade union movement, which has been described above, in exchange for trade union adherence to a 'voluntary' (i.e. non-statutory) incomes policy. But it will be suggested that such a characterization of the Social Contract is misleading. In its conception, at least, the Social Contract was both more and less than an exchange of new labour laws for acceptance of an incomes policy.

It is certainly true that labour legislation was from the beginning an important ingredient of the Social Contract. The TUC–Labour Party Liaison Committee, which consisted of six representatives each from the leadership of the Parliamentary Labour Party, the National Executive of the Labour Party, and the Trade Union Congress, and which was the institution which begat the Social Contract, was established in 1970 in order to co-ordinate the campaign of opposition, both within Parliament and outside, to the Industrial Relations Bill. In 1971 it was agreed in the committee that a future Labour government would repeal the Industrial Relations Act. However, more than a bald repeal was already envisaged. The General Council's report to the Special Congress, held in Croydon in March 1971 in order to determine the TUC's policy towards the 1971 Act, called upon the parties represented on the Liaison Committee to 'develop a constructive alternative which would ensure that a workable accord between a future Labour Government and the unions and their members could be put to the electorate as a firm basis for the repeal of the Bill'.[4] This alternative was quickly developed. The General Council's report to the 1973 TUC Congress could state that agreement had been reached within the Liaison Committee on the basic strategy for labour law to be followed by a future Labour government. This was the famous three-stage approach. First, there was to be a 'Repeal Bill', then an Employment Protection Bill to 'extend the rights of workers and unions', and finally, industrial democracy legislation.

The role of the TUC, however, went beyond participation

[4] TUC, *Annual Report 1971*, 348.

through the Liaison Committee in the debate on the principles of future labour law policy. As the General Gouncil's Report to the 1974 Congress put it, once the Liaison Committee had agreed (in September 1973) on the proposals which would be contained in the Repeal Bill, 'the General Council asked TUC counsel to draft them in the form of a Bill so that the agreed proposals could be enacted speedily by a Labour Government'[5]—and, no doubt, though this is unsaid, so that any scope for Civil Service advice to a future Labour government, tending to water down the Liaison Committee's proposals, would be reduced to a minimum. The General Election, which Labour won, was held on 28 February 1974, and on 5 March 'the General Council sent to the Employment Secretary the draft Bill prepared by counsel together with the Liaison Committee documents on which it had been based'.[6] The draft from the General Council was substantially followed in the Government's Trade Union and Labour Relations Bill, published on 30 April 1974.

The TUC also had considerble influence on the scope of the Employment Protection Bill. This had been considered within the Liaison Committee, which continued to meet even after a Labour Government was elected. No draft Bill was produced by the TUC in this case, but as early as May 1974 the General Council sent to the Employment Secretary a detailed document (of some 51 paragraphs) setting out the Council's proposals for inclusion in the Bill.[7] The Government produced a Consultative Document in September 1974, which was clearly strongly influenced by the TUC's proposals and which was, accordingly, 'strongly welcomed by the TUC', although the General Council felt 'disappointment' about some aspects of it.[8] The General Council's detailed response to the Consultative Document (of some 47 paragraphs)[9] produced some further changes in the direction the TUC wished to go by the time the government produced its first version of the Employment Protection Bill in March 1975. Consultations between the government and the TUC continued during the Bill's progress through Parliament.

[5] TUC, *Annual Report 1974*, 68.
[6] Ibid.
[7] Ibid. 74.
[8] TUC, Annual *Report 1975*, 91.
[9] Ibid.

The result, in the TUC's words, was an Act which introduced 'valuable new rights for workers'.[10]

There is, thus, no doubt about the influence that the TUC exercised over government labour law policy in the period 1974 to 1976 or about the centrality of labour law reform in the relations between the TUC and the government. During the period the TUC achieved an influence over legislative policy towards labour law which has not been equalled, before or since. However, it is important not to overestimate this influence, powerful though it was. There was never a one-to-one relationship between what the TUC wanted and what Parliament enacted. Even in respect of the Trade Union and Labour Relations Bill, where the TUC's influence was at its maximum, the Labour government's lack of an overall majority in the Commons and of any majority at all in Lords resulted in an Act that was rather different from the Bill of April 1974. Before the Bill was ever published, certain matters were dropped from the TUC's draft Bill and deferred to the Employment Protection Bill, in order to speed the government Bill's passage through Parliament.[11] Nevertheless, that passage was not smooth. In the Commons two opposition amendments were passed which were intended to increase the range of situations in which dismissal of an employee, in a closed shop, for non-membership of the appropriate union would be an unfair dismissal. Further amendments to the government's Bill followed in the Lords, notably amendments providing legal protection for those arbitrarily or unreasonably excluded or expelled from a trade union and confining the protection of those engaged in industrial action against the common law tort of inducing breach of contract to situations where the contract in question was a contract of employment.[12] As we have seen, it was only with the Amendment Act of 1976 that these restrictions were removed. Perhaps even more significant, as indicating that the government did not regard itself as incapable of exercising independent judgment over the TUC's proposals, was the one significant proposal in the government's Bill with which the General Council did not agree. Again, this concerned the

---

[10] TUC, *Annual Report 1976*, 404.

[11] TUC, *Annual Report 1974*, 68.

[12] For the details of the parliamentary process see K. W. W., (1974) 37 MLR 525, 529, 549.

closed shop. The TUC wished dismissal of an employee for non-membership of the appropriate union always to be, in law, a fair dismissal, with compassionate cases being dealt with through unions' own machinery. The government, however, included in the Bill a provision making a dismissal in such cases unfair where 'the employee genuinely objects on grounds of religious belief to being a member of any trade union whatsoever'.[13]

That the Department of Employment remained an independent centre of decision-making on labour law matters was demonstrated even more clearly in relation to the Employment Protection Bill. Here there was, in any event, probably less agreement within the TUC and the Liaison Committee on the basic strategy of this Bill to create 'positive rights' than had been the case with the Repeal Bill. Although the content of the Bill very much reflected the TUC's proposals, the fact that the government issued a Consultative Document before the Bill was promulgated enabled other interest groups to have a greater chance to influence policy formation than had been the case with the Repeal Bill. Consequently, the Act sometimes differed in detail, often important detail, from what the TUC had proposed. For example, the TUC had originally proposed that redundancies should not be permitted to employers without the prior approval of the relevant government agency and of the trade unions concerned. The Act ultimately required only that the relevant unions be consulted and the government informed. Again, the TUC proposed that a union should be able to complain to the CAC 'where it considers that an employer is "undercutting" by not complying with the prevailing rate for the district as a whole'. Ultimately, schedule 11 to the Act considerably circumscribed the circumstances in which complaint could be made that an employer was not complying with the 'general level' of terms and conditions of employment. Or again, the provisions controlling the granting of interlocutory injunctions in trade disputes did not restore the prima-facie case test which the *Ethicon* case had recently removed (although this was what the TUC had asked for), but rather threw the strength of the defendants' case into the balance of convenience, as one only of the factors to be considered there.[14]

[13] TUC, *Annual Report 1974*, 71; TULRA 1974, sched. 1, para. 6(5).
[14] TUC, *Annual Report 1975*, 96 and 102.

Thus some matters were not legislated upon in the precise way the TUC had suggested. A small number of TUC proposals were not taken up at all. Private fee-charging employment agencies were not prohibited. 'Bogus' self-employed workers were not brought within the definition of employee. The enforcement of industrial tribunal awards was left as a matter for individual applicants to pursue in the county court. More important, the government failed to enact legislation conferring upon pickets the right peacefully but effectively to communicate with others, especially when those others were in vehicles.[15] This was a major defeat for the TUC, for legislation to this end was originally envisaged as one of the items for the Repeal Bill. The item was deferred to the Employment Protection Bill, but was ultimately dropped from that Bill too when the government failed to find a formula that would satisfy both the TUC and the police. As we shall see, the TUC proved far from invincible when it came up against another interest group as powerful (in its own way) and as well organized as the police. Or to put it another way, the TUC's special relationship was with the Department of Employment. The Home Office lay to some extent outside its sphere of special influence. Thus the TUC made equally little progress when it tried to achieve the release from prison of the 'Shrewsbury three' pickets, who had been convicted of criminal conspiracy in connection with a sometimes violent building workers' strike in 1973. In spite of motions passed at the TUC's annual congresses, meetings with the Prime Minister, and a national lobby of Parliament, the Home Secretary refused to budge.[16] The TUC's relative lack of influence was even discernible when the Home Office was not resisting TUC initiatives, but promoting its own progressive legislation. Thus one cannot detect the same degree of TUC influence on the Sex Discrimination and Race Relations Bills, even though they dealt in part with employment issues, as on the Employment Protection Bill. Whilst welcoming both Bills as contributions towards producing a fairer society, the TUC would have wished the Acts to provide greater scope for the

---

[15] Ibid. 91, 100.

[16] Ibid. 105–12. 'I had the impression that the bulk of the deputation [from the TUC] was not so much angry as amazed that I would not accede. The climate of the time was that of ministers finding out what the TUC wanted and giving it to them' (Roy Jenkins, *A Life at the Centre* (London, 1991), 392).

parties' own machinery to deal with complaints of discrimination than the Acts in fact allowed.[17]

In assessing the TUC's influence on labour legislation in the two or three years after the return of the Labour government in 1974, a number of caveats therefore have to be entered against the view that the law of the land was being written in Congress House. Indeed, the biggest piece of evidence against this view has not yet been mentioned. This was the total failure of the government to enact the legislation on industrial democracy envisaged in 1973 as the third stage of the legislative programme of a future Labour government. That story will be examined in more detail below, but it shows how short was the period of very high influence by the TUC over the labour law proposals of the Labour government: by the end of 1975, when the Bullock Committee was established, it was already beginning to wane. Nevertheless, the TUC's influence over legislation and governmental policy in general was an issue out of which the Opposition was able to derive considerable political capital, for any form of corporatist bargaining is always open to rather unsophisticated challenges on the basis that it bypasses Parliament and subverts the democratic process. Certainly, one consequence of this period seems to have been to put the legislation relating to trade unions' political activities back on to the policy agenda. This area of law had been something of a backwater since the Conservative government, elected in 1951, had decided not to disturb the restoration of 'contracting out' of the political levy by the previous Labour government in the Trade Disputes and Trade Union Act 1946. In the 1980s, however, as we shall see, this and related issues were re-assessed in the Trade Union Act 1984.

(b) The Failure of the 'Wider' Social Contract

However one assesses the TUC influence, there is anyway the more fundamental criticism that it is inadequate to view the Social Contract as simply favourable labour legislation in exchange for trade union acceptance of an incomes policy, because, at least in origin, the social contract was both more and less than that. We also need to examine more carefully the notion of 'contract' or 'exchange' that is implicit in this statement. The Social

[17] Ibid. 69–70.

Contract very quickly became something more than a policy on labour law which would provide an alternative to the Industrial Relations Bill. As early as 1972 the General Council's report to Congress could state that 'the Liaison Committee intends to continue its work in the Autumn when among the issues for discussion will be the wider economic and industrial policies of the next Labour Government.'[18] Putting flesh on the bones of the 'wider' social contract (in contrast with the labour law focus of the 'narrower' social contract) did not take long. In January 1973 the Committee agreed upon a document, *Economic Policy and the Cost of Living*,[19] which called upon a future Labour government to adopt a range of radical economic and social policies. Personal incomes would be affected by subsidies to food production, price controls over the items important for the family budget, subsidies to transport and public sector housing rents, a large-scale redistribution of income and wealth, and increases in pensions. These policies were to be paid for by increases in investment, employment, and economic growth, themselves to be brought about by 'new public enterprise and effective public supervision of the investment policy of large private corporations', controls on overseas investment, and a new regional policy 'spearheaded by effective manpower subsidies, a massive expansion in training and re-training, and investment funds for industry linked to greater accountability'. Finally, there should be 'much greater democratic control in all aspects of our national life', part of which would be the industrial democracy legislation proposed as the third stage of the legislative response of a Labour government to the Industrial Relations Act. With the industrial democracy legislation, therefore, the line between the 'narrower' and 'wider' social contracts became blurred.

In the eyes of the Liaison Committee, at least, the Social Contract was thus an over-arching programme of economic and social reform, of which labour legislation was only a small part. Consistently with the radical cast of these policies, the Committee's programme contained no commitment by the trade union movement to even a voluntary incomes policy (in contrast, therefore, to the commitment given by the TUC in the period

---

[18] TUC, *Annual Report 1972*, 107.
[19] The document is set out in TUC, *Annual Report 1973*, 312–15.

before the election of the Labour government in 1964). What the TUC asked negotiators to do, for example in its 1974 document, *Collective Bargaining and the Social Contract*,[20] was 'to take account of the general economic and industrial situation and of the economic and social policies being pursued by the Government' and to 'recognize that the scope for real increases in consumption is limited'. There were, in 1974, no norms or guidelines, merely a general appeal for restraint in the context of a government which was pursuing 'a coherent economic and social strategy—one designed both to overcome the nation's grave economic problems and to provide the basis for co-operation between the trade unions and the Government'.

So the Social Contract was not, in the conception of the early 1970s, favourable labour legislation in exchange for a voluntary incomes policy, but a programme of radical social and economic policies, of which favourable labour legislation constituted an integral part and with which a rigid incomes policy, even of a voluntary nature, was regarded as inconsistent. Such an analysis also eliminates the notion of an exchange being at the heart of the Social Contract. It was, in any case, always slightly odd to regard the Labour Party and then government as being in a position analogous to that of a buyer under a contract for, say, the sale of goods. Such an analogy would suggest that the government saw no intrinsic merit in enacting the policies described in the Social Contract. They were merely a price to be paid for income restraint, a price that any rational buyer would wish to minimize or even reduce to a peppercorn. Although there were clearly wide divisions of opinion within the parliamentary party and then the government over the wisdom of some of the Social Contract policies, it is difficult to believe that even the strongest critics within the government of the Social Contract policies regarded, say, the repeal of the Industrial Relations Act or a strengthening of regional policy simply as a cost to be incurred in order to obtain some other desired benefit.

However, we would not wish to deny that, at a deeper level, the Social Contract contained an important element of political bargaining between the industrial and political wings of the labour movement. In broad terms, by the adoption of a radical

[20] Set out in TUC, *Annual Report 1974*, 284–91.

programme of economic and social policies the Labour Party was able to secure the continued support of the trade union movement. It will be recalled that the failure by the Labour Government of 1964 to 1970 to pursue its original idea of a National Plan, its imposition of a series of statutory incomes policies, and, above all, its attempt to implement the restrictive labour law proposals from *In Place of Strife* had all brought relations between the unions and the parliamentary leadership to a very low ebb. This period had also destroyed the traditional demarcation agreement between the industrial and political parts of the labour movement, namely, that the government's task was to guarantee full employment and abstain from interference in collective bargaining, whilst the unions gave the Labour Party political support but abstained from interfering in political issues. This arrangement, always implicit rather than explicit and always subject to qualification, depended for its coherence upon the possibility of drawing a firm line between the 'economic' and the 'political' spheres. In the modern state any such distinction was open to the criticisms which Kahn-Freund so forcefully made of the attempt to draw a similar line in the statutory definition of a 'trade dispute'. The distinction was based, he said, 'on a theory of society and of politics . . . which to-day is plainly untenable'.[21]

That the arrangement would cease to be followed in practice was, therefore, perhaps inevitable. What was not necessarily predictable was the bitterness that would accompany the move away from the old way of doing things. Anyway, the TUC (and indeed the more left-wing elements of the Labour Party) responded to the Labour government's resort to statutory incomes policies and attempt at restrictive labour legislation in the period 1966 to 1970 by concluding that it should come to a much firmer and more detailed agreement with the party in opposition about the policies that should be followed when the party was returned to power. The institutional expression of this development was the Liaison Committee and the substantive results of the process were embodied in the various Liaison Committee documents, notably *Economic Policy and the Cost of Living*.

---

[21] O. Kahn-Freund, 'Legal Framework', in A. Flanders and H. Clegg, eds., *The System of Industrial Relations in Great Britain* (Oxford, 1954), 127.

What has been said so far does not, however, explain the particular radical balance of policies that emerged in the Social Contract. Soskice and his colleagues argue that this resulted from the fact that Mr Wilson after his defeat in the General Election of 1970 and the limited success of his policies over the previous six years 'had no real choice but to move towards the unions' in order to recapture their financial and political backing. He made the move at a time when 'the centre of equilibrium of the unions ... was significantly to the left', especially in the case of the TGWU under Jack Jones and the AUEW under Hugh Scanlon.[22]

Thus the Labour Party went into the 1974 General Election with a considerably more radical programme (in relation both to labour law and more general issues of economic and social policy) than that with which it had entered the 1964 election. It challenged a Conservative government which had itself over the previous years adopted a much more radical (right-wing) approach to labour law and economic management than any of its predecessors since the Second World War. The process of political polarization over such issues was now well under way: the early 1960s cross-party consensus on employment legislation seemed to belong to another age. However, in spite of the efforts of the Liaison Committee, the programme of the Social Contract was put into operation to no greater extent than the principles of indicative planning which had informed the Labour Party's 1964 programme, and it is in the failure to implement in full the Social Contract, especially the 'wider' Social Contract, that one can detect the emergence of the view, criticized above, that the Social Contract consisted of no more than favourable labour legislation and a tough incomes policy.

For a year or so after the first election of 1974 all went well for the proponents of the Social Contract. The General Council could list at the 1974 Congress the achievements of the Labour government as being, besides the repeal of the Industrial Relations Act, an increase in pensions, tax reform, an increase in food subsidies, and a freeze on rents.[23] During this period, however, there was building up the most serious economic crisis for

[22] R. Flanagan, D. Soskice, and L. Ulman, *Unionism, Economic Stabilization, and Incomes Policies: European Experience* (Washington, DC, 1983), 419.

[23] TUC, *Annual Report 1974*, 287–8.

Britain in the post-war period. The economic crisis was international in origin, stemming from the very large increases in the price of oil brought about by the oil-producing countries in 1973. The crisis hit Britain very hard, pushing up inflation to an annual rate of 27 per cent in mid-1976 and causing investment and output to fall sharply. These in turn led to higher unemployment, a return of balance-of-payments problems, and a sharp fall in the value of sterling. The drafters of the Social Contract had not foreseen that the economy would be subject to such a large external source of inflation and had assumed a steady growth in international trade, an assumption which the energy crisis also falsified. In effect, the economic conditions in which the Social Contract could have had a chance of success no longer obtained.[24]

The more immediate question was what policies the government would adopt to deal with economic crisis. The government resisted the proponents of an 'alternative economic strategy' (based upon the idea of a 'seige' economy), and instead a conventional answer emerged: a tough (but voluntary) incomes policy and cutbacks in government spending (a condition imposed by the International Monetary Fund as part of a large loan to the UK). The TUC responded to the government's intention to impose a limit on incomes by itself proposing and securing acceptance by trade unions of a £6 per week limit for 1975/6 and 5 per cent (subject to a maximum of £4) for 1976/7. The cutbacks in government expenditure (coupled with a change to a less radical mood in the depths of crisis) meant that many items of the wider social contract (including, as we shall see, industrial democracy legislation) were never implemented or were reversed. Writing in 1978 Robert Taylor could conclude that 'it is hard to say that the TUC had much impact on the government's general economic strategy, except perhaps during its first period of office between the two 1974 elections',[25] and he thought the same was true of industrial strategy. This left the first two items of the narrower Social Contract (the Trade Union and Labour

[24] For further analysis of this period, see Flanagan, Soskice, and Ulman, eds., *Unionism, Economic Stabilization, and Incomes Policies*, 418–36, and P. Gourevitch *et al.*, *Unions and Economic Crisis* (London, 1984), 46–64.

[25] R. Taylor, *Labour and the Social Contract*, (Fabian Tract 458; London, 1978), 13.

Relations Acts and the Employment Protection Act) as its main monument. The rest was overtaken by events.

The incomes policy of the 1970s, though voluntary, proved as destructive of relations between Labour government and the trade union movement as had the statutory policies of the 1960s. The first two stages of the policy were largely followed by bargainers and resulted in a significant decline in real wages. This generated such pressures at grass-roots level that in 1977 the TUC Congress voted for 'a planned return to free collective bargaining', and the TUC did not agree to, but did not oppose, a stage 3 limit of 10 per cent for 1977/8. For 1978/9 the government set a unilateral limit of 5 per cent. This led to a rash of major disputes, mainly but not entirely in the public sector, which are usually known collectively as the 'winter of discontent' and which are usually regarded as having significantly contributed to the Labour government's defeat in the 1979 General Election. Once again, the government proved incapable of either building upon trade union acceptance in a time of crisis of the need for an incomes policy in such a way as to make income restraint part of an agreed overall policy or, on the other hand, of managing the economy without an incomes policy once the immediate crisis was over.

In the sections that follow we shall look in turn at the three legislative stages of the 'narrower' Social Contract and then at some of the legislative initiatives, not foreseen in the Social Contract but nevertheless brought to prominence by the economic crisis, especially the 'special measures' designed to support employment levels.

8.2. THE REPEAL OF THE INDUSTRIAL RELATIONS ACT

As we have seen, the overriding political objective of the Labour government when it was elected in 1974 was to repeal the Industrial Relations Act. Since, however, in addition to the unfair industrial practices which the 1971 Act contained and which the government wished simply to repeal, it also contained the immunities against the common law doctrines which had previously been part of the Trade Union Act 1871 and the Trade Disputes Acts 1906 and 1965 and which the Government needed to re-enact if trade unions and industrial action were to be lawful, the government in the 'Repeal Bill' perforce had to define its legislative policy in the two areas of industrial action and trade union law. The policy was relatively easy to formulate, although its implementation involved a bravura technical performance on the part of the draftsman. In relation to industrial action the policy was that peaceful economic sanctions applied in the context of industrial disputes were always to be lawful, and this meant the exclusion from this area of the economic torts— including breach of contract, intimidation, interference with business by unlawful means, conspiracy—that would otherwise have rendered such sanctions unlawful. In relation to trade union law, again the common law doctrines, notably restraint of trade, that might have rendered trade unions illegal organizations were to be excluded, but the main thrust of the policy in this area was simply to dismantle the statutory structure of trade union law— including the system of registration—that had been contained in the 1971 Act.[26] The common law rights of members and (such as they were) applicants for membership as against trade unions were to be left in full force.[27]

As we have also seen, these policies were very controversial in Parliament. The minority Labour government of 1974 suffered opposition amendments to its Trade Union and Labour Relations Bill which it was able to remove only in 1976 with an Amendment Act, which itself created further controversy. (Unless we indicate otherwise we shall be referring for simplicity to the Act in its amended 1976 form.) But why did these legislative policies

[26] Registration was replaced by a simple system of 'listing', which carried no powers of control over the internal affairs of trade unions by the state official, ultimately the Certification Officer, who was in charge of compiling the list. See TULRA 1974, ss. 8–9. Listing was supplemented in 1975 by a process whereby the CO could certify unions as independent of employer domination and control, independence being a prerequisite for union access to certain rights and procedures, notably the recognition procedure, created for unions by the 1975 Act. See Subsect. 8.3(c) below. However, the government did continue in an expanded form the statutory duties upon trade unions, which could be traced back to 1871, to keep accounting records and make annual returns to the CO. See TULRA 1974, ss. 10–12 and now TULRECA 1992, pt. I, ch. 3.

[27] Opposition pressure secured the inclusion in the Act of a statutory right for individual members to resign from the union. That right, reformulated in 1976 as an implied term in the contract of membership, remains part of the current law. See now TULRECA 1992, s. 69.

arouse such opposition? By 1974 the Industrial Relations Act 1971 was largely discredited. The fact of its repeal was not the real basis of opposition to the Trade Union and Labour Relations Act, for by this time it had few committed supporters even amongst the Conservatives. Nor could it be argued with much conviction that the legislative policies of the 1974 Act were novel. On the contrary, they were a conscious attempt to restore what were understood to have been the policies underlying the law from the beginning of the century until 1971 (with the exception of wartime). In relation to industrial disputes the policy which might be called the policy of 'unrestricted legality short of violence'[28] was seen to be the one that underlay the Trade Disputes Act 1906, whilst the primacy in trade union law of the union's rule-book and of the union's autonomous control over its rule-book were seen to be the principal bases of the Trade Union Acts of the 1870s. In this scheme the union member's main legal right against his union was thus his contractual right to insist upon observance by the union of its rule-book, supplemented by the requirements of natural justice, and the Trade Union and Labour Relations Act did not attempt to abridge this right.

This attempt to restore the legislative policies of the earlier part of the century was reflected even in the drafting techniques which emerged to effectuate the policies. This was especially evident in relation to industrial conflict law. In 1906 Parliament had chosen to achieve its ends by granting immunities against the economic torts to the participants in industrial disputes. This 'negative' form of the law can be contrasted with the creation by law of a positive 'right to strike'. The 1906 Act did not create such a legal right; instead, the social right to strike was given effect by means of legal provisions which removed the common law liabilities which would otherwise have rendered the taking of industrial action unlawful. The absence, in legal terms, of a right to strike is an important point of contrast between the British

---

[28] The law has never managed to bring within the scope of protection even peaceful sanctions that infringed upon employers' property rights or public rights, for example, peaceful occupation of an employer's premises or peaceful picketing that obstructed the highway. Indeed, during the 1970s the procedural obstacles that faced an employer wishing to evict workers engaged in a work-in or sit-in were (at least in England and Wales) progressively reduced, especially by the introduction in 1970 of new expedited procedures in both the High Court (RSC, Ord. 113) and County Court (CCR, Ord. 26).

legal system and that of many other European countries. The peculiar British approach to the 'right to strike' via immunities has been explained by the absence in the late nineteenth and early twentieth centuries of a political wing to the British Labour movement—the Labour Party was created only in 1906. A political movement might have articulated a demand for a legal right to strike; as it was, a largely non-ideological trade union movement asked for and obtained simply the removal of the obstacles to the unrestricted operation of the collective bargaining system.[29] What is interesting from our point of view is that even in 1974, with a Labour government in power for the third time since the end of the Second World War and seeking the co-operation of the trade union movement, there was never any serious question of the immunities approach being abandoned for legal rights. The debate over rights and immunities emerged only in the 1980s, partly because the 1974 structure received such a rough handling from the judiciary in the late 1970s and some of those sympathetic to trade unions thought that legal rights might prove more robust, and partly because those who wished to restrict the freedom to take industrial action thought that embodying such a policy in legal rights might make it more palatable to trade unions and workers.[30] In 1974, however, as we shall see further in the next section, there was considerable scepticism among trade unions about the value of positive legal rights in the area of collective labour relations, and the old approach of the 1906 Act seemed in consequence a more appealing one.

The parallelism of the 1974 and 1906 Acts can be traced, beyond the decision to give effect to the social right to strike by way of legal immunities, to the differing methods of giving immunity to trade unions, on the one hand, and individuals, whether full-time officials, shop stewards, or ordinary employees, on the other. Largely for reasons of historical and doctrinal accident, immunity was granted to trade unions in the 1906 Act by saying that, with limited exceptions, they could not be sued in tort at all, whereas individuals were given immunity only in

---

[29] See K. W. Wedderburn, 'The New Structure of Labour Law in Britain' (1978) 13 *Israel Law Review* 435, at 436–9.

[30] On this debate see readings 35 and 37 in W. E. J. McCarthy, ed., *Trade Unions* (2nd edn. Harmondsworth, 1985) and K. Ewing, 'The Right to Strike' (1986) 15 ILJ 143.

respect of certain specified heads of tortious liability and only when acting 'in contemplation or furtherance of a trade dispute'. This approach was followed in the Trade Union and Labour Relations Act, the union's broad immunity being in section 14, the protection for individuals in section 13, and the definition of trade dispute in section 29.[31] This further degree of parallelism was perhaps surprising, given that the Donovan Commission had recommended that the union's immunity be confined to situations where it was acting in contemplation or furtherance of a trade dispute.[32] Moreover, there clearly was, on the other hand, a case for giving an equivalent protection to individuals by defining the torts in respect of which they could be sued rather than defining these in respect of which they could not, on the grounds that the former method was a better protection against unforeseen developments in the common law.[33]

Instead, the Government attempted to confer adequate protection upon individuals by extending the heads of tortious liability, as compared with the 1906 Act, in respect of which they could not be sued when acting in coutemplation or furtherance of a trade dispute and by extending the statutory definition of trade dispute. The former was necessary because of developments in the common law since 1906, notably the extension of the scope of the tort of inducing breach of contract and the emergence (or resuscitation) of the torts of intimidation and interference with business by unlawful means,[34] whilst case-law and, indeed, the definition contained in the 1971 Act itself suggested various deficiencies in the 1906 definition of trade dispute.[35] The commitment on the part of the government was, thus, to the policy

[31] Strictly the protections provided in s. 13 applied to 'an act done by a person' (including trade unions), but trade unions would in practice rely on the broader protections of s. 14. However, when, in 1982, s. 14 was repealed, trade unions could be brought within s. 13 without the need to amend that section. See below, ch. 9.4(c). Ss. 13 and 29 were both heavily amended by the legislation of the 1980s, as discussed below in Ch. 9, and appear in their amended forms as ss. 219 and 244 respectively of TULRECA 1992.

[32] Cmnd. 3623, paras. 902–11.

[33] As was done, in relation to trade unions, by s. 14(2) of TULRA 1974, though a different formulation would have been needed in respect of individuals.

[34] P. Elias and K. Ewing, 'Economic Torts and Labour Law: Old Principles and New Liabilities' [1982] CLJ 321.

[35] R. Simpson, '"Trade Dispute" and "Industrial Dispute" in British Labour Law' (1977) 40 MLR 16.

perceived to underlie the 1906 Act and to its drafting techniques, but not to its *ipsissima verba*.

The extension of the catalogue of torts against which individuals were protected, especially the extension of protection from inducing breach of contracts of employment to all forms of the tort of inducing breach of contract, was a main focus of attack upon the Bill in Parliament. It led to a rather inconclusive debate between the Opposition, which alleged that this was a major extension of the 1906 Act, which had applied only to contracts of employment, and the government, which alleged that commercial contracts had been omitted from the 1906 Act only because inducing breach of them played no significant role in the case-law of the 1900s, which the 1906 Act was designed to overturn, and that they would have been included had this not been so.

Underlying this debate, however, was a more fundamental one, which really was about the acceptability of a policy of collective *laissez-faire* in the fields of industrial conflict and trade union law. One must not suppose that, because the Labour government's ambitions in the 1974 Act did not go beyond the re-assertion of policies lying behind statutes going back in some cases over a century, the policies were thought acceptable on all sides. The 'settlement' of the relationship between the law and industrial conflict laid down in the 1906 Act was a matter of great controversy at the time. It had achieved a considerable level of acceptance in the period of trade union weakness between the two World Wars, but, as we have seen, increasingly in the post-war period the question was asked whether, in changed economic and social circumstances, the policy of collective *laissez-faire* was any longer the right one. This was the central question the Donovan Commission was set up to answer. Its answer was, in effect, in the positive in relation to industrial conflict law and, with rather more qualifications, in relation to trade union law, where the Commission recommended the creation of a statutory independent review body to hear complaints of unreasonable treatment of union members and applicants for membership and to deal with complaints of malpractice in internal union affairs. That the Donovan Commission's answers, especially in the area of industrial conflict law, did not carry conviction in all quarters was demonstrated both by the then Labour government's White Paper, *In Place of Strife*, and by the Conservative government's

Industrial Relations Act.[36] Although the particular forms of intervention contained in the 1971 Act had become discredited by 1974, the fierceness of the parliamentary opposition to the 1974 Act indicated that it was naïve to suppose that the underlying policy question was to be regarded as settled. The arguments about the 1974 Bill may have constituted a debate very familiar to labour lawyers, but the importance of the issues and the lack of consensus about them were still central features of the political debate.

Having said that, however, it is important not to exaggerate the differences between Labour Government and Conservative Opposition over industrial conflict law in the wake of the perceived failure of the Industrial Relations Act 1971. The Opposition did not argue strenuously against the restoration of the complete protection for trade unions or even against the broad protection to be conferred upon individuals, except where that protection exceeded what had been provided in 1906 by embracing inducement of breaches of commercial contracts. No doubt the Opposition found it a convenient debating-point to argue that, in respect of commercial contracts, the government was going beyond even the 1906 Act, but it was also a point of substance. So long as liability for inducing breaches of commercial contracts remained, the organisation of secondary action by workers remained very much at risk of being held illegal. Protecting secondary employers from being brought into industrial disputes had been a main objective of the industrial conflict provisions of the 1971 Act. Having secured the removal from the 1974 Act of the extension of the protection to commercial contracts (and various other changes in other areas of law), the Opposition was prepared to accept the Act. Its manifesto for the second election in 1974 was remarkably candid on the point:

As we have said elsewhere, we still believe that our own legislation was soundly based and unfairly attacked, but in view of the hostility it aroused we will not re-introduce it. We accept the Trade Union and Labour Relations Act, introduced by the present government and sen-

---

[36] On the Donovan Report and its aftermath, see above, chs. 6.2, 6.3, and 7.1.

sibly amended by Parliament, as the basis for the law on trade union organization and as the legal framework for collective bargaining. We hope that our decision will help create a better climate for industrial partnership.[37]

However, the Labour government, returned with a small over-all majority in the second election of 1974, rejected the offer of a new 'settlement' of the labour law questions. It proceeded in the 1976 Act to extend the trade dispute protection to inducing breaches of commercial contracts, and to remove various other amendments, notably those bearing upon the closed shop (see below), that the Opposition had inserted in the 1974 Act. It is, of course, a matter of speculation whether the new settlement, if achieved, would have proved durable into the changed economic and social conditions of the 1980s.

Thus, once the 1976 Amendment Act was on the statute-book, a pretty thorough policy of collective *laissez-faire* was implemented in relation to industrial conflict and trade union law. The only clear failure was in the area of picketing, where section 15 of the 1974 Act did repeat, virtually intact, the wording of the 1906 Act. This meant, however, that, against the opposition of the police, the TUC had failed in its aim of extending the policy of peaceful persuasion, which underlay the 1906 Act, so as to embrace a right of access to people in vehicles, a problem which had not concerned the legislator in 1906. This problem was postponed to the 1975 Act, which also failed to solve it.[38] Apart from this, in the area of industrial conflict law, the broad immunity of trade unions was restored, protection against an extended catalogue of tortious liabilities was accorded to individuals, the definition of trade dispute was widened, some controls were placed on *ex parte* injunctions, and collective agreements were declared not to be intended to be legally enforceable unless both parties chose legal enforcement. This last change was not controversial in view of the small use that had been made of the

---

[37] E. W. S. Craig, *British General Election Manifestos, 1900–1974* (1975), 434.

[38] It proved impossible to achieve agreement on anything other than a very anodyne clause, so that in the event nothing at all was included on picketing in the 1975 Act. See HC Deb., Standing Committee F, 28th Sitting on the Employment Protection Bill, 17 July 1975, cols. 1485–1526. S. 15 was much restricted in its scope by the Employment Act 1980 (see ch. 9.3(*d*) below) and in its amended form appears now as TULRECA 1992, s. 220.

contrary presumption in the 1971 Act. In the area of trade union law statutory rights of members and applicants to complain of unreasonable treatment were removed, as was statutory control of the union's rule-book. Such provisions had been contained in the 1971 Act and were continued by opposition amendment in 1974 until removed in 1976.

In this general context of 'going back to 1906' (if not 1871), however, one novel issue presented itself. How did the policy of collective *laissez-faire* intersect with the new individual employment rights that had been created in recent years, notably the right not to be unfairly dismissed? The problem presented itself in two areas in particular. If an employee was dismissed for non-membership of a union—either because he refused to join or because he had been expelled—where his employment was covered by a closed shop, was such a dismissal to be fair or unfair? Again, was an employee dismissed because he was on strike or involved in other industrial action or locked out to be regarded as fairly or unfairly dismissed? These questions had, of course, arisen under the 1971 Act, and the policy preferences of the drafters of that Act indicated pretty clearly the answers to be given. The desire to restrict the closed shop meant that, usually, dismissals for non-membership were unfair under the 1971 Act, and the aim of restricting industrial action meant that dismissals of those engaged in industrial action or locked out were normally fair. Under the 1974 Act, with commendable consistency, the precepts of collective *laissez-faire* were applied to answer both questions. In respect of the closed shop it was thought that the freedom of unions and employers to secure and maintain closed shops required a reversal of the 1971 Act position, so that an employer would be free to dismiss a non-member without fear of unfair dismissal liability. After enormous controversy in Parliament this position was achieved in 1976, with unfair dismissal protection being offered only to those who objected on religious grounds to being a member of any trade union whatsoever. Thus, where the new individual rights clashed with collective freedoms, it was the former that were to give way. This somewhat ungenerous result was defended by saying that in practice closed shops were operated quite flexibly, and the TUC agreed to establish its own Independent Review Committee to hear complaints from those who were in principle willing to join a trade union but who had lost job opportunities as a result of being excluded or expelled.[39]

With equal rigour the principles of collective *laissez-faire* were applied to the question of 'strike dismissals' and here, at first sight surprisingly, they led to an endorsement of the position adopted under the 1971 Act. One might have supposed that implementing a right to strike in legal terms would have required some protection against dismissal for those who actually engaged in the industrial action. In many legal systems such a proposition would be regarded as axiomatic. It was argued against such laws in Britain, however, that 'the Industrial Tribunals would be led inevitably into pronouncing upon the reasonableness of the strike in order to ascertain whether the employer had acted "reasonably" in dismissing the strikers. This result would deeply offend the philosophy behind a non-interventionist collective labour law . . .'[40] The objection to having the legitimacy of industrial action determined by courts was so strongly felt that, again, individual rights had to give way to collective considerations. Only if not all the strikers were dismissed or not all were offered re-engagement would the industrial tribunal have jurisdiction to consider the fairness of the dismissals; if there was no suggestion of victimization the industrial tribunals were to be excluded. A confident labour movement in 1975 may have felt few qualms about forgoing a protection it had never previously had—since before 1971 the issue could not have arisen—and choosing instead the pure milk of collective *laissez-faire*. However, the potential disadvantage of relying solely on industrial action to secure protection for dismissed strikers was demonstrated in the Grunwick dispute of 1976 and 1977, when an employer did sack all the strikers and months of sometimes violent picketing failed to cause him to change his mind.[41] A similar dispute a decade later over the movement of newspaper

---

[39] For a review of the work of the IRC, see P. Davies and M. Freedland, *Labour Law: Text and Materials* (1st edn. 1979), 548–57 and K. Ewing and W. Rees, 'The TUC Independent Review Committee and the Closed Shop' (1981) 10 ILJ 84.

[40] Wedderburn, 'New Structure of Labour Law', at 450.

[41] See J. Rogaly, *Grunwick* (Harmondsworth, 1977), 136–40.

printing from Fleet Street to Wapping did much to bring about a change in trade union attitudes on this point.[42]

Thus by 1976 a strongly *laissez-faire* policy was in place in relation to industrial conflict and trade union law. Exclusion of the courts from the area of industrial conflict did not mean, however, a complete absence of a role for the state. The state always had had a role in the collective *laissez-faire* system of. trade dispute law: namely, one of making facilities for conciliation and arbitration available to the disputing parties, should they wish to use them. These powers can be traced back in their modern form to statutes of 1896 and 1919. However, traditionally these facilities had been provided by the Department of Employment, and in the 1960s the Department's functions of acting as impartial conciliator and enforcing incomes policies began to conflict. In 1974,[43] therefore, the function of providing conciliation and arranging arbitration was hived off from government to a government-funded but independent agency, controlled by a tripartite governing council of TUC and CBI representatives and independent persons. This was ACAS (the Advisory, Conciliation, and Arbitration Service), which was to have an important role under the 'positive laws' discussed in the next section and whose tripartite controlling body was to be an important sign of the new philosophy in labour law.

8.3. EMPLOYMENT PROTECTION LEGISLATION

The second stage of the Labour Government's legislative programme in the field of labour law was the Employment Protection Act 1975, described in the Consultative Document on the Employment Protection Bill as designed to enact 'more positive and far-reaching proposals for the extension of employees' rights and for the strengthening of collective bargaining' than had been possible in the 1974 Act, which had been 'deliberately limited in scope'.[44] However, whereas, as we have seen, the 1974 Act

[42] K. Ewing and B. Napier, 'The Wapping Dispute and Labour Law' [1986] CLJ 285.

[43] ACAS was established in 1974, although it was only with the 1975 Act that it was placed on a statutory basis and its powers given statutory definition. See EPA 1975, ss. 1–6 and sched. 1 and now TULRECA 1992, ss. 209–14.

[44] Department of Employment, *Employment Protection Bill: Consultative Document* (1974), Introduction.

contained an essentially coherent overall plan, namely, the restroration of legal abstentionism in the field of industrial conflict and trade union law, the 1975 Act is much more difficult to characterize. Indeed, Brian Bercusson, in his entertaining and provocative annotations to the Act, described it as comprising 'some warmed up relics from the previous Labour Government's 1970 Industrial Relations Bill and the Industrial Relations Act 1971 . . . with the belated implementation of various benefits already provided employees in other member states of the EEC'.[45]

The Act had two broad objectives: first, to use the law to support and extend the processes of collective bargaining and, second, to extend the employment rights of individual employees. The line dividing the two is not entirely clear-cut. Some rights conferred upon individuals (for example, not to be discriminated against by employers on grounds of trade union membership or activities) were clearly also intended to support collective bargaining, and we deal with them under the latter heading. It is in relation to the purely individual rights created by the Act that the charge of lack of boldness and even of an underlying strategy can be made. As one of the present authors said at the time, the aims of the individual employment aspects of the 1975 Act seemed to be 'to up-date the law, to close loopholes, to remedy infelicities revealed by the operation of the law in practice and to superimpose some new initiatives and legislative patterns'.[46] This worthy catalogue of aims hardly amounts to a fundamental reorientation of individual labour law. In this respect, as we shall see, the Sex Discrimination Act 1975 and the Race Relations Act 1976 have much greater claims to theoretical interest. In relation to collective bargaining the Act showed much greater signs of coherence and underlying strategy, but there were also indica-

---

[45] Current Law Statutes Annotated, 1975, c. 71, General Note. The 1975 Act is no longer on the statute-book. The parts relating to the rights of individuals were consolidated into the Employment Protection (Consolidation) Act 1978 and the collective provisions which survived the 1980s—together with some provision that had previously been regarded as 'individual' and so been put into the 1978 Act—were consolidated into the Trade Union and Labour Relations (Consolidation) Act 1992.

[46] M. R. Freedland, 'Employment Protection Act 1975: Individual Aspects' (1976) 39 MLR 561, 562.

tions of a certain hesitation about assigning to the law an important role in supporting collective bargaining.

Why should the 1975 Act have appeared, on the one hand, to be rather inconsequential, and on the other, to lack in some sense the courage of its convictions? There is no doubt that it was intended by the Liaison Committee to be something more substantial than this and, indeed, that it did in fact mark a turning-point in trade union attitudes towards the role of labour law. The Employment Portection Act 1975 was intended to demonstrate the 'positive' use of labour law, as against its largely 'negative' role in the Trade Union and Labour Relations Act 1974. Thus whereas the 1974 Act was intended to sweep away the common law doctrines that impeded the taking of effective industrial action by workers and trade unions, and thus to produce a legal situation in which the social institution of collective bargaining could operate freely, the 1975 Act had substantive goals of its own which were to be realized by means of legal rather than social mechanisms. The 1975 Act was therefore, in intention at least, a considerable break on the part of trade unions with the tradition of relying upon their own efforts to achieve substantive goals. Indeed, to the extent that the 1975 Act was concerned with 'the strengthening of collective bargaining', it was the social system of regulation that was to become, in part at least, dependant upon the support of the legal system.

It is perhaps the audacity of this last thought that reveals the Achilles' heel of the Employment Protection Act 1975, for, whether one is thinking of those aspects of it that related to 'the extension of employees' rights' or those that related to 'the strengthening of collective bargaining', it is doubtful whether trade unions in general thought that the law had a major role to play in these areas. There is, of course, a perfectly respectable case to be made, even—perhaps especially—in a system that relies upon collective bargaining to regulate terms and conditions of employment, for the use of the law in an auxiliary way to support the collective bargaining system, especially, but not solely, by securing that employers recognize and bargain with the representatives of their employees.[47] Equally, there is a respect-

---

[47] It would also be wrong to suppose that, before the 1970s, no examples of the use of the law in a role auxiliary to collective bargaining could be found. See e.g.

able case to be made in such a system—since collective bargaining will never cover all establishments—for the use of the law to provide at least minimum guarantees to all employees and even to stimulate the growth of collective bargaining. However, in the context of the early 1970s, with union membership growing and the unions confident of their industrial strength, neither case was one the unions were centrally concerned to press. Had not the unions achieved a very wide measure of recognition without help from the law? Should not employees who wanted better terms and conditions of employment join unions rather than rely upon the law? It would be more than a decade before, in very different economic and political circumstances, some union leaders would begin to see the enforcement on behalf of individuals of their employment rights as giving the union a sustainable role in establishments where union recognition was not forthcoming—and perhaps even where it was.

If trade unions did not press hard for such legislation it was not the case in 1975 that a lead would come from elsewhere. The Government would not do *more* than the unions wanted, and most employers regarded such legislation with suspicion. There was, therefore, a fundamental ambivalence about the role of the law at the heart of the 1975 Act. It represented an acceptance in principle by trade unions of a 'positive' role for labour law, but demonstrated also their inability to identify in legislative terms precisely what that role should be. The result was on the employee rights side of the Act its rather miscellaneous character and, on the collective bargaining side, its lack of rigour and innovation.

(a) Individual Employment Law

What was the content of the Act on the individual rights side? Some new, relatively minor, if useful, rights were introduced: to a trial period in a new job without loss of one's right to treat the change as a dismissal for the purposes of the redundancy payments legislation; to a (minimal) guarantee payment when an employee is suspended by the employer for lack of work or on medical grounds; to time off with pay for employees given notice of redundancy to look for alternative work; to a statement in

above, pp. 27–34, 38–43, 67–71. But the 1975 Act proposed a major extension and systematization of this aspect of labour law.

writing of the reasons for a dismissal. The most significant new rights, closely linked to the new Sex Discrimination Act, were probably those for pregnant employees: rights to maternity pay, to reinstatement in the job after childbirth, and to protection against dismissal on grounds of pregnancy. Although far from generous in scope, they were the most interesting innovations in terms of extending the compass of the employment protection legislation. None of these new rights was, however, as great an innovation as the introduction of protection against unfair dismissal in 1971 (continued by the Trade Union and Labour Relations Act 1974) or even, perhaps, as the introduction of the redundancy payments scheme in 1965.

A number of existing individual rights were extended, of which the following were the most important. The minimum periods of notice required for lawful termination of the contract of employment were extended. The remedies for unfair dismissal were upgraded by the introduction of a basic award (a lump sum based on years of service) to supplement the existing compensatory award (based on loss suffered by the dismissed employee) and by provisions, almost wholly ineffective in practice, designed to make reinstatement or re-engagement, as opposed to compensation, the primary remedies for unfair dismissal. The security of the employee's entitlements as against an insolvent employer was strengthened. Finally, the employee became entitled to more detailed written particulars from the employer of the terms and conditions of the employment. These extended rights and the new rights described in the previous paragraph were later consolidated in the Employment Protection (Consolidation) Act 1978, and as such they remain part of the current law, although the conditions for the exercise of some of them, notably the unfair dismissal and maternity rights, were made more restrictive in the 1980s.

(b) Anti-Discrimination Legislation

The rather miscellaneous and, in some cases, inconsequential character of the individual rights contained in the Employment Protection Act 1975 can be contrasted with the bold and comprehensive legal scheme to be found in the Sex Discrimination Act 1975 and the Race Relations Act 1976. Yet this latter legislation, although supported by the TUC, lay rather outside the Social

Contract programme as such. This legislation was under the general control of the Home Office, although the Department of Employment naturally had an important input into its employment aspects. Its main governmental support came from the then Home Secretary, Mr Roy Jenkins, and his advisers, and they were responding to a decade or more of lobbying from the women's movement and the various race relations groups. The TUC, although long a supporter of equal-opportunity policies, was only a late convert to the full-blooded use of the law to achieve these goals. It is significant from our point of view that it proved easier to identify a coherent and comprehensive 'positive' role for the law where the primary aim of the legislator was not to fit the law around the existing structures of collective bargaining but to vindicate rights to equality of treatment even if those rights cut across established industrial practices, and where it was agreed that those benefiting from the law would make little headway without legal support.

The Sex Discrimination Act 1975 and the Race Relations Act 1976, which, as a matter of deliberate legislative policy, contained largely parallel provisions, although the social problems with which they dealt might be thought to be rather different, were not of course the first legislative enactments in this area. As we have seen, the Equal Pay Act 1970 (although it did not come into full force until the end of 1975, on the same date as the Sex Discrimination Act) provided for equal pay for like work and work rated as equivalent under a (voluntary) job evaluation scheme (compulsory evaluation of jobs was not introduced until 1983). Dismissal on grounds of race or sex was capable of being dealt with under the general unfair dismissal legislation after 1971. Finally, racial discrimination in employment had been brought within legislative purview by the Race Relations Act 1968, but in a very limited way. The 1968 Act was premised upon securing legal rights by conciliation[48] rather than enforcement—the individual complainant indeed had no *right* of access to the courts; then Act dealt only with what later came to be known as 'direct' discrimination, that is, discrimination on grounds of race; and the Race Relations Board, which administered the Act, had only

---

[48] See J. Jowell, 'The Enforcement of Laws against Sex Discrimination in England and Problems of Institution Design', in R. Ratner, ed., *Equal Employment Policy for Women* (1980) and above ch. 5.4.

limited powers of initiative in the absence of an individual complaint. By contrast the 1975 and 1976 Acts contained a very thorough-going implementation of the principle of non-discrimination on grounds of gender (including discrimination against married persons—a very important extension) and race. Four aspects of the legislation deserve comment.

First, the two anti-discrimination Acts cover all the stages of the employment relationship in a way that was and remains unparalleled by any other employment protection law. They apply to access to jobs (including promotion to new jobs and access to vocational training), to the terms of employment (in so far as not covered by the Equal Pay Act in the case of gender) and to non-contractual benefits, and to the termination of the employment relationship. The unfair dismissal legislation, the doyen of individual employment law, may apply to wider categories of unfairness, but it attaches itself to only one aspect of the employment relationship, normally not even catching unfair disciplinary treatment falling short of dismissal unless the employee chooses to resign in response to the unfair action. Second, the two Acts are not confined to the employment relationship,[49] for they apply, *mutatis mutandis*, to discrimination by trade unions *vis-à-vis* members and applicants for membership, by vocational training bodies, by employment agencies, by professional bodies or trade associations which confer qualifications or authorizations needed for particular types of employment, and by partnerships *vis-à-vis* actual or potential partners.

Third, the Acts contain a particularly rigorous definition of discrimination. Building on US experience they cover not only direct discrimination but also indirect discrimination: that is, they render unlawful practices which have unfavourable effects upon women or ethnic minority groups because they create barriers which, although placed in the way of all employees, are such that it is more difficult for women (as opposed to men) or members of ethnic minority groups (as opposed to whites) to surmount them.[50] Examples might be imposing a height requirement for a

[49] Both Acts also apply to discrimination in the fields of education, the provision of goods, facilities, and services, and in the disposal and management of premises, but these aspects of the Acts are not within the scope of this book.

[50] See L. Lustgarten, 'The New Meaning of Discrimination' [1978] PL 178 and C. McCrudden, 'Institutional Discrimination' (1982) 2 OJLS 303.

particular job (a barrier more difficult for women to surmount) or a requirement of being born in this country (more difficult for members of ethnic minority groups). It is important to see that such requirements may be rendered unlawful even though they were not imposed *in order to* exclude women or members of ethnic groups and even though some women or members of ethnic minority groups may be able to comply with them. Actual disadvantage to the group[51] as a whole caused by the requirement may render it unlawful without any intention on the part of the perpetrator of the requirement to bring this result about. Of course, if the intention behind the requirement is not to disfavour members of the group in question (although it has this effect), the purpose of the requirement must lie elsewhere—it may, indeed, be a legitimate purpose—and so the discriminator is allowed to attempt to justify the discriminatory effects of the practice by reference to a non-discriminatory purpose (e.g. the need to produce imposing police officers). A crucial issue in the legislation, on which it gives little guidance, is thus the balance to be struck between furthering legitimate business objectives and the elimination of the discriminatory effects of particular practices.

However that issue may ultimately be resolved in the courts—and its proper resolution may require some legislative re-drafting of the definition of indirect discrimination[52]—the crucial point is that in 1975 Parliament accepted that established industrial practices should be capable of judicial scrutiny for their discriminatory effects. The significance of this is that the law can intervene where discrimination in employment is of such long standing and is so deeply seated that it seems unlikely that discrimination on grounds of sex or race is the major barrier—which is not to say that it does not exist—but rather that the greater obstacle is the institutionalization of discriminatory attitudes in customary practices and procedures whose operation guarantees continua-

---

[51] An individual (as opposed to the CRE or EOC) will not, however, be able to complain about the practice unless he or she is disadvantaged by it.

[52] The legislation applies the indirect discrimination test only to conditions or requirements, and one of the reforms that has been mooted is whether the definition should not be amended so as to avoid the doubt whether it also applies to policies and practices. See CRE, *Review of the Race Relations Act 1976: Proposals for Change* (London, 1985), 3–6; EOC, *Legislating for Change? Review of the Sex Discrimination Legislation* (Manchester, 1986), 10–14.

tion of discriminatory effects without the need for prejudiced decision-making. In reliance on the definition of indirect discrimination, such customary practices as recruiting new employees by word of mouth among an existing, predominantly white, workforce; dismissing part-timers (mainly women) on grounds of redundancy ahead of full-timers; refusing part-timers access to occupational pension schemes; refusing to create part-time jobs; applying upper age limits for recruitment to certain categories of jobs (thus disadvantaging women who have been engaged in child-rearing) have all been held to be unlawful.[53] The legislation can thus be seen as an ambitious challenge to established industrial practices and an attempt, by law, to produce an awareness of the discriminatory potential of traditional patterns of behaviour, including patterns of behaviour (like making part-timers redundant first) that were embodied in collective agreements.

How successful this challenge has been in practice is something we shall consider later in this chapter. For the moment we need only note that the more sophisticated definition of discrimination contained in the 1975 and 1976 Acts was accompanied by more sophisticated enforcement machinery. The individual obtained a right of direct access to the industrial tribunal for the redress of unlawful discriminatory acts, whilst the two agencies set up under the Acts, the Equal Opportunities Commission and the Commission on Racial Equality, acquired their own powers of strategic law enforcement. They were empowered to give financial support to individual litigants (particularly important in the sex discrimination area, where (expensive) appeals to the European Court of Justice in order to take advantage of the European principles in this area have been an important way of developing the law) and were given the sole power to initiate legal proceedings in respect of discriminatory practices, instructions to discriminate, pressure to discriminate, and persistent discrimination. More important in practice, the legislator, again influenced by the US model of the administrative agency, gave the EOC and CRE the power to initiate formal investigations into organizations, which investigations might result in the issuance of a 'non-discrimination notice'

---

[53] CRE, *Report of an Investigation into Massey Ferguson* (London, 1982); *Clarke* v. *Eley Kynoch Ltd.* [1983] ICR 165; *Bilka-Kaufhaus* v. *Weber von Hartz* [1987] ICR 110; *Home Office* v. *Holmes* [1984] ICR 678; *Price* v. *Civil Service Commission* [1978] ICR 27.

by the EOC or CRE requiring the organization to cease discriminating and remedy the effects of past discrimination. The idea of combining investigative and law enforcement powers in the hands of a single agency was a novel one in the British context.[54]

(c) Strengthening Collective Bargaining

We have seen that the individual employment law provisions of the Employment Protection Act 1975 seemed to be more part of a tidying-up process than part of a coherent, independent strategy of legislation. It would be too harsh to view the provisions of that Act which were designed to strengthen collective bargaining in the same light. On the contrary, these did fit together into an overall design for the legal support and promotion of all stages of the collective bargaining process. The Act contained, first, provisions protecting employees against acts of discrimination against them by their employers for joining or taking part in the activities of independent trade unions. Legal protection of the right to associate in trade unions was intended to aid the recruitment of members by trade unions and, in particular, to protect those who were active on the union's behalf. Second, the Act contained a procedure which could result in an employer being put under a duty to negotiate with a union representative of the employees—the so-called 'recognition' procedure. Third, assuming collective bargaining to be established either as a result of social or of legal pressures, the Act contained a number of provisions aimed to 'improve its quality' or to extend its scope. The employer had to disclose to the recognized union information which it possessed and which was relevant to the collective bargaining between employer and union. Union officials (including shop stewards) were given the right to time off with pay for the performance of duties in connection with the conduct of industrial relations between employer and union, and all union members had the right to time off (without pay) in order to take part in trade union activities. Whether an employer negotiated with a recognized union about redundancies or not, it was now obliged to consult with the relevant recognized union over proposals to make even a single employee redundant. These

---

[54] See generally McCrudden, 'Legal Remedies for Discrimination in Employment' [1981] CLP 211.

provisions supplemented the regulations on consultation over health and safety made under an Act of 1974 and over pensions contained in another Act of 1975.[55] Finally, by schedule 11 to the Employment Protection Act 1975 the results of collective bargaining could be extended by law to other employers who did not pay the going rate, thus both benefiting non-unionized or weakly organized employees and protecting the well organized from undercutting by less well-paid competitors.[56]

The above provisions have some title to be regarded as a grand plan for the promotion by legal means of the system of collective bargaining. Certainly that was how these provisions were presented in 1975, and it is at that date we should judge the legislative intentions. The subsequent repeal of the recognition procedure in 1980 (along with schedule 11) in many ways removed the linchpin of the scheme and reduced the remaining collective bargaining provisions to the same miscellaneous status as the individual employment rights of the 1975 Act. In this form they have survived, largely unchanged, into the current law as contained in the Trade Union and Labour Relations (Consolidation) Act 1992. However, the repeal of the recognition procedure and schedule 11 shed light on the policy priorities of the 1979, rather than the 1974, government. Looking at matters, then, as they appeared whilst the recognition provisions were still on the statute-book, what can we say about this grand plan? Again, there is no doubt that in principle it marks a considerable change of view on the part of trade unions towards the role of the law in collective labour relations. As Professor Wedderburn has put it:

But the Employment Protection Act went further and ventured directly into the territory of collective labour relations. It did so at the request of the trade unions to a Labour Government. Having suffered at the hands of the Industrial Relations Act 1971, the unions saw no reason why 'our' Government should not pass new laws to help them in collective

---

[55] Health and Safety at Work etc. Act 1974, s. 2(4); Safety Representatives and Safety Committees Regulations 1977 (SI 1977, No. 500); Social Security Pensions Act 1975, s. 31; Occupational Pensions Regulations 1975 (SI 1975, No. 1927).

[56] Sched. 11, a complex provision, could apply to extend either the results of national or regional multi-employer collective agreements to 'non-federated' employers—this was called the 'recognized' level of terms and conditions—or the 'general level' of terms and conditions resulting from plant or company bargaining in a particular local area, the preference being for the former. See B. Bercusson, 'The New Fair Wages Policy' (1976) 5 ILJ 129.

bargaining. This was a new attitude, a bequest undoubtedly of the 1971
Act. It was also, however, part of the 'social contract' between the
unions and the Labour Government from 1974 to 1977 . . .[57]

The change of attitude on the part of the trade unions was both
real and important, but it was accompanied still, as we have
suggested, by considerable tentativeness about the use of the law
to promote collective bargaining. Signs of this approach can
be detected in the sources of the legislation, the formulation of
the substantive rules, the sanctions for breach of the rules, and
the nature of the agencies concerned with administering the
legislation. First, although the trade unions may have wanted
'new laws' from the Labour Government, in fact the collective
bargaining provisions of Employment Protection Act 1975 were
not in general new—or, at least, not very new. The Industrial
Relaitons Act 1971 contained provisions on freedom of association and on the disclosure of information and a recognition
procedure, whilst schedule 11 built on two even earlier legal
instruments, one dating from the late nineteenth century and the
other from the Second World War.[58] Except in relation to disclosure of information, there were significant differences between
the 1975 Act's provisions and those of the 1971 Act. The former's
recognition procedure, for example, was aimed straightforwardly
at extending collective bargaining, whilst the latter's had as part
of its design (though it was not much so used in practice) the idea
that the procedure could also be used to promote the reform of
bargaining structures. In fact the recognition procedure of the
1975 Act drew as much on the recommendations of the Donovan
Commission as on the 1971 Act. Nevertheless, the point to be
made is that the change in trade union attitudes was in the
direction of accepting proposals for the use of the law to support
collective bargaining that were already well established in public
debate rather than in the direction of producing wholly new
modalities of intervention.

[57] Wedderburn, 'New Structure of Labour Law', at 450.
[58] Sched. 11 generalized principles to be found in the Fair Wages Resolution,
the first version of which had been adopted by the House of Commons in 1891
and which had been most recently revised in 1946, and in s. 8 of the Terms and
Conditions of Employment Act 1959, whose origins were to be found in the
Conditions of Employment and National Arbitration Order 1940 (SR&O 1940,
No. 1305). See above pp. 31, 88 and 102.

Second, there were certain weaknesses in the drafting of the substantive rules which, one suspects, were due to a lack of a wholehearted commitment to the use of the legal process. Perhaps the most remarkable lacuna, at least with the benefit of hindsight, was the failure to extend the freedom of association provisions to applicants for employment. Dismissal for trade union membership or activities was declared to be automatically unfair and action short of dismissal on these grounds was also made unlawful, but an applicant was not brought within the provisions of the law. Thus, the operation of blacklists of known trade union activists was able to continue, for the central method of implementing the blacklist was screening out 'undesirable' applicants at the stage of selection for employment. This practice was particularly well established in the construction industry, the very nature of which means that many employees will be seeking employment with a succession of employers on a series of different projects.[59] This omission is particularly striking, since the equivalent provisions of the 1971 Act had protected applicants for employment and since the principle of controlling employers' hiring processes was being acknowledged and implemented in the Sex Discrimination and Race Relations Acts, at the same time as the Employment Protection Act was being passed. Nevertheless, there is no evidence that the TUC pressed the Government to widen the scope of the legislation on this point. On the contrary, their main concern seems to have been with the evidence provided by the experience of the freedom of association provision of the 1971 Act to the effect that such provisions could be used by non-recognized unions (often not affiliated to the TUC) to secure a foothold in plants where established collective bargaining arrangements (usually with TUC affiliated unions) existed. The TUC pressed, without much success, for the right to take part in trade union activities to be limited to recognized trade unions. In this context, at least, the TUC was as much concerned with what it saw as the possible disadvantages of legal protection of freedom of association as with its potential benefits.[60]

---

[59] See S. Evans and R. Lewis, 'Anti-Union Discrimination Practice, Law and Policy' (1987) 16 ILJ 88. The Employment Act 1990 now provides protection at the hiring stage to those refused employment on grounds of union membership (but not activities) or non-membership.

[60] TUC, *Annual Report 1975*, 88–9. For the same reasons the TUC pressed, unsuccessfully, for the right to refer recognition cases to ACAS to be confined to

(d) The Problem of Sanctions

Undoubtedly more symptomatic of a cautious approach towards the legal process, however, were the provisions concerning the sanctions to be applied for non-compliance with the legislation. The best-known example of the distaste for 'legal penalties'. because it was highlighted in the *Grunwick*[61] case, concerned the powers of ACAS when investigating a recognition claim. Under the 1975 Act a union with a recognition claim reported it directly to ACAS. If ACAS could not settle the matter by conciliation, it carried out an investigation into the industrial relations situation and might, after the investigation, 'recommend' that the employer recognize the union in question. ACAS was given a very free hand as to the nature of the inquiries it might think fit to make, but it was required to 'ascertain the opinions of workers to whom the issue relates'.[62] By the simple expedient of withholding the names and addresses of its employees, Grunwick prevented the Service from discharging its duty with the result, so the House of Lords eventually held, that ACAS had no statutory power in this case to make any recommendation. The decision seems to have had a significant adverse effect upon ACAS's work in this area, not simply in the eleven cases in which, because of its inability to establish the employees' views, ACAS decided it could make no recommendation, but also in encouraging a growing reluctance by employers to co-operate with the Service's investigations; by the end of 1979 ACAS estimated that full co-operation was not forthcoming from employers in a quarter of all cases.[63]

But why was the legislation drafted so as to rely upon voluntary co-operation by employers with the Service's investigations? Under the Industional Relation Act 1971, where recognition claims were under the control of the National Industrial Relations Court, it would no doubt have been a contempt of court for the employer not to co-operate in the inquiries that the NIRC asked the Commission on Industrial Relations (in many ways ACAS's

---

unions affiliated to the TUC. In the end this right was conferred upon all 'bona fide' (i.e. independent) trade unions. Ibid. 95-6.

[61] *Grunwick Processing Laboratories Ltd.* v. *ACAS* [1978] ICR 231 and see generally P. Elias, B. Napier, and P. Wallington, *Labour Law: Cases and Materials* (London, 1980), 29-59.

[62] EPA 1975, s. 14(1).

[63] ACAS, *Annual Report 1979*, 27.

predecessor) to carry out. Under the 1975 Act recognition claims went directly to ACAS, and this seems to have reflected not merely a policy of excluding courts from the area of collective labour relations and of using instead an administrative agency whose main functions were voluntary conciliation and arbitration, but also a policy of excluding 'legal penalties' from collective labour law. In Rogaly's view 'the result was another flawed piece of legislation'.[64] In Lord Scarman's more measured prose:

The law favours collective bargaining and encourages the use by workers of independent trade unions for the purpose. The policy of the law is to exclude 'trade disputes' from judicial review by the courts and to rely not on the compulsory processes of law but on the voluntary approach backed by advice, conciliation, and arbitration to promote good industrial relations. The efficacy of such a law depends upon good will. If men act unreasonably, by which we mean in obedience to the letter but not the spirit of the law, it will not work.[65]

But was it not naïve to draft recognition legislation on an assumption of goodwill? For what is often in dispute in such cases is whether the employer will accept the principle of collective representation of his employees, and the scope for compromise is accordingly limited.

However, the lack of sanctions against non-co-operation with an ACAS investigation into a recognition claim was only one example of a general policy of excluding 'legal penalties' from this area of labour law, a policy adopted very much by way of reaction to the unfair industrial practices created by the 1971 Act and the contempt sanctions that attached to them. 'Legal penalties' meant sanctions which had as their main aim the punishment of the person who had infringed the legal rules as opposed to the compensation of the person who had suffered thereby. In those areas of collective bargaining law which operated by conferring rights upon individuals—to freedom of association or time off—the problem was thought to be overcome by giving the individual the right of complaint to an industrial tribunal, which could award the applicant such compensation as it considered 'just and equitable in all the circumstances having

---

[64] *Grunwick*, 144.
[65] Report of a Court of Inquiry into a dispute between Grunwick Processing Laboratories Limited and members of the Association of Professional, Executive, Clerical and Computer Staff, Cmnd. 6922 (1977), para. 72.

regard to the employer's breach of the law and to any loss sustained by the complainant'.[66] A modified version of this approach was even used in the case of the employer's failure to consult with the recognized union over proposed redundancies. Here the tribunal was empowered to make a monetary award in favour of individual employees, but the right of complaint to the industrial tribunal was vested solely in the trade union.[67]

However, even in the industrial tribunal, the problem of 'legal penalties' was not completely avoidable. The TUC felt strongly that reinstatement should be the normal remedy for an employee dismissed on grounds of union membership or activity, and it successfully argued to the government for an amendment to the Bill so as to introduce a speedy interlocutory procedure in such cases—called interim relief—which was designed to keep the contract of employment alive, at least as far as payment was concerned, until the full tribunal hearing.[68] The reasoning was that, where the contract was prolonged, the employee would not be forced to seek employment elsewhere and so would be in a position to ask for reinstatement at the hearing. But suppose the employer would not comply with the tribunal's reinstatement order. The legislators balked at making infringement of such orders a contempt of court and the TUC did not press for this. Instead the tribunal was to make the non-reinstated employee 'an additional award of compensation' of between six months' and a year's pay. This infelicitous phrase reveals the ambiguity of the legislator's stance. Since the award did not require proof of loss (the compensatory award was payable as well) and had a fixed minimun amount, it would normally operate as a penalty upon the non-reinstating employer. Terminological consistency, however, was maintained by calling the penalty an award of compensation and making it payable to the employee. Even when

[66] See e.g. EPA 1975, s. 56(1), now TULRECA 1992, s. 149(2). Interpreting this phrase the EAT said in *Brassington* v. *Cauldon Wholesale Ltd.* [1978] ICR 405: 'So, for the infringement of . . . right, compensation for the employee, not a fine on the employer however tactfully wrapped up, is the basis of the discretionary monetary award.'

[67] Again, the purpose of the 'protective' award in favour of the individual is to compensate for loss of the opportunity for consultation, even if the amount of the compensation is not necessarily measured by the employee's loss of wages: *Spillers-French (Holdings) Ltd.* v. *USDAW* [1980] ICR 31 (EAT).

[68] TUC, *Annual Report 1975*, 93–4.

correctly viewed as a private penalty, however, the additional award technique shows the reluctance of the legislator to provide, or the TUC to ask for, effective enforcement of reinstatement orders, even in this area where the demonstration effect of such orders could be expected to be at its greatest.

With regard to those rights not thought of as suitable for adjudication by industrial tribunals—rights to recognition, to disclosure of information, and to the recognized or general level of terms and conditions of employment under schedule 11—the problem of non-penal sanctions was solved by the use of compulsory arbitration by the Central Arbitration Committee on a claim brought by the union that the terms and conditions of the relevant employees be improved. The arbitration was compulsory both in the sense that one party to the issue, normally the union, could invoke the arbitral process without the other party's consent and in that the CAC's award was a compulsorily implied term in the contracts of employment of the employees to whom the award related and so was enforceable, ultimately, by the individual in the ordinary courts. With regard to schedule 11 compulsory arbitration was a natural enforcement mechanism, since the substantive right related to certain levels of terms and conditions of employment, and the Industrial Court, the CAC's predecessor, had since the 1940s fulfilled such a role in relation to schedule 11's precursors. It was much less obvious that arbitration on a claim for improved terms and conditions of employment was the appropriate sanction where an employer had refused to recognize a union after having been recommended by ACAS to do so or had failed to disclose the information the union was entitled to for collective bargaining purposes. Yet as against contempt sanctions, as used in the USA since 1935 to enforce the duty to bargain in good faith, or criminal penalties, as used in the more recent French laws, compulsory unilateral arbitration had in the eyes of the legislators in 1975 the advantage of avoiding 'legal penalties'.

There was, of course, a price to pay. In relation to recognition, for example, the use of compulsory arbitration amounted to an admission that the procedure did not at the end of the day purport to compel the employer to bargain with the union, but rather it took away from the employer the right to determine unilaterally the terms and conditions of its employees' employment and vested that power instead in a third party, the CAC. Since the CAC, in discharging its arbitral function, saw its role 'as fulfilling the negotiating function which the company, by its refusal to recognize the union, is failing to undertake',[69] rather than as penalizing the employer for its refusal, the sanction held few terrors for employers already observing good terms and conditions of employment. *Mutatis mutandis* the same comments can be made about the method of enforcing the duty to disclose. As Wedderburn commented in 1978, 'This may have already been a source of disillusion to some unions who have found that the end of the road after an ACAS recommendation is not enforced recognition and bargaining with the union, but only an award of individual employment rights.'[70] But the disappointment was inherent in the design of the legislation, for individual rights were at the centre of the legal forms, no matter how much the social purpose of the legislation was the collective one of furthering the trade unions' goal of extended collective bargaining. This is obvious enough where the substantive rule took the form of an individual right—to freedom of association or time off— but if one pursued to the very end the enforcement processes attached to the apparently collective substantive rights—to recognition, to disclosure of information, to consultation over redundancy, to recognized or general levels of terms and conditions of employment—one again discovered rights conferred upon individual employees. It is suggested that the explanation of this apparent paradox was an overwhelming commitment on the part of the Government and the TUC to monetary compensation as the sanction for breaches of legal rules. Individual rights to compensation in the industrial tribunals or damages for breach of the contract of employment in the ordinary courts fitted the legislators' requirements very well.

(e) The Choice of Adjudicatory Body

Closely associated with the legislators' rejection of 'legal penalties' in 1975 was the fourth and final aspect of the collective bargaining law that we wish to comment on. This was the deep distrust of courts as the means of determining disputes in the area of col-

---

[69] CAC Award No. 78/808.
[70] 'New Structure of Labour Law', at 454.

lective labour relations, a policy very much of reaction to the activities of the National Industrial Relations Court in the period 1972 to 1974. In the area of industrial conflict law this policy was thought to be achieved, as we have seen, as an adjunct to the process of excluding the common law liabilities from the area of trade disputes. If there were no liabilities which those taking peaceful industrial action could incur, the role of the courts would be reduced to declaring, when asked, that this was the case. This was a task, it was thought (in the event erroneously), that could be safely left to the ordinary courts. What, however, was to be done in this respect about the new 'positive' rights created by the 1975 Act to promote collective bargaining? Some body would have to adjudicate upon allegations that the new obligations had been infringed. Where those obligations were, in legal form, cast as individual rights, it was thought acceptable to entrust adjudication to the industrial tribunals, and tribunals were even given, as we have seen, the task of adjudication over redundancy consultation. The fact that the industrial tribunals were in fact courts—or, at least, 'court substitutes'[71]—simply had to be swallowed with good grace, for was not the use of courts an inevitable consequence of a policy of legal regulation? In fact, the individual employment and collective bargaining aspects of the 1975 Act together meant an enormous expansion in the jurisdictions and case-loads of the tribunals.[72]

The problem did not seem so easy of solution in respect of those collective rights where adjudication was not thought appropriate for the industrial tribunals. The experience with the NIRC ruled out asking the Employment Appeal Tribunal—in part the NIRC's successor—to undertake this task. The EAT, a tripartite body like the industrial tribunals and with the same status as the High Court, was to have no original jurisdiction; its role was to be purely appellate, mainly the hearing of appeals from the industrial tribunals. The solution that emerged, almost without anyone noticing it, was dictated by the decision to use compulsory arbitration as the sanction in recognition, disclosure, and schedule 11 cases. The arbitral body, the CAC, became in effect

---

[71] B. Abel-Smith and R. Stevens, *In Search of Justice* (London, 1968), 224–8.
[72] The number of applications to industrial tribunals increased from just over 15,000 in 1974 to just over 42,000 in 1976.

the British collective labour court in the period 1975 to 1980 (when the recognition procedure and schedule 11 were repealed). ACAS might have the power to recommend union recognition, but before the union's claim for improved terms and conditions could be subject to arbitration, it had to be determined that the employer was not complying with the recommendation. Almost *faute de mieux* the task of determining whether the employer was bargaining in good faith with the union was entrusted to the CAC, as also were the decisions whether the employer had complied with the obligation to disclose or had a good defence for not so doing or whether the employer was observing the recognized or general levels of terms and conditions of employment. Added to the CAC's jurisdiction under section 3 of the Equal Pay Act to amend discriminatory collective agreements, these jurisdictions meant an enormous increase in the case-load of the CAC in the late 1970s.[73]

In fact, the CAC turned out to be probably the most successful and innovative of the institutions established by the Employment Protection Act 1975 (the others being ACAS and the EAT). The CAC had the benefit that its decisions were not subject to appeal to the ordinary courts (thought it was, of course, subject to judicial review), but the crucial element in its approach was the application to its statutory jurisdiction of techniques it had developed as a voluntary arbitration body. Two aspects of this stand out in particular. First, as far as its statutory powers allowed, it placed the legal issue that had arisen within the over-all context of the parties' industrial relations situation and attempted to produce in appropriate cases a solution not merely to the legal problem but to the underlying social problem of which the legal issue might be only a symptom. 'Its attitude is one of problem solving, in that it is much more active and interventionist than a court.'[74] Second, the CAC sought to asso-ciate the parties as far as possible with the process of adjudication or, as it preferred to call it, 'the actual construction of a solution'. Adjudication was not something that came from on high but was, as far as possible, to be negotiated between the

---

[73] 132 cases were referred to the CAC in 1976 (it came into existence on 1 Feb. 1976); in 1978 the number of new references to the Committee was 1,065.

[74] Sir John Wood (Chairman of the CAC), 'The Central Arbitration Committee: A Consideration of its Role and Approach' (1979) 87 *DE Gaz.* 9.

parties, with the CAC acting as a facilitator, and as adjudicator only in the last resort. Whether such an approach would have survived a sustained period of judicial review we cannot know, given the changes in the law in 1980, but the CAC in the late 1970s can be given the credit for developing a genuinely novel approach to the process of adjudication which may serve as a model in future proposals for reform.[75]

8.4. INDUSTRIAL DEMOCRACY[76]

The third, in the event unfulfilled, stage of the legislative programme for labour law envisaged by the Liaison Committee involved proposals to legislate for greater industrial democracy. 'Industrial democracy' is a term capable of bearing a myriad of meanings, but, although perhaps initially a little more broadly conceived by the Liaison Committee, it came in the context of labour law reform at this time to refer to precise and concrete proposals for employee representation on the boards of directors of large, private-sector companies. These proposals, developed largely by the TUC and the then leadership of the Transport and General Workers' Union, were both radical and innovative, though they came rather less out of the blue and were rather more related to the other stages of labour law reform than some observers at the time were prepared to recognize.

The issue of employee representation at board level had been a minor, indeed often submerged, theme in trade union thinking at various times earlier in the century, admittedly usually in respect of companies that were not in the private sector. In its evidence to the Donovan Commission in 1966, however, the TUC argued for a system of board-level representation for employees in the private sector, and a Labour Party working party report in 1967 made somewhat similar proposals. However, the TUC's proposals

[75] See further, P. Davies and M. Freedland, 'Labour Courts and the Reform of Labour Law in Great Britain', in A. Barak et al., eds., In Memorian Zvi Bar-Niv: Collection of Essays on Labour Law (Tel Aviv, 1987), 58–65.

[76] For more extended discussions of developments in this area at this time see J. Elliott, Conflict or Cooperation? The Growth of Industrial Democracy (London, 1978); P. Davies, 'The Bullock Report and Employee Participation in Corporate Planning in the U.K.' (1978) 1 Journal of Comparative Corporate Law and Securities Regulation 245; and J. Clark et al., Trade Unions, National Politics and Economic Management (London, 1980), pt. III.

at this time were fairly imprecise and, in particular, did not entail that such representation should be compulsory. Nevertheless, a majority of the Donovan Commission were unable to recommend even a voluntary system.[77] The opportunity for the TUC to raise the matter again came when in the early 1970s the then Conservative government sought reactions to proposals that had been made within the EEC (which the UK was about to join) for a generalization of the German and Dutch systems of board-level representation throughout the Community.[78] The TUC had now had the opportunity to develop its ideas more fully and they were set out, in particular, in two reports to the annual Congresses, an interim report on Industrial Democracy to the 1973 Congress and a final report to the 1974 Congress, and in the TUC's evidence to the Bullock Committee that was subsequently established by the government to examine the issue. A compulsory system was now envisaged.

Given the much stronger political position of the TUC *vis-à-vis* the Labour Party and government in the late 1970s, as compared with the late 1960s, it is not surprising that the proposals contained in the 1973 and 1974 documents were taken more seriously than the earlier ones. What is of importance, however, is to understand why the TUC was now pressing so hard on this issue. In the TUC's eyes, at least, there was a real link between the industrial democracy proposals and the other two stages of labour law reform, especially the second. We have already noted, in connection with the Employment Protection Act, the General Council's view that, although 'the main method [of conducting industrial relations] is voluntary negotiations between employers and unions', nevertheless, 'legislation should ensure that all workers have certain minimum rights and should encourage the development of voluntary collective bargaining and supplement it where necessary'.[79] This view is, at the very least, a recognition

---

[77] Cmnd. 3623, para. 1002.

[78] See, in general, on the genesis of the proposals, Clark *et al.*, *Trade Unions*, 75–6 and 80–1. The European proposals, notably the Draft Fifth Directive on harmonization of the company laws of the member states, have still not, in 1991, achieved sufficient consensus among the member states to be adopted. The process of company law harmonization has in effect left this awkward issue to one side and continued with matters of a more traditional character, which involve no cross-subject problems.

[79] Above, p. 353.

that collective bargaining cannot by itself achieve all that is desirable in the way of regulation of industrial relations. Some workers do not, and cannot realistically be expected to, benefit from effective protection via collective bargaining, and so the law should try, no doubt inadequately, to plug the gap. In other cases, collective negotiations will not develop to their full extent (or at all) without legal support. These seemed to be the implications of the strategy behind the legislation contained in the 1975 Act.

However, the debate on the Employment Protection Bill was about effective joint regulation (by employers and trade unions) of the traditional subject-matters of industrial relations, essentially terms and conditions of employment, procedures for handling disputes, and the regulation of jobs. Here collective bargaining was, of course, to remain pre-eminent, even if the voluntary machinery was thought capable of improvement by a judicious application of the appropriate blend of legal oil. The case that the TUC was concerned to argue in its industrial democracy proposals was that, once one moved outside the traditional subject-matters of industrial relations, collective bargaining became an inadequate method for promoting joint regulation. An alternative to collective bargaining needed to be found, but an alternative whose function was the same as that of collective bargaining, namely the joint regulation of the new subject areas. Employee representation on the board was to be the new machinery, but, as we shall see, the particular form of representation proposed faithfully reflected the principles of joint regulation. To put the matter another way, both collective bargaining and employee representation were seen as methods of achieving industrial democracy and each was to be employed in the appropriate circumstances.[80]

Thus the radical nature of the TUC's proposals can be seen to have consisted in the idea that major new areas of managerial decision-making should be subject to the principle of joint regulation rather than, perhaps, in the particular nature of the machinery proposed to be established to achieve that aim, although proposals to place employees on the boards of companies had, no doubt, in themselves a strong symbolic signifi-

[80] See esp. 'Industrial Democracy', Report by the TUC General Council to the 1974 Trades Union Congress, Supplementary Report B, paras. 84–5.

cance, for both employees and employers. But what were these new areas of managerial decision-making to which the principle of joint regulation was to be extended? The answer was the areas comprised in the notion of 'strategic corporate planning', for instance, decisions about major investments, location of plant, pricing, or product diversification. Decisions by management on these matters were not 'new' in one sense; they had always been the major preoccupation of the central management of large companies. What was new was the perception by the TUC of the importance of these decisions for more mundane matters of industrial relations—bargaining rights over terms and conditions of employment meant little if investment decisions led to the closure of the plant in question—and the confidence on the part of the TUC that trade unions could effectively participate in this larger area of decision-making. The industrial democracy proposals were, thus, a major push to extend trade union influence over managerial decisions—hence employers' bitter hostility to them—but, from another perspective, they were as much defensive as offensive. They were a response to what the TUC saw as the growing concentration and centralization of capital in large—often multinational—companies and to its fear that traditional collective bargaining was being confined to ever more marginal aspects of corporate strategies.

Why could collective bargaining not be developed to embrace these areas of decision-making? Why did a new mechanism of joint regulation need to be devised? In small part the answer was that collective bargaining, although well developed at industry and plant level, was generally less well developed at enterprise level, but that answer only raises the further question of why the TUC proposals did not focus themselves upon a major push to establish collective bargaining at enterprise—or company—level. The answer to *that* question was that in collective bargaining it is ultimately the unions' ability to make a credible threat of effective industrial action that moves the employer further towards the unions' position than it would otherwise, consulting only its own interests, be prepared to go. The TUC's doubts about the effectiveness of collective bargaining in the area of corporate planning seem to have been as to whether employees would be prepared to take industrial action, with its certain and immediate costs to the employees, over an issue of corporate planning, the significance of which for the workforce might appear only in the medium term and whose precise significance for any particular section of the employees might be very difficult to predict. A position of institutional power on the board was intended to solve this dilemma.

However, not any and every system of employee representation on the board would guarantee the principle of joint regulation over corporate planning. The system, in the TUC's view, would have to be carefully tailored to achieve the desired effect, and in designing the system the analogy with collective bargaining was kept firmly in mind. This analogy appears even if, as one must, one examines, not the TUC's proposals as such, but the variation on them recommended in the Report of the Committee of Inquiry on Industrial Democracy, set up by the government under the chairmanship of Lord Bullock in 1975 and reporting in January 1977.[81] The report of the majority of the Committee, which largely endorsed the TUC's position, had two significant features from the present point of view. First, it recommended equality of representation for employer and employee representatives on the board, with a smaller number of independent members being jointly appointed by the employer and employee representatives. This was the famous $2x + y$ formula, which decisively rejected the dissentients' view, that employees should have only a minority position on the board, in favour of the idea of joint regulation. Second, the method of selecting the employee representatives was to be determined by a 'joint representation committee' of all the unions recognized by the employer for the purposes of collective bargaining. If there were no such unions, there could be no JRC and so no employee representation. The link between board-level representation and collective bargaining could hardly have been more strongly asserted.

As we have suggested, employer opposition to the extension of trade union influence, which was implicit in the report of the majority of the Bullock Committee, was to be expected, and the CBI in fact mounted a strident but also very effective campaign of opposition. The government's response to the Bullock Report did not appear until May 1978,[82] and it proposed a system

---

[81] Cmnd. 6706.
[82] Industrial Democracy, Cmnd. 7231 (1978).

of minority representation for employees and placed primary emphasis upon voluntary moves towards even this limited goal, with compulsion having only a fall-back role in the rather distant future. However, a General Election intervened before legislation along even these modest lines could be brought forward. In practical terms, the only significant consequence of the Bullock Report was the introduction of board-level representation into the Post Office,[83] a somewhat ironic result, since the public sector had been excluded from the scope of the Bullock Committee's remit. Even this scheme was terminated after a few years.[84]

However, it would be wrong to ascribe the very limited results of the Bullock Report simply to strong employer opposition, even when combined with a lack of support for it in some quarters of the Labour government. The trade union movement itself was deeply divided on the issue. We have described the industrial democracy proposals as the 'TUC's proposals' and, indeed, the main support for them was located there and amongst the leadership of the powerful Transport and General Workers' Union, especially its then General Secretary, Jack Jones. It was very unclear how far support for the proposals extended to the leaderships of other trade unions or among the membership of trade unions in general. Indeed, Clark and his colleagues ascribe a major part of the explanation for the Bullock Committee's lack of success to the fact that 'during the main period of policy development, little attempt was made [by the TUC] to promote internal discussion on the issue and the initiative remained extremely centralized'.[85] The report of the Committee itself, which was required to be produced quickly, did not play much of a role in building a consensus on the central issues, since its terms of reference required it to proceed 'accepting the need for a radical extension of industrial democracy in the control of companies by means of representation on boards of directors and accepting the essential role of trade union organizations in this process . . .'.[86]

[83] And some amendments to an already existing scheme in the British Steel Corporation.
[84] For an analysis of the Post Office scheme see E. Batstone, A. Ferner, and M. Terry, *Unions on the Board* (Oxford, 1983).
[85] Clark *et al.*, *Trade Unions*, 83 and 122–6.
[86] Cmnd. 6706 (1977), page v.

However, it would be inadequate simply to record the fact of disagreement among trade unions and trade unionists about the value of the Bullock proposals. Although the proposals had few immediate consequences, an analysis of the trade union views on industrial democracy sheds light on their attitudes towards the larger question of the role of trade unions in society, an issue which we shall pick up again in the next section of this chapter. Before looking at the various attitudes adopted by trade unions towards the Bullock proposals, we need to make one general point which has significance for the concerns of this chapter.

No one in the union movement seems to have expressed any significant opposition to the Bullock proposals simply on the grounds that they would involve yet more legal intervention in industrial relations. Abstentionism in the sense of not creating positive rights for workers and unions seemed to have lost its attraction as a rallying-call, as our analysis of the Employment Protection Act has already suggested. People might disagree as to whether employee representation on the board was a good thing or not or whether it would give employees an effective say in corporate planning,[87] but the fact that representation would be put in place by virtue of legislation was not, as such, thought to be objectionable. One may surmise that trade unions in the mid-1970s were willing to support legal interventions in industrial relations now that their increased political power gave them greater control over the sort of interventions that might occur, especially as one lesson of the Industrial Relations Act 1971 seemed to be that the abstentionist arguments of the 1960s had not rendered the traditional negative trade dispute immunities proof against legislative change. 'What the law gave the law might take away' was a maxim that could be applied to negative labour law as much as to positive labour law, and so was not an argument against introducing the right type of positive law, given the long-standing acceptance of negative laws.

What trade unions divided over was the substance of the Bullock Report, not the mechanisms for its implementation. That substance was the extension of joint regulation to, and therefore

[87] Much debate revolved around the issue of whether employees should be represented on the traditional 'single tier' boards known to UK company law or on the supervisory board of a two-tier board structure, as was the case in Germany. See Davies, 'The Bullock Report', at 254–7.

of some degree of joint responsibility for, corporate planning. Some unions, on the political left, objected to such a role for trade unions in a capitalist economy, because it meant acceptance of industry being run for profit. Such unions were, however, generally prepared to accept worker representation schemes in the nationalized industries, since these were said to be run in the public interest, perhaps a somewhat rosy view of the way in which nationalised industries actually functioned in the 1970s but, no doubt, a view in line with much of the nationalisation rhetoric of the 1940s. Other unions, on the political right of the union movement, rejected employee representation on the board (whether in public or private sectors) because they saw the traditional role of the union as one of opposition, of being able to veto managerial decisions, rather than of co-operation in the running of the enterprise. The view of the TUC and the unions supporting them was that unions, by participating in traditional collective bargaining, had already departed from a policy of pure opposition, for the signing of a collective agreement involved some responsibility for the union in the administration of the enterprise. Just as collective bargaining specified no particular resolution of the tension between management and unions' conflicting interests, on the one hand, and congruent interests, on the other, nor would a system of employee representation on the board that was based upon the principle of joint regulation.[88] Attractive though this argument might be, suggesting that no new principle lay behind the Bullock proposals but rather the radical extension of an existing one, it could not be denied that what was being proposed was an extension of trade unions' responsibilities as a concomitant part of the extension of their powers. As we shall see in the next section, the questions of whether trade unions were ready for such an extension of power and responsibility and whether such an extension was desirable lay behind

---

[88] Assuming that any company law impediment to the functioning of the board in this way was removed. Curiously, the only legislative change in the private sector to flow from the Bullock proposals was one to achieve this end. S. 46 of the Companies Act 1980 (now s. 309 of the Companies Act 1985), introduced by the Conservative government, requires directors 'to have regard in the performance of their functions . . . [to] the interests of the company's employees in general, as well as the interests of its members'. In the absence of any scheme of employee representation on the board, it is not clear that any change in board-level decision-making has flowed from this change in the law.

the whole 'wider Social Contract' and not just the Bullock proposals.[89]

8.5. CORPORATISM, JURIDIFICATION, AND JUDICIALIZATION

We have now described the outcomes of the three stages of labour law reform proposed by the TUC–Labour Party Liaison Committee in the early 1970s, as part of its policy of developing an alternative set of legal, economic, and social policies to those being pursued at that time by the Conservative government of Edward Heath. It now seems appropriate to try and set these labour law reforms in some sort of broader context and, in particular, to ask whether they signified any permanent changes in the role and functions of labour law. It has been suggested by various writers that the period under consideration demonstrated tendencies to incorporate trade unions into the governmental process, to juridify industrial relations, and to judicialize the settlement of industrial disputes. We will look at each contention in turn.

(a) Corporatism

The notion of corporatism has been developed in recent years with considerable sophistication by political sociologists.[90] For our limited purposes we take the two crucial features of corporatism as a system of government to be (1) that the rigid distinction between politics and economics is abandoned and government seeks to control economic results rather than leaving them to be determined by market forces, and (2) that government seeks to use organized interest groups to control activities in the economy so that these coincide with the government's plans. In relation to trade unions this means that government seeks to use them to control the actions of their members, as opposed to the situation

[89] For the above analysis of trade union attitudes we are indebted to Clark et al., *Trade Unions*, 88–91.

[90] See esp. C. Crouch, *Class Conflict and the Industrial Relations Crisis* (London, 1977), esp. pt. I, and *The Politics of Industrial Relations* (2nd edn. London, 1982), chs. 6 and 9; G. Lehmbruch and P. Schmitter, eds., *Patterns of Corporatist Policy-Making* (London, 1982) and *Trends Towards Corporatist Intermediation* (London, 1979).

where the primary function of trade unions is to represent the interests of their members against, *inter alia*, government. Obviously, a number of rather different forms of arrangement might meet these two criteria, ranging from a corporatism in which trade unions have no existence independent of government and where their sole function is control of their members in the government's interest, to a system which Crouch has labelled 'bargained corporatism'. Here trade unions, which are independent of the state, agree 'to sacrifice some of their entrenched but narrow and unambitious achievements in exchange for the possibility of greater political influence and more and broader power for their members at the workplace, but at the same time to accept more restraint, a more obvious role for the unions in restraining their members, more state interference and fuller acceptance of the industrial order and its priorities'.[91] With bargained corporatism unions maintain their autonomy but agree, in exchange for concessions by government in the areas under the latter's control, to accept certain restrictions on the full exercise of their autonomous powers. The nature and scope of the exchange could, no doubt, vary from time to time.

How useful is the notion of bargained corporatism in analysing the labour law developments in the period 1974 to 1979? Two initial points can be made. First, the possibility of some sort of arrangement between the TUC and a Labour government whereby the unions' industrial power is not exercised to the full in order to give the government the scope to introduce economic and social policies favoured by both government and union movement did not arise for the first time in the 1970s. We have argued[92] that such an arrangement was implicit in the relations between government and trade unions in the period 1945 to 1951, and that these relations did involve some restraint by trade unions of their members' wage claims. There was an attempt to re-create such an arrangement in the early 1960s—the TUC accepted the idea of a voluntary incomes policy as part of the Labour Party's commitment to engage in indicative economic planning when returned to power—though we have seen that the arrangement did not work out as intended. From this perspective

---

[91] Crouch *Politics of Industrial Relations*, 212–13.
[92] Above, ch. 2.3(*a*)(iii).

the Social Contract of the early 1970s was novel mainly because it was a more explicit and radical statement of aims than anything that had occurred previously. As we have argued earlier,[93] the commitments it contained were mainly on the part of a future Labour government. What the Labour Party secured in exchange was mainly a re-confirmation of the trade unions' political and financial support for the party rather than strong commitments by the unions to control their members' activities (though some moderation in wage claims was no doubt implicit in the arrangement arrived at by the Liaison Committee).

Second, as we have also seen,[94] after a year or so in government the economic crisis produced a *bouleversement* in the power relations between government and union movement such that the trade unions, anxious to avoid the return of a Conservative Party now committed to a *laissez-faire* philosophy, agreed to exercise very strong control over wage claims. At the same time and by the same token, however, the government dropped many of its social contract commitments. The exchange was now weighted very much in favour of the government, and, perhaps not surprisingly, this built up such discontent among the grass roots that the TUC ceased formally to support incomes restraint after two years. This experience may be said to be rather ambiguous on the question of whether a sustained system of control by trade unions over wage claims is possible in Britain. It might be thought that the experiment failed because the exchange for wage constraint was (or was perceived by union members to be) so meagre or, alternatively or in addition, because the structure of the union movement is such that the TUC exercises little real control over its affiliated unions, which in turn lack the degree of control over their members that a lasting corporatist system would require. The former problem could be susceptible to a new political initiative; the latter might be more difficult to resolve.[95]

It may be said, however, that, whether or not the Social Contract, at any of its stages, was an example of bargained corporatism, the analysis so far has said nothing about the reflection of corporatist ideas in legal structures during the period under

[93] Above, Subsect. 8.1(*b*).
[94] Above, p. 364.
[95] For an exploration of these possibilities, see Crouch, *Politics of Industrial Relations*, 212-22.

review. It should be conceded at once that in fact the Social Contract gave rise to few distinctive legal structures, partly because it was designed to operate though extra-legal institutions to a large extent, and partly because some of its more far-reaching proposals were never implemented. On the former point, the central institutional expression of the Social Contract was the Liaison Committee, which brought together in regular meetings the TUC leaders and the Prime Minister and other leading members of the Cabinet. But the Liaison Committee operated outside the ordinary machinery of government, and there seems not to have been any suggestion that a formal constitutional body be established in which government and the organized economic interests could co-ordinate their policies (on the lines, for example, of the Social and Economic Council in the Netherlands). Again, the incomes policies adopted by the TUC were voluntary in the sense that they relied upon social sanctions (notably those at the disposal of trade unions and the TUC) rather than legal sanctions for their enforcement. Statute was essentially confined to relieving those who did comply with the 'voluntary' policies from any consequent liability for breach of contract.[96] Except in this respect no special legal status was conferred upon the policies agreed between government and TUC as to the permitted level of wage increases, even though, in the years 1975 to 1977, these effectively determined that issue for the overwhelming majority of workers in the country, in both public and private sectors.[97]

[96] See the Remuneration Grants and Charges Act 1975. The policy was clearly not voluntary in the sense that its adoption was the TUC's imitative. On the contrary, on 1 July 1975 the then Chancellor of the Exchequer (Mr Healey), 'gave the TUC and CBI until the end of the following week to come to an agreement acceptable to the Government', otherwise he 'would be obliged to introduce a statutory policy': Clark *et al.*, *Trade Unions*, 34. Moreover, the government had contingency legislation in draft for use if the 'voluntary' policy failed. Dell comments: 'This (the 1975 Act), together with the co-operation of the TUC, contingency powers in draft, and the use of the Government's powers to control settlements in the public sector, made it as effective as a fully statutory policy could have been, possibly even more effective' (E. Dell, *A Hard Pounding* (Oxford, 1991), 172).

[97] The combination of voluntarism and pressure that produced the incomes policy is perhaps appropriately reflected in the embodiment of the policy in a series of White Papers. See especially *The Attack on Inflation*, Cmnd. 6151 (July 1975) (as an appendix to which appears an extract from the TUC document, *The Development of the Social Contract*, which sets out the £6 a week policy).

As to the latter point, had the Social Contract been fully implemented, some statutes with a distinctly corporatist flavour would, no doubt, have reached the statute-book. A case can be made, for example, for viewing the proposals of the majority of the Bullock Comittee as capable of leading to a form of 'bargained corporatism' at enterprise level, which would have paralleled developments occurring at the level of the whole economy. Through their representatives on the board the employees would have obtained a say in the development of corporate strategies, and it was argued by some that implicit in this was an understanding that unions would restrain the exercise of their collective bargaining powers. Again, in the initial concept of the Social Contract, employee representation on the board was to be part only of a broader system for extending trade union influence over corporate planning. It had been proposed that large companies should enter into 'planning agreements' with the government concerning their investment policies, and trade unions were to be involved in the drawing-up of these agreements.[98] These proposals did in fact achieve legislative status in the Industry Act 1975, but in a very watered-down form. In particular, the agreements were not compulsory (and, indeed, only two were ever signed—by companies in dire need of the government's financial assistance) and, more important from our point of view, in the implementation of the Act 'the trade unions were elbowed out into a sort of consultative status to a main game that was usually played inconclusively by civil servants and companies'.[99]

Perhaps because of the matters discussed in the previous two paragraphs, those looking for symbols of the Social Contract have tended to focus on what came to be known as 'tripartism', that is, the hiving-off from government to quasi-governmental organizations of certain areas of administration. The governing

However, the 'voluntary' or non-statutory basis of the incomes policy gave rise potentially to problems of administrative law in relation especially to the use by government of its contracting powers to enforce the policy. See the notes by G. Ganz and by R. Ferguson and A. Page in [1978] *Public Law* 333 and 347.

[98] In *The Development of the Social Contract* (Supplementary Report to the General Council's Report to the 1975 Trades Union Congress) it was stated that 'the General Council was looking for speedy progress in the formulation of planning agreement between trade unions, management and Government, in all the major firms in U.K. industry' (para. 25).

[99] Elliott, *Conflict or Co-operation?*, 38.

bodies of those organizations consisted of employee representatives (nominated by the TUC), employer representatives
(nominated by the CBI), in some cases representatives of other
interest groups, and non-affiliated, 'independent' persons. Such
quasi-governmental institutions were the Advisory Conciliation
and Arbitration Service (ACAS), the Manpower Services Commission (MSC), the Health and Safety Commission (HSC), the
Equal Opportunities Commission (EOC), and the Commission
for Racial Equality (CRE).[100] They differed from earlier tri-
partite bodies, like the National Economic Development Council
(NEDC), in that these newer organizations had administrative
and policy-making functions and were not merely places for
discussion and research. They clearly also reflected a policy of
involving trade unions in certain areas of activity which a purist
might think should be the sole preserve of government. In this
general sense, however, the policy was not unique to the Labour
government of 1976 to 1979. The HSC and MSC, indeed, were
established by the previous Conservative administration, at a
time when it was seeking a *rapprochement* with the trade unions.
Whether these tripartite bodies were expressive of a corporatist
philosophy is less clear. In some cases, their origins suggest the
opposite, namely an attempt to resurrect the voluntarist system in
which government kept out of industrial relations. Thus ACAS
was created largely because trade unions (and many employers)
had lost confidence in the impartiality of the conciliation and
arbitration services offered by the Department of Employment,
given that Department's responsibility for running various types
of incomes policies over the previous decade. To a large degree
ACAS was an attempt to re-create the old Ministry of Labour, an
impartial body in which both employers and unions could have
confidence, by *excluding* government from these areas of activity.

Thus it would seem fair to conclude that corporatist ideas did
not implant themselves to any great extent in the labour legislation of 1974 to 1979. However, this does not amount to a denial
of the corporatist tendencies, or indeed actualities, contained in
the Social Contract considered more broadly in terms of a system
of government. Although the specific provisions of the labour

[100] However, neither the EOC nor the CRE is required to be constituted in
this way by the relevant legislation.

legislation that reached the statute-book during this period, notably the Trade Union and Labour Relations Acts and the Employment Protection Act, reflected little in the way of corporatist ideas—one can easily imagine them as elements in a governmental strategy that was content to leave the conduct of industrial relations entirely in the hands of employers and trade unions—the Social Contract did in fact provide the indispensable context for their enactment. It is by no means clear that the government in 1974 and 1975 would have been prepared to re-enact the broad immunities against liability for industrial action or to create positive rights for unions and their members were it not in the expectation of co-operation in some form or another from the union movement in other areas of governmental activity, notably in the area of wage restraint. To abstract the labour laws of 1974 to 1976 from their political context can lead to a misreading of their significance, and to a tendency towards seeing the Trade Union and Labour Relations Acts in particular as reflecting some 'natural state' of British labour law rather than being, as we would assert, highly contingent upon the balance of political forces that obtained during the period in question.

(b) Juridification

The observations made in the last paragraph have relevance, as we shall see, also to the recent debates about 'juridification' of industrial relations. First, however, it is necessary to define the meaning of that term. We adopt that put forward by Clark and Wedderburn, who see juridification 'as a process (or processes) by which the state intervenes in social life . . . in ways which limit the autonomy of individuals or groups to determine their own affairs'.[101] On this definition corporatist policies are examples of juridification, since their aim (in the context in which we have been discussing them) is to limit the autonomy of organized economic interest groups, such as trade unions. On the other hand, not all examples of juridification involve the use of corporatist techniques. As we have seen, an essential feature of corporatism is the use by government of organizations to control the actions of their members. But the state might intervene

[101] J. Clark and Lord Wedderburn, 'Juridification: A Universal Trend? The British Experience in Labour Law', in G. Teubner, ed., *Juridification of Social Spheres* (Berlin, 1987), at 165.

directly to control the freedom of individuals to determine their own affairs, rather than indirectly through the agency of organizations which represent the individuals. Thus whereas corporatist policies would always seem to be examples of juridification, juridification is in fact a broader idea, embracing any method of state intervention in social life to limit individual or group autonomy. It might be, therefore, that the period under consideration shows greater tendencies toward juridification than towards corporatism.

Clark and Wedderburn also distinguish, we submit correctly, between juridification and state intervention more generally. 'All juridification involves state intervention, but not all state intervention necessarily involves juridification.'[102] Thus state intervention designed to remove an obstacle to individual or group autonomy would not be an example of juridification. This, perhaps rather obvious, point has particular significance, as we shall see, for the period under review. Finally, we need to make it clear that juridification raises the question of where the line between state control and individual or group autonomy is drawn and of the pressures tending towards greater state intervention. In labour law terms the question is usually put as to where the line between legislation and collective bargaining is to fall, though the issue could be conceived of in other ways (for example, in terms of the line between legislation and individual freedom of contract). What the concept of juridification does *not* in terms address itself to is the question of what the correct balance between state control and individual or group autonomy ought to be or, therefore, the question of whether a particular example of state intervention is to be approved of or not. In fact, the examples of juridification are legion, ranging from state interventions of which few people would disapprove (for example, controls over the use of child labour) to those which are much more controversial (for example, affirmative action requirements placed on government contractors). We are concerned in this section with the identification of the extent of the process of juridification in the period 1974 to 1979 and not with saying whether the process was to be welcomed or not.

The debate on juridification was launched, in the field of

[102] Ibid.

labour law, by a stimulating article published by Professor Simitis in 1984,[103] to which the article by Clark and Wedderburn, referred to above, is in effect a reply. Simitis's contention was the broad statement of comparative law that, since industrialization 'was and is not a specific national phenomenon', juridification can be identified as a universal trend in industrialized economies: 'where . . . the industrialization process begins there is no alternative to juridification'.[104] Britain necessarily receives considerable attention from Simitis as he attempts to establish this broad proposition, because of its abstentionist tradition in the field of labour law, and he pays particular attention to the developments of the Social Contract period, because of its apparent break with the abstentionist tradition.[105] We do not propose to follow Simitis in his broad comparative sweep, but, like Clark and Wedderburn, to concentrate upon the question of how well the British system fits in with the overall proposition.

The contention of Clark and Wedderburn is that 'the volatile and uneven development of British labour law and industrial relations does not in fact represent a "single confirmation of progressive juridification". Instead, the development of juridification, even since the late 1960s, will be shown to be much more contradictory, complex and open than suggested, and to have been at times a reversible process.'[106] How well do these competing views apply to the period 1974 to 1979, a period central in the arguments of both Simitis and Clark and Wedderburn? Both views accept that, at least at the level of government policy, the period in question saw a considerable juridification of the individual employment relationship by direct, regulatory legislation, a contention that appears to be true if one is prepared to extend the period under consideration back to 1971 so as to embrace the introduction of unfair dismissal legislation.

Clark and Wedderburn, however, correctly consider that, in view of the importance of collective bargaining in the British system, an assessment of the extent of the process of juridifica-

---

[103] 'Zur Verrechtlichung der Arbeitsbeziehungen', in H. Zacher et al., Verrechtlichung von Wirtschaft, Arbeit, and socialer Solidarität: Vergleichende Analysen (Baden, 1984). A somewhat shorter English version appears in G. Teubner, ed., Juridification, 113–62. Our references are to the English version.

[104] Ibid. 115.

[105] Ibid. 115–16, 120–1, 135–7, 139–40.

[106] Juridification, at 164.

tion crucially depends upon forming a view of how far collective labour relations were subject to the process in the period 1974 to 1979. Here, it does seem correct to conclude that employment protection legislation, by conferring rights upon individual employees, only rather marginally restricted the freedom of the parties to collective bargaining to arrive at the agreements they themselves thought best. We do not say this because this legislation aimed to regulate the individual employment relationship rather than collective relations, for this would be to ignore the extent to which regulatory individual legislation reduces the scope for regulation via collective agreements. Thus legislation and collective agreements can be competing methods of regulating the individual employment relationship, a competition which, in formal terms, legislation must always win. Rather, we regard the individual employment legislation of this period as intended by government not greatly to impinge upon collective bargaining freedom, because of the type of legislation enacted. Some subject-matters of collective bargaining were simply not touched up at all by the legislation. In other cases (as with guarantee pay) the purpose of the legislation was to extend generally forms of regulation already existing in and, indeed, pioneered by collective bargaining. In yet other cases, besides the generalizing function, the aim of the legislation was to speed up trends already incipient in collective bargaining but whose development was regarded by government as too slow and too uncertain. This was true of unfair dismissal legislation and, for that matter, of the earlier redundancy payments law. Indeed, as we have seen, in those areas (the closed shop and dismissals in the case of industrial action) where individual rights appeared likely openly to clash with collective patterns of behaviour, the legislation sharply curtailed the scope of these rights.[107] We do not intend by these arguments to deny the juridificatory purposes *vis-à-vis* collective bargaining of individual employment law, only to question their extent. In one respect, however, Clark and Wedderburn seem to overplay their hand, for they virtually ignore the equal pay and discrimination legislation. As we argued earlier,[108] these laws did in fact cut across traditional patterns of collective bargaining.

[107] For our earlier discussion of individual employment rights see above, Sect. 8.3.

[108] See above, Subsect. 8.3(*b*).

Simitis's observation in respect of such laws that they 'reflect the inability of the existing procedural mechanisms and particularly of collective bargaining to correct practices deeply rooted in a series of social prejudices and well established attitudes' seems apposite.[109]

The argument so far is that the test for juridification of British industrial relations in the period 1974 to 1979 should be seen primarily in terms of the juridification of collective employment relations, and that the juridificatory aims in this regard of the individual employment legislation were relatively slight (though not insignificant). How does the matter appear if one considers the aims of the collective labour legislation passed in this period? Here Clark and Wedderburn, looking at the Trade Union and Labour Relations Acts, take the view that the process of juridification was in fact thrown into reverse: 'One of the first acts of the Labour Party after its return to government in March 1974 was to "intervene" to restore the traditional non-interventionist framework of voluntary collective bargaining . . . The state intervened to recognize or sanction a "non-juridified" system of negotiating, concluding and enforcing collective agreements . . .'[110] As our discussion above would indicate,[111] we would agree with this analysis of the Trade Union and Labour Relations Acts, but as an analysis of the Social Contract legislative policy as a whole, it seems to be inadequate on two grounds. First, it ignores the collective provisions of the Employment Protection Act, and other statutes of the period, dealing with matters such as trade union recognition, disclosure of information, time off, consultation over redundancies, health and safety, etc. The fact that such legislation was designed to extend rather than restrict collective bargaining, or was auxiliary rather than directly regulatory, is not to the point in respect of the juridification thesis. The crucial

---

[109] *Juridification*, 145. See also P. Davies, 'European Equality Legislation, U.K. Legislative Policy and Industrial Relations', in J. C. McCrudden, ed., *Women, Employment and European Equality Law* (1987), ch. 1.

[110] *Juridification*, at 173–4. They add: 'When this is taken together with other provisions in the 1974–76 legislation . . . there appears to be powerful evidence in support of the view that the Social Contract labour legislation reaffirmed the non-interventionist voluntary framework of the industrial relations system as a whole.'

[111] Above, Sect. 8.2.

matter is that the legalisation aimed to remove the legal freedom of employers to decide whether or not to recognize unions or to consult with recognized unions over proposed redundancies, and so on. As such these are clear examples not merely of state interventions, but of intervention designed to restrict the autonomy of one of the actors in collective bargaining.

The second ground, we would suggest, for not seeing the period under review simply as one in which the trend of juridification was reversed, is that this view seems to depend upon abstracting the Trade Union and Labour Relations Acts from their broader Social Contract context. We have criticized above[112] some of the cruder views that have been put forward about the nature of the Social Contract, but we have also made it clear that the Social Contract was a political arrangement, part of which always was restraint to be exercised by trade unions over wage claims, and in the event the commitments which the trade unions gave and enforced in this respect in the period 1975 to 1977 were far-reaching and severe. We would wish to argue, therefore, that among the forms of state intervention to which regard must be had in considering the juridification thesis are these 'extra-legal' forms which produced such a severe control over wage increases in the period 1975 to 1977 that real incomes fell by nearly 6 per cent. As Simitis suggests, legislation is merely one form of intervention to which the state may resort for the implementation of its policies: besides legislation, one must look at administrative measures, court decisions, and 'indirect steering based on a carefully delegated decision-making power',[113] a rather apt description, one might think, of the process whereby the TUC, under threat of something much worse from the government, produced its 'own' incomes policies in the mid-1970s. We would go so far as to argue that the period 1975 to 1977 saw a remarkable degree of loss of autonomy for the collective bargaining parties. The fact that this loss of autonomy was reflected in large degree outside the area of traditional labour law is an immensely important fact—both by way of comparison with the period 1971 to 1974 and for the general role of labour law in industrial relations—but it is not a refutation of the juridification thesis.

[112] Above, Subsect. 8.1(a).
[113] *Juridification*, 122.

The point that the linkages between labour law and other areas of government policy need to be closely examined can be taken further. We have suggested so far that narrow concentration upon the Trade Union and Labour Relations Acts gives one a false view of government policy as a whole. We would also wish to argue that it can give one a false view of the legislation itself, by disguising the conditional nature of the government's commitment to the policies embodied in the Trade Union and Labour Relations Act 1974 and 1976. We would argue that the government in 1974 was prepared to restore the broad legal freedoms of trade unions and workers to engage in industrial action because it took the view that the Social Contract contained other mechanisms—outside the field of labour law or outside the field of law altogether—that would enable it to achieve its economic goals. The Social Contract contained a set of economic and social policies that were to be achieved in co-operation with the trade unions and employers, in contrast with the immediately preceding period in which policies were to be imposed on trade unions and where the law, in the shape of the Industrial Relations Act in particular, played a predominant role. But this form of collective *laissez-faire* is somewhat different from that of the 'golden age' from 1906 to the Second World War, which, in Fox's words, was characterized by 'the long persistence of the limited state, which allowed the pace of much, though not all, social and legislative change to be set by "voluntary" (that is, non-state) associations, groups or movements, either acting by themselves or bringing pressure to bear upon the governments'.[114] Governments now had their own economic and social objectives, though the methods they used to implement them, and the prominence of law in the processes of implementation, varied from time to time.

Moreover, even Labour governments might shift their views on the desirability of collective *laissez-faire* in relation to industrial conflict law if these other mechanisms of control did not work. So much had already been indicated by *In Place of Strife*[115] in the late 1960s. Some hints in the same direction were contained in *The Economy, the Government and Trade Union Responsibilities*, a document put together by government and TUC shortly before

[114] A. Fox, *History and Heritage* (London, 1985), 373.
[115] See above, ch. 6.3.

the 1979 General Election in the wake of the final breakdown of the Social Contract in the 'winter of discontent'. On the economic side it floated the idea of a 'national economic assessment' to guide pay negotiations; in relation to industrial conflict, the document gave relatively unequivocal support to the use of pre-strike ballots and said that secondary picketing should not occur 'save in exceptional circumstances'. Neither of these restrictions on collective *laissez-faire* was proposed to be enforced by legislation, but the 1979 document represented a clear shift in government policy on the virtues of collective *laissez-faire*. Both forms of control were, of course, to be given legislative expression by the Conservative governments in the 1980s.

We have thus sought to argue against the view that the period 1974 to 1979 saw the process of juridification thrown into reverse. Do we, then, take the opposite view: that 1974 to 1979 was a period of simple intensification of the tendencies at work in the period 1970 to 1974? This is an equally difficult proposition to accept, especially as the period 1970 to 1974 was not one in which government policy was homogenous.[116] It began with the emphasis being placed upon controls upon industrial relations imposed in the traditional areas of labour law (via the Industrial Relations Act), but shifted towards primary importance being attached to an incomes policy at least half-agreed with the trade union movement, with the Industrial Relations Act being downplayed. This may suggest that Simitis's thesis is misleading in so far as it implies that the trend towards juridification is a simple, unilinear one. As Clark and Wedderburn suggest, the process is, at least over relatively short periods of time, more complex and contradictory. We would wish to assert that this is because of the fundamental disagreements in the British context since the mid-1960s about the aims and objects of state intervention and about the most appropriate methods of intervention. These are not issues upon which the juridification thesis tells us very much, but we shall want to take them up elsewhere in this book.

(c) *Judicialization and Effectiveness*

The debate about the juridification of labour relations in the period 1974 to 1979, which so far has been considered at the level

[116] See above, ch. 7.1.

of legislative policy, leads naturally to a discussion of the effectiveness or the impact in practice of the laws enacted at this time.[117] In large part the issue of effectiveness can be equated with that of judicialization: how far have courts (and tribunals) replaced voluntary procedures as dispute-settlement machinery and how far, even within voluntary procedures, are decisions now taken by reference to legal criteria rather than to criteria developed autonomously by the parties? These questions are a good deal easier to pose than to answer, because the empirical evidence that is available is incomplete and not always easy to interpret.

Let us take as an example[118] the question of the impact of the unfair dismissal legislation, paying particular attention to the impact of the legislation upon collective labour relations. There is evidence that a disproportionate percentage of claims filed in industrial tribunals comes from weakly unionized industries—indeed, three such industries, construction, distribution, and miscellaneous services, accounted for over 50 per cent of the claims in the 1970s—whereas strongly unionized industries, such as mining, shipbuilding, and public services, were underrepresented in tribunal claims.[119] This evidence might suggest that the impact of the legislation was almost wholly in the non- or weakly-unionized sectors, and that where effective voluntary procedures existed, they proved more attractive to all parties in industrial relations. One might attribute the apparent failure of the industrial tribunals to take business from the voluntary

---

[117] Simitis (*Juridification*) 117 sharply distinguishes between the aims of the state and the effectiveness of its intervention: 'But the choice of a particular regulation at no point entails its effectiveness. Consequently, effectiveness considerations have always been understood as challenging the means, not the aims, of an interventionist policy. They reflect the search for better means of implementation and thus implicitly accept the motives and purposes of intervention.' However, in Britain at least, the question raised is not merely a technical one of the most efficient means of intervention, but goes to the potential instability of an industrial relations system regulated, as was attempted in the Social Contract period, partly by collective bargaining and partly by legislation. Cf. Wedderburn's oft-quoted statement that the statutory recognition procedure contained in the 1975 Act proved to be 'too strong a burden for the traditionally "voluntary" system of collective labour law to bear' (13 *Israel LR* at 456).

[118] For an attempt to analyse the evidence on the impact of the equal pay and discrimination legislation, see Davies, 'European Equality Legislation'.

[119] P. Davies and M. Freedland *Labour Law: Text and Materials* (1st edn. London, 1979), 391.

procedures to the refusal of the former to make effective use of the remedies placed at their disposal and their adoption of a 'managerialist' approach to the definition of 'fairness'.[120] There is also little evidence that the number of strikes over dismissal and disciplinary issues declined after the introduction of the legislation, though this was one of the aims of the legislators.

On the other hand, there is evidence that after the introduction of the legislation there was considerable growth in the number of voluntary dismissal and disciplinary procedures in existence and this growth was higher in unionized than in non-unionized sectors of the economy.[121] A recent survey concluded that 'it would seem likely that the extensiveness of both dismissals and health and safety procedures is in part due to the impact of legislation and the accompanying codes of practice in each of those areas.'[122] This would suggest that the unfair dismissal legislation had a differential impact in strongly and weakly unionized sectors, not that its impact was confined to the latter. In the former the effect was to encourage management and unions to institute or develop formal procedures for dealing with these matters so as to reduce the chances of a dispute reaching the industrial tribunal. However, it would be over-simple to ascribe the growth of disciplinary procedures wholly to the legislation. The tendency to formalize plant-level industrial relations was a general tendency in the 1970s—indeed this was part of the Donovan Commission's (non-legal) prescription for changing British industrial relations. Hence the surveys note also a widespread development of individual grievance procedures—separate from disciplinary procedures—and procedures for dealing with pay and conditions.[123] These procedures seem to have no direct relationship

---

[120] Out of a voluminous literature on these issues see L. Dickens et al., *Dismissed* (Oxford, 1985); K. Williams (1983) 12 ILJ 147; H. Collins (1982) 11 ILJ 78, 170; H. Glasbeek (1984) 13 ILJ 133.

[121] W. Daniel and E. Stilgoe, *The Impact of the Employment Protection Laws* (London, 1978), 49; W. Brown, ed., *The Changing Contours of British Industrial Relations* (Oxford, 1981), 43 ff.; Dickens et al., *Dismissed*, 236; W. Daniel and N. Millward, *Workplace Industrial Relations in Britain* (London, 1983), ch. 7; N. Millward and M. Stevens, *British Workplace Industrial Relations, 1980–1984* (Aldershot, 1986), ch. 7. For the relatively undeveloped state of disciplinary procedures before the legislation was introduced, see National Joint Advisory Committee of the Ministry of Labour, 'Dismissal Procedures' (1967).

[122] Millward and Stevens, *British Workplace Industrial Relations*, 170.

[123] Ibid.

with any particular legislative initiative, but rather to reflect the general trend towards formalization of industrial relations procedures. However, it is no doubt the case—and this illustrates well the complexity of the relationships between legal norms and autonomous social developments—that the general trend towards formalization of industrial relations procedures, which has its basis in industrial relations pressures, is reinforced and consolidated by the development of a corpus of individual employment laws, no matter what the precise content of these laws may be.

The suggestion implicit in the above discussion, that individual employment legislation is more easily effective in the area of collective labour relations where it is pushing in the same direction as social and economic pressures operating in this field, is of significance also when one is discussing the effectiveness of legislation designed directly to influence collective relations. The 1970s saw legislation designed both to restrict trade union power (Industrial Relations Act 1971) and to expand the scale of collective bargaining (Employment Protection Act 1975). By the end of the 1970s the view had emerged in some quarters that neither type of legislation was capable of having a substantial impact upon the voluntary system of British industrial relations. This may be too apocalyptic a view. Failure may be explicable by reference to more precise and limited criteria, namely, defects in the design of crucial parts of the legislation, the shortness of time that each legislative strategy was in operation, and its lack of support from contemporaneous social and economic developments. As we have suggested above, in the Industrial Relations Act the government put its main reliance upon the law in order to deal with what it saw as the problems of industrial relations, without having any substantial evidence that employers were enthusiastic to use the weapons the government was placing in its hands. It was opposed by a union movement confident of its economic and industrial strength. The legislation was on the statute-book for only three years and it had become clear long before the three years were up that the government's strategy had developed so as to place less reliance upon purely legal controls. Finally, the defects in the legislation, most notably the exposure of individuals to penalties for contempt of court, had hardly enough time to be identified let alone remedied (by a shift

to emphasis being placed upon trade union liability)[124] before the
Act was repealed. The history of the 1980s, as we shall see, might
suggest that all these 'problems' are capable of being solved, and
that the British system, for good or bad, is not in some magical
way impervious to restrictive regulation, imposed in the appropriate way at the appropriate time.

When one turns to the collective provisions of the Employment
Protection Act, it is in fact much less clear that one is dealing
with a failed piece of legislation. Substantial parts of its collective
provisions are still on the statute-book. Debate has concentrated,
however, upon the effectiveness or otherwise of the recognition
procedure, which can be said to have been at the centre of
the Act's strategy for promoting collective bargaining. It was
abolished in 1980 and had been disavowed by ACAS, the body
which operated it, as early as June 1979, on the grounds that
ACAS found it difficult to combine the operation of this compulsory mechanism with the provision of voluntary conciliation
and arbitration services.[125] Although ACAS handled some 1,610
cases under the recognition procedure, it estimated that recognition covering only 65,000 employees was achieved as a result.
However, as Dickens and Bain have pointed out, an assessment
of the effects of the legislation cannot stop at this point. There
was in the mid-1970s a clear 'public policy favourable to union
organisation and collective bargaining ... which indirectly
promoted union recognition not only by making employees more
aware of the feasibility of collective representation, but also by
encouraging employers to recognise unions voluntarily in order to
safeguard orderly bargaining structures and to avoid the public
scrutiny which would result from a reference under the statutory
procedure'.[126] The compulsory recognition procedure was only
part of this public policy. There was also the general obligation
placed upon ACAS in all its activities of 'encouraging the
extension of collective bargaining',[127] not to mention the central

[124] See P. Davies and S. Anderman, 'Injunction Procedures in Labour
Disputes' (1974) 3 ILJ at 33–40.
[125] See the letter from the Chairman of ACAS to the Secretary of State, app. C
to ACAS, *Annual Report 1979*.
[126] L. Dickens and G. S. Bain, 'A Duty to Bargain? Union Recognition and
Information Disclosure', in R. Lewis, ed., *Labour Law in Britain*, at 93.
[127] EPA 1975, s. 1(2). Now TULRECA s. 209, but proposed to be repealed by
the Trade Union Reform and Employment Rights Bill 1992.

role accorded to trade unions under the Social Contract in developing government policy. What was perhaps clear was that by 1979, with the collapse of the Social Contract on a general political level and the exposure in the courts of the defects of the recognition procedure,[128] legal procedures could no longer be expected to operate almost alone so as to induce a climate favourable to union recognition. Perhaps one can say that a recognition procedure of the type contained in the 1975 Act was dependent upon the development and institutionalization of corporatist governmental structures in a way that, in the end, failed to occur in the period 1974 to 1979.

8.6. CONCLUSION

The period 1974 to 1979 was a rich one for labour legislation. If one looks at the enactments of this period through the model developed at the beginning of this book, however, the legislation appears to have a paradoxical feature. That model of collective *laissez-faire*, it will be recalled, suggested analysis along two dimensions. The first was the extent to which government or the industrial relations actors controlled the individual employment relationship; the second was the degree of control the government exerted over the collective social institutions of industrial relations, through which the non-governmental regulation of individual employment relationships was effectuated. In Kahn-Freund's strong version of collective *laissez-faire*, governmental regulation was largely excluded along both dimensions.

The paradoxical feature of the legislation of the period considered in this chapter might at first sight appear to be that governmental intervention directly to regulate the individual employment relationship continued apace, building upon the developments analysed in Chapter 5, whilst legislative regulation of the structures of industrial relations was rolled back with the repeal by the Trade Union and Labour Relations Acts 1974 and 1976 of the Industrial Relations Act 1971. The first limb of this argument appears sustainable. The Sex Discrimination Act 1975,

---

[128] See above, p. 389, and R. Simpson, 'Judicial Control of ACAS' (1979) 8 ILJ 69.

and the associated maternity provisions of the Employment Protection Act, and the Race Relations Act 1976 did substantially add to the corpus of legal rules aimed at furthering one important facet of the policy of promoting industrial justice in the individual employment relationship. The unfair dismissal laws were also to some extent upgraded. There also appears much to be said for the second limb of the argument. Indeed, it could be said that the second policy was the stronger one, for, where collective autonomy clashed with individual protection, the policy of promoting the former tended to prevail over that of securing the latter. This was certainly true in respect of the provisions of the law of unfair dismissal regarding dismissals in a closed shop or for taking part in industrial action, and of the legislation relating to the protection of members against arbitrary treatment by trade unions, though not, it is suggested, of the discrimination legislation, where few concessions to collective autonomy were made.

Yet our analysis earlier in this chapter suggests there are considerable difficulties in accepting the straightforward view that governmental policy was simply to remove the controls on collective autonomy. Just in terms of the positive law one can identify the confirmation of one of the legislative interventions into collective autonomy introduced by the 1971 Act, namely the use of the law to promote collective bargaining. The centrepiece of that policy, the statutory recognition procedure, was, as we have argued, a less than full-blooded use of the law to this end, but its presence at all on the statute-book is highly significant. More important, we have sought to argue that it is wrong to view the apparently purely 'negative' provisions of the Trade Union and Labour Relations Act, restoring the autonomy of trade unions and workers in the field of industrial action, in isolation from the broader context of relations between government and trade unions at this time. In this broader context the restoration of the tort immunities appears to be not so much a reaffirmation of the liberal model of collective *laissez-faire*, in which the conduct of industrial relations is delegated by government to the parties, as an attempt to construct a corporatist relationship. Certainly the legal freedom of action of unions was restored by and large, but that was accompanied by a set of policies designed to encourage trade unions not to exercise their industrial power to the full, such restraint opening up to the unions greater influence over the government's legislative and executive policy-making than they had been accustomed to exercise.

Such a policy was not entirely novel. As we shall argue in the final chapter of the book, one of the central issues of post-war labour law in government's eyes has been how to adapt what was seen as the pre-war legacy of only very limited restraints upon the autonomy of the industrial relations parties to the post-war environment of an enormously enhanced governmental respon-sibility for the performance of the economy. All the post-war Labour governments were to some extent alive to the advantages of attempting to square this circle by incorporating trade unions and employers more closely into the enterprise of government, but of doing so largely by political rather than legal mechanisms, so that the formal legal structure of collective autonomy could remain intact. This was, we suggest, the true significance of the government's anti-inflation policies in the immediate post-war period, under the Prices and Incomes Acts of the 1960s and again in the Social Contract period. What was erected in the second half of the 1970s was, however, clearly the most elaborate and explicit of these corporatist arrangements, and yet it proved no more capable of even medium-term success than its predecessors. Its collapse in the shambles of the so-called 'winter of discontent' in 1978/9 dealt an enormously heavy blow to the perceived political feasibility of this type of strategy and paved the way for the very different governmental policies of the 1980s.[129]

---

[129] 'This shambles was of course a triumph for Mrs. Thatcher. The cowardice and irresponsibility of some union leaders in abdicating responsibility at this time guaranteed her election; it left them with no ground for complaining about her subsequent actions against them. On the other hand, we in the Cabinet should have realised that our five per cent norm would be provocative as well as unattainable. If we had been content with a formula like "single figures", we would have had lower settlements, have avoided the winter of discontent, and probably have won the election too" (Denis Healey, *The Time of My Life* (Harmondsworth, 1989), 462–3).

9

REDUCING THE POWER
OF TRADE UNIONS,
1979–1990

9.1. ECONOMIC POLICIES and TRADE UNION POWER

In this chapter and the next, we describe the history of labour legislation and government policy relating to labour legislation from 1979 to 1990. This means that we are concerned with the labour legislation policy of the three successive Conservative governments elected in 1979, 1983, and 1987, and with the period during which Margaret Thatcher was the Prime Minister.[1] One of the main concerns of this book is to relate the developments of these years to those of the period from the end of the Second World War down to 1979. That relationship appeared to re-define itself as the 1980s progressed, and as the changes in labour legislation policy appeared to be more and more fundamental, and greater and greater in their cumulative effect. Hindsight seemed increasingly to confirm that 1979 had been a watershed, and to illuminate the enormity of the transformation brought about since then. However, such an analysis is apt to be simplistic, neglecting important continuities between the 1970s and the 1980s—there was a good deal of monetarism in later 1970s governmental practice, for instance, although it was not yet the credo which it was to become in the 1980s. We are in search of a more significant relationship between the 1945–79 and the 1979–90 phases of labour legislation policy.

---

[1] This narrative does not extend systematically beyond Nov. 1990 when Margaret Thatcher was replaced by John Major as Prime Minister. The legislative developments of this period, in the field of the present chapter, are treated in S. Auerbach's *Legislating for Conflict* (Oxford, 1990). The political and economic developments are usefully gathered together in P. Riddell's *The Thatcher Era and its Legacy* (Oxford, 1991).

That relationship is more effectively explained by looking closely at the texture of post-1979 labour legislation than by thinking of it as a broad canvas from which we have to stand at a distance in order to see the picture. From a distance, we may think we see a bold and simple design, depicted in broad brush-strokes—the picture seems to consist of a few vivid motifs such as 'reducing the power of trade unions' and 'freeing the labour market'. From that perspective, the picture seems to represent an *art nouveau*, deliberately shocking to traditional sensibilities and making no concessions to earlier styles. There is indeed a kind of pattern to post-1979 labour legislation which can be viewed in that way; but if we stand up close to the picture we see it in a more complex light. It becomes apparent that the measures and policies, rather than being the implementation of grand strategies, are more in the nature of a series of initiatives and experiments having cumulative effects. Our method of proceeding will be to identify the main items in that series, and to try to relate them to the economic and ideological developments which occurred during the 1980s.

We have found it useful to organize our discussion of the 1980s in two parts—thus far, following the broad-brush approach. So we distinguish between, on the one hand, measures and policies concerned specifically with reducing trade union power, and, on the other hand, measures and policies concerned more generally with the restructuring of the labour market. This is primarily a division made for clarity of presentation, rather than a sharp theoretical distinction. The measures and policies for reducing trade union power are really a subset of the larger category of measures and policies for the restructuring of the labour market. In the early 1980s in particular the reduction of trade union power was probably the most significant of the legislative means for restructuring the labour market; the aims became larger and the means by which it was sought to achieve them became more diverse in the course of the 1980s. Sometimes we shall find it necessary to consider a given measure in both aspects, because it can be seen as operating at both levels. A good example is the abolition by the Employment Act 1980 of the statutory trade union recognition machinery established, as we saw in the last chapter, by the Employment Protection Act 1975. It is nevertheless useful to make a working distinction between the two categories, and to seek to isolate a group of themes in the narrower category of reducing trade union power.

We shall find that there are three main themes which run through the relevant measures and policies, and which intersect with the chronological development from one Employment Act or Trade Union Act to the next. The first theme is that of the reversal of corporatism and the de-politicization of the trade unions. This theme is mainly expressed in administrative measures, rather than in legislation; we shall see that it was expressed in a distancing of the unions from the corridors of power from 1979 onwards, and by a progressive downgrading of tripartism in the processes and agencies of government. It was sometimes a theme of legislation; thus, in aspiration at least, it was an aim of part III of the Trade Union Act 1984, which required periodical balloting to maintain trade union political funds. It was a theme which produced a sharp contrast between this era and the previous, Social Contract, phase of government policy in which the role of the trade unions in the political process had been positively enhanced. We shall describe the reduction of trade union political power in greater detail in the next section.

The second theme of the measures and policies which reduced or sought to reduce the power of trade unions was that of empowering employers to resist trade union demands and providing employers with countervailing sanctions. In a general sense, the empowering of employers to resist trade union demands was part of a wider phenomenon, which was the reversal of the public policy of supporting collective bargaining and effective trade union representation in collective bargaining. Thus the repeal in 1980 of the statutory trade union recognition provisions of the Employment Protection Act 1975 both signified the reversal of the prevailing policy of the Social Contract era and gradually empowered some employers to display resistance towards the basic demand of the trade union to represent the workforce in a collective bargaining process.

The more positive measures for encouraging employer resistance to trade unions—the reducing of trade union industrial power in a narrower sense—consisted of those which extended the sanctions available to employers against industrial action or the threat of it. We shall see that a whole series of measures in the 1980s both restricted the legality of industrial action, extended the liability of trade unions, and accorded employers an enhanced freedom to dismiss workers involved in industrial action. These measures were very largely targeted upon trade unions, and, even when their immediate target was the organizing of unofficial industrial action, they were aligned so as to empower employers to resist trade unions in particular, and to deploy sanctions which would weaken the position of trade unions in industrial relations.

There was a third theme, which was associated with the second but distinct from it. This consisted of an attack on expressions of solidaristic behaviour by trade unions and by workers, and the encouragement of individualistic attitudes. This was to reduce trade union industrial power indirectly, not so much by directly deterring trade unions from using that power as by fostering patterns of behaviour which would isolate trade unions and workgroups from each other, and which would cause individual workers to define their own interests against participating in industrial action. We shall see that this theme had a number of different manifestations. Firstly, the restrictions placed on the legality of industrial action were concentrated, especially in the early 1980s, upon discouraging external trade union action of a solidaristic kind in industrial disputes, such as picketing away from one's own workplace, or the imposition of secondary boycotts; and the concept of 'industrial dispute' was re-defined along similar lines to exclude disputes other than those between workers and their own employers, and certain international disputes.

Secondly, the conduct of the internal affairs, decision-making, and government of trade unions was restructured in such a way as to encourage individualistic behaviour and to override perceptions of solidarity on the part of trade union members. Thus (in one of the most widely supported reforms in the era) secret balloting was imposed as a required substitute for mass meetings; it was also required for the election of trade union officials. Much more contentious would be the move in the late 1980s to ensure that trade union members could not be disciplined by their unions for refusing to take part even in industrial action validated by support in a secret ballot; this, as we shall see later, was to take to very extreme lengths the policy of atomizing trade union behaviour into continuous individual decision-making by each member of the union.

The third aspect of this theme was an attack on traditional patterns of trade union organization at the workplace. The major form of this attack, we shall see, was to consist in a progressive placing of restrictions upon the closed shop to the point where it was accorded no legal protection at all. There were associated measures, which were also progressively elaborated, for joinder of contractors and trade unions as defendants to claims of unfair dismissal, and eventually for direct sanctions upon trade unions to control efforts by trade unions to establish closed shops, or even recognition for bargaining purposes, in hitherto non-union workplaces.

These three aspects of the attack upon solidaristic behaviour did not develop sequentially; we shall see that each of them, and indeed each of the other two themes, affects or explains to some degree all of the measures for reducing trade union industrial power which were taken in the 1980s. Before proceeding to a more or less chronological survey of those measures, it will be useful to bring together in the next section the measures and policies which struck particularly at trade union political power. Even before we begin to do that, however, it is important to consider the framework of economic policy within which the exercise of reducing the power of trade unions was undertaken.

Most of the phases of the post-war history of labour legislation so far described have required an introduction describing the economic policy background against which the labour legislation has been enacted. This is particularly necessary in approaching the post-1979 period, because in the post-1979 decade economics and economic policies had a more direct and overt impact upon labour legislation than was previously the case. Previous governments, for reasons we shall examine, were more inclined to treat economic policies as part of the background of labour legislation; after 1979, the government put them in the foreground so far as labour legislation was concerned. By the mid-1980s, it had become customary to announce the coming year's labour policy, and even proposals for labour legislation, in the Chancellor's Budget Speech.[2] How and why did this considerable change in

[2] HC Deb., 6th ser., vol. 75, cols. 787–90 (19 Mar. 1985); vol. 94, cols. 171–3 (18 Mar. 1986)—Nigel Lawson as Chancellor of the Exchequer.

governmental style come about, and how was it related to the policies which shaped post-1979 labour legislation?

The single most important and prioritized policy commitment of post-1979 governments was the control of inflation. It was their main undertaking to the electorate in 1979 to achieve that goal in a way that previous governments had seemed increasingly unable to do. (One might argue that their main undertaking was to bring the unions under control and prevent a recurrence of the Winter of Discontent of 1978–9, but this was less prominently undertaken than controlling inflation. It was also less prominently undertaken than it had been by the incoming Conservative government in 1970: the new Prime Minister clearly regarded the example of 1970–4 as one to avoid at all costs so far as the handling of the trade unions was concerned.[3]) As we have seen, it was nothing new for a British government to be crucially preoccupied with the control of inflation—the Achilles' heel of every government since the mid-1960s. But it was new for the government to be disposed to give this goal overriding priority over a number of social goals the pursuit of which had come to be regarded as a non-displaceable feature of the post-war state. This was full of consequence for labour legislation.

The giving of overriding priority to the control of inflation provides the outline of an economic policy, but fails to provide its details. In the early 1980s, in particular, the government identified its economic policies as those of 'Monetarism'.[4] The term has no very precise significance. It refers to economic policies of which the leading theoretical exponent was Milton Friedman. In its simple basic form, it stands for an emphasis on the importance of controlling money supply, and for the view that a failure to control the supply of money to the economy is an irresponsible failure to control inflation.[5] The mechanics of controlling—indeed, of measuring—money supply need not concern us very much, beyond our making the point that it is much more complex than measuring and controlling the quantity

---

[3] Cf. P. Riddell, *The Thatcher Government* (updated edn. Oxford, 1985), 36–7.

[4] See, generally, D. Robinson, *Monetarism and the Labour Market* (Oxford, 1986).

[5] Ibid., ch. 1 sets out a brief explanation of monetarism, 'emphasising its central tenet that inflation is determined by changes in the money supply'

of notes and coins in the economy; it is not simply about 'not printing bank-notes'. The main instrument, in the British context, of restricting money supply is that of keeping interest rates high, which discourages the growth of credit and debt. In the early 1980s, the government was at pains to publish money supply figures (according to various measures, of which M3—money in circulation plus sterling deposits held by UK residents—was regarded as the most significant) and to show how it was using its levers of control in response to those measurements. In 1980 this process had been institutionalized as the Medium-Term Financial Strategy, which set a target of limiting money-supply growth to 6 per cent per annum by 1983/4 and announced an intention of increasing interest rates as necessary to achieve this.[6]

The other main feature of the Medium-Term Financial Strategy, and an important aspect of Monetarism in the wide sense of that term, was the declared intention severely to restrict public expenditure—to reduce the annual deficit of public expenditure compared with public revenue, known as the Public Sector Borrowing Requirement. Monetarism as thus embodied in this two-pronged Medium-Term Financial Strategy was a direct—and consciously direct—reversal of the Keynesian economic policies which had, by and large, been dominant throughout the post-war period. Where Keynesian economists urged positive demand management—that is to say, concentrating on bringing about demand-led growth in the economy—Monetarists now instead insisted on restriction of money supply to implement a 'sound money' policy. Where Keynesians regarded public expenditure as necessary and desirable even if that meant running an annual public sector deficit. Monetarists regarded public sector deficit financing as the worst kind of collective self-indulgence.[7]

All this was, of course, far more than a theoretical disputation between rival academic schools of economists; it was fraught with political and social consequences. As we have seen, Keynesian economic policies were, from the 1940s onwards, the essential

---

[6] The nature and significance of MTFS is usefully analysed by A. Gamble, *The Free Economy and the Strong State* (London, 1988), 100 ff.

[7] Cf. D. Marquand, *The Unprincipled Society* (London, 1988), 17 ff., 'Keynesian Social Democracy'; Robinson, *Monetarism*, 422 ff., 'Public Expenditure'.

underpinnings of the two great social goals of the post-war state—full employment and adequate universal welfare provision. The change to Monetarism in the early 1980s represented—indeed was part and parcel of —an allocation of lower priority to those goals than they had hitherto been accorded. For the governments of the 1980s, Monetarism involved—some would say, was defined as—the subordination of those goals to the control of inflation so far as was necessary and politically possible. The latter assessment was made, as we shall see, in a markedly bold and robust fashion. The rate of unemployment doubled between 1979 and 1981; the numbers of the unemployed passed the 2 million mark in 1980 and the 3 million mark in 1981. This increase is partly attributable to the recession suffered by industrial economies throughout the world at that time; the point is that Monetarism involved the government in being, to say the least, visibly prepared not to combat the rise in unemployment, where previous post-war governments had assumed they could not survive if they pursued such a strategy.[8]

Just as the Monetarism of the post-1979 governments should not be seen as merely theoretical, so it should also not be seen as purely global and macro-economic in its operation. Post-1979 governments understood Monetarism to require sound financial management—good housekeeping—at the micro-economic level also. According to their version of Monetarism, each unit of the public or publicly subsidized sector of the labour economy should be subjected to the same monetary restrictions in the form of 'cash limits' as the macro-economy itself. To quote from Robert Hall,[9]

Thatcher put a set of ruthless industrialists in charge of the nationalized industries and instructed them to render the firms profitable at any cost in terms of lost employment or foregone capital investment . . . Their relations with the government were not without friction, as Ministers attempted to impose strict financial limits on the capital expenditure of these firms while their managers argued for greater freedom of action and investment in longer-term growth. . . . As a result, reorganization

---

[8] This was especially true of Edward Heath's government in the early 1970s—see M. Holmes, *Political Pressure and Economic Policy: British Government 1970–1974* (London,1982), 40–4, 'The Political Pressure of Rising Unemployment'.

[9] R. Hall, *Governing the Economy* (London, 1986), 112.

schemes, involving the loss of over 250,000 jobs between 1979 and 1985 were implemented in steel, coal, the national airline, automobiles, the railways and shipbuilding.'

The Government's monetarist economic policies, taking the form just described, had and were perceived to have major repercussions upon the government's relations with trade unions—and therefore upon labour legislation. Monetarism involved nothing less than a complete re-alignment of the government's perception of the trade union movement. Post-war Keynesian economic policies had basically been benevolent towards, and had been so regarded by, the trade union movement. Governments had, of course, experienced mounting difficulties in securing trade union self-restraint, or restraining trade union militancy, as they had to do if the favourable conditions for the sale of labour created by Keynesian economic policies were to be sustainable. These difficulties had loomed large in the 1960s and reached crisis proportion in the 1970s. But even at the high points of crisis, the economic policies of the governments concerned had envisaged a positive role for trade unions; the search—however illusory—was for a way to make or persuade the trade unions to play that appointed role (and no larger part).

It was altogether different under post-1979 monetarist economic policies. After 1979, it was clear to the Government that the trade unions represented a straightforward obstacle to their monetarist aims. This was true at both macro- and micro-economic levels. At the macro-economic level, the whole admission of the trade unions to the counsels of the corporatist state was premised upon the assumptions that they would insist upon the priority of full employment and that it was acceptable for them to do so. The new economic policies challenged those assumptions and made it necessary either to reformulate the corporatist state to the exclusion of trade unions or to resile from corporatist commitments. After 1979, there were clear tendencies in both those directions, and those tendencies had a major effect on the orientation of labour legislation.

That is to say, after 1979 labour legislation was directed towards the reducing of trade union power, and this re-direction was linked to the government's desire to effectuate its economic policies at micro-economic level. It was fully expected that trade unions would resist the sort of reorganizations and redundancies that monetarist economic policies enjoined directly—via cash limits—upon the public sector and indirectly upon the private sector of the labour economy. It was perceived by post-1979 governments as necessary to fragment and to reduce trade union power so far as it constituted a resistance to their economic goals. In the early 1980s, the trade unions seemed less able, even in the view of some less motivated, to provide that resistance than was predicted in the foregoing scenario. But the government continued to modify labour legislation on the assumption that their economic policies necessitated doing so; and in 1984 the National Union of Mineworkers—with hindsight one would say obligingly—set off down the road to Armageddon so far as trade union resistance to Monetarism in the labour economy was concerned. It is easy to overlook the fact that the Miners' Strike of 1984/5 was not about pay or directly about terms and conditions of employment; it was precisely a challenge to the outcome of Monetarism in that particular public sector industry, namely threatened—and eventually actual—extensive pit closures, especially in depressed regions of the country.[10] The defeat of the miners in 1985 represents the watershed of this kind of interaction between the trade unions and the government's economic and labour market policies, and it is that interaction—continuing well beyond 1985 in one form or another—which forms the essential subject-matter of this chapter on the Reduction of Trade Union Power.

If we have here the makings of an account of the economic policy background to the reducing of trade union power in the 1980s, this is by no means to say that we are offering an explanation for the trade union and industrial conflict legislation of the 1980s in terms of monetarist policies. Significant interactions do not amount to complete explanations, and we do not offer them as such. Indeed, there are important reasons for *not* regarding monetarism as providing complete explanations for this particular set of developments in labour law. First of all, we have already seen in a number of earlier chapters abundant evidence

[10] See, generally, M. Adeney and J. Lloyd, *The Miners' Strike 1984–85: Loss without Limit* (London, 1986).

that the search for a body of trade union and industrial conflict law which would moderate and control the power of trade unions long antedated the monetarist policy formulations of the early 1980s; and we shall see that, particularly during Mr Prior's period as Secretary of State for Employment, the evolution of labour legislation owed as much to the debate about labour law as to the post-1980 rhetoric of monetarism. Secondly, the fit between monetarist policies and post-1980 strategies for labour legislation is also an imperfect one is substantive terms, to the extent that the monetarist policies bear much more obviously on the public sector, while the legislative measures were in no way specific to the public sector and were even at some points predominantly concerned with the private sector.

This leads on to the third and most important reason why we are not advancing monetarism as a comprehensive explanatory framework, and only as one historical starting-point, for post-1980 legislative developments. This reason is that monetarism receded quite rapidly into the background as an account of governmental economic policies, becoming little more than an episode in a larger and longer programme of restructuring the economy so as to realize the ideal of a free and unconstrained labour and product market. It is in those latter terms, in the discourse of the free labour market, that we can start to find an explanation and a structure for the developments in labour law and employment policy with which we are concerned both in this chapter and the next.

From this wider perspective, it is apparent that 1980s government fairly continually perceived the freeing of the labour market as necessitating the reduction of the power of trade unions to impose collectivist constraints upon the functioning of the labour market. There was thus a real sense in which the first priority of those governments, in terms of labour law and employment policy, was to free both private sector employers and themselves as the ultimate employer in the public sector from the shackles of trade union power. It is with that central and continual element of free labour market policy that we are essentially concerned in this chapter. Lying behind that concern was an even more fundamental set of questions about how the participants in the labour market were supposed to operate when freed from the constrictions of trade union power—how, in other words, the free market was to be maintained as an efficient market. Here again, governments would address these questions both as the formulators of labour law and employment policy for the labour economy as a whole, and in the role of public sector employers. In the latter role they would take the view that they had greater leverage upon the course of events than in the former role, but also a greater need to take positive action if their overall economic aims were to be achieved. The restructuring of the labour market which resulted from those imperatives took a number of forms, and came to include both a series of transformations of public sector institutions and systems, and a new (and hostile) stance towards European Community labour law and social policy. Those developments are explored in the next chapter; in both chapters we shall thus be looking in different ways at the interaction between labour law and governmental free market economic policies.

9.2. REDUCING TRADE UNION POLITICAL POWER

Before we embark on an examination, in some detail, of the measures for reducing trade union industrial power, we shall consider the other important aspect of the reduction of trade union power, namely, the series of developments tending to reduce the political power of the unions and to push them out of the national policy-making process and policy agenda. As we indicated in the previous section, these developments constituted a reversal of corporatism in the sense that they denied the inclusion of trade unions in the political structure of the state, rather than simply seeking to minimize the power of trade unions in industrial society.

This was the underlying implication, for instance, of part III of the Trade Union Act 1984, which tightened the conditions on which trade unions might maintain a political fund (normally in support of the Labour Party), conditions which had been settled by the Trade Union Act 1913. The provisions of part III aimed to demonstrate and give effect to a supposed lack of enthusiasm on the part of many trade union members for the political dimension to their trade unions, by requiring balloted support for the maintenance of a political fund at least every ten years. At one level, this could be seen simply as a direct attack upon trade union financial support for the Labour Party, the traditional recipient of trade union political funds. Indeed, the Green Paper *Democracy in Trade Unions* had proposed an even more direct attack, consisting in the replacement of contracting-out of the political fund by the system of contracting-in which had been imposed by the Trade Disputes and Trade Unions Act 1927 until its repeal in 1946.[11] The government decided not to press for contracting-in, on the strength of an undertaking by the TUC to ensure that trade union members would be made fully aware of their statutory right to contract out and would be enabled to exercise that right freely. The more limited strategy of requiring periodic ballots which was in fact adopted in part III was not very effective in eliminating political funds, for the ballots held in pursuance of part III produced, in the short term at least, far greater support for the funds in the ballots than might have been predicted.[12]

The controversy over this aspect of part III of the 1984 Act diverted attention from the fact that part III also re-defined the political objects of trade unions in such a way as to enlarge them, bringing within their scope, for instance, expenditure on the production, publication, or distribution of any literature, document, film, sound recording, or advertisement the main purpose of which is to persuade any person to vote or not to vote for a political party or candidate.[13] The enlargement of the definition of political objects has the effect of cutting down the objects the unions can finance out of their general funds; it would seem the government's target was an advertising campaign conducted by NALGO in 1983 against public sector financial cuts

[11] Green Paper, *Democracy in Trade Unions* , Cmnd. 8778 (1983), paras. 88–98, 'Contracting-out'.

[12] Details are given by P. Elias and K. Ewing in *Trade Union Democracy, Members' Rights and the Law* (London, 1987), 182–3. For a full study of the outcomes and implications of pt. III, see M. Steele, K. Miller, and J. Gennard, 'The Trade Union Act 1984: Political Fund Ballots' (1986) 24 BJIR 443. They conclude that 'If . . . the real intention of the authors of the Act was that the ballots would result in fewer unions having political funds, fewer political fund contributions and a weakening of trade union influence in the Labour Party, then the Government can be said to have scored "an own goal".'

[13] Substituted s. 3(3)(f) of the Trade Union Act 1913, now TULRECA s. 72(1)(f).

and privatization.[14] The aim of reducing trade union participation in the political policy-making process was fairly clear.

It is worth noting here that later in the decade a somewhat analogous legislative attack was made upon the activities in the public employment sector of, as it were, the political wing of the labour movement. This was carried out by part I of the Local Government and Housing Act 1989 which placed restrictions on the political activity of local government officers and staff.[15] Part I consists mainly of measures taken in response to the Widdicombe Committee of Inquiry into the Conduct of Local Authority Business,[16] and to that extent can be regarded as non-partisan. Nor was it specifically aimed at trade union political power. However, the Act did adopt a wider category of politically restricted posts than that recommended by the Widdicombe Committee,[17] thus extending the political disqualifications (from being a Member of Parliament, *inter alia*) downwards from the most senior grades of local authority employment to include, for instance, posts where the duties include giving advice on a regular basis to the authority or speaking on behalf of the authority on a regular basis to journalists or broadcasters.[18] Such a measure is, of course, fully consistent with the broad aim of the Widdicombe Report of ensuring 'political impartiality' or 'neutrality' in local government;[19] but the provisions of part I in general mainfest the government's more contentious concern to challenge what they perceived as the conjunction of political activism and trade union militancy in the public employment sector.[20]

Alongside these legislative measures there occurred a general distancing of trade unions from the policy-making process by the

[14] See K. Ewing, 'Trade Union Political Funds: The 1913 Act Revised' (1984) 13 ILJ 227 at 238.

[15] See annotation by K. Ewing, (1990) 19 ILJ 111 and, on the Local Government Officers (Political Restrictions) Regulations 1990 (SI. 1990, No. 851), (1990) 19 ILJ 192.

[16] Report: Cmnd. 97997 (1986); Government Response: Cm. 433 (1988).

[17] See Ewing, (1990) 19 ILJ. 111.

[18] Local Government and Housing Act 1989, s. 2(3).

[19] See Widdicombe Report, paras. 6. 205–17, and the valuable annotation in *Current Law Statutes* (1989), 42, 29 ff.

[20] Cf., in general, K. Young's reflections on developments in Local Government which form ch. 9 of D. Kavanagh and A. Seldon, eds., *The Thatcher Effect: A Decade of Change* (Oxford, 1989).

government. Thus Martin Holmes, writing in 1985 from a point of view by no means wholly unsympathetic to the policy concerned, noted that in the period from 1979 to 1983,

The attempted close relations between governments and unions that had dominated the post-war period of consensus Keynesianism was simply jettisoned. The idea that the unions had a role to play in formulating government policy—the essence of the corporatist approach—was repudiated. This change of attitude was arguably more fundamental a change than that proposed in the 1979 Conservative manifesto to amend trade union law. The significance of the end of the corporatist approach cannot be overstressed in understanding both economic policy sources and the nature of contemporary Conservatism under Mrs. Thatcher's first administration.[21]

A good example of this withdrawal from corporatism is provided by the decline in importance of the tri-partite National Economic Development Council in the 1980s, and by the marginalizing of the trade unions within the NEDC. In 1981 James Prior, an advocate of the very sort of tripartism which the NEDC embodied, urged in the Green Paper on the reform of trade dispute law that the practice whereby employers, unions, and government met to discuss 'questions of the day' in the NEDC could with advantage be expanded.[22] But he was moved out of the Department of Employment, not least because the Prime Minister was suspicious of his corporatist policies, and by 1985 all the trade unions could claim for the NEDC consultative process was that it showed that, 'with the support of the CBI, not all doors were closed to TUC representations to the Government'.[23] However, in 1992 the government took what from their point of view was the logical next step and abolished the Council.

In the next chapter, moreover, we shall see a vivid specific example of this marginalization of trade unions in the development of the policy-making institutions concerned with training for employment.[24] In the course of that development, as we shall

[21] M. Holmes, *The First Thatcher Government, 1979–1983* (Boulder, Colo., 1985), 34. See id., 'Trade Unions and Governments', in H. Drucker *et al.*, eds., *Developments in British Politics* (London, 1985), ch. 10.

[22] Green Paper, *Trade Union Immunities* (1981), Cmnd. 8128, para.32.Cf. James Prior, *A Balance of Power* (London, 1986), 170.

[23] TUC, *Annual Report 1985*, 293. The NEDC did not meet between June and Dec. 1984, attendance of the TUC representative being suspended following the GCHQ episode—see NEDC, *Annual Report 1984–5*, 1.

[24] See below, ch. 10.5.

see, perhaps the grandest of all post-war tri-partite experiments, the Manpower Services Commission, was disbanded, and control of training activities was transferred to employer-led Training and Enterprise Councils on which trade unions had no formal representation and in which they were to have little or no practical role to play.

It was symptomatic of this engineered breakdown of corporatist structures that the TUC should have been driven to take the crucial step of deciding to withdraw from participation in the government's Employment Training Scheme in 1988, thus paving the way for Norman Fowler as Secretary of State for Employment to abolish the Training Commission—the already downgraded remnant of the Manpower Services Commission.[25] That episode serves as a reminder of the extent to which the moves away from corporatism weakened not just the trade unions in general but in particular the TUC, which had grown important as the agent for the trade union movement in all the post-war phases of expansion of corporatist activity. It was significant that Norman Fowler should confirm this development in 1989 by withdrawing the recognition of the TUC as, hitherto, the sole channel of selection of employees' representatives on such tripartite bodies as had survived the 1980s, thus driving home the point that the TUC was no longer to be regarded as an 'estate of the realm' in the way that it had been for much of the post-war period.[26] It was at this stage that the TUC distanced itself crucially from the government by providing a platform for Jacques Delors's promotion of the Social Dimension of the European Single Market; that the TUC should move in that unaccustomed direction was a reflection of the extent to which it had been marginalized by the Government in the national policy-making process.

These matters are mentioned at this point in order to indicate that the measures of the 1980s concerned with reducing trade union industrial power should be seen in the context of a wish on

[25] K. Middlemas, *Power, Competition and the State, iii. The End of the Postwar Era: Britain since 1974* (London, 1991), refers at p. 332 to 'this absurd decision' on the part of the TUC; that view underestimates the difficulty of the position in which the TUC had been placed. Cf. below, p. 611.

[26] B. C. Roberts makes this point, not entirely without relish, in his chapter on Trade Unions in D. Kavanagh and A. Seldon, eds., *The Thatcher Effect* (Oxford, 1989), at pp. 74–5.

the part of the government to negate the constitutional role of trade unions as a whole.[27] At the same time, those measures concerned with the political role of trade unions and their members have been referred to relatively briefly in order to emphasize that it is the industrial power of trade unions which the government was centrally concerned to challenge from 1979 onwards, and it is the measures taken to that end which we now proceed to describe in greater detail.

9.3. REDUCING TRADE UNION INDUSTRIAL POWER: THE 1980 MEASURES

The measures taken between 1979 and 1990 to reduce the industrial power of trade unions amounted to a cumulative reformulation of the role of labour law in relation to industrial conflict. These measures were shaped by an often unspoken assumption that the government had a clear mandate to weaken the control exercised by the unions over the industrial economy and to reassert public order. This was, in itself, nothing new; the Conservative government of 1970 had come into office with the same assumptions and had acted upon those assumptions for at least its first two years in office. But from 1979 onwards the government felt progressively more and more free of any countervailing need to maintain collective bargaining as a central institution of the industrial economy, or, therefore, to ensure that trade unions were strong and effective participants in the processes of industrial relations. They could and did view their electoral victories in 1983 and 1987 as an affirmation that this departure from the central tradition of post-war industrial relations was based on a politically correct assessment.

It would not, however, be correct to view the government as having pursued a single line of argument, or as having had a preconceived programme for the reduction of trade union industrial power, during the decade 1980–90. A series of initiatives took place, under a succession of ministers, apparently with

---

[27] See, generally, K. Ewing's chapter on 'Trade Unions and the Constitution' in C. Graham and T. Prosser, eds., *Waiving the Rules: The Constitution under Thatcherism* (Milton Keynes, 1988), esp. at p. 152 where he refers to 'the revival of constitutional fundamentalism'.

the Prime Minister maintaining the momentum. From about 1985 onwards, these initiatives had a visible cumulative effect; the changes in the legal regime governing industrial disputes were seen to be accelerating that reduction in trade union power which was in any case being brought about by increased unemployment especially affecting those sectors of the labour economy in which trade union strength had been concentrated. Although this cumulative effect was certainly something radically new, each individual step was not; many of the individual measures had starting-points in various earlier episodes of labour law history, most but not all within the period 1945–79. So we need to consider each of the measures both for its own particular rationale and for its contribution to the general reduction in industrial power and influence sustained by trade unions in this decade.

During the period 1979–90, the government brought forward measures having the aim, in one way or another, of reducing trade union industrial power, with almost complete regularity at two-yearly intervals. The Employment Act of 1980 was followed by the Employment Act of 1982 and the Trade Union Act of 1984. There was relevant legislation in the Public Order Act 1986, and the full cycle was resumed with the Employment Acts of 1988 and 1990.[28] This regularity was not, on the whole, conscious or deliberate; it did not indicate that the whole sequence of legislation was programmatic. It is true that James Prior, the first in the post-1979 succession of Secretaries of State for Employment, characterized the approach to this legislation in the early 1980s as a 'step by step approach'; but this, as we shall see, implied an intention to legislate no further than was necessary at any given moment, rather than a plan of arriving at a preconceived goal by a series of measured steps.[29] The regularity and frequency of these legislative interventions in fact reflects two things: firstly, the high priority which the control of trade

---

[28] The Employment Act 1989 was not part of this cycle, as it was not concerned with the law of industrial conflict or with trade union law. Its concerns were with labour market issues, which are discussed in the next chapter.

[29] See Jim Prior's memoirs, *A Balance of Power*, (London, 1986), 158: 'It would have been easy for the Government to go too far in changing the law and to do so too fast: we would then find that not only the unions but also business and most of the country would unite in saying that we had produced a scheme of law which was unworkable.' The spectre of the Industrial Relations Act evidently shapes that comment.

union industrial power had in the government's policy-making process throughout the 1980s, and secondly, the continuing need which the government felt to re-formulate its strategies in the face of that trade union power, in response to their experience of current industrial disputes or perceptions of the ways in which industrial relations were developing. In order to assess how far each of those roughly biennial bursts of legislative activity was either pre-emptive or opportunistic or merely reactive, we need to ask, in relation to each of them, how far and in what ways each one developed along the two thematic lines we sketched out earlier in this chapter, namely the empowering of employers to resist trade union industrial power and the encouragement of individualistic over solidaristic behaviour on the part of workers and trade unions. We begin by asking those questions of the first set of measures, of which the core was the Employment Act 1980.

Like the Industrial Relations Act 1971, the Employment Act 1980 was legislation whose main features were determined by the experience of the Conservative Party while still in opposition. This is important to an understanding of the policy-making process by which it was designed. The main features of the policy framework formed during those years were, firstly, a determination shared by both moderates and radicals within the Conservative Party not to repeat what was now seen as the mistake of attempting a single comprehensive legislative re-structuring of industrial relations.[30] Secondly, there was a common perception that the labour legislation of the Social Contract phase was over-protective of trade union industrial power, especially so far as trade union and trade dispute immunities from economic tort liability were concerned. Thirdly, there was an emerging tension between the radical monetarists, particularly Margaret Thatcher herself and Keith Joseph, and the moderates—represented in this field by James Prior—over the question of how fundamentally the corporatist framework of the Social Contract period was to be attacked.

Although that tension was still basically unresolved when the Conservative government came into office in May 1979, it was

---

[30] Thus M. Holmes, *The First Thatcher Government, 1979–83: Contemporary Conservatism and Economic Change* (Boulder, Colo., 1985), 11.

deflected by the events of the so-called 'winter of discontent', the
winter of 1978 to 1979, events which enabled Conservative
policy-makers to agree upon immediate objectives, to embody
those objectives in firm political commitments, and to conclude
that they had a specific mandate from the electorate for proceeding rapidly to proposing the Employment Bill once in office.
The 'winter of discontent' episode consisted of a cumulative
succession of large wage claims by trade unions in both the public
and private sectors and large-scale industrial action in support of
those claims which disrupted or threatened to disrupt essential
services in a wide range of different ways. Some of the industrial
action concerned could be seen to symbolize oppressive use of
industrial power affecting the community at large, as where the
road haulage workers controlled and rationed the movement of
essential supplies, or where the local authority manual workers'
industrial action extended to grave-diggers and caused delays in
burials.[31] The Opposition were able to capitalize politically upon
the inability of both the Labour government and the TUC to
control this situation; and was able to agree to concentrate upon
an industrial relations strategy which would promise legislation to
curb the abuses of trade union power which were perceived to
have occurred during the 'winter of discontent,' in particular the
extension of picketing beyond the premises and the workers of
the employers involved in an industrial dispute, and the use of
the closed shop to coerce workers into participation in industrial
action.[32] So strategies directed especially against coercive trade
union solidarity were crystallized at that juncture.

The new government after May 1979 did not, however, claim
in the short term to be doing more than remedying specific
abuses. The changed regime for industrial relations was ushered
in, with an almost defensive supporting rhetoric, by the Employment Act 1980 and its accompanying two Codes of Practice, one
on Picketing and the other on Closed Shop Agreements and
Arrangements. James Prior, introducing the Employment Bill in
December 1979[33] as Secretary of State for Employment, was

[31] See Middlemas, *Power, Competition and the State*, iii. 162–5: 'The "winter
of discontent" was not . . . an isolated or unexpected episode, except to the
Opposition and the public'
[32] See, for details of this development, Auerbach, *Legislating for Conflict*,
24–9, especially the account of Mr Prior's responses to the picketing aspect of the
events of 1978–9.
[33] Working Papers were issued for consultation in July 1979: see ibid. 32–6.

more of an adherent to the traditions of industrial relations than his successors in that office, or than his Prime Minister, and therefore at some pains to depict his proposals as being continuous with those traditions:

Our proposals are designed to improve industrial relations, but to do so by working with the grain rather than against it.[34]

This 'working with the grain' was presented as a self-restraint on the part of the government, which commanded a corresponding self-discipline from the industrial relations partners:

Our proposals do not change the need for bargainers to behave sensibly, nor do they in any way absolve those who lead them from their responsibility of providing practical voluntary guidance on the use of the powerful weapons in their bargaining armoury.[35]

This was to understate the challenge to a consensual and corporatist tradition which the measures themselves represented; but it nevertheless provides some explanation of the strategy which it introduced.

In presenting the Employment Bill, Mr Prior located it in the line of descent of a fifteen-year-long search, conducted by both Labour and Conservative governments, for a legal solution to the problems of industrial society:

The incomes policies of the early 1960s, the statutory policies of 1966 and 1972, 'In Place of Strife' in 1969, the Industrial Relations Act 1971, Trade Union and Labour Relations Acts of 1974 and 1976, and Employment Protection Act 1975 have all attempted to tackle the problem, and any minister who presents proposals to change law . . . must be mindful of that record.[36]

It was claimed that this Bill was seeking that balance which had been the elusive goal of all those measures:

Let me reiterate that we have sought a balance. I do not believe that what we have witnessed in the last 20 years has been a balance. It is that which has worried successive Governments and this House throughout the whole of this unsettled period.[37]

---

[34] HC Deb., 5th ser., vol. 976, col. 60 (17 Dec. 1979).
[35] Ibid., col. 60.
[36] Ibid., col. 58.
[37] Ibid., col. 60.

Through this caution, and this appeal to the idea of continuity, there nevertheless appear some hints of the ideologies which are to become dominant in the ensuing years. Thus, although it is said that 'the rights of an individual as an individual need to be balanced by the right of individuals to act together',[38] it is asserted that

Our guiding principle has been ... to ensure that the rights of the individual are respected and upheld, at the place of work as in every other facet of our lives.[39]

And included in the 'limited' category of circumstances seen as justifying legislative change are those cases 'where privilege is being abused and suffering results, where the creation of new jobs is being inhibited by fear of the present law and what it means'.[40] The pursuit of individualism, and the opposition to what was perceived as the negative effect of trade union activity upon job creation, were to become increasingly open and prominent later in the decade. Both in rhetorical and in practical terms, the Employment Act 1980 made important initial contributions to the themes, which we specified earlier, of empowering employers to resist trade union industrial strength, and of encouraging individualism at the expense of solidarity within the workforce and within trade unions.

So we can begin to identify in the 1980 measures a tension between two approaches in Conservative governmental policy-making at that period. The 1980 measures were poised between, on the one hand, the industrial politics of the 1970s and, on the other hand, the new set of policies and prevailing attitudes which the 1980 measures themselves started to usher in. The policy-makers shared a commitment to a general need to reduce trade union industrial power; they also shared a conviction that this could not be accomplished by a sudden comprehensive reworking of the whole of labour law such as had been attempted by the Industrial Relations Act in 1971. They diverged about whether the ultimate goal was to establish a new, readjusted, equilibrium between trade unions and employers—which was what the moderates, represented by Mr Prior, wanted—or, on the other

---

[38] Ibid., col. 59.
[39] Ibid.
[40] Ibid., col. 60.

hand, fundamentally to restrict trade union power, perhaps eventually destroying it. The Prime Minister's aims were of the latter, more fundamentalist, kind; and although the 1980 measures reflected the temporary ascendancy of the more moderate approach, they also had a number of radical components which were the starting-points for later, unequivocally radical, developments.[41] From the original collective *laissez-faire* position of labour law, the first watershed had been its attempted replacement by regulated collective bargaining in the 1970s, in which attempt the Industrial Relations Act had been central. The second watershed, that of the 1980s, was going to be the loss of faith in collective bargaining even in a regulated form. Some control of industrial action was consistent with both regulated collective bargaining and the destruction of collective bargaining, and it was not clear in 1980 in which direction the new measures were pointing. Mr Prior probably wanted the former—hence his emphasis on controlling abuses; the Prime Minister already probably aspired to the latter aim.

The tension between the two approaches was manifested in the dichotomy between, as it were, hard rules contained in the Employment Act itself and soft rules contained in Codes of Practice issued under the authority of the Act. The issue by the Secretary of State for Employment of Codes of Practice, for which provision was made by section 3 of the 1980 Act, was a central feature of the 1980 measures; but because of this underlying tension, their status was somewhat equivocal. The Codes so issued, on Picketing and on Closed Shop Agreements and Arrangements, gave rise to concern because of their constitutional implications; the Goverment seemed to regard this code-making power as including the making of informal delegated legislation—which would have coercive effects not provided for by the statute.[42] The Codes were radical not just in that constitutional sense but also specifically in a labour law context.

---

[41] See R. Lewis and B. Simpson, *Striking a Balance? Employment Law after the 1980 Act* (Oxford, 1981) for a very perceptive contemporary assessment of the 1980 measures in similar terms. They concluded that the 1980 Act was attempting to force new patterns of behaviour and attitudes; their prediction was that the attainment of those goals might generate social and political costs of an unpredictable nature (p. 231).

[42] Cf. Lord McCarthy, ' Closed Minds and Closed Shops' (1980) *Federation News* 145.

The Codes of the 1970s, whether emanating from the Department of Employment, from the Commission for Industrial Relations, or from ACAS, had on the whole been the subject of a commitment to reflect existing good industrial relations practice, however selectively that was assessed.[43] The new Codes of the 1980s, by contrast, were entrusted solely to the Department of Employment rather than to the tri-partite ACAS, and quite often attempted to establish new normative patterns which were only very tenuously, if at all, grounded in existing law or industrial relations practice. Earlier Codes were located in the territory occupied by the existing conventions of collective and individual employment relations; these latest ones seemed to blur the lines between existing labour law and radical new approaches to industrial conflict and trade unionism. At a number of points, the Codes developed the attack upon solidaristic behaviour by workers and trade unions significantly further than the legislation itself did.

Given that these were the general policies and strategies which shaped the 1980 measures, what specific changes did the 1980 measures make to the law and practice affecting the exercise of trade union industrial power? The centrally relevant measures taken by or under the Employment Act 1980 fell into five groups, respectively concerned with:

1. Encouragement of secret balloting as the method of decision-making by trade unions;
2. Controls upon closed shop practices and union membership clauses;
3. Restrictions upon coercive recruitment;
4. Restrictions upon picketing;
5. Restrictions upon secondary action.

While each of these groups can be seen as being to some extent concerned with the encouragement of individualistic over solidaristic behaviour, it is the latter three, and more especially the last two, which are concerned with empowering employers to resist trade union industrial power. We shall look at these five groups in turn; there is a certain sequence of ideas between them in the order in which we have set them out. In order to complete the picture of the impact of the 1980 measures upon trade

[43] Compare above, pp. 306–7.

union industrial power, we shall also look at two further sets of measures, namely:

6. the abolition of statutory procedures available to trade unions under the Employment Protection Act 1975; and
7. the curtailment of supplementary benefit to strikers' dependants.

The inspiration for the measures in these two groups was rather different from that which generated the measures in the former five groups; their effect, as we shall see, was arguably just as great.

(a) Encouragement of Secret Balloting

The most moderate and consensualist of all these groups of measures was that concerned with the encouragement of secret balloting. There were two measures in this group. Section 1 of the 1980 Act authorized the Secretary of State for Employment to make regulations for a scheme to provide for payments by the Certification Officer towards the cost of trade union secret ballots about the calling or ending of industrial action, elections of officers or shop stewards, rules amendments or amalgamations. When the regulations were made, they extended only to postal ballots, and did not include elections of shop stewards.[44] Section 2 of the Act placed a duty on employers to permit trade union secret ballots to take place on their premises. The latter provision, which seems to have been less central than the former to the strategy of the 1980 Act as a whole, was apparently designed to stress to employers that the encouragement of workplace secret balloting (as preferable to decisions by workplace mass meetings) represented good industrial relations practice.[45]

The former provisions, on state funding for secret (postal) ballots, bespoke a more continuing concern to give effect to moderate rank-and-file opinion within trade unions both in elections of trade union officers and in decisions about industrial action.[46] This had been a concern of the Conservative Opposition

[44] These were the Funds for Trade Union Ballots Regulations 1980 (SI. 1980, No. 1252). See, for a detailed discussion, Lewis and Simpson, *Striking a Balance?*, 127–31.

[45] See Lewis and Simpson, *Striking a Balance?*, 132–3; Auerbach, *Legislating for Conflict*, 120.

[46] See R. Undy and R. Martin, *Ballots and Trade Union Democracy* (Oxford, 1984), 17.

from 1974 onwards, which had been heightened by the events of the 'winter of discontent'.[47] Their controversy had been how far to made secret balloting compulsory, either in addition or as an alternative to providing state funding for it; the preference for state funding over compulsion seems to have been the result of Mr Prior's preference for the most voluntarist of the options presented by the Conservative policy debate of the 1970s, though this did not prevent an attempt on the part of the TUC to secure concerted trade union refusal to accept state funding in the style of earlier concerted resistance to the Industrial Relations Act.[48] The sort of procedural reform which was attempted by section 1, and the Regulations made under it, did not go to the lengths of discouraging solidaristic behaviour on the part of trade union members; but the attempt to proceduralize trade union decision-making in such a way as to promote a paradigm of rank-and-file moderation tends towards a policy of encouraging individual trade union members to define their interests against supporting industrial action, as later policy developments would amply demonstrate.

(b) Controls upon Closed Shop Practices and Union Membership Clauses

The 1980 measures in relation to the closed shop further illustrate the way the 1980 measures in general served as a bridge between the debates of the 1970s and the outcomes of the 1980s. The closed shop had been a matter of fairly acute controversy in the 1970s. The legislators of the Industrial Relations Act had declared pre-entry closed shop agreements to be void, and had attempted to make post-entry closed shops conform to specific statutory models. Moreover, the introduction of unfair dismissal legislation by the 1971 Act brought with it a continuing need for special legislation about the closed shop where there had been no such need before, if employers were to be protected from remedies for unfair dismissal where they enforced a closed shop by dismissing a worker for not belonging to a trade union. The

[47] See Auerbach, *Legislating for Conflict*, 119–20; Lewis and Simpson, *Striking a Balance?*, 126.

[48] See Prior, *A Balance of Power*, 159: 'An objective observer might have thought that this would be relatively uncontroversial, but it took six years for the unions to come to terms with it.'

adjustment of the unfair dismissal legislation dealing with the closed shop to the policies of the Social Contract era, which was effected by the Trade Union and Labour Relations Acts 1974 and 1976, was a matter of bitter and prolonged controversy, which had as its sequel the ultimately successful challenge to that legislation, as it related to the closed shop in British Rail, before the European Court of Human Rights in the case of *Young, James and Webster* v. *UK*.[49]

So in 1979, proposals for further changes to the law about the closed shop could plausibly be located against a background of continuing debate about the right legal regime for closed shop practices. The rhetoric with which the measures were introduced was certainly a cautious one; it was asserted that the government wished merely to safeguard individuals in an effective way; that the government had resisted pressures from its own backbenchers to go further and outlaw the closed shop; and that the law was merely replicating good industrial relations practices such as were being adopted voluntarily in relation to new closed shops.[50]

However modest the proclaimed intentions of the closed shop provisions of the 1980 Act, they nevertheless contained important encouragements for individualistic resistance to trade union solidarity in the workplace, for example in the way that the re-casting of the unfair dismissal legislation in relation to the closed shop was effected by section 7 of the Act. Essentially, the conditions upon which a dismissal in pursuance of a closed shop agreement or arrangement would be exempt from unfair dismissal liability were narrowed. The agreement or arrangement would now have to tolerate non-membership on the part of all those objecting to belonging on any ground of conscience or deeply held personal conviction (whereas previously only religious objection needed to be tolerated) and also on the part of non-members forming part of the relevant workforce when the

---

[49] [1981] IRLR 408. Essentially, the European Court of Human Rights held that the UK was in breach of art. 11 of the European Human Rights Convention in that UK legislation, as it then stood, failed to protect freedom of association in allowing a union membership agreement to be imposed upon existing employees who wished not to belong to any of the specified unions. (For the view that 'rarely has such a strange judgment been so misunderstood and misrepresented', see Lord Wedderburn, *The Worker and the Law* (3rd edn. 1986), 376–8,: 'The Railwaymen's Case'.) See above, pp. 357–8.

[50] HC Deb., 5th ser., vol. 976, col. 66 (James Prior, 17 Dec. 1979).

closed shop in question was first established.[51] Moreover, any new closed shop agreement or arrangement could only thereafter be the basis of exemption from unfair dismissal liability if approved in a ballot in which at least 80 per cent of the employees voted in its favour.[52] This could be seen as enforcing existing best practice, though the qualifying majority was notably high. Sections 4 and 5 of the Act further provided a right for someone employed or seeking employment where there was a closed shop (in the shape of an operative union membership agreement) not to be unreasonably excluded or expelled from a trade union, and enabled industrial tribunals to award compensation for the violation of that right. This revived, in the context of the closed shop, a controversial legislative pattern which the Conservative Opposition had briefly imposed on the Trade Union and Labour Relations Act 1974 until its repeal by the Amendment Act of 1976.[53]

If the measures relating to the closed shop in the 1980 Act, thus far described, were not strikingly innovative, the same could not be said for the contents, whatever their normative status, of the Code of Practice on the Closed Shop. The Code gave indications of an underlying individualism and distrust of the authority and power of trade unions which had been discernible on the fringes but not in the mainstream of the debates of the 1970s. Two inter-related new themes stand out. Firstly, it was apparent, from the suggestion that all union membership agreements should require periodic revalidation by overwhelming support of the workforce in a ballot,[54] that there was a greatly increased preoccupation with giving an effective voice and set of options to workers who were unwilling to belong to trade unions. Secondly, when the Code indicated how the new statutory right to challenge arbitrary trade union disciplinary action might be invoked in the case where the individual refused to take part in industrial action called for by the union, or crossed a picket line which the union had not authorized or which was not at the member's place of work,[55] it was embarking on the project of

---

[52] S. 7(3).
[53] See above, p. 374.
[54] *Code of Practice*, paras. 42, 43, and 45, cross-referring to 35.
[55] Ibid., paras. 54, 55.

breaking the link between trade union external or industrial power and trade union internal or workforce power which the closed shop increasingly represented to 1980s governments.

Further evidence that this was the underlying project is to be found in rather arcane joinder and double joinder provisions of the 1980 Act. Section 10 of the Act made elaborate provisions for joinder by employers, for contribution to compensation, of those (including trade unions) putting industrial action pressure on them to dismiss an employee for non-membership of a trade union. There was a precedent for doing this in the Industrial Relations Act of 1971; but there was no such precedent for the further, and even more elaborate, provisions for double joinder—a contractor could join a company or public authority contracting with him, which could in turn join a person (including a trade union) exerting such industrial action pressure for the dismissal of an employee. This latter measure was directed against union membership clauses in commercial contracts, whereby a company or public authority putting work out to a contractor would require that contractor to ensure that the work in question was carried out entirely by trade union members, thus as it were extending the one contractor's own closed shop arrangements to the other contractor for the purposes of the contracted work. Although the double joinder provisions resulted from an amendment in the House of Lords, rather than being proposed by the government itself, in retrospect we can see this measure as the first of a series of attacks on solidaristic employment practices on the part of local authorities, who were the principal source of the union membership clauses against which the double joinder provisions were aimed.[56]

It was widely thought at the time that, as the government asserted, this whole set of measures would not fundamentally alter closed shop practice (just as the Industrial Relations Act, though overtly more ambitious in relation to the closed shop, had failed to do so).[57] Perhaps not; but the measures were in an

---

[56] For discussion of the extent of use of union membership clauses by local authorities in the early 1980s, see S. Fredman and G. Morris, *The State as Employer: Labour Law in the Public Services* (London, 1989), in their ch. 12 on Contract Compliance at pp. 458, 463.

[57] In their contemporary assessment, however, Roy Lewis and Bob Simpson were very clear about the radical aims of the closed shop provisions (*Striking a*

underlying sense highly significant, for they involved the notion of the primacy of the preferences of the individual worker over the preferences of the collective trade union majority—a notion which was to emerge as quite central to the government's strategy for labour law. To dismiss this as mere ideological posturing irrelevant to industrial society would have been, indeed was, to underestimate the new brand of Conservatism which was emerging through the interstices of Mr Prior's generally collectivist discourse.

(c) Controls upon Coercive Recruitment

There was a further provision in the 1980 Act which, like the joinder and double joinder provisions, was both about controlling certain kinds of closed shop activity and about sanctions upon industrial action, and which, also like the joinder provisions, was a first initiative along lines which were to be followed with increasing vigour in later legislation. Section 18, which dealt with coercive recruitment, was not of very great practical significance (at least in the sense that it gave rise to very little litigation); but the thinking which underlies it is of very notable importance. Ostensibly the section was no more than a response to a report by Andrew Leggatt QC,[58] who had been commissioned by the Department of Employment to look at certain specific problems about trade union recruitment practices in the printing industry and had expressed concern at the practice whereby the printing union SLADE had been coercively recruiting members in non-union artwork printing shops by blacking or threatening to black work coming from those non-union shops if those employed in them did not become union members.[59] Both the form and the objective of industrial action of this kind were particularly suspect in the view of the government; and the combination of unacceptable form with unacceptable objective was felt to present an especially strong case for legislation. The unacceptability of the form of industrial action lay in its being taken by

Balance?, 122): 'the Employment Act seeks to make the closed shop—and also the right to organise—maintainable only at a considerable cost for the unions, for their individual members and even for the employers who favour the practice.'

[58] Andrew Leggatt, QC, Report of Inquiry into Certain Trade Union Recruitment Activities, Cmnd. 7706 (1979).

[59] Cmnd. 7706.

workers not employed by the employer with whom the dispute existed against their employers with whom no dispute existed; it was entirely secondary action. The unacceptability of the objective consisted in the aim of recruiting into a trade union members of a workforce none of whom might wish to belong to a trade union; to try to create a closed shop entirely without the support of the workforce.[60] The section withdrew trade dispute immunity from industrial action taken or threatened with that purpose in those circumstances.

This provision, while apparently so specific to the particular area covered by the Leggatt Report, embodies or foreshadows many of the government's wider objectives for the restriction of the role and power of trade unions. This is true in three senses. Firstly, it challenged a tradition which accepted that trade union recruitment and trade union claims to be recognized in all workplaces were legitimate goals which the law should support or at least not impede. Secondly, it identified the freedom of choice of the individual worker as an overriding priority for the legal regulation of industrial relations. Thirdly, it enabled the employer to derive rights and expectations from that freedom of choice on the part of the individual worker—both in the sense that it protected the employer's opportunity to create and maintain a non-union workforce, and in the sense that it enabled him to bring a civil action derived from the freedoms of the individual non-union workers whom he had chosen. The Working Paper which gave rise to section 18 made it clear that the employer was to be the real beneficiary of the government's concern over coercive recruitment of workers:

Mr Leggatt's report confirms that, under the law as it stands, there is often no remedy for someone whose business or livelihood is threatened with destruction by the application of economic pressure through industrial action taken by employees of another company for the purpose of coercing the employees of that business into membership of a particular union. . . . The government consider this to be an unacceptable situation.[61]

---

[60] Cf. Auerbach, *Legislating for Conflict*, 30: 'This activity attracted particularly widespread condemnation because of the way in which employees rather than employers were seen to be its target.'

[61] Working Paper, *Statutory Protection against Certain Trade Union Recruitment Activities* (Oct. 1979) (set out in IRLIB 149 (21 Nov. 1979), 11), Para. 4.

Hence the government saw a special case for enabling an employer to bring a civil suit when coercive recruitment occurred against both the employer's wishes and those of the whole of his workforce (though the employer might deliberately have recruited and maintained a wholly non-union workforce). This measure reflects both the themes underlying the whole sequence of measures reducing trade union industrial power; it was directed against solidaristic trade union behaviour when solidarity was sought to be achieved by coercive intrusion upon non-union workforces, and it sought to empower a particular set of employers to resist trade union pressure to organize their workforces, and to counter that pressure with civil sanctions derived from the common law of economic torts. In different ways, both those themes, and especially the latter one, were writ even larger in the provisions of the 1980 Act concerning picketing and secondary action which we now turn to consider.

(d) Restrictions upon Picketing

As we have seen, the perceived need to assert greater control over picketing was one of the central starting-points for the 1980 Act, and the measures which were taken for that purpose typify the way in which the 1980 legislation in general moved from the rapidly crumbling but still real consensualism of the post-Donovan era and towards the deliberate reduction of trade union power. On the one hand, the 1980 measures, and the policy formation process leading up to them, reflect the debates about picketing which had become more and more urgent in the post-Donovan era as picketing grew, and seemed more of a threat, with the increase in major confrontational nationwide industrial disputes and stoppages. On the other hand, section 16 of the 1980 Act was one of the centrally important points of development of the new themes in industrial dispute legislation; it attacked solidaristic trade union behaviour by a drastic curtailment of the scope of lawful picketing, and it empowered employers to resist industrial action by making common law sanctions available to them.

In some respects, then, the picketing measures of 1980 reflected an agenda of the 1970s.[62] Major issues of the 1970s

---

[62] Cf. Auerbach, *Legislating for Conflict*, 23–5, identifying in detail the events of the 1970s which influenced Conservative policy, and the types of activity which raised policy concerns. See above, ch. 7.2.(a).

reflected in the 1980 measures were, firstly, whether trade union self-regulation according to a voluntary or at least participative code of conduct could limit the adverse effects of picketing upon the community more effectively than the use of police power could; secondly, how the traditional right to picket should be interpreted in an era in which an effective right to picket was claimed to involve a right to stop vehicles entering or leaving an employer's premises and, thirdly, how to insulate from the adverse effects of picketing those perceived as innocent third parties to an industrial dispute, whether as non-involved employers or simply as consumers and citizens.

In some respects, the 1980 measures can be seen as falling within the range of the orthodox responses to those questions in the 1970s. For instance, Mr Prior's enthusiasm for a Code of Practice on Picketing partly reflects his view that voluntary codes of practice promulgated by trade unions, particularly the National Union of Mineworkers in 1974, had played a useful part in moderating behaviour on the picket lines in the 1970s.[63] This and other traces of the 1970s debate about picketing are clearly visible in the Working Paper in which the government set out its proposals for legislation on picketing, and indeed in the relevant part of the Conservative Election Manifesto of 1979 which the Working Paper takes as its starting-point.[64] The statement, for instance, that:

The Government believe that the function of the law in the case of picketing as in the case of other forms of industrial action is to describe with clarity the rights immunities and liabilities of those who take part.[65]

comes squarely within the discourse of the 1970s about picketing.

On the other hand, the government felt that it had a clear mandate to 'reflect the widespread public concern at recent developments in the use of picketing as a weapon in disputes',[66] and its manner of doing so foreshadows many of the great shifts which were to take place in the 1980s, not just in industrial conflict law but in labour law as a whole. The events of the 'winter of discontent', the great industrial disputes of late 1978

---

[63] See ibid. 26-7: 'Labour having dropped the proposal, the Conservatives duly picked it up.'

[64] The Working Paper of July 1979 is set out in full in IRLIB 142 (8 Aug. 1979), 5.

[65] Working Paper, para. 1.

[66] Ibid., para. 3.

and early 1979, were a turning-point and contributed to a number of these ideological transformations. For instance, the concern with the impact of mass picketing and flying picketing, which was a recurring one in the 1970s, was intensified and concentrated by the events of the 'winter of discontent' to the point where it provided the rationale for the crucial decision implemented by section 16[67] of the 1980 Act, to confine lawful picketing to picketing at one's own place of work (or the place of work of members of a trade union whom one is representing as a trade union official).[68] This was the first major instance of the new trend to reduce the power of trade unions by fragmenting the processes both of industrial conflict and of collective bargaining, and by curtailing inter-enterprise and inter-workplace co-ordination on the part of the workforce.

The measure was presented as one merely to protect the non-involved victims of secondary picketing to the extent that the industrial action of the 'winter of discontent' had gone beyond the bounds of 'traditional picketing'.[69] This presentation obscured two critical features of section 16. Firstly, by confining lawful picketing, as we have seen, to picketing at one's own place of work, the section excluded from the ambit of legality a good deal of the picketing activity traditionally regarded as industrially justifiable and therefore as lawful. For example, such a claim of industrial justification would be made for 'following the struck work', that is, secondary picketing of other enterprises acting as suppliers to or customers of the production process which is the subject of the dispute.[70] There was also a second sense in which section 16 fundamentally changed the direction of the law of industrial conflict, and the events of the 'winter of discontent' again provided the starting-point. The United Biscuits Company, by bringing a successful claim for an injunction against picket organizers for interfering with employment contracts and commercial contracts during the road haulage dispute,[71] seem to

[67] Now TULRECA s. 220.

[68] The Working Paper, in para. 8, proposed to go further and also to confine lawful picketing to that carried out by employees party to the trade dispute.

[69] HC Deb., 5th ser., vol. 976, cols. 64–5 (17 Dec. 1979).

[70] Cf. the facts of the Wapping dispute—see below, p. 498; see *News Group Newspapers Ltd.* v. *SOGAT 1982* [1986] ICR 716.

[71] *United Biscuits (UK) Ltd.* v. *Fall* [1979] IRLR 110. See Auerbach, *Legislating for Conflict*, 28, for details of the litigation and its political impact.

have given a powerful boost to the idea of controlling picketing by making *civil* sanctions available against it, rather than by strengthening the already comprehensive criminal sanctions and police discretions which were applicable. By depriving unlawful picketing of civil immunity, the section invited the use of common law civil actions within the area of industrial action taken in contemplation of furtherance of a trade dispute. This was in its way as important a change as the House of Lords had made in 1963 when, in *Rookes* v. *Barnard*,[72] they had recognized a tort liability not covered by trade dispute immunity; and whereas in 1965, Parliament had stepped in to repair the defences of collective *laissez-faire* against judicial interventionism, in 1980 it was Parliament itself that was creating the breach.

It was easy in the aftermath of the 1980 Act to underrate the importance of the new measures against picketing; with hindsight one can see that they renewed the legislative retrenchment upon the post-war settlement of the law of industrial conflict, which had been embarked upon by the Industrial Relations Act 1971, and that they changed the legal norms about picketing in a way that the Act of 1971 had not attempted to do. It is true that in the ensuing couple of years, with very little major national industrial action, and with trade unions still enjoying their general immunity from tort liability for industrial action, employers did not make a great deal of direct use of the new opportunities for civil actions.[73] But section 16 had broken with tradition in its handling both of the idea of lawful picketing and of the idea of exclusion of the courts from industrial disputes. A major challenge had been mounted to the abstentionist conclusions about industrial conflict law which had been drawn from the political failure of the Industrial Relations Act, and, according to an important empirical assessment in 1983, a departure had been invited from customary managerial practice in the handling of industrial disputes to which employers, influenced by the contemporary changes in the economic and wider industrial relations environment, made a significant response.[74] The cracks thus opened

---

[72] [1964] AC 1129.

[73] See, for details, S. Evans, 'The Labour Injunction Revisited: Picketing, Employers and the Employment Act 1980' (1983) 12 ILJ 129; and 'Research Note—The use of Injunctions in Industrial Disputes' (1985) 23 BJIR 133.

[74] S. Evans, 'The Labour Injunction Revisited' (1983) 12 ILJ 129 at 146: 'Quite clearly, the seeking of an injunction or the threat to seek an injunction has been a

in the consensualist edifice were to be widened rapidly in the ensuing few years.

It is also tempting, with hindsight, to assess the Code of Practice on Picketing as an example of the transition from traditional approaches to radical new approaches to industrial conflict which the measures of the 1980s as a whole represent, though it is always important to bear in mind that only modest and cautious first steps were being taken in 1980. Thus the Code seems to have grown out of enthusiasm, which had built up in the 1970s, for regulation of picketing by voluntary codes of practice, and the proposal to issue this Code was originally conditional upon 'the absence of comprehensive and effective voluntary guidance'[75] which the government hoped (or professed to hope) that the TUC would provide. On the other hand, it was originally seen, and envisaged in the Working Paper of July 1979, as having the function of 'helping to bring about a more consistent interpretation of the law by police and magistrates';[76] this would have made it an exercise in co-ordination of policing and legal administration which would have marked it out as something much more than an analogue of the voluntary codes of practice of the 1970s.[77]

The government's main aim for the Code, whether it was to be achieved by quasi-voluntary guidance or by more coercive means, was to limit the intimidatory impact of picketing on workers otherwise willing to cross picket lines in order to go to work or move supplies. Their particular concern in this respect was to avoid the intimidatory effect of mass picketing by limiting picketing numbers. The original idea seems to have been one of using the Code to make it clear to all concerned that the police had the power to limit picket numbers according to a specific numerical guideline. In the event, it would seem that the Association of Chief Police Officers successfully opposed the couching of this rule in a form in which it could be seen as in any

significant feature of the handling of a number of recent industrial disputes, if not as a grand strategy then at least as a tactic deserving serious consideration.'

[75] Working Paper, para. 14; cf. para. 5, 'The importance of voluntary guidance'.

[76] Ibid., para. 13. Auerbach, *Legislating for Conflict*, 33 points out the slight irony that the same suggestion had been canvassed in Labour's Jan. 1979 Consultation paper. See above, p. 416.

[77] Cf. Lewis and Simpson, *Striking a Balance?*, 173: 'This possibility alarmed the police as well as the TUC.'

way limiting the powers or discretions of the police to control the numbers of pickets.[78] As a result, it seemed that the Code of Practice on Picketing would have hardly any significant legal effect, and that its restriction of picketing numbers to six pickets at each gate was little more than the expression of a pious hope.[79] However, during the litigation arising out of the Miners' Dispute of 1984–5, the limit of six to a gate in the Code acquired positive legal force when it was used to distinguish intimidatory from non-intimidatory picketing in an injunction granted to a working miner to compel his union to refrain from organizing picketing which was tortious in unreasonably harassing working miners in the exercise of their right to free passage along the highway.[80] This remarkably creative development of the common law and of the use of the injunctive remedy vindicated, albeit in an unexpected way, the suspicions that the Code had greater potential effects than were acknowledged by those responsible for it.

(e) Restricting Secondary Action

Although the picketing provisions of the 1980 Act and the Code of Practice on Picketing addressed the form of extra-enterprise industrial action which was most prominent when the 1980 measures were first being formulated, they did not deal with the whole range of questions about sympathetic industrial action. Picketing had been a prominent topic of debate in the 1970s; but the secondary action provisions which were added to the Employment Act in the course of its passage through Parliament addressed a wider issue which had lain at the heart of discussions about industrial conflict law from the mid-1960s onwards, namely, how far could industrial action legitimately be extended outwards beyond workers and their employers with whom they had an industrial dispute. Once the decision of the House of Lords in *Rookes* v. *Barnard*[81] in 1963 had made an initial breach in the

---

[78] Ibid., describing the discussions in the House of Commons Select Committee on Employment, 1979–80.

[79] Section E. of the Code, on Limiting Numbers of Pickets, concluded with an assertion (*in vacuo*, so far as legal sanctions were concerned) that 'pickets and their organisers should ensure that in general the number of pickets does not exceed six at any entrance to a workplace' (para. 31).

[80] *Thomas* v. *NUM (South Wales Area)* [1985] IRLR 136.

[81] [1964] AC 1129.

legal fortifications of trade dispute immunity, the subsequent litigation, from *Stratford* v. *Lindley*[82] onwards, concentrated not on the closed shop practices which had been the subject of that case, but rather on the question of what civil liabilities might now be invoked against secondary industrial action; that is to say, industrial action operating upon employers other than the primary employer with whom the dispute exists, most obviously though not necessarily by the involvement of those working for the secondary employers. Concern about secondary action, though real enough, tended to be ambiguous. Was it a concern for the primary employer, in that illegitimate means of industrial action were being used against him, or was it a concern for secondary employers in that they were being adversely affected in consequence of industrial disputes which had nothing to do with them? The former concern tends to be a commercial or an economic concern; the latter tends to be an ethical or communitarian concern. Practical measures could be taken to limit industrial action without disentangling those two concerns; the Industrial Relations Act 1971 provides a good example of that happening.[83]

In the Social Contract period, as we have seen,[84] the aim of the legislation was to restore trade dispute immunity to the intact condition in which it had been before the litigation and legislation which had occurred from 1963 onwards. Because the legislation about trade dispute immunity followed a reactive pattern, it had to respond to those intervening developments which had created open-ended possibilities of liability for secondary action. Two particular measures were at the time judged necessary for this purpose; section 13(3) of the Trade Union and Labour Relations Act 1974 sought to eliminate, firstly, actions themselves identified as covered by trade dispute immunity, and, secondly, simple breach of the contract of employment, from the category of unlawful means, so that they could not contribute to the novel tort liabilities; and then in the Amendment Act of 1976, the basic trade dispute immunity of section 13(1), which covered inducing or threatening interference with contracts of employment, was extended to cover commercial contracts as well.

[82] [1965] AC 269.
[83] Esp. s. 98; see above, p. 295.
[84] See above, pp. 366–73.

This did not bring about the hoped-for reconstruction of the consensus which had, for the most part, existed before the Industrial Relations Act about the trade dispute immunities. It left a tension between those who accepted that the new formulation followed the spirit of the earlier formulation in the changed legal circumstances, and those who, on the other hand, felt that the new immunities broke the bounds of the traditional understanding of the legal freedom to organize or threaten industrial action. Apart from the Conservative Opposition in Parliament, the most important protagonist of the latter view was Lord Denning, who as Master of the Rolls led the Court of Appeal into several decisions which sought to reassert what were viewed as the appropriate limits on trade dispute immunity, particularly so far as secondary action was concerned.[85] The Conservative Party Manifesto for the 1979 Election placed the incoming Government squarely in the same camp, declaring that

We shall ensure that the protection of the law is available to those not concerned in the dispute but who at present can suffer severely from secondary action (picketing, blacking and blockading). This means an immediate review of the existing law on immunities in the light of recent decisions, followed by such an amendment as may be necessary of the 1976 legislation in this field.

When the proposals leading to the Employment Act 1980 were first publicly formulated in the Working Papers of August 1979, there seemed to be an intention to exclude secondary picketing from trade dispute immunity, but no proposals in relation to other forms of secondary action; and when the Employment Bill was first published, even secondary picketing was addressed only in so far as it consisted in picketing other than at one's own place of work. This reticence seems to have been displayed because Mr Prior hoped that the desired restrictions would be realized by judicial interpretations of the existing legislation;[86] the style of

---

[85] *Express Newspapers Ltd.* v. *Keys* [1978] ICR 582; *Star Sea Corporation of Monrovia* v. *Slater* [1979] 1 Lloyd's Rep. 26; *Express Newspapers Ltd.* v. *McShane* [1979] ICR 210; *Associated Newspapers Group* v. *Wade* [1979] ICR 664. See P. L. Davies and M. R. Freedland, ch. 8 of J. Jowell and P. McAuslan, eds., *Lord Denning, the Judge, and the Law* (London, 1984), 367 at 388–99.

[86] This is asserted in terms by Jim Prior in his memoirs, *A Balance of Power* (London, 1986) at p. 158. The hope was that the House of Lords would uphold the judgment of the Court of Appeal in *Express Newspapers Ltd.* v. *McShane* [1979] ICR 210.

government had not yet become as declaratory as it was to do later in the 1980s. So when the 1980 legislation was originally framed, it was not intended to alter the law in relation to secondary action generally.[87] It was intended to deal with secondary picketing; but it was thought that the measure contained in what is now section 16 (which we have looked at) was sufficient for that purpose.

However, while the Bill was going through Parliament, the steelworkers, who were engaged in a major industrial dispute with the British Steel Corporation, extended their industrial action to include secondary action against the private steel companies. This was, in fact, simply sympathetic action; the union called out its members working for the private steel companies not because there was movement of goods or services between the British Steel Corporation and the private producers (though there may have been a little of that), nor even because the private producers were seen as an alternative source of supply which was jeopardizing the success of the primary industrial action, but rather because the union simply felt that the pressure on the government to secure a settlement of the public sector dispute would be increased by these means. It was clear that the Bill would leave this sort of secondary action still subject to trade dispute immunity, especially as the House of Lords had refused to follow Lord Denning's Court of Appeal in curtailing the trade dispute immunity by judicial means.[88] In particular, it was clear that the extension of trade dispute immunity to include interference with commercial contracts as well as with contracts of employment, which had been effected in 1976, was an important shield for trade unions wishing to extend their industrial action out into a wider commercial or social community.

The private steel producers, who could credibly present themselves as unjustifiably damaged by industrial action in a dispute from which they were quite remote, effectively lobbied the government with their grievance. In the early months of 1980, while the Bill was going through its parliamentary stages, the government decided to deal with this problem by introducing

---

[87] For the detailed chronology of the interaction between the legislative process and the judicial one, see Auerbach, *Legislating for Conflict*, 45–6.

[88] The crucial decision was *Express Newspapers Ltd.* v. *McShane* [1980] ICR 42. The private steel producers tried and failed to escape from the consequences of this case in *Duport Steels Ltd.* v. *Sirs* [1980] ICR 161.

a new clause to deal with secondary action. But rather than proposing a sweeping provision removing immunity from all secondary action in the way that their proposals removed immunity from all picketing away from one's own place of work, they produced a much more complex and qualified proposal which sought in essence to remove immunity from tertiary action while conceding immunity to immediate secondary action in the sense of action against a first supplier or first customer of the employer with whom the dispute existed,[89] or against an associated employer providing substitute goods or services,[90] or taking the form of lawful picketing.[91]

It had proved very difficult to draft a provision which would achieve this highly specific aim.[92] Perhaps the most eloquent testimony to the delicacy of the balance which section 17 sought to achieve is the fact that Lord Denning, whose underlying view was that the 1976 extension of immunity to interference with commercial contracts should simply have been revoked, saw fit to disregard its detailed provisions and to accord it a blanket effect upon all secondary and even some primary industrial action.[93] The House of Lords had to assert the fact that this was not what had been intended or done by section 17.[94] Thus section 17 reflected an approach on the part of Mr Prior as Secretary of State for Employment which was more cautious and traditional than, for example, the approach taken to picketing in section 16. Nevertheless, section 17 was to prove in practice as important a gateway to civil suits as section 16. It made an important contribution to the breaching of the dam of trade dispute immunity, because it often provided the most straightforward path to obtaining an interlocutory injunction in a trade dispute case.[95]

[89] S. 17(3).

[90] S. 17(4).

[91] S. 17(5).

[92] Cf. Auerbach, *Legislating for Conflict*, 49: 'the immense difficulties which the Government faced in translating its objectives into a clear and precise measure'.

[93] *Hadmor Productions Ltd.* v. *Hamilton* [1981] ICR 114 in the Court of Appeal.

[94] [1982] ICR 114, 129D–130B (Lord Diplock).

[95] S. Evans, in his research notes on 'The Use of Injunctions in Industrial Disputes' (1985) 23 BJIR 133, and 'The Use of Injunctions in Industrial Disputes May 1984–April 1987' (1987) 25 BJIR 419. Evans lists 34 cases where employers sought injunctions in industrial disputes between Sept. 1980 and Sept. 1984, of which 17 related to picketing and 11 to unlawful secondary action. For the period from May 1984 to Apr. 1987, the corresponding figures were 11 and 16.

Although a convoluted provision, it did much both to discourage extra-enterprise extensions of industrial action and to empower employers to counter industrial action.

(f) Abolition of Statutory Procedures Available to Trade Unions

Even outside the immediate area of trade dispute law, the 1980 legislation included other measures which tended to oust the trade unions from the position which they had previously enjoyed in the legal framework of industrial relations. This is true of the repeals of the statutory trade union recognition procedure and, more peripherally, perhaps, to our present concerns, of schedule 11 of the Employment Protection Act 1975. Schedule 11, it will be recalled, provided a process for the compulsory extension of the results of multi-employer collective bargaining, or of generally observed terms and conditions of employment, to employers who were falling below those standards. We shall see that the government's main concern with schedule 11 was the fact that it tended to inflate wages, and that it constituted an artificial regulation of the labour market. But not the least of their objections to schedule 11—and, one suspects, a more prominent reason for getting rid of it than was admitted—was the position that it accorded to (independent) trade unions as in effect the sole competent claimants under the schedule's procedure.

If the curtailing of the industrial power of trade unions was a factor in the repeal of schedule 11, so it was, even more directly, in the repeal of the statutory recognition procedure, again a creation of the Employment Protection Act 1975. In this case, the repeal was justified on the ground that the difficulties which ACAS had encountered in operating the statutory procedure had been so great as not only to stultify that procedure but also to reduce the effectiveness of the use by ACAS of its powers of voluntary conciliation and arbitration.[96] ACAS itself had contributed powerfully to the general acceptance of this view of the working of the statutory procedure, by placing on record its own misgivings to that effect.[97] But whereas ACAS had been

---

[96] Mr Prior, HC Deb., 5th ser., vol. 976, col. 69 (17 Dec. 1979).

[97] The letter in which this is done is reproduced in the ACAS *Annual Report* for 1980, and reproduced in part in P. Davies and M. Freedland, *Labour Law: Text and Materials* (2nd edn. 1983), 202–3.

partly concerned with the obstacles which judicial review had placed in the way of their desired way of operating the procedure, the government in taking the same tone was actually much more concerned to get rid of the special protections for unions in the legal framework inherited from the previous administration. Mr Prior when introducing the proposal added the interesting rider that:

I should say that I am not wholly unsympathetic to the idea of some statutory recognition provision. I appreciate the problems for smaller unions, including the EMA—there are other unions even smaller—but I feel, on balance, that such was the damage to ACAS that it would be better to proceed as we propose.[98]

If this revealed an interest in policies which would protect the position of small unions while reducing the power of the large, and, in the government's perceptions, over-mighty ones, it was an initiative which was not pursued by Mr Prior's successors. The upshot was that, although these repeals of parts of the 1975 Act were not especially controversial at the time, the 1980 Act was in fact almost as significant in its dis-empowerment of trade unions as in its empowerment of employers.

(g) Social Security and Strikers' Dependants

Thus far, we have been concerned with 1980 measures strictly within the sphere of labour law. As in 1971, however, a major upheaval in labour law was accompanied by a set of social security measures intended to realign the role of supplementary benefits in trade disputes. As in 1971, a Conservative government was again concerned that the supplementary benefit system could be used by trade unions to help to finance industrial action. The government brought forward a proposal which was enacted as section 6 of the Social Security (No. 2) Act 1980 of which the purpose was 'to implement the pledge which this party gave at the last election to deal with the payment of supplementary benefit to the families of strikers'.[99] This involved a significant redefinition of the conception of neutrality which the supplementary benefit system was supposed to maintain towards

[98] Ibid.
[99] HC Deb., 5th ser., vol. 982, col. 1033 (15 Apr. 1980): Mr Partrick Jenkin as Secretary of State for Social Services introducing the Bill on Second Reading.

industrial disputes. The 1971 measures, as we have seen,[100] reflected the view that the trade unions were unduly favoured if strikers could receive strike pay from the union while their dependants received supplementary benefit; strike pay, previously disregarded, was therefore set against dependants' supplementary benefit.[101]

This had the result, however, that the unions had no incentive to pay strike pay to strikers with dependants, for the strike pay would make the strikers and their dependants no better off. This meant that trade unions, though limited in the extent to which they could support strikers with dependants, could run strikes without depleting their own union funds by paying strike pay.[102] By 1980, the government felt that this, too, must be avoided if the supplementary benefits system was not to be open to abuse by trade unions. But how were they at once to impel unions to pay strike pay and yet ensure that this did not benefit strikers via their dependants? The solution adopted by section 6 of the 1980 Act and the regulations associated with it was (in slight simplification[103]) firstly to ensure a total discounting of strike pay against dependants' supplementary benefits,[104] then secondly to discount against dependants' supplementary benefits up to a fixed amount—originally £12 per week—for strike pay whether actually paid or not;[105] and finally almost to eliminate urgent needs payments to strikers or their dependants.[106] This scheme would on the one hand place unions under pressure to pay strike pay up to the fixed limit, while on the other hand making it inordinately expensive[107] for them to increase strikers' resources over that fixed limit. So by adjusting the level of the fixed limit,

[100] See above, pp. 327–8.

[101] Except for £1 per week, increased to £4 per week from 1976.

[102] Mr Patrick Jenkin listed as evidence of his concerns a number of instances since 1971 where this had occurred: ibid., col. 1050.

[103] Useful fuller accounts are given by M. Partington, 'Unemployment, Industrial Conflict and Social Security' (1980) 9 ILJ 243 and K. Ewing, *The Right to Strike* (Oxford, 1990), 104–10.

[104] Social Security (No. 2) Act 1980, s. 6(1)(a).

[105] Ibid., s. 6(1)(b), coupled with the Supplementary Benefit (Trade Disputes and Recovery of Earnings Regulations) SI 1980, No. 1641.

[106] Ibid., s. 6(1)(c) coupled with the Trade Dispute Regulations cited in the above note.

[107] In that a further very high threshold, originally set at £45, would have to be surmounted before actual strike pay was not discounted.

governments would henceforth be able to define the neutrality of the supplementary benefits system in pecuniary terms at the point of maximum discouragement of industrial action as between those different variables.

It is interesting that this set of measures could be presented as a withdrawal by the state from the subsidizing of strikers and hence as the assertion of neutrality and a limited role for the state over what, by implication, was a previously partisan interventionism on the part of the state. That rhetoric concealed a more secular and instrumental definition of the role of social security law in trade disputes than had previously been attempted. Cutting social security benefits for strikers had been one of the methods suggested by Mr Nicholas Ridley in 1978 for equipping a future Conservative government to confront trade union power in a major industry-wide dispute—the other main method being preparing a large mobile force to deal with violent picketing.[108] In this there was a parallel with, for example, the new role assigned to trade dispute law by the Employment Act 1980 in relation to picketing or secondary industrial action. That particular tension between rhetoric and underlying aims was to recur in different forms throughout the course of the industrial conflict measures of the 1980s.

9.4. THE SECOND STEP: THE EMPLOYMENT ACT 1982

The reduction of trade union industrial power by curtailment of trade union and trade dispute immunities was not initially conceived of, at least by Mr Prior as its formal initiator, as a continuing and cumulative process. If it was described by him as a 'step by step approach', it was, as we commented earlier in this chapter, to emphasize the intention to proceed no further than necessary, rather than to identify a specific goal and an inexorable march towards it. As he later put it himself,

'I wanted to hold some shots in my locker, so that the unions would know that if they continued to abuse their power, tougher measures would follow.[109]

[108] See Ewing, *The Right to Strike*, 107. This was the so-called Ridley Report.
[109] Prior, *A Balance of Power*, 158.

But that caution was not the prevailing sentiment within the government as a whole, and Mr Prior became engaged in an uneasy compromise with the Prime Minister's more forceful ambitions, which formed the background of the Green Paper on *Trade Union Immunities* in which the options for further legislative changes were canvassed.[110]

The scope, content, and methodology of the Green Paper were all shaped by its political function of enabling Mr Prior to temporize in the face of pressure from the Prime Minister and the right-wing members of her Cabinet for more radical legislative restrictions upon trade union power. The scope was a wide one, ranging across the whole agenda of the post-Donovan discussion of industrial conflict law and of the law relating to the closed shop, and even extending to consideration of 'an alternative system of positive rights' which was deliberately linked to the wider question whether Great Britain should have a Bill of Rights.[111] Given the extent to which the adverse experience of the Industrial Relations Act had discredited the idea of a comprehensive single legislative reform of industrial relations, the width of the range of competing alternatives for piecemeal legislation identified by the Green Paper thus served to emphasize the desirability of caution and empiricism in selecting from among those numerous options.

This was accentuated by the fact that the Green Paper explored some of the more acute controversies of the Industrial Relations Act period, such as whether to make collective agreements legally enforceable,[112] or whether the aim of protecting the community from the damaging effects of industrial action should be achieved by giving the government emergency powers to impose a statutory cooling-off period or make strikes unlawful, or by means of restrictions on workers in essential industries.[113] The sense that the Green Paper was more con-

---

[110] Cmnd. 8128 (Jan. 1981).

[111] Ibid., para. 345.

[112] Ibid., ch. 3E. The discussion was angled towards the preoccupations of the 1980s in that it was specifically directed to the question whether to remove tort immunity from industrial action taken in breach of a collective agreement (paras. 220–3).

[113] Ibid., ch. 3H. The Industrial Relations Act itself had caused controversy by *revoking* certain existing restrictions on industrial action in the gas, water, and electricity industries; the question in the Green Paper was whether to return to an industry-specific approach to strikes affecting essential services (paras. 330–7).

cerned to pose questions than to propose answers was enhanced by the methodology of the Green Paper, which consisted of counterpoising pros and cons for each of the main options under consideration, and of invoking comparative data relating to other Western industrial countries[114] to show how other systems interrelated their choices among those options in very different ways.

To very much the same purport was the substantive content or conclusions of the Green Paper; having at a number of points emphasized the difficulties involved in further restrictions upon trade union and trade dispute immunities, the document concluded that each of the proposals for change which it had canvassed must be evaluated by a balancing process between the interests of employers, trade unions, individual workers, and the community at large.[115] The Green Paper finally confirmed its preference for a principled long-term debate about the future role of the law in industrial relations, rather than an opportunistic move towards further restrictive legislation in the short term, by identifying the issue of whether to move to a system of positive rights as the basic unanswered question.[116]

Mr Prior was clearly aware that the studied moderation and spirit of inquiry and debate which informed the Green Paper was distancing him from his Prime Minister.[117] It was also clear enough that Mr Norman Tebbit, who succeeded him as Secretary of State for Employment later in 1981, was a new broom intent upon sweeping this area very clean. By contrast with Mr Prior, he did intend to reduce trade union industrial power by means of cumulative legislative steps.[118] He was, however, as much concerned as his predecessor to avoid the pitfalls of over-ambitious legislation as illustrated by the fate of the Industrial

[114] Ibid., Appendix: 'Industrial Relations in Other Countries'; the countries were Australia, West Germany, France, Sweden, and the USA.

[115] Ibid., ch. 5: Conclusion.

[116] Ibid., para. 385. Cf. in general, Auerbach, *Legislating for Conflict*, 69–71, where the Green Paper is viewed, even more strongly than in our argument, as a manifesto against further legislation.

[117] Thus Prior, *A Balance of Power*, 171, referring to the position in Summer 1981: 'I was not expecting to stay on as Secretary of State for Employment.'

[118] Norman Tebbit, *Upwardly Mobile* (London, 1989), 233: 'I had a clear game plan for my programme of reform before I made the first move but . . . I had no intention of exposing more than one move at a time.'

Relations Act.[119] So, starting as he did with the rather measured tones of the Green Paper as his political stock-in-trade, he was not on the whole concerned to heighten its rhetoric when introducing his proposals for further restrictions on trade union and trade dispute immunities, and on closed shop activities.

Hence, when presenting the 1982 Employment Bill, Mr Tebbit supported it with texts rather mischievously selected from Labour Party pronouncements to show how uncontroversial a Bill it was;[120] and when introducing the particular clauses which were to restrict trade union immunities, he was at pains to disclaim any far-reaching aims and to justify these clauses as little more than the tidying-up of an archaic anomaly bequeathed to us in the aftermath of the *Taff Vale* case. The political judgment involved was quite sound; by 1982, the Conservative Party was ready for the removal of the cornerstone of the arch which had on the whole protected trade unions since 1906—so ready, indeed, that they required no promises of a brave new world in industrial relations, and preferred the old order to be laid to rest with the minimum of ceremony. The full extent to which burial of the old order had in fact occurred was to reveal itself gradually over the next few years.

For the goal of reducing the industrial power of trade unions in the framework of labour law was in fact pursued much more directly and forcefully in the Employment Act 1982 than in the 1980 Act. Where Mr Prior had stood for caution and for some concession to the traditions of collective *laissez-faire*, his successor mounted a more aggressive onslaught upon the trade unions, though even in 1982 the redefinition of the role and powers of trade unions was carried out in a way which contrasted deliberately with the comprehensiveness of the Industrial Relations Act 1971. Both the two themes which we have identified as characterizing the 1980s legislation in this area were strongly articulated in Mr Tebbit's proposals; he was concerned to attack what in his perception was the oppressive aspect of trade union solidarity manifested by closed shop practices, and to empower employers to resist trade union industrial power

[119] Ibid.: 'I was determined not to enact unenforceable legislation—the memory of the collapse of the 1972 Industrial Relations Act [*sic*] was very much in my mind.'

[120] HC Deb., 6th ser., vol 17, col. 737 (8 Feb. 1982).

by withdrawing what he saw as unwarranted legal privileges protecting that power. We shall consider in turn the two main groups into which the relevant measures in the 1982 Act divide themselves; the first is concerned with the closed shop and the second with trade union and trade dispute immunities.

(a) Further Restrictions on Closed Shop Activity

Towards the closed shop, the Act represented a move from the conditional tolerance extended by the 1980 Act to a barely qualified intolerance. Mr Tebbit was later to say of the closed shop measures in the 1982 Act that,

I rejected the pressures to 'ban' the closed shop—it simply would not have worked—but I did set out to undermine it.[121]

Both at a practical and a psychological level, this led to quite a severe displacement of trade unions from their existing position in the framework of labour law.

The first of the measures dealing with the closed shop was almost wholly symbolical. Section 2 of the Act empowered the Secretary of State for Employment to pay compensation to workers dismissed for non-membership of a union between 1974 and 1980 who were not able to claim remedies for unfair dismissal as the law then stood, but who would have been able to do so if the provisions of the 1980 Act had been in force. The government based its case for this measure on the judgment of the European Court of Human Rights in the case concerning the closed shop at British Rail.[122] But that judgment, while indeed indicating that some amendment of the law as it had stood between 1974 and 1980 had been necessary, did not in itself render the British government liable to compensate individuals for the deficiencies in the legislation. Although it is possible that the retroactive compensation scheme was designed to control the amount of compensation by preempting a possible subsequent larger award from Strasbourg, it seems more likely that it was an emphatic gesture of abhorrence directed against the legal regime for the closed shop which the Labour government had created in 1974 and endorsed in 1976.

---

[121] Tebbit, *Upwardly Mobile*, 234.
[122] *Young, James and Webster* v. *UK* [1981] IRLR 408 (see above, p. 451).

The other measures of 1982 in relation to the closed shop were much more severely practical. The conditions in which a dismissal for non-membership of a trade union would be exempt from liability for unfair dismissal (conditions which identify in practice the lawful closed shop) were so far narrowed as to preclude the disciplinary, or even the solidaristic, use of the closed shop in support of trade union power. Thus, approval in a ballot was made necessary for pre-1980 as well as post-1980 union membership agreements (with a requirement, in the pre-1980 case, that at least 80 per cent of those entitled to vote or 85 per cent of those voting should be in favour).[123] Further circumstances were specified in which non-membership of a union was protected; this protection was now extended to the case of continuous non-membership from the date of a ballot in the case of a post-1980 closed shop, the case where the individual had obtained or was seeking a declaration of unreasonable exclusion or expulsion from the union, and the case where the individual concerned refused to take part in industrial action and that refusal implemented a written code of conduct for his profession.[124] The right, as against the employer, not to belong to a trade union was made into a general right subject only to the very narrow exceptions that we have described;[125] and very large mandatory awards of compensation were introduced for dismissals which violated that right (or which violated the positive right of freedom of association—ironically, more awards were in the event to be made in this latter category than in the context of claims to disassociate, for which the new awards were primarily intended).[126]

There were also in the 1982 Act two directions in which initiatives which had been directed against the closed shop practices in the 1980 Act were taken so much further as to produce a change in kind and not just degree. In the 1980 Act, as we saw, there had been a procedure for joinder, whereby an

[123] Employment Act 1982, s. 3, substituting new ss. 58 and 58A of the EPCA 1978.

[124] Ibid., new s. 58(6), (7), and (8) respectively.

[125] Ibid., new s. 58(1)(c), relating to dismissal; this was carried through to action short of dismissal by s. 10(4) of the 1982 Act; see now TULRECA, ss. 152, 146.

[126] Employment Act 1982, s. 4, creating a new mandatory element in the Basic Award and adding new EPCA s. 72(4A) and (4B), and s. 5, creating the New Special Award; see new EPCA ss. 72, 75A, now TULRECA ss. 156–8.

employer sued for unfair dismissal who claimed to have been induced to dismiss by industrial pressure, exerted because of the non-membership of a union of the worker concerned, could join those exerting the pressure so that they could be ordered to contribute to compensation.[127] There had also been, as we saw, a double joinder procedure whereby a contractor could join a company or public authority on the other side of a commercial contract which had necessitated the dismissal by requiring union labour only for the performance of the contract, and whereby that other party in turn could join those who had exerted industrial pressure to cause the union-labour-only requirement to be imposed.[128] In the 1982 Act, the joinder procedure was extended to enable the claimant worker himself to join those exerting the industrial pressure, thus in effect giving him a cause of action in unfair dismissal directly against, for instance, the trade union which brought about the dismissal by threatening industrial action.[129]

The double joinder procedure of the 1980 Act underwent an even more radical transformation under the 1982 Act. Both the double joinder provision and the coercive recruitment provision of section 18 of the 1980 Act were repealed, their content being subsumed into an elaborate free-standing body of legislation which imposed prohibitions upon union membership or union recognition requirements in commercial contracts,[130] and which withdrew trade dispute immunity where there was pressure to impose such requirements.[131] That legislation, justified as a control upon contracting practice by local authorities which the government saw as an abuse of contracting power, did much to promote an ideology in which claims to maintain high levels of union membership and even union recognition would increasingly be identified as anti-social. As we shall see in the next chapter, this was a step along a road which led to the abolition of fair wages measures—measures which had underpinned an almost

[127] See above, p. 453.
[128] Ibid.
[129] Employment Act 1982, s. 7 substituting new s. 76A of EPCA 1978 ('Awards against third parties'). This provision was itself in due course to be overtaken by the more far-reaching provision of s. 10 of the Employment Act 1988, now TULRECA s. 222(1), (2), (4), (5).
[130] Employment Act 1982, ss. 12–13, now TULRECA ss. 114–15, 186–7.
[131] S. 14, now TULRECA ss. 222(3), 225.

diametrically opposed tradition of regarding union membership and recognition as crucial components in an apparatus designed to ensure that public authorities discharged a social responsibility for protecting fair labour standards.

The erosion of the role of trade unions which is implicit in this change of legislative direction is quite evident. In describing these provisions of the 1982 Act, we have deliberately linked together, as the legislators themselves did, provisions dealing with, on the one hand, practices strictly speaking concerned with the closed shop, and, on the other hand, a wider range of associated practices known as 'union-only' or 'recognition-only' or 'fair-list' practices. A contemporary commentary identified the way in which all those practices formed part of a structure which served to maintain union organization and recognition, and upon which the system of collective industrial relations therefore depended.[132] Its authors concluded that the Employment Act 1982 was intended to weaken some of the major elements of this infrastructure, and that the provisions by which it sought to do so exemplified an overall trend towards individualism in labour law policy.[133] In the course of developing these individualistic policies, the 1982 Act had, in the shape of the provision of section 14 dealing with pressure to impose union membership or recognition requirements, made one particular new breach in trade dispute immunities; we turn to consider the many other modifications of trade dispute and trade union immunities which the Act effected.

(b) Trade Union and Trade Dispute Immunities

There was thus, as we have seen, a continuity between the aspect of the 1982 Act which related to closed shop activity and the aspect of it which involved a radical curtailment of trade union and trade dispute immunities. Although it was the restrictions on closed shop activity which seemed more important to Mr Tebbit himself,[134] it was the curtailment of immunities which probaly

---

[132] R. Lewis and B. Simpson, 'Disorganising Industrial Relations: An Analysis of sections 2–8 and 10–14 of the Employment Act 1982' (1982) 11 ILJ 227.

[133] Ibid. 227, 244.

[134] In his own account of the 1982 Act, the closed-shop measures are accorded priority: see Tebbit, *Upwardly Mobile*, 234. Moreover, it would seem that the provisions for state compensation to past closed-shop victims were the result of a personal initiative on his part; his memoirs certainly imply this: ibid. 240.

had greater practical impact on trade union industrial power. In this respect, we must regard the curtailment of the two types of immunity—trade union and trade dispute immunity—as entirely interconnected, and as between them constituting a single strategy. That was a strategy of empowerment of employers to resist trade union pressure—especially, though not solely, of empowering employers who were not parties to an industrial dispute to resist its extension to them. This strategy can best be understood by looking first at the new restrictions on trade dispute immunities, and then at the restrictions on trade union immunity which, we shall argue, were complementary to them both in the intentions of the legislators and in the practical outcome.

Thus, in the 1982 Act, not for the first time in the history of labour law, the imposition of tort liability upon trade unions was associated with an enlarging of the scope of that liability. In this case, the enlargement took the form of a narrowing of trade dispute immunity; in particular, a re-definition in more restricted terms of the 'golden formula' of acts done in contemplation or furtherance of a trade dispute. The most important element in the re-definition was the requirement that the dispute must 'relate wholly or mainly to' the matters specified as trade dispute matters in section 29 of the 1974 Act, instead of simply being 'connected with' those matters.[135] In effect, in order to bring industrial action or the threat of industrial action within the trade dispute formula, it would now be necessary to show that the dispute, in contemplation or furtherance of which the action was taken or threatened, had an industrial subject-matter as identified by section 29, not just as part of its subject-matter or objective but as its sole or primary subject-matter or objective. Lord Denning had attempted to bring about an equivalent restriction by judicial interpretation;[136] but the House of Lords had thought otherwise.[137] That conflict of judicial opinion enabled this change to be represented as an exercise in tidying up confusion in the

---

[135] Employment Act 1982, s. 18(2)(c); the whole of s. 18 operated by way of amendment of s. 29 of TULRA 1974, now TULRECA s. 244.

[136] See esp. *Express Newspapers Ltd.* v. *McShane* [1979] ICR 210.

[137] See the trilogy of decisions, *NWL* v. *Woods* [1979] ICR 867; *Express Newspapers Ltd.* v. *McShane* [1980] ICR 42; *Duport Steels Ltd.* v. *Sirs* [1980] ICR 161.

case-law; but it was rather more than that. It meant that any more-than-negligible presence of reasons which were not trade dispute reasons would now negate trade dispute immunity, where previously their presence had been immaterial as long as there was some positive basis for finding a trade dispute. This would tend to exclude from the ambit of trade dispute immunity a broad category of disputes which could be regarded as political disputes; thus, whether or not this was a deliberate part of its purpose, the case-law would soon illustrate that disputes arising out of privatization or other public sector restructuring could easily be excluded by the new formulation.[138]

The further changes in the definition of a trade dispute were also momentous enough; they too were generally directed to narrowing the ambit of trade dispute immunity in relation to the various dimensions of solidaristic behaviour on the part of trade unions and their members. Disputes between workers and workers would no longer qualify,[139] thus excluding inter-union disputes about recognition; and disputes must, in order to qualify, be between workers and their employer, rather than between workers and somebody else's employer.[140] This did not deny immunity to all sympathetic industrial action, for it remained possible for the workers employed by employer *A* to claim immunity for industrial action taken in furtherance of a trade dispute between employer *B* and his workers—provided, of

---

[138] The *cause célèbre* in this respect was *Mercury Communications Ltd.* v. *Scott-Garner* [1984] ICR 74, where a dispute arising out of the ending of the British Telecom telephone monopoly was held not a trade dispute because it failed the 'relates wholly or mainly' test, despite the fears of job losses involved. Cf. the discussion of the trade dispute issue in the judgment of Millet J. in *Associated British Ports Ltd.* v. *TGWU* [1989] IRLR 291, a case which related to the dispute about the abolition of the Dock Work Scheme. Here Ron Todd, the leader of the TGWU, managed to keep the trade and non-trade disputes separate, but only at great tactical cost: see B. Simpson, (1989) 18 ILJ 234 at 236–7.

[139] Employment Act 1982, s. 18(2)(*b*). Moreover, a dispute with a trade union was no longer necessarily to be treated as a dispute to which workers are a party: s. 18(5).

[140] Employment Act 1982, s. 18(2)(*a*) (carried through to civil servants by s. 18(3)). The employer and own worker restriction was aimed particularly at the International Transport Workers' Federation and its industrial action directed against shipowners operating under flags of convenience (see the elaborate discussion of this particular issue in the Green Paper, *Trade Union Immunities* (Cmnd. 8128, Jan. 1981), paras. 210–13: 'International Shipping').

course, that they were within the limits of immune secondary action as set by section 17 of the 1980 Act. But it meant—and was precisely intended to mean—that the workers employed by A could not claim a qualifying dispute with employer B if none of B's own workers was party to that dispute. This would be a crucial restriction where employer B refused to grant trade union recognition or freedom of association and had ensured that the whole of his own workforce was acquiescent in that regime. This tended to encourage a process of fragmentation and restriction of workplace trade unionism and collective bargaining.

Indeed, the encouragement of that process was one of the major themes of the 1982 Act, and was taken further, as we have seen, by the withdrawal of trade dispute immunity (by section 14 of the Act) from industrial action aimed at securing the imposition of requirements of trade union membership among the workforce of a contractor or of trade union recognition by the contractor. These provisions were directed particularly against the public authorities—especially local authorities—who sought to secure trade union membership and collective bargaining to the employees of outside contractors to the same extent as they conceded those things to their own directly employed workers. As such, they were part of a wider attack on various kinds of political and trade union activity within local authorities, an attack which, as we have already seen,[141] was a recurring theme of the legislation of the 1980s. There was yet another dimension in which the 1982 Act restricted solidaristic trade union action; trade disputes occurring abroad would no longer give rise to trade dispute immunity unless those taking action within the UK were likely to be affected by the outcome of the dispute, and affected, moreover, in respect of one or more of the industrial matters specified by statute;[142] in other words, an element of self-interest was required on the part of those taking the industrial action in the UK.[143]

(c) Trade Union Liabilities

Thus far, we have argued for the view that the main purpose of these reductions in the scope of trade dispute immunity was the

---

[141] See above, s. 9. 2, esp. at p. 438 (LGHA 1989, pt. I).
[142] Employment Act 1982, s. 18(4), amending s. 29(3) of TULRA 1974.
[143] See Davies and Freedland, *Labour Law, Text and Materials*, 813.

discouragement, in various ways, of trade union and worker solidarity. If this purpose was to be achieved in practical rather than merely declaratory terms, the government—and the Secretary of State for Employment in particular—were persuaded that employers must be empowered to pursue their enlarged common law claims against trade unions as such, rather than merely against individual trade union officers, shop stewards or members. If trade union immunity had formerly been justified as part of the general logic of dis-empowering employers from invoking the civil law in industrial disputes,[144] it presented itself as no more than an outmoded privilege in the face of the new policy of empowerment of employers to make use of the civil law—which was the policy underlying the trade dispute provisions of both the 1980 and 1982 Acts. This serves to explain not only the fact of repeal by the 1982 Act of the tort immunity of trade unions at that stage contained in section 14 of the Trade Union and Labour Relations Act 1974, but also the rhetoric which accompanied that repeal, and also, more important still, the reasons for the measures consequent upon that repeal.

For the bare repeal of trade union immunity (by section 15(1) of the 1982 Act) seemed to be significantly softened by an apparently restricted definition of trade union liability for the activities of members or officers: the activity had to be authorized or endorsed by specified categories of 'responsible persons', unpaid shop stewards being outside those categories.[145] There was also a facility for repudiation, even of acts otherwise authorized or endorsed by a responsible person, by the president or general secretary or executive committee of the union.[146] Moreover, fairly tight limits were placed on damages against trade unions according to the size of their membership (in a range between £10,000 and £250,000).[147] If the legislation did not attempt to make unions liable for the actions of unofficial shop-floor activists, it was probably because the framers of the legislation saw the main need as being that of withdrawing an un-

---

[144] Simon Auerbach offers a detailed argument to this effect in relation to the original trade union immunity provision, i.e. s. 4 of the Trade Disputes Act 1906 (*Legislating for Conflict*, 87–91).

[145] S. 15(2)–(6), now (as amended by EA 1990, s. 6) TULRECA ss. 20–1.

[146] Employment Act 1982, s. 15(4)(*b*).

[147] S. 16, now TULRECA s. 22.

warranted legal privilege in relation to official union policy decisions, and regarded the shop-floor members of trade unions as readier to accept a new realism than the official leadership was. If they restricted the quantum of damages against trade unions, it was probably to secure political consent to the empowerment of employers to use civil sanctions, given the fears of overkill which must still have been lurking in the aftermath of the Industrial Relations Act.[148]

It was to become apparent, moreover, that the shields for the unions were less substantial than they appeared. The restricted definition of trade union liability applied only where the tort action was of a kind capable of attracting trade dispute immunity (though that immunity would have, of course, to be unavailable on the facts of the case). Where the tort was outside the ambit of trade dispute immunity—for example, inducing breach of statutory duty—the significantly wider common law test of trade union vicarious liability derived from the *Heatons* case[149] could be applied. Furthermore, the restriction on the quantum of damages in tort against trade unions did not protect them in any way from liability to injunctions, and did not apply to fines awarded for contempt consisting in failure to comply with such injunctions. Whether or not this open-ended liability of trade unions was an anticipated feature of the legislation, it would become very prominent, as we shall see, during the Miners' Dispute of 1984–5.[150] Finally, it should be added that trade union liability for contempt of an injunction could still be based on a concept of vicarious liability for the actions of members which was not in any way restricted to the statutory concept of trade union liability.[151]

(d) Overall Assessment

What, then, was the overall significance of the 1982 Act in terms of the reduction of trade union industrial power? For all the

---

[148] Cf. Auerbach, *Legislating for Conflict*, 98–9: 'The Government was no doubt sensitive to the charge that it might otherwise be exposing some unions to financial destruction.'

[149] *Heatons Transport Ltd.* v. *TGWU* [1973] AC 15.

[150] See below, pp. 492 ff.

[151] It was so held by the Court of Appeal in *Express & Star Ltd.* v. *NGA* [1986] ICR 589. This was probably not, however, intended by the framers of the 1982 legislation. The situation was eventually clarified by s. 6(8) of EA 1990, inserting new ss. (9) into s. 15 of EA 1982, now TULRECA s. 20(6).

trenchancy of Mr Tebbit's claims for 'his' Act, it actually left the law of industrial conflict and industrial relations in a somewhat transitional and indeterminate state. As we have seen, the law relating to the closed shop was left in a position in which closed shop practices were neither wholly accepted as legitimate nor totally restricted. So far as the law of industrial conflict was concerned, the complex compromise of the 1980 Act in relation to secondary action had been retained. Trade union immunity had been abolished, but trade union liability was defined in a rather equivocal way. As one contemporary commentator put it,

The industrial conflict provisions in particular are astonishing for the uncertainty which they leave in their wake and for the extent to which Parliament has abdicated its duty to legislate to the courts.[152]

There were other ways in which the 1982 Act left great un- certainties about the future directions in which the law con- cerning trade union industrial power would develop. The 1982 Act started to extend the employer's immunity from unfair dismissal liability where employees were dismissed in the course of industrial action; section 62 of the Employment Protection (Consolidation) Act 1978 was amended to assert the employer's freedom to dismiss workers currently on strike at a particular establishment without also dismissing all those who had at any stage participated in the industrial action in question, or those still on strike at other establishments of the same employer.[153] While the declared purpose was mainly to correct an anomalous interpretation of section 62 by the House of Lords,[154] it was apparent that the government was becoming dissatisfied with the extent of the individual freedom to strike which that section upheld, and might in due course wish to press this dissatisfaction further.

The 1982 Act also left areas of uncertainty by staying right out of certain contemporary areas of debate about the role of the law in relation to trade union industrial power—areas in which changes had been canvassed in the Green Paper on Trade Union Immunities in 1981. Thus the 1982 Act did not concern itself at

---

[152] K. Ewing, 'Industrial Action: Another Step in the "Right" Direction', (1982) 11 ILJ 209, 226.

[153] Employment Act 1982, s. 9. See now TULRECA s. 238.

[154] In the case of Stock v. Frank Jones (Tipton) Ltd. [1978] ICR 347.

all with the legal enforcement of collective agreements and, perhaps more surprisingly, did not directly address the issue of special measures to protect essential services, or to secure restrictions upon industrial action in key public sector areas. These various omissions and equivocations are largely explicable in terms of the concern not to repeat the mistakes of the Industrial Relations Act. Nevertheless, the general effect is that the overall direction of legislative policy in this field had not been fully determined by the end of this phase in its development; it remains to be seen how far clear general strategies were subsequently articulated, or how far, on the other hand, the later phases of development were mere tactical responses to short-term needs corresponding to the latest fashion in industrial dispute behaviour. Predictably, the answer lies between those two extremes; in the immediately succeeding phase, the development would, on the whole, be strategic rather than tactical.

9.5. BALLOTED DEMOCRACY AND THE TRADE UNION ACT 1984

The restrictions on trade union industrial power imposed by the cumulative effect of the 1980 and 1982 Acts, immensely significant as they were, thus seemed to lack a clear specific direction. By the beginning of 1983, however, the government had settled upon a theme for further activity in this field, and declared its new aims in the Green Paper entitled *Democracy in Trade Unions*.[155] Having just deprived trade unions of the protection from civil suit conferred on them first in 1906 and again in 1974, the Government nevertheless declared in the Green Paper that,

Unions have important legal immunities and privileges not afforded to other organisations, and the public as well as their own members need to be assured that the affairs of trade unions are properly conducted.[156]

---

[155] Cmnd. 8778 (Jan. 1983).

[156] Cmnd. 8778, para. 1. The underlying point was that, with the immunity of trade unions, as such, having been abolished, the stigma of 'unwarranted privilege' was now being transferred to the trade *dispute* immunities, although they were not confined to trade unions.

And the essence of that proper conduct was seen to consist in guarantees that the decisions and actions of trade unions fully and directly reflected the views and interests of the members.

The slogan, then, was that of 'handing the unions back to their members'. The main method of achieving this was by requiring important union decisions to be taken by secret ballot of the members at large; the Green Paper envisaged this as the way to approach trade union elections and trade union decisions to take industrial action; by the time the Trade Union Act 1984 had been enacted, it had also become the main approach to the political activities of trade unions, the third area under consideration in the Green Paper. This was to prove an effective way of restricting the industrial power of trade unions; not so much because the unions were accustomed to act in despite of their members' wishes or even without ascentaining the views of their members as because the requirement to submit decisions to secret ballot seemed eminently reasonable and yet tied the hands of unions quite tightly.

It was, moreover, a strategy which linked together the two main themes underlying the legislative reduction of trade union power. On the one hand, the individual interest of each trade union member is deliberately prioritized, as against any collective interest to which the trade union might claim to accord higher importance. On the other hand, there is seen to be a wider public interest in ensuring that trade unions do not use their industrial power where they would not be truly representing their members' preferences by doing so; and the Green Paper is the first major policy document, of all those we have considered, which strongly contemplates mobilizing employers to enforce that representativeness upon trade unions. Thus the Green Paper considered, and considered sympathetically, the arguments for strike ballots to be 'triggered' by employers—which it equated with requiring a strike ballot as a condition of trade dispute immunity.[157] That was a misleading way to describe what was really a proposal to empower employers to deploy the sanctions for failure to hold a strike ballot, rather than to empower employers to trigger the ballot itself; the important point remains that both the Green Paper, tentatively, and the 1984 Act, unequivocally, identified

[157] Cmnd. 8778, para. 67.

employers as the most appropriate enforcers, so far as industrial action decisions were concerned, of trade union democracy secured by secret ballots.

The 1984 Act in fact pursued the goal of balloted democracy within trade unions in three quite distinct ways—and for three quite different specific purposes, purposes so different as to reveal how much diminution of trade union power could be effected under the banner of the democratic rights of trade union members. The three purposes are indicated by the titles of the three substantive parts of the 1984 Act; part I deals with Secret Ballots for Trade Union Elections; part II with Secret Ballots before Industrial Action; and part III with Political Funds and Objects. We shall examine each part in turn.

(a) Trade Union Elections

The purpose and effect of part I of the 1984 Act was to require trade unions to hold elections by secret ballot for all voting positions on the executive of the union at intervals of no longer than 5 years.[158] The sanction consisted of a right on the part of members of the union to apply to the Certification Officer or to the High Court for a declaration of non-compliance and an enforcement order.[159] This meant that many unions some or all of whose principal officers were appointed other than by direct election, or were elected for long terms of office or even for life, had to change their rules accordingly. The purpose of the measure was to increase the accountability of trade union leaders and governing bodies to their members, and to foster a sense that secret balloting was the preferred mode of taking decisions within trade unions. As we have seen, the government had pursued that goal since 1979, and to that end had included in the Employment Act 1980 provisions making public funds available to trade unions for the expenses of holding postal ballots. By the beginning of 1983, in the Green Paper on *Democracy in Trade Unions*, they had felt in a position to accuse trade unions of having 'refused the opportunity to reform themselves voluntarily',[160] and so to impose this duty of 5-yearly secret balloted elections for union

---

[158] TUA 1984, ss. 1–3, now TULRECA ss. 46–7, 50–1, 53.
[159] TUA 1984 ss. 5–8, now TULRECA ss. 54–8.
[160] Cmnd. 8778, para. 2.

executives. The government seems to have been moved by a sense that support for, or at least acceptance of, their philosophies and policies in industrial relations would be more extensively manifested within trade unions as the result of this new requirement. To put it another way, they calculated that the rank-and-file members of trade unions would subscribe to 'the new realism' more readily than would their leaders, and that those leaders would be more likely to reflect that attitude if they were subject to the discipline of periodical elections. As a contemporary study concluded, the main function of this legislation was to seek to alter the perception of union members and of the public as to the proper function of trade unions.[161]

(b) Trade Union Ballots

Part II of the 1984 Act was ostensibly as much devoted as part I was to getting trade unions to reform themselves from within. In fact there are a number of features of part II which identify it as a restriction upon the industrial power of trade unions which would, in an immediate sense, be imposed from outside. Part II provided, in effect, that industrial action which would otherwise enjoy trade dispute immunity from tort liability would not enjoy that immunity if it was action for which a trade union was liable and if there had not been a majority vote in favour of it in a secret ballot.[162] This meant that it was employers, as the potential claimants in tort, who were given control over the sanction for failure to obtain majority approval of the industrial action in a secret ballot. It did not, contrary to what was asserted in the Green Paper on *Democracy in Trade Unions,* enable an employer to 'trigger a ballot',[163] for the employer only controls the sanction, not the original obligation itself. That curious misdescription in the Green Paper may, however, reveal a good deal of the thinking that lay behind this measure.

For part II of the 1984 Act is in effect a way of enabling employers—whether primary or secondary in relation to an industrial dispute—to require majority support in a ballot as a

---

[161] R. Kidner, 'Trade Union Democracy: Election of Trade Union Officers' (1984) 13 ILJ 193 at 211.

[162] TUA 1984, ss. 10-11, now (as amended by EA 1990) TULRECA ss. 226-32.

[163] See above, p. 484.

condition for the initiation or continuation of industrial action by which they are adversely affected. Part II was a way of meeting the demand upon the Conservative government—both self-imposed and imposed by employers—for tighter control over industrial action, which had continued to exist despite the measures of 1980 and 1982. The demand had sometimes asserted itself in terms of a renewal of the suggestion for making observance of collective procedure agreements a condition for trade dispute immunity, sometimes in the form of suggested restrictions on the freedom to take industrial action in essential services whose interruption would seriously disrupt the life of the community. Indeed, as we have seen, the Green Paper of 1981 indicates how diffuse this demand was at that time, and how little agreement there then was about the best way to meet it. Part II of the 1984 Act harnessed that potent but imprecise demand to the equally potent but rather more specific notion of internal trade union democracy. The result, as we shall see, was a considerable transformation of the role of the civil law as a control upon industrial action.

The provisions of part II of the 1984 Act show, at the levels both of strategy and of tactics, how far the government's aims in the field of industrial conflict law had crystallized into one of reducing, specifically, trade union power, as contrasted with the idea of reducing the industrial power of the workforce in general. This is not to say that the government was specially well disposed towards the industrial power of the workforce in general; but they perceived that power as being in a broad sense amenable to the economic discipline of Monetarism. The power of trade unions, on the other hand, was not so directly influenced by monetarist policies, and had to be addressed by reform of the law of industrial conflict. We have already seen how the 1982 measures were directed at the trade unions rather than at unofficial industrial action; there is woven into the texture of the 1984 measures not only that same set of priorities, but also a tactic of using the—as it were—economically disciplined workforce to constrain trade union power from within.

This becomes evident when one considers certain choices among available options which are embodied in part II of the 1984 Act. The loss of immunity arising from failure to obtain balloted support for industrial action could have been attached to any industrial action, but was attached only to trade union industrial action.[164] The scope of trade union industrial action could have been defined to include action organized by union shop stewards, but its scope was limited by reference to the 1982 definition of trade union liability whereby, as we have seen, shop stewards' actions did not *per se* count as actions of their union.[165] Again, the constituency to be balloted could have been defined as the whole workgroup within which the industrial action was to take place, but was in fact defined as the members of the trade union who it is reasonable, at the time of the ballot, for the union to believe will be called upon in the industrial action to break or interfere with the performance of their contracts of employment.[166] The question to be put to a ballot among the members of that constituency could have been left to the trade union to formulate, but in fact had to ask whether those in favour of industrial action were prepared to take that action in breach of their contracts of employment.[167] By these various means the legislation emphasizes that the union is calling on members to implement a strategy formulated by the union which will involve them in contract-breaking, which they are free to vote down. A useful contemporary evaluation of all this by John Hutton was that:

Behind the Secretary of State's broad appeal to democracy there lies a partisan assessment of how to reduce the number of strikes. This assessment rests on the expectation that current fears and concerns over mass unemployment among trade unionists can be converted into a surging tide of negative results in strike ballots.[168]

The fact that this expectation turned out, as we shall see, to be ill-founded in the short term does not detract from the validity of the explanation of the intentions of the legislation.

(c) Political Funds

It is appropriate to mention part III of the 1984 Act in the context of a discussion of restriction of trade union industrial

---

[164] TUA 1984, s. 10(1)–(2).

[165] TUA 1984 s. 10(3)(c), referring to 'authorization or endorsement', and s. 10(5), defining authorization or endorsement by reference to s. 15 of the Employment Act 1982.

[166] TUA 1984, s. 11(1).

[167] TUA 1984, s. 11(4).

[168] 'Solving the Strike Problem: Part II of the Trade Union Act 1984' (1984) 13 ILJ 212, 226.

power; but it is necessary to acknowledge that part III only contributes to that discussion in a rather special sense, and that it is significantly, as we have seen,[169] concerned with goals rather distinct from that of the restriction of the industrial power of trade unions. The main effect of part III, it will be recalled, is to require the maintenance of separate political funds by trade unions under the Trade Union Act 1913 to be validated by a resolution passed by a ballot of members at least every 10 years. In the outcome, as we saw earlier, the political funds were much more fully supported in ballots of the membership than had been expected. It might be tempting to conclude that part III was unimportant, and unsuccessful in achieving its aims. This, however, would be to overlook its importance to the strategy of the Act as a whole. For part III contributes to the idea that the ballot, whether *ad hoc* or periodic, is the unique basis of validity for any policy or major decision of the trade union. The Act pursued a unified aim in that sense; and, if part II was its vanguard, part III nevertheless had a significant rearguard role.

The 1984 Act was thus probably the most schematic and coherent of all the measures of the 1980s directed against trade union political power. Its effects were, in the short term at least, somewhat masked, and certainly complicated, by the great confrontation between the government and the National Union of Mineworkers which dominated industrial society from mid-1984, and the equally stark confrontation at News International between Mr Rupert Murdoch and the printworkers on *The Times* newspaper from late 1986. The legislative developments which followed after the 1984 Act have to be understood in relation to those disputes.

9.6. LABOUR LAW, PUBLIC ORDER, AND INDUSTRIAL DISPUTES, 1984–1986

The developments of 1984–86 illustrate the dangers of trying to reduce the legislative history of labour law to symmetrical patterns. One can, admittedly, by treating section 14 of the Public Order Act 1986 as if it were a piece of trade dispute or trade union legislation, arrive at a neat biennial sequence of such measures: the Employment Acts of 1980 and 1982, the Trade

---

[169] See above, pp. 436–8.

Union Act of 1984, and the Employment Acts of 1988 and 1990. (The Wages Act 1986 and the Employment Act 1989 belong to a distinct chronology, not being trade dispute or trade union legislation in the above sense.) This would, however, be a false symmetry in a number of respects. The implication that the Public Order Act was as important to the law of trade disputes as those other measures would be a false one; it has proved considerably less important. If, on the other hand, one drew the conclusion that this was therefore a relatively quiet period in the 1980s saga of the reduction of trade union power, that would be even more false; it was an absolutely central phase mainly because of the Miners' Dispute of 1984–5 and the News International Dispute at Wapping in 1986, about both of which we shall have a good deal to say. It was a central phase, moreover, in terms of the development and implementation of governmental policy towards trade unions, thus reminding us that the extent and significance of governmental action and policy formulation cannot be measured solely or even primarily in terms of legislative activity. Finally one must make the point that assessments of programmes of legislation are apt to understate the importance of judicial activity (just as case-law-based accounts of legal topics are apt to overstate it); this was a phase in which civil litigation was a major primary source of new labour law, quite apart from its importance as an interpretative source of trade dispute and trade union legislation.

If these were the misconceptions one wishes to avoid, what was the real significance of what happened in the period between the enactment of the Trade Union Act 1984 and the General Election of 1987? By, let us say, the autumn of 1984 (the 1984 Act having reached the statute-book and been brought into force, for the most part, in July of that year), the government had succeeded in transforming trade dispute and trade union law out of all recognition from its condition in 1979. They had not, however, yet managed fundamentally to alter employers' strategies towards trade unions. Changes in industrial relations practice were more obviously attributable to conditions of severe recession and high unemployment than to the widened availability of labour injunctions.[170] Admittedly, by Autumn 1984, Mr

---

[170] See S. Evans, 'The Labour Injunction Revisited: Picketing, Employers and the Employment Act 1980' (1983) 12 ILJ 129.

Eddie Shah had set a significant example, in the Messenger Newspapers Dispute, of how a small employer might use the labour injunction,[171] and its enforcement against a union by sequestration of its assets, to challenge the dominant position of the print unions in the newspaper-printing industry; and the Austin Rover Group, under the management of Michael Edwardes, was in the course of using the 1984 Act so effectively against the union side of its Joint Negotiating Committee[172] that in the end, 'Whoever was right or wrong in the dispute, the unions lay like skittles bowled out into the corners of the industrial arena.'[173]

At the time, however, it was far from obvious that the actions of those employers presaged a general trend. The government had not, moreover, provided a decisive example in the public sector of the successful use of strategies for reducing trade union power. There had been only qualified victories over the steel-workers (ISTC) in 1981 and the train-drivers (ASLEF) in 1982, and the government had emerged with, at best, a draw, from the Civil Service strike of 1981, and as the fairly clear loser from the Water Industry dispute of 1983. Nor, by late 1984, had the government succeeded in identifying trade unions as a general threat to national security, as they were trying to do in their action relating to trade union membership among civil servants employed at the Government Communications Headquarters ('GCHQ').[174]

In December 1983, the Prime Minister in her capacity as Minister for the Civil Service gave an instruction for the imme-diate variation of the terms and conditions of GCHQ staff so that they would no longer be permitted to belong to national trade unions. This action was a response to the action of the Civil Service unions in calling upon their members at GCHQ to take industrial action on a number of occasions since 1979, and in particular in March 1981 during a national dispute between those unions and the government about the pay and conditions of civil

---

[171] See *Messenger Newspapers Group Ltd.* v. *NGA* [1984] IRLR 397.

[172] See *Austin Rover Group Ltd.* v. *AUEW (TASS)* [1985] IRLR 162.

[173] Lord Wedderburn, *The Worker and the Law* (3rd edn. 1986), 78.

[174] See generally, Lord Wedderburn, 'Freedom of Association and Philosophies of Labour Law' (1989) 18 ILJ 1 (based on the 'GCHQ Lecture' for 1988 sponsored by The First Division Association of Civil Servants).

servants generally. The validity of this executive action was eventually upheld by the House of Lords,[175] and found by the European Commission of Human Rights not to be in breach of its Convention,[176] on the grounds that the Minister could legitimately claim to be acting to protect national security, though the action was identified by the Freedom of Association Committee of the ILO as being in breach of ILO Conventions.[177] It represented a direct challenge to a political consensus which upheld the legitimacy of public service trade unionism, and it did some damage to the strength and self-confidence of public sector trade unions, not least by demonstrating the ineffectiveness of trade union solidarity to close such a gaping breach in its defences. It did not, however, effect a fundamental shift in the balance of power between the government and the trade unions.

(a) The Miners' Dispute

That fundamental shift did occur as the outcome of the Miners' dispute, which ran from mid-1984 to March 1985. The Miners' dispute was of crucial significance firstly because of what was at stake in terms of the goals of the two sides as to the way in which this public sector industry should be run and managed.[178] The dispute was about pit closures and redundancies: the National Coal Board under the chairmanship of Sir Ian MacGregor from mid-1983 onwards was moving towards an acceleration of pit closures in an attempt to make the industry commercially competitive with its foreign rivals; the National Union of Mineworkers under the leadership of Arthur Scargill was seeking to preserve the post-war understanding that the coal industry could not be run down without regard to the local unemployment this

---

[175] *Council of Civil Service Unions* v. *Minister for the Civil Service* [1985] ICR 14.

[176] *Council of Civil Service Unions* v. *United Kingdom*, Application 11603 of 1985 to the European Commission of Human Rights: see S. Fredman and G. Morris, (1988) 17 ILJ 105.

[177] ILO, *234th Report of the Committee on Freedom of Association, Case No. 1261* (Geneva, 1984); see S. Corby, 'Limitations on Freedom of Association in the Civil Service and the ILO's Response'(1986) 15 ILJ 161.

[178] See esp. the account of the dispute given by K. Middlemas, *Power Competition and the State, iii* (London, 1991), 296–303, upon which this passage draws.

would cause in mining communities and without acquiescence of the union—an understanding embodied in its latest version in the tripartite *Plan for Coal* of 1974.[179]

The ultimate defeat of the NUM in this dispute meant that the government could, for the rest of the 1980s, be confident that corporatist understanding with trade unions would not pose an obstacle to the restructuring of public sector industries or the abolition of constraints upon the free labour markets such as the Dock Labour Scheme, as we shall see in more detail in the next chapter. More immediately, the defeat of the NUM demonstrated conclusively that unions were vulnerable even when taking nationwide industrial action in defence of jobs and the employment base of whole communities, and not just when they were pursuing claims for terms and conditions of employment which could be more readily represented as the selfish and self-defeating pursuit of narrow sectional interests.

This brings us to the second crucial aspect of the Miners' dispute from the point of the development of labour law and government policy towards trade unions, namely that the defeat of the union was to a significant extent attributable to isolation and division of the striking miners. This was in part due to the demagogical leadership style and intransigent strategy formation of Arthur Scargill; but it also has important interconnections with the way that labour law was developing at the time. Thus a great source of weakness for the leadership of the NUM was the fact that the strike had not been preceded by a national ballot[180]— one of the things which encouraged the growth of a working miners' movement against the strike, and the formation of a breakaway union, the Union of Democratic Mineworkers. The government could use this as ammunition in support of its Trade Union Bill, which was passing through the parliamentary process in the early months of the strike.[181] In a sense, however, it was fortunate from the government's point of view that the Bill was

---

[179] See, for a most valuable detailed account, W. Rees, 'The Law, Practice and Procedures concerning Redundancy in the Coal Mining Industry' (1985) 14 ILJ 203–14.

[180] See, for a detailed discussion of the impact of the strike on the Bill, Auerbach, *Legislating for Conflict*, 151–2.

[181] For details of the process by which the strike was initiated, see K. Ewing, 'The Strike, the Courts and the Rule Books' (1985) 14 ILJ 160–1.

not yet law when the dispute began, because part II of the Act, as we have seen, would place the onus on employers to invoke the union's failure to obtain a balloted majority before taking strike action.

As it was, the National Coal Board, after an initial foray, decided not to use the opportunities opened up by the 1980 and 1982 Acts to enforce labour injunctions against the NUM. This significant decision[182] seems to have been prompted at least by the calculation that such litigation would alienate miners who were minded to remain at work,[183] and possibly even by some degree of collusion between the NCB and the working miners.[184] It was a strategy which yielded handsome dividends; not only did it make it easier for the TUC not to support the strike directly,[185] but it produced, to a far greater extent than could have been predicted, litigation against the NUM by working miners,[186] who succeeded in establishing that the strike was unlawful at common law in that it involved violations of the union rule-books by a number of the NUM Areas (which are in fact distinct unions, federated into the NUM itself). The failure of the NUM to comply with various judicial rulings so obtained resulted in the sequestration of its funds in October 1984, and in its being put into receivership at the end of November 1984. Not only did this litigation indicate the scope for reducing trade union power by promoting internal fragmentation in the name of trade union democracy—a lesson which, we shall see later, the government was quick to learn—but it also reduced Mr Scargill and his colleagues to more and more desperate measures to keep the strike going. When this involved moving funds to foreign banks and accepting subsidies from the Miners' Union of the USSR,[187] the NUM could easily be depicted as acting against the national interest, thus increasing their growing isolation from the rest of the trade union movement, let alone from the mainstream of public opinion.

---

[182] Aptly compared by Roger Benedictus to Sherlock Holmes's 'curious incident of the dog in the night time': see 'The Use of the Law of Tort in the Miners' Dispute' (1985) 14 ILJ 176.

[183] Benedictus, 'Use of the Law of Tort', at 177.

[184] Cf. Wedderburn, *The Worker and the Law*, 90.

[185] See Middlemas, *Power, Competition*, 300, 328–9.

[186] For details see Ewing, 'The Strike', at 161 ff.

[187] See Middlemas, *Power, Competition*, 300.

(b) Trade Unions and Public Order

This brings us to what was, perhaps, the most important aspect of the shift in the balance of power between the trade union movement and government which resulted from the Miners' dispute. Before that dispute, the government had not really succeeded in identifying trade union industrial action as a general threat to national security and public order, or at least as a *controllable* threat to public order, which was the most important thing from the government's point of view. Before this dispute, the government was still significantly constrained by a public perception of the legitimacy of trade union economic action in the form of picketing—a perception which had survived, somewhat weakened, the events of the 'winter of discontent' of 1978–9. For instance, as we have seen, the government in 1979–80 encountered a reluctance on the part of the police to be overtly entrusted with the enforcement of a more stringent criminal law of picketing, a reluctance which had to do with their wish to be seen as neutral in the policing of picketing as between strikers and employers.

There was, on the other hand, among the senior ranks of the police forces of the UK and on the part of the government, dissatisfaction with the relative ease with which cohorts of flying pickets could block access to the sites which they chose to target, a tactic developed particularly by Arthur Scargill himself, who had led the mass pickets who had closed the Saltley Coke Depot during the 1972 Miners' strike, to the enormous discomfiture of the West Midlands Police, who had been obliged to withdraw and leave the site in the control of the pickets for some hours. In the aftermath of that dispute, the police forces of the UK had set up a National Reporting Centre to organize and co-ordinate mutual support operations if such events should recur. The Miners' dispute of 1984–5 probably provided the first occasion on which the police had the positive assurance of the government that full political and financial support would be available to sustain such operations. An immense police operation took place to maintain access to collieries, and to combat the violence of picketing miners.[188] The high point was a set-piece confrontation at the

---

[188] See generally, Peter Wallington, 'Policing the Miners' Strike' (1985) 14 ILJ 145–59.

Orgreave Colliery in 1984, in a sense a return match for the Saltley Coke Depot incident, which may have resulted from pre-emptive action on the part of the police.

The success of the policing strategy in the Miners' dispute had its consequences in terms both of changes in public and political attitudes and in specifically legislative terms. Previously, there had been an assumption that it was not practicable to use the police directly to challenge and contain the full might of trade union industrial power. The events of 1984-5 demonstrated that this was not a necessary assumption. That meant that mass picketing in the course of industrial disputes could now be regarded as simply a public order problem which it was within the remit of the police to deal with in the same way as they were to deal with the other (rapidly growing) public order problems of inner city riots and football hooliganism. So, in effect, mass picketing could be directly equated with other anti-social threats to public order, could be denied any vestige of industrial legitimacy, and could be overwhelmed by aggressive policing without the traditional inhibition of loss of industrial neutrality on the part of the police.

Various legal developments maintained this trend. The decision in *Moss* v. *McLachlan*[189] confirmed the legality of the use of roadblocks by the police to prevent striking miners from travelling to join picket lines where the roadblock could be shown to be honestly and reasonably believed to be necessary to avert a risk to the peace which was proximate both in place and time. This was to endorse an important preventive power, although the endorsement was in less sweeping terms than that given by the Attorney-General in his statement on the criminal law of picketing made at the outset of the dispute.[190] The Divisional Court also refused judicial review of the use by magistrates of bail conditions whereby miners charged with public order offences were restrained from going to places other than their usual place of employment to picket or demonstrate in connection with the Miners' dispute.[191] It was also significant that, in the climate of the time, Scott J. should judge it appro-

---

[189] [1985] IRLR 76. See G. Morris, (1985) 14 ILJ 109.

[190] HC Deb., 6th ser., vol. 56, cols. 279-80w (Written Answers, 16 Mar. 1984).

[191] *R.* v. *The Mansfield Justices ex parte Sharkey* [1984] IRLR 496; see (1985) 14 ILJ 109.

priate, in one of the civil actions brought by working miners,[192] to identify mass picketing as amounting to a tort of unreasonable harassment, and to treat the Code of Practice guideline on picket numbers as indicating that picketing in greater numbers than six at a gate would amount to that tort—thereby according that provision of the Code a legal status in a way that those responsible for the Code, as we have seen, had hesitated to do.

This new attitude towards mass picketing found expression in the Public Order Act 1986. That Act was partly an exercise in rationalizing the common law public order offences along lines recommended by the Law Commission. But it also had the purpose of implementing a series of government reports which were themselves responses to the various major infractions of public order occurring since 1979. The culmination of these reports was a Home Office White Paper of May 1985,[193] upon whose discourse the miners' strike had had an obvious and heavy imprint. Thus the offences connectecd with picketing specified in section 7 of the Conspiracy and Protection of Property Act 1875 were made arrestable without warrant; but, even more significantly, mass picketing was treated both as a major justification for and a major target of section 14 of the Public Order Act, which conferred upon senior police officers new powers to issue directions imposing limiting conditions upon the holding of public assemblies. Both in the White Paper and in the government's presentation of the Public Order Bill, this new power was identified as being directed equally against mass picketing and against other (implicitly equivalent) disorderly gatherings. Thus the White Paper gives the instances where preventive action might be or might have been useful: National Front rallies; picketing at Grunwick's or Warrington; and football matches.[194] Mr Hurd as Home Secretary, introducing clause 14 on Second Reading in the House of Commons, cited the examples of the gatherings at Greenham Common, the 'Stop the City' campaign, and the picketing at Grunwick's, Warrington, and during the Miners' dispute.[195] This rhetoric, both in policy documents and in parliamentary debates, confirms the extent to which the

---

[192] *Thomas v. NUM (South Wales Area)* [1985] ICR 886.   [193] White Paper, *Review of Public Order Law,* Cmnd. 9510.

[194] Cmnd. 9510, Para. 5.7.

[195] HC Deb., 5th ser., vol. 89, cols. 797–8 (13 Jan. 1986).

government wished to identify a continuity of concern between street violence, political militancy, and industrial action. As this approach was being propounded, the events of another major industrial dispute seemed to confirm and reinforce that set of ideas.

(c) The Wapping Dispute

In a number of ways, the News International dispute of 1985–6[196] was a sort of sequel to the Miners' dispute which confirmed, in a very different context, many of the developments which had occurred in the course of, or as a consequence of, the latter dispute. The News International dispute revolved around Rupert Murdoch's introduction of a radical new management strategy for the production of the newspapers he owned—a change of pattern at least as far-reaching as that sought by the National Coal Board in 1983–4—namely the transfer of production from Fleet Street to new premises at Wapping, where new technology would be operated in processes free from the restrictive practices applied by the print unions in Fleet Street. In order to achieve this, Mr Murdoch was prepared for the whole existing workforce of more than 5,000 people to be dismissed *en masse*, and for the new premises to be run in a physical state of seige.

It reflects the new atmosphere created by the 1984 Act and by the Miners' Dispute that the employers in this dispute could make full use of the civil law against the print unions NGA and SOGAT without thereby appearing to be particularly maverick among employers.[197] It also reflects those changes in attitudes, and in relative strength of competing positions, that the employers' strategy succeeded not least because they were able to divide the trade union movement and recruit a new workforce with the co-operation of the electricians' union, the EETPU, which was expelled from the TUC in 1986. Finally, the changed climate is perhaps most powerfully reflected by the way in which the Metropolitan Police, sustained by perceptions about the

---

[196] See K. Ewing, *The Right to Strike* (Oxford, 1991), 1–3; K. Ewing and B. Napier, 'The Wapping Dispute and Labour Law (1986) 45 CLJ 285; British Journal of Industrial Relations Chronicle, 'News International', (1986) 24 BJIR 479.

[197] For details see Ewing and Napier, 'The Wapping Dispute', at 294–5; 'As has become common in trade disputes, writs began to fly like confetti at a wedding.'

primacy of public order, could bring to bear aggressive policing tactics at Wapping which gave rise to pitched battles between police and demonstrators in January 1987, to which the Home Secretary responded by announcing that section 14 of the new Public Order Act would be brought into effect.[198]

Thus, at that point, there seemed to have been major successes in curtailing trade union industrial power in a number of different respects. The forces of public order seemed to have gained an ascendency over trade union power which they had not enjoyed since before the 1970s. Employers seemed to have been effectively empowered to use the legal process to support a newly aggressive set of managerial strategies. The trade union movement had been very significantly divided and fragmented, and solidarity between trade unions and between workgroups had been visibly undermined. Nevertheless, there was still to be extensive further legislation in the fields of industrial conflict law and trade union law before the end of the decade. What were the factors bringing about this continuing legislative interventionism?

9.7. THE AFTERMATH OF THE MINERS' DISPUTE: THE EMPLOYMENT ACT 1988

We have just seen that in the years 1985 to 1987, the problems of industrial conflict were addressed primarily in terms of the protection of national security and public order. However, the experience of the Miner's dispute also stimulated the government to continue to seek a transformation of the civil law so that it would provide an effective framework of restriction upon trade union industrial power. In particular, the events of that dispute suggested that the most significant opportunities for further legislative change lay in the direction of activating members of trade unions to constrain the exercise of trade union power from within their own unions. It was this thinking which underlay part I of the Employment Act 1988, the development and enactment of which is described in this section.

We saw in the previous section that, at the time of the Miners' dispute and in its immediate aftermath, the dominant perception

---

[198] HC Deb., 6th ser., vol. 111, col. 36w (23 Feb. 1987), announcing that the section would come into effect on 1 Apr. 1987.

was that the civil law had played less of a part than might have been expected in the containment of the miners' industrial action—that it had been 'a surprising defeat for the advocates of a more active use of the civil law in industrial disputes'.[199] This view was based particularly on the decisions of the National Coal Board and the major nationalized enterprises affected by the industrial action such as the Central Electricity Generating Board not to invoke the causes of action which they presumably had in abundance in respect of much of the picketing that occurred. Those decisions do indeed seem to have reflected a strategy which saw active policing as a more effective and less counter-productive tactic than corporate civil action.

On the other hand, we have seen that the government had several strong reasons for regardding the experience of the period from 1984 to 1986 as fundamentally encouraging towards further development of the civil law. Firstly, civil ligation did have a crucial role in weakening the National Union of Mineworkers, albeit that it was for the most part litigation generated by dissident union members by way of enforcement of the union rule-book,[200] rather than litigation generated by employers invoking the 1980 and 1982 legislation. Secondly, part II of the 1984 Act had not been passed and implemented in time to be invoked against the failure of the National Union of Mineworkers to hold a national ballot before initiating strike action. The fact that the failure to hold a ballot was widely perceived as the fatal flaw in the strategy of the National Union of Mineworkers served to legitimate part II of the 1984 Act, and probably helped to produce a climate in which part II was aggressively invoked by employers—most notably by Austin Rover Ltd. in mid-1985. That aggressive use of the 1984 Act in turn brought about a state of affairs in which the legislation of 1980, 1982, and 1984 operated cumulatively to consummate the government's long-term aim of offering substantial sanctions within the civil law with which to contest trade union industrial action. The initiation of litigation from within trade unions, although happening to be

[199] Benedictus, 'Use of the Law of Tort', at 176.

[200] See K. Ewing, 'The Strike'. Centrally significant decisions, in addition to that in *Thomas* v. *NUM (South Wales Area)*, discussed earlier, were those in *Taylor* v. *NUM (Yorkshire Area)* [1985] IRLR 445. *Taylor* v. *NUM (Derbyshire Area) (No.1)* [1985] IRLR 440 and *Clarke* v. *Chadburn* [1985] 1 WLR 78.

independent of the government's own legislation, was entirely in accordance with the government's policies; it seemed logical to provide legislative stimulus to further development of such initiatives.

Early in 1987, the government produced a Green Paper entitled *Trade Unions and their Members* which confirmed that this was their thinking and advanced these policies further.[201] The proposals advanced for discussion in the Green Paper showed not only that the government wished to pursue still further what it saw as a programme for restoring a proper balance of bargaining power between trade unions and employers, but also that they now envisaged the creation of constraints upon trade unions from within the unions and enforced by trade union members as an important way of carrying out that programme. Thus the proposals included not only removing legal immunity from strikes called to enforce a closed shop, and taking away the remaining legal protection for the closed shop, but also the requiring of secret postal ballots under independent supervision for the election of members of union executive bodies (including non-voting members such as the President of the National Union of Mineworkers), the enabling of trade union members to require ballots about industrial action, and the creation of a right exercisable against the trade union to choose to go to work or cross a picket line despite a strike call. Moreover it was proposed to create a special Commissioner for Trade Union Affairs to provide advice and support to complaining individual trade union members and to take legal action against unions or officials failing to comply with statutory duties. The Secretary of State for Employment could well say of these proposals that 'These next steps are wholly consistent with our whole approach to trade union reform through the period of office of this government'; it was equally pertinent for him to remark that 'the Green Paper is based on our experience of events since the last legislation.' The Miners' dispute was, of course, prominent among those events.

Although the evolution of the Green Paper, and its subsequent implementation by the Employment Act 1988, seem with hindsight to follow logically from previously formed government

---

[201] Cm. 95 (Feb. 1987).

policy, nevertheless this development came as something of a surprise to many at the time it occurred. By the beginning of 1987, it appeared, as we have observed, that the government had achieved its main aims in this area. The cumulative effect of the industrial conflict provisions of the Employment Acts 1980 and 1982 and the Trade Union Act 1984 had been, as we have seen, to create the legal machinery whereby employers might gravely weaken trade industrial action, and to create a climate in which many employers regarded themselves, and were regarded, as acting legitimately in deploying their new sanctions. This latter achievement was specially attributable to the balloting provisions of the 1984 Act, which created a more cogent rationale for civil liability for trade union industrial action than had previously existed. It was widely predicted that the government would be content to consolidate these gains by minor measures; when the Green Paper appeared in February 1987, canvassing a set of far from minor proposals for further reforms, there was some sense that this represented electioneering propaganda rather than concrete intentions. There certainly seems to have been an electoral factor in the Green Paper proposals to give trade union members the right to sue for a ballot before industrial action. The Labour Party made a similar proposal in its 1987 Election Manifesto, though in their case the proposal was to be in sub-stitution for the employer's cause of action, not in addition to it.

It remains a matter for speculation how specific were the government's plans to legislate along the lines of the 1987 Green Paper at the time of its publication. It is also an interesting question what effect the undoubted shift in Labour Party policy towards an acceptance of some aspects of Conservative industrial conflict legislation of the earlier 1980s had upon the development of government policy at this stage and in subsequent years. At all events, it is now clear enough that its re-election later in 1987 encouraged the government towards more extreme and ideologically driven measures even than those it had adopted in the early and mid-1980s, in the field of labour legislation as in other areas of government activity. When part I of the 1988 Act implemented the Green Paper proposals, it represented the weaving together of several strands of late 1980s governmental ideology; in particular (1) the perceived need to complete the reduction of the power of trade unions; (2) the desire to complete the creation of a full, derigidified labour market; and (3) the intention to use the individual worker and trade union member as the agent for the realization of both these goals. This requires elaboration in relation to the detailed provisions of part I of the Act.

(a) Employment Act 1988 Part I

The first aim of part I, as we have seen, was to press home the advantage, in terms of the reduction of trade union power, which the government perceived itself to have gained in the 1984–6 period from the defeat of the Miners' strike and the coming into effect and use of the balloting provisions of the 1984 Act. The events of that period had signalled to the government that individual workers and trade union members held the key to the reduction of trade union power in two respects. Firstly, the accountability of trade unions to the opinions, obtained by secret ballot, of their own members was the most widely acceptable, and therefore powerful, rationale for the curbing of trade union industrial power. Secondly, the events of the Miners' dispute had suggested that dissident trade unionists, exponents of the 'new realism' in industrial relations, would be at least as willing litigants against trade unions to enforce this kind of accountability upon them as ever employers would—litigants, moreover, armed with a stronger moral claim to uphold internal trade union democracy than the employers had.

So section 1[202] of the 1988 Act, in conferring on trade union members a right to apply for a court order requiring the union to revoke any inducement to industrial action which has not yet received support in a ballot, as required by the 1984 Act, was building on a perceived success in both law reform and political terms. As the 1987 Green Paper had put it:

Such a right, if introduced, could be exercised by directly affected members who do not wish to strike, both those who supported the principle of balloting and were not prepared to accept the loss of the right to vote and those who supported the proposed action but were reluctant to see union funds jeopardised through the loss of immunity which unballoted action would entail.[203]

---

[202] Now TULRECA s. 62.
[203] Cm. 95, para. 2.4.

That latter category of trade union members was also mobilized by other provisions of part I which were responding to the experience gained in the 1984–6 period, especially *vis-à-vis* the National Union of Mineworkers. Section 8[204] made it unlawful for the property of a trade union to be applied to indemnify individuals against a penalty imposed by a court for a criminal offence or for contempt; and enabled an individual member, claiming an unreasonable failure on the part of the union to enforce this restriction, to apply for a court order authorizing the member to pursue proceedings at the union's expense. This strengthened the hand of any trade union members who might wish to repeat the claim of Mr Thomas to restrain the NUM in this respect.[205] Similar reinforcement was offered to the successors of Mr Taylor[206] seeking to restrain unlawful use of union property, who are enabled by section 9[207] to apply for a court order which may result in the appointment of a receiver of the union's property and the removal of the trustees of the union.

A further measure by way of reinforcement of the existing legislation in the light of the experience of the Miner's dispute consisted of the extension of the duty to hold elections to the principal executive committee of the union at least every 5 years. Mr Scargill having taken advantage of a loophole whereby that duty did not include non-voting members of the executive, section 12 extended the duty to non-voting members of the executive, and specifically to the president and general secretary of the union in any event. This was labour law at its most casuistical, comparable to the manœuvring of tax-avoiders and the Inland Revenue; part I of the 1988 Act nevertheless made further provisions of strategic rather than merely tactical significance.

Thus the industrial dispute of 1984–5 in the coal industry corresponded exactly with a stereotype, which certainly fitted the preconceptions of 1980s governments, in which a militant leadership was vulnerable to attack from moderate or 'realistic'

---

[204] Now TULRECA s. 15.

[205] See *Thomas v. National Union of Mineworkers (South Wales Area)* [1985] ICR 886.

[206] See *Taylor v. National Union of Mineworkers (Derbyshire Area)* [1985] IRLR 440

[207] Now TULRECA s. 16.

rank-and-file members suitably armed to pursue claims of denial of their democratic rights within the union. Although the government regarded many subsequent lesser industrial disputes as also fitting that stereotype, they could see that requiring balloted support for industrial action was not invariably a method of reducing the industrial power of the union; it was capable of reinforcing solidarity as well as of fragmenting it. There are two groups of provisions in part I of the 1988 Act which reflect the government's concern about this counter-effect.

The first group consists of measures to make the requirements for balloted support more stringent. This was done not by requiring postal ballots or independent scrutiny, conditions applied to political fund ballots and union elections by sections 14 and 15, but instead—in section 17[208]—by requiring balloted support for industrial action to be demonstrated by a majority in a separate ballot in each separate workplace concerned. This is the general principle—there was a curiously complex set of excepted cases where ballots may be aggregated across workplaces; the strategy was apparently to prevent unions producing an artificial majority for a strike in one key workplace by dilution of the constituency with more militant workers from another workplace.[209] This defensive strategy was supplemented by the addition, in section 18, of a power conferred on the Secretary of State for Employment to issue codes of practice 'for the purpose of promoting what appear to him to be desirable practices' in relation to the conduct by trade unions of ballots and elections. It would seem that this was especially aimed at strike ballots, and late in 1988 the Secretary of State produced a draft code for ballots relating to industrial action which proposed a remarkably restrictive and hostile set of rules of practice for such ballots. (The final version, which was produced in 1990, was slightly less specific and coercive; this was perhaps some acknowledgement of the extent to which the 1988 draft had been almost universally felt to be outrageously partisan.[210])

[208] See now TULRECA s. 228.

[209] See E. McKendrick (1988) 17 ILJ 145–7. It is not entirely clear why this strategy was preferred to that of imposing postal balloting (as now proposed by the Trade Union Reform and Employment Rights Bill 1992).

[210] Department of Employment, *Code of Practice on Trade Union Ballots on Industrial Action* (HMSO, 1990): see, for details and evaluation, B. Simpson, (1990) 19 ILJ 29–32.

That group of measures was something of an afterthought, a sign of growing misgivings about the backlash effect of the ballot requirements.[211] Far more fundamental to the concept of part I of the 1988 Act was another set of measures which indicated the real nature of the government's thinking underlying their democratization of trade unions. This group of measures displayed the intensity of the government's objection to trade union discipline whereby the individual members and workers generally might be pressed into acting in conformity with the collective decisions made or collective interests represented by trade unions. They showed a deep concern lest their own democratization of trade unions be seen as in any way legitimating collective discipline of that kind. Thus further measures were taken against the closed shop: section 10[212] withdrew trade dispute immunity in tort from all acts for which the reason includes belief that an employer is, in effect, not implementing a closed shop. Section 11,[213] its counterpart in individual employment law, removed all remaining licence from employers to dismiss or take action against employees short of dismissal to enforce a closed shop in the form of a union membership agreement. The Green Paper sought to articulate a case for doing this despite its own admission that the measures of 1980 and 1982 had already meant that virtually all closed shops were without legal sanction, in the sense that the dismissal of any employee on the grounds of non-union membership would automatically be unfair.[214] Interestingly, the nearest the Green Paper comes to a specific justification is the suggestion that 'The closed shop has traditionally been associated with restrictive practices, not least in the printing industry', and that

Further restrictions on the closed shop would provide greater flexibility in the labour market and increased freedom of choice for employers when recruiting.

This indicated how, in the formation of part I of the 1988 Act, the aim of reducing trade union power had become combined

---

[211] For statistics indicating the trade unions' success with strike ballots, see ACAS *Annual Report 1985*, 15, *1986*, 13–14, *1987*, 11.

[212] Now TULRECA s. 222.

[213] See now TULRECA ss. 146, 152.

[214] Cm. 95, para. 4.6.

with that of creating a free and flexible labour market—with the development of the printing industry visibly regarded as an example of positive progress in this respect.

That same approach underlay what was, perhaps, the most extreme—but philosophically central—provision of part I of the 1988 Act—namely that of section 3,[215] giving the individual member of a trade union the right not to be 'unjustifiably disciplined'—which turned out to focus upon the right not to be disciplined for refusing to participate in or support industrial action. The right conferred by section 3 was to apply even though the industrial action in question was balloted and otherwise lawful. There has been a certain amount of incredulity towards a provision so apparently inconsistent with the barrage of measures designed to control and validate duly arrived at decisions of the trade union; but it should in reality occasion no surprise. The anti-collectivism underlying part I was quite resolute enough to produce this outcome, and to be untroubled by what is apt to appear an arbitrary inconsistency from any different perspective. Again, it is interesting to look at the rationale for this provision which is offered in the Green Paper; it comes to this, that,

Every union member should be free to decide for himself whether or not he wishes to break his contract of employment and run the risk of dismissal without compensation.[216]

All the strands of part I of the 1988 Act were woven together in this; trade union power was to be reduced by the agency of the worker and union member taking decisions which appear rational in his own individual interest in a free and flexible labour market (constituted, *inter alia*, by laws enabling employers freely to dismiss a workforce taking part in industrial action). Section 3 was supplemented by an apparatus of complaint to an industrial tribunal and remedies of declaration, and compensation by the union, as provided by sections 4 and 5; and sections 19 to 21 set up a Commissioner for the Rights of Trade Union Members with the function and power of assisting individuals in enforcing this right, and also the other main rights to trade union democracy as conceived of and provided by the post-1980 legislation—in

---

[215] Now TULRECA ss. 64–5.
[216] Cm. 95, para. 2.22.

which, as we have seen, trade union law and industrial conflict law were combined and integrated towards the goal of reduction of trade union power. As we shall see, it was precisely that coalescence which was identified and censured by the ILO Committee of Experts as involving extensive and multifarious inconsistency with ILO Convention No. 87 on Freedom of Association and Protection of the Right to Organise.[217]

9.8. THE OLD LOGIC AND THE NEW: THE EMPLOYMENT ACT 1990

The succession of measures from 1980 onwards directed at reducing trade union power which have been discussed in this chapter continued into the 1990s; a further measure in the sequence was the Employment Act 1990. That Act both re-echoed most of the important themes of the 1980s trade dispute legislation, enabling them to be more clearly understood, and also introduced some new points of departure. The discussion of the provisions of the 1990 Act is therefore a convenient way of starting to draw together the discussion about the reducing of trade union power in the 1980s, and to evaluate where that process was tending at the beginning of the 1990s.

The lengths to which the reduction of trade union power had already progressed before the 1990 legislation was passed can be judged from the relative absence of public controversy surrounding an Act whose provisions would in 1979 have seemed absolutely revolutionary. As it was, both Government and Opposition seemed to dismiss the Bill somewhat lightly as probably the last in the series of Acts about trade dispute and trade union law, and hence in the nature of a tidying-up operation.[218] It was really far more significant than that, both in ideological and practical terms.

In fact the 1990 Act was shaped by the particular combination of prominent ideology with pragmatic opportunism which was very typical of the legislation of the late 1980s. At the end of

---

[217] ILO Committee of Experts, *Observations 1989*.

[218] Cf. the presentation of the Bill at Second Reading in the House of Commons by the Secretary of State for Employment, Michael Howard, with the speech by the Opposition spokesman on employment matters, Tony Blair (HC Deb., 6th ser., vol. 165, cols. 38 ff. (29 Jan. 1990)).

1988, the Department of Employment published a White Paper, entitled *Employment for the 1990s*,[219] which presented all the employment measures of the 1980s as a coherent programme directed at creating employment by removing barriers to jobs. This was, of course, a rationale for taking further measures along the same lines, and it was notable that trade unions and patterns of industrial relations were one of the targets identified by the White Paper for further reform.

In that context, it is noticeable that the White Paper stressed the importance of the control of the closed shop to their programme of 'curbing the abuse of trade union power'. The freedom of the individual worker not to belong to a trade union had loomed large in the Conservative government discourse throughout the 1980s; it was now put forward as a major obstacle to the improvement of the efficiency of the labour market. Research findings from the Centre for Labour Economics of the London School of Economics were cited for the view that 'trade unions do particular damage to jobs where a closed shop is in operation.'[220] The government's view seems to have been that a concentration of closed-shop practices upon the pre-entry closed shop had rendered the previous amendments to the unfair dismissal laws an insufficient set of controls, because the pre-entry closed shop operated at the point of hiring. Hence the White Paper indicated that the government would look particularly at the operation of the pre-entry closed shop and would 'take any further legislative steps that are needed on this or any other aspects of industrial relations which constitute a barrier to emlployment'.[221]

Thus we find that the first tranche of proposals for legislation which led to the Employment Act 1990 was couched in a rhetoric of promoting further growth in employment, yet accorded priority to the libertarian cause of abolishing closed-shop practices. The proposals were presented in March 1989 in a Green Paper entitled *Removing Barriers to Employment*[222]—a sort of title hitherto

[219] Cm. 540
[220] Ibid., para. 2.23. The two LSE/CLE papers relied upon were D. Blanchflower, N. Millward, and A. Oswald, 'Unionisation and Employment Behaviour' (July 1988) and D. Metcalf, 'Trade Unions and Economic Performance' (Aug. 1988).
[221] Cm. 540, para. 2.24.
[222] Cm. 655.

reserved for deregulation proposals rather than proposals 'for the further reform of industrial relations and trade union law' as these were sub-titled. This Green Paper went so far as to assert that: 'The main economic effect of the closed shop is to destroy jobs by raising labour costs and depressing profitability',[223] and canvassed a proposal to provide a right of complaint to an industrial tribunal for any individual whom an employer refuses to engage on the grounds of non-membership of a trade union or of any particular trade union, or on the ground of refusal to agree to become a member after the employment has started.[224] This proposal, which the government later (prudently in the face of earlier findings by the ILO's Committee of Experts about the inadequacy of protection of freedom of association in the United Kingdom[225]) decided to couple with equivalent rights to belong to a trade union,[226] was eventually implemented as section 1 of the 1990 Act.[227] The government presumably felt they also had evidence that the pre-entry closed shop might be maintained indirectly by the refusal of the services of an employment agency on the grounds of non-membership of a trade union, as that refusal of services was made unlawful and the subject of complaint to an industrial tribunal by section 2 of the Act.

The government's second priority for the 'further reform of industrial relations law' lay in the area of trade dispute law; it was to place further restrictions on the trade dispute immunity in relation to secondary industrial action. Thus the first two priorities for the 1990 Act lay in the same areas as those of the 1980 Act. In both cases, the 1990 Act swept away what remained of the compromises contained in the 1980 Act. So far as secondary industrial action was concerned, this meant abolishing all the remaining gateways to immunity for secondary action except the one for action in the course of peaceful picketing by workers employed by the employer in dispute or the trade union officials representing them. The resulting formula, making no allowance for anything except primary industrial action, was contained in section 4[228] of the 1990 Act.

---

[223] Ibid., para. 2.9.   [224] Ibid., para. 2.37.

[225] See, for details, B. Napier, 'The International Labour Organization and GCHQ' (1989) 18 ILJ 255.

[226] Employment Act 1990, s. 1(1)

[227] Now TULRECA s. 137. See, generally, R. Townshend Smith, 'Refusal of Employment on Grounds of Trade Union Membership or Non-membership: The Employment Act 1990' (1991) 20 ILJ 102.

[228] Now TULRECA s. 224.

The main justification for it was the possibility that secondary action might 'deter employers from starting up for the first time in this country with harmful effects on new investment and on jobs',[229] the example given being the threat of industrial action at Ford of Great Britain plants which the American Ford Motor Company asserted had deterred them from establishing a new plant in Dundee. For the government itself, and, in its judgment, for the country generally, this incident made it appropriate to have as draconian a formulation of the law relating to secondary action as that relating to picketing which was introduced in 1980 in the aftermath of the 'winter of discontent'.

The government's third priority was to expand the regulatory structure designed to enforce trade union ballots and promote trade union democracy as they perceived it. To this end, balloting on trade union industrial action was extended to those doing work under contracts 'for services' by section 5 of the Act; and by section 10 the scope was extended of the proceedings by members against trade unions in which the Commissioner for the Rights of Trade Union Members could provide assistance, so as to include a wide range of actions to enforce the union rule-book. It is significant that, in pursuit of this third priority, the government was prepared to depart from its own general preference for minimizing the scope of legal regulation—especially in relation to the self-employed—and, in expanding the powers of the CROTUM, to breach its declared principle that 'the use of legal proceedings to prevent or restrain unlawful acts should be left to those directly affectly by such acts.'[230]

(a) The Re-emergence of Unofficial Action

Even before the Green Paper of March 1989 had given rise to a Bill, it had become manifest that, in a larger sense, the government could not press on with its drive against trade union power without sacrificing the coherence of legislative principles which they laid claim to. On the whole, the legislation of the 1980s had been fairly uniformly shaped by the idea that the main need was to curb the industrial power of trade unions and their leaders, as far as possible by using the leverage of a more 'realistic' work-force against that power. However, as the so-called 'summer of

---

[229] Cm. 655, para. 3.10.
[230] Ibid., para. 2.37. See K. Ewing, *Britain and the ILO* (1989), 31 ff.

discontent' of 1989[231] revealed, the recurring continuity between official trade union industrial action and unofficial industrial action suggested that repression of the former might simply generate more of the latter—the experience, particularly, of the London Underground and British Rail disputes pointed in this direction[232]—so the government began to diversify from this line of legislation.

Hence in the later part of 1989 the government abruptly identified the control of unofficial industrial action as a further leading priority. In October 1989, the Department of Employment produced a further Green Paper entitled *Unofficial Action and the Law*,[233] with very different aims and preoccupations from those which had shaped the earlier one. This Green Paper, considerably diverging from the very up-beat account of the industrial relations scene which had been given by its predecessor, presented the industrial relations context in terms almost laughably reminiscent of the discourse of the 1960s in its emphasis on unofficial industrial action as the major problem.[234] Indeed, the Green Paper explicitly relates itself to the 'unofficial action in the 1950s and 1960s [which] was serious enough to influence the decision to set up . . . the Donovan Commission'.[235]

One of the two main solutions proposed to the problem thus perceived, which were both implemented in the 1990 Act, indeed marked a return to one aspect of the Donovan debate; the other took off in a new direction along which employment law policy had not previously developed. The first of these two projects was that of extending trade union responsibility for unofficial industrial action; the second was that of reducing the protection from dismissal of employees taking unofficial industrial action.

The first of those projects involved a fundamental reformulation of the nature of the tort liability of trade unions. The experience of the Industrial Relations Act 1971 and of the Employment

---

[231] The events are usefully chronicled and analysed by Ian Beardwell in the *British Journal of Industrial Relations* Annual Review Article for 1989: see (1990) 28 BJIR 114 at 120–4: 'The Resurgence of Industrial Conflict'.

[232] For discussion of these disputes and of the case-law which they generated, see B. Simpson, 'The Summer of Discontent and the Law' (1989) 18 ILJ 234–41.

[233] Cm. 821.

[234] Cf. H. Carty, 'The Employment Act 1990: Still Fighting the Industrial Cold War' (1991) 20 ILJ 1.

[235] Cm. 821, para. 1.4.

Act 1982 had shown how, once the tort immunity of trade unions is removed, their liability has to be defined both positively and negatively. If the legislation does not provide this definition, the courts have to supply it. The positive definition consists in identifying those persons or committees whose actions or acquiescence may render the union liable for the industrial action in question; the negative definition consists in identifying what steps those persons or committees have to take if they are not to be identified with industrial action taken or threatened by members of the union. Section 15 of the 1982 Act imposed a fairly moderate version of trade union liability in which the two modes of definition were interlocked. The union was made liable for actions authorized or endorsed by 'responsible persons'. There are five categories of such persons (or groupings) extending from the president or general secretary through the principal executive committee down to employed officials or any committee to which an employed official regularly reports; but liability for the latter two categories is subject to repudiation by the former two categories.[236] The Green Paper argued that this pattern of definition left scope for connivance at unofficial industrial action which was in substance trade union industrial action.[237]

Section 6 of the 1990 Act therefore extended trade union liability in both dimensions of the definition. In the dimension of responsibility, it extended the category of responsible persons to include all officials whether employed or not—which brought shop stewards into the definition. It also extended the category of liability-creating committees to include, in effect, workplace multi-union shop stewards' committees, even if the shop stewards of the union in question were absent when the relevant decision of the committee was taken or even voted against it.[238] In the other dimension, the new section considerably tightened the requirements for repudiation, including with them an obligation for the union to do its best to give individual written notice of the repudiation to all members actually or potentially involved in the industrial action formally warning them of the lack of support they can expect from the union and of their consequential greater

---

[236] See above, p. 480.
[237] Cm. 821, paras. 2.7–2.9.
[238] This was the effect of s. 6(3) of the 1990 Act, adding new s. 15(3A)(b) to the 1982 Act. See now TULRECA s. 20(2), (3).

exposure to dismissal (a matter to which we shall return shortly). The stringency of these conditions amounts to an attempt to override the operational distinction (which the framers of the 1982 legislation had broadly respected) between trade union industrial action and unofficial industrial action by ensuring that unofficial action will normally amount to trade union industrial action for the purposes of establishing trade union liability in tort. The net result was that unions would first have to repudiate 'unofficial' industrial action in order to preserve their funds from liability for that action, and secondly, if they wished to adopt the industrial action in question, would have to hold a ballot before providing any encouragement to the members of the union in respect of that action. This was a fairly crippling set of operational requirements.

It is difficult to modify an elaborate regulatory structure at any one point without threatening its cohesion at a number of other points. The authors of the Green Paper realized that industrial action falling within the new larger ambit of trade union liability would in consequence be subject to the balloting requirements of part II of the Trade Union Act 1984.[239] They perhaps did not fully contemplate the difficulty of bringing unofficial industrial action within institutional mechanisms designed to test the very question which their own legislation was largely pre-empting, namely whether the unofficial action should be supported as trade union official action. During the passage of the Bill through Parliament, and apparently prompted by observation of the course of an industrial dispute at the Ford Motor Company of Great Britain, the government brought forward amendments eventually enacted as sections 7 and 8[240] of the 1990 Act which sought to respond to this difficulty. The response consisted in imposing stricter conditions than before to define the circumstances in which trade union industrial action would count as having the support of a ballot. These stricter conditions sought to address the new relationship between official and unofficial action by requiring that the trade union must not have called, authorized, or endorsed the action before the ballot, and that the ballot must confine the authority to call the action to a specified person. By

---

[239] Cm. 821, para. 2.11.
[240] Now TULRECA s. 237.

altering the context in which it operates, section 7 accorded a much harsher significance to the rule that the action must be called within four weeks of the ballot, albeit that section 8 provided a new procedure for stopping time from running against the four-week limit during the currency of a court order or undertaking to a court.[241] It rather looked as if the logic of coercing all industrial action into the framework of official industrial action had come to prevail over the earlier, and, in industrial relations terms, rather different priority of ensuring that moderate opinion in the rank-and-file of trade unions was fully expressed in a ballot before industrial action was identified as trade union official action.

(b) Dismissal of Unofficial Strikers

That first project, even if pressed to fairly extreme lengths, can be seen as lying within a range of options which had been under exploration since the time of the Donovan Commission. Indeed, it was not the first time that policy-makers had found those different patterns of control of industrial action hard to reconcile fully with each other. The second project, that of exposing those taking unofficial action to selective dismissal, lay outside any range of options which had been seriously considered before the late 1980s. Ever since unfair dismissal legislation was introduced in 1971, it had been sought on the one hand to exclude issues of the merits of industrial action from industrial tribunals by treating dismissals of a whole body of strikers as non-justiciable under the law of unfair dismissal while on the other hand leaving within jurisdiction the selective dismissal of strikers, at least where the selection was on the ground of trade union membership or activity.[242] And it is pretty clear that the preparedness in 1975 to leave even non-selective dismissals of strikers outside unfair dismissal jurisdiction was based on the premiss that trade unions would almost invariably be able to guarantee that this theoretical employers' sanction was not in practice used.

---

[241] For explanation of the details of this provision, and of its origins in the 1989 Docks Dispute, see H. Carty, 'The Employment Act 1990: Still Fighting the Industrial Cold War' (1991) 20 ILJ 1 at 11–12.

[242] The latter restriction prevailed from 1971 to 1975. The 1975 provision was embodied in s. 62 of the Employment Protection (Consolidation) Act 1978. See above, p. 375.

By 1982, the government must have contemplated a somewhat more active use of the sanction of non-selective dismissal, for, as we have seen, they promoted legislation to enable employers to dismiss those currently taking industrial action without having to dismiss all those who had at any stage participated in the industrial action concerned.[243] This, however, was to do no more than to abrogate a rather extreme version of the principle of non-selectivity, rather than to encroach fundamentally upon that principle. When section 9 of the 1990 Act introduced the proposition that,

S. 62A.(1) An employee has no right to complain of unfair dismissal if at the time of dismissal he was taking part in an unofficial strike or other unofficial industrial action,[244]

a truly new direction was being taken in labour law. The new Section 62A, taken as a whole, exposed those participating in industrial action to selective dismissal unless they belonged to a union which had authorized or endorsed the industrial action in question and had not repudiated it by the time of the dismissal.[245] By 1990 it was, moreover, merely routine that the few remaining statutory immunities available for organizing industrial action should be withdrawn from action one of the reasons for which is the fact or belief that an employer has carried out dismissals of which those dismissed have no right to complain by virtue of that new provision of Section 62A.[246]

That such a provision should scarcely[247] attract surprise indicates the depth of the legal transformation which had been cumulatively wrought in the law of industrial conflict since 1979. Nor, as we shall see, did the government regard that transformation as necessarily being complete, or the 1990 Act as necessarily the last such legislation they would wish to promote. In the next and final section of this chapter, we shall nevertheless attempt to reach some overall conclusions about the significance of the

---

[243] See above, p. 482.
[244] Now TULRECA s. 237.
[245] See H. Carty, 'The Employment Act 1990', at 10.
[246] S. 9(2) of the 1990 Act, now TULRECA s. 223.
[247] Foremost in drawing attention to the importance of these provisions is ch. 4 of K. Ewing's study, *The Right to Strike* (Oxford, 1991): 'Section 62 of the EPCA, even without the 1982 and 1990 amendmends, is a truly remarkable measure' (p. 62).

measures which had been taken in this field between 1980 and 1990.

9.9. REDUCING TRADE UNION POWER: ATTEMPTS AT EVALUATION

Considerable risks are involved in trying to assess the over-all significance of the measures of 1979 to 1990 at such close quarters. It must be fairly rare for the immediate assessment of a programme of legislation to appear valid some years later. Never-theless, enough material exists at least to identify some relevant criteria or methods of evaluation, and to indicate some tentative conclusions from their short-term application.

The government itself produced a useful starting-point for this exercise in July 1991 by producing a Green Paper, entitled *Industrial Relations in the 1990s*,[248] whose main purpose was to set out proposals for further reform of industrial relations and trade union law, but which offered an analysis of the reforms of the 1980s as a starting-point for those further proposals.[249] The Green Paper proposals indicated that in the view of the govern-ment, the process of reform undertaken in the 1980s was not complete, and that certain debates which had been relatively dormant in the 1980s still deserved to be actively pursued: thus, proposals were advanced, *inter alia*, to promote the right of mem-bers of the general public to seek the protection of the civil law to prevent unlawful industrial action affecting public services,[250] and to reverse the statutory presumption that collective agree-ments are not legally enforceable between their parties.[251] The important point, however, for our present purpose, is that the Green Paper, while asserting the need for further reform, nevertheless claimed that enormous improvements in industrial relations had occurred in the 1980s, and that the measures dis-

---

[248] Department of Employment Green Paper, *Industrial Relations in the 1990s: Proposals for Further Reform of Industrial Relations and Trade Union Law*, Cm. 1602 (July 1991).

[249] The analysis is mainly contained in Cm. 1602, ch. 1. 'Industrial Relations in the 1980s: The Achievement of Reform'.

[250] Cm. 1602, ch. 4.

[251] Ibid., ch. 8 not in the event proceeded with in the 1992 Bill.

cussed in this chapter had been very major contributors to those improvements.[252]

Thus the Green Paper claimed that in the 1980s there had been a dramatic reduction in strikes,[253] the elimination of many restrictive practices and virtual disappearance of abuses of industrial power such as the flying picket,[254] and a consequential improvement of Britain's industrial reputation among potential inward investors.[255] The legislation of the 1980s was asserted to have contributed to these improvements by 'providing practical remedies and effective protection against real problems and abuses', thus producing a general acceptance 'both by employers and by employees that the law has a necessary and legitimate role to play in protecting businesses, jobs, the individual and the community as a whole against the abuse of industrial power.'[256] The argument of this section will be that the Green Paper advances an essentially subjective analysis, derived from the perspective of convinced protagonists of the very policies which it claims to evaluate; the conclusions so reached may be wholly or largely correct, but more objective methods of evaluation can be devised, and can be usefully applied to the experience of the 1980s. We begin that attempt by summarizing the main findings of this chapter about the way the legislation developed during that period.

In the early years of the decade, and to some extent throughout, the main preoccupation of the Government in this field of legislative activity was to find ways of reducing trade union power while avoiding what they perceived as the mistakes—the fatal mistakes—of the Industrial Relations Act 1971. The error they chiefly wished to avoid was that of making the operation of the legal framework dependant upon, or even capable of bringing about, a continuing government involvement in its enforcement. For example, an immediate priority in 1979 was to secure control over mass picketing and secondary picketing. Yet it was quickly decided that it would be counter-productive to seek to achieve this by amendment of the criminal law, because of the tensions

---

[252] Ibid., ch. 1.
[253] Ibid., para 1.6.
[254] Ibid., para. 1.7.
[255] Ibid., para. 1.8.
[256] Ibid., para. 1.19.

this would produce about the role of the police. Post-1979 governments, moreover, for similar reasons felt a reluctance to legislate
directly against industrial action in essential service occupations.
From time to time flirting with the idea of such legislation
because of its apparent popularity, they would draw back from it
because it would visibly involve them in deciding whether to take
executive steps to control each situation of industrial action in
essential service industries.

There were positive as well as negative reasons for minimizing
the role of the government in implementing a reduction of trade
union power. The government perceived after 1979 that it was
necessary to get management to think in terms of using the
law against trade union power, something that the 1971 Act
had signally failed to achieve, especially in relation to large and
mainstream employers. At least in the early 1980s, as Simon
Auerbach had demonstrated, there was in this respect a clear
divergence between the government's aspirations and those of
many employers and their associations, who were decidedly
reluctant to be sent forth as champions[257] and would, for instance,
have preferred 'automatic' sanctions against unlawful industrial
action.

In the early 1980s, the government's intuition was that the best
way to achieve these positive and negative objectives was to
subject the trade unions to the ordinary law of the land, in the
form of the common law of economic torts. This avoided the
risks which experience under the Industrial Relations Act had
shown to be attached to special labour courts implementing
special labour laws. The process of bringing the common law into
play could be represented as one of de-regulation in so far as it
swept away a complex superstructure of statutory trade dispute
immunities, and one of abolishing unjustifiable privileges when it
involved depriving trade unions of their general immunity from
liability for economic torts.

However, even in the early 1980s, the legislation about industrial
conflict and trade union power never quite fitted into this simple
analysis. There was a preoccupation with controlling the closed
shop which was in part a libertarian crusade, relevant but somewhat tangential to the process of redressing the balance of power

[257] Auerbach, *Legislating for Conflict*, 65–6.

between trade unions and employers. Controlling the closed shop required complex legislation; it could not be achieved by simply increasing the availability of common law remedies. Moreover, even in the area of trade dispute law itself, the rolling back of trade dispute immunities could not be accomplished without the formulation of intricate statute law, especially so far as secondary action was concerned, where James Prior as Secretary of State for Employment was politically committed to a highly delicate compromise between liability and immunity which produced the unusually tangled provisions of section 17 of the 1980 Act.

Partly because of this great complexity, the legislation of 1980 and 1982 did not in itself seem to give employers a clear lead towards an abandonment of their ingrained habit of not normally involving the courts in their industrial disputes. The government's response to this represented a gradual shift away from the objectives of a simple common-law-based structure in which employers would enforce the law against trade unions. From 1984 onwards, the legislation depended on a structure which admittedly still operated by limiting trade dispute immunities in order to create common law liabilities, but which did so according to principles of internal trade union democracy and the necessity for balloted support for industrial action which were purely statutory and not continuous with any common law principles.

Moreover, although this shift towards statutory requirements for internal union democracy did reinforce and help to develop employers' willingness to invoke legal remedies, the government came to realize—especially in the light of the experience of the Miners' dispute of 1984 to 1985—that trade union members were important agents in enforcing these requirements against their unions. So in 1988 a series of special statutory causes of action were created to enable trade union members to do that; and the involvement of the government in the enforcement process was increased by the creation of a Commissioner for the Rights of Trade Union Members with the function of assisting that enforcement process.

All these trends towards an elaborate and autonomous statutory body of industrial conflict law were intensified in the 1990 Act. That Act also sought to achieve control over unofficial industrial action, and to make trade unions themselves exert that control, thus further increasing the complexity of the whole structure. The whole programme began to resemble the Industrial Relations Act 1971 in the sense that it began to encounter the problems of comprehensiveness, though it was still the case that the government had firmly eschewed a separate labour court, and had not accorded the Commissioner for the Rights of Trade Union Members the central role assigned to the Registrar of Trade Unions under the 1971 Act.

The major remaining question, to which we must now return, is what impact all these measures actually had in practice. We have been primarily concerned with the development of legislative policy rather than with the actual impact of these measures on industrial relations practice. As labour law became more and more politicized—really from 1968 onwards—so the assessment of its impact also became more and more a matter of political rather than empirical perception. One consequence of that, in the 1980s, was that it became increasingly difficult to decide whether proposals for legislation were shaped by ideological considerations or by pragmatic ones. Lord Wedderburn has argued that ideological considerations were to the forefront—that the realizing of the ideals of Hayek was the central determinant.[258] Auerbach has written a history of the industrial conflict legislation of the 1980s which asserts the primacy of short-term practical considerations—the political need to respond to a particular major industrial dispute or an intervention on behalf of small employers feeling under-represented in associations of large employers. These views depend in part on the particular aspects of the legislative programme on which they are concentrated. We have argued in this chapter that the measures against the closed shop have been more ideologically driven while the measures aimed directly at trade union (and now unofficial) industrial action have been more opportunistically devised. This serves to explain why the development of legislative policy cannot be directly related to an assessment of the impact of the legislation itself—why neither can be derived from the other. It still evades the questions of what impact the legislation in fact had, either in terms of how much it was invoked or, more significantly, in terms of its indirect impact on the behaviour of employers, trade unions, and workers generally.

[258] Lord Wedderburn, 'Freedom of Association and Philosophies of Labour Law' (1988) 17 ILJ 1.

As we saw earlier, the Green Paper of July 1991 asserted that there were clear answers to those questions, and that they were answers which testified to the success of the legislative measures. Essentially, it was felt to be clear that the legislation had been successful in persuading employers and dissident trade union members to consider invoking trade dispute law where previously they would have regarded it as unthinkable to do so. The government's gamble upon the possibility of stimulating the impulse to self-help was seen to have succeeded in large measure, and was seen to have brought about a basic improvement in the functioning of industrial relations, in the sense of a maximizing of efficiency, productivity, and competitiveness.

This account of the impact of the measures discussed in the present chapter is, however, open to a double critique. The first question posed by that critique is whether the Green Paper evaluation correctly identified the nature and extent of changes in patterns of behaviour in the field of industrial relations and in the use of legal processes in industrial relations—and in particular the permanence or transience, the depth or superficiality of apparent changes in patterns of behaviour. That is the critique in terms of identification. The second question is whether the Green Paper evaluation sufficiently addressed the assumptions about causation which are made when the legislative changes are credited with bringing about changes in behaviour. That is the critique in terms of attribution. Some useful arguments have been advanced, particularly from the discipline of industrial relations, which enable this double critique to be developed somewhat further.

If one starts with the first of the two critiques, that relating to identification of the extent and dimensions of changes in industrial relations behaviour, it is useful to distinguish between trade union and worker behaviour on the one hand and management behaviour on the other—something which the Green Paper analysis on the whole fails to do when it asserts very generalized 'improvements in industrial relations'. More specific analyses, which single out some particular aspect of the behaviour of the parties to industrial relations, tend to cast doubt on the extent, and above all on the permanence, of changes in behaviour. Thus, particular empirical studies concentrating on trade union behaviour have suggested the following conclusions: firstly, that legislation requiring ballots failed to undermine collective decision-making within unions to the extent that it was expected to do;[259] secondly, that the imposition of changes on trade union decision-making procedures had less effect on outcomes than might be expected;[260] and thirdly, (perhaps more tangentially) that trade unions were becoming more popular in public opinion when they might have been expected to become less so.[261]

If one asks equally specific questions about changes in the behaviour of management, commentaries in the fields of industrial relations and industrial politics raise similar doubts as to whether there were changes in behaviour which were more than superficial or transient. John MacInnes, writing in 1987, argued that it was important to distinguish between 'espoused' or formal and 'operational' or informal policies of management, and that there was little evidence of basic change at the more significant operational level:

Thus beyond the espoused managerial strategy of total prerogative over work organisation has lain the operational policy of admitting limits to it in practice, and in effect submitting the organisation of work to a process of low trust bargaining, mostly local and informal, about what will be acceptable to both sides.[262]

MacInnes was looking at the period down to 1986; surveying the whole of the 1980s, Middlemas asserted rather greater changes in managerial behaviour, in particular that 'legalism and formalism intruded, and institutional modes of behaviour shaped themselves to adversarial court proceedings, whether or not court action ensued'.[263] However, Middlemas accurately captures the essentially reactive rather than proactive character of the

[259] R. Martin et al., 'The Decollectivisation of Trade Unions? Ballots and Collective Bargaining in the 1980s' (1991) 22 Industrial Relations Journal 199–208.

[260] W. Brown and S. Wadwhani, 'The Economic Effects of Industrial Relations Legislation since 1979' (CLARE Group Paper, 1989).

[261] P. K. Edwards and G. Sayers Bain, 'Why are Unions Becoming More Popular? Trade Unions and Public Opinion in Britain' (1988) 26 BJIR 311–26. The argument is elaborated by D. Marsh, 'Public Opinion, Trade Unions and Mrs Thatcher' (1990) 28 BJIR 57 in a way which challenges the explanation advanced by Edwards and Bain, but, if anything, supports its citation in the present context.

[262] J. MacInnes, Thatcherism at Work (Milton Keynes, 1987), 132.

[263] K. Middlemas, Power, Competition and the State, iii, The End of the Post-war Era: Britain since 1974 (London, 1991), 334.

behaviour of most managers, in a way that suggests that their responses would turn out to be ephemeral in the face of different policy directions set by government.[264]

If we turn to the second critique of the Green Paper, which concerns attributability, we find even greater reason to doubt the Green Paper analysis which, as we saw earlier, while not claiming the 'improvements in industrial relations' of the 1980s as solely due to industrial relations legislation, nevertheless takes a markedly optimistic view of its causative impact. We saw in an earlier section that the real reduction in the political power of trade unions was scarcely attributable to the main legislative attack upon it in part III of the Trade Union Act 1984. The position so far as trade union industrial power is concerned is somewhat more complex; there is, for instance, an unresolved debate about the attributability of the fall in trade union density (that is, the rate of membership in the workforce) in the 1980s to industrial relations legislation.[265] However, powerful and persuasive cases have been developed both by those who welcome the changes of the 1980s, and by those who are sceptical about their value, to the effect that those changes (for example in industrial dispute behaviour) are vastly more attributable to economic conditions, especially to increased unemployment and the decline in the absolute and relative importance of manufacturing industry, than to the impact of industrial relations legislation.[266]

The use of that double critique enables us to attempt an overall

---

[264] 'Management collectively avoided going to court, letting bold individual entrepreneurs take the initiative as Eddie Shah did against the NGA in 1984, but they did not shun the results. The CBI followed the new rules of engagement whether these were set by court decisions or by unilateral action by entrepreneurs such as Rupert Murdoch and Sir Jeffrey Sterling, Chairman of P.&O. Ferries, just as peak organizations were doing in the rest of Europe' (Middlemas, *Power, Competition and the State*, iiii. 334). For discussion of the P & O Dispute and the use of the law in that dispute, see S. Auerbach, 'Injunction Procedure in the Seafarers' Dispute' (1988) 17 ILJ 227.

[265] Contrast R. Freeman and J. Pelletier, who argue for very high attributability, 'The Impact of Industrial Relations Legislation on British Union Density' (1990) 28 BJIR 141–64, with R. Disney, who argues for negligible attributability, 'Explanations of the Decline in Trade Union Density in Britain: An Appraisal', ibid. 165–77.

[266] See, e.g. D. Metcalf, 'Water Notes Dry Up: The Impact of the Donovan Reform Proposals and Thatcherism at Work on Labour Productivity in British Manufacturing Industry' (1989) 27 BJIR 1–32; and, more generally, Brown and Wadwhani, 'The Economic Effects of Industrial Relations Legislation'.

assessment of the legislation discussed in this chapter; it is an assessment which ends up by relating the foregoing discussion to developments in the labour market, and to the government's aims to restructure the labour market. On the whole, we have tended to argue in this chapter that the rhetoric of the policy-making process sped ahead of the realities of industrial society, but it did not lose contact with those realities in the way that the Industrial Relations Act 1971 turned out to have done. To that extent, the legislation directed at reducing trade union power had a greater gradual and cumulative impact than earlier attempts had done, especially in transforming perceptions of the goals which industrial conflict law might properly pursue and means which might be used to achieve them. That widespread change in people's outlook upon trade dispute and trade union law did not necessarily have a clear transforming effect upon industrial society or industrial relations themselves.

However—and this is a crucial point—we have seen that the extent of change and the determinants of change in industrial society and industrial relations cannot be understood simply in terms of changes in trade dispute and trade union law. We have referred to the argument that changes in the underlying economic conditions were important, and we began this chapter by show-ing the close interelationship between the monetarist economic policies of the government, particularly in the early 1980s, and their aims of reducing trade union power. Moreover, the government's programme of labour legislation and employment measures in the 1980s involved, in aspiration at least, a restructur-ing of the labour market in ways not directly connected with the reduction of trade union power. Those other aspects of the labour legislation and government employment policy of the 1980s are considered in the next chapter; the final assessment of the impact of the legislation discussed in this chapter is to an important extent dependent on what is said there.

10

RESTRUCTURING THE LABOUR ECONOMY, 1979–1990

10.1. INTRODUCTION: FROM MONETRIASM TO THE MARKET ECONOMY IN LABOUR LAW

In the previous chapter, we described the doctrine of Monetarism as developed and practised by post-1979 Conservative governments, and showed how that doctrine was seen to require a transformation of labour law towards the function of restricting trade union power, particularly industrial power. At various stages in the description of that development, we made the point, deferring it for later discussion, that the political doctrine of those governments certainly did not assert that the reduction of trade union power was the sole function of labour law. In this chapter, we shall argue that labour law and employment policy were also directed towards an increasingly ambitious restructuring of a number of central features of the labour economy—a restructuring which gradually focused upon the notion of a market economy as the ideal for industrial society. Throughout the 1980s, legislation aimed at restricting trade union power was accompanied by legislation aimed at restructuring the labour market, though they were developed at varying levels of intensity at different points in the decade. In this introductory section, we consider the nature of the economic policy which underlay these attempts to restructure not only the labour market but also industrial society itself.

(a) The Economic Background

As we saw at the beginning of the previous chapter, there is considerable scope for debate about the nature and significance of the Monetarism of the post-1979 governments.[1] As the doctrinal basis of 1980s governmental economic policy, it seemed to diverge from the pure theory of Monetarism, because it was attempting to pursue or reconcile a wider range of policy objectives, and was using a more complex set of techniques, than the pure theory would allow for.[2] Thus if the pure theory concentrates wholly or primarily on the control of inflation, governmental policy in the 1980s tended to elevate the reducing of public expenditure (expressed as the Public Sector Borrowing Requirement) to a separate policy goal rather than seeing it as simply a means to the end of controlling inflation. And if the pure theory envisages control of money supply as the chief or sole policy instrument, governmental policy (as defined in the Medium-Term Financial Strategy) relied much more on combining monetary with fiscal regulators of the economy.

From this starting-point, which was in itself a complex one, post-1979 economic policy was modified and compromised by a whole series of political considerations and political expedients (including electoral tactics).[3] Strict Monetarism, and even the more loosely defined MTFS, gradually ceased to be practicable in the face of the international mobility of capital which the government was committed to promote or sustain. Although, as we shall see in more detail later, the government rejected the pre-1979 commitment to full employment, it nevertheless had to respond to rising unemployment in the early to mid-1980s—especially youth unemployment—more extensively than strict Monetarism might allow or than it had itself originally hoped. The control of public expenditure was less stringent in the mid-1980s than in the early 1980s, and inflation, including wage inflation, was notoriously allowed to rise faster in the later 1980s. If political expediency led to those relaxations of Monetarism, political rather than narrowly economic considerations also sometimes

---

[1] The most accessible discussion is probably ch. 1 of D. Robinson's *Monetarism and the Labour Market* (Oxford, 1986), 'What is Monetarism?'

[2] For two excellent overviews, see chs. 2 and 4 of G. Maynard, *The Economy under Mrs. Thatcher* (Oxford, 1988) and chs. 1, 2, and 8 of C. Johnson, *The Economy under Mrs. Thatcher, 1979–1990* (London, 1991).

[3] This argument is stressed in chs. 1 and 2 of P. Riddell, *The Thatcher Era And its Legacy* (Oxford, 1991); see esp. p. 5: '[M]any of the most important new policies have been the result of the failures of initial policies and in response to circumstances.'

militated against the observance of monetarist principles—for example, in making the government profoundly reluctant to join or accept the full rigours of the European Monetary System and Exchange Rate Mechanism.

Throughout these various policy shifts around the Monetarism of the 1980s, certain significant continuities nonetheless present themselves. The governments of the 1980s fairly consistently wished to avoid Keynesian demand management—they did not wish to increase demand in the economy in order to reduce unemployment. They preferred, therefore, to develop micro-economic policies rather than macro-economic policies; they were thus committed to operating on the supply side of the economy, that is to say (broadly speaking) to controlling inflation in the costs of production. Moreover, as we shall see in greater detail towards the end of this chapter, they wished to do that while avoiding engaging in formal incomes policy as practised (disastrously in their view) in the late 1960s and 1970s.

The important thing, from our present perspective, is that the governments of the 1980s understood, and indeed proclaimed, that supply-side control, espcially if it was to avoid formal incomes policy, had to involve some degree of actual restructuring of the labour economy. Thus, as we saw in the last chapter, they consistently asserted the need to reduce the industrial power of trade unions. But they also accepted, both at the rhetorical and at the practical level, the necessity for other sorts of restructuring. This was expressed, for example, in policies of 'de-regulation', in particular, policies for alleviating the impact of labour legislation upon the individual employment relationship. Such policies came to be seen as part of a process of 'de-rigidification', whereby rigidities of all sorts would be removed from the labour economy— especially rigidities arising out of collective bargaining procedures and patterns. Eventually, these policies in turn would be conceived of and presented in terms of a grand design of turning the labour economy into an enterprise or *market* economy. The remainder of this section is devoted to describing those three themes, of de-regulation, de-rigidification, and the market economy, in greater detail.

(b) De-regulation and De-rigidification

We should begin by stating what we understand by the distinction between de-regulation and de-rigidification. By de-regulation we mean the reduction of the impact of state-generated regulation upon the employment relationship and the labour market. Employment legislation is the major but not the only source of such regulation. By de-rigidification, on the other hand, we mean the reduction of all sorts of socially generated structural constraints upon the labour market and the employment relationship, of which collective bargaining is an important but far from the only example. It would be misleading to present this as an entirely mutually exclusive pair of categories, or, moreover, to seek to assign any given measure or intervention wholly to one or other of them. Public sector collective bargaining directed by a Whitley Council would be an illustration of a form of intervention which is ambivalent between the two categories. Nevertheless, the distinction is a valuable one in helping to refine our understanding of policy developments in the 1980s, not least because it points up the way in which the ambitions of 1980s governments on the one hand included, but on the other hand extend beyond, the de-regulatory aim of retrenching upon the legislative advances of the 1960s and (more particularly perhaps) the 1970s. The extension beyond that aim was towards a de-rigidificatory restructuring of the labour market which would extend to the fundamental collective structures of post-war industrial society.

De-regulation of the individual employment relationship, in the sense of reducing the impact of employment protection legislation, was a prominent objective of post-1979 governments right from the beginning; as we shall see, one of Mr Prior's first actions as Secretary of State for Employment in 1979 was to accomplish as much of this kind of de-regulation as could be achieved by powers of delegated legislation. From 1985 onwards a series of White Papers was devoted to writing one aspect of the past history of the government, and setting out a prospectus for the future, in terms of de-regulation of business activity on a large number of fronts, with employment as one of the most important of them. The co-ordinating initiative was first proclaimed in a Report in March 1985 by the Department of Trade and Industry under Mr Tebbit.[4] This Report identified options for de-regulatory action in ten priority areas, of which three

---

[4] *Burdens on Business: Report of a Scrutiny of Administrative and Legislative Requirements.*

directly concerned employment. They were statutory sick pay, terms and conditions of employment, and health and safety at work. Within the second of these areas, the particular items singled out for attention were the Unfair Dismissal legislation and the Wages Councils legislation.[5] We shall see that these were the areas of employment legislation which were the most directly affected by the de-regulation initiative.

The themes of *Burdens on Business* were taken up and pursued by Lord Young at the stage when he was Minister without Portfolio (but effectively responsible for stimulating moves towards an 'enterprise economy'). He published a White Paper entitled *Lifting the Burden* in July 1985[6] which pursued the de-regulation initiative and introduced proposals to institutionalize the de-regulation process within government departments and at Cabinet Office level. In May 1986, by now Secretary of State for Employment, Lord Young published another White Paper, entitled *Building Businesses . . . not Barriers*,[7] which took stock of the progress of de-regulation, especially but by no means solely in the employment sphere, and set out a further programme of de-regulatory action. It was of some significance that the central task force for carrying out the de-regulation programme throughout the whole range of government departments, called the Enterprise and Deregulation Unit, was now located in the Department of Employment itself,[8] and that in the Preamble to this White Paper in which the objectives of the Department of Employment were identified, there was included the aim to 'help businesses to grow and jobs to multiply by cutting "red tape"'. We shall see that the de-regulatory activity in the area of labour law was extensive and significant, and we shall look at a number of measures in those terms.

However, as we have already indicated, the government's policies and measures in relation to the labour market were not presented entirely in terms of de-regulation, and cannot be understood solely in terms of de-regulation. As time went on, a more openly interventionist presentation of the government's policies and measures within this area was offered. Thus,

---

[5] Ibid., s. 4.3.
[6] Cmnd. 9751.
[7] Cmnd. 9794.
[8] Ibid., para. 1.19.

Mr Tom King, by way of conclusion of his period of office as Secretary of State for Employment, presented a White Paper,[9] in March 1985, which well exemplifies a more underlyingly significant set of policies. Entitled *Employment, the Challenge for the Nation*, it attempted to establish an equivalence between the policies of the government and the aims and policies identified in the 1944 White Paper on *Employment Policy*[10] which, as we have seen, ushered in the post-war era of full employment.

The specific sense in which the 1985 White Paper claimed that the government was revalidating the 1944 White Paper was as follows. The claim was that the government was maintaining the very balance that the 1944 White Paper stipulated, by, on the one hand, 'directing Government policy to bringing about conditions favourable to the maintenance of a high level of employment', but, on the other hand, recognizing, as the 1944 White Paper enjoined, that the success of such a policy direction depended primarily not on government intervention nor on legislation but on the efforts of the community in general and on the pursuit of industrial efficiency by employers and workers.[11] This way of legitimating the policies of 1985 by reference to those of 1944 conceals the fact that everything depends upon the sense in which government policy is 'directed to bringing about conditions favourable to the maintenance of a high level of employment' and to 'helping to set the framework for the nation's effort'. In the 1985 White Paper, that policy direction was defined in terms of de-rigidifying the labour market. This needs some illustration.

The 1985 White Paper at one point sums itself up in these terms:

The key contribution of Government in a free society is to do all it can to create a climate in which enterprise can flourish, above all by removing obstacles to the working of markets, especially the labour market.[12]

This would amount to no more than de-regulation of the labour market, as long as the removing of obstacles was envisaged as the sole, rather than just the chief, means of creating the desired climate, and if the obstacles were viewed as consisting entirely of

[9] Cmnd. 9474.
[10] Cmd. 6527. See above, ch. 2.3.
[11] Cmnd. 9751, para. 1.5.
[12] Ibid., para. 1.4.

over-elaborate legislation or administrative measures. In fact, the promotion of enterprise was envisaged in rather more positive terms, and in particular it was thought necessary to free the labour market of rigidities which were not imposed entirely by legislation but rather by wider behavioural and attitudinal constraints. This is made clear, for instance, at the passage in the White Paper which enumerates the government action taken since 1979 'to lay a firm foundation for lasting recovery' in labour market policy.[13] The action which is here specified consists only partly of de-regulation; it also includes a wider category of de-rigidification; thus: (1) 'providing a surer and better balanced framework of law for responsible and constructive industrial relations'. This refers to the measures for restricting the industrial power of trade unions, which was regarded as a great rigidity in the labour market.

Some of the remaining heads were also more in the nature of de-rigidification than of de-regulation, thus:

(4) stimulating the reform of our education and training systems to meet the needs of a competitive modern economy;
(5) financing major new efforts in training for young people and adults;
(6) programmes which give unemployed people not just short-term help but better chances of getting jobs afterwards;
(7) modernizing the information and support services for those seeking work.

Few could quarrel with these latter aims; the important thing is to ascertain the larger goals to which they were directed. This would become easier when the next employment White Paper appeared in 1988.

By December 1988, when Norman Fowler (another in the long list of Secretaries of State for Employment to serve in Mrs Thatcher's governments) issued his employment White Paper,[14] both the programme and the rhetoric had become more ambitious—and, in their way, more sophisticated. This was typical of the radical and ideological phase which followed the Conservative election victory of 1987. In this White Paper,

---

[13] Ibid., para. 4.4.
[14] *Employment for the 1990s*, Cm. 540 (Dec. 1988).

the government's whole past and future labour law and labour market policies were seen as tending towards the promotion of employment. This was seen as a vast exercise in removing 'barriers to employment'—a phrase heavily charged with the values of de-regulation and de-rigidification. The labour law measures which we considered in the last chapter (down to and including the Employment Act 1988) were claimed as major successes in this direction, which had broken through the barrier of poor industrial relations.[15] So also were a number of measures which we shall consider in the course of this chapter, which were directed against the 'barrier to jobs' created by 'excessive pay increases and inflexible pay arrangements'.[16] This, as we shall see, involved a general attack upon collective bargaining, especially industrywide bargaining and comparability bargaining.[17] It also involved an attack on legislation supporting collective bargaining or directly maintaining labour standards; thus, having radically curtailed the powers of Wages Councils by the Wages Act 1986, the government now questioned whether there should be any future at all for them.[18]

Superficially, the final employment White Paper of the 1980s, entitled *Employment for the 1990s*, seemed to continue in the same vein; two further 'barriers to employment' are identified, namely the inadequacy of existing training arrangements[19] and 'the attitudes of employers to recruiting unemployed people and the attitudes of unemployed people to finding work'.[20] However, the proposals made by the White Paper to surmount those barriers show in what directions, and to what lengths, the culture of enterprise was being refined by the policy-makers of the Department of Employment. The 'attitudes to employment' which the White Paper wishes to modify turn out to consist almost entirely in what is perceived as the failure of the unemployed to seek work as actively as they should.[21] This failure, for which no specific evidence was cited,[22] is seen to justify a

---

[15] See ibid., paras. 2.5–2.10.
[16] Ibid., para. 3.1.
[17] See e.g. ibid., para. 3.5.
[18] Ibid., para. 3.16–3.17.
[19] Ibid., ch. 4, *passim*.
[20] Ibid., para. 7.1.
[21] Ibid., para. 7.6–7.13.
[22] Ibid., para. 7.7 is a blatant example of unsupported assertions.

proposal, which we shall see was implemented in 1989, to make unemployment benefit conditional upon the claimant's actively seeking work.[23] This, as we shall also see, would return the law of unemployment benefit to its condition during an illiberal phase in the Great Depression of the 1930s. So the ostensibly positive and forward-looking rhetoric of de-rigidification and employment growth had come to support a specifically retrogressive approach to social legislation associated with the labour market. In a wider sense, this explains the intensifying conflict between the government's employment policies and the social policies of the European Community, which we shall consider in detail in the course of this chapter.

It was, however, the training proposals in the White Paper which displayed most clearly the radical direction in which governmental strategies for de-rigidification of the labour market were now tending. We shall look later in this chapter at the details of the plan for transfer of responsibility for training to Training and Enterprise Councils, the local groupings led by employers which the Government proposed first to create and then to entrust with its own functions of providing and co-ordinating training for employment. This plan, and the underlying rationale for it, indicate the crucial features of late-1980s radical de-rigidification. The essence of that consisted in maximizing the freedom of action of private sector employers, and their control over the labour market. This freedom and this control would be achieved at the expense of, and over against, not only the rigidities imposed by trade unions, by collective bargaining, by labour standards legislation, and by social legislation, but also the centralized powers and responsibilities of the government of the state itself, whether as employer or as the direct bearer of political, economic, and social functions in relation to the labour market. That is why an understanding of the development of employment and training policy is central to an understanding of the government's restructuring of the labour market during the 1980s; and it is also why a discussion of training arrangements leads on to a consideration of the government's strategies for the public employment sector, and hence to the whole relationship between governmental labour market policies and policies for

[23] Ibid., para. 7.18. See below, p. 612.

controlling inflation—a sequence therefore followed in the later part of this chapter.

We shall thus be concerned in the course of the present chapter to examine in detail the various measures of de-rigidification of the labour market to which the White Papers refer, though first we should locate those measures within a broader analysis of the policies of the post-1979 governments. The analysis of post-1979 labour law measures in terms of de-rigidification of the labour market is a useful one in showing the continuity between many of those measures (though be it noted that we do not seek to coerce all the measures into that framework—a point to which we return shortly). It is an analysis which transcends the distinction between collective and individual labour law—for instance, by indicating that altering the law relating to trade disputes and the closed shop came to be regarded as part of a process of de-rigidification and to that extent on an equal footing with partial repeal of employment protection legislation. It is also an analysis which emphasizes the Government's aim of creating a reformed labour market in which labour would be traded on a more flexible and a more mobile basis and—let us not mince our words—more cheaply; for many of the rigidities which the government wished to challenge were whose which tended to maintain the price of labour at levels which the government increasingly stigmatized as artificially high and thus in their view inhibitive of demand.

(c) *The Enterprise Economy*

This last reflection, about the nature of the de-rigidified labour market which the post-1979 governments sought to bring about, leads on to a further analysis of the ideology which underlay this process of de-rigidification of the labour market. This ideology was hinted at in both the de-regulation White Papers and the employment White Papers which we have looked at, when they refer to the need to create a labour economy characterized by enterprise, or in which enterprise can flourish. This ideology of enterprise had obvious connotations of *laissez-faire* and free trade, and reflects an underlying commercialism towards the labour economy. It was closely related, as we have seen, to the philosophy of Monetarism that the government had espoused in the early 1980s. The transition from early 1980s Monetarism to the more ambitious policies of the later 1980s can be clearly observed in Nigel Lawson's Budget Statement of March 1985.[24] In a context in which formal incomes policy had been eschewed by the government since 1979, the Treasury had nevertheless been significantly concerned with the containing of wage inflation in the course of its pursuit of the government's monetarist strategies. From that point of departure, the Treasury became involved in the business of seeking to reconcile the pursuit of monetarist anti-inflation strategies with the combating of unemployment.[25] In the 1985 Budget Statement the fully forged link between monetarist fiscal and public spending policy on the one hand and labour market strategy on the other hand was proclaimed as being at the heart of the Chancellor's policy formulation. He said,

my Budget today has two themes: to continue the drive against inflation and to help create the conditions for more jobs.[26]

It was in the course of the parliamentary debate on that Budget that the Secretary of State for Employment (Tom King) announced the publication of the employment White Paper[27] and also announced some important measures for the de-rigidification of the labour market, such as an expansion of the Youth Training Scheme[28] and a further extension of the qualifying period for unfair dismissal rights.[29]

The Budget Statement of 1985 was also important in particularizing the labour market philosophy on the strength of which it purported to reconcile Monetarism with job creation. Thus under the heading of the Medium-Term Financial Strategy, the Chancellor said:

The Government's economic strategy has two key components: a monetary policy designed to bring down inflation and a supply side policy designed to improve the competitive performance of the economy.

The supply side policy is rooted in a profound conviction, born of practical experience both at home and overseas, that the way to improve

[24] HC Deb., 6th ser., vol. 75, col. 783.
[25] That is evidenced by the Review by Treasury Officials of the Relationship between Employment and Wages which was published at the beginning of 1985.
[26] HC Deb., 6th ser., vol. 75, col. 783.
[27] Ibid., col. 1022.
[28] Ibid., col. 1013.
[29] Ibid., col. 1020.

economic performance and create more jobs is to encourage enterprise, efficiency and flexibility; to promote competition, de-regulation and free markets; to press ahead with privatisation and to improve incentives.[30]

It would be hard to encapsulate more neatly the ideology of enterprise within a free market which came to underlie the measures taken or proposed by way of the restructuring of the labour market.

Thus we are able to identify, in its ideological context, the broad prescription according to which the post-1979 Governments sought to restructure the labour market. The prescription had the following main elements:

(1) The restructuring would take place against a background in which employing enterprises both public and private would be pressed by the government to become more commercially effective and efficient, with greater control over their expenditure. (In the public sector this would be achieved by a combination of imposition of firm spending limits, privatization, liberalization, and increased contracting-out of specific functions to private contractors.)

(2) The labour market would be restructured in its wage-setting aspect by the removal of what were seen as rigidities maintaining wages at artificially inflated levels tending to limit labour demand. This would be achieved by legal restriction of the industrial power of trade unions, destruction of the legally supported or protected position of trade unions in the collective bargaining process, repeal of minimum wage legislation and fair wage legislation, and an attack upon institutional factors promoting or maintaining relativity pay-bargaining.

(3) The labour market would also be restructured in its aspect of determining the patterns in which labour was requisitioned and provided. This restructuring would aim to secure the provision of employment on a more entrepreneurial basis, that is to say, on a basis which is more risk-allocative towards the worker. This would be achieved by an attack upon states of security of employment and tenure of employment, and by encouraging workers to present their labour to the market in more flexible or risk-bearing forms, and present themselves to the market on the basis of greater

[30] Ibid., col. 748. For details of the extent of privatization, see below, p. 619.

mobility and with more developed and mobile skills derived from training.

We devote the remainder of this chapter to an examination in more detail of the measures or proposals which implemented this programme of restructuring of the labour market. Certain preliminary points remain to be made. Firstly, the three elements identified above are to some extent interactive with each other, so we shall not adhere slavishly to distinctions between them. Secondly, the post-1979 governments, however single-minded they appear or present themselves as being, could not and did not pursue labour market restructuring to the exclusion of all other objectives or by the overriding of all constraints. Our account of the process will at various points display the pursuit of other objectives, such as the containment of unemployment or the reduction of public expenditure on employment beyond the point where those goals were achievable by labour market restructuring. Our account will also show that part of the process was a reconciliation of restructuring goals with constraints or countervailing forces such as the requirements of EEC law in matters such as transfer of employment, and equal pay and treatment as between men and women. It is convenient to begin with the de-rigidifying of pay-bargaining; we shall be initially concerned with measures relating to collective bargaining and legal fair wage and labour standards.

10.2. RESTRUCTURING PAY-BARGAINING

An increasingly central feature of the labour market policies of post-1979 governments was an attack upon the legal supports for collectively bargained terms of employment and upon the legal protection of minimum wage standards and fair labour standards. These were attacked because they were seen as responsible for rigidities which distorted the working of the labour market and caused people to 'price themselves out of jobs'. The attack was closely linked with the attack upon the industrial power of trade unions which we examined in the previous chapter; but the two can nevertheless usefully be distinguished from each other. We suggest that the governments of the 1980s had a preoccupation with the elimination of certain patterns of wage determination and wage-bargaining which was distinct from, though certainly associated with, their concern to curtail the industrial strength of trade unions. In pursuit of that latter concern, certain measures were taken which bore directly upon the position of trade unions in collective bargaining, and particularly upon the legal protection accorded to their position in collective bargaining. Thus we saw in the previous chapter how the Employment Act of 1980 abolished the statutory trade union recognition machinery, and how the Employment Act of 1982 affected the freedom to take commercial or industrial action to secure or maintain trade union recognition by subcontractor-employers. Those measures were not directly concerned with challenging the legal protection accorded to certain patterns and levels of wage payment. There has, however, been a sequence of measures having that latter goal which we examine in this section. We also try to relate the post-1979 governments' pursuit of that goal to their general hostility towards and action against relativity pay-bargaining and national pay-bargaining.

(a) The Abolition of Fair Wage Standards

In this subsection, we shall show how the first of the post-1979 exercises in the restructuring of pay determination consisted in the abolition of the legal protection accorded to Fair Wage standards. We have already looked at the first step that was taken down this road, namely the repeal of schedule 11 of the Employment Protection Act 1975 by the Employment Act 1980.[31] At that stage, we were interested in the repeal as part of an attack on the position of trade unions in collective bargaining; the repeal was also important in terms of the restructuring of the way that wage levels are determined in the labour market. It will be recalled that schedule 11 had extended to the whole of the labour market the legal protection of Fair Wage standards which had before 1975 applied only in certain situations where the government was involved as a contracting party to or a licensor of a private employing activity under the Fair Wages Resolution of the House of Commons and the legislation dependent thereon.[32] And it will further be recalled that the Fair Wages standard

[31] See above, ch. 8, s. 3.
[32] See above, p. 387.

consisted of a claim to parity either with the terms and conditions achieved by the relevant collective bargaining process elsewhere in the industry in the district concerned or with the general level of terms and conditions prevailing in the industry in the district.

This was the sort of parity claim that post-1979 governments were increasingly to challenge as representing an upward distortion of the pay levels that the labour market view would, and in their view should, determine. In September 1979, as part of the process of preparation of the Employment Bill, the Department of Employment published a Working Paper on schedule 11 and on the Fair Wages Resolution. With hindsight, one can see displayed there the full extent of the government's misgivings about existing structures of pay determination. The main expressed reasons for proposing the repeal of schedule 11 and the longer-term reconsideration of the Fair Wages Resolution were fairly uncontroversial ones, such as that schedule 11 failed to achieve its declared objective of eliminating 'pockets of low pay' and instead benefitted higher-paid groups; and that the schedule was extensively, and sometimes collusively, used as a means of circumventing the restrictions of pay policy.[33] But among the criticisms of schedule 11 which the Department of Employment described and ultimately accepted in the Working Paper appears, ominously, the following one:

The procedure for arbitration on the general level of terms and conditions observed for comparable workers of employers whose circumstances are similar does not allow all the considerations which should help to determine terms and conditions to be fully considered, e.g. market prospects, profitability, labour efficiency, prices.

In the succeeding years, many more changes were to be rationalized in that way.

The government moved on from the repeal of schedule 11 to the rescission of the Fair Wages Resolution of the House of Commons which, as we have seen, was foreshadowed in the Working Paper of 1979. They had first to resile from (the technical term is to 'denounce') the ILO Convention which had—once a proud boast—itself been based on British Fair Wage measures.[34]

---

[33] Dept. of Employment Working Paper on sched. 11 of the Employment Protection Act 1975 and the Fair Wages Resolution (25 Sept. 1979; set out in IRLIB 416 (10 Oct. 1979) at pp. 7–9), para. 4(a), (b).

[34] ILO Convention No. 94 (1949).

This was done in 1982; when the government then proceeded to propose the rescission of the Fair Wages Resolution, Mr Tebbit reminded the House of Commons that 'only 51 countries have ratified the convention, and 95 have not done so because they had too much sense to get involved.'[35] So much for any claim, thereafter, of the UK to be a leader in the maintaining of international labour standards. The government was now in a position to assert, disingenuously it may be thought, that with the repeal of schedule 11, the Fair Wages Resolution now appeared as an isolated relic of the days of sweated wages, an anomalously sectional treatment of government contractors. The Fair Wages Resolution was duly rescinded and the fair wages provisions of four Acts which referred to the Resolution therefore ceased to have effect.[36] So the government disclaimed responsibility for maintaining Fair Wage standards in its capacities as contractor or licensor; and was, as we shall see in a later section, to go on to legislate to prevent local authorities from enforcing those standards in their contracting capacity.[37] In the end, the government was prepared to justify its withdrawal from the protection of Fair Wages by a simple deregulationist argument. As Mr Tebbit put it, 'We believe in doing away with artificial controls and barriers because they are usually counter-productive.'[38] The concept of 'artificiality' may be thought at best an unclear one, and at worst a rationale for the sweeping away of many widely perceived social rights. It was certainly one which, as we shall see, the post-1979 governments were to use to justify much more restructuring of the whole process of pay determination in the ensuing years.

(b) The Attack upon Minimum Wages and Youth Wages

If those aspects of the system of pay determination which directly protected pay relativities were to come under increasing attack

[35] HC Deb., 6th ser., vol. 34, col. 507 (16 Dec. 1982).

[36] These were the Housing Act 1957, the Films Act 1960, the Public Passenger Vehicles Act 1981, and the Independent Broadcasting Authority Act 1973.

[37] In a Consultative Document issued early in 1985 on the topic of 'Competition in the Provision of Local Authority Services', the Department of the Environment floated a proposal to legislate, in relation to local authority contracts or invitations to tender, to declare void any term or condition not directly related to the required performance by the contractor, in respect of the quality, timing, or cost of the specified goods or services (ibid., para. 16a). This was implemented by pt. I of the Local Government Act 1988: see below, sect. 6.

[38] HC Deb., 6th ser., vol. 34, col. 507 (16 Dec. 1982).

after 1979, so also were those aspects which did so indirectly by maintaining minimum wage rates. The Government in 1979 inherited and perpetuated a system which had always resisted a national minimum wage,[39] and one might have expected that the industry-by-industry system of Wages Councils would scarcely have been seen as creating 'rigidities in the labour market' at a level where they would be viewed as other than necessary and minimal protections for the very lowest-paid workers. But from the beginning of the 1980s, the government maintained a concern with the way that wages, especially youth wages, even at the bottom end of the spectrum were high enough to 'price workers out of jobs'.[40]

This preoccupation was displayed—it seemed an isolated phenomenon then—in the introduction by the Department of Employment in 1981 of the Young Workers Scheme.[41] That was perhaps the first of a large number of schemes in which, as we shall see, the government sought to combine the provision of a subsidy to alleviate unemployment or provide training with some restructuring of the system of pay determination or of the labour market in a larger sense. The Young Workers Scheme provided allowances for employers who took on workers under 18 years of age at a certain rate provided the gross wages were less than £40 per week, and at a reduced rate between £40 and £45 per week, over which no allowances were payable. Those limits were such as to give employers an economic incentive to pay markedly low youth wage rates; the government had to battle with accusations that this scheme undercut some Wages Councils' rates of pay, and it seems to have determined that young workers should not enjoy the protection of Wages Councils' adult rates of pay.[42] At all events, the rhetoric of 'young workers pricing themselves out of jobs' started to become prominent at this point. It was also, as we shall see, to loom large in the development of the Youth

---

[39] A useful account of the recent history is provided by F. Bayliss, *Making a Minimum Wage Work* (Fabian Pamphlet 545; July 1991).

[40] This concern was the subject of active lobbying on behalf of small businesses in particular; cf. the pamphlet produced by the National Federation of the Self-Employed and Small Businesses, *Priced Out! The Effect of Wages Councils on Jobs* (London, 1981).

[41] See M. Freedland, (1982) 11 ILJ 41 for an account of the scheme.

[42] For discussion of the relationship between YWS wage maxima and Wages Councils wage minima, see Freedland, ibid., at 42.

Training Scheme, where the government was concerned to keep the level of the allowance paid to trainees below the wage rates afforded to young workers, and particularly below adult wage rates obtainable in the labour market, and sought to limit the availability of social security benefits to young people eligible for the Youth Training Scheme but unwilling to participate in it.[43]

Early in 1985, the Department of Employment issued a Consultative Paper on Wages Councils, which revealed the extent to which they were prepared to justify the curtailment of minimum-wage protection on the basis of an alleged gain in job creation. Thus the Paper stated that:

The Government attaches the highest priority to removing unnecessary obstacles to the creation of more jobs. Wages Councils have been increasingly criticized as such an obstacle and the Government therefore believes that it is now right to consider whether the system should be retained and, if so, what reforms are needed.[44]

The Treasury Paper on the Relationship between Employment and Wages was relied upon for the view that slower rises in real pay would lead to significant increases in job opportunities;[45] and it was said that there was a growing body of evidence that the employment prospects of young people are adversely affected by the level of their wages relative to adults.[46] The powers of Wages Councils to protect holidays and other conditions of work, and to maintain wage differentials between different grades of workers, were dismissed as 'a proliferation of requirements...that are difficult for both employers and employees to understand, unnecessarily burdensome, and detrimental to flexibility and efficiency'.[47] In a succinct sweeping-away of a good century of social progress, the Paper concluded bleakly that 'there can be no case for the legal prescription of pay rates which have the effect of making it difficult for those who wish to take up employment to do so.'[48]

It was perhaps a matter for relief that the government did not

[43] See Freedland, (1983) 12 ILJ 220, and see below, Sect. 5.
[44] Dept. of Employment, Consultative Paper on Wages Councils (21 Mar. 1985; see details in IRRR 341 (2 Apr. 1985) at p.12), para. 1.
[45] Ibid., para. 9.
[46] Ibid., para. 11.
[47] Ibid., para. 7.
[48] Ibid., para. 11.

adopt the option of total abolition of Wages Councils which had been favourably identified in the Consultative Paper. However, the Wages Act 1986 did curtail the operation of the Wages Councils system to such an extent as radically to alter its character. The system had developed in such a way as to enable the Wages Councils not merely to set an overall minimum rate of wages for the trade or industry concerned, but also to establish a protective superstructure including higher minimum rates for particular occupations within the trade or industry, overtime and premium rates, and minimum holiday entitlements.[49] The 1986 Act repealed all the existing Wages Councils legislation,[50] thus removing the possibility of creating any new Wages Councils, or extending the scope of existing ones, by ministerial order, and merely left existing Wages Councils with the single power either to set a single minimum hourly rate of remuneration or a single minimum hourly basic rate coupled with a single minimum hourly overtime rate.[51] The government's claim was that this was to reduce complexity and an administrative burden upon business. The more immediate effect was to remove obstacles to the employment of cheap labour. That this was the real aim is suggested by the further provisions depriving Wages Councils of any powers in relation to workers under the age of 21,[52] and requiring them to have regard to the effect the rate they fix will have on the level of employment among the workers to whom it will apply 'in particular in those areas where the remuneration received by such workers is generally less than the national average for such workers'.[53] So full force and effect was to be accorded to any downward pressure on wages which fragmentation of the labour market might exert even in the former, and potentially future, sweated trades.

The government nevertheless returned to the suggestion of total abolition of Wages Councils in 1988, this time as part of the grand strategy for destroying all remaining 'barriers to

[49] Wages Councils Act 1979, s. 14, consolidating, *inter alia*, the Holidays with Pay Act 1938.

[50] Section 12(1) of the 1986 Act begins, 'The Wages Councils Act 1979 shall cease to have effect, but . . .'.

[51] Wages Act 1986, s. 14.

[52] Ibid., s. 12(3).

[53] Ibid., s. 14(6)(a).

employment' which was laid out in the White Paper *Employment for the 1990s*.[54] It was suggested that the Wages Act 1986 had done no more than reduce the burdensome complexities of the Wages Orders and clarify the role of Wages Councils; doubt was cast on whether the councils had been carrying out their new duty of giving weight to the impact of settlements on jobs, and it was questioned whether the whole system was 'relevant to pay determination in the 1990s'.[55] Hence the White Paper announced that the government believed the time had come to reconsider the Wages Councils' future; and a consultation document followed later in 1988 proposing abolition of all remaining councils.[56] It was on the face of it surprising that this intention was not carried out by the Employment Acts of 1989 or of 1990. We must assume that employers' reactions to the consultation document persuaded the government that more was to be lost by overriding employers' fears of undercutting of wage rates if the councils were abolished than was to be gained by destroying the councils' negligible remaining impact on collective bargaining after the curtailment of their powers (which the government stigmatized as powers to set 'going rates'[57]) by the Wages Act 1986.

(d) The Attack on National and Relativity Bargaining

The developments which we have examined in the course of the present section involved removing features of the process of pay determination which improved or protected the position of workers therein. Those features tended to be stigmatized by the government as distortions of the functioning of the labour market. Implicit in these happenings and in the rhetoric with which they were supported was the conclusion that collective bargaining itself could be regarded as a kind of rigidity constraining or distorting the operation of the labour market, and therefore as something to be attacked. We have already in this and the

---

[54] Department of Employment, Cm. 540 (Dec. 1988).

[55] Ibid., paras. 3.14–3.17.

[56] Consultative Document on Wages Councils, 1988. The Agricultural Wages Boards, which under the Agricultural Wages Act 1948 have similar powers to those of the Wages Councils before the Wages Act, were not affected by the legislation of the 1980s; this may have been attributable to the existence of a separate ILO Convention relating to them.

[57] Cm. 540, para. 3.15. However, abolition was proposed in the Trade Union Reform and Employment Rights Bill 1992.

previous chapter considered a number of ways in which the government from 1979 onwards sought to reduce the power of trade unions in collective bargaining. But the government also sought to challenge, at an even more fundamental level, some of the assumptions underlying the very process of collective bargaining itself. In particular, so far as pay-bargaining is concerned, the government was more and more openly hostile to collective bargaining in so far as it tended to generate (1) claims of fair pay relativities and (2) nationwide pay standards.

Let us first of all consider the government's hostility to these aspects or effects of collective bargaining in terms of the principles they formulated, or the rhetoric they developed, in relation to pay-bargaining. In a general sense, we have seen that opposition to the sort of pay-bargaining which imported notions of comparability and fair relativities was an inherent part of the economic policies which the government sought to implement at the micro-economic as well as the macro-economic level.[58] In the micro-economic context, the rhetoric of Monetarism was supported by that of the free, unrestricted, and therefore efficient working of the labour market.[59] In this framework of argument, it was not surprising that the government should not only maintain a general hostility towards comparability bargaining but should also develop a specific attack upon national pay-bargaining. That attack was formally launched in November 1986 by the Chancellor of the Exchequer, Nigel Lawson, in a speech at the National Economic Development Council which argued that common pay rates throughout an industry impede labour mobility and so promote unemployment.[60] The maintaining of the rhetorical attack upon national pay-bargaining became the particular task of Kenneth Clarke as Minister of State for Employment in the period preceding the General Election of 1987.[61] The theme was taken up in the Employment White Paper of December

[58] See P. Hall, *Governing the Economy* (Cambridge, 1986), 100–1, 108–9; D. Robinson, *Monetarism and the Labour Market* (Oxford, 1986), 426–30.

[59] The Budget Statement of Mar. 1985 provides a good illustration—see HC Deb., 6th ser., vol. 75, cols. 783 ff., esp. at cols. 787–8 (The Chancellor of the Exchequer, Nigel Lawson, 19 Mar. 1985).

[60] The episode is documented in Incomes Data Report 495 (Apr. 1987), see esp., p. 25.

[61] Most notably in a speech at the City University Business School on 12 Feb. 1987.

1988, where ' "the going rate", "comparability" and "cost of living increases" ' were denigrated as 'outmoded concepts', and where it was complained that national agreements set levels of earnings which failed to reflect local unemployment rates even where those were 'particularly high'.[62]

This is not to say that the attack upon comparability bargaining was or remained at the level of rhetoric alone. On the other hand, severely practical though this attack was, much of it took the form of administrative measures in the public sector which did not require legislation of any sort. This was true, for example, of the Civil Service, where patterns of pay determination were fundamentally altered by purely administrative action. A watershed event in this development was the suspension in 1981 of the Civil Service Pay Research Unit, whose function was to provide the data for the relating of Civil Service pay levels to those of equivalent jobs in the private sector. Having thereby effectively abandoned the existing collective bargaining system— and so precipitated the civil servants' pay dispute of 1981–2— the government appointed a Committee of Enquiry under the chairmanship of Lord Justice Megaw to consider the future of Civil Service pay determination. That Committee produced its Report in 1982[63]—a Report which, although widely regarded at the time as inimical to collective bargaining, should perhaps be seen as attempting to reconstitute Civil Service pay-bargaining in politically and economically realistic terms.[64] Be that as it may, the subsequent conduct by the government of Civil Service pay determination more resembled the subordination of collective bargaining to cash limits than any reconstituting of it.[65] Administrative measures also brought about the curtailment of public sector collective bargaining in another important dimension, in the sense that the government's extensively effective pressure, exerted from the early 1980s onwards, upon local authorities and upon the National Health Service authorities to contract out to private contractors the performance of services such as cleaning and laundry resulted in the removal of the workforce performing those functions from the ambit of public

[62] Cm. 540, para. 3.5.
[63] Cmnd. 8590.
[64] See W. Brown, (1982) 11 ILJ 266–7.
[65] See Robinson, *Monetarism and the Labour Market*, 426–7.

sector pay-bargaining.[66] That this was one of the chief objects of that exercise was only lightly concealed beneath the rhetoric of market efficiency with which the operation was cloaked. By the same token, the campaign against nationwide pay-bargaining could be prosecuted in the National Health Service by a purely administrative process of fragmentation of pay determination into regional units, carried out from the mid-1980s onwards.

Sometimes, on the other hand, the attack upon nationwide or comparability pay-bargaining assumed legislative form. For instance, the Water Industry Act 1983 was a measure which, among other things, by abolishing the National Water Council simply removed the level of operation at which national collective bargaining was conducted in that industry.[67] In terms of its impact upon collective bargaining structures, this measure was as significant as the subsequent Water Act 1989 which implemented the privatization of the water industry by transferring the regional water undertakings from water authorities to public limited companies, shares in which were then offered for public sale.[68] Another, more notorious, piece of legislative intervention against nationwide collective bargaining was the Teachers' Pay and Conditions Act 1987 which, again in the aftermath of a major industrial dispute, dismantled the statutory framework for collective bargaining for the primary and secondary teaching profession, replacing it with a mechanism for government imposition of terms and conditions of employment upon both parties to the teachers' contracts of employment.[69] The ILO Committee on Freedom of Association concluded that the Government was no longer offering arrangements for the teaching profession which

[66] See ibid., 453–4.

[67] A point which is sedulously concealed in the presentation of the Bill for Second Reading by Tom King as Minister for Local Government and Environmental Services, but extensively developed in the Opposition speech of Denis Howell (HC Deb., 6th ser., vol. 32, cols. 150–62).

[68] For a useful account of the impact of these events upon industrial relations in the water industry, see S. Ogden, 'The Trade Union Campaign against Water Privatisation' (1991) 22 *Industrial Relations Journal* 20–35.

[69] See S. Fredman and G. Morris, 'The Teachers' Pay and Conditions Act 1987' (1987) 16 ILJ 107 and 'The Teachers' Lesson: Collective Bargaining and the Courts' (1987) 16 ILJ 215. The 1987 Act did not in itself destroy nationwide pay-setting for teachers, but it changed the process away from that of collective bargaining. The Education Reform Act 1988, by making arrangements for schools to opt out of local authority control, and for local management of those within local authority control, set up long-term trends towards localized pay-setting.

implemented ILO Convention No. 98 on the Right to Organize and Bargain Collectively.[70] By the time of the General Election of 1987, the extensiveness and ferocity of the government's attack upon public sector collective bargaining was all too obvious, though with no obviously adverse consequences for the government from an electoral point of view.

In the third Conservative government of the 1980s, these and other assaults upon existing patterns of public sector collective bargaining would be enlarged into a more general restructuring of public sector employment relationships. This will be discussed as a separate theme towards the end of this chapter.[71] We shall there see, for instance, how the pressure upon local authorities to contract out the performing of services such as refuse collection was elaborated, by part I of the Local Government Act 1988, into a system of compulsory competitive tendering for the performance of, in effect, all local government services capable of being contracted out. If the restructuring of pay-bargaining gradually concentrated itself upon the public sector, that was because there was no direct way for the government to bring about the restructuring of private sector collective bargaining— though they were, of course, doing this indirectly by their measures to reduce trade union industrial power which we examined in the previous chapter. Industrywide and comparability bargaining proved more tenacious in the private sector than the government probably hoped. On the other hand, the trend towards single employer plant or enterprise level pay-bargaining, which was a general post-Donovan trend but which the government was actively encouraging, did continue right through the 1980s, and did facilitate a tighter internal control by employers over pay and productivity and a relegation of trade unions more to a consultative than negotiatory role on non-pay matters.[72] Moreover, there was an associated set of aims and policies at the level of the individual employment relationship; the government aspired to promote, especially in the private sector, a new and more

[70] See S. Fredman and G. Morris, *The State as Employer: Labour Law in the Public Services* (London, 1989), 189.

[71] See below, sect. 10.6.

[72] W. Brown and S. Wadwhani, *The Economic Effects of Industrial Relations Legislation since 1979* (CLARE Group Paper, Nov./Dec. 1989); cf. P. Gregg and A. Yates, 'Changes in Wage-Setting Arrangements and Trade Union Presence in the 1980s' (1991) 29 BJIR 361 at 370–3, where similar conclusions are reached.

market-sensitive set of stereotypes for the individual employment
relationship, and it is to their efforts to restructure employment
relationships primarily at the individual level that we turn our
attention in the next section.

10.3. THE RESTRUCTURING OF THE INDIVIDUAL EMPLOYMENT RELATIONSHIP

(a) Restructuring, Flexibility, and De-regulation

In the previous section, we saw how a restructuring of the labour
market took place from 1979 onwards in terms of the creation of
a much more hostile legal regime for collective bargaining. In this
section, we shall see how there was a corresponding transformation in both the legal and the social regime for the individual employment relationship. This dual transformation of the
employment relationship was an attempt to bring about a general
restructuring of the labour market.

The transformation or attempted transformation of the individual employment relationship was clearly observed and well
documented both by labour lawyers and by labour economists.[73]
The analysis concentrated upon employers' acquisition, by means
both of legal and social changes, of greater flexibility in their
employment of labour. This flexibility takes various forms, but is
of two principal types, often distinguished as 'functional' and
'numerical'.[74] The employer acquires the first type of flexibility
by widening the range of tasks that members of the workforce
can each be required to perform, and the second type by arranging
to be able to vary the amount of labour employed as needs
fluctuate. The second type might perhaps better be styled volume
flexibility, as it need not depend upon adjusting the size of the
workforce; it may consist in adjusting the length of time for
which the members of the workforce are employed each week or
month or year.

[73] See e.g. S. Deakin, 'Labour Law and the Developing Employment
Relationship in the UK' (1986) 10 *Cambridge Journal of Economic* 225–46;
J. Atkinson, 'Employment Flexibility and Internal and External Labour Markets',
in *New Forms of Work and Activity* (Documentation for Brussels Colloquium
of the European Foundation for the Improvement of Living and Working Conditions, 1986); R. Tarling, ed., *Flexibility in Labour Markets* (London, 1987).

[74] See Atkinson, 'Employment Flexibility', 7.

By the later 1980s, it was a widely held view that employers, both in the public and private sectors, had had such success during the 1980s in acquiring greater flexibility than they had had before, that a real qualitative change in individual employment relationships had occurred across a wide section of the labour market. Thus, in relation to the private sector, the Institute of Manpower Studies identified a new model of labour market behaviour called the 'flexible firm'.[75] In this model, the pursuit of flexibility brings about a segmentation of the workforce into a core and a periphery. The core consists of fully employed workers who are, as it were, 'on the establishment'—who thus enjoy relatively high security of employment—but of whom functional flexibility is increasingly required. The periphery consists of those workers in relation to whom the enterprise enjoys numerical flexibility—because, for instance, they are on short-term contracts, or because the employer has distanced those workers from him by sub-contracting for the performance of their work or hiring them with an agency as intermediary. The employer has greater freedom in relation to the peripheral work-force than in relation to the core workforce to vary the amount of labour he is employing according to the demand for the output of the enterprise.

There was, and continues to be, a real debate about whether the 'flexible firm' model provided an accurate or useful account of the way the labour market was developing; some thought that it was an actively misleading model, and produced cogent arguments in support of that view.[76] At all events, the attention of labour lawyers focused upon the peripheral workers in the 'flexible firm' model.[77] It was realized that, in order to maximize

[75] See National Economic Development Office, *Changing Working Patterns: How Companies Achieve Flexibility to Meet New Needs: A Report Prepared by the Institute of Manpower Studies for the NEDO in Association with the Department of Employment* (London, 1986), esp. paras. 1.13–1.16, where the analytical construct of the 'flexible firm' is set out.

[76] See esp. A. Pollert, *The 'Flexible Firm': A Model in Search of Reality (or a Policy in Search of a Practice)?* (Warwick Papers in Industrial Relations, 19 Dec. 1987.) The thesis is expanded into a more general critique of the whole concept of flexibility in A. Pollert, ed., *Farewell to Flexibility* (Oxford, 1991), esp. Introduction and ch. 1.

[77] See generally, P. Leighton, 'Marginal Workers', ch. 18 in R. Lewis, ed., *Labour Law in Britain* (1986); Deakin, 'Labour Law and the Developing Employment Relationship in the UK'.

volume flexibility, employers were constituting employment relationships more and more often in the forms hitherto regarded as
atypical or 'marginal'; they were employing on a temporary, part-
time, casual, home-working, agency or self-employed basis, or
even combining more than one of these bases in a given case. It
was widely asserted that, where ten years before there had been a
failure to extend the legal regime of employment protection to
certain small groups of workers, such as homeworkers in, for
instance, the toy-making industry, there was now a much larger
failure to respond in any systematic way to the growth of an
enormously larger marginalized workforce.

The main purpose of this section is to examine that assertion,
and to try to identify the policy choices that were made by
governments in this connection after 1979. Essentially, the argument will be that government policy favoured the de-rigidification
of employment patterns. The rigidities, however, consisted largely
of social and economic restrictions rather than legal ones. Therefore flexibility could be encouraged and could develop apace
without extensive changes in individual employment law. But the
law had a crucial constitutive role in this development in that it
allowed employers freedom to adopt or devise more or less any
form of work contract they chose;[78] and where changes in the law
did take place, they generally had the purpose and the effect of
taking this development further.

In this section, we are therefore concerned with examining the
impact both of legal passivity in the face of social change and
of certain legal developments which positively conduced to
that change. In order to understand both types of impact more
clearly, it may be helpful to analyse the dynamics of change in
the structure of individual employment relationships during the
period in question. It could be said that during this period, many
employment relationships came to look more like the relationship
between employer and independent contractor. We noted above
that self-employment was one of the marginalized forms of work

---

[78] In contrast with many Continental European systems; for appreciations of
the importance of this contrast, see e.g. Otto Kahn-Freund, 'Blackstone's
Neglected Child: The Contract of Employment' (1977) 93 LQR 508–28;
U. Mückenberger and S. Deakin, 'From Deregulation to a European Floor of
Rights: Labour Law, Flexibilisation and the European Single Market' (1989)
Zeitschrift für ausländisches und internationales Arbeits- und Sozialrecht (ZIAS)
153, esp. at 159–60.

found on the periphery of the flexible firm. Some of the other types of marginalized employment also display characteriztics of self-employment. Indeed, it has long been difficult to decide how to classify casual workers, for instance, or home-workers, as between employment and self-employment. It was entirely consistent with the 'enterprise culture' of the post-1979 governments that self-employment should be to some extent a preferred model for work relationships.[79]

We do not suggest, however, that the restructuring of individual employment relationships primarily took the form of re-classifying employees as independent contractors, nor even of steering employment relationships into the formal legal category of self-employment. The changes occurred mainly under the umbrella of the contract of employment rather than by exporting workers from that category. The mechanics of this process will be clearer if we isolate certain key features of employment relationships, features which determine their social and economic character. In their social dimension, employment relationships take up differing positions on a spectrum which has the worker fully integrated into the employing enterprise at one end of the spectrum and fully autonomous at the other end of the spectrum. In their economic dimension, employment relationships sit upon a different spectrum with high security for the worker at one extreme, and high risk-bearing by the worker at the other end. The distinction between employment and self-employment is drawn in these two dimensions; but it is not drawn at any clearly defined point on the two spectra we have isolated. Moreover—and this will turn out to be very important—a given employment relationship may sit at different points on the two spectra; and it may be shifted on one spectrum without any corresponding shift on the other. An example of an unequal shift would be the case of a fully employed worker enjoying full employment protection rights who, having been paid a fixed monthly salary, is changed to a commission basis of payment. Such a worker may remain just as fully integrated as before in the social dimension, but he will have moved towards greater risk-bearing in the economic dimension. His situation is now more like that of the independent

---

[79] Cf., generally, H. Collins, 'Independent Contractors and the Challenge of Vertical Disintegration to Employment Protection Laws' (1990) 10 OJLS 353–80.

contractor, though it by no means follows that he will have moved out of the legal category of employee under a contract of employment.

The above analysis enables us to cast some extra light upon the process of restructuring the individual employment relationship which occurred after the end of the 1970s and was encouraged by governments and by legal measures. In the post-war period until the 1980s there was general movement of employment relationships both on the social spectrum—towards greater integration— and on the economic spectrum—towards greater security. Both movements were actively promoted by legal measures; both movements occurred in tandem, for instance, in the Employment Protection Act 1975.[80] From the end of the 1970s onwards, the impulse is in the opposite direction on both spectra—more especially on the economic one, which became the leading edge of employment restructuring as employers gained the upper hand in the labour market. Many workers became in various ways more risk-bearing. In terms of the flexible firm model, that movement was concentrated upon the periphery; indeed, in many cases, the movement towards greater risk-bearing took the form of shifting workers to the periphery. But that movement was not confined to the periphery; many workers who remained fully integrated core workers also became more risk-bearing. In such a case, we could say that the movement on the economic spectrum was the significant one, and did not need to be accompanied by a parallel move on the social spectrum. There could even be a move in the other direction on that spectrum. That would be the case, for instance, where core workers were given profit-related pay to make them more risk-bearing than before, but were also more closely integrated into a group production process in return for an increase in individual functional flexibility. We proceed to examine the relevant legal and governmental measures of the post-1979 period in light of this thesis that the predominant trend was towards greater economic risk-bearing on the part of the workforce. In terms of the discussion at the beginning of this chapter,[81] these were measures of de-rigidification and of de-

---

[80] Thus the improvement of rights in respect of unfair dismissal was a measure of social integration, while the provision of guaranteed pay during short-time working (now EPCA 1978, ss. 12–18) was a measure of economic integration.

[81] See above, p. 528.

regulation; we look first at measures of de-regulation and then move on to those in the nature of de-rigidification.

(b) Reducing the Impact of Employment Protection Legislation

From 1979 onwards, there were a number of legislative measures designed to reduce the impact of the employment protection legislation—especially, though not solely, the unfair dismissal legislation. The declared purpose was one of de-regulation; the beneficiaries were identified as businesses, especially small businesses, whose burdens were to be alleviated. This was to remove disincentives to the employment of labour in times of recession. It was a process of transferring some of the economic risks of employment from employers to the workforce. Some post-1979 labour law developments were made to seem programmatic only retrospectively. This particular development could fairly claim to be systematic from the very outset, though as we shall see the programme was elaborated and upgraded as the years went on.

(i) *Unfair Dismissal.* The outset was the 1979 Conservative election manifesto, which stated an intention to amend laws such as the Employment Protection Act 'where they damage smaller businesses—and larger ones too—and actually prevent the creation of jobs'.[82] The new government moved with some speed to start to carry out this promise, using delegated powers of amendment to make statutory instruments to lengthen the qualifying period of service for complaints of unfair dismissal from six months to one year,[83] and to reduce the compulsory period for consultation with recognized trade unions about impending redundancies.[84] The latter measure was not of enormous practical significance; but the former was the first step in a partial dismantling of the unfair dismissal jurisdiction which was of importance both in an immediate and in a symbolical sense.

The next steps were proposed in the Working Paper of

---

[82] As quoted in the Department of Employment, Working Paper on *Proposed Amendments to the Employment Protection Legislation* (Sept. 1979), para. 1, set out in IRLIB 146 (10 Oct. 1979) at p. 3.

[83] Unfair Dismissal (Variation of Qualifying Period) Order (SI 1979, No. 959).

[84] Employment Protection (Handling of Redundancies) Variation Order (SI 1979, No. 958).

September 1979 and for the most part implemented in the Employment Act 1980. The onus of proof of the reasonableness of dismissals, which had previously lain upon employers, was made neutral as between employer and employee, and industrial tribunals were specifically required to take into account the circumstances, such as the size and resources, of a firm when considering whether or not an employer had carried out a dismissal reasonably.[85] There was a tendency at the time to view this measure as not immensely significant; but in retrospect at least it is apparent that this legislative endorsement of an essentially passive view of the unfair dismissal jurisdiction—passive in the sense that it militated against a reformist use of the law of unfair dismissal—must have encouraged a new reserve among the judiciary towards unfair dismissal claims which was to become marked as the 1980s progressed. Moreover, this measure also indicated the extent to which small businesses both formed an effective lobby or pressure group at this period,[86] and commanded the active sympathy and support of 1980s governments as being a prime source of the kind of spirit of free enterprise which they wished to foster and encourage. (This link between enterprise and small businesses would later be stressed in the series of policy documents about de-regulation which were produced in the mid-1980s.[87]) Furthermore, the qualifying period for unfair dismissal rights was extended to two years where the employer had no more than twenty employees; the small firms turned out to be the stalking-horse for all employers in this respect. And the capacity of employees on fixed-term contracts to waive unfair dismissal rights on the expiry of their contracts was extended to include contracts of duration of one year or more, where the lower limit had previously been two years—an obvious extension of risk-bearing by employees.[89]

[85] Employment Act 1980, s. 6, amending s. 57(3) of EPCA 1978.
[86] The National Federation for the Self-Employed and Small Businesses was their main institutional representation; cf. above, n. 40.
[87] Cf. below, p. 561, and see e.g. the White Paper, *Lifting the Burden*, Cmnd. 9571 (July 1975), para. 1.10: 'The burden is that much greater on small businesses where the owner/manager is wholly responsible for all aspects of the business . . . It is the small and new businesses which are precisely those we need to encourage.'
[88] Employment Act 1980, s. 8(1), adding new s. 64A to EPCA 1978.
[89] Employment Act 1980, section 8(2), amending EPCA 1978 s. 142(1).

The Working Paper also contained proposals which were implemented in the 1980 Act which had the aim of subjecting the basic award of compensation for unfair dismissal to the same limitations and qualifications as the compensatory award. The basic award had been introduced in 1975 with the aim of ensuring that an award of compensation for unfair dismissal would have a guaranteed minimum value and a scale value corresponding to that of a statutory redundancy payment. The judicial House of Lords had objected to the prospect of this basic award being made to employees who turned out to have been undeserving.[90] The 1980 Act abolished the two weeks' pay minimum for the basic award, and provided for the basic award to be reduced by reference to any conduct of the employee before his dismissal, or by his unreasonable refusal of an offer of reinstatement.[91] Here again, the expressive effects of these changes were considerable; they encouraged the industrial tribunals and the appellate courts to regard unfair dismissal adjudications as the striking of a balance, in pecuniary terms, between the imperfections of the employer and those of the employee.

This was a significantly different process from the stern vindication of the interests of the unjustly dismissed employee which the legislators of 1975, and even 1971, had had in mind. The same shift of emphasis took place at the procedural level; in the Working Paper of September 1979, it was observed, not without some sympathy, that there was 'a widespread belief among employers that many cases which reach the stage of a tribunal hearing are without merit and should have been sifted out earlier'.[92] Accordingly in 1980 new rules of procedure for industrial tribunals were introduced, which provided for a pre-hearing assessment at which the tribunal could advise either party that their case appeared weak and that costs could be awarded against them if they chose to pursue their contentions to a hearing; and the rule on costs was widened to provide for the award of costs against applicants bringing or conducting their case not just frivolously

---

[90] In the case of *Devis* v. *Atkins* [1977] ICR 662.

[91] Employment Act 1980, s. 9, amending s. 73 of EPCA 1978 (also certain words of s. 73 repealed by EA 1980 s. 20 and sched. 2).

[92] Department of Employment, *Working Paper on Proposed Amendments to the Employment Protection Legislation* (Sept. 1979), annexe 2, para. 1. The Working Paper is set out in IRLIB 146 (10 Oct. 1979) at pp. 3 ff.

or vexatiously but also 'unreasonably'—a much more inclusive criterion.[93] Bringing a claim for unfair dismissal was becoming a more risky affair; and so was being dismissed. The scaling-down of employment protection rights by the Employment Act 1980 was not, moreover, entirely confined to the law of unfair dismissal; thus, the conditions for the exercise of the right to reinstatement after maternity leave were made more stringent, apparently on the basis that this was an especially onerous obligation for small employers.[94]

(ii) *Maternity Rights and Sick Pay*.   It is pertinent to consider at this point whether we can regard the individual employment law measures of the first Conservative government of the 1980s (1979–83) as being entirely concerned with reducing legislative employment protection. The answer is that we can do so, subject to one genuine exception and one apparent exception. As the one genuine exception is quite a minor one, and the apparent exception turns out not to be real, we can conclude that the individual employment legislation of this period was almost uni-directional in favour of de-regulation, though it did display a caution and restraint comparable with the contemporary 'step by step' approach to the reform of trade dispute and trade union law. The genuine exception consisted in the creation by section 13 of the Employment Act 1980 of a new right to time off with pay for antenatal care. Although a minor entitlement in the sense that it conferred no more than the right not to be unreasonably refused permission to keep appointments with a doctor, midwife, or health visitor for the purpose of receiving antenatal care which most employers would allow as a matter of course, this seems to have been a response to evidence that low-paid women workers were begin adversely treated in this respect[95]—a kind of response which was hardly to recur later in the 1980s.

The apparent rather than real exception to the trend of de-

---

[93] Industrial Tribunals (Rules of Procedure) Regulations 1980 (SI 1980, No. 884), rules 6 and 11.

[94] Employment Act 1980, s. 11, amending s. 47 of the EPCA 1978.

[95] See G. Pitt, 'Individual Rights under the New Legislation', (1980) 9 ILJ 233 at 242: 'Section 13 offers one sop [to opinion offended by the reduction of maternity rights elsewhere in the Act] introduced at a late stage and stimulated by the shocking evidence that the UK has one of the worst perinatal infant mortality rates in the Western World.'

regulation consisted of the introduction of the obligation upon employers to pay Statutory Sick Pay, followed later in the decade by parallel provision for Statutory Maternity Pay. It was an apparent exception, because the aim and effect was not to increase the protection to which employees were entitled, but rather to transfer the administrative responsibility for and administrative costs of existing protections from the state social security system to employers, while actually reducing the value of the benefits to employees by subjecting them to income tax and National Insurance contributions, which were not deducted from National Insurance Sickness Benefit.[96] Moreover, existing state social security levels of income replacement during absence due to sickness were low enough to ensure that no significant new labour standard was being imposed on employers. Statutory sick pay was introduced by social security legislation passed in 1982,[97] having been proposed in a Green Paper issued by the Department of Health and Social Security in 1980.[98] In 1985, the statutory sick pay scheme was extended to cover the first 28 weeks of sickness[99] instead of the 8 weeks initial sickness it had covered since it came into effect in 1983, so it would henceforth cover the whole period for which state sickness benefit had normally been paid. The employer was to be entitled to recoup the cost of statutory sick pay by setting it against National Insurance contributions; so the position was that a state social security benefit would be administered by employers as, nominally, a statutory incident of the employment relationship.

This, then, was an instance where, not for the last time in the 1980s,[100] the government gave greater priority to reducing public expenditure than to reducing employers' employment-related costs; the latter goal seemed to be an overriding one only where it could be pursued at the expense or risk of the workforce rather than of the public purse. It was consistent with this that in 1991

[96] See Richard Lewis, 'The Privatisation of Sickness Benefit' (1982) 11 ILJ 245 at pp. 246–8: 'Comparing Statutory Sick Pay with Sickness Benefit'. (The government's declared aim of subjecting National Insurance Sickness Benefit to income tax was not implemented within the period under consideration.)

[97] Part I of the Social Security and Housing Benefit Act 1982.

[98] *Income During Initial Sickness: A New Strategy*, Cmnd. 7864.

[99] By pt. III of the Social Security Act 1985.

[100] Cf. e.g. the restriction to small businesses in 1986 and abolition in 1989 of the employer's redundancy rebate: see below, nn. 117, 125.

the Statutory Sick Pay Act[101] reduced the proportion of statutory
sick pay which the employer could recoup from the state social
security scheme from 100 per cent to 80 per cent (subject to a
minor concession to small employers). In the same year, moreover, a statutory order[102] held the higher rate of SSP down,
where previously it had been uprated in line with inflation, and
raised the minimum earnings threshold to qualify for that higher
rate, thus dispelling any remaining illusion that SSP ran counter
to a general de-regulatory scaling down of statutory protections
for employees.

The introduction of statutory sick pay was followed by a
parallel reform of provision for income support during maternity
absence. The DHSS issued a Consultative Document on *Statutory
Maternity Allowance* in 1985, and added proposals for Statutory
Maternity Pay to the Social Security Bill which was enacted as
the Social Security Act 1986.[103] The provision previously made
had consisted of a maternity allowance scheme administered by
the DHSS and a statutory maternity pay scheme (created by
the Employment Protection Act 1975) imposing a maternity pay
obligation upon employers, and enabling them to recoup themselves from a Maternity Pay Fund financed out of National
Insurance contributions and administered by the Department of
Employment. Essentially the new scheme combined both sets of
payments to employees, made employers responsible for both
of them, and enabled employers to recoup themselves, as with
statutory sick pay, by setting off their payments against National
Insurance contributions and tax payments.

These reforms were effected with the aims of saving administrative costs to the DHSS and subjecting income replacement
benefits to income tax.[104] Both of these had long been aims of the
DHSS; the new development was that post-1979 Conservative
governments were prepared to give practical effect to this new
kind of restriction on welfare provision. Indeed, they were pre-

---

[101] See Richard Lewis, 'The Statutory Sick Pay Act 1991: Who Pays for
Sickness?' (1991) 20 ILJ 159 for a most valuable annotation.

[102] The Statutory Sick Pay (Rate of Payment) Order 1991 (SI 1991, No. 506):
see Lewis, 'The Statutory Sick Pay Act'.

[103] Pt. II, ss. 46–50; which came into force in Apr.1987.

[104] Green Paper, *Income During Initial Sickness: A New Strategy* (1980), paras.
3–4; HC Deb., 6th ser., vol. 96, cols. 137–8 (Tony Newton, Minister for Social
Security).

pared to do so by transferring primary responsibility for the benefit provision to employers, even though this ran counter to their general aim of reducing administrative burdens on employers. This perhaps indicates the primacy accorded to the general aim of retrenching upon state social security activity in order to reduce public expenditure both on benefits and on administrative manpower. At all events, it shows that neither statutory sick pay nor statutory maternity pay would be regarded as intended to benefit employees, for whom this was at best a 'zero sum game'.

As we have indicated, as the 1980s progressed, the aim of deregulation in favour particularly of small businesses became more programmatic. In March 1985 the Department of Trade and Industry published, under the title of *Burdens on Business*, the Report of a Scrutiny of Administrative and Legislative Requirements which assessed the 'burden of regulation' and suggested remedial action. Employment protection law was seen as part of the burden, as for that matter were health and safety at work requirements.[105] The proposals for employment protection law were to increase employees' qualifying periods in unfair dismissal cases from one to two years in firms employing over twenty (on the ground that 'the present one year period is too short for many smaller businesses, and is distorting dismissal decisions'; and to 'redress the balance in unfair dismissal cases by further action to discourage ill-founded complaints, (e.g. a scheme for cash deposits from some or all complainants to be refunded or forfeited at the discretion of the tribunal)'.[106] Action to implement the former proposal was announced in the Budget Statement of March 1985,[107] and was taken with effect from June 1985 in the shape of the Unfair Dismissal (Variation of Qualifying Period) Order 1985.[108]

The latter proposal (ultimately implemented in 1989) remained an active one through two White Papers in similar vein to that of *Burdens on Business*, namely Lord Young's White Paper of July

---

[105] *Burdens on Business*, para. 2.2.1.
[106] Ibid., para. 4.3.
[107] HC Deb., 6th ser., vol. 75, col. 794 (Nigel Lawson, 19 Mar. 1985).
[108] Unfair Dismissal (Variation of Qualifying Period) Order 1985 (SI 1985, No. 782). Debated in the House of Commons, HC Deb., 6th ser., vol. 79, cols. 423 ff. (15 May 1985).

1985 entitled *Lifting the Burden*[109] and his further White Paper, presented by him this time as Secretary of State for Employment in May 1986, entitled *Building Businesses . . . not Barriers*.[110] The later of these White Papers, having indicated a somewhat grudging assent to the continuance of employment protection legislation, rather chillingly qualified that assent with the proposition that 'in each case the Government have to consider why it is necessary to depart from the basic principle that terms and conditions of employment are matters to be determined by the employer and the employees concerned (where appropriate through their representatives), in the light of their own individual circumstances'.[111] At a theoretical level, this seemed to offer the basis for a direct challenge to the whole *raison d'être* of employment protection legislation.

(iii) *The Wages Act 1986.*   The mid-1980s were in fact a period of fairly intense activity in terms of the de-regulation of the individual employment relationship; apart from the Order varying the qualifying period for Unfair Dismissal rights, the legislative centrepiece of this activity was the Wages Act 1986,[112] the impact of which on collective bargaining and labour standards (via its provisions on Wages Councils) we considered earlier in this chapter. On the individual employment law side, the Wages Act was concerned with reforming the Truck legislation and with reducing the significance of statutory redundancy rebates. The government announced in July 1983 its intention to repeal the Truck Acts 1831–40 and the Payment of Wages Act 1960 'in order to facilitate the trend towards cashless pay'. Two consultative documents were issued by the Department of Employment in order to decide what if any replacement system of protection for employees was appropriate. The provisions which were ultimately made stress the general necessity for, but sufficiency of, prior contractual authorization for deductions from wages.[113] That requirement, less exigent than the previous requirements

---

[109] Cmnd. 9571.
[110] Cmnd. 9794.
[111] Ibid., para. 7.2.
[112] See Second Reading Debate on the Wages Bill in the House of Commons (HC Deb., 6th ser., vol. 91, cols. 796 ff.); introduced by Kenneth Clarke as Paymaster-General and Minister for Employment.
[113] Wages Act 1986, s. 1.

that deductions also be fair and reasonable, does extend to non-manual workers as well as to the manual workers, who alone were protected under the previous Acts. Moreover, a distinct protection was conferred upon retail workers, consisting of a provision that deductions from that remuneration made on account of cash shortages or stock deficiencies are not to exceed 10 per cent of the gross amount of the wages payable on a particular pay-day.[114] This was in response to evidence of swingeing deductions of this kind from the wages of workers such as forecourt attendants at petrol stations.[115] However, the modernization in this respect of the provisions of the Trucks Acts should not obscure the fact that the Wages Act restored to employers a general contractual freedom to stipulate for deductions from wages and financial penalties for employees. If the Truck Acts were archaic and complex,[116] that was because employers' abuses of that contractual freedom had been multifarious for many decades.

The opportunity was also taken in the Wages Act to withdraw employers' entitlement to rebates on statutory redundancy payments where the employer employs ten or more persons.[117] It was asserted that,

these rebates were designed to encourage employers to shed labour in the 1960s when labour shortages . . . were a major impediment to growth. Today the rebates provide a perverse public subsidy to redundancy in an age when . . . unemployment is our major economic and social problem.[118]

It was not explained why small employers were henceforth to be differently treated; but the fact of their continuing to enjoy the entitlement to rebate until 1989 (when it was universally abolished by the Employment Act of that year) reminds us that in the early and mid-1980's phase of de-regulation, the small employers were the primary beneficiaries, while larger employers, like their employees, tended to be regarded by the policy-makers

[114] Wages Act 1986, s. 2.
[115] See T. Goriely, 'Arbitrary Deductions from Pay and the Proposed Repeal of the Truck Acts' (1983) 12 ILJ 236.
[116] See O. Kahn-Freund, *Labour and the Law* (3rd edn. 1983), 50. See also above, p. 133.
[117] Wages Act 1986, s. 27.
[118] HC Deb., 6th ser., vol. 91, col. 796 (11 Feb. 1986) (Kenneth Clarke).

as unduly protected from the discipline of the labour market.

From these proposals for and measures of de-regulation in the mid-1980s, two common themes emerge. The first is an under-lying purpose of reducing labour costs and costs associated with employment, whether for the state or for individual employers. The second is that the distributive effects of cost-cutting measures could be concealed under an increasingly pervasive rhetoric of efficiency and job creation. The rhetoric rises to a triumphant crescendo in the Minister for Employment's peroration to his presentation of the Wages Bill:

This is a Bill to promote employment. It will do this by easing the regulation of the labour market and removing burdens on employers. It will have a modest but significant effect on the employment level. It is a Bill to enable employers to employ workers under modern conditions without being hamstrung by legislation and controls that are a legacy of yesterday's problems and yesterday's social attitudes, whether the problem was the Victorian 'tommy shop', the Edwardian sweatshop or the overmanned shopfloor of the 1960s. Few Bills can claim such a wide sweep of simplifying and clarifying the accumulation of over 150 years of different sorts of controls dealing with quite different problems.[119]

(iv) *The Employment Act 1989.* The Wages Act 1986 had marked the high point of straightforward de-regulation in the simple sense of the cutting-down of legislative protection in employment. There was one final burst of that activity in the late 1980s in the shape of the Employment Act 1989, which seems to have resulted partly from a stock-taking within the Department of Employment of its de-regulatory progress.[120] That process gave rise to some further moves along by then well-established de-regulatory lines. The qualifying period of service for the employee's right, upon request, to a written statement of reasons for dismissal was extended from six months to two years, as the qualifying period for unfair dismissal rights had earlier been extended.[121] The employer's obligation to give employees particulars of disciplinary procedures applicable to them was

---

[119] Ibid., col. 806.

[120] The starting-point for this part of the 1989 Act was the White Paper, *Building Businesses . . . Not Barriers* Cmnd. 9794 (1986). See generally, S. Deakin, 'Equality Under a Market Order: The Employment Act 1989' (1990) 19 ILJ 1 ff.

[121] Employment Act 1989, s. 15, amending EPCA 1978, s. 53.

abolished in favour of employers of fewer than twenty employees, thus further reinforcing the policy of 'lifting legislative burdens' in particular from small employers.[122] The conditions for making unfair dismissal claims were made more strict by the strengthening of the controls imposed at the pre-hearing review stage, which as we have seen was itself introduced in the early 1980s.[123] The right of employee trade union officials (such as shop stewards and convenors) to take time off for trade union duties was circumscribed so as, in effect, to exclude purposes extending beyond that of collective bargaining with one's immediate employer,[124] thus severely localizing the collective dimension of this individual employment protection right just as collective rights or freedoms had themselves been confined to disputes with one's own employer by the trade dispute legislation of the early 1980s. Finally, so far as this group of measures is concerned, redundancy rebates were abolished for small employers, having previously been abolished for all other employers by the Wages Act 1986.[125] Technically this was to remove an entitlement of employers rather than employees; but the measure was in the de-regulatory mode in the sense that the government had come to regard these rebates as a public subsidy which was underpinning the making of redundancy payments to employees.

If the Employment Act 1989, as the last major exercise in de-regulation of the 1980s, was wide-ranging in its scope, it was nevertheless far from exhaustive. The Unfair Dismissal legislation had been left broadly intact, and the Act had notably failed to pursue the proposal made in 1986 to raise the general weekly hours threshold for employment protection rights from 16 to 20 hours.[126] All this was in part explicable by the fact that the 1989

[122] EA 1989, s. 13, adding a new s. 2A to EPCA 1978.

[123] EA 1989, s. 20, adding new para. 1A to sched. 94, EPCA 1978. Regulations could now be made to ensure that the pre-hearing review could result in a requirement upon the applicant to make a deposit of £150 as a condition of proceeding to full hearing.

[124] EA 1989, s. 14, amending EPCA 1978, s. 27, now TULRECA ss. 168–9, and reversing by statute the interpretation of s. 27 by the Court of Appeal in *Beal v. Beecham Group Ltd.* [1982] IRLR 192.

[125] EA 1989, s. 17, repealing EPCA 1978, ss. 104, 104A, sched. 6.

[126] The proposal was made in the White Paper, *Building Businesses . . . Not Barriers*, Cmnd. 9794. For discussion of the impact of the existing and proposed thresholds, see C. Hakim, 'Employment Rights: A Comparison of Part-time and Full-time Employees' (1989) 18 ILJ 69, followed by R. Disney and E. Szyszczak, 'Part-Time Work: Reply to Catherine Hakim' (1989) 18 ILJ 223.

Act was not straightforwardly a measure of de-regulation in the way that the Wages Act 1986 was. As we shall see in the next section, the programme of de-regulation had become complicated by the various needs to comply with EEC requirements of equal treatment between men and women, and by the Government's perception that if they were thus required to remove gender-based defects in protection—such as women's loss of unfair dismissal protection at a lower retirement age than that of men—it must be appropriate also to abolish all positive gender-based protections for employees as well. That perception in turn reflected the enlargement in the later 1980s of mid-1980s policies of de-regulation into a fundamental opposition to the development of a Social Dimension to the Single European Market. It is that general development with which we shall be concerned in the next section of this chapter. In the meantime, we turn to consider the ways in which, apart from reducing the impact of employment protection legislation, the governments of the 1980s sought to restructure the individual employment relationship.

(c) *Enterprise Promotion and Risk Transfer in the Individual Employment Relationship*

From the mid-1980s onwads, the government sought ways of positively achieving patterns of flexibility in individual employment relationships—of attacking, in other words, not just the rigidities imposed by protective legislation but the rigidities, as they saw it, of the wage–work bargain itself. This meant pursuing forms of the wage–work bargain and of its ancillary features which would better realize the ideal of the free and enterprise-led labour market. Closely associated with those ideological aims was the idea of transferring employment-related economic risks to the individual in the labour market, whether by way of transfer from the employer or from the state social security system. Two sets of measures are especially interesting in this context; firstly those concerning profit-related pay and secondly those concerning personal pensions.

(i) *Profit-Related Pay.* The idea of encouraging the development of profit-related pay was a particular enthusiasm of Nigel Lawson as Chancellor of the Exchequer in the mid-1980s. He seems to have been influenced[127] by the arguments advanced by Professor Martin Weitzman of the Massachusetts Institute of Technology in 1984 that partial payment of employees by a share of company profits could help to combat wage inflation without adversely affecting levels of unemployment by reducing the costs to employers of workforce expansion when profits are high or of workforce reduction. Thus in his 1986 Budget Speech, the Chancellor developed his general assertion of the responsibility of employers and management for controlling wage costs into a specific case for profit-related pay:

The problem we face in this country is not just the level of pay in relation to productivity but also the rigidity of the pay system. . . . One way out of this might be to move to a system in which a significant proportion of an employee's remuneration depends directly on the company's profitability per person employed.[128]

In other words, it was wished to transfer some of the financial risks, hitherto carried by the employing enterprise, to its workforce. The case for doing this by encouraging profit-related pay was developed in a Green Paper issued by the Treasury, Department of Employment, and Department of Trade and Industry in July 1986.[129] In that document, two advantages were claimed for profit-related pay:

(a) if part of pay moves up and down with profits, it gives employees a more direct personal interest in their company's success, as existing employee share schemes do; and (b) reducing the rigidity of the pay system brings benefits for employment.[130]

The Green Paper presented the policy of encouraging profit-related pay as continuous with earlier measures to encourage employees' involvement in their companies by means of employee share-ownership.[131] Indeed, the government was a bit reluctant, in moving from those measures to profit-related pay, to forego the change in ownership structures which the earlier measures had produced.[132] But the integrative possibilities of employee

[127] See R. Chote, 'Profit-Related Pay Proves No Panacea', *The Independent*, 24 May 1991, p. 25.
[128] Ibid.
[129] *Profit Related Pay: A Consultative Document*, Cmnd. 9835.
[130] Ibid., para. 1.
[131] Ibid., para. 15.
[132] Cf. ibid., para. 15.

share-ownership had become less attractive to them than the possibilities of breaking down the rigidities in pay structures which they thought profit-related pay offered; and, besides, it was available to small and unincorporated businesses in a way that employee share-ownership schemes were not. It was asserted that the introduction of PRP schemes could make an important contribution to 'breaking the "going rate" psychology' which was thought to afflict pay bargaining.[133]

By the time of his 1987 Budget speech, the Chancellor was persuaded that profit-related pay (although no panacea) was 'a tool to help British business gradually to overcome one of our biggest national handicaps—the nature and behaviour of our labour market'.[134] It was therefore thought appropriate to introduce a scheme of tax relief for profit-related pay broadly along the lines floated in the Green Paper, but with the proportion of an employee's profit-related pay that would be tax free doubled from a quarter to a half, and with the upper limits on the relief raised.[135] This proposal was put into legislative effect, after the 1987 General Election, by chapter I of the Finance (No. 2) Act 1987.[136]

By the late 1980s, the government had probably appreciated the lack of significant effect that their profit-related measures would have, and their policy had shifted towards the encouragement of performance-related pay rather than profit-related pay— that is to say, remuneration quantified by reference to personal performance rather than to the performance of the enterprise. No legislative measures were taken to encourage performance-related pay, though the repeal of the Truck legislation by the Wages Act 1986 may have removed some obstacles to such schemes in relation to manual workers. However, the government was certainly committed to imposing performance-related pay in the public sector when they had the opportunity, especially by linking marginal elements in pay, such as incentive bonuses, to schemes for appraisal of the performance of individual employees.[137] In many ways these schemes fitted in better with

---

[133] Ibid., para. 22.
[134] HC Deb., vol. 112, col. 823 (17 Mar. 1987).
[135] Ibid. Tax relief was extended to the whole of PRP by the 1991 Budget.
[136] The key provision is that of s. 3.
[137] Cf. IDS, *Focus on Performance Pay*, IDS Quarterly 61 (Dec. 1991).

the government's individualistic and entrepreneurial model of the employment relationship than profit-related pay schemes did. Of much greater significance than the profit-related pay measures in promoting that model was their treatment of pensions legislation.

(ii) *Pensions.* As the 1980s progressed, Conservative governments became increasingly intent upon manipulating the development of individual employment law towards their own model of the individual employment relationship, with the development of the law relating to occupational pension schemes as the most powerful example. There were various pressures towards the reform of this body of law; the government steered the process of reform towards their own concept in which occupational pensions were seen as realizable and transferable investments in the hands of the individual worker, who would thereby ideally acquire something of the independence and self-reliance of the self-employed worker. The rhetoric concealed the extent to which this also transferred considerable downside risk to individual workers—especially those less well placed to operate as individual investors or as if they were in business on their own account.

The governments of the 1980s inherited a pensions regime which, having been contested in the early 1970s, seemed to command considerable consensus across the political spectrum.[138] The Social Security Pensions Act 1975, for which Barbara Castle was the Minister responsible, had for the most part replaced the pensions provisions of the Conservative government's Social Security Act 1973. The 1975 Act had provided a state earnings-related pension which had considerably improved the pension prospects especially of relatively lower-paid workers, while providing a tri-partite specialist agency, the Occupational Pensions Board, to oversee the functioning of the occupational pension scheme sector, that is, the sector which was contracted out of the state scheme. The Board had the function of considering whether the regulatory framework for occupational pension schemes adequately vindicated the legitimate expectations of employees as pension scheme members. By the early 1980s, the Board was producing reports which cast doubt on that, in par-

---

[138] See G. Moffatt, 'Provision for Retirement: Some Recent Developments' (1985) 14 ILJ 134.

ticular suggesting that there was insufficient protection of the interests of early leavers,[139] that is, employees leaving an occupational pension scheme before retirement, typically in order to work for another employer, and in general indicating that the existing legal structure of occupational pensions schemes, still very largely based upon the general law of trusts, provided scant guarantees of the security of members' rights and expectations, failing to address issues such as that of security of the real value of pensions, or disclosure of information to pension scheme members.[140]

In the course of the 1980s, the priorities which had shaped the 1975 Act and these proposals for further reform were very significantly altered. The governments of the 1980s had little enthusiasm for the protective policies embodied in the two OPB reports to which we have referred, though they were prepared to improve the position of early leavers on the rather different ground that this would enhance workers' job mobility, thereby improving the efficiency of the labour market,[141] and were prepared to require greater disclosure of information partly as a milder alternative to more extensive statutory regulation and partly because it fitted in with a sort of workers' consumerism which the government was, as we shall see, keen to encourage.[142]

This transitional phase between the employment protection policies of the 1970s and the free labour market policies of the later 1980s is perfectly represented by the pensions provisions of the Social Security Act 1985. The key provisions were those of section 2 dealing with the rights of early leavers and of section 3 dealing with information about occupational pension schemes. Before 1973, employers had been free to stipulate that early leavers in an occupational pension scheme would enjoy no greater rights than a return of their own contribution to that scheme. The Social Security Act 1973 had conferred upon early leavers a right to a preserved pension—that is, a pension at

---

[139] Occupational Pensions Board, *Improved Protection for the Occupational Pension Rights and Expectations of Early Leavers*, Cmnd. 8271 (1981).
[140] Occupational Pensions Board, *Greater Security for the Rights and Expectations of Members of Occupational Pension Schemes*, Cmnd. 8649 (1982).
[141] See Moffatt, 'Provision for Retirement', at 135.
[142] See the various DHSS Consultative Documents referred to by Moffatt, ibid., at 136, 138.

retirement age in respect of their employment before their early leaving; but the real value of those preserved pensions was not protected. The 1985 Act now guaranteed that those preserved pensions would be increased in line with prices up to a ceiling of 5 per cent compound.[143] Early leavers were also given the right to transfer out of their occupational pension, taking the actuarial cash equivalent of rights built up in the scheme into another scheme, or buying insurance policies with it.[144] Furthermore, rights to be informed of the constitution and about the administration of occupational pension schemes were accorded to interested parties, including[145] independent trade unions recognized in relation to members and prospective members of the scheme.[146]

Even while these modestly protective reforms were taking place, the government was engaged in a much more fundamental reformulation of its pensions strategy, which was shaped by very different priorities; this was implemented by the Social Security Act 1986, the pensions part of which is a distinctly different animal from the corresponding part of the 1985 Act.[147] From the early 1980s onwards, the government had been moving in the direction of a retreat from the state earnings-related pension commitment embodied in the Social Security Pensions Act 1975, because they felt that it would develop into an unacceptably burdensome state liability. Yet from the outset they wished to make this retreat without an equivalent advance in employers' labour costs. This would mean transferring part of the liability for retirement provision back to the workforce itself. The government initially, early in 1985, proposed an extreme measure along these lines, which would have involved the abolition of the earnings-related part of the state pension provision, with a requirement for money purchase pensions to be provided by employers instead.[148] (Money purchase pensions are those in

---

[143] Social Security Act 1985, s. 2 and sched. I.

[144] Ibid. See Annotations by K. Ewing in *Current Law Statutes* (1985), 53. 4.

[145] Surprisingly, as Ewing pointed out, ibid.

[146] 1985 Act, s. 3 and sched. 2.

[147] Though one element at least of the 1985 Act, the transfer rights for early leavers, was in part a preparation for the 1986 measures: see Ewing, *Current Law Statutes* (1985), 53. 4.

[148] Department of Health and Social Security Green Paper, *The Reform of Social Security*, Cmnd. 9517 (Feb. 1985). See R. Nobles, 'Retirement Provision and the Social Security Act: The Prospects for Radical Change' (1986) 15 ILJ 209.

which pensions contributions are used to build up a fund for the purchase of an annuity upon retirement, but where the size of the fund—and thus of the annuity—is not guaranteed to relate to the earnings of the worker in question. This means that a lower level of insurance is provided by money purchase schemes than by earnings-related or final salary pension schemes; the premiums to secure that insurance are correspondingly smaller.)

Perhaps the consultation process which then ensued suggested that this would involve an unacceptably extensive transfer of pensions liability from the state to employers or even to employees. At all events, the proposals were modified, by the time the White Paper stage was reached,[149] so that the State Earnings-Related Pension Scheme would be retained, albeit at a somewhat downgraded level, and so that state liability would be reduced by creating new incentives to contract out of the state system. It was this plan which was implemented by part I of the Social Security Act 1986. The central strategy consisted in extending the arrangements for contracting out of the state pension scheme, which had hitherto existed only in respect of occupational pension schemes (that is, pensions provided by employers). Contracting-out would now be possible in favour of personal pension schemes certified as appropriate schemes by the Occupational Pensions Board; this meant that employees acquired the right, as against the employer, to choose to contribute to a personal pension scheme run by, as it might be, a bank or building society or life assurance company, instead of contributing to the employer's occupational pension scheme.[150] The legislators, intent on ensuring that the financial institutions would find it worthwhile to offer personal pensions and that employees would find these equally as attractive as occupational pensions, were prepared for both personal and occupational schemes to involve a greater degree of risk-taking by employees than occupational pension schemes had hitherto been allowed to involve. Hence personal and occupational schemes could now obtain the contracted-out rebate from the national insurance system by offering money purchase pensions, where previously occupational schemes had had to offer

---

[149] Department of Health and Social Security White Paper, *The Reform of Social Security*, Cmnd. 9691 (Dec. 1985).

[150] See ss. 1–5, and s. 15 (terms of contracts of service or schemes restricting choice to be void).

salary-related benefits; and the government rejected the argument that money purchase pensions should be required to provide guaranteed minimum pensions for the member and his or her widow or widower, as contracted-out salary-related occupational schemes had to do.[151] Moreover, contracting-out by employers into occupational pension schemes was further encouraged by abolishing certain benefit requirements for salary-related occupational schemes;[152] and provision was made for the social security system to make an incentive payment equivalent to 2 per cent of reckonable earnings either to a personal pension scheme (as an incentive to provide a personal pension) or to a newly contracting-out occupational scheme (as an incentive to contract out).[153] On the basis of all this, Norman Fowler, when presenting the Social Security Bill as the Secretary of State for Social Services, could pass lightly over the reductions in pension expectations, and could claim that:

Each person will be able to choose the kind of pensions savings scheme that he wants, and the kind of body that he wants to run his savings scheme.[154]

This measure involved a significant conceptual transformation, which went beyond its immediate practical importance. The government could now, as Norman Fowler's statement shows, regard pensions primarily as a form of savings rather than as deferred earnings. In other words, the individual contributor to a pension scheme (whether a personal or occupational one) could be regarded as an investor rather than as a worker. This would make the rhetoric of freedom of choice more convincing and compelling. It would also make more acceptable, to the government, measures to safeguard the (admittedly reduced) pension expectations of those concerned, the government being much more comfortable with 'investor protection' than with 'employment protection'.

Hence we find in the pensions provisions of the Social Security

[151] S. 2, and see Annotation thereto by K. Ewing and D. Brodie, *Current Law Statutes* (1986), 50. 7; also s. 6 (money purchase contracted-out occupational pension schemes).
[152] S. 8 abolished the existing 'requisite benefit' requirements, leaving only the lower 'guaranteed minimum pension' requirements in place.
[153] Ss. 3, 7.
[154] HC Deb., 6th ser., vol. 90, col. 819 (28 Jan. 1986).

Act 1990[155] a new readiness on the government's part to take such protective measures. These measures involved an extensive acceptance of recommendations made by the Occupational Pensions Board for the safeguarding of pension benefits;[156] they established a Pensions Ombudsman and a Registrar of Occupational and Personal Pension Schemes, and they put in place a general requirement to increase the amount of salary-related pensions to take account of inflation (up to a maximum of 5 per cent per annum) once the payment of the pension has commenced.[157] (Employers would presumably be less hostile to this indexation of salary-related pensions now that the alternative of money purchase schemes existed, and, as we have seen, the government was at least content if not positively anxious for all concerned to be under incentives to move from salary-related to money purchase pension provision.) Provision was also made for protecting pensions in the event of the employer's insolvency, including a requirement for the appointment of an independent pension fund trustee in that event.[158] In general (although later events were abundantly to demonstrate how limited a degree of protection was in fact provided[159]), the government seemed solicitous of the interests of pension scheme members in relation to company mergers and takeovers;[160] this concern for pension scheme members perceived of as investors stands in some contrast with the government's hostility, displayed earlier in the 1980s, towards European Community measures designed to increase the protection of *employees* in relation to transfers of undertakings or corporate insolvencies.[161]

(*iii*) *Restructuring and the Law.* In fact, that very contrast provides a focal point for understanding the significance of the

[155] Ss. 11–14.
[156] Occupational Pensions Board, *Protecting Pensions: Safeguarding Benefits in a Changing Environment*, Cm. 573 (Feb. 1989).
[157] See Annotation by J. Mesher, *Current Law Statutes* (1990), 27. 28.
[158] S. 14 and sched. 4, pt. I.
[159] Cf. the Parliamentary Social Security Select Committee Report on the Maxwell/Mirror Group Newspapers Pensions affair: HC Session 91/92, Social Security Committee, 2nd Report, *The Operation of Pension Funds*, HC 61/II (4 Mar. 1992).
[160] See e.g. the presentation of the Bill by Tony Newton as Secretary of State for Social Services, HC Deb., 6th ser., vol. 165, cols. 637–9 (22 Jan. 1990).
[161] See below, pp. 577–80.

restructuring or attempted restructuring of the individual employment relationship during the 1980s. In so far as the individual
worker acquired the benefits of 'flexibility' or acquired new
choices of an entrepreneurial character, this seemed to depend
on reclassifying the relevant relationship as one of investment—
whether as a shareholder in a privatized enterprise for which
the individual worked, or as the purchaser of pension policies;
in other words, it depended on taking the activity in question
outside the scope of the employment relationship. Within the
employment relationship, 'flexibility' consisted very largely in
conferring or confirming a widely defined freedom of managerial
control of that relationship,[162] and of transferring economic risks
to the workforce from employers (or, to some extent, from the
state itself).

If we understand the restructuring or attempted restructuring
of the individual employment relationship in that way, how far
should we see the measures of the 1980s as having achieved such
a restructuring by means of de-rigidification or de-regulation?
The answer would seem to be that those measures encouraged
and marginally reinforced trends in the development of the
labour market which were present well before the 1980s, and
which were intensified in the 1980s more by general economic
developments than by changes in labour legislation. Thus the
shift from a primarily manufacturing economy to a primarily
service economy was of fundamental significance, and served
to increase the importance of the patterns of part-time, temporary, and casual employment, and of the employment of a
predominantly female workforce in relatively low-paid and low-
status jobs, which had long been characterizing features of parts
of the service sector of the labour economy;[163] as, of course, had
been low trade union density and under-developed collective
bargaining. Inasmuch as this state of affairs depended upon
legislative intervention, it probably depended at least as much

---

[162] Cf. A. Pollert, ed., *Farewell to Flexibility?* (Oxford, 1991), a symposium
book in which a similar thesis is stated and explored from a number of different
points of view—see esp. ch. 1, 'The Orthodoxy of Flexibility' (Anna Pollert), and
pt. II, chs. 4–6 'Restructuring Rationales: Productivity, Cost Controls or
Flexibility?' (Peter Fairbrother, Richard Whittington, Tim Walsh).

[163] This is powerfully argued, for instance, in relation to the Retail and Hotel
Trades by Tim Walsh in ch. 6 of Pollert, ed., *Farewell to Flexibility?*

upon the legislative social security regime as on changes to employment protection legislation.[164]

Within this context, governmental measures and policies of de-regulation and de-rigidification of the individual employment relationship had the importance, not so much of being the primary engines of change in the way that the labour economy developed, but rather of being a decisive form of resistance to further growth of the juridification and legislative socialization of the employment relationship which had been such a feature of the previous decade or decade and a half. As that resistance developed and intensified, the social policy of the European Community was increasingly identified as the primary or sole countervailing force. How far that polarization was apparent and how far it reflected a real orientation and impact of an emerging body of labour law at European Community level is a question to be addressed in the next section.

10.4. THE IMPACT OF MEMBERSHIP OF THE EUROPEAN COMMUNITY

So far we have considered the labour market restructuring measures of the 1980s in terms of the developing policies of Conservative governments during those years—as the evolution and working-out of the ideology of those governments. That policy development was itself in some measure a response to the necessities created by the UK's membership of the European Community. This was true in practical terms throughout the 1980s, in the sense that the government had to make specific policy decisions and to take specific measures in fulfilment of its obligations to the Community from 1979 onwards. It was also increasingly the case as the decade progressed that the government's labour market ideology developed by way of reaction to the perceived ideology of the Community. The European Community came to represent the main countervailing force seeking to perpetuate 1960s and 1970s styles of industrial justice legislation. By 1990, indeed, the government had come overtly to

[164] See, for a very valuable development of this thesis, S. Deakin and F. Wilkinson, *Labour Law, Social Security and Economic Inequality* (London, 1989).

maintain that the two ideologies were in conflict with each other, and that it was committed to resisting the encroachment of the Community's policies upon the working of the labour market in the UK. These battle-lines were not fully drawn up until the late 1980s; but these matters were approached in a somewhat adversarial way even in the early 1980s.

(a) Transfers of Businesses

This description is borne out by the first episode in the saga, which was the enactment in 1981 of the Transfer of Undertakings (Protection of Employment) Regulations.[165] These were made under the authority of the European Communities Act 1972—the first piece of employment legislation to be so—in implementation of the EEC Acquired Rights Directive of 1977.[166] Admittedly the preceding Labour government had not hastened to implement that Directive; indeed, they had contributed to the weakening of the draft directive originally published in 1974.[167] But the Conservative government after 1979—which was the year appointed for implementation of the Directive—tarried until the European Commission had begun non-implementation proceedings against the UK in the European Court of Justice, and even then gave effect to the Directive only with an openly expressed 'remarkable lack of enthusiasm'.[168]

That remarkable lack of enthusiasm is both eminently comprehensible and highly significant in view of the policy underlying the Acquired Rights Directive. The Directive was one of the products of the Social Action Programme adopted by the Council of Ministers in 1974. The general aim of the Social Action Programme was to ensure that the development of social policy within the Community kept pace with the economic integration which the Community was bringing about.[169] One specific product of that general aim was the policy of recognizing

---

[165] SI 1981, No. 1794.

[166] Directive 77/187 on the approximation of the laws of the Member States relating to the safeguarding of employees' rights in the event of transfer of undertakings, businesses, and parts of businesses.

[167] See Hepple, (1976) 5 ILJ 197 and (1977) 6 ILJ 106.

[168] HC Deb., 6th ser., vol. 691, col. 680 (David Waddington for the government).

[169] See M. Shanks, 'The Social Policy of the European Communities' (1977) 14 CML Rev. 375.

the interests of employees in changes of ownership or control of the enterprises employing them, these being changes which the EEC had the aim and effect of facilitating. This is the rationale for the acquired rights approach; a rationale which can sustain either a narrow approach to acquired rights which says that employees should enjoy the same rights against the new owner or controller of the enterprise as they enjoyed against the old one, or a broad approach which goes on to say that they should also be able to influence the decision whether to transfer ownership or control.[170] Both approaches were at best foreign to, at worst antithetical to, the labour law of the UK. The narrow approach challenged a conscious denial in the common law of the contract of employment of the unilateral transferability of contracts between employers—a doctrine evolved in the context of company amalgamations, and expressed in the decision of the House of Lords in 1940 in *Nokes* v. *Doncaster Amalgamated Collieries Ltd*.[171] The broad approach seemed to involve the adoption of different patterns of industrial relations from those current in the UK; it threatened to require processes of consultation with directly elected representatives of the workforce via Works Councils and, in the Draft Directive of 1974, envisaged compulsory arbitration of employment issues arising out of proposed takeovers and mergers, where British unions still strongly preferred a voluntarist approach.[172]

The fact that both approaches are evident in the Acquired Rights Directive of 1977 helps to explain its reception in the UK. The Labour Government was cool towards it, probably because they felt that the tendency to require changes to patterns of industrial relations had been successfully resisted in the implementation of the Collective Dismissals Directive of 1975 by part IV of the Employment Protection Act 1975; they saw little point in a further traversal of what they regarded as very much the same ground.[173] They nevertheless got as far as producing,

[170] See P. L. Davies, 'Acquired Rights, Creditors' Rights, Freedom of Contract and Industrial Democracy' (1989) 9 *Yearbook of European Law* 21.

[171] [1940] AC 1014. This was a decision protective of the employee; it meant that the amalgamated company which was the *de facto* employer could not sue the employee for breach of his contract of employment made with the original company.

[172] See Hepple, (1976) 5 ILJ at 208–9.

[173] See above, pp. 385–6.

in 1978, draft regulations to implement the Acquired Rights Directive, which Member States were supposed to do by 1979. For the incoming Conservative government, however, both the narrow and the broad aspects of the Directive must have seemed deeply challenging to their aims of de-regulating and de-rigidifying the working of the labour market. In a broad sense it must have seemed to challenge free transfer of capital and freedom of contract; in a narrow sense it impeded the sale of businesses in difficulty—this was an important consideration in the conditions of severe recession prevailing by the early 1980s. Although representations made by the UK government among others had secured the result that the Directive itself, unlike the draft Directive, did not extend to takeovers and mergers by transfer of share control (the typical form of takeover transaction in the UK), the government in making the Transfer Regulations in 1981 made no secret of the fact that they were acting under the compulsion of their EEC Treaty obligations. Their revised version of the 1978 draft included a partial relaxation in favour of sales of the viable parts of insolvent businesses by receivers—the so-called 'hiving-off' transactions—which came to the very brink of non-compliance with the Directive, indeed over the brink in the views of some.[174]

In the event, the Transfer Regulations contained three key provisions. Regulation 5 had the effect that the contracts of employment of employees of an undertaking or part of an undertaking are transferred with the undertaking or part. Secondly, Regulation 8 amended the unfair dismissal legislation by requiring employees to be treated as unfairly dismissed if dismissed by reason of the transfer, though not if dismissed for an economic, technical, or organizational reason entailing changes in the workforce of either the transferor or the transferee. This was to prevent Regulation 5 from being frustrated by dismissals effected as part of the transfer process. Thirdly, Regulation 10 imposed a duty on both the transferor and the transferee to inform and consult the trade union representatives of employees potentially affected by the transfer or by measures taken in connection with it, where the employer recognized a trade union in respect of the

---

[174] Regulation 4. See P. L. Davies and M. R. Freedland, *Transfer of Employment* (London, 1982), General Note, 'Hiving down'.

employees concerned. This was to be the last major occasion on which the labour legislation of the 1980s followed the mid-1970s pattern of conferring representative status upon recognized trade unions.

The experience of the Transfer Regulations in practice is interesting in relation to the government's rather hostile perceptions at the time they were made. Regulation 10 was deprived of much of its significance, even before it was made, by the repeal in 1980 of the statutory trade union recognition procedure, which, as we have seen,[175] meant that employers could avoid obligations which assumed the presence of a recognized trade union. Moreover, there was no effective remedy for failure to consult as required by Regulation 10.[176] Hence Regulations 5 and 8 were the most significant provisions, though they in turn appeared to be capable of being defeated by dismissals carried out by insolvent transferors before the transfer took effect, for in those circumstances the transferee was not liable for those dismissals and the transferor had no assets with which to meet such liabilities. It was not until the late 1980s that the House of Lords restored some effectiveness to the Regulations by their decision in *Litster* v. *Forth Dry Dock and Engineering Co. Ltd.*[177] Here they interpreted, indeed re-fashioned, Regulation 5 in particular, so as to give effect to the Acquired Rights Directive by ensuring that employees were not excluded from the scope of the Regulations by being dismissed before, but by reason of, a transfer. It has been argued that this purposive construction, in seeking to implement the aims of the EEC Directive, went so far counter to the aims of the government in this area as to 'subvert the Government's strategy of facilitating the sale of insolvent businesses'.[178] Certainly the government appeared content for the Regulations to wither on the vine, had not the House of Lords intervened in this way. The government was offering little prospect that there would be UK legislation to reinforce the Regulations or give full effect to the Directive.

[175] See above, pp. 427, 466–7.

[176] This was mainly due to the limit, upon the compensation which can be awarded for failure to consult as required by Reg. 10, of 2 weeks' pay for each employee affected (Reg. 11(11)).

[177] [1989] ICR 341. (See H. Collins, 'Transfer of Undertakings and Insolvency' (1989) 18 ILJ 144.)

[178] Collins, 'Transfer', at p. 157.

(b) Equal Pay for Work of Equal Value

There are significant parallels between the history of the Transfer Regulations and that of the second UK labour law measure to be generated by the EEC in the 1980s, namely the Equal Pay (Amendment) Regulations of 1983 which introduced the right to equal pay for work of equal value as between men and women.[179] The 1983 Regulations were also the implementation of a Directive made as part of the Social Action Programme—in this case, the Equal Pay Directive of 1975, which confirmed an interpretation of Article 119 of the Treaty of Rome as extending to include an equal value concept.[180] Equally, they were made only under the pressure of proceedings against the UK by the EEC Commission— this time pursued through to judgment against the UK in the European Court of Justice;[181] and equally they were deliberately made within the contained framework of section 2(2) of the European Communities Act 1972, rather than by means of new parliamentary legislation. On this occasion, more was at stake than there had been in relation to the Acquired Rights Directive, for the Equal Pay Directive challenged a central tenet of 1980s Conservative labour market policy, namely that there should be no general legal norms constraining the free operation of that market, and particularly no norms capable of generating wide-ranging comparability claims in the way that a right to equal pay for work of equal value threatened to do.

So it is not surprising that the Equal Pay (Amendment) Regulations were a particularly minimal implementation of their parent Directive. The claim to an equal value assessment by an independent expert which they introduced[182] was hedged about with qualifications such as that precluding such an assesssment where an existing (non-discriminatory) job evaluation scheme had assessed the jobs as unequal in value.[183] Moreover, though this was to turn out to be more symbolically than practically significant, the new equal value claim was subjected to a some-

---

[179] SI 1983, no. 1794, which were accompanied by procedural changes made by the Industrial Tribunals (Rules of Procedure) (Equal Value Amendment) Regulations 1983 (SI 1983, No. 1807).

[180] Council Directive 75/117 of 1975. See above, p. 218.

[181] *Commission of the European Communities* v. *UK*, Case 61/81 [1982] ICR 578.

[182] Reg. 2(1), introducing new s. 1(2)(c) into the Equal Pay Act 1970.

[183] Reg. 3(1), introducing new s. 2A of the 1970 Act.

what wider defence—genuine material factor as opposed to genuine material difference—than the defence applicable to the previously existing claims;[184] and that greater width was thought to permit greater account to be taken of external labour-market considerations.[185] Underlyingly, as one of us has argued elsewhere, the Regulations addressed only one of the compromises of which the Equal Pay Act 1970 was composed, thus leaving in place very significant qualifications upon the principle of equal pay—for example, the confinement to workers in the 'same employment', whch brought geographical limits into play.[186] Again, moreover, as with the Transfer Regulations, it fell to the House of Lords to rescue the new measure from the threat of nullification. This they did in their decision in *Pickstone* v. *Freemans plc.*;[187] though this time the threat to the efficacy of the Regulations came not so much from the inherent restrictiveness of their design as from an egregiously narrow interpretation of them which—probably contrary to the intention of the Department of Employment in drawing up the Regulations—would have denied an equal value claim to a member of a mixed gender workgroup engaged upon like work with each other. Had this narrow interpretation been upheld, employers could have frustrated equal value claims from women workers by ensuring the presence of token male workers doing like work with them. Again, although the comparison with the Transfer Regulations is not exact, the driving force behind the decision of the House of Lords was the parent EEC measure—in this case article 119 of the Treaty of Rome itself—and there is no reason to think that the UK Government would have moved to repair the breach if the House of Lords (and for that matter the Court of Appeal in this instance) had not done so. Indeed, the government seemed scarcely troubled by the fact that the process of getting an independent equal value assessment and getting the assessor's

---

[184] Reg. 2(2), introducing a reformulated s. 1(3) of the 1970 Act. Cf., however, the discussion of the relationship between the two defences in *Rainey* v. *Greater Glasgow Health Board* [1987] ICR 129 (HL).

[185] See C. McCrudden, 'Equal Pay for Work of Equal Value: The Equal Pay (Amendment) Regulations 1983' (1983) 12 ILJ 197, esp. at 216–17.

[186] See P. L. Davies, 'European Equality Legislation, U.K. Legislative Policy and Industrial Relations', in C. McCrudden (ed.), *Women, Employment and European Equality Law* (London, 1987) and above, p. 213.

[187] [1988] ICR 697.

report accepted by an industrial tribunal turned out to be so lengthy and cumbersome as to frustrate all but the most determined, well-resourced, and patient of claimants.

(c) The Sex Discrimination Act 1986

As the 1980s wore on, and the government became more confident in and assertive of its aims of de-regulating and de-rigidifying the labour market, so its divergence from the mainstream of European Social Policy became the more marked. In a sense this was evident in the next major measure in the chronological sequence of measures generated by UK membership of the European Community, which was the Sex Discrimination Act 1986. Here the government sought to combine the by now routinely minimalist response to pressure from the Community with a deliberately counterpoised abandonment of important legislative protections applying specifically to women workers. It was largely in order to accomplish the latter, pointedly de-regulatory, aim that the government adopted the mode of proposing a Bill, rather than making regulations under the European Communities Act 1972 as they had done in 1981 and 1983 in comparable situations. A decision of the European Court of Justice had identified areas in which the government had to take steps to comply with their obligations under the Equal Treatment Directive of 1976 (a further product of the Social Action Programme);[188] in *European Commission* v. *UK*, Case 165/82,[189] the Court had found that the Sex Discrimination Act 1975 failed to comply with the Equal Treatment Directive, firstly in excluding workers in small undertakings and private households from its coverage, and secondly in failing to provide for the declaring void or amending of discriminatory provisions in collective agreements or the rules of undertakings, or of professional bodies. Section 1 of the 1986 Act dealt with the first of those two findings, repealing the existing exclusion and replacing it by a new genuine occupational qualification (that is, a case where it is legitimate to choose a worker according to gender) relating to employment in a private home involving physical or social contact with a person living there or knowledge of intimate

---

188 Directive No. 76/207.
189 [1984] ICR 192.

details of the person's life—the Court having recognized the case for a privacy exception of this kind.

The response to the second of those two findings of the European Court of Justice is particularly interesting, especially so far as collective agreements were concerned. The government had contended vigorously that the European Commission had been making a misconceived claim of non-implementation in so far as collective agreements in the context of the UK had their legal impact via the individual contract of employment, to which the protection of the Sex Discrimination Act 1975 already applied. Thus feeling that they were being required to legislate for form's sake, the government proposed a measure which provided only for the declaring void of discriminatory provisions and not for their amendment, and which provided no remedial mechanism to give any practical significance to this nullification process.[190] Moreover, the making of this minimalist proposal was put forward as the justification for the repeal by the 1986 Act of the only existing mechanism, itself severely limited in scope, for amending collective agreements to remedy discriminatory provisions, namely section 3 of the Equal Pay Act 1970.[191] This had, by giving collective access to an arbitral tribunal (latterly the CAC), constituted a practical implementation of the fair labour standard of non-discrimination in terms and conditions of employment determined by single employers or by collective bargaining.[192]

The attack on labour standards was further pursued by this Act; for, not content on this occasion to confine themselves to Regulations having the sole purpose of implementing EEC obligations, the government took the opportunity to propose the repeal of the legislation imposing restrictions on the working hours and conditions of women—legislation affecting mainly factory work which prevented women working nights and limited their shift-working and starting and finishing hours.[193] The government

[190] S. 6, amending s. 77 of the Sex Discrimination Act 1975.
[191] See above, pp. 214–15.
[192] See P. L. Davies, 'The Central Arbitration Committee and Equal Pay' [1980] CLP 165.
[193] The repeal was effected by s. 7 of the 1986 Act. The restrictions on women's night work had been contained in the Hours of Employment (Conventions) Act 1936; see above, p. 25.

could point to the fact that exemption from the requirements of this legislation had become very readily obtainable from the Factory Inspectorate. But their reaction to unsystematic regulation was crudely de-regulatory. The repeal of the legislation on women's hours of work would have resulted in restrictions on night working by men but not by women in the baking industry. The response was to repeal the Baking Industry (Hours of Work) Act 1954.[194] Lord Young asserted robustly that:

The alternative course which was put to us of extending the Act's provisions to cover women as well as men working in the baking industry would have been totally inconsistent with the need to avoid unnecessary and burdensome restrictions on enterprise. There is no justification for singling out the baking industry for this sort of statutory underpinning of collective bargaining on hours of employment.[195]

As we have seen earlier in this chapter, the attitudes there revealed towards collective labour standards were to be expressed in many other instances.

(d) Equality and Retirement

The 1986 Act also contained the first major UK response to the European Community's attack upon the discriminatory consequences of the inequality between the ages at which men and women qualify for a state pension—65 and 60 respectively. The Community Social Security Directive recognized the freedom of each member state to choose its own pensionable ages;[196] but the consequences of the British differential ages for employers' retirement and occupational pension provisions were inherently vulnerable as the Community pursued the goal of equal pay and treatment for men and women in employment more vigorously under the Social Action Programme. In the *Marshall* case,[197] the European Court of Justice held that there was a violation of the Equal Treatment Directive where a woman worker was required to retire at the state pensionable age when a male worker in the same employment would not have been required to

---

[194] See below, p. 587.
[195] HL Deb., 5th ser., vol. 471, col. 1182 (2nd Read. Deb.; 27 Feb. 1986).
[196] Directive 79/7, art. 7.
[197] *Marshall* v. *Southampton and South-west Hampshire Area Health Authority*, Case 152/84 [1986] IRLR 140.

retire until his state pensionable age of 65. The Court went on to hold that the Directive was directly applicable to claims by state employees—among whom this claimant was counted. It was, however, clear that the government would in due course be required to amend the law as it applied to employees in the private and public sectors alike. Sections 2 and 3 of the 1986 Act sought to bring the law relating to equal pay and sex discrimination, and the law of unfair dismissal, into compliance with the Equal Treatment Directive in this respect with the minimum of consequences for occupational pension and retirement provisions generally.

It fairly soon became clear that this was only one aspect of a larger movement towards equality of treatment, as between men and women in relation to retirement. For instance, there had been in 1986 a deliberate omission to bring the redundancy payments legislation into line with the amended unfair dismissal legislation, apparently on the ground that statutory redundancy payments came within the scope of the Social Security Directive, which, as we have seen, protected differential state pensionable ages. However, it subsequently appeared, and indeed was held by the Employment Appeal Tribunal, that a redundancy payment would count as 'pay' so as to attract the application of article 119 of the Treaty of Rome,[198] so section 16 of the Employment Act 1989 repaired the omission and assimilated upper age limits for men and women in relation to statutory redundancy payments. In the following year, the European Court of Justice would take the momentous, if by now predictable, step of holding that unequal pensionable ages for men and women under contract-based occupational pension schemes were in violation of article 119.[199] This evoked no short-term legislative response in the UK, despite (or was it in part because of?) the enormous uncertainty as to how far the ruling in the *Barber* case applied to pensions accruing, or based on contributions made, before that decision was given.[200]

[198] *Hammersmith and Queen Charlotte's Special Health Authority* v. *Cato* [1987] IRLR 483 (EAT).

[199] *Barber* v. *Guardian Royal Exchange Insurance Group*, Case C262/88 [1990] ICR 616.

[200] See V. Shrubsall, (1990) 19 ILJ 244.

(e) Repeal of Protective Legislation

There was another, and much more significant, sense in which the Employment Act 1989 (the last of the series of UK measures of the 1980s which are in whole or in part related to the employment law of the European Community) completed a programme of measures which the 1986 Act had embarked upon. As we saw earlier, the 1986 Act had a partly de-regulatory purpose; section 7 removed the existing statutory restrictions on women's working hours, and section 8 completed the destruction of gender-based controls on night work by repealing the Baking Industry (Hours of Work) Act 1954—the enactment of which was described in an earlier chapter.[201] The Employment Act 1989 proceeded much further along that path of de-regulation; sections 9 and 10 removed or modified many protective restrictions on the employment of women and young people. The dramatic example was the removal of the prohibition on women working underground in the mining industry; in order to free itself to propose this legislation, the government had first to denounce its obligations under an ILO Convention and an article of the European Social Charter, both of which required such a prohibition to be maintained.[202] Another Article of the Charter had to be denounced in order to make way for the repeal of the provision of the Employment of Women, Young Persons, and Children Act 1920 which prohibited the employment of young people on night work in industrial undertakings.[203]

The relationship between the policy of de-regulation which underlies those measures, and the policy of (reluctant) compliance with European Community employment law is a complex and interesting one. We have seen how the Sex Discrimination Act 1986 combined measures reflecting both those policy objectives. So also did the Employment Act 1989; its first eight sections have the aim of amending the Sex Discrimination Act 1975 to complete the implementation of the Equal Treatment Directive (while still preserving certain legislative protections for the special treatment of women in employment in situations where that was felt to be

---

[201] See above, pp. 102–3.
[202] ILO Convention 45—Underground Work (Women)—and art. 8(4)(b) of the European Social Charter.
[203] Art. 7(8).

appropriate and consistent with the Directive).[204] The amendment of the 1975 Act included the conferring upon the Secretary
of State of Employment of a formidable set of powers to override
or repeal statutory provisions granting positive protection to
women in employment or in vocational training arrangements,
and these cannot be seen in isolation from the de-regulatory
measures of sections 9 and 10 of the Act.

From 1986 onwards, the government saw the possibility of
linking its own programme of de-regulation (as outlined in the
1986 White Paper, *Building Businesses . . . Not Barriers*[205]) with
the need to amend in particular section 51 of the 1975 Act to
implement the Equal Treatment Directive. That was evident from
the Department of Employment's Consultative Document issued
in 1987 on the portmanteau topic of *Restrictions on Employment of Young People and the Removal of Sex Discrimination in
Legislation*, and it is that which explains the shape of the 1989
Act and its analogy to the 1986 Act. It is of course the case
that those concerned with the elimination of sex discrimination
in employment find themselves confronted with the problem of
what to do with existing provisions designed specially to protect
women from conditions of employment historically considered
imappropriate for them; and that they are cast in the role of
de-regulators where they decide to discard those protective provisions. Such an analysis, however, conceals the choice between
levelling-up and levelling-down which the policy-makers have
to make in operations of this kind. Simon Deakin has argued
cogently that the 1989 Act represented a different choice in this
respect from that which the European Commission wished for, as
evidenced by its Communication on this subject issued in 1987,
where it was emphasized that:

the obligation to ensure equal treatment must be seen in the context of
the need to improve working conditions set out in Article 117 of the
Treaty. Equality should not be made the occasion for a dis-improvement
of working conditions for one sex, and it would be insufficient to simply

---

[204] The compliance of some of those exemptions with the Directive was a
matter of some controversy, e.g. that of s. 5(3) which enabled women's colleges at
Oxford and Cambridge Universities to continue by their statutes to restrict their
academic appointments to women.
[205] Cmnd. 9794.

take away necessary protections which are presently limited to one sex.[206]

(f) Community Social Policy in the 1980s

The difference in balance and emphasis which is thus indicated between the British government's approach to equal treatment and that of the European Community as a whole is symptomatic of a larger development which was occurring during the 1980s. As British policy moved towards an ever more ambitiously conceived de-regulation and de-rigidification of the labour market, important countervailing tendencies emerged at Community level. In a much less dramatic way than in Britain, the employment law and labour market policy of the Community also moved in new directions in the 1980s. The impetus of the Social Action Programme had been largely lost by the end of the 1970s. In particular, the various initiatives towards greater involvement of workers in the management of companies seemed to be encountering an insuperable lack of enthusiasm on the part of the member states. As Bob Hepple starkly put it,

The draft 'Vredeling' directive on procedures for informing and consulting employees in large national and multinational enterprises had the misfortune to be presented to the Council on October 24, 1980, just as the steam had run out of the moves for greater worker involvement.[207]

In the early 1980s, therefore, the social action of the Community tended to be confined to the rather limited pursuit of humanitarian concerns (as Bob Hepple put it) for industrial safety, for training and employment growth, and for equal opportunities for women.[208]

In this period, moreover (and this cannot be dissociated from the developments to which we have just referred), there was a strong trend within the member states—with the UK in the vanguard—towards legal and collective bargaining regimes which would confer an increased flexibility upon employers in their use of labour; this was undoubtedly a reaction to the recessionary

---

[206] S. Deakin, 'Equality Under a Market Order: The Employment Act 1989' (1990) 19 ILJ 1 at 17, quoting from European Commission, *Protective Legislation for Women in the Member States of the European Community*, Communication of 20 Mar. 1987, COM (87) 105 final.

[207] B. Hepple, 'The Crisis in EEC Labour Law' (1987) 16 ILJ 77 at 80.

[208] Ibid. at 83.

condition of the labour economies of many European countries at that time. The move towards flexibility was in general terms a move towards de-regulation of the labour market; but it is important to realize that the extent and nature of the de-regulation involved differed as between member states. These differences were in part at least a reflection of the differences between the legal base-lines from which flexibility was to be increased. For example, in France and West Germany (as it then was), there was far tighter legal regulation of the permitted patterns of employment (as to weekly hours, for instance, or duration of the employment relationship) than in the UK. Where the legal regime was relatively *dirigiste* in that way, flexibility could be achieved by relaxing the legislation so that it became as permissive as that of the UK. In the case of the UK itself, given that there was that much less scope for legislative manœuvre, greater flexibility could be achieved only by cutting deeper into the foundations of employment protection legislation or by seeking to curtail the scope and effectiveness of collective bargaining. It was thus no accident that, as we have seen, the government came in the course of the 1980s increasingly to define its objectives in precisely those ways.

In all those circumstances, it was not unnatural that the European Community should tend to become the focus of moves to place social restraints upon the more extreme forms of deregulation of the labour market. For a number of the member states, the aggressive versions of de-regulation seemed both worryingly extreme in absolute terms—because so remote from the fairly intensely regulated structures to which they were accustomed—and threatening in competitive terms, as exercises in 'social dumping' whereby a member state could confer an unfair advantage upon its entrepreneurs by lowering the social protection costs of employment for them. It was not, of course, the first time the Community had been called upon to act in this way; it was for comparable reasons that Article 119 was included in the Treaty of Rome, mainly at the instance of France.[209] From late 1981 onwards, the European Commission began to advance to the Council of Ministers proposals in the form of draft Directives to respond to the growth of a disadvantageously

---

[209] See P. L. Davies, 'European Equality Legislation'.

employed workforce of temporary and part-time workers by guaranteeing basic employment protections, and treatment for workers in those categories comparable with that accorded to full-time and permanently employed workers.[210] In 1983 the Commission proposed a Council Recommendation on the reduction of working time and its reorganization to make it less anti-social from the point of view of the worker.[211]

It was not long before the British government identified these developments—whose progress it obstructed in the Council of Ministers—as directly contrary both to its own principles of deregulation and to what it conceived to be the proper liberal common market function of the European Community. By late 1984, a Minister in the Department of Employment could publicly describe the temporary work proposals as 'an irrelevant piece of European busybodying' which 'would probably introduce rigidities into the labour market, undermine competitiveness and actually reduce the number of jobs on offer'.[212] In 1986, the UK used its period of presidency of the Council of Ministers to persuade the Council to adopt an 'Employment Action Programme' which was distinctly more de-regulatory in its tone than was by then customary in Community policy statements.[213] By the end of 1986, it looked as if the UK had achieved considerable success in halting the development of Community employment law in many of the areas in which the government wished to maintain a free and de-regulated labour market.

Thus the Community in February 1986 had taken major steps, in the shape of the Single European Act, towards enabling itself to pursue its objectives by qualified majority decisions of the Council, where hitherto measures had required unanimous decisions of the Council; but the two crucial new articles of the Community Treaty inserted by the Single European Act were so framed as not to apply qualified majority decision-making to

---

[210] The original proposal for a Directive on Voluntary Part-Time Work was submitted to the Council by the Commission in Dec. 1981 (OJ C62/82—see 97 EIRR 6). The original proposals for a Directive on Temporary Work was submitted in Apr. 1982 (OJ C128/82—see 101 EIRR 24).

[211] OJ C290/83.

[212] Peter Morrison, 15 Nov. 1984 (see Department of Employment Press Notice of that date).

[213] See B. Hepple, 'The Crisis in EEC Labour Law', at 82. The Programme was adopted on 11 Dec. 1986.

employment matters except so far as Health and Safety were concerned. That is to say, new article 100A allowed a qualified majority for the approximation of measures having as their object the establishment and functioning of the internal market; but paragraph 2 of that article reimposed the requirement of unanimity for provisions 'related to the rights and interests of employed persons'. New article 118A created a legislative power, which the Council could exercise by qualified majority vote on a proposal from the Commission, to adopt Directives imposing minimum requirements for gradual implementation to encourage improvements, especially in the working environment; but this article was limited in its scope to the health and safety of workers rather than to employment matters in general. These limitations upon the scope of these two articles seem to have been secured in part at least by insistence upon them by the UK government.

(g) *The Community Social Charter*

So in the early and mid-1980s, there was quite a pattern of frustration by the UK of Community employment measures attempting to go much beyond the areas of health and safety and equal treatment for men and women at work. However, despite this frustration at a practical level—or perhaps as a result of it—there were highly significant developments in the later 1980s in the discourse of the European Community about social action in the employment field; these developments would drive quite a deep wedge between the employment and Community policy of the UK government and those of many other member states. They grew out of a 'social dialogue' conducted initially by the European level trade union and employers' organizations, starting with talks at Val Duchesse in 1985; the Commission was placed under a duty to develop this social dialogue between management and labour at European level by the new article 118B of the Community Treaty, another product of the Single European Act of 1986. The essence of this new discourse, as distilled, for instance, in the report of an interdepartmental working party of the Commission in 1988 entitled *The Social Dimension of the Internal Market*,[214] was the insistence that social policy has an independent value in contributing to the achievement of the

---

[214] *Social Europe*, Special Edition, 1988.

complete internal market within the Community and should not be continually regarded as subordinate to economic policy objectives.[215] That Report, rejecting on the one hand the extremes of harmonization policy of the 1970s but on the other hand the severely de-regulatory policy advocated by the UK government, involved a considerable acceptance of the idea of controlling 'social dumping' which we saw earlier as a rationale for social action by the Community. This idea was moderated, though not fundamentally compromised, by a 'principle of subsidiarity' which was accorded the meaning that 'the level at which a function is administered is the lowest at which it can be effectively carried out',[216] and amounted to a mild presumption in favour of national rather than Community legislation as the appropriate means of realising social policy—but a presumption readily rebuttable by evidence of the sort of unwillingness to implement Community social policy which the UK government only too clearly displayed. The Report also put forward another moderating principle, consisting in a preference for collective agreements over legislation as the method of implementing social policy; but this was less significant than the subsidiarity principle so far as relations between the UK and the Community over employment matters were concerned.

The culmination and focal point of these developments was the adoption as a political commitment in December 1989 of a European Community Charter of Fundamental Social Rights of Workers by the eleven member states other than the UK at a meeting of the heads of government in Strasbourg.[217] The Charter identified—in fairly general terms—a series of fundamental social rights of workers under the headings of Freedom of Movement (articles 1–3), Employment and Remuneration (articles 4–6), Improvement of Living and Working Conditions (articles 7–9), Right to Social Protection (article 10), Right to Freedom of Association and Collective Bargaining (articles 11–14), Right to Vocational Training (article 15), Right of Men

[215] See P. L. Davies, 'The Emergence of European Labour Law', ch. 10 in W. McCarthy, ed., *Legal Intervention in Industrial Relations: An Assessment of Losses and Gains* (Oxford, 1992).
[216] *Social Europe*, 68.
[217] See B. Bercusson, 'The European Community's Charter of Fundamental Social Rights of Workers' (1990) 53 MLR 624 for a valuable detailed analysis.

and Women to Equal Treatment (article 16), Right of Workers to Information, Consultation, and Participation (articles 17–18), Right to Health Protection and Safety at the Workplace (article 19), Protection of Children and Adolescents, Elderly Persons, and Disabled Persons (articles 20–7).

The speedy progress from the 1988 Social Dimension Report towards the adoption of this Charter was to some extent a product and outcome of the polarization within the Community about the speed and extent of the development of the Community—with the UK conducting an increasingly vigorous rearguard action. It must, for instance, have produced a certain hardening of the position of the proponents when Norman Fowler as Secretary of State for Employment said in September 1989:

We believe that the draft Social Charter points in the wrong direction— towards a Europe of greater regulation and additional restrictions on business growth and not towards a Europe of increased employment opportunities and falling unemployment.[218]

So although the Charter is a political rather than a legislative pronouncement, and although its provisions reflect many compromises, it did make significantly bold statements, for instance on collective matters such as that workers should be assured of an equitable wage sufficient to enable them to have a decent standard of living, that trade unions and employers' associations should have the right to negotiate and conclude collective agreements, and that the right to resort to collective action in the event of a conflict of interests should include the right to strike.[219]

By the year 1990, a central issue—perhaps even *the* central issue—for employment law in the UK was how far the new discourse of Community social action would be translated into practical measures affecting the UK. No doubt the temperature of the discussion of this issue had been raised by the welcome accorded to Jacques Delors, the President of the European Commission, and to his policies, by the Trades Union Congress in 1988, and by the adoption of markedly pro-Community policies by the Labour Party in its policy review completed in 1989.[220]

[218] Department of Employment Press Notice 237/89 of 28 Sept. 1989.
[219] See for an evaluation P. L. Davies, 'Emergence'.
[220] See TUC, *Annual Report, 1988*, 567 ff.

The government had kept up its practical as well as its rhetorical opposition to the growth of Community employment law right through the later years of the 1980s. It had successfully delayed progress on a number of social policy initiatives, such as the draft Directives on Parental Leave and on the Burden of Proof of Discrimination.[221] It had opposed the inclusion of provisions about workers' participation in the proposals for a Statute to permit incorporation as a European Company (Societas Europa), and had opposed progress on the draft Fifth Directive on the Harmonization of Company Law and on the Vredeling Directive because of their implications for mandatory workers' participation.[222]

On the other hand, the institutions of the Community were clearly in quite a vigorously progressive state so far as the development of Community employment law was concerned. In May 1990, as we have seen, the European Court of Justice took the crucial step in the *Barber* case[223] of holding that most occupational pension scheme benefits fell within the scope of article 119 of the Treaty. Moreover, the European Commission in November 1989 published an Action Programme for the Implementation of the Community Charter (the Charter which was adopted, as we have seen, by eleven member states in the following month). This indicated the Commission's intention to bring forward a number of draft Directives to implement various aspects of the Charter, including the sensitive areas of working time and workers' participation.[224] By the end of 1990, a number of such proposals had been made by the Commission,[225] with a

---

[221] The draft Directive on Parental Leave was first submitted by the Commission in 1983 and submitted in revised form in 1984 (COM (84) 631 Final). The draft Directive on the Burden of Proof was submitted in 1988 (COM (88) 269 Final).

[222] The government's generally negative position was set out in a Department of Employment Report entitled *People and Companies: Employee Involvement in Britain* (Nov. 1989).

[223] *Barber* v. *Guardian Royal Exchange Assurance Group*, Case C262/88 [1990] ICR 616. See above, p. 586.

[224] COM (89) final (Nov. 1989). See (Jan. 1990) 192 EIRR 11.

[225] A Proposal for a Council Directive complementing the Statute for a European Company with regard to the involvement of employees in the European Company was made in Aug. 1989: see (Feb. 1990) 193 EIRR 29. A Proposal for three Council Directives relating to Part-Time and Temporary Work was made in June 1990 (COM (90) 228): see Department of Employment Consultative Document of 3 Aug. 1990 on those Draft Directives. A Proposal for a Directive on Working Time was made in July 1990: see (Oct. 1990) 201 EIRR

significant potential impact upon various aspects of employment protection legislation in the UK.

The deepening antithesis between the employment law policies of the UK government and the European Commission has to be seen as part of the government's general resistance to the significant growth of European Community federalism—which was to become a dominant preoccupation in British political life in the course of 1990. In the employment law context, the divergence over substantive policies became inextricably linked with a contest about the extent of the legislative power of the Community *vis-à-vis* the member states. The crucial question was how constraining would prove to be the limitations, which we considered earlier, upon the new Treaty articles 100A and 118A, which provided the main possibility of Community employment legislation by qualified majority vote. Despite the ingenious interpretations advanced by Eliane Vogel-Polsky,[226] it was always clear that the limitations would be formidable; the UK government would presumably not have assented to the Single European Act with any lesser assurances.

In the course of 1989 and 1990, the Commission became adept at advancing proposals so framed as to sidestep these limitations. By 1989, the Commission—with the concurrence of the UK government—had made substantial proposals for the expansion of Community legislation on health and safety at work, and in June 1989 the Council approved the central 'framework' Directive for the introduction of measures to encourage improvement in the safety and health of workers at the workplace.[227] By the end of 1990, the Commission had seen fit to follow up this mainstream development of health and safety legislation by proposals sometimes rather contrivedly couched in terms of health and safety in order to be presented under article 118A.[228]

14; text at (Nov. 1990) 202 EIRR 27. A Proposal for a Council Directive on the protection at work of pregnant women and women who have recently given birth was made in Nov. 1990—COM (90) 406 final; text at (Nov./Dec. 1990) 34 EOR 32—and later adopted as Directive 92/85.

[226] 'What Future is there for a Social Europe Following the Strasbourg Summit?' (1990) 19 ILJ 65.

[227] Directive 89/391 of 12 June 1989. See R. F. Eberlie, 'The New Health and Safety Legislation of the European Community' (1990) 19 ILJ 81.

[228] A good instance is provided by this passage in the preamble to the Directive on protection of pregnant women (see above, n. 225): 'Whereas the risk of

Tactics of this kind reached a high point in the June 1990 proposals concerning part-time and temporary work, where three Directives were proposed—one under article 100, one under article 100A, and one under 118A[229]—with the fairly palpable aim of ensuring that legislation would occur on whatever basis of legislative power was found acceptable in due course by the European Court of Justice. The Department of Employment in its Consultative Document on these proposals[230] concentrated on challenging their legal base as much as on advancing substantive arguments against them. This was hardly a satisfactory way in which to develop or fail to develop employment law in crucial areas of social concern.[231]

The rift between the UK Government and the EEC Commission continued to deepen in the early 1990s, a development which for the purposes of this narrative we can see as culminating in the events of the Maastricht Summit Conference of December 1991. At this meeting, the heads of the member states agreed to bring forward for ratification various revisions of the Community Treaties which tended towards a more powerfully federal structure for the Community; but because the UK alone would not agree to the revised Social Chapter which had been proposed to form part of the Maastricht Treaty, the revisions in question were instead embodied in the Maastricht Protocol on Social Policy which was agreed between the other eleven member states of the Community. This meant that there would be in effect two sets of Treaty provisions in the field of Community Social Policy, one binding all member states and the other binding all member states except the UK. The provisions of the Social Protocol, as one might imagine, were mainly directed towards increasing the legislative competence and facility of the Community in the sphere of Social Policy; probably its most significant provision

dismissal for reasons associated with their condition may have harmful effects on the physical and mental state of pregnant workers . . .'.

[229] The third of these was enacted vis-à-vis temporary workers as Directive 91/383.

[230] See above, n. 225.

[231] The government was, of course, unable to prevent existing Community law from continuing to affect UK law, or the adoption of all new Community proposals. See Part II of the Trade Union Reform and Employment Rights Bill 1992.

was the extension (by Article 2 of the Social Chapter) of the principle of qualified majority voting beyond health and safety matters into a more widely defined (though by no means open-ended) range of social policy concerns.

It became a matter of speculation how such a 'two-track' system might operate—or, indeed, whether such a system was juridically or practically viable in the first place; but we shall not attempt to chart or pursue those speculations here. Suffice it to observe that the very fact that the 'two-track' system was embarked upon at Maastricht showed how far, for the UK government, de-rigidification of the labour market and opposition to European Community federalism had become mutually reinforcing policies. At that point, the government distanced itself from EEC social policy formation and concentrated upon opposition to that whole policy development. This had ironical consequences, because it meant that the government deprived itself of the opportunity properly to exploit both the real doubts within other member states about the desirability of overactive Community social policy and what one of us has described as 'the continuing precariousness of the Community's legislative powers in the social field'.[232]

Both chronologically and in terms of substance this has brought us to the appropriate point at which to conclude the present section. By the end of the 1980s, the government was convinced that there was an inexorable logic to a programme of restructuring the labour market which it saw itself as having pursued right through the decade. With this went the conviction that the European Community was a countervailing force, threatening the future of the restructured labour market which the Government had laboured to create. In the policy document in which the government had proclaimed both their past achievements and future intentions in the matter of restructuring—the White Paper *Employment for the 1990s*, published in December 1988[233]—they had declared that:

For their part the Government are ready to take whatever further legislative steps may prove necessary and will resist European Community regulations which would make the operation of the labour market more inflexible.[234]

[232] Davies, 'The Emergence of European Labour Law'.
[233] Cm. 540.
[234] Ibid., para. 2.26.

By the early 1990s, there did indeed seem to be a real opposition between the extreme economic liberalism which had come to inform the employment law of the UK, and ideals of social citizenship in industrial society of which the European Community had become the most important champion—or, at least, the most obvious rallying-point. From a standpoint in 1950, 1960, 1970, or even 1980, this would have seemed a scarcely predictable state of affairs, an unlikely way in which the government would be defining its policy objectives for employment law.

10.5. THE EMPLOYMENT AND TRAINING LEGISLATION OF THE 1980s

Thus far, our discussion of the restructuring of the labour economy during the 1980s has been focused upon the determining of pay and of other terms and conditions of employment, and upon the making and termination of employment relationships. This does not, however, provide a complete picture of the impact of governmental measures and policies upon the supply side of the labour economy during that period; for one thing, it fails to take account of the importance of governmental activity in the field of employment and training—by which we mean measures and policies directly concerned with the creation and maintenance of employment, or concerned with the provision of training for employment. The development of employment and training measures in the 1980s in fact provides a central case-study of governments' increasingly ambitious efforts to restructure the labour market during that decade. There is scarcely an area of labour legislation which better illustrates the interplay between political dogma, pragmatic opportunism, and economic constraints that we have been considering, in one form or another, throughout this book. At the beginning of the decade, a certain kind of corporate statism appeared to be still dominant, even if under threat. By the end of the decade, free market philosophy was triumphant in this area, for the time being at least. By charting the details of this transition, we can hope to contribute materially to understanding the movement of labour legislation and labour market policy during the 1980s. The later years of the decade will be seen to have a very different aspect from the earlier years.

(a) Inheritance and Retrenchment, 1979–1981

The government's inheritance in 1979 of employment and training policies and measures nicely reflected the layers of post-war employment policy development so far considered in this book. Thus from the later 1940s until the early 1960s, the prevailing policies were essentially voluntaristic; they were a good example of collective *laissez-faire* in operation. The provision of training was very largely left to the apprenticeship system, which was to some extent a vehicle of trade union power, and not in general the subject of statutory regulation. The creation and maintenance of employment was also largely left to the market, and to the extent that there was state intervention, it was primarily organized on a regional basis with the effect and perhaps even the aim of minimizing the appearance of state control of the labour market as a whole. In the 1960s, as we have seen, the government addressed itself in a number of ways, in an attempt to modernize the labour economy, to regulating the behaviour of employers in the labour market. Such measures included the Selective Employment Payments Act 1966, the Redundancy Payments Act 1965, and, most significantly from our present point of view, the Industrial Training Act 1964—a bi-partisan recognition that voluntarist means would fail to remedy an already serious skill shortage in the workforce. The 1964 Act, as we have seen, regulated employers' training practices by imposing a training levy on them, the use of which was administered by Industrial Training Boards on an industry-by-industry basis.[235]

In the next phase, a new kind of initiative was taken, which we have examined in relation to the Employment and Training Act 1973.[236] This represented a shift away from the regulation of employers' training practices, towards the assumption by the state of direct responsibility for the provision of training and the creation and maintenance of employment opportunities. As we have seen, two agencies were separated from the Department of Employment to discharge these enlarged direct responsibilities of the state—the Training Services Agency and the Employment Service Agency; and a major tri-partite body, the Manpower Services Commission, was created to supervise their conduct of this task.

[235] See above, p. 145.
[236] See above, pp. 336–8.

The extent to which this was a shift of direction away from that of the Industrial Training Act 1964 is well indicated by the changes which the 1973 Act made to the Industrial Training Board system which that Act set up. On the one hand, as we have previously pointed out, the 1973 Act made a minor retrenchment upon the regulation of employers, by moving from a levy/grant system to a levy/exemption system. This was intended to enable small firms in particular to be exempt from the training levy. On the other hand, the government made a commitment to finance the deficit which the Industrial Training Boards had started to incur. Thus the state was accepting in this way a partial transfer of responsibility for industry-based training, while embarking on an ambitious programme of tri-partite activity in the job-creation and training field as a whole.

The reactions of post-1979 governments to this complex legacy is a highly interesting one. On the one hand, it was entirely consistent with the programme of de-regulation undertaken by the government in the early 1980s that they should secure the enactment of a major retrenchment upon the statutory industrial training system. This was carried out by and under the Employment and Training Act 1981, which enabled the Secretary of State for Employment to abolish Industrial Training Boards without the requirement of a proposal from the Manpower Services Commission which had been imposed by the 1973 Act.[237] The declared purpose was to enable the Secretary of State to reduce the number of Boards from twenty-three to seven.[238] This wholesale dismantling of the statutory framework of industrial training destroyed the bi-partisan consensus about training which had prevailed in relation to the 1964 and 1973 Acts. It was a return to voluntarism as significant as any de-regulatory measure within the traditional employment-law field.

(b) *The Rise of the Manpower Services Commission*

On the other hand, the legacy of the 1973 Act, so far from being wound down, was vigorously built upon in the early 1980s. The

---

[237] The procedure for the winding-up of Industrial Training Boards was consolidated by s. 4 of the Industrial Training Act 1982.

[238] HC Deb., 6th ser., vol. 13, col. 30 (16 Nov. 1981)—Secretary of State's statement (Norman Tebbit).

very statute which prepared for the substantial dismantling of the Industrial Training Boards greatly enhanced the power of the Manpower Services Commission. This was the Employment and Training Act 1981, which by abolishing the Employment Service Agency and Training Services Agency transformed the role of the MSC from a supervisory one to a directly executive one. Moreover, in the first half of the 1980s the employment and training activities of the MSC expanded so greatly that the Commission became, in Peter Hennessy's description, a kind of super-ministry of unemployment comparable in importance to the overarching ministries which were created to deal with the needs of the wartime economy.[239] The apparent paradox between the Government's actions in scaling-down the Industrial Training Board system but at the same time building up the programmes of the MSC is at least partly explicable in terms of a shift of emphasis from training those in work to training the unemployed. This was to some extent a shift from the concerns of employers and unions to the concerns of the state; the aim was to associate employers and unions in those primarily governmental concerns by means of the tri-partite institutional structure.

At first sight, or at least with hindsight from the end of the decade, this expansion of statist, tri-partite, and in a certain sense corporatist governmental activity appears surprising. It seems to accord ill with what one would expect of 1980s Conservative governments, which were in general anti-statist and certainly anti-corporatist, especially *vis-à-vis* trade unions. This apparent anomaly can be explained on two levels. Firstly, it reflects the fact that in the early 1980s the policies of the New Right did not yet enjoy the full ascendancy they were to obtain in the later 1980s. On the one hand, there were still powerful forces within the Conservative Party which would favour the pursuit of consensualist—if necessary, corporatist—solutions to the growing problems posed by economic recession and rapidly rising unemployment. James Prior as Secretary of State for Employment from 1979 to 1981 was a centrally placed representative of those forces. On the other hand, the proponents of New Right policies within the government were not yet as confident of the acceptability of those policies to the electorate as they were to become

[239] P. Hennessy, *Whitehall* (London, 1989), 453–6.

in the later 1980s; they were still, accordingly, prepared to com-promise with a more traditional set of Conservative policies and attitudes.

At the second level, it turns out, on a detailed examination of the way employment and training policies developed in the early to mid-1980s, that the apparent predominance of tripartism and, broadly speaking, welfare state attitudes conceals a real tension between competing goals, and institutions pursuing divergent goals. In particular, there were significant differences of emphasis and of priorities between the Manpower Services Commission and central government as represented by the Department of Employment. These explanations can best be illustrated by refer-ence to the most important training measure of the period—the Youth Training Scheme initiated in 1983.

(c) The Youth Training Scheme

The Youth Training Scheme was initiated and administered by the Manpower Services Commission, and marks the high point of the commission's power and importance. The Scheme was the fruition of the policies embodied in the Employment and Training Act 1973. During the later 1970s, a series of schemes had been devised and run by the MSC, under the powers con-ferred by the 1973 Act, as augmented by the Employment Subsidies Act 1978, to subsidise employment training, and the creation and maintenance of jobs in the face of rising unemploy-ment. In the early 1980s, with the enormous growth in unem-ployment, there were reasons for concentrating on training rather than job subsidies. Firstly, straightforward employment subsidies such as the Temporary Short-Time Working Compensation Scheme had run up against objections from the European Com-mission that they distorted competition between employers in the UK and those in other member states.[240] Secondly, training measures were perceived to be more constructive than employ-ment subsidies, especially so far as the (particularly acute) prob-lem of rising unemployment among school leavers and other young people was concerned. Hence in 1981 the Manpower Services Commission published two policy documents which

---

[240] See M. R. Freedland, 'Leaflet Law: The Temporary Short Time Working Compensation Scheme' (1980) 9 ILJ 254.

envisaged the transformation of the existing Youth Opportunities Programme into a scheme whose primary emphasis would be on the training of young people;[241] and by 1983 these proposals were implemented in the form of the Youth Training Scheme.

Before this could happen, however, there was a highly significant interplay of policies between the Manpower Services Commission and the government itself. The MSC was, from the outset, more committed to expansion of state training activity than the government. In the view of the latter, the great increase in public expenditure which this involved ran counter to their monetarist aims. Moreover, although they were not oblivious of the good supply-side case for expanding the provision of training, especially of youth training as an extension of vocational education, nevertheless the whole concept aroused their suspicion of undue intervention in the free working of the labour market. Norman Tebbit as Secretary of State for Employment would eventually agree to the MSC's proposals;[242] but the Department of Employment's initial response showed that its priorities were different from those of the MSC.[243] The Department of Employment wanted the participants in the new scheme to contribute to the cost of their training by receiving an allowance which would be lower than the remuneration-based allowance currently paid to young people taking part in the Youth Opportunities Programme.[244] This would ensure that the new scheme would tend to keep down the wage expectations of young entrants on to the labour market. The White Paper also sought to promote an associated policy to which the government attached great importance, namely that of ensuring that young people could not bid up their position in the labour market by relying on social security benefits to support them during periods of voluntary unemployment. Hence the White Paper proposed that unemployed minimum-age school leavers, being guaranteed a place on the new scheme, should not have access to supplementary benefit in their own right (rather than as dependent on their parents).[245]

---

[241] *A New Training Initiative: A Consultative Document* (MSC, May 1981); *A New Training Initiative; an Agenda for Action* (MSC, Dec. 1981).

[242] In 1982 (HC Deb., 6th ser., vol. 26, cols. 22 ff.).

[243] White Paper, *A New Training Initiative; a Programme for Action*, Cmnd. 8455 (Dec. 1981).

[244] Ibid., paras. 34, 38. See M. R. Freedland (1983) ILJ 220 at 222 n. 15.

[245] Cmnd. 8455, para. 35.

In the face of the MSC's determination not to see its initiative subverted in these ways and in the circumstances that the MSC was the only organization by which the government could realistically promise the electorate that a major new youth training scheme would be delivered, the Department of Employment gave ground in these respects in advance of the 1983 General Election. But there were already indications that the victory of tripartism might be a transient one and was at best partial. For example, it would seem that the MSC considered making consultation and negotiation with recognized trade unions a condition of approval of particular youth training schemes by Area Manpower Boards, but that they decided not to do so because of the likelihood that this would involve violation of the principle, which had by then been enacted in Section 13 of the Employment Act 1982, that selection of employers tendering for commercial contracts should not be confined to those willing to recognize trade unions.[246]

There were further senses in which the Youth Training Scheme, although generally rather a corporatist and counter-monetarist— even a Keynesian—sort of measure, nevertheless in some aspects reflected the philosophies of the New Right. The Youth Training Scheme consisted, in legal terms, of the administrative framework for a series of interlocking contracts. The MSC offered to make contracts with Managing Agents who in turn could make contracts with employers or educational institutions for the provision of training.[247] The young people who participated in the scheme entered into training arrangements with employers or other providers of training which could be but generally were not contracts of employment. This provides a still slightly imprecise but nevertheless clearly recognisable paradigm which would in due course emerge, as we shall see, as the supremely preferred legal and conceptual formula for the provision of public services so far as the New Right was concerned. The paradigm was that in which the public service is procured by central government on a contractual basis, and also provided on a contractual basis to the consumer or recipient of the service concerned. In the perception of the New Right, this was conducive to commercial efficiency in

---

[246] See above, p. 475.
[247] See Freedland, (1983) ILJ 220 at 228–9.

the procurement process and to freedom of choice at the consumption stage. Even if both these apparent gains were in reality
illusory, the paradigm was to become a dominant one in ensuing
years.[248]

The Government had other reasons for feeling that the Youth
Training Scheme had worked out to some extent as they wished
rather than as the MSC wished. The MSC had insisted on there
being two bases on which young people could participate in the
scheme—either as trainees on a fixed allowance or as employees,
on such remuneration as might be agreed by the ordinary processes of wage determination (with, in both cases, a capitation
payment from the MSC to the employer or provider of training).
The MSC wanted the employment alternative to limit the undermining effect of YTS upon young workers' wages. But in the
event, employers were generally unwilling to choose the employment alternative, and the Department of Employment insisted
that the allowance to trainees was kept at a low level. So, although
participation in the Scheme was not compelled by denial of social
security benefits, the Scheme did have some of the negative effect
on young workers' wages which the government wanted (and
which the tripartist MSC feared). Hence by the time of the 1985
Budget, Nigel Lawson as Chancellor of the Exchequer could
announce proposals to extend YTS so that it would offer two
years of training instead of one as hitherto and, very significantly, he could present these as positively serving the Government's economic objectives despite the extra public expenditure
involved:

Since it was first launched in 1983, the Youth Training Scheme has
proved to be a very successful bridge between school and work. It has
also helped to make young people's pay expectations more realistic. But
too many trainees are still reluctant to accept rates of pay which reflect
their inexperience, and too many employers still fail to recognise that
training is an investment in their own commercial interest. This is in
marked contrast to our major competitors overseas. The Government
have therefore decided to provide a substantial expansion of the Youth
Training Scheme. Provided employers contribute a major share of the
cost, the Government are prepared to provide further funds to launch
this new initiative, over and above the existing £800 million a year of
public expenditure on the YTS.[249]

[248] See below, pp. 625–35.
[249] HC Deb., 5th ser., vol. 75, col. 788 (19 Mar. 1985).

(d) The Fall of the Manpower Services Commission

By the mid-1980s, then, the policies promoting better training and vocational education of young people seemed to have gained some predominance over monetarist and free labour market policies. The Government seemed content for the former policies to be pursued as long as the latter policies were firmly asserted at the rhetorical level—as witness the statement we have just cited by the Chancellor of the Exchequer. Perhaps the high point of this constructive approach to training occurred in 1986; it was marked by a White Paper produced jointly by the Department of Employment and the Department of Education and Science, entitled *Working Together: Education and Training*.[250] This White Paper envisaged a complementary and coherent approach to education and training policies. It presented, as linked proposals, (1) measures to ensure the quality of training on the two-year Youth Training Scheme, (2) the extension into a nationwide scheme of hitherto pilot ventures under the Technical and Vocational Education Initiative (TVEI) whereby local education authorities promoted technical and vocational education in schools and colleges of further education, and (3) the creation of a new national framework of vocational qualifications called the National Vocational Qualification. Although hedged about with indications of the government's determination to obtain value for money,[251] these proposals fall squarely within the best progressive traditions of both government departments concerned.

Even by 1986, there were already pointers towards the development of less progressive employment, education, and training policies. In 1982 the Department of Employment introduced a Young Workers' Scheme, apparently suggested by Professor Alan Walters (later to become famous as the Prime Minister's arch-monetarist economic adviser). This scheme had the overt aim of keeping young workers' wages down; it offered subsidies to employers for employing otherwise unemployed young workers, provided their wages conformed to stated maximum amounts.[252] The restructuring of the labour market which the Government hoped to bring about by its employment and

---

[250] Cmnd. 9823 (July 1986).
[251] Ibid., paras. 1.2, 1.9, 2.11, 2.18, 7.7.
[252] See Freedland, (1983) ILJ 220 at 221.

training policies in the first half of the 1980s is less crudely but nevertheless significantly illustrated by the various schemes which favoured self-employment and the creation of very small or one-man businesses, in particular the Enterprise Allowance Scheme.[253]

From 1987 onwards, employment and training measures reflected more extreme New Right policies. Somewhat ominously, the government introduced in January 1988 a Job Training Scheme which offered employment training to the long-term unemployed—the political legacy of the recession of the early 1980s—but did so on what was arguably a low-cost and low-quality basis. With a General Election in the offing, it looked as if there was the same opportunism as had motivated the introduction of the Youth Training Scheme in time for the 1983 election, but this time without the idealism which the Manpower Services Commission had injected into that Scheme. After the 1987 election was successfully won, the new Conservative government set about applying a new strain of radical idealism to employment and training measures—the full force of which was scarcely appreciated at the time. As was often to occur in the period 1987 to 1990, ideology was applied alike to reformulation of policies and to restructuring (or destructuring) of institutions. There were two White Papers about employment and training in the course of 1988 which deserve to be seen in this light. The first of them, issued in February 1988 and entitled *Training for Employment*,[254] seemed innocuous enough on the face of it. Its main proposals consisted in the elaboration of a decision, announced by the Secretary of State for Employment in November 1987,[255] to bring all post-18 employment and training programmes together into a simple unified programme of training for employment—which came into operation in September 1988 under the title of Employment Training.

This measure implemented two lines of policy which were not articulated in the White Paper, but which were to be major themes of government in the period 1987–90. The first was to transfer power away from local authorities wherever possible;

---

[253] Cf. e.g., the claims advanced for this scheme in the White Paper, *Employment: The Challenge for the Nation*, Cmnd. 9474 (1985), 36.

[254] Cm. 316.

[255] HC Deb., 6th ser., vol. 122, col. 1067 (18 Nov. 1987) (Norman Fowler).

post-18 employment and training measures had been dominated by the Community Programme, which had been largely controlled by local authorities. The second was to ensure that this power was exercised as efficiently as possible and on as commercial a basis as possible. It was sought to achieve this by reproducing, on a grand scale, the contractual pattern of procurement which had been used for the Youth Training Scheme, in this case by setting up a network of Approved Training Agents and Training Managers. This time, according to a pattern which we shall see was to become widespread throughout the public services, the White Paper indicated that:

The Government are asking the Commission to develop quantifiable performance indicators which could apply to Approved Training Agents and Training Managers. These will include such matters as recruitment and occupancy rates, length of stay against . . . the percentage of leavers who get a job, and the percentage who secure vocational qualifications or credits. The performance indicators will be published.[256]

The anxiety to establish an analogue of commercial pressures upon the Agents and Managers is evident enough.

The White Paper also pursued a major line of government policy which, as we have seen,[257] manifested itself in relation to the planning of the Youth Training Scheme in the early 1980s but was then subordinated to other priorities. This was to put pressure on the unemployed to engage in training or actively to seek employment by making that a condition of support from the social security system. The White Paper did not go so far as to propose that participation in the Youth Training Scheme or in Employment Training should be compulsory in that sense. But it did proclaim a major concern with making sure that the social security system was not abused;[258] it defined abuse (a concept which is strongly associated with outright fraud) as including claiming social security when not genuinely available for work,[259]

---

[256] Cm. 316, para. 5.21.
[257] See above, p. 604.
[258] Cm. 316, para. 71.
[259] Ibid., para. 7.11. Cf. N. J. Wikely's comment that 'The first White Paper devoted an entire chapter to the question of availability for work, which is notable for its construction of the problem as one of fraud and abuse', (1989) 16 *Journal of Law and Society* at 209.

and it included among the proposed remedial measures making claimants aware of training available to them.[260]

In the event, in the course of 1988 and 1989 a number of measures were taken which moved a long way in the direction in which the White Paper had pointed. Section 4 of the Social Security Act 1988, by largely withdrawing income support from all young people under 18, in effect made participation in YTS compulsory, in the sense described above, for young people who are not in employment or continuing with their education.[261] Section 27 of the Employment Act 1988 extended the voluntary unemployment disqualification from social security benefits to cover all aspects of non-participation in training schemes approved by the Secretary of State for Employment.[262] The Youth Training Scheme was already an approved scheme for this purpose; and Nicholas Wikely has drawn attention to evidence that the government had it in mind also to designate the Employment Training Programme as an approved scheme,[263] and has concluded that 'the statutory framework for a system of "workfare" [the American term for welfare provision to those in work] is thus in place.'[264]

These important shifts into new policy directions were accompanied by, and associated with, major institutional reforms. As Nicholas Wikely has argued, the policy of enforcing the rules governing availability for work more rigorously against benefit claimants had already in 1987 led to a transfer of responsibility for Job Centres and other employment services back to the Department of Employment from the Manpower Services Commission.[265] The latter was no doubt regarded as less committed to the new rigour against benefit claimants; section 24 of the Employment Act 1988 renamed it the Training Commission 'to emphasize its now more specific remit', as Wikely puts it.[266] That

---

[260] Cm. 316, para. 8.15.

[261] See N. J. Wikely in 'Training, Targeting and Tidying up: The Social Security Act 1988' (1989) 5 *Journal of Social Welfare Law* 277 at 277–9.

[262] See N. J. Wikely, 'Unemployment Benefit, the State, and the Labour Market' (1989) 16 *Journal of Law and Society* 291 at 302–4.

[263] Ibid. at 302–3.

[264] Ibid. at 303.

[265] N. J. Wikely, 'Training for Employment in the 1990s' (1990) 53 MLR 354 at 356.

[266] Ibid. at 357.

section also transferred the underlying statutory function of the MSC back to the Department of Employment, so that the Training Commission would be no more than the delegatees of the Department's powers; and enabled the Secretary of State for Employment to dilute the Commission's membership by appointing new employer members. Policy changes further interacted with institutional changes later in 1988; in September of that year, the TUC withdrew trade union support for the Employment Training Scheme because they thought is was aimed at reducing wages, and the Secretary of State for Employment responded by transferring the functions of the Training Commission to a new training agency within the Department of Employment. The Training Commission was formally wound up by section 22 of the Employment Act 1989, thus bringing this particular wheel round full circle to where it had stood before the Employment and Training Act 1973. The most significant institutional survivor of the tripartite corporation of the 1970s had been abolished.

Even before that happened the government had felt confident enough, by December 1988, to present a further White Paper, entitled *Employment for the 1990s*,[267] in which the whole of the government's handling of industrial relations and the labour market was envisaged as a grand strategy for 'removing barriers to employment'. In the field of employment and training measures, policies which had been evident in the earlier White Papers were developed in a far more radical way. Even more prominently on this occasion, the development of new substantive policies and the process of institutional reform went hand in hand. A good case in point is that of the changing approach to social security benefits for the unemployed. The second White Paper took up the theme of abuse and fraud from the first White Paper and generalized it into a perception that the whole problem of unemployment had ceased to be attributable to the functioning of the economy and had become largely a function of the attitudes of employers to recruiting unemployed people and of unemployed people to finding work.[268] At the institutional level, the Employment Service, back under the control of the

---

[267] Cm. 540; see above, pp. 509, 533.
[268] Ibid. at para. 7.1, 7.4–7.13.

Department of Employment rather than the Manpower Services Commission, was increasingly envisaged as having the task of challenging such attitudes among the unemployed. The White Paper claimed that:

By March 1989, arrangements will be in place for ensuring that all new claimants for benefit are interviewed by senior staff of the Employment Service who can advise them on jobs and give them other help to enable them to return to work as well as detecting anyone whose claim to be available for work is doubtful.[269]

At the substantive level, the White Paper proposed that, to break down the attitudinal barrier to employment growth, there would be legislation to provide that unemployed benefit claimants, in addition to being capable of work, should actively be seeking work.[270] This was implemented by section 10 of the Social Security Act 1989. This was to restore to the statute book a provision whose earlier counterpart had been notorious for its inhumanity to benefit claimants during its period of operation from 1924 to 1929.[271]

(e) The Rise of Employer-Led Training

The system of provision of training and particularly the new Employment Training programme were seen as important to bringing about the desired changes in the attitudes of employers and the unemployed.[272] It was in relation to the provision of training that the White Paper proposed its most extensive set of further institutional reforms to ensure that the training system would serve the labour market in the way the Government thought it should. This consisted essentially in subjecting the training system to commercial or quasi-commercial disciplines— an enterprise upon which the first White Paper of 1988 had embarked, as we have seen, in relation to the Employment Training Scheme. The second White Paper sought to achieve this more ambitiously at three distinct levels—the national, the industry, and the local levels. At the national level, two institu-

---

[269] Ibid. at para. 7.16.
[270] Ibid. at para. 7.18.
[271] See R. Lowe, *Adjusting to Democracy: The Role of the Ministry of Labour in British Politics 1916–1939* (Oxford, 1986), 137–9, 146–7.
[272] Cm. 540, para. 7.3.

tional developments were proposed: the Training Agency which, as we have seen, was by December 1988 in the course of taking over the operation of the Training Commission, would in due course be separated off from the Department of Employment as 'an agency of the kind described in The Next Steps'.[273] This meant that it would become separately financially accountable and expected as such to answer to commercial standards of efficiency. Moreover, the function of planning training at national level, which had hitherto been entrusted first to the Manpower Services Commission and then briefly to the Training Commission, would now be given to a National Training Task Force, two-thirds of which was to be appointed 'from leading figures in industry and commerce'.[274] This had the overt purpose of identifying employers as the partners of the government in planning training arrangements, to the total exclusion of trade unions.[275]

These preoccupations were also fully evident in the proposals for institutional reform at the lower levels. At industry level, the ideal was identified as being that of having standard-setting bodies created and run by employers themselves—in other words, a state of voluntary self-regulation.[276] In pursuit of this ideal, it was proposed that the seven remaining Industrial Training Boards should be pressed to transform themselves into 'independent non-statutory training organisations, fully supported by employers in their sectors'.[277] This was a kind of privatization of the ITBs; and the White Paper went on directly to propose the privatization of the Skills Training Agency, which ran the sixty government training centres known as Skillcentres.[278] This proposal was later implemented by means of a management buy-out which caused controversy by reason of the high profitability of the transaction to the civil servants who bought out the Skills Training Agency.[279]

The most ambitious proposal for privatization of the training

---

[273] Ibid., para. 4.14. The policy document referred to is *Improving Management in Government: The Next Steps* (1988). See further below, pp. 628–35.

[274] Cm. 540, para. 4.17.

[275] Ibid., para. 4.15.

[276] Ibid., paras. 4.21 ff.

[277] Ibid., para. 4.25.

[278] Ibid., para. 4.36.

[279] See HC Deb., 6th ser., vol. 149, col. 23 for Norman Fowler's statement of intention, and vol. 170, cols. 157–8 (written answers) for subsequent controversy.

system was, however, made in relation to the local level. Here it was proposed to encourage employers to establish Training and Enterprise Councils which would 'contract with Government to plan and deliver training and to promote and support the development of small businesses and self-employment within their area'.[280] The White Paper went on to stipulate that:

At least two-thirds of TEC members should be employers at top management level drawn from the private sector. Others on the Councils will include senior figures from local education, training and economic development activities and from voluntary bodies and trade unions *who support the aims of the Council* [emphasis added].[281]

It was further stipulated that:

[TECs] will be responsible for promoting and directing more private sector investment in training, vocational education and enterprise activities designed to strengthen the local skill base and to spur economic growth.[282]

And it was also projected that:

TECs will operate on the basis of a contract with the Employment Department's Training Agency. The contract will specify programme and management standards and will contain quantitative outcome measures . . .[283]

Here, then, was the groundwork—which could be built upon by administrative action without the need for any legislation—for a fully privatized local training administration. It would be run largely by private sector employers, was dedicated to developing training activity within the private sector, and was to be entrusted with large public resources[284] on the basis of quasi-commercial contractual arrangements. Standing in sharp contrast in all these respects with the tri-partite Area Manpower Boards which had existed under the Employment and Training Act 1973, the

---

[280] Cm. 540, para. 5.7.
[281] Ibid., para. 5.10.
[282] Ibid., para. 5.9.
[283] Ibid., para. 5.15.
[284] Ibid., para. 5.13: 'The resources available to each TEC will range between £15 million and £50 million [s.c. per annum] depending on size.'

Training and Enterprise Councils provide one of the clearest illustrations in this chapter of the lines along which the government aimed to restructure the labour market in the latter part of the 1980s. In the next section, we consider the general restructuring of the public sector of the labour market, of which the treatment of governmental manpower and training institutions was a vivid example.

10.6. THE RESTRUCTURING OF THE PUBLIC EMPLOYMENT SECTOR IN THE 1980s

In the foregoing discussion of the employment and training legislation of the 1980s, we saw how developments occurring in that field in the later 1980s intensified and heightened certain policies which had been present, though accorded less priority, throughout the decade—the policy, for example, of applying benefit sanctions to compel people to undertake training rather than be unemployed. This perspective upon the 1980s was found to be a revealing one, but subject to the risk that it might make opportunistic responses to short-term needs assume the appearance of programmatic pursuits of long-term policies. Similar insights, attended by similar risks, are to be gained by putting together a large number of measures and policy developments occurring between 1979 and 1990 which cumulatively amounted to a fundamental restructuring of the public sector of the labour economy. This restructuring of the public employment sector illustrates in their most significant form the main themes which have been emerging in the course of this whole chapter—in relation both to the restructuring of pay bargaining discussed in section 10.2 and the restructuring of the individual employment relationship which was the subject of section 10.3.

Why was restructuring of public sector employment so important to the government's labour market strategies from 1979 onwards? There were two main sets of reasons why this was so. The first set can be summarized by saying that those features of the labour market which 1979 governments regarded as problems and styled as rigidities were to be found most pre-eminently in public sector employment and industrial relations practice. Sandra Fredman and Gillian Morris have convincingly argued that there was a 'traditional' model of employment practice in public services which 'conflicted directly with the Thatcher Government's free market ideology, which views public services as inefficient, uncompetitive and an obstacle to the market'.[285] We have seen in an earlier chapter how the doctrine of Whitleyism had ensured that effective national-level collective bargaining and vigorous trade unions were incorporated into public sector employment structures—that this was one of the assumptions upon which post-war collective *laissez-faire* rested.[286] However, the presence of a large public sector created a progressively increasing problem for traditional collective *laissez-faire* policies. As we saw earlier in this chapter, by the beginning of the 1980s public sector national-level bargaining had come to embody many implemented expectations of comparability[287] of pay and conditions between workers within the public sector and with workers in the private sector—expectations which 1980s governments regarded it as important to challenge.[288] At a more basic level, both central government and local authorities were committed to observing, and securing the observance by contractors of, the Fair Wages Resolution of the House of Commons until its rescission in 1983.[289]

There were other conventions prevailing in the public employment sector which conflicted with the goals of post-1979 governments. Public sector white-collar workers—civil servants and local authority public servants—on the whole had greater expectations of job security than their private sector counterparts. For example, the justification which was advanced for the unwillingness of successive governments to resolve the doubt whether civil servants had contracts of employment was that, in any event, civil servants, in practice, enjoyed job security at least as extensive as that prevailing outside the Civil Service.[290] More-

[285] S. Fredman and G. Morris, 'The State as Employer; Is it Unique?' (1990) 19 ILJ 142 at 145.

[286] See above, pp. 38–40.

[287] See above, pp. 119–21 for the role of the Priestley Commission in establishing the comparability principle.

[288] See above, pp. 545–50.

[289] See above, pp. 539–41 and Fredman and Morris, 'The State as Employer', at 144.

[290] This was formally asserted in Estacode, the code of terms and conditions for established civil servants: see S. Fredman and G. Morris, *The State as*

over, we have remarked in an earlier chapter that where there had to be compulsory redundancies (arising from parliamentary decisions) in the public sector—including nationalized industries —those made redundant could expect to benefit from a set of statutory regulations providing compensation for loss of office on a scale significantly more generous than that provided either by statute law or most employers' practice in the private sector.[291] Not only was the notion of job property thus more fully developed in the public than the private sector; so also, in a broad sense, was the notion of the representation of the workers' interests in the running of the enterprise more deeply embedded in public sector employment policy and practice than in the generality of private sector employment relations. As we have seen, it had a formal status in nationalization statutes,[292] and, certainly in the perception of post-1979 Conservative governments, it was an entrenched feature of the employment practice of, at least, Labour-controlled local authorities, if not local authorities in general.

There was a second set of reasons why restructuring the public employment sector should be a high priority for 1980s governments. These reasons arose from the monetarist goals which those governments set themselves. When we examined the Monetarism of post-1979 governments at the beginning of the previous chapter, we saw how it demanded that each unit of the public or publicly subsidized sector of the labour economy should be subject to the same monetary restrictions, in the form of cash limits, as the macro-economy itself.[293] Although the desire to subject the public sector of the economy to market forces was distinct from Monetarism in its pure theoretical form, by the mid-1980s that desire had increased in importance to the point where it was effectively the main tenet of government Monetarism.[294] This, however, involved the government in a process very much akin to a formal public sector incomes policy—especially when cash limited allocations to government

Employer: Labour Law in the Public Services (London, 1988), 68–71, 'Civil Servants and Dismissal at Will'.

[291] See above, pp. 63–4.
[292] See above, pp. 68–71.
[293] See above, p. 432.
[294] See D. Robinson, *Monetarism and the Labour Market* (Oxford, 1986), 422.

departments came to be expressed as being to provide for specific percentage average increases in wages and salaries bills.[295] Yet 1980s governments were strongly committed to avoiding involvement in incomes policies, which would falsify their claims to be letting the labour market operate freely. The public sector specially threatened those claims, not least because the government would be seen as directly political responsible for inflationary wage and salary movements occurring within it. This was perceived within the government as the very dilemma which the 1970–4 Conservative government had disastrously failed to resolve; as we have seen earlier, the policy 'U-turn' of 1972 towards formal incomes policy, which the government was so determined to avoid repeating, had been a response to precisely this set of pressures in an acute form.[296] Ironically, this problem had been heightened by the commitment of the Labour government in the late 1970s to the imposition of financial targets, determined by central governments, upon nationalized industries.[297]

Hence it was the case that, right from the beginning of the 1980s, the government was in search of methods of restructuring the public employment sector in such a way as to shake off its rigidities, and to make it behave according to sound monetarist principles of its own volition without the need for close and obtrusive governmental control along incomes policy lines. Many measures taken and policies pursued in the 1980s were explicable in these terms; in earlier sections we have referred to the attack on national and relativity bargaining in the public sector, and to the use, for these purposes, of privatization and compulsory putting-out of work to tender.[298] These developments can be described in terms of approaches to a free labour market; they have been so described by the Department of Employment itself.[299] The argument of this part of the chapter will be that the restructuring of the public employment sector was more positive

[295] See ibid. 423.

[296] See above, pp. 329–31.

[297] Cf. the White Paper, *The Nationalized Industries*, Cmnd. 7131 (1978): see C. Veljanowski, *Selling the State: Privatization in Britain* (1987), 59–60, 'The nationalised industries were clearly being used to promote government's macro-economic policy [in the 1970s].'

[298] See above, pp. 545–9.

[299] Cm. 540, para. 1.1–1.3.

and more specific than is implied in the free market description of it. In particular, there was a series of moves to re-cast the role of management in public sector employment; this profoundly affected the whole employment regime with which public services are provided.

(a) Privatization

In the early and mid-1980s, the most prominent form of restructuring of the public employment sector consisted of privatization of nationalized industries and public utilities. Between 1979 and 1987, according to the calculations of one of the leading writers about privatization, 20 per cent of the state sector and over 400,000 jobs had been transferred to the private sector by the privatizing of twelve major companies and a larger number of smaller ones.[300] By 1991, it was recorded that major flotations had raised to two-thirds the proportion of previously state-owned industries which had been sold to the private sector, and that as significant a change in ownership had occurred as between 1945 and 1951.[301] In one sense the privatization programme completely restructured the relevant parts of the public employment sector, simply by removing them from that sector. But the change from public ownership does not in itself bring about a restructuring of the way the enterprise in question is run and managed. We need therefore to look behind the rhetoric of privatization and consider its practical consequences. In particular, the reasons or justifications advanced for privatization in the early 1980s are somewhat misleading in terms of its actual effects upon the enterprises concerned. The expressed rationale emphasized the importance of exposing the enterprises in question to commercial competition. Thus, the first really massive privatization, that of British Telecom, was presented as the logical end of the process of liberalization which had preceded it. Liberalization consisted in abolishing the state monopoly in telecommunications; this was carried out by the British Telecommunications Act 1981. It has been argued that privatization was more of a fortuitous than a

---

[300] C. Veljanowski, *Selling the State: Privatization in Britain* (London, 1987), 4.
[301] P. Riddell, *The Thatcher Era and its Legacy* (Oxford, 1991), 86, 87. The following post-war nationalizations had been reversed: the gas, water, and electricity industries, cable and wireless, civil aviation, road haulage, steel production.

logical outcome of liberalization, occurring when the government saw the opportunity to recoup an enormous amount of public expenditure by these means and to minimize a future source of pressure on the public sector borrowing requirement.[302] At all events, whether logically or fortuitously, privatization was strongly associated with achieving the discipline of commercial and capital market structures. By the later 1980s it was reasonably apparent that, even if privatization could occasionally be justified as a form of liberalization, it certainly could not in all cases. The difficulties over the privatization of the electricity industry were proof enough of that; the manœuvrings preceding the Electricity Act 1989 demonstrated the impossibility of liberalizing the supply of electricity by nuclear power.[303]

The liberalizing rationale for privatization in itself made no overt claims to restructuring employment relationships within the industries concerned. Claims about the restructuring of employment relationships were made independently of the liberalizing rationale, though such claims were somewhat misleading as to the kind of restructuring that was involved. The claim was that the employees in the industries concerned were being brought into a more participative relationship with the employing enterprise by the mechanism of share-ownership. This was prominent, for instance, in the privatization of the gas industry. Within the larger aim of encouraging wider share-ownership among the population as a whole, priority was given to transforming employees into financial participators in the profits of their industry—with a corresponding interest in guaranteeing its high productivity. This claim was rendered partly illusory by the tendency of employees who had bought shares on privileged terms to realize their profits as quickly as possible; this was hardly surprising in view of the extent to which the value of shares was discounted in order to ensure the success of the massive share sales involved in the privatization process.

There was one perceptible employment restructuring effect which was much less illusory and which privatization had in

---

[302] Veljanowski, *Selling the State*, 66: 'It was the frustration he encountered while devising a method of doing this [i.e. controlling borrowing by public enterprises] . . . that caused Patrick Jenkin to hit on the idea of privatising B.T.'

[303] See Statement on Electricity Privatization by the Secretary of State for Energy, John Wakeham, HC Deb., 6th ser., vol. 159, col. 1171 (9 Nov. 1989).

common with liberalization; in a labour market in which terms and conditions of employment were quite tightly controlled by collective bargaining, privatization tended to lead to net workforce reductions in the industries concerned, and often to compulsory redundancies to achieve those reductions. The employees of British Telecom at the time of liberalization gave rise to a leading case in trade dispute law by refusing to connect the network of the private company Mercury Communications Ltd. into the British Telecom system;[304] one of the main issues in the case was how far this refusal could be attributed to fears of job losses as the result of the breaking of British Telecom's monopoly towards the end of the decade. Job losses were generally expected to result from putting nationalized industries into the private sector, either because privatization was accompanied by increased competition or because newly privatized industries were now subject to shareholder and regulator control. The privatized British Telecom was to engage in employment restructuring of the very kind that privatization might be expected to encourage, when it later decided to remove an entire layer of its existing management structure. It was significant that, by the grudging nature of its implementation of the EEC Acquired Rights Directive in the 1981 Transfer Regulations, the government had ensured that public sector employees would frequently not carry their accumulated employment protection rights with them when transferred into the private sector as the result of privatization.[305]

Other measures taken early in the 1980s in relation to the public employment sector also involved fairly harsh labour-shedding—somewhat parallel to that being effected in the private sector by the prevailing condition of employment recession. From

---

[304] *Mercury Communications Ltd.* v. *Scott-Garner* [1984] ICR 74. It is possible that the re-formulation of the definition of a trade dispute by the Employment Act 1982—see above, pp. 477–8—was to some extent designed to facilitate privatization or liberalization; this decision shows how that was the outcome. Cf. Auerbach, *Legislating for Conflict*, 84 n. 47.

[305] Cf. above, pp. 581–2. The clearest illustration of this phenomenon has been provided where the contracting-out of part of its operation by a public sector employer has been held not to amount to a transfer of an undertaking 'in the nature of a commercial venture'—a restriction imposed by the Transfer Regulations but not authorized by the Directive. The restriction is now proposed to be removed by the Trade Union Reform and Employment Rights Bill 1992.

1979 onwards, the Prime Minister made a special concern of the pursuit of efficiency in the Civil Service, of which the early manifestation was heavy job losses. Efficiency studies were conducted under the direction of Sir Derek Rayner, a senior director of Marks and Spencers. By May 1980, the Prime Minister could announce to the House of Commons that:

When the Government took office, the size of the Civil Service was 732,000. As the result of the steps that we have already taken it is now 705,000. We intend now to bring the number down to about 630,000 over the next four years.[306]

Apart from liberalization, privatization and the operations of the Efficiency Unit in the early 1980s, there were other policy developments which tended to bring about restructuring of public sector employment relationships. We have considered in an earlier section the various attacks on relativity bargaining and national-level collective bargaining, which were concentrated upon the public sector.[307] We noticed that one form of attack consisted in putting pressure upon local authorities, and National Health Service employing authorities, to contract out the provision of services such as cleaning, laundry, or refuse collection, so removing that workforce from the ambit of public sector collective bargaining.[308] This policy culminated in the provisions of part I of the Local Government Act 1988, which require that if a local authority is to engage in any of a list of activities including refuse collection, cleaning, catering, or ground or vehicle maintenance, it must do so only if there has been the opportunity for competitive tendering for the performance of the function or the obtaining of the contract in question, and if the authority's own direct labour organization has won or survived any competition thus offered to it, without restricting, distorting, or preventing competition from other contenders.[309]

---

[306] HC Deb., 5th ser., vol. 948, col. 1050 (13 May 1980).

[307] See above, pp. 545–9.

[308] Fredman and Morris, *The State as Employer*, 145. For the failure of the Transfer Regulations to maintain statutory employment protection in this situation, see above, n. 305.

[309] Cf. Fredman and Morris, *The State as Employer*, 145. The strategy of part I of the Act is to permit 'defined authorities' either to enter into works contracts or to carry out functional work falling within the 'defined activities' only if elaborate conditions, designed to make the authorities act competitively, are satisfied. The

(b) Removal of Security of Tenure

A further set of measures restructured employment relationships which were actually or in effect in the public sector, and which were governed by protective regimes for the employees concerned, originally created because of some perceived public interest which justified them. Within this category came the abolition of university teachers' academic tenure by the Education Reform Act 1988, and the abolition of the Dock Labour Scheme by the Dock Work Act 1989. Although technically employed for the most part in the private sector, both university teachers and registered dock workers operated under employment regimes which, from the perspective of 1980s governments, displayed the worst features of the public employment sector in conferring unusually great security of employment upon the employees concerned. University teachers were generally employed under university statutes or regulations which ensured that, once having survived a period of probation, they could not be dismissed before reaching retirement age except by reason of their own misconduct or dereliction of duty—often narrowly defined; in particular, they could usually not be dismissed by reason of redundancy. Dock workers in ports within the Dock Labour Scheme were protected from dismissal by their employers by regulations requiring the approval, for such dismissal, of the Local Dock Labour Board. The local boards were joint bodies of representing employers and trade unions which maintained an effective veto upon redundancies in the scheme ports, a state of affairs upon which the trade union members of the boards strictly insisted. In both cases a specialized public interest provided the rationale, or at least the historical reason, for the special protection in question; in the case of university teachers, the purpose was to secure academic independence, while the dock workers had become a protected category by reason of their crucial importance to the wartime industrial economy. The Scheme ports had been so designated in or just after the Second World War; a competing sector of non-scheme ports had grown up alongside them and had been better placed to exploit technical developments such as containerization.

conditions in effect involve competitive tendering—see s. 4 (work contracts) and ss. 7–8 (functional work—which means the carrying-out of work by a local authority by direct labour).

In both cases, 1980s governments came to attach great importance to displacing these special protections in the interest of bringing about more efficient—in the sense of economical—patterns of employment in the occupations concerned. The abolition of academic tenure was effected by sections 202–8[310] of the Education Reform Act 1988, which set in train a process of mandatory revision of the statutes and regulations of all universities to ensure that all academic and related staff appointed or promoted after a cut-off date in 1987 would be susceptible to dismissal for redundancy, and that all academic and related staff would be liable to be dismissed on defined grounds amounting to 'good cause'—it being thought that some had previously been liable to be dismissed only for extreme misconduct very narrowly defined.

More immediately controversial was the government's plan, suddenly announced in a White Paper in April 1989,[311] to abolish the Dock Labour Scheme. This plan was swiftly implemented by the enactment of the Dock Work Act 1989,[312] which was effective in time to stultify the industrial action which the Transport and General Workers Union sought to organize to oppose abolition of the scheme. That industrial action was held up, firstly by lengthy steps the union took to ensure that the action would attract trade dispute immunity from tort action brought by the port employers, and then by the interlocutory injunction obtained by the port employers, despite these precautions, on the strength of an egregious development of the tort of interference with business by unlawful means.[313] The Dock Work Legislation of 1989 offered compensation of up to £35,000 to registered dock workers made redundant in the ensuing three years. By June 1990, the official estimate of up to 2,000 redundancies resulting from the Act had been largely exceeded: 4,840 dockers—more than half the number of registered dock workers

[310] See G. Pitt, 'Academic Freedom and Educational Reform: The Tenure Provisions of the Education Reform Act 1988' (1990)18 ILJ 33.

[311] *Employment in the Ports: The Dock Labour Scheme*, Cm. 664.

[312] See D. Brodie, 'The Dock Work Act 1989 and the Dock Work (Compensation Payments Scheme) Regulations 1989' (1989) 18 ILJ 230.

[313] See B. Simpson, 'The Summer of Discontent and the Law' (1989) 18 ILJ 234 at 236–9 commenting on *Associated British Ports Ltd.* v.*TGWU* [1989] ICR 557.

in July 1989 when the Act took effect—had been made redundant.[314] The port employers, freed from the constraints of the Dock Work Scheme, very rapidly transformed their operations to reproduce the commercial practices of the existing more prosperous non-scheme ports such as Felixstowe. Thus an area of employment which was functionally in the public sector had been effectively privatized and wholly restructured.

The measures towards restructuring the public employment sector which we have so far considered have been largely negative rather than positive ones, more concerned with getting rid of existing (protective) regimes than imposing new regimes; this is on the whole true not just of the abolition of academic tenure and the Dock Work Scheme, but also of liberalization, privatization and compulsory contracting-out. A partial exception, however, was the Local Government Act 1988 which, as we have seen,[315] not only intensified the pressure towards contracting-out of the performance of local authority services but also sought radically to alter the framework within which local authorities would provide the services which were not contracted out. It is no coincidence that this measure was a product of the third Conservative government of the 1980s, that one which took office in 1987. That administration was notable for taking a more radical approach to the restructuring of the public employment sector than had hitherto been attempted. We shall look in turn at two sets of such radical measures: firstly those concerning delegation of management and opting-out of local control in the education and health services and, secondly, in close parallel, those concerned with the hiving-off of Civil Service functions to agencies—the so-called 'Next Steps' programme.

(c) Restructuring Employment in the Education and Health Services

The first of the two measures concerned with local delegation and opting-out was the Education Reform Act 1988. It was apparent from the time that it was first proposed that the Education

---

[314] Report of the Comptroller and Auditor General's National Audit Office for 1989/90 on Appropriation Accounts Class VIII Vote 3, Transport Industries—see *The Independent*, 1 Nov. 1990, p. 5.

[315] See above, pp. 549, 622.

Reform Act was an extremely radical measure—we have already seen that it abolished academic tenure. It was less immediately obvious, but turned out to be the case, that it would fundamentally restructure employment patterns throughout the public education service—even more profoundly than the obviously employment-oriented Teachers' Pay and Conditions Act 1987 had done by substituting the imposing of terms and conditions of employment decided upon by the Department of Education and Science in place of the previously existing statutory collective bargaining mechanisms.[316] In the school part of the public education service, the structures which the government wished to challenge were employment regimes which they regarded as overly protective of teachers and insufficiently financially rigorous by reason of local authority control. One method of challenging those structures was to provide for schools to opt out of that local authority control, becoming self-governing trusts financed directly by the Department of Education and Science.[317] The staff of opted-out schools would be employed by the self-governing trusts on terms and conditions determined by each of them within the framework of the 1987 Act.[318]

Scarcely less destructive of local authority control was the system of local management of schools which the 1988 Act instituted for those schools which did not opt out. Under this system, the financial management of each school was to be delegated by the local education authority to the governing body of the school concerned. The schools thereby became independent financial units whose ability to remain within their budgets would depend partly upon the number of pupils they managed to enrol and partly also upon their decisions about the employment of staff. The Act and statutory regulations made under it modified the general law of employment to ensure that the governing body of each school would have the power to require the dismissal of those employed at that school, while the financial liability for doing so remained with the local authority as nominal employer.[319] Significantly, the regulations also modified the

[316] See above, p. 548.
[317] Education Reform Act 1988, pt. I, ch. 4.
[318] Ibid., s. 75.
[319] Ibid., ss. 44, 46 and the Education (Modifications of Enactments Relating to Employment) Order 1989 (SI 1989, No. 901). See M. R. Freedland, (1989) 18 ILJ 231.

general law of trade dispute immunity so as to limit immunity to action relating to contracts the performance of which affects the school in question—in effect identifying the governing body as the sole primary employer for the purpose of the limits on secondary action.[320] The school governing body seemed to get the best of both worlds, being treated as the real employer for the purpose of acquiring rights, but not for the purpose of being subject to financial liabilities.

There were close parallels between the way that the public education service was restructured by the Education Reform Act and the way that the National Health Service was restructured by the National Health Service and Community Care Act 1990. In particular, the arrangements for schools either to opt out of local authority control or to receive delegated budgets within the local authority framework have strong analogies with the provisions whereby ownership and management and staff of hospitals could be transferred to National Health Service Trusts,[321] and whereby doctors' practices could seek recognition as fund-holding practices within the framework of the Regional Health Authorities and the Family Health Services Authorities with which the Act replaced the Family Practitioner Committees.[322] Just as the Education Reform Act aimed to place schools in a competitive relationship with each other, so the NHS and Community Care Act aimed to create an 'internal market' in the provision of publicly funded health care. Both measures sought to ensure a more commercial-minded approach to the employment of staff, and both pursued strategies designed to replace national-level collective bargaining by localized setting of terms and conditions of employment. In so far as both sets of measures tended to de-centralize control of the services concerned, they could be seen as being aimed at reducing the power of local authorities—that is, area health authorities and, especially, local education authorities. That this was not the primary aim, however, is suggested by the fact that a very comparable development was occurring within the Civil Service itself, in the shape of the 'Next Steps' programme. That programme had intentions and implica-

---

[320] 1989 Order, art. 5.
[321] NHS and Community Care Act 1989, ss. 5–11.
[322] Ibid., ss. 12–17.

tions which enable us to identify important underlying features common in some degree to all these restructuring measures.

(d) Restructuring Civil Service Employment

We have already seen that, from 1979 onwards, the government was attempting to increase the efficiency with which the Civil Service was conducting its operations, and was maintaining an Efficiency Unit, reporting directly to the Prime Minister, for that purpose. In the later 1980s the Efficiency Unit devised a general strategy with which to pursue its task; that strategy is identified with the idea of executive agencies and was presented in the policy document entitled *Improving Management in Government: The Next Steps* in 1988. The 'Next Steps' strategy was based upon the premises that a distinction should be drawn between the 'policy advice' and the 'executive functions' aspects of the work of the Civil Service—a distinction which received a wide measure of acceptance across the political spectrum, but whose full commercializing implications were perhaps not fully appreciated. In the 'Next Steps' document, a series of defects were identified in the existing organization of the Civil Service. The findings were that senior management was dominated by people whose skills were in policy formulation and who had relatively little experience of managing or working where services were actually being delivered; that civil servants respond to the priorities set by their ministers, which tend to be dominated by the demands of Parliament and of communicating government policies, in which situation it is easy for the task of improving performance to get overlooked; that there was still too little attention paid to the results to be achieved with the resources available and relatively few external pressures demanding improvement in performance; and that the Civil Service was too big and diverse to manage as a single entity.[323] These led up to the conclusion that:

At present the freedom of an individual manager to manage effectively and responsibly in the Civil Service is severely circumscribed[324]

and to the key recommendation that:

[323] *Improving Management in Government: The Next Steps* (Efficiency Unit, London, 1988), paras. 2.3–2.10.
[324] Ibid., para 2.11.

'agencies' should be established to carry out the executive functions of government within a policy and resources framework set by a department.[325]

The 'Next Steps' programme of devolution of Civil Service functions to agencies within government proceeded apace, and had produced over thirty agencies by the end of 1990, with a further thirty candidates for agency status under consideration.[326] Agency status had already been conferred upon the Employment Service, involving over 33,000 staff, and was contemplated for the Social Security Benefits operation, involving over 68,000 staff.

It is important to identify what 'Next Steps' agency status involved. It was a half-way house towards privatization, and an exercise in creating market analogues in relation to the activities concerned; its central significance is as a reform of the management of employment within the Civil Service. This reform can best be understood as a combination of localisation and contractualization. In the course of the 1980s, Government policy-makers came increasingly to perceive the private sector of the labour economy not just as the location of healthy competition and the discipline of commercial pressures but, more specifically, as providing the best model of efficient management. That is not to say that they saw the private sector as universally more efficient than the public sector, but rather that it contained within it the most efficiently managed enterprises. These were perceived as those enterprises where there was a powerful local management at the level where goods were manufactured or delivered, or services were provided, and where that powerful local management was fully accountable to any higher levels of the enterprise. In the 'Next Steps' Report, the managerial culture of the Civil Service is implicitly contrasted with this model:

The culture of the Civil Service is cautious and works against personal responsibility. The culture of the Civil Service puts a premium on a 'safe pair of hands' not on enterprise. It does not reward the person who says 'I have saved money.' It does not penalise the person who ignores the opportunity to get better value.[327]

[325] Ibid., para 4.19.
[326] For the situation by mid-1991, see the White Paper, *Improving Management in Government: The Next Steps Agencies: Review 1991*, Cm. 1760 (Nov. 1991).
[327] *Next Steps*, annexe B (Findings), para. 5.1.

Elsewhere in the Report, it is made clear that it is the managers who are to shoulder this sort of personal responsibility and to do so in the way they handle employment matters:

At present, the freedom of an individual manager to manage effectively and responsibly in the Civil Service is severely circumscribed. There are controls not only on resources and objectives, as there should be in any effective system, but also on the way in which resources can be managed. Recruitment, dismissal, choice of staff, promotion, pay, hours of work, accommodation, grading, organisation of work, the use of IT equipment [i.e. computerisation[328]] are all outside the control of most Civil Service managers at any level.[329]

Within the concept of efficiency which is embodied in the 'Next Steps' programme, the notions of personal responsibility and enterprise have, as we have indicated, to be reconciled with notions of accountability and the ensuring of value for money. The policy-makers who were concerned with the pursuit of efficiency gravitated towards contractualization as the method of trying to achieve this reconciliation. In this framework, both the empowering of local managers or agencies and the securing of their accountability were sought to be achieved by the defining of relationships in contractual terms. Employment relationships were defined in terms which were more unequivocally contractual, more specific, and more individuated than they had previously been.[330] This would tend to give local managers greater control over their staff; but they in turn would be subjected to essentially contractual controls by which efficiency standards would be defined and enforced. We return shortly to the effects of this programme upon terms and conditions of employment and upon employment practices, those being our central concerns in this whole discussion. First it is useful to try to understand the contractual method of controlling Next Steps operations, because of its crucial bearing upon employment in the Civil Service and elsewhere in the public sector.

The process of putting in place those mechanisms of control

---

[328] Cf. the impact, on staff, of computerization of the PAYE operation of the Inland Revenue, as discussed in *Cresswell* v. *Board of Inland Revenue* [1984] ICR 508.

[329] *Next Steps*, para. 2.11.

[330] Cf. the 'Next Steps' agreement for the employment of prison officers, which was under consideration in *McClaren* v. *Home Office* [1990] ICR 824.

and accountability was described and developed in a Treasury White Paper of 1989 entitled *The Financing and Accountability of Next Steps Agencies*.[331] The purpose of this White Paper was to introduce a proposal for a Government Trading Bill—which in due course became the Government Trading Funds Act 1990. The earlier Government Trading Funds Act 1973 had enabled independent trading funds to be given to government operations in the nature of trading; the restriction to operations in the nature of trading was to be removed by the 1990 Act. This needed to be justified by guarantees of accountability; the White Paper stressed the importance for this purpose of the Framework Document which would apply to each Next Steps agency:

The Framework Document for each Agency is a new and key element in the accountability process. Objectives for units of Civil Service work have existed since the Financial Management Initiative, but they have usually been for internal management purposes. Framework Documents, which are normally made available to Parliament and published more widely, set out explicitly for each Agency its aims and objectives, and the boundaries between policy and service delivery functions. They also describe the monitoring, accountability and reporting patterns between the Agency and the parent department, the financial and personnel management flexibilities that the Agency will have and the Accounting Officer status of the Chief Executive.[332]

This is an attempt to reconcile strong management with accountability by structures of an essentially contractual character. The Framework Document is the central contract, as it were, in a contractual hierarchy or network by which a certain kind of public demand, for goods or services, is related to a process of supply. Within this organizing framework lie various kinds of contracts of employment—with senior managers, local managers, and those personally engaged on producing goods or providing services. At the core of the whole set of arrangements is the separation of the demand function and the supply function and their location on the two sides of what is, in all but name, a contractual transaction.

This contractual dividing of the public employment sector into, on the one hand policy-makers, procurers, and purchasers of

<hr>

[331] Cm. 914 (Dec. 1989).
[332] Ibid., para. 5.8.

goods and services and, on the other hand, the deliverers of those goods and services turns out to underlie not just the 'Next Steps' programme but also many of the other public sector restructuring exercises of the later 1980s. For example, it is this, rather than supposed market-type competition, which was at the heart of the strategy of the Education Reform Act 1988, at least for primary and secondary if not for tertiary education. Schools were turned into discrete units for the delivery of education services both by the arrangements for opting-out of local authority control and by the system of local management of schools. Polytechnics and universities were placed in a deliberately and overtly contractual relationship with the new Funding Councils. The managerial ideology underlying this restructuring was identified very clearly in the following terms in a Report to the Department of Education and Science on the Local Management of Schools prepared by Coopers and Lybrand, a leading firm of chartered accountants:

The underlying philosophy of financial delegation to schools stems from the application of the principles of good management. Good management requires the identification of management units for which objectives can be set and resources allocated; the unit is then required to manage itself within those resources in a way which seeks to achieve the objectives; the performance of the unit is monitored and the unit is held to account for its performance and for its use of funds. These concepts are just as applicable in the public sector as they are in the private sector.[333]

That is a discourse in terms of management by contractualization, and we find that this process of contractualization is developed even further in the National Health Service and Community Care Act 1990 to which we have already referred. This emerges clearly from the White Papers containing the proposals which gave rise to the Act. Thus, the White Paper *Working for Patients*[334] made it clear that it was pursuing a strategy of creating strong local managerial authorities to fill an essentially contract-making and contract-enforcing role—for example, the new Family Health Service Authorities which were to replace the existing Family Practitioner Committees as the authorities exercising local control over the provision of general practitioner services:

[333] (HMSO, 1988), para. 1.5.
[334] Cm. 555 (Jan. 1989).

The Government does not believe that a Committee with 30 members can lead the management of the Family Practitioner Service as effectively as the changes now envisaged will require. Further, it is difficult for the management of contracts with practitioners to be the responsibility of the bodies on which half the members are nominated by representatives of the practitioners whose contracts are to be managed.[335]

In the White Paper which made proposals for the restructuring of the welfare and social services functions of local authorities— entitled, perhaps predictably, *Caring for People*[336]—the con- tractualization of the role of the public authority is even more forcefully developed:

The Government . . . endorses Sir Roy Griffiths' vision of authorities as arrangers and purchasers of care services rather than as monopolistic providers. In future social services departments will have the following key responsibilities

. . . [assessing individual needs]
. . . [designing packages of services]
    securing the delivery of services not simply by acting as direct providers but by developing their purchasing and contracting role to become 'enabling authorities'.[337]

These various intentions are fully reflected in the detailed pro- visions of the 1990 Act.

So the restructuring of the public employment sector thus came to concentrate more and more upon the contractualization of local management functions. The local managers and managing bodies would be expected to carry out their contractual obliga- tions by the use of efficient employment practices—which would mean making and implementing tightly structured and indi- viduated contracts of employment, whereby personal perform- ance would be closely monitored, and levels of payment would tend to depend increasingly on assessments of personal perform- ance.

A report to the Prime Minister by the Efficiency Unit in May 1991 provides strong evidence of the extent to which the Next Steps programme had already given a new breed of managers a greater freedom to alter the employment conditions of the work-

---

[335] Ibid., para. 7.24.
[336] Cm. 849 (Nov. 1989).
[337] Ibid., para. 3.1.3.

force, and evidence also of the aspirations that this state of affairs would become a general one throughout the Civil Service and the executive agencies of government.[338] In July 1991, the Chancellor of the Exchequer announced[339] a re-negotiation of the Civil Service pay agreements which was intended to enable responsibility for pay-bargaining to be delegated to Agencies and to achieve a closer link between performance and reward.[340] The following main employment outcomes of the Next Steps initiative were becoming evident:

1. overall workforce reductions, achieved presumably to some extent by means of redundancies, especially in central departments of government;[341]
2. extensive delegation of managerial responsibility from central Departments to chief executives of Agencies, whose remuneration and job tenure was heavily dependent on the performance of their Agencies; and
3. localization of the setting of pay and other terms and conditions, and therefore of pay-bargaining, to Agency level, with resulting divergences especially in pay and grading structures and in patterns of performance-related pay—which tended to become a more and more significant element in remuneration.

The complete fragmentation of Civil Service employment structures and the erosion of the concept of the 'Civil Service career' became real medium-term prospects. As an ideological and practical restructuring of public sector employment relationships, these measures amounted to changes in employment law and policy as significant as the more general measures such as the Wages Act 1986 or the rescission of the Fair Wages Resolution in 1983 which we examined earlier in this chapter. Since we can therefore see this as a culmination of the restructuring of the labour economy which took place during the 1980s, it is thus

---

[338] Efficiency Unit, *Report to the Prime Minister: Making the Most of Next Steps: The Management of Ministers' Departments and their Executive Agencies* (HMSO, May 1991).

[339] HC Deb., 6th ser., vol. 195, cols. 604–5w (24 July 1991; Written Answers).

[340] See Cm. 1760, p. 6.

[341] This is advocated, at the level of a 25 per cent reduction in staff of the personnel and finance divisions of central departments, in Efficiency Unit, *Making the Most of Next Steps*, para. 2.14.

appropriate to turn to an evaluation of that whole process of restructuring, which is attempted in the next, and concluding, section of this chapter.

10.7. THE RESTRUCTURING OF THE LABOUR ECONOMY AND THE CONTROL OF INFLATION, 1980–1990

In each of the pre-1979 phases of post-war labour legislation which were considered in earlier chapters of this book, we found it necessary to discuss the impact of governmental incomes policies. Thus we looked at the Wage Freeze of the late-1940s, at the Pay Pause of the early 1960s, and at the formal or statutory Incomes Policies of the middle and later 1960s, of the early 1970s, and of the later 1970s. We observed the way in which general governmental strategies for the control of inflation were transformed by events into specific incomes policies; this was the fate, in particular, of the Joint Statement of Intent on Productivity, Prices, and Incomes and the National Plan of 1964, of Edward Heath's industrial and industrial relations strategies of the early 1970s, and of the Social Contract strategy of the Labour Government from 1974 onwards. In the 1980s, however, events did not follow that pattern, and nor accordingly did our discussion of those events in this and the previous chapter follow that pattern. By seeking to identify why that was the case, we can hope to find a focal point for conclusions about the significance and the effectiveness of the restructuring of the labour economy which was achieved or attempted during the 1980s.

The governments of the 1980s did, as we have seen, fully share their predecessors' pre-occupation with the control of inflation; indeed, it is arguable that they pursued that concern more single-mindedly than those predecessors had done in any part of the post-war period, for they were less committed to the maintenance of full employment than their predecessors had been. As we have seen, both their monetarist policy of the early 1980s and the Medium-Term Financial Strategy which was maintained, with various changes, through the 1980s, were, essentially, counter-inflation strategies. Moreover, those counter-inflation strategies extended into the micro-economic sphere; many of the policies and measures described in this chapter and the previous one, under the general head of restructuring of the labour economy, can be regarded as supply-side counter-inflation policy amounting to informal undeclared incomes policy.

Thus, writing in 1983, Derek Robinson could effectively identify most of the policies described in these two chapters as 'indirect' or 'partial' pay policy measures.[342] These were contrasted with comprehensive pay policies; measures available to a government seeking to influence pay might be 'partial' in applying only to parts of the employed population, or might be 'indirect' in avoiding a direct impact on the settlements or the results of collective bargaining or of other forms of pay determination, and in choosing to operate on other factors affecting pay movements.[343] Thus, Robinson includes among indirect measures, firstly, measures influencing the behaviour of workers as individuals, particularly measures tending to lower individual reservation wages, secondly, measures to remove 'artificial' wage floors, and thirdly, measures to discourage collective action either by altering the balance of power against trade unions or by reducing the militancy of their membership. Robinson's category of partial measures consisted essentially of measures applying various pressures to different parts of the public sector. It requires no ingenuity and involves no artificiality to place most of the labour legislation and associated measures of the 1980s within that framework.

A similar analysis could, however, be advanced, as we have seen, for much of the initial set of policies and measures of Edward Heath's government from 1970 to, say, 1972, or, allowing for a different orientation, of the Social Contract phase of the Labour government's term of office in the 1970s—from 1974 to, say, early 1976. Why, then, was there no comparable transition in the 1980s to comprehensive or formal incomes policy? Even if the governments of the 1980s were disenchanted with the 'traditional' incomes policies of the 1960s and 1970s, there were, after all, proposals for new forms of incomes policy which would more closely accord with their general economic policies, or at least avoid some of the obvious pitfalls of those earlier experiments in formal incomes policy. For instrance, Professor Meade suggested a system of arbitration of disputed wage settlements, which

[342] D. Robinson, ch. 7, 'Indirect and Partial Measures', in D. Robinson and K. Mayhew, eds., *Pay Policies for the Future* (Oxford, 1983).
[343] Ibid. 105.

would operate within a monetarist framework, and would consider whether a settlement was conducive to increasing employment within a set target for growth of nominal national income, while Professor Layard proposed a tax-based system which would tax employers on increases of earnings above a fixed norm.[344] 1980s governments remained, however, impervious to any such initiatives, or to any intervention in the nature of general co-ordination of pay-bargaining.

There are several ways of explaining why that was the case. One such explanation is that 1980s governments simply regarded the measures they took to reduce trade union power and to restructure the labour economy as amounting to a successful counter-inflation strategy on the supply side of the labour market. If indirect and partial measures could be judged to be successful, there was no need to move to comprehensive or formal incomes policy measures. This is a useful explanation, but an incomplete one; further explanatory factors need to be brought into play. In particular, it is necessary to consider what were the criteria which governments used in judging that their counter-inflation strategies in the labour market were successful, or that there was no necessity for formal incomes policy. There was no simple criterion such as the achievement of a negligible level of wage inflation; that was not achieved in the 1980s, but neither that failure, nor indeed the moderately serious problems of inflation experienced towards the end of the 1980s, were seen as compelling the adoption of formal incomes policy in the way that previous governments had done. Admittedly 1980s governments could conclude that their indirect and partial measures seemed *more* successful than those of their predecessors, but that is not the whole story.

An important point is that the criteria of success adopted by 1980s governments differed significantly from those of their prdecessors. Firstly, 1980s governments were, as we have seen, much less committed to regarding the limitation of unemployment as a criterion of the success of counter-inflation strategies; the existence of a moderately high rate of unemployment was not merely accepted as a consequence of their counter-inflation

---

[344] See G. Maynard, *The Economy under Mrs. Thatcher* (Oxford, 1988), 133–4.

strategies, but seemed to form an integral part of those strategies.[345] Secondly, the governments of the 1980s were significantly more reluctant than any of their recent predecessors to operate within the corporatist framework which they regarded as the inevitable framework of formal incomes policy. They were, in other words, deeply averse to policies or measures which would operate directly and comprehensively upon the outcomes of the pay-bargaining process, because that involved accepting the legitimacy of a collectivised system of pay-bargaining. That aversion meant that they were heavily committed to regarding indirect and partial measures as successful, not perhaps at all possible costs but certainly at greater costs than had previously been accepted.

There is another line of explanation for the absence of formal incomes policy in the 1980s, which should be followed alongside the foregoing one. This consists in recognizing that, from the point of view of 1980s governments, the measures for reducing trade union power and for restructuring the labour economy were important not solely as counter-inflation strategies. The development of effective counter-inflation strategies was highly important to 1980s governments, but only as part of, and not as the whole of, a search for a viable governmental role in relation to the labour economy, and the political economy itself. This meant that strategies for the labour economy would not ultimately be judged solely, or even perhaps primarily, in terms of their counter-inflationary effectiveness. A clear but slightly tangential example is to be found in the government's policies, in the middle and later 1980s, towards the Exchange Rate Mechanism of the European Monetary System. Entering the ERM was an attractive counter-inflation strategy, in so far as it offered a way of convincing those participating in the wage-setting process that they would have to make supply-side adjustments which recognized that there was no alternative of depreciating the currency to compensate for poor international competitiveness on the part of the labour economy. However, the government's considerations of its loss of political control over the economy militated against joining the ERM, and, in the view of many, resulted

---

[345] For discussion of the role of the 'Non-Accelerating Inflation Rate of Unemployment' (NAIRU) in the economic strategies of the 1980s, see e.g. C. Allsopp and A. Graham, 'The Assessment: Policy Options for the UK' (1987) 3: 3 *Oxford Review of Economic Policy* at pp. viii–xiii.

in the UK joining at such a late time and on such relatively unfavourable terms that considerable counter-inflationary potential was sacrificed and the whole operation proved ultimately unsustainable.[346]

A less clear-cut but more central statement of the thesis that indirect and partial measures were not judged solely as counter-inflation strategies can be made in relation to the whole body of measures discussed in this and the previous chapter. We have argued that most if not all those measures tended towards implementing an ideologically determined view of a de-rigidified labour market economy. Many economists would argue that it requires excessive 'market optimism' to view that as a counter-inflation strategy of enduring effectiveness.[347] It would seem that 1980s governments were, ultimately, attracted to these measures and strategies not only because they really experienced that 'market optimism', but rather because those measures and strategies seemed to offer the possibility of a viable non-interventionist position for the government and for the state itself in relation to the labour economy—a position where they would be free of the network of corporatist compromises in which 1980s governments viewed their predecessors as having been enmeshed. The measures for the restructuring of the labour economy can better be understood as a disengagement of government from a collectivized industrial society than as counter-inflation strategy. In the next and final chapter, we shall offer an assessment of the forty-five year sequence of development which culminated in that attempt to curtail the role of the state by transforming the nature of the labour economy.

[346] Cf. Johnson, *The Economy under Mrs Thatcher 1979–1990*, 214–15.
[347] Cf. e.g. Allsopp and Graham, 'The Assessment', at pp. xiv–xvii.

11

CONCLUSION: A POST-WAR PERSPECTIVE

In Chapter 1 of this book, we examined the policy of collective *laissez-faire* as the dominant ideology of British labour law in the 1950s. This involved showing the terms in which Otto Kahn-Freund put forward the theory, and the ways in which labour law and the employment policy of the government corresponded to that theory. We suggested that the application of collective *laissez-faire* theory was not a simple or straightforward matter even at the very moment at which the theory was proposed as a general account of British labour law. There were already the makings of a set of pressures and tensions under the stress of which collective *laissez-faire* was to collapse by the end of the 1960s. The fact that collective *laissez-faire* never worked in a neat simple way, and the fact that it went through a process of collapse, did not, however, lessen its importance as a starting-point for the history of labour legislation in the period 1945–90. On the contrary, we suggested that the development of labour law throughout this period, in the later years as much as in the early years, should be understood as being intimately bound up with the destiny of collective *laissez-faire* policy.

This was not to say that the development from collective *laissez-faire* would be a simple linear one, or that its outcomes could be directly contrasted, one to one, with the original propositions of collective *laissez-faire* theory. We should expect the various determinants of change away from collective *laissez-faire* to filter through the system at different speeds, and to interact in complex ways with each other. This approach, we argued, would involve exploring two main themes in the course of this book. The first related to the impact of changes in governmental policy towards the economy upon the policy of abstentionism. This concentrated upon the effects of the post-war political commitment to achieving both full employment and continuing economic growth. The second concerned the stresses *placed upon* abstentionism by an emerging new set of ideals of industrial justice. We embarked upon the exploration of those themes with the suggestion that we would find successive governments becoming more and more radical in their responses to these various pressures and in their reactions to each perceived failure to devise a lasting solution to this complex of problems. We emerge from the attempt to explore these themes with the feeling that the hypothesis of growing radicalism has been substantiated. Over the period with which we are concerned, this was reflected partly in major shifts of priority in government policies towards industrial society—for example, away from full employment towards attaching a higher importance to the control of inflation, or away from collectivism towards individualism. It was also manifested in increasingly titanic efforts to shift and to re-model the sources of regulation of industrial society—away from voluntary collective bargaining via regulated bargaining towards, ultimately, market-disciplined employers. This, however, is to anticipate a series of conclusions which this chapter will seek to articulate in greater detail.

11.1 THE CHALLENGES TO COLLECTIVE *LAISSEZ-FAIRE*

Let us begin by going back to the definition and discussion of collective *laissez-faire* which was put forward in Chapter 1. Our point of departure for that discussion was Otto Kahn-Freund's presentation of a theory of British labour law in terms of the doctrine of collective *laissez-faire*. What thus began as an account of the seminal academic theory became, however, more of a description of how the state viewed itself in relation to labour law and to industrial society. (Perhaps unusually, the state turned out to have an articulated consciousness of its own role, expressed, for example, in the *Industrial Relations Handbook* of the Ministry of Labour,[1] which for its own reasons shared Kahn-Freund's views.) It was important that collective *laissez-faire* was a governmental stance, because it emphasized the extent to which col-

---

[1] See above, pp. 43–4.

lective *laissez-faire* was a specific manifestation of a broader theory and practice of self-limitation by the state in its dealings with society in the first half of the twentieth century. Alan Fox has described this relationship in the following terms:

Central to this body of contingent circumstances [which provided the context for collective *laissez-faire*] was the long persistence of the limited state, which allowed the pace of much, though not all, social and legislative change to be set by 'voluntary' (that is, non-state) associations, groups, or movements, either acting by themselves or bringing pressure to bear upon governments.[2]

So in a sense we are looking at a special case of the continuing dominance at this time in the UK of Gladstonian liberal theories of the role of government.

We found, on examining collective *laissez-faire* as a specific example of self-limitation by the state, that it was a particularly strong form of liberalism in that it was doubly abstentionist in relation to collective bargaining. That is to say, it was abstentionist firstly in leaving the establishment and regulation of terms and conditions of employment to collective bargaining between employers and trade unions, rather than regarding that regulation as a matter for the state. In that respect, it stands in contrast, for example, to systems of labour law in which the state restricts or controls the forms in which, or the terms on which, employment relationships may be constituted. It was abstentionist, secondly, in leaving to employers and trade unions the control of their own procedures and processes of collective bargaining and industrial relations. Here the contrast is with labour law systems in which, on the one hand, the state imposes patterns of representation (such as works councils or compulsory recognition procedures), or, on the other hand, extensively restricts the parties' freedom to take industrial action. Under collective *laissez-faire* the state treats employers and trade unions as the source of control both of the procedures and, at least equally significantly, of the *outcomes* of collective bargaining. In its pure form, collective *laissez-faire* would thus imply, among other things, that the state would impose neither maximum nor minimum limits upon the gains secured to the workforce by the processes of collective bargaining,

---

[2] A. Fox, *History and Heritage: The Social Origins of the British Industrial Relations System* (London, 1985), 373.

nor would it control the use of the peaceful industrial sanctions available to either employers or employees and their unions.

We concluded, of course, as the above description hints, that the pure form of collective *laissez-faire* existed in the realm of ideals rather than in the real world even of the 1950s. But even if, as Otto Kahn-Freund undoubtedly did, we build in enough by way of modification of the pure theory to make it square with reality, we still have a serious problem in reconciling it with apparently inconsistent major policies and tendencies in Britain at that period. No serious student of British history could suppose that Gladstonian liberalism was still intact at the beginning of the First World War, let alone at the end of the Second; it had already been modified into Asquithian liberal theories and the growth of socialist ideas, and had been heavily qualified by the growth of state social security provision. In the course of the Second World War, moreover, we saw that major new political responsibilities were assumed on behalf of future governments as part of the plans for post-war Britain. This promised an enhanced notion of citizenship, envisaging minimum standards of welfare and protection for all, and in particular adopting the goals of full employment and sustained economic growth. But if these things required an interventionist government and an active state, how could they co-exist with a regime of collective *laissez-faire*, alleged to have reached its zenith almost exactly at this historical moment?

Thus, even at the time of its maximum impact in the late 1940s and early 1950s, collective *laissez-faire* was already a slightly surprising reconstruction of a pre-war approach to industrial society, which was really in conflict with a number of pressures towards greater *dirigisme* in the post-war world. The enactment by the post-war government of Beveridge's plan for a comprehensive welfare state meant that in the adjacent area of the regulation of the position of those out of work, state provision became paramount and the role of private associations in this field was reduced. Whether people were out of work because they were too young or too old, because they were not available for work or work was not available for them, the state was to make provision; and it made provision through a legal and administrative structure which brought with it an extremely high degree of juridification and bureaucratization of this area. Private —individual or collective—supplementation of the state scheme was not forbidden—in respect of pensions, indeed, it was encouraged—but the aim was to provide a decent basic standard of state provision upon which all could rely. There was thus created a strong contrast with the state's role in determining the conditions of those in work. The Wages Councils, Order 1305, and the provisions relating to government contractors were a far cry from an effective, legally enforceable, general system of terms and conditions of employment, even when supplemented by the laws regulating the hours of work of women and children. Of course, it could be said in relation to the provision of social security that the mixed system of state provision and reliance upon voluntary non-state activity (for example, via charitable hospitals) had not worked well in the inter-war period, whereas for those in work there were effective organizations of employees and employers which could discharge the regulatory task. But this argument served to underline the contingent nature of the state's reliance upon collective bargaining. If it ceased to regulate terms and conditions of employment effectively—perhaps because of a failure to keep abreast of new expectations about what such regulation should achieve—the government might wish to modify its policy of abstention.

Equally challenging to the premises of collective *laissez-faire* were the commitments the government undertook during the war and the period thereafter in relation to the goals of economic management. There was the specific commitment, undertaken in the 1944 White Paper, that the government would take steps to ensure a high and stable level of employment. More enduring in the long run was the general commitment governments acquired in this period to ensure a steady increase in the wealth of the nation and in particular of those at work. It is important not to underestimate the novelty of this undertaking. In the inter-war period it would not have been expected that the real standard of living of workers should increase year in, year out, or that government, by adopting appropriate policies, could ensure sustained increases in people's economic well-being. These commitments were, of course, political rather than legal ones—the post-war government toyed with, but rejected, the idea of enacting a Labour Law (Full Employment) Act—but they challenged the assumptions upon which the doctrine of collective *laissez-faire* was constructed, in two fundamental ways.

First, these new developments had an impact upon the traditional function which the state viewed the collective bargaining system as performing, namely the articulation and resolution of conflicts between employers and workers. From government's point of view, a highly prized feature of the autonomous system of collective bargaining was its institutionalization of the inevitable conflicts of interest created by the labour market and the subordinate position of the employee in the employment relationship. The disruption caused by strikes, lock-outs, and other forms of industrial action was a price to be paid for a system which resolved the majority of such conflicts without resort to either overt industrial action or state intervention. As Wellington has put it:

The effect of a work stoppage is a cost traditionally paid by the public for the benefits of private ordering in labor–management relations.[3]

There clearly was an issue as to whether full employment and the higher expectations raised by continuous economic growth might not reduce the dispute-settling efficiency of the collective bargaining system, especially if, as in fact occurred, as we have seen, in the 1950s and 1960s changes in the location of bargaining power developed ahead of reforms in the collective dispute-settling machinery. Putting the matter more provocatively, Professor Wedderburn suggested in 1972 that:

the traditional framework of British labour law really rested upon a middle-class acquiescence in the current balance of industrial power. That framework was already under severe attack before 1971 because middle-class opinion . . . no longer acquiesced in the 1950s in the new muscles which trade unions had, but rarely efficiently flexed, in days of full employment.[4]

So far we have suggested that the government's commitment to full employment and continuous economic growth raised employee and trade union expectations in a way that employers,

[3] H. H. Wellington, *Labor and the Legal Process* (New Haven, Conn., 1968), 272.
[4] K. W. Wedderburn, 'Labour Law and Labour Relations in Britain' (1972) 10 BJIR at 275.

in the relatively enfeebled state of the British economy, found it difficult to meet. One response by employers was at times to resist those demands in bargaining more strenuously than had previously been the case, thus raising the incidence of unsettled issues and of industrial conflict over them, and in turn reducing the benefit to government of the conflict-resolving function of the collective bargaining system. As lower rates of dispute settlement increased the disruption experienced by the public as a result of collective bargaining, the government came under political pressure to modify parts of the abstentionist system of labour law, pressures which, as we saw, bore legislative fruit in the Industrial Relations Act 1971.

However, one can also identify a second impact that higher levels of industrial conflict had upon government. They rendered —or were perceived by government to render—the UK a less effective competitor in the international market, an important point for government given the traditional dependence of the UK economy on a high level of exports and given the increasing levels of international competition in the world economy throughout the post-war period. In other words, in the new context, collective bargaining might come to be seen as not only achieving less effectively its traditional objective of institutional-izing conflict but also as rendering more difficult the discharge by government of its commitment to economic growth. Far from being seen as an instrument through which, as in the Second World War, government achieved its labour market goals, col-lective bargaining, or at least some versions of it, was seen increasingly as an obstacle.

The second challenge to the state's policy of abstention stemmed from the possibility that employers might respond to the in-creased bargaining strength of trade unions in a situation of full employment by conceding improvements in terms and conditions of employment that exceeded the increases in productivity achievable through new investment or changed working methods. If employers in other countries were able to continue operations without making such concessions, then again the competitive position of British goods and services would deteriorate, and the discharge by government of its new economic commitments would be rendered that much more difficult. For that reason also, government came to feel itself under pressure to seek some relief through a modification of the principle of collective *laissez-faire* in relation to labour law.

As we saw in chapter 2, those who promoted the governmental commitment to full employment were aware of its potential impact upon the state's policy of collective *laissez-faire* towards collective bargaining. In these circumstances, as we have already remarked, it was slightly surprising that the wartime apparatus of labour-market control was so thoroughly dismantled, although such a dismantling was wholly consistent with the political commitments that had been given in the early stages of the war to secure the consent of employers and trade unions to the wartime regime. The tension between the newly reasserted policy of collective *laissez-faire* towards collective bargaining and the newly adopted activism on the part of the state in the areas of welfare and economic management was, if not resolved, at least rendered less apparent by delineating a distinct sphere of operations within which collective *laissez-faire* could prevail, while other, more statist, policies could operate outside that sphere without apparently impinging upon collective *laissez-faire*. That is to say, there was a certain separation of the sphere of industrial relations —within which collective *laissez-faire* policy was dominant—from the rest of the domain of economic and social planning and management. This was clearly reflected in the way that the institutions of government developed in relation to industrial society. The Ministry of Labour emerged from the Second World War with a dominant role in the government, and could conceivably have assumed a central responsibility for the whole direction of the labour economy, and by extension the national economy. In the event, it was accorded a much more limited role as, in effect, the ministry servicing the voluntary processes of collective bargaining and industrial relations. Within this sphere of operation, it was natural that its institutional ethos should be that of collective *laissez-faire*. Outside that sphere, the directing of the economy would tend to revert back to the Treasury, as the apparatus of wartime economic management was gradually dismantled; and, as David Marquand has argued,[5] the Treasury's enthusiasm for Keynesian demand management was largely born

---

[5] D. Marquand, *The Unprincipled Society: New Demands and Old Politics* (London, 1988), ch. 1.

of the fact that it seemed to offer a method of controlling the economy *without* active involvement in the detailed working of industrial society. Hence the acceptability of a compartmentalization which created a protected territory for collective *laissez-faire*.

11.2. THE LEGISLATIVE RESPONSES

(a) *Corporatist Policies*

That analysis makes it sound as if collective *laissez-faire* found a well-designed niche, a natural home, in the ordering of post-war industrial society. It was, indeed, distinctly convenient for the government that the leaders of the trade union movement were willing to co-operate with its reconstruction policies, provided that the system of collective *laissez-faire* was formally reconstructed. However, it should not be supposed that this accommodation could be achieved without cost, or that it could be achieved on a really durable basis. The cost was paid in those areas where the impetus to social or economic advance was provided neither from within the system of voluntary collective bargaining nor by the machinery of government outside the sphere of collective *laissez-faire*. A good example of that is the relative neglect of vocational training between 1945 and 1964.

So far as the durability of the structure is concerned, we have seen that the architects of the policy of full employment, certainly William Beveridge himself, clearly foresaw the difficulty of reconciling it with voluntary collective bargaining. They contemplated, in other words, that the political commitment to full employment would require a more centralized control of the collective bargaining process, though Beveridge himself hoped that control could be exercised by the TUC rather than the government. A major question for the immediate post-war period was whether the close wartime co-operation between employers, unions, and government would translate itself into a permanent overall framework within which the voluntary system of bargaining could flourish. As we saw in Chapter 2, although a notable feature of that period was the strength of the corporatist arrangements between government and trade unions, those arrangements were tacit rather than explicit and, ultimately, not sustainable.

We are using the term 'corporatist arrangement' here as defined in the following way by Colin Crouch and Ronald Dore:

An institutionalized pattern which involves an explicit or implicit bargain (or recurring bargaining) between some organ of government and private interest groups (including those promoting 'ideal interests'—'causes') one element in the bargain being that the groups receive certain institutionalized or *ad hoc* benefits in return for guarantees by the groups' representatives that their members will behave in certain ways considered to be in the public interest.[6]

Of particular importance were the corporatist arrangements between the government and the TUC which had evolved during the Second World War and which were maintained in peacetime. The arrangements were expressed, for instance, in Ernest Bevin's move from the front rank of the TUC to the central position which he held in the wartime Cabinet as Minister of Labour and National Service, and in Attlee's confidence during the late 1940s that the Labour Government could count on the leaders of the TUC to ensure that restraint was exercised in trade union wage demands. It was the process, which Keith Middlemas styled 'corporate bias',[7] whereby, as he put it, equilibrium was maintained because trade unions (and employers' associations) were elevated from the status of interest groups to that of governing institutions and as such came to share some of the political power and attributes of the state.

For the purpose of explaining the effect of these corporatist arrangements upon the development of labour law, and in order to understand how they contributed to collective *laissez-faire*, it is important to observe how diffuse and implicit these arrangements were at this time. This point can be made by means of an analysis of the impact of corporatist arrangements on the sources of regulation of industrial society. Where a corporatist arrangement is sufficiently tacit and diffuse to lie mainly below the formal horizon and to be invisible or only dimly visible above that horizon, that arrangement will not affect the formal allocation of regulatory power; it will leave the sources of regulation

---

[6] C. Crouch and R. Dore, 'Whatever Happened to Corporatism?', in *Corporatism and Accountability: The Role of Organized Interests* (Oxford, 1990), 1–45.

[7] K. Middlemas, *Politics in Industrial Society* (London, 1979), ch. 13.

apparently distinct from each other in their respective spheres. The informal corporatism of the late 1940s left the government to govern in the political and macro-economic sphere, free of overt challenge from the trade unions, while trade unions and employers, in their own sphere at least, enjoyed an equivalent freedom to be the source of regulation of industrial society. So the corporatist arrangements actually helped sustain the voluntarist sources of regulatory power; although inconsistent with the true theory of collective *laissez-faire*, they were, in practical reality, part of the structure of collective *laissez-faire*. It would be very different if, as later happened, those corporatist arrangements became specific and formal. That would affect the sources of regulation; the government would be visibly intervening in the working of industrial relations, and the trade unions would be seen to behave as one of the estates of the realm. The corporatist arrangements, so far from sustaining collective *laissez-faire*, would have become the instruments of its destruction, and would re-shape the whole pattern of labour law.

In spite of the relative lack of success of the implicit corporatism of the immediate post-war period, it was a strategy that subsequent governments were attracted to again and again in later decades as a way of reconciling a substantial degree of autonomy for the bargainers with the achievement of the government's economic policy objectives. A somewhat weaker version of the post-war relations between government and TUC continued to operate, for example, in relation to the newly elected Conservative government of 1951, at least until the middle of that decade. It was, however, not surprisingly Labour governments that developed corporatist strategies to the fullest extent—and thus Labour governments that sought to impose the greatest restraints upon the bargainers in terms of incomes policies, whether voluntary or statutory. Given the close links between the Labour Party and the trade unions, it was Labour governments that found it both feasible and desirable to attempt to persuade the bargainers to restrain to some degree the full exercise of their industrial power provided this was counterbalanced with the adoption by government of legislative and administrative policies that were perceived to be in the interests of trade union members. The exercise could be presented as a relatively technical re-balancing of the respective functions of the industrial and political wings of the labour movement or, in the Webbs' terms,[8] as a slight shift in favour of the method of legislation and away from the method of collective bargaining. As, however, the demands the government thought it needed to make of the bargainers increased in the post-war period, and the willingness and, above all, the ability of the TUC to satisfy those demands decreased, except in times of palpable economic crisis, the process of bargaining between government and trade unions needed to be made more and more explicit.

Thus when Labour returned to power in 1964 it wished to secure from the trade union movement a commitment to a permanent incomes policy, rather than a temporary freeze of the 1948–50 style. It was able to secure this commitment because it was sought in the context of explicit undertakings, given by government, to accelerate the rate of economic growth, the whole deal culminating in the signature by government, employers, and trade unions of the National Plan. Thus restraint on incomes could be presented as a restraint only on nominal incomes and as facilitating the growth of real incomes, and as part of a coherent plan of economic management. When, in the event, the government preferred the policy objective of defending the value of the pound to economic growth, it was shown that not even the attachment of criminal sanctions to the incomes policy was an adequate substitute for agreement between government and unions on the fundamentals of an incomes policy.

The rift between party and unions that the 1960s incomes policies produced ensured that the re-constitution of corporatist policies in the early 1970s, in anticipation of a Labour government's return to power, had to be on a more far-reaching basis, and one that was more favourable to the trade unions than had been the case in the early 1960s. The Labour Party/TUC Liaison Committee produced agreement on the part of a future Labour government to follow a range of policies beneficial to trade union members, whilst committing the unions to only rather vague expressions of restraint in relation to the exercise of their bargaining power. In practice, as we saw, the economic crisis produced by the oil shocks reversed the balance of advantage:

---

[8] S. and B. Webb, *Industrial Democracy* (London, 1920), pt. IV, chs. 2 and 4.

the TUC followed, for at least a couple of years, a very tight, if non-statutory, incomes policy, whilst, outside the repeal of the Industrial Relations Act and the enactment of an Employment Protection Act, rather few of the government's prior commitments were met. Finally, the rift produced between government and unions at the end of the 1970s by the failure of the Social Contract was as profound as that of the late 1960s.

Thus the corporatist mechanism, aimed at preserving or, in the case of the 1970s Social Contract, restoring the formal legal framework of collective *laissez-faire* in respect of collective labour law by securing voluntary restraint on the part of the trade union movement in the exercise of its bargaining strength, has proved not to be a durable one on any of the three occasions upon which it was used in the post-war period. Neither party to the arrangement proved able to deliver its side of the bargain, except over the short term: the government had insufficient control over the economic environment in which the UK had to operate and the TUC over the behaviour of the bargainers.

(b) Regulated Bargaining

For Conservative governments the chances of securing an arrangement along corporatist lines with the trade union movement were necessarily more limited; the objectives of the two potential parties to any agreement constituted a less good fit than in the case of a Labour government, at least from the mid-1950s onwards. Nevertheless, some limited forays were made in this direction by Conservative governments. The process of 'modernization', embarked upon by Mr Macmillan's government in the early 1960s, involved participation by the TUC in the running of the National Economic Development Council, a body with policy functions, though not executive responsibilities, in relation to economic planning, and participation by trade union officials at lower levels in the organization of industrial training. The TUC, however, refused to agree to any restraint on its pay-bargaining activities. Again, Mr Heath, in the latter part of his administration, after it became clear that the Industrial Relations Act 1971 would not achieve the goals initially set for it, tried, but failed, to reach agreement with the TUC on a voluntary incomes policy.

Thus a Conservative government, finding itself blocked from the route of preserving the formal structure of collective *laissez-*

faire through an extra-legal, but in fact highly interventionist, control over the results of bargaining, was more likely to be persuaded of the merits of direct changes to the legal structure, especially that part of it that preserved the autonomy of the collective bargaining parties. This was one reason why the Industrial Relations Act 1971 was such a significant statute. The government proceeded through a breach in the walls of collective *laissez-faire* created by the Labour government itself, at the nadir of the success of its corporatist policies of the 1960s, by its proposals in *In Place of Strife* to use the law to regulate strikes.

However, the Conservative government was influenced above all by the US model of reliance upon a legally regulated system of collective bargaining to set terms and conditions of employment, and so imposed the first post-war restrictions, upon the peaceful use of economic sanctions in trade disputes, for which there was no shadow of a claim that this was part of an agreement with the TUC. The aim was to render unlawful (and to impose the sanctions of the civil law upon) industrial action leading to a national emergency, secondary action, and unofficial action, though, as we saw, the back-firing of the registration system meant that this third set of provisions came close to rendering all industrial action unlawful. However, the imposition of legal sanctions upon a confident labour movement, still buoyed by high employment, proved no easier than the erection of sustainable corporatist structures, especially as employers and the courts were rather slow to learn the lesson that individuals were as often raised up as cast down by being made defendants in legal actions and that trade unions themselves were in fact potentially more attractive targets.

(c) *Industrial Justice*

The period of the later 1960s and early 1970s was, however, a watershed not only for the autonomy of the bargaining parties but also for that limb of the doctrine of collective *laissez-faire* which counselled abstention by the state from regulation of the terms and conditions of the individual employment relationship. Individual employment law in the UK during this period moved fairly rapidly and fundamentally away from a liberal and con-tractualist approach towards a variety of commitments to ensure, at least at the level of principle, protection against arbitrary treatment. The pressures for these changes were not principally derived from difficulties perceived by government in reconciling the tenets of collective *laissez-faire* with the goals of economic management, but from the need to achieve more purely social goals. In some cases the policy imperatives could be identified rather specifically. The race relations legislation of 1968 and 1976 stemmed from government's desire to promote a legitimate place in society for the newly arrived immigrant groups (whilst at the same time making it very difficult for additional immigrants to join them). An important part of 'society' was bound to be the world of work, and the need, in the government's eyes, for swift and effective action overrode the underlying notion of collective *laissez-faire* that it was for the bargaining parties to determine the pace and direction of social change within the industrial relations system.

In other areas of individual employment law the pressures were more diffuse and more international. The pressures of the women's movement, operating both within and outside the trade union movement, helped to secure the passing of the Equal Pay Act 1970 and the Sex Discrimination Act 1975, and the view of at least some of the proponents of that legislation, that collective *laissez-faire* operated in practice so as to protect bastions of male privilege, did not dispose them in favour of arguments against the legislation that were based upon the principle of industrial autonomy. Finally, and most generally, we saw that the enactment of unfair dismissal legislation in 1971, action which many similar countries took during the 1950s and 1960s, seemed to be a response to the growth of large organisations and of what Hugh Collins subsequently termed 'bureaucratic power',[9] and to a fear that the dominance of such organisations was so great that collective bargaining, unaided, would not be able to counteract it. Of course, the line between the social pressures on collective *laissez-faire* and those stemming from considerations of economic management was not entirely clear-cut. Thus an argument in favour of unfair dismissal legislation was that it would reduce the incidence of strikes over disciplinary issues. However, that line

---

[9] H. Collins, 'Against Abstentionism in Labour Law', in J. Eekelaar and J. Bell, eds., *Oxford Essays in Jurisprudence*, 3rd ser. (Oxford, 1987), ch. 4.

of justification for unfair dismissal legislation has tended to be emphasised by those generally unsympathetic to the notion of using the law to promote the goals of industrial justice, often because such use was thought to lead to the judicialization of issues, to the disadvantage of employees. More important, the pursuit of industrial justice brought the law into conflict, in places, with collective structures, and the conflict was not always happily resolved. One might point, on the one hand, to the excessive protection afforded to discriminatory collective agreements by the Equal Pay Act, and, by way of contrast, to the use in the Industrial Relations Act of the individual right to dissociate to undermine union security arrangements.

(d) The Demise of Collectivism

Thus the Industrial Relations Act 1971 contained elements derived from both the social and economic pressures upon collective *laissez-faire* as well as displaying some of the difficulties of determining their proper reconciliation. But that Act also contained a third policy. Once the taboo on the use of the law had been broken, it might be asked whether the law should be used, not only to control strikes or to advance industrial justice for the individual, but also to advance the spread of collective bargaining. Traditionally, public policy had been said to favour the promotion of collective bargaining, albeit by government encouragement rather than by legislation. If legislation was now to be an appropriate tool for advancing governmental policy, should it not be deployed to promote collective bargaining? That this argument received some recognition in the 1971 Act was shown by the inclusion in it of a statutory recognition procedure and of provisions protecting freedom of association in (registered) trade unions. Such provisions were carried on, in rather different form, into the Social Contract legislation of the later 1970s and were added to, notably through provisions for 'extending' collective agreements to workers outside the original bargaining unit. That the Social Contract legislation should have contained such provisions was perhaps less surprising than their presence in the 1971 Act. What this demonstrated was that in 1971 government saw collective bargaining as still the central and legitimate method for settling terms and conditions of employment, but wished to regulate the operation of the bargaining process, especially the consequences of a failure to agree in the collective negotiations.

It is here that one finds the sharpest possible contrast with the policies of the Conservative governments of the 1980s. The Industrial Relations Act sought to put in place a type of regulated collective bargaining; the legislation of the 1980s to replace collective bargaining by individual bargaining in the name of exposing bargaining over employment contracts to the full rigour of the labour market. As *Employment for the 1990s* put it, 'the consistent theme of the Government's reforms has been to enlarge the freedom of employers and employees to make their own decisions', both needing to be protected against 'the balance of power between trade unions and employers and between trade unions and their own members [which] was weighted heavily in favour of the unions'.[10]

By early 1992, the government could go so far as to claim that, as a result of the changes in the 1980s,

traditional patterns of industrial relations, based on collective bargaining and collective agreements, seem increasingly inappropriate and are in decline . . . [Individual workers] want the opportunity to influence, in some cases to negotiate, their own terms and conditions of employment, rather than leaving them to the outcome of some distant negotiations between employers and trade unions.[11]

Thus, if the late 1960s and early 1970s were a watershed, as collective *laissez-faire* collapsed, the period after 1979 was another, as collective bargaining lost its central role in governmental policy towards industrial relations (which is not the same as saying that in fact the influence of collective bargaining in the setting of terms and conditions declined to the same extent). It would probably be wrong to suppose that the government anticipated that its stress on individual bargaining would lead in fact to systematic negotiations between individual workers and their employers. The disparity in bargaining power between employer and employee would remove this possibility in the normal case, though exceptional cases can easily be imagined where some significant bargaining might take place. Nor prob-

[10] Cm. 540 (1988), para. 2.5.
[11] White Paper, *People, Jobs and Opportunity*, Cm. 1810 (1992), para. 1.15 and 1.18.

ably did the government suppose that employers would take advantage of their new freedom of action to impose unilaterally upon employees of the same class different terms and conditions of employment, although the encouragement of performance-related pay did mean that common contractual provisions might well produce different outcomes for different individuals. The attraction for the government, it may be thought, of 'individual bargaining' was that it enabled the employer to reflect more rapidly in the terms and conditions of its workforce the changing pressures upon the employer which emanated from the product market. Collective bargaining interposed the mediating influence of the union between the competitive pressures upon employers and their ability to respond to them by re-shaping terms and conditions of employment. Individual bargaining, on the other hand, was an important method of facilitating and even en-couraging flexibility in the labour market.

After two spectacularly unsuccessful attempts at preserving the centrality of collective bargaining in the 1970s, first by placing it in a context of legal controls designed to regulate, above all, resort to industrial action, and second, by surrounding the restored formal autonomy of the collective parties by an extra-legal agreement between government and TUC, designed to control the results of bargaining, it was not surprising that the Conservative government elected in 1979 decided to set off in a third direction. What *was* surprising was the extent of and thoroughness with which the new path was pursued. The last equivalent period of unchanging political control at Westminster had been in the 1950s when, as we saw, the Conservative govern-ment was only beginning to think about questioning the post-war framework of labour law. From the outset, however, the govern-ment elected in 1979 was determined to change labour law, though it would probably be wrong to suppose that there was a fixed master-plan determining what the end-point would be.

The government began with legislation relating to strikes, which could be reconciled with the policies of the Industrial Relations Act, but as statute succeeded statute, restriction was piled upon restriction, as the immunities against the common law torts were decreased and the possibilities of individual members suing their trade unions were increased, it became clear that this process had no logical stopping-point, because government saw

no legitimate place for collective bargaining in the regulation
of labour relations, except perhaps at enterprise level to help
management achieve its goals. The White Paper *Employment for
the 1990s* endorsed the view that in the past,

trade unions tended to push up the earnings of the people they represented while blocking improvements in productivity which are needed
to pay for those higher earnings.

For the future,

trade unions must recognize that their members' interests are not served
by conflict, and that efficiency, profitability and flexibility in working
practices are the best guarantee of jobs.[12]

In the circumstances, it was not surprising that collective
bargaining, that engine for the articulation and resolution of
conflict, should be held in low esteem, as little regarded as that
motor of collective bargaining, the right to strike. By 1989 the
Committee of Experts of the International Labour Organization,
which was the institutional embodiment of the fundamental right
of workers to bargain collectively, could identify six ways in
which Conservative legislation had breached Convention No. 87
on Freedom of Association and Protection of the Right to
Organize. It felt bound 'to express its concern at the volume and
complexity of legislative change since 1980'. Many of the individual changes might be consistent with the Convention, but they
'may nevertheless, by virtue of their complexity and extent,
constitute an incursion upon the rights guaranteed by the
Convention'.[13]

As we have seen, the disfavour into which collective bargaining
fell in the 1980s not only led the government to impose one of the
most restrictive regimes of strike law in Europe, but also, and not
surprisingly, to repeal the legislation that promoted collective
bargaining (the statutory recognition procedure went in 1980) or
extended the results of collective bargaining to workers outside
the bargaining unit (schedule 11 of the 1975 Act was repealed in
the same year). Multi-employer collective bargaining was a par-

---

[12] Cm. 540, paras. 2.4 and 2.12.
[13] Observation of the Committee of Experts on Convention No. 87,
Observations 1989, quoted in K. Ewing, *Britain and the ILO* (Institute of
Employment Rights, London, n.d.), 36.

ticular subject of attack because it was seen as restricting the freedom of individual enterprises to adjust to market conditions, and, *a fortiori*, legal structures perceived as having a similar effect (such as the Wages Councils) were removed or extensively modified.

(e) Individual Employment Relationships and the Market

However, although dramatic, these changes were at one level no more than a ground-clearing exercise. Employers were to be freed from the incubus of collectively bargained or legislatively set requirements in order to negotiate contracts with their workers that reflected the conditions of their enterprise. As the 1989 White Paper put it,

Management has regained the freedom to manage, and the incentive, and will do so.[14]

But what sort of employment relationships did government expect management to create? As far as the private sector was concerned, that was a matter largely for management to decide (though like all governments the Conservative administrations of the 1980s found it impossible to refrain from criticising managements which, under labour market rather than trade union pressure, awarded pay increases above the rate of inflation). However, some indications of what the government would like to see could be gleaned from the legislation providing tax incentives for the adoption of profit-related pay or employee share-ownership schemes (not that either in fact became a major element in non-executive remuneration packages). The individual, too, was to be encouraged to find protection in the labour market, so that the drag on labour mobility created by occupational pension schemes was reduced by entitling early leavers to something like an adequate transfer value (a long overdue reform), and the system of personal pensions was encouraged, and individual tax incentives to re-training were provided (at the same time as state promotion of industrial training through the industrial training boards was wound down).

It was, however, in relation to those employments remaining in the public sector that the governmental model of the employment

---

[14] Cm. 540, para. 2.6.

relationship was most fully displayed, partly because there was so much to react against. In the public sector, government, as always, not only set the legislative framework but was also the employer exercising whatever freedoms that framework created (subject to some special, but usually not intrusive, controls imposed by public law). In the heyday of collective *laissez-faire* the public sector had in many ways displayed an ideal version of that system. Trade unionism and collective bargaining were then encouraged (by extra-legal means) by governments committed to collective regulation of terms and conditions of employment, whilst *vis-à-vis* individual employees the government was committed to acting as a good employer in providing, for example, as the NJAC discovered in 1967, much more adequate protections against arbitrary discipline than was generally the case in the private sector at that time. In the 1980s there was a deliberate dismantling of these collective and individual protections in order to expose the public sector to the control by the market or by market-analogues, as we saw in chapter 10.

The vision of individual contracting in an atomized market presented, however, almost as profound a challenge to individual labour law as to collective labour law. In some ways the *bouleversement* in relation to individual employment law was even more surprising. Before 1979 there was evidence for an optimistic view that, whatever party was in power and whatever policy was being pursued as regards collective labour relations, there would be a steady expansion of the industrial justice laws. There was much greater (though not complete) party political agreement as to the policies underlying such legislation, and individual employment law displayed an almost linear development, in contrast with the sudden shifts and changes of collective labour law reform (only where individual rights and collective structures collided had the heights of controversy been reached). But the new insistence upon the hegemony of individual contracting led to the question being asked of why such protection as the employee wished to have could not be provided by striking a bargain with the employer to provide it. Why should the state play a paternalistic role, especially if the result of such paternalism might be to make employers less willing to hire workers?

In each case the Government have to consider why it is necessary to depart from the basic principle that terms and conditions of employment

are matters to be determined by the employer and employee concerned
... in the light of their own individual circumstances. The rights of
people in employment have to be balanced against the needs of those
who are unemployed.[15]

Perhaps because downgrading the rights of individuals was
perceived to be less politically popular than similar action in
relation to trade unions, the governments of the 1980s were more
circumspect in relation to individual employment law. However,
the unfair dismissal legislation was considerably weakened by a
policy of extending the qualifying period for protection to two
years and of allowing the compensatory remedy for unfair dismissal to drift into gross inadequacy (except in cases where unfair
dismissal law could be used to undermine collective structures, in
which case specially enhanced remedies could be awarded). On
the other hand, pressure from outside the country, in the shape
of European Community commitments entered into in the 1970s,
led to some modest expansion of industrial justice legislation,
especially in the areas of equal pay and sex discrimination,
although the UK government made full use of the rhetoric of de-
regulation to block most new Community legislation in the
employment field.

(f) Community Labour Law

Indeed, by the end of the decade, Community labour law, actual
and, more important, potential, was being used by those within
the UK who were opposed to the market ideology of the UK
government in a much more fundamental way than merely as a
counterbalance to government policy in specific areas of individual employment law. Community (and to some extent international) labour law policy was being pressed into service to fill a
vacuum of a general ideological character, namely to provide a
counter-theory to the government's vision of a labour market
consisting of a multitude of individual bargains. The traditional
alternative theories—collective *laissez-faire*, legally regulated
bargaining, and bargained corporatism—all appeared tarnished
in the 1980s. Rightly or wrongly, they were the subject of a
thorough-going loss of political confidence brought about largely
by economic crisis and economic decline.

[15] *Building Businesses . . . Not Barriers*, Cmnd. 9794 (1986), para. 7.2.

In this situation, the European Community came to appear as the most important and effective source of a countervailing discourse to that of the government. In the later 1980s, as in the mid-1970s, the expansionism of the European Community gave rise to an activism in the sphere of social policy, culminating in the Social Charter agreed upon by the other eleven member states at the end of 1989, and the Social Chapter added to the Treaty of Rome at Maastricht at the end of 1991, but again in a protocol not applicable to the UK. The Social Charter and the policies underlying it were anathema to the government both because the expansionism of the Community was felt to challenge national sovereignty, and because the social activism was seen to challenge free labour market policies. The TUC in particular was prepared to embrace Community social activism wholeheartedly because it seemed to be the only effective focus of practical opposition to the government's onslaught upon their whole position; a whole new alignment of social forces was symbolized by the visit of Jacques Delors as President of the EEC Commission to the TUC Conference in 1988. It had, indeed, become easier for the TUC and the Labour Party in opposition each to conduct a dialogue with the European Commission than for them to conduct a dialogue with each other; the latter would ultimately have forced them to confront the continuing difficulty within the trade union movement about how far incomes policy would ever be acceptable, a difficulty manifested in the internal divisions about proposals for a national minimum wage, and for a national pay forum.

It remains profoundly open to question whether the Social Charter and the European Commission's Social Action Programme really do offer the promise of an overall external reference point for socially active labour law which opponents of government labour market policies within the UK in the 1980s have attributed to it. It is true that these initiatives promised to build upon the relative success which the Community has had in developing a concern for industrial justice, especially in relation to sex discrimination, and in off-setting the cruder manifestations of extreme de-regulation in the member states during the 1980s. It was not, however, realistic to think that this amounted to a coherent body of principles of European labour law. In particular, the experience of the 1970s and 1980s provides a potent reminder that the Community was unable to evolve a framework of collective labour law or an agreed structure for employee participation in corporate management.

11.3. CONCLUSION

All this amounts to the conclusion that there were no easy answers to be found, either within British experience or by looking to the European Community, to the ever-intensifying problem of how to reconcile the various demands upon governments in relation to industrial society, within a framework of reasonably acceptable, democratic, representative, and humane labour law. The post-war experience of the UK has been that, in a relatively unsuccessful and declining economy, reconciliation could not be accomplished within the tradition of autonomous collective bargaining and legal abstention from intervention in industrial relations and the individual employment relationship. As we saw, governments began to realise the force of this view by the early 1960s and it had been fully borne in on them a decade later. Twenty years after that, however, agreement on the appropriate set of replacements for collective *laissez-faire* seemed as far away as ever. In large part, as Kahn-Freund himself recognized, the very strength of the abstentionist tradition made the development of a more extensive role for labour law more difficult.[16] The 1950s system of predominantly negative labour law provided few pointers as to how law could be used more constructively in this field. The wholesale adoption of an unsuitable foreign model of regulation in 1971 and the over-reliance on corporatist policies, for which the necessary substructure did not exist, in the 1960s and 1970s, were false starts at a point when time was running out for the values of collectivism. Nevertheless, it cannot be said that the policies of the 1980s have produced a more successful reconciliation of the desirable goals: perhaps a better, but still patchy, record on inflation and productivity, but higher levels of unemployment and less protection against arbitrary treatment and less democracy in industry. Do the last two decades really represent the best that can be done?

[16] O. Kahn-Freund, *Labour Relations: Heritage and Adjustment* (Oxford, 1979).

It is tempting to consider whether there existed, at the beginning of our period, an alternative path from the path of collective *laissez-faire* which was taken. We think there probably was not, in that the post-war government was not in a position to assume that additional political burden of confronting the demand for a return to free collective bargaining. However, if we think there was such a possibility then, should we not rather be asking, is there a corresponding possibility at the end of the period to evolve a system of labour law which will be sufficiently strongly based in principles of industrial justice, and yet sufficiently recognizing of the need for effective representation of the workforce in collective bargaining if industrial justice is to be realized, for that system of labour law to be able to be disengaged from the economic crisis to which there is no obvious resolution in sight?

It is to be hoped that the framers of an ultimately more stable yet juridified system of labour law would interpret the experience of 1945 to 1990 as demonstrating the need to legislate for an effective combination of individual industrial justice with collective representation, and the further need to integrate that combination with the responsibility of the state to achieve a socially balanced and reasonably humane political economy. By the end of the period which we have surveyed, it seemed that other European countries operating in broadly the same economic and social environment were capable, or at least more capable, of achieving the balance we postulate, between the demands of industrial justice, of representation, of responsibility, and of autonomy. Nor could those comparisons be dismissed as irrelevant to the situation of the UK, as it was clear that all European Community countries would be operating in an increasingly similar economic and political structure.

Does this mean that one is forced to conclude in a pessimistic sense about the outcome, in labour law terms, of the whole post-war period and the post-war settlement itself, with no more to offer on the positive side than encouragement to follow the preferable examples of other European states? Certainly it must be admitted that by the end of the period, the post-war settlement seemed in great disarray, totally discredited in the eyes of many people. This seemed to be the conclusion reached by David Marquand when he surveyed political society generally over this period,[17] by Keith Middlemas in his monumental survey of the political economy over the same period,[18] and by Alan Fox in his long-term history of the industrial relations system which concluded with the post-war period.[19]

On the other hand, each of those writers sought to offer some sort of prescription for more positive future development, and the suggestion that some elements in the post-war history offered the prospect of movement, however gradual, towards implementing such a prescription. David Marquand offered a prescription built around the idea of politics as mutual education, that education being a means of re-identifying and re-stablishing communitarian values.[20] Keith Middlemas, more reluctant to propose positive solutions, nevertheless offers the similar notion of 'the competitive symposium', a civilized discourse between competing but mutually acknowledging interests in society.[21] Alan Fox asserted the need for 'a reconstruction towards greater equality that might make it just possible for the concept of community needs to have some practical behavioural significance for everyday life';[22] though he, the most sceptical of the three writers, actually hoped for, at best, no more than the retention of as much of the characteristic structures and textures of British society as is compatible with the necessary minimum of adjustment to a rapidly changing world'.[23]

Can we make these prognoses, and these aspirations to salvage the best features and discard the worst features of the recent past, any more concrete and specific in terms of labour law? Let us start by summarizing what we found to be the strengths and weaknesses of the system of collective *laissez-faire*. Its main strengths lay in the relatively high degree of worker participation in the setting of terms and conditions of employment, and in the commitment which it embodied to providing decent levels of protection at the workplace. Its weaknesses, on the other hand, consisted in a failure to integrate industrial relations into general

[17] Marquand, *The Unprincipled Society*, esp. ch. 7.
[18] K. Middlemas, *Power, Competition and the State*, esp. iii, *The End of the Post-war Era: Britain since 1974* (London, 1991).
[19] Fox, *History and Heritage*, esp. ch. 8.
[20] Marquand, *The Unprincipled Society*, ch. 8, 'The Public Realm'.
[21] Middlemas, *Power, Competition and the State*, iii. 479–87.
[22] Fox, *History and Heritage*, 450.
[23] Ibid. 452.

governmental economic policy goals, and in its failure to protect those outside the reach of the collective bargaining system—or, indeed, those pushed to the bottom of the labour market by the collective *laissez-faire* system itself.

The history we have recounted suggests that it would be impracticable to return to the collective *laissez-faire* system, and we are not advocating doing so. However, achieving the sort of reconciliation between competing goals which we postulated above depends on capturing those strengths of collective *laissez-faire*, as a particularly British tradition of industrial relations and labour law, while learning from the post-Donovan experience of active labour law, including the experience of European Community Social Policy. We have depicted the history in terms of moves first from collective *laissez-faire* towards policies of achieving regulated collective bargaining, and then secondly from those policies towards policies aimed at the total or partial destruction of collective bargaining. We have indicated that the middle one of those three states seems to us to provide the best starting-point for future policy prescriptions, though we have not underestimated the imperfections of the experiments with regulated collective bargaining in the 1970s.

The question at the time of writing is whether regulated collective bargaining can be reconstituted in a viable form after the changes of framework and of attitudes which occurred during the 1980s. There are some optimistic signs; by the early 1990s there were few defenders left of earlier totally abstentionist views of labour law even on the trade union side. Effective exploitation of the possibilities which are thus created depends on a combination of imaginative and constructive formulation of positive labour law, and on the creation of a set of attitudes conducing to its successful implementation. The history and theory of labour law may have something to contribute to the latter process, and certainly seem relevant to the former process of formulation of future labour law.

At the very least, that history and theory can suggest an appropriate agenda for labour law—in the way that the Report of the Donovan Commission did in the 1960s. We would conclude by arguing that a socially adequate agenda for reconstituting a system of regulated collective bargaining would have to include some treatment of the following concerns:

1. Fair labour standards, including minimum wage standards;
2. Rights of workplace representation and participation;
3. Equal treatment in relation to employment as between groups, especially those differentiated by gender, race, or religion;
4. The provision of training both for those in employment and outside it;
5. The securing of industrial justice in the management and termination of the employment relationship;
6. The integration of policies to control inflation with autonomous pay-bargaining;
7. The protection of freedom of association;
8. The guaranteeing of democratic procedures for trade union decision-making, and the protection of individuals against abuse of power by trade unions;
9. The guaranteeing of rights to take industrial action subject to appropriate limitations;
10. The provision of an autonomous system of adjudication by industrial tribunals and Labour Courts, and of autonomous machinery of conciliation and arbitration of disputes.

It is for our readers to judge how far this history might help with the elaboration and specification of that agenda.

INDEX